The Aviation Consumer
USED AIRCRAFT GUIDE

The Aviation Consumer
USED AIRCRAFT GUIDE

Richard B. Weeghman, Editor

BELVOIR PUBLICATIONS, INC.

ISBN 0-9615196-5-7

The authors of this book were Richard B. Weeghman, David B. Noland, and Kas Thomas. Carolyn A. Magruder was the managing editor, and the production assistant was Rosemary Royer.

CONTENTS

Twin-Engine

Turbine Aircraft

Helicopters

For information about the editorial content of this publication or regular subscriptions to *The Aviation Consumer* magazine for pilots and aircraft owners, contact *The Aviation Consumer*, 1111 East Putnam Avenue, Riverside, CT 06878; (203) 637-5900.

Introduction

This is actually our second edition of the Used Aircraft Guide. We published the first one in 1981, and the entire run went like the proverbial hotcakes, and has been sold out for some time.

This time we have analyzed, in depth, squadrons of different models, and in some cases updated articles on popular aircraft included in the first issue. Since we figure the safety record of each make and model is of such high concern among potential buyers, we have included an introductory section that analyzes the accident rates of two major classes of aircraft: the single-engine retractables and the light twins. And we have explored the always provocative topic—are twins or singles safer?

As before, in the tradition of *The Aviation Consumer*, we have let the facts fall as they may, and spared no model complete details about any nasty faults that may jeopardize either the flying safety of the readers or their pocketbooks, in their quest for the "perfect plane." We have gone to some effort to dig out the real-world strengths and weaknesses of each aircraft. To do this we have scoured National Transportation Safety Board accident records and Federal Aviation Administration Service Difficulty Reports. But perhaps most importantly, we have also secured the comments of owners who have been through good and bad with each aircraft.

We think the reader will find nuggets of information here that are in very short supply elsewhere. Along with the safety record and maintenance history of each aircraft, we have provided what we believe is a unique feature: graphs of their resale value. This allows the buyer to calculate whether his purchase is likely to shrink horribly in value through the years, or actually enhance his equity. For a court of last resort on information about the various models, we have listed the various owner associations. Note that the prices we have provided were the latest we could obtain, for the most part 1985 figures—but these change with the flux and flow of the economy and inflation. The articles in this volume are adapted from regular monthly issues of *The Aviation Consumer* and were written by its editors.

Richard B. Weeghman, Editor

SAFETY ROUNDUPS

Single-Engine Retractables: Which are the Safest?

The strutted Cessna Skylane RG, a relative newcomer, leads the pack with the lowest fatal accident rate of them all.

When's the last time you heard a new plane buyer ask the salesman, "What are the accident and fatality rates of this Arrow compared to a Skylane RG?" Probably never. Human beings seem almost programmed not to think about nasty things like airplane accidents. Oh, sure, most pilots give lip service to safe piloting techniques, and some even practice them. But few ever stop to think that the design of the airplane they're flying may determine whether that day's flight ends safely.

Most pilots think about planes the way they think about cars: safety-wise, there's not much difference between a Ford and a Chevy, so there's probably not much difference between a Cessna and a Beech, either. But the accident rate of general aviation aircraft, on a passenger-mile basis, is at least ten times higher than that of passenger cars. And various types of aircraft have accident rates that differ widely—sometimes by as much as three or four hundred percent. In some cases, it turns out, there's a very big difference indeed between a Cessna and a Beechcraft.

There's much debate about the safety merits of various types of aircraft. Which is safer, a high-wing or a low-wing? Twins or singles? Is centerline thrust safer than the standard twin-engine setup? Is centerline thrust safer than the standard twin-engine setup? Does the low stall speed of a Cessna make it safer than, say, a Mooney? Aircraft manufacturers like to brag about safety advances like simplified fuel systems, stronger structures, fool-proof stall traits and so forth, and the aviation press is quick to praise those features that theoretically improve safety.

The Bottom Line

But the bottom line of all this debate is one simple question: How often does each type of aircraft crash, and how likely are the occupants to be killed? Theoretical safety is born in the minds of industry engineers and FAA bureaucrats, but real safety is reflected only in cold, hard accident statistics.

Unfortunately, such statistics simply don't exist for the most part. Neither the FAA nor the NTSB assembles accident rate data on a regular basis. In 1979, the NTSB published a special study of accident rates by aircraft type covering the years 1972-76. (Ironically, *The Aviation Consumer* pulished its own study, based on essentially the same data, at about the same time). But except for that one-time study, the government simply does not have any accident rate data for individual aircraft types. The plane buyer who asks his salesman about accident rates will get a blank stare in return—not because the salesman is trying to hide something, but because good numbers simply do not exist.

Filling the Vacuum

We have attempted to fill this statistical vacuum. Using raw data supplied by the NTSB and FAA (and in some cases estimated or projected, when no such data exists) we have calculated accident rates for seventeen popular aircraft types. The numbers show conclusively that not all airplanes are created equal—not by a long shot. If you fly the lowest-ranking aircraft on our list, you are nearly four times more likely to have a fatal accident than if you fly the highest.

To establish a *rate* of accidents, it's necessary to know two things; first, the number of accidents; and second, a measure of the exposure to accident risk in terms of flight hours, aircraft in the field, or some other measure. The standard industry measure of exposure is flight hours, with rates normally expressed in terms of accidents per 100,000 flight hours.

Digging out the number of accidents is no problem. The NTSB keeps careful records of all accidents, and its computer can sort them according to types. The NTSB also published for several years an annual document called "Listing of aircraft accidents/incidents by make and model." We culled through these lists for the years 1977-79, the last years the lists were published, and obtained individual computer printouts of accidents by type for 1980 and

1981. So our numbers for fatal accidents are virtually bulletproof, coming directly from NTSB files. Our figures of total accidents may have slight room for error, due to the grey area between what is classified as an accident and what's labeled an incident. We feel confident that our numbers for total accidents are accurate to within a percent or two, barring some NTSB computer sorting error in the printouts supplied to us.

Unfortunately, the hours-flown numbers we used to measure exposure are much less certain. Most of the numbers come from the FAA, which sends out questionnaires to a random sampling of aircraft owners, and from that projects a fleet total for various aircraft types. At best, the hours-flown numbers are estimates, albeit U.S. Government approved ones.

The Mooney 201 has only a fair to middling accident rate, but that is quite a bit better than the poor rate of the turbocharged 231 in total and fatal accidents.

Even more unfortunately, the FAA does a lousy job of sorting out the various aircraft types. Until 1977, the FAA hours-flown data was very detailed, and with enough hours spent hunched over squinting at computer printouts, it was possible to come up with some decent figures. (That's just what one of out bleary-eyed reporters did for the last study we did, covering the years 1972-1976).

Change in Procedures

But in 1977, the FAA changed its data-gathering procedures. Since then, hours-flown numbers are published only for very broad categories. For example, after 1976,

the FAA publishes only one annual hours-flown number for all Piper PA-28s. That grouping happens to include everything from a primary trainer (the Cherokee 140) to a retractable turbocharged T-tailed business aircraft (the Turbo Arrow). For our purposes, these numbers are essentially useless. Likewise, the latest FAA hours-flown numbers fail to distinguish between, for example, the 185-hp 1947 Model 35 Bonanza and the 285-hp 1982 V35B model built 35 years later; the Cessna Cardinal and Cardinal RG, not to mention the Skylane and Skylane RG or the 210 and the P210.

We complained to the FAA about these problems back in 1979, while researching our first accident-rate study, and were promised that things would improve shortly. They never did. As a result, we were forced to estimate hours flown for certain aircraft types in our listing. This was done mostly by analyzing fleet totals and projecting trends from the 1972-76 period, when good data was available.

For example, the FAA has hours-flown data for the Cessna 177 series, which includes both the retractable and straight-leg Cardinal. We determined that the RG made up 32 percent of the total 177 fleet. Therefore we assumed the

Accident Rate Summary 1972-1981

Aircraft	Hours Flown	Total Accidents	Total Rate	1972-1976 Total Rate	Fatal Accidents	Fatal Rate	1972-1976 Fatal Rate
Beech 24 Sierra	774,000	94	12.1	15.2	24	3.1	4.0
Beech 33 Debonair/Bonanza	2,567,000	118	4.6	4.6	35	1.4	1.0
Beech V-tail Bonanza (35-P35)	5,989,000*	638	10.7	11.8	199	3.3	3.6
Beech V-tail Bonanza (S35-V35B)	3,808,000*	221	5.8	7.0	66	1.7	2.0
Beech 36 Bonanza	1,905,000	98	5.1	4.7	28	1.5	1.7
Bellanca 17-30/31 Viking	1,413,000	156	11.0	16.8	39	2.8	4.2
Cessna 177 Cardinal RG	1,450,000*	128	7.8	8.2	21	1.5	1.6
Cessna R-182 Skylane RG	533,000*	37	6.9	—	4	0.8	—
Cessna 210	7,461,000	843	11.3	15.0	171	2.3	3.1
Cessna P210	255,000*	25	9.8	—	4	1.6	—
Mooney M-20B-G	6,266,000	599	9.6	11.3	137	2.2	2.4
Mooney M20J (201)	630,000*	41	6.5	—	15	2.4	—
Mooney M-20K (231)	189,000*	21	11.1	—	6	3.2	—
Piper PA-24 Comanche	4,660,000	698	15.0	16.8	133	2.9	2.9
Piper PA-28R Arrow series	6,984,000*	583	8.3	11.3	149	2.1	3.2
Piper PA-32R Lance/ Saratoga	1,191,000	127	10.7	14.1	39	3.3	5.9
Rockwell 112/114	1,413,000	156	11.0	—	39	2.8	—

* Hours-flown data based on projections from FAA data.

RG to have flown 32 percent of the total hours flown by the 177 fleet. Multiplying the FAA figure for the total 177 fleet by 0.32, we arrived at an estimate for RG hours flown.

We also double-checked our estimates by dividing them by the known fleet totals to get an average number of hours flown each year by each airplane. GAMA and FAA figures show that the average general-aviation aircraft flies between 150 and 200 hours per year. If our estimated number didn't yield a per-plane average in this range, we went back to the drawing board. In almost every case, the numbers agreed reasonably well.

How Accurate?

How accurate are our hours-flown numbers? We'd estimate they're within 20 percent. That means our final accident rates are also accurate to within about 20 percent. Readers should not panic and immediately trade in their old Mooney (fatal accident rate 2.2 per 100,000 flight hours) for an Arrow (2.1 per 100,000 hours) for the sake of the wife and kids. Comparing two planes, we wouldn't worry about a difference less than 50 percent or so. There's that much statistical "slop" in the numbers.

Because of this inherent imprecision, we have rounded off the accident rate numbers to the nearest tenth. Greater mathematical precision is possible from the raw data, but we feel that level of precision is not justified.

The Standings

Here's how the 17 most popular single-engine retractables stack up for the period 1972 through 1981. The numbers listed are accidents per 100,000 flight hours, the standard industry yardstick for measuring accident rates.

Cessna Skylane RG

The retractable version of Cessna's familiar Skylane didn't debut until 1978, too late for it to appear in our earlier study that covered the years 1972-1976. But the newcomer swept to the top of the chart with a

Fatal Accident Rates 1972-1981		Total Accident Rates 1972-1981	
Aircraft	Fatal Accident Rate*	Aircraft	Total Accident Rate*
1. Cessna Skylane RG	0.8	1. Beech 33 Bonanza/ Debonair	4.6
2. Beech 33 Bonanza/ Debonair	1.4	2. Beech 36 Bonanza	5.1
3. Cessna Cardinal RG	1.5	3. Beech V-tail Bonanza (S35-V35B)	5.8
4. Beech 36 Bonanza	1.5	4. Rockwell 112/114	6.5
5. Cessna P210	1.6	5. Mooney 201	6.5
6. Beech V-tail Bonanza (S35-V35B)	1.7	6. Cessna Skylane RG	6.9
7. Rockwell 112/114	1.8	7. Cessna Cardinal RG	7.8
8. Piper PA-28R Arrow	2.1	8. Piper PA-28R Arrow	8.3
9. Mooney M-20B-G	2.2	9. Mooney M-20B-G	9.6
10. Cessna 210	2.3	10. Cessna P210	9.8
11. Mooney 201	2.4	11. Beech V-tail Bonanza (35-P35)	10.7
12. Bellanca Viking	2.7	12. Piper PA-32R Lance/ Saratoga	10.7
13. Piper PA-24 Comanche	2.9	13. Bellanca Viking	11.0
14. Beech 24 Sierra	3.1	14. Mooney 231	11.1
15. Mooney 231	3.2	15. Cessna 210	11.3
16. Piper Lance/Saratoga	3.3	16. Beech 24 Sierra	12.1
17. Beech V-tail Bonanza (35-P35)	3.3	17. Piper PA-24 Comanche	15.0
*Fatal accidents per 100,000 hours		*Accidents per 100,000 hours	

sterling fatal accident rate of just 0.75 per 100,000 flight hours—nearly twice as good as the next best airplane. The Skylane RG's low fatal rate may be partly a statistical anomaly, since it has accumulated fewer hours than most of the other aircraft in the chart. But the undeniable fact is that NTSB records show only four fatal accidents in five years in a fleet of nearly 2,000 airplanes. That's a remarkable record.

The RG's total accident rate is not the best of the lot, but is still a low 6.9 per 100,000 hours. What's remarkable is the RG's low percentage of fatal accidents: four out of 37, or eleven percent. That's the lowest of any aircraft in the chart.

Our previous studies showed that, generally speaking, high-wing Cessnas have the best accident records, and the Skylane RG seems to carry on that trend. Apparently Cessna's design philosophy of low stall speed, docile stall characteristics, rock-solid handling qualities and strut-braced wings pays big safety dividends.

Cessna Cardinal RG

Cessna's retractable Cardinal also finished high in the pack with a fatal rate of 1.5 and an overall acci-

dent rating of 7.8. That's good for third place in fatals and seventh overall. Both numbers are slightly better than those for the 1972-76 period. (In fact, virtually every airplane on the list has improved its safety record substantially compared to our earlier 1972-76 study. This reflects the general trend of improving safety over the past decade; NTSB figures show a fatal accident rate for all of general aviation of 1.7 in 1983, compared to 2.7 in 1972).

Cessna 210

The big six-place 210 is the one Cessna that doesn't have an excellent safety record. In fact, the unpressurized C210 and T210 rank a dismal 15th out of 17 in fatal accidents and a mediocre tenth overall. Why the poor showing?

In an attempt to explain the 210's high accident rate, we closely examined all 210 accidents for the years 1975 and 1976 (about the middle of the 1972-1981 period for the entire study. Conclusion: Engine stoppage is the single most common cause of 210 accidents during those years (58 out of 181 accidents). About half the engine failures were mechanical problems—four crankshaft failures, for example—but the rest were fuel exhaustion or starvation. The notorious vapor lock syndrome likely played a role in the 210's high accident rate; a 1980 NTSB document cites 87 fuel starvation accidents in 200 series Cessnas through 1978, and suggests that many may be the result of vapor lock.

In-flight Breakups

Another factor may be in-flight breakups. Of the 171 fatal 210 accidents recorded during our sample period, 24 were in-flight breakups—about one in seven.

Surprisingly, the pressurized P210, widely known for numerous powerplant problems, has a good safety record in its first four years on the marketplace. Fatal rate was 1.6, number five in the rankings, and overall accident rate was 9.8, in the middle of the pack. Both are better than the standard 210's numbers.

Two cautions before we begin cheering, however: first, the P210 had only four years of exposure and 255,000 flight hours of exposure during the study period —among the lowest on our list. Therefore, the statistical validity of the number is also comparatively low. With only four fatal accidents, one more or less fatal P210 crash would have changed its rate by 20 percent. Secondly, we're aware of at least three P210 fatals in 1982 and 1983, just after the period of our study. As time goes on, it appears, the P210's fatal rate is rising from its initial very low level.

The V-tail Bonanzas

We divided the venerable Beech 35 into two categories, since it seems unwise to group a 37-year old 185-hp ''straight 35'' Bonanza with thin wing skins and an antiquated fuel system and instrument panel with a 3400-lb 285-hp 1982 V35B with radar and RNAV. A natural cutoff point seemed to lie between the 1963 P35 and the 1964 S35. With the S35 came the change to the 285-hp engine and a 175-pound gross weight increase, essentially identical to the last model V35B configuration in production.

How safe is the Bonanza? It all depends on which model you're talking about. Late models like the three shown here all show up well in our statistics, sweeping the top three positions for total accident rates and three of the top six places in fatality rates. Straight-tail 33 (rear) is best of the trio.

We were not surprised to find the huge difference in the accident rates of the 35-P35 and S35-V35B models, The answer to the question, ''How safe is the V-tail?'' immediately begs a second question: ''Are you talking about an old one or a new one?''

Old is Awful

The old V-tails have the worst fatal accident rate of any of the 17 single-engine retractables we measured. At 3.3 fatal accidents per 100,000 hours, the 35-P35 series was statistically four times more likely to have a fatal crash than the top-ranked skylane RG, and nearly twice as likely as the newer V-tails. Overall accident rate was 11th out of the 17 planes, and still nearly twice as bad as the newer Bonanzas.

Why the terrible safety record of the old V-tails? Statistics don't tell why, of course, but the old Bonanzas have several safety problems that may contribute to their high accident rate. Among them:

• In-flight breakups. The well-known V-tail breakup syndrome applies mostly (although by no means exclusively) to the older aircraft. Of the 230-odd V-tail breakups, roughly 90 percent have involved the 35-P35 models. The original 1947 35 in particular has a horrendous breakup count—about 75 in all—due primarily to the very thin wing skin, absence of a shear web on the outer portion of the wing, and very light pitch forces in that model. Of the 199 fatal accidents accumulated by the ''old'' V-tails during our study period, we estimate that about 50 were in-flight breakups.

• Fuel sloshing. Most old Bonanzas were built without baffles in the fuel tanks to prevent sloshing in turbulence, uncoordinated flight or during turning takeoffs. By 1971, the FAA had identified 16 accidents caused by fuel sloshing, and an AD was issued. Baffles were made available for retrofit, but few of the old Bonanzas have them.

• Fuel mismanagement. A 1964 CAB report on fuel mismanagement showed that the Bonanza had the second highest rate of fuel mismanagement accidents of any light aircraft that year. A later

NTSB study covering the years 1965-69 rates the Bonanza as having the highest incidence of fuel starvation among lightplanes. This is probably the result of the poor placement of the fuel selector valve in the older Bonanzas (on the cockpit floor, out of sight), which encourages some pilots to switch tanks by feel. Selector detents are poorly defined in some old models, and the fuel gauging systems are not the best.

• Stall/spin accidents. According to an earlier *Aviation Consumer* study covering the years 1965-1973, the Bonanza had the highest Stall/spin accident rate of any modern light aircraft still in production at that time. The Bonanza's stall/spin rate was triple that of the Cessna 210's in the NTSB study. (That study covered all Bonanzas, but in those days the vast majority of V-tails flying were 35-P35 models).

By contrast, the late-model 285-hp V-tails have an excellent safety record. Fatal accident rate was 1.6 per 100,000 hours, sixth best among the 17 planes in the survey, while overall accident rate was 5.8, third best of the group.

Straight-tail Bonanzas

The 33 and 36 model Bonanzas rank in the top four in terms of fatality rates, and first and second in the total accident standings. The late-model V-tail ranks third in overall accidents, making it a clean one-two-three sweep for Beech. The straight-tail airplanes virtually never break up in flight (about 24 times less often than the V-tails, according to an *Aviation Consumer* study) and most have improved fuel systems. The Straight-tail airplanes also have wider center-of-gravity envelopes than the V-tails, heavier pitch forces and improved yaw stability. All of these factors provide improved stability and handling qualities.

The Also-Rans

We studied three different types of Mooneys: the older M20B-G models (variously known as Super 21, Chaparral, Mark 21, Ranger,

The old V-tail Bonanzas have the worst fatal accident rate of all.

Statesman, etc.) and the new-generation 201 and 231, both currently in production. We should caution that the 201 and 231—particularly the latter—have a low exposure because of their newness and therefore their numbers are less certain, statistically. Also, in both cases, hours flown were estimated according to fleet ratios.

The older M-20s and the 201 showed up about average in both total and fatal accident rates. The 231,

however, ranked poorly: 15th out of 17 in fatal accidents, and 14th overall. This may well be a statistical aberration, but it might also reflect the lower reliability of the 231's Continental TSIO-360 engine compared to the four-cylinder Lycomings in the other Mooneys. The 201, incidentally, has a startlingly high ratio of fatal accidents to total. However, this may be due as much to an unexpectedly low number of non-fatal accidents as to an unusually high incidence of fatals.

The Piper Arrow, middle-of-the-roader that it is, has a nice middle-of-the-road accident rate: eighth out of 17 in both fatal and total-accidents.

The Lance's Poor Record

The other Pipers fare poorly. The PA-32R Lance and Saratoga have the second highest fatal accident rate of all, and the overall accident rate is sixth worst. The Lance

Fatality Ratio

We've also listed what we call the fatality ratio: the percentage of the total accidents that are fatal. We advise caution in the interpretation of this number, however. The fatality ratio almost certainly reflects both the severity of the typical crash and the crashworthiness of the aircraft (its ability to protect the occupants from impact and fire during the crash itself). The severity of the accident is affected by things like approach speed, (impact goes up by the square of the speed) and the way the aircraft is used. (An IFR weather crash is likely to be more serious than a primary training accident.)

But the fatality ratio may be deceptively low if one type of aircraft tends to have a lot of minor non-fatal accidents—gear-up landings, for example—which add to the accident totals but rarely hurt anybody. It's probably no coincidence that four of the top five airplanes (in terms of fatality ratio) are Cessnas that share the same basic landing gear system, a system that has had its share of problems, to put it mildly.

On the other hand, the Cardinal and Skylane RGs have lower stalling

Fatality Ratios 1972-1981
(Percentage of total accidents that are fatal)

Aircraft	Percentage Fatal
Cessna Skylane RG	11
Cessna P210	16
Cessna Cardinal RG	16
Piper Comanche	19
Cessna 210	20
Mooney M-20B-G	23
Bellanca Viking	25
Piper PA-28R Arrow	26
Beech 24 Sierra	26
Rockwell 112/114	28
Mooney 231	29
Beech 36 Bonanza	29
Beech 33 Bonanza/ Debonair	30
Beech V-Tail Bonanza (S35-V35B)	30
Piper PA-32R Lance/ Saratoga	31
Beech V-tail Bonanza (35-P35)	31
Mooney 201	37

speeds than the other airplanes on the chart, which lowers crash impact in certain types of accidents and could well generate a lower fatality ratio. And since neither of the two high-ranking Cessnas have a disproportionately large number of total accidents, we can infer no huge rash of ''cheap'' gear-up accidents.

showed up very bad in our earlier study for the years 1972-1976, but we dismissed the poor numbers because of low exposure. (The Lance had only been out one year at that point, and had just 85,000 hours of flight time.)

To see how the Lance/Saratoga SP measured up, we looked at NTSB accident records and FAA hours-flown estimates for the years 1977-1983. This time span encompasses every known PA-32R breakup (except for one that occurred early in 1984) and provides a reasonable statistical base for comparison with the 210 and Beech V-tail and conventional tail.

Worse than the Bonanza

Combining FAA hours-flown estimates and NTSB accident data, we figured the 32R's breakup rate to be 6.5 per million flight hours. Surprisingly, this is higher than the V-tail Bonanza's breakup rate (4.8) and more than twice as high as the 210's (3.3) during the same time span. The Lance/Saratoga is more than 10 times worse than the leader in this class, the straight-tailed Bonanza models 33 and 36. Only two straight-tails broke up in flight during our 1977-1983 sample period, for a rate of just 0.5.

We should point out that the total number of PA-32R breakups is not large—11 in our 1977-1983 sample period—and that the number of hours flown is small compared to that of the Bonanza and 210 (1.68

The Bellanca Viking, with the benefit of constant wing inspections and an improved fuel system design, has bettered its safety record in recent years.

million, compared to about seven million and six million for the 210 and Bonanza, respectively). Therefore, the rate figure is not as statistically significant as those for the Bonanza and 210.

The venerable Comanche ranks dead last—or worst—in total accidents and 13th out of 17 in fatals. The poor overall accident rate may be partly due to the antiquated landing gear system in the PA-24s, which result in a good number of gear-up landings. During the period 1971-1975, in fact, the Com-

In terms of total accident rate, the Piper Comanche has the most terrible record of all 17 aircraft. In fatal accidents it is merely worse than average.

anche led all single-engine aircraft with 114 gear-up accidents, according to an earlier *Aviation Consumer* study.

Beech's Sierra ranks a surprisingly bad 16th out of 17 in total accidents, and 14th in fatals. The Sierra has rather wicked porpoising tendencies and a high rate of overrun accidents, according to the 1972-76 NTSB study. *Aviation Consumer* figures also show the Sierra (along with its fixed-gear siblings, which are essentially identical aerodynamically) to have a high stall/spin accident rate.

The Bellanca Viking, while making a rather mediocre showing (12th and 13th in fatal and total rates, repectively) has at least made a big improvement from our earlier study, in which it ranked dead last in both categories. The Viking's fatal rate has improved from 4.2 to 2.7, and the total rate dropped from 16.8 to 11.0. Part of this may be due to the 1976 AD requiring inspection for wood rot in the aircraft's wing spar. Seven fatal in-flight airframe failures (most of them due to wood rot) occurred before the AD, but we're aware of only one Viking wing failure since then. (That occurred in 1983, too recently to be included in our study.)

One other factor may be the complex fuel system in older Viking; one out of four non-fatal Viking accidents is the result of fuel starvation. This is an extraordinarily high proportion. Perhaps the improved fuel systems in later Vikings is partly responsible for the lower accident rates.

Step-Up Decision: Heavy Single or Light Twin?

Analyzing the trade-offs in performance, cost and safety.

Airplane ownership is a step-up game. Start with a simple, cheap, easy-to-fly aircraft like a Cherokee or a skyhawk. As cockpit experience and bank account grow, trade up to a faster, bigger plane that demands more piloting skill and money. If you're skilled enough and rich enough, you could end up owning a Learjet some day.

Not everybody climbs to the peak of the step-up pyramid, of course. But thousands of plane owners work their way up into the middle regions, the sphere of big, fast retractable singles and light twins. With new prices currently running between $150,000 and $400,000, this class of aircraft—typified by the Bonanza, the Cessna 210, and the Piper Seneca—is the mainstay of the small business run by the hard-driving entrepreneur who likes to do the flying himself.

The step from heavy single to light twin is a perplexing one. Performance and load-carrying of the twins are usually a little better than that of the big singles. But the purchase price and operating costs are much higher. Is the bit of extra speed, range and load worth the megabucks it costs?

And then there's the question of safety. The second engine—along with the second vacuum pump and alternator—are a potent psychological crutch. But are twins really safer than singles?

And finally, there is the matter of style and status. Some pilots use their aircraft primarily to impress other people, and perhaps themselves. Ego plays a big role in aircraft sales, and there's little doubt that the twin is the better ego-massager and status symbol.

Guinea Pig Aircraft

For comparison, we've picked three single-vs.-twin matchups, one each from the Big Three manufacturers. Our task was made simpler by the parts-bin engineering philosophy of Beech and Piper, who "designed" their light twins by simply removing the engine from the nose of a well-proven

Beechcraft A36 Bonanza (top) is virtually identical to the 58 Baron (below), except for the number of engines. Price tag is half.

Baron does not hold its resale value nearly as well as the A36. A four-year-old 58 has lost more than $100,000 in value.

single-engine model and grafting a pair of motors onto the wings. In these cases, precise single-vs-twin comparisons are easy.

For Beech's pair, we selected the Bonanza A36 and 58 Baron, virtually identical airplanes except for the number of engines. Piper's Turbo Saratoga SP and Seneca III are also virtually identical except for the engine count.

Cessna has no such derivative twin, so we selected the Turbo 210 and the T-303 Crusader for comparison.

Purchase Price

Generally speaking, a light twin has a list price anywhere from half again to double that of a comparable single. For example, a 1985 Piper Seneca lists for about $270,000, compared to $190,500 for a Turbo Saratoga. That's a 42 percent difference.

A 1985 Beech A36 Bonanza goes for $246,000; a new 58 Baron lists for $446,000, a whopping 81 percent increase. A 1984 Cessna Turbo 210 went out the door at $182,000, while its stablemate light twin, the Crusader, would set you back $329,000. Difference: 81 percent.

In terms of dollars, the penalty of moving up to two engines in these examples ranges from $82,000 to $187,000, sums that would make most of us ponder.

Used Aircraft

For late-model used aircraft, the step-up penalty is less. For 1980 models of the same aircraft pairs, the cost of stepping up ranges from $10,000 to $52,000.

Oddly, the percentage step-up penalty is much smaller for the used airplanes, ranging from 23 to 66 percent in our sample pairs. (The new-plane figures ranged from 47 to 86 percent.) This suggests that the light twins tend to be overpriced when new, and depreciate more rapidly than the singles.

Take for example the Baron and the Bonanza. The 1980 Baron has re-

With nearly an identical cabin, Piper's Saratoga SP can fly nearly 200 nm farther than its Seneca counterpart.

tained 59 percent of its value, while the A36 has retained 82 percent. Both the Piper and Cessna singles in our comparison also beat their twin rivals handily in the resale value derby, 70 to 59 percent and 68 percent to 57, respectively. (Incidentally, we used the Cessna Turbo 310 rather than the Crusader in this example, since the Crusader didn't exist in 1980.)

These numbers foreshadow the answer to the central question of this article: is the extra cost of a twin worth it? In essence, the resale marketplace is saying no.

The depreciation numbers are telling us that the extra intrinsic value of a light twin doesn't justify the new-plane price difference—that the buyer of a new light twin, so hopeful and optimistic when he handed over the check to Cessna or Piper or Beech, is apparently sadder and wiser after using the airplane for a few years, and is willing to dump it at a significant loss.

On the other hand, the twin's faster loss of value can work in favor of the used-plane shopper. "I bought a 1976 Turbo 310 because it was a lot of airplane for the money," one pilot told us. "For my $60,000, I could have gotten a five-year old Mooney 201 or the 310. For me, it was no contest. The 310 can carry six people, it can fly 40 knots faster than the Mooney, and it's got radar, de-ice and dual systems. Sure, it costs more for gas

and maintenance, but I fly less than 100 hours a year, so I can manage it. And all that stuff is tax deductible anyway."

Performance

One buys an airplane, of course, to carry a load over a distance during a time. Generally speaking, a light twin climbs better, cruises quite a bit faster, hauls a bit more load, and can fly a little farther than a heavy retractable single. (See the comparison chart for details of our six example aircraft.)

Speed advantage of the twin ranges from 13 to 27 knots (we're comparing 65-percent cruise figures), and the extra engine helps get the twin up to cruising altitude sooner. On a typical 500-nm trip, the twin gets there quicker than its single-engine counterpart by anywhere from 17 to 36 minutes.

One would think that with nearly double the power, the twin would have a big advantage in load-carrying. Not necessarily so. Useful loads of our sample twins run 84 to 544 pounds higher than their single-engine counterparts. That averages out to an extra couple of people. But there's a catch.

Fuel consumption is nearly twice as high in the twin-engine airplanes, and extra fuel cuts into payload. For example, a Seneca has 345 pounds more useful load than a Turbo Saratoga SP. But to fly a 500-nm trip, the Seneca requires 128 pounds more fuel than the SP. Payload advantage is reduced to only 217 pounds—about one person and a travel kit.

The longer the trip, the smaller the payload advantage of the twin. For example, in the case of a 725-mile trip—the max for a Seneca III with tanks full—payload advantage over the Saratoga would be just 164 pounds.

The Turbo 210 can actually carry more payload than the Crusader on a longish trip. Useful load advantage of the Crusader is only 84 pounds, and on any trip longer than about 200 nm, the T210 has a *higher* payload than the gas-guzzling Crusader. On a long 750-mile trip, the T210 has a 180-pound payload advantage, enough for an extra passenger.

And of course the twin's appetite for fuel cuts into absolute range with full tanks. The Seneca, in fact, falls short of the Saratoga by nearly 200 miles. Only the Baron 58 has a significant range advantage over its single-engine counterpart.

In sum, the typical twin doesn't exactly overwhelm the heavy single in performance. On the average, if you fly a twin, you'll carry an extra passenger over the same distance and save 15 or 20 minutes.

Safety

All of these highfalutin performance numbers and economic analyses go up in smoke, however, when the pilot (or his wife) says, "You know, I'd really feel safer with two engines."

In the eyes of the general public, the simple fact that an airplane has two engines makes it safer. And most pilots agree. Yet there's been a growing debate in recent years about the safety of singles vs. twins.

It's beyond dispute that that the second engine has prevented many accidents and saved many lives when the first one quits. But what about the classic twin-engine Vmc stall/spin crash, which is virtually always fatal?

A growing school of thought believes that twins are actually more dangerous than singles if an engine quits—particularly on take-off—because of the airplane's roll/yaw tendency with an engine out. In a single, according to this line of reasoning, the pilot who suffers an engine failure will face up to the inevitable and bring the plane down to hit the ground level and under control, and perhaps walk away from it. The multi-engine pilot faced with an engine failure will make every attempt to keep flying. If he's not up to snuff, he may lose control entirely and hit the ground upside down—an event that nobody walks away from.

A 1980 NTSB study of engine-failure accidents in twins revealed that a person involved in an engine-failure crash in a twin is four times more likely to die than one who has an engine-failure crash in a single.

Crusader is only 13 knots faster than the T210. Useful load and maximum range are very close.

This debate will probably rage endlessly. But we can say one thing for sure: in terms of all accidents—not just engine-failure crashes—light twins have a better record than retractable singles. Past *Aviation Consumer* studies, based on NTSB accident records and FAA hours-flown data for the years 1972-1982, show that a representative sample of 18 popular twin-engine aircraft chalked up a combined fatal accident rate of 1.7 per 100,000 flight hours. The comparable figure for a group of 17 single-engine retractables is 2.3—about 35 percent higher.

In terms of total accidents, the rate is 6.5 for twins and 9.6 for retractable singles, an advantage for the twins of nearly 50 percent.

Single Vs. Twin Comparison

Aircraft	Equipped New Price	Equipped Used Price (1980 model)	65% Cruise Speed (kts)	500-nm Trip Time	Rate of Climb (fpm)	Equipped Useful Load (lbs)	Max Range (nm)
Beech 58 Baron	$446,000	$150,000	192	2:39	1,750	1,844	1,131
Beech A36 Bonanza	$246,000	$110,000	167	3:03	1,210	1,300	720
Piper PA-34 Seneca IV	$270,000	$84,000	175	2:55	1,400	1,708	725
Piper PA-32 Turbo Saratoga SP	$190,000	$78,000	148	3:26	1,120	1,363	895
Cessna 303 Crusader	$329,000	$160,000*	170	2:59	1,480	1,675	816
Cessna 210 Centurion	$182,000	$69,000	157	3:16	930	1,591	782

*1982 model

Singles vs. Twins Safety

Cessna Turbo 210 has a useful load very close to that of the twin Crusader.

Our sample aircraft matchups followed the overall pattern. In each case, the twin has a better record than the single. The Baron 58 beat the A36 in fatal rate, 1.1 to 1.5, and in total rate, 4.5 to 5.1. The Seneca's numbers were 1.2/5.8, compared to 3.3/14.1 for the single-engine PA-32R series. And the Cessna 310 beat the 210 by a margin of 2.0/8.3 to 2.3./11.3.

These numbers may not be precise apples-to-apples comparisons, however. Keep in mind that the pilots of twins tend to be more experienced than those who fly retractable singles. And quite a few light twins are air taxi and charter aircraft flown by professional pilots. Pilot proficiency plays a big role in accidents, so the differences may not be all due to the airplanes themselves.

And keep in mind that twins are generally better equipped than heavy singles. Weather radar, for example, is almost exclusively the province of twins, and singles as a rule have only rudimentary de-ice equipment (with the exception of the Turbo 210 and P210, which are approved for flight into known icing conditions).

To pilots who habitually fly into heavy weather, the availablity of top-quality radar and de-ice equipment in a twin is often the deciding factor in the safety equation, quite

The old Piper Apache had the worst engine-failure accident rate in an NTSB study.

apart from the question of one engine vs. two.

Until a few years ago, a twin's dual vacuum pumps and alternators were a major plus. But the recent proliferation of standby vacuum systems and alternators for singles has mooted that advantage to some degree.

NTSB Report

The 1980 NTSB report on engine-failure crashes in twins sheds some unexpected light and skewers a few sacred cows. The report's most startling conclusion, as previously mentioned, is that engine-failure crashes are four times as likely to be fatal in twins than singles.

But notice that we said engine failure *crashes*, not engine failures. The multi-engine pilot who lost a motor and cruised uneventfully

home on the other one never appears in the NTSB statistics. No one knows what proportion of engine failures end up as crashes. Half? A third? Ten percent? There simply are no such statistics.

Likewise, no one knows what percentage of engine failures in singles result in accidents. Obviously, it's going to be much higher than in twins. But some fortunate and/or skillful pilots do manage to land successfully —either on an airport or off—when the only engine aboard gives out. What this proportion is, we have no idea. But we wouldn't be surprised if an engine failure resulted in a crash four times more often in a single than in a twin. But if the twin accident is four times as likely to be fatal, as the NTSB reported, then the whole thing might be a wash.

Crash From Cruise

The NTSB report does reveal some surprising facts about engine failures in twins. First of all, the engine failure in cruising flight is not the piece of cake that most pilots believe it to be. Theoretically, it shouldn't be so difficult to shut one down and bring it home when the failure occurs in cruise, with plenty of speed and altitude in the bank. But the NTSB found that a failure in cruise was more likely to result in an accident than in any other phase of flight—even takeoff.

Used Aircraft Guide

Furthermore, the NTSB found a high correlation between engine-failure accident rate and power loading. The implication is that pilots may not be losing control of the airplane as much as they are simply unable to maintain altitude.

The twin with the worst engine-failure accident rate—by far—is the Piper Apache, which is notoriously underpowered and actually has a negative single-engine climb rate under some conditions.

Marginal Multis

But even the best single-engine climbers are very marginal. Unfortunately, this fact is almost mandated by the FAA certification regulations. The rules set down various performance standards, one of which is the ability to climb on a single engine at a certain minimum rate figured by a formula based on stall speed. (For a 75-knot stall speed, the minimum works out to about150 fpm at 5,000 feet.) Manufactureres typically use this standard as a way to set gross weight. If a plane beats the climb requirement at a certain weight, the manufacturere usually responds by raising the weight until the requirement is just barely met.

As long as useful load numbers are deemed a better selling tool than single-engine climb numbers, it's likely that every light twin you can buy will, almost by definition, have marginal single-engine climb.

The only exceptions are the souped-up conversions like the Colemill Navajo Panther, Miller Twin Comanche and various Riley mods. These aircraft have bigger engines, but the small companies that produce them are usually unwilling or unable to go through all the testing and redesign of wing and landing gear that might be necessary to raise gross weight. The result is a big safety bonus for owners: the planes climb well on a single engine because gross weight remains the same as in the unmodified airplanes.

The Safety Equation

Summing up, there is no clear

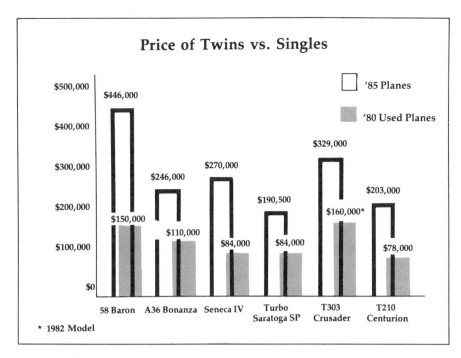

answer to the safety question in the great debate of single vs. twin. Multis definitely have a better overall accident rate (both fatal and non-fatal), but this may be due as much to better pilots and equipment as the airplanes themselves.

If an engine quits, are you better off in a single or a twin? Nobody really knows. Clearly, you're less likely to crash in a twin, but if you do crash, you're more likely to die. Our feeling is that a twin is safer than a single in the hands of a cool, skillful, practiced pilot, and less safe in the hands of a mediocre pilot.

Operating Costs

While purchase price can be precisely nailed down, operating costs can't. Certain of the expenses of running an airplane—fuel, insurance and tiedown—are fairly predictable, but maintenance costs are a maelstrom of uncertainty. An owner knows the lower limit of his maintenance costs—the price of a flat rate annual or 100-hour inspection—but there is virtually no upper limit.

Fuel costs are quite predictable, and are usually about double for the twin-engine airplanes. A Baron, for example, will burn about 30 gallons an hour, the A36 about 15. (No surprise, the engines are the same.) But the Baron will

make the trip a bit faster and therefore beat the two-to-one ratio slightly.

Over a year, assuming 300 hours of flying, the typical light twin will use about $8,000 more fuel than a comparable single. If you plan to keep the airplane a while, it adds up at a frightening rate. At current fuel prices, a retractable single or light twin may well use up its new purchase price in fuel over a busy 20-year lifetime. That adds up to a $100,000-plus advantage for the single.

Insurance costs also run about double for a twin, since they are based on hull value. One insurance broker we talked to said that a new 36 Bonanza and a 58 Baron would have about the same percentage rate for hull insurance (two percent is a typical figure), assuming that both pilots were equally qualified for their type of aircraft. Liability insurance costs for each would be about $500 per year.

So total annual premium for a new Baron would run around $8,500 per year, compared to about $5,000 per year for the Bonanza.

Hangar costs would be fairly inconsequential compared to the vast amounts spent on fuel and insurance, but the single once again has the advantage. At one suburban airport we checked, fees were

$100 per month for a single and $185 for a light twin. That's a thousand-dollar-a-year advantage for the single.

Overall, assuming 300 hours a year of flying, the predictable operating costs of a twin run about $12,500 a year higher.

Maintenance

The monster that has shredded the checkbook of many a plane owner is maintenance. On the average, over the long haul, maintenance costs can be fairly well predicted. But try consoling the owner of a P210 who needs a top overhaul after 300 hours with Cessna's predicted hourly maintenance costs. It's sort of like telling a guy who just lost his job to cheer up because the unemployment rate dropped a half a percent last month.

Aviation Consumer owner surveys illustrate the unpredictability of maintenance costs. Owners of light twins reported hourly maintenance bills ranging from $30 to $50, while retractable single owners paid $20 to $35.

The manufactures figure estimated hourly maintenance costs for most of their aircraft. Piper and Beech did not respond to our requests for information, but Cessna estimates an hourly routine maintenance cost of $17.60 for the Turbo 210 and $20.48 for the Crusader. Assuming 300 hours per year, that's an $864-a-year advantage for the single.

We must also consider engine overhaul reserve. Naturally, this cost is about double for the twin—$15 per hour for the Baron, for example, compared to $7.50 for the A36. That's another plus for the single, this time to the tune of about $2,250 per year.

So, at the very least, the typical light twin will cost about $3,000 more per year to maintain than a heavy single. Almost certainly, the real cost penalty will be higher. And the potential for the stunning financial disaster in a twin is higher, too. A gear-up landing in a

Piper Seneca fatal accident rate is less than half of the PA-32R's. Is it due to the second engine, or perhaps better pilots?

twin, for example, will require two engine teardowns instead of just one, at a cost of $5,000 to $10,000 additional.

Summing Up

If you make your buying decision on the basis of coldly rational cost-effectiveness, it looks to us like the big single is the better deal in most cases. For a small sacrifice in performance, you'll save a hundred grand or better when you buy it, suffer less depreciation loss, and save at least $15,000 a year in operating expenses. The economic argument for the single is rather persuasive.

(Tax considerations blunt the single's economic advantage in many cases. Owners of this class of

Though twins are less likely than a single to crash when an engine fails, the chance of a fatal accident is more likely. Here NASA probes the crash characteristics of an Aztec.

aircraft usually find ways to make them tax deductible. And the investment tax credit can actually produce short-term positive cash flow. Some people make an up-front profit when they buy an airplane, and the more expensive the airplane, the bigger the profit. This generous arrangement has helped to sell a lot of twin-engine airplanes.)

For overall utility, a twin equipped with first-class radar and full de-ice equipment has the edge in heavy weather. There will be occasions when the twin flies and the single stays on the ground.

In terms of safety, there's no clear choice. Twins have lower accident rates, but this may be due to better pilots as much as the airplanes themselves. In case of an engine failure, the second engine can be a mixed blessing; a crash is less likely in a twin, but more likely to be fatal if it occurs.

On the other hand, the status and ego value of a twin are very persuasive. As much as GAMA and NBAA like to tout the practical utility of business aircraft, many airplanes are bought primarily as accoutrements of success and power. To the man on the street, a Piper Seminole is probably more impressive than a Malibu.

Our recommendations: If money matters a lot, buy the single. If it doesn't, and you are a cool, skilled and practiced pilot who wants to fly in virtually any weather, or over rough terrain at night, go with the twin.

Light Twin Accident Rates

A statistical look at the real-world safety records of the most popular twin-engine general aviation aircraft.

After poring over reams of NTSB accident printouts and FAA estimates of hours-flown data, we have figured the accident rates of light and medium twins in terms of accidents per 100,000 hours.

These numbers allow apples-to-apples comparisons of competitive aircraft. One can debate the merits of centerline thrust and counter-rotating props and good handling qualities and how they affect accident rates, but our hard numbers unequivocally answer the question, "How often does this type of plane crash, and how likely is the accident to be fatal?"

Our survey in most cases covers the most recent decade for which data is available, from 1972 through 1982. Several years ago, the NTSB published accident rate data for the years 1972-76. We have updated these numbers through 1982 in most cases, to give a full decade's worth of data.

In some cases, the NTSB made bad selections of aircraft in its 1972-76 study. For example, it groups the Cessna 401, 402, 411 and 414 together. As we discovered, this can be very misleading, for the 411 has a dramatically higher accident rate than the other Cessna twins

(and all other twins, for that matter) and distorts the composite accident rates.

Therefore, we have in some cases changed the groupings for our own study. As a result, we were unable to use the 1972-76 data in those cases, and our numbers will apply only to the years 1977-82.

We have also included newer aircraft like the Beech Duchess and Piper Seminole, which didn't exist at the time of the NTSB study. Obsolete aircraft like the Twin Bonanza, Queen Air and the Aero Commander 560 and 680 were eliminated. The FAA hours-flown estimates showed that these planes flew so little that any calculated accident rate would not be statistically significant.

Winners and Losers

No clear winner emerged from our figures. A trio of cabin-class Cessnas and the Piper Seneca all had less than one fatal accident per 100,000 hours to top the fatal accident rankings. But most of the rest of the light twins weren't too far behind. There seems to be a much narrower spread between the various twins than between the single-engine retractables, where the best were four times safer than the worst. Among the twins, the best seem to be only about twice as safe as the worst.

There's one glaring exception: the Cessna 411, a cabin-class twin built in the sixties. Astoundingly, the

Piper Seneca, a favorite of commercial air taxi operators, ranks among the safest in fatal accident rates.

411 had a fatal accident rate three times higher than the next-worst twin. This is most likely due to its atrocious single-engine handling qualities. A 1981 *Aviation Consumer* study showed that the 411 had a fatal engine-failure accident rate 10 times higher than the Cessna 401, a generally similar aircraft.

We did notice one pattern. Owner-flown "step-up" twins seemed to have higher accident rates than the big iron. The Cessna 337 Sky-master, touted as a "safety" twin for step-up pilots by virtue of its center-line thrust, and the Twin Comanche ranked poorly, while the big Cessnas, the Piper Navajo and the Baron 58 all looked good. Perhaps the type of pilot and the typical mission plays a larger role in an aircraft's accident rate than the inherent safety of the design.

Improvement

General aviation accident rates have improved steadily over the years. For example, the fatal accident rate in 1972, the first year of our study period, was 2.7. By 1982, the last year of the study, the fatal rate had improved to 1.8. Keep this in mind when evaluating the accident rates of certain types for which we had data only for the 1977-82 period. Even though an airplane's accident rate declines slightly from 1972 to 1982, it may

actually be losing ground, since the rest of the field has improved even more.

The Barons

Beech's popular twins ranked about in the middle of the pack. From 1972-76, the entire Baron/Travel-Air series scored 2.8 and 8.3, respectively, for fatal and total accident rates. The same group improved to 1.4 and 5.3 in 1977-82, for overall scores of 2.0 and 6.5 for the entire decade.

We decided to separate the 58 and 55 models out of the group to see if there was a difference between the long-body 58s and their smaller forebears. The answer: not much. For the period 1977-82 only, the 58 had a low 1.1 fatal rate, while the 58 was a not-quite-so-low 1.4. The 58 also had a better overall accident rate, 4.5 to 6.4.

The Baron's accident rate might have been better without a bunch of stall/spin accident. An earlier study commissioned by *Aviation Consumer* showed that for the years 1970-74, the Baron had a much higher stall/spin rate than other light twins. In fact, about a quarter of all fatal Baron accidents during that period were stall/spins. Eliminate those, and the Baron's accident rate would improve noticeably.

The Baron stall/spin rate has apparently declined in recent years, however, as more attention has been focused on the subject and Beech has mailed Baron owners handbook supplements warning of

Beech Baron 58 had a fairly good fatality rate, somewhat better than the short-body 55 Baron.

the problem. That may be a big part of the Baron's improved accident rate during the last half of the decade.

Beech Duke

The Baron's macho big brother also showed up in the middle of the safety standings, ranking ninth out of the 17 planes in both fatal and overall accidents. Note that the Duke figures cover only the years 1974-82, and that hours flown for the years 1974-76 were projected from FAA data for later years.

Some people may be surprised at the Duke's reasonably good showing. The rich, aggressive achiever-types who typically own and fly Dukes are often blamed for the high accident rates of planes like the Learjet and MU-2, but Duke pilots seem to hold their own among their supposedly more conservative fellow pilots.

Beech 76 Duchess

The Duchess light-light twin has flown too few hours to establish a good statistical base, but we have included it anyway out of curiosity. Over 151,000 flight hours (1978-81), the Duchess has had two fatal and five non-fatal accidents, for rates of 1.3 and 4.6.

Interestingly, the Duchess's chief marketplace rival, the Piper PA-44 Seminole, has virtually identical numbers: 1.2 and 4.8. The two

planes, quite similar in design and used for the same purpose (multi-engine training) have achieved virtually identical accident rates with only a few hundred thousand flying hours beteween them.

Cessna 310

Among the "big three" classic light twins—the Baron, 310 and Piper PA-23 Apache/Aztec—the 310 ranks best by a smidgin in fatal accidents, but worst of the three in total accident rates. Comparable fatal rates for all three aircraft is so close that it hardly matters: 1.95 for the 310, 2.02 for the Baron series, and 2.12 for the PA-23s. (These numbers have been rounded off to the nearest tenth in our tables.)

In overall accidents, the Baron/Travel-Air and Apache/Aztec, at 6.5 and 6.6 respectively, lead the 310, which registers 8.3.

All three of these popular aircraft started in the 50s as low-powered four-seaters, gradually evolving into high-performance six-seaters. About 3,500 of each of them are currently flying. And each flew more than six million hours during the last decade. It seems only appropriate that each has a virtually identical fatal accident rate.

The 310, like virtually all other twins in our study, improved its accident rate as time went on. The original 1972-76 study listed the 310 fatal and total rates as 2.2 and 9.8. Our figures for 1977-82 were 1.8 and 7.1. This is probably due to better avionics, systems, pilot training and perhaps more safety awareness among pilots.

Cessna 337

Cessna's unique "push-pull" Skymaster was designed as an easy-to-fly step-up twin for single-engine pilots. The centerline thrust eliminated the deadly engine-out roll/yaw reaction that has killed hundreds of pilots who couldn't cope with engine failures in conventional twins. If an engine quits, the Skymaster keeps flying straight by itself while the pilot identiifes and feathers the prop on the failed engine. The plane may not climb heroically on a single engine (though it does better than many other twins), but at least it will go down level and under control. Theoretically, that's a lot safer.

But the statistics show that theoretical safety features don't necessarily improve accident rates in the real world. The Skymaster's fatal rate of 2.5 and total accident rate of 9.5 are both among the worst of any light twin. The fatal rate is worse than any other twin except for the awful Cessna 411. (That's like saying that the Hindenburg was a lot safer than the Titanic. Ironically, both of those famed vehicles, like the Skymaster, were touted as major advances in safety.) The Skymaster's total accident rate was 15th out of 17 planes, better only than the 411 and the Twin Comanche.

Why does the Skymaster fare so poorly? Is centerline thrust actually more dangerous than the conventional arrangement? We think not. Admittedly, in the early days, some Skymasters crashed on takeoff when the rear engine quit and the pilot didn't notice—something that couldn't possibly occur in a 310. But better pilot awareness has apparently almost eliminated this type of accident. Still, the Skymasters keep crashing. Why?

Examining this question in 1979, we analyzed a five-year rundown of accident briefs on the aircraft. A close look at the causes of the fatal accidents—29 of them, amounting to 27 percent of the total number of crashes—showed that most were unrelated to the design of the aircraft, in our opinion. The largest single accident cause was weather-related, with seven fatals. None of the pilots involved could be described as an inexperienced pilot of the type who might be expected to select the Skymaster as a safe, easy stepup twin. All were commercial pilots with instrument ratings, and four were flight instructors.

Twelve of the other fatals were a mixed bag—like gyro failure, low flying, hit wires, pilot fatigue, nose-over—that could have occurred in any twin. In three accident categories, however, fatal crashes were obviously aircraft related. There were three fatal accidents caused by loss of power on takeoff and climbout. Two of those involved failure of the rear engine—the bugaboo that haunted the "push-pull" aircraft through the years. Also, there were two fatal accidents from engine failure because of fuel exhaustion and two attributed to stall/spins.

Most of the stall/spin or mush accidents appeared unrelated to any particular aircraft deficiency. Of the two fatals, one occurred during a buzzing incident, the other was attributed to pilot fatigue. We noticed however, that surprisingly often pilots who lost just one engine were unable to bring the aircraft back to a safe landing despite operating without the handicap of assymetrical thrust.

The Cabin-class Cessnas

If the bottom-of-the-line Cessna twins have less-than-sterling accident rates, the big machines make up for it. By our numbers, the Cessna 414, 340 and 401/402 have the best fatal accident rates on our list, and the 421 is not far behind.

Overall leader is the Cessna 414, the "small-engine" version of the pressurized 421. Its fatal and total accident rates of 0.8 and 3.2 both rank the best of the 17 aircraft we studied. One word of statistical caution, however: the 414 numbers cover only eight years (1974-82) and include three years of projected hours-flown data. Oddly, the 414 suffered half of its fatal accidents in just one year, 1974. If we consider only the 1977-82 period for which we have complete hours-flown data, the 414's fatal rate is a phenomenally low 0.5.

Close behind in the fatal accident rankings is the Cessna 340, a smaller "owner-flown" pressurized twin. Again, the 340's rate is based only on the years 1977-82, since the FAA did not include the 340 in its 1972-76 study.

Accident Rate Summary 1972-1982

Accident Rate Summary 1972-1982

Aircraft	Hours Flown	Fatal Accidents	Fatal Rate*	Total Accidents	Total Rate*
Aero Commander/Rockwell 500**	665,000	14	2.13	38	5.80
Beech 55 Baron	2,514,000	37	1.47	161	6.40
Beech 58 Baron**	1,886,000	20	1.11	84	4.45
Beech 55/56/58/95	8,149,000	165	2.02	528	6.47
Beech 60 Duke	659,000	9	1.36	37	5.61
Beech 76 Duchess**	151,000	2	1.32	6	4.63
Piper PA-23 Apache/Aztec	8,598,000	182	2.12	572	6.65
Piper PA-30/39 Twin Commanche	2,766,000	58	2.09	295	10.66
Piper PA-31 Navajo	6,155,000	69	1.12	227	3.69
Piper PA-34 Seneca	4,019,000	43	1.07	213	5.84
Piper PA-44 Seminole**	337,000	4	1.19	16	4.75
Cessna 310	6,664,000	130	1.95	555	8.33
Cessna 337 Skymaster	951,000	49	2.51	186	9.53
Cessna 340**	1,202,000	11	0.92	62	5.16
Cessna 401/402**	2,170,000	21	0.96	132	6.08
Cessna 411**	185,000	14	7.56	31	16.76
Cessna 414**	1,711,000	14	0.82	55	3.21
Cessna 421	3,018,000	36	1.19	164	5.43

*Accidents per 100,000.

**Data not available for full 1972-82 period.

Light Twin Accident Rates

The Cessna 401 and 402 rank third in fatality rates with an excellent 0.9 rate. (We combined the 401 and 402 into one category. Both are non-pressurized and use the same engine; the 402 is a slightly stretched "commuter" version.) In overall accidents, the 401/402 ranks 10th out of 17. We have some confidence in the 401/402 numbers; they are based on more than 2 million flight hours. However, they cover only the period 1977-82, since the NTSB unwisely lumped the 401 and 402 together with the 411 and 414 in its 1972-76 study.

The top-of-the-line pressurized 421 ranked seventh out of 17 in fatal accidents with a 1.2 rate, and eighth in total accidents with a 5.4. Why does the 421 rate less safe than the nearly identical 414? We don't know for sure, but virtually the only difference between the two aircraft is the engines. The 421's souped-up GTSIO-520 engines have had a spotty history, and engine problems may play a role in the 421's slightly higher accident rate. The difference may also be statistical; the 421 data starts in 1972, while the 414 numbers start in 1974. Also, the 421 was introduced before the 414, so the 421 fleet is, on the average, older than the 414 fleet.

The deadly 411

Cessna's very first cabin-class 400-series twin holds the dark distinction of the worst accident rate of any twin—by far. The 411's 7.6 fatal rate is three times worse than any other twin, and the total accident rate is 50 percent worse. These numbers are so bad that, quite frankly, we would hesitate even to get into a 411.

To put things in perspective, the 411 has had 14 fatal accidents since 1977. That's double the number of fatal accidents of the 414 in the same period. Yet the 411 flew only 185,000 hours during those five years, compared to more than one million hours for the 414.

It's no big secret why: the 411 has truly awful single-engine handling qualities. Look at the size of the 411 tail and rudder in the picture

below. Compare it to the tail of the 421, which replaced the 411 after three years on the marketplace. Apparently, Cessna learned its lesson on the 411. Pilots should heed that lesson, too.

An earlier *Aviation Consumer* study showed the 411 to have a fatal engine-failure accident rate 10 times higher than the Cessna 402. In fact, nearly 10 percent of all 411s ever built have crashed after engine failures. The accidents began as soon as the 411 was introduced in 1965, and in 1969, the FAA, in cooperation with Cessna, supposedly did a complete certification review of the airplane, with special attention to single-engine handling. The FAA gave the airplane a clean bill of health, but it turns out that the FAA "evaluation" was, in our opinion, a sham, virtually made up out of thin air. Only one brief test flight was made, in gusty conditions.

Some years later, Cessna hired a test pilot to do single-engine tests in a 411. (The videotaped tests were to be used as evidence in a lawsuit against Cessna filed after the fatal engine-failure crash of a 411 in Minnesota.) The test pilot was Al White, former North American test pilot who flew the XB-70 and F-100, among other ex-

otic aircraft. White, in a carefully rehearsed intentional engine shutdown with cameras rolling, failed to feather in time and crashed ignominiously. (He was unhurt, but Cessna lost the case.)

Another test pilot hired by the plaintiff's lawyer in the same case found that rudder pressures required to keep the 411 straight at blue-line speeds were 270 pounds, nearly double the maximum allowed by FAA regulations.

The 411's engine-out problems are especially critical because the engines themselves were not very reliable. The 340-hp GTSIO-520-C Continentals were the first of the big geared engines, fearsomely complex, with a TBO of only 1,200 hours. After 20 years of refinement, the GTSIO-520s have become reasonably reliable in the current 421 models, but the 411 engine had its problems.

Complicating the picture even more are the current economics of the 411. The planes are very cheap on the used-plane market—as little as $30,000 in some cases—but the engines are horribly expensive to maintain. ($40,000 for a pair of remanufactured engines). As a result, 411s are often flown by shoestring operations that can't af-

Fatal Accident Rates 1972-1982

Aircraft	Fatal Accident Rate*
Cessna 414**	0.8
Cessna 340**	0.9
Cessna 401/402**	0.9
Piper PA-34 Seneca	1.1
Beech 58 Baron**	1.1
Piper PA-31 Navajo	1.1
Cessna 421	1.2
Piper PA-44 Seminole**	1.2
Beech 60 Duke	1.3
Beech 76 Duchess**	1.3
Beech 55 Baron**	1.5
Cessna 310	2.0
Piper PA-30/39 Twin Comanche	2.1
Piper Pa-23 Apache/ Aztec	2.1
Aero Commander/ Rockwell 500**	2.1
Cessna 337 Skymaster	2.5
Aerostar	3.8
Cessna 411**	7.6

*Accidents per 100,000 hours

**Data available for 1977-82 only

Total Accident Rates 1972-1982

Aircraft	Accident Rate*
Cessna 414**	3.2
Piper PA-31* Navajo	3.7
Beech 58 Baron**	4.5
Beech 76 Duchess**	4.6
Piper PA-44 Seminole**	4.8
Cessna 340**	5.2
Cessna 421	5.4
Beech 60 Duke	5.6
Aero Commander/ Rockwell 500**	5.8
Piper PA-34 Seneca	5.8
Cessna 401/402**	6.1
Beech 55 Baron**	6.4
Piper PA-23 Apache/ Aztec	6.6
Cessna 310	8.3
Cessna 337 Skymaster	9.5
Piper PA-30/39 Twin Comanche	10.7
Aerostar	11.1
Cessna 411**	16.7

*Accidents per 100,000 flight hours

**Data not available for entire 1972-82 period

ford to maintain the engines properly. It all adds up: a cheap old plane with expensive, unreliable engines and very poor engine-out handling qualities. Maybe it should come as no surprise that the 411, which probably should never have been certified in the first place, has the worst accident record of any twin.

Piper Seneca

The best of the Piper twins turns out to be the workhorse Seneca, which over the past decade has emerged as the runaway best-selling multi-engine aircraft. More than 2,000 are currently flying. The Seneca's 1.07 fatality rate (rounded to 1.1 in the table) is the best non-400 Cessna in the bunch, and its total rate of 5.8 ranks ninth best.

These good numbers come despite the fact that many Senecas are flown by relatively low-time pilots and multi-engine students—factors often blamed for the high accident rates of aircraft like the Cessna 337 and Piper Twin Comanche.

The Seneca's accident rates, like most other aircraft, improved over the years. For the first half of the decade, 1972-76, the PA-34 had fatal and total rates of 1.5 and 10.0. For the 1977-82 time span, the numbers were 1.1 and 5.8. Unfortunately, neither the NTSB nor the FAA distinguishes between the original Seneca and the improved Seneca II and III, which have better handling but less reliable turbocharged engines.

Piper Navajo

The venerable PA-31 Navajo series ranks just behind the Seneca in fatal accidents, with a fine 1.12 rate. The Navajo's total accident rate is a superb 3.7, second only to the Cessna 414. The Navajo is one of the few aircraft that didn't improve its accident rate as the decade went on; first-half and second-half crash numbers were virtually identical.

The NTSB didn't sort out accidents for the pressurized PA-31P Navajo, a rather different airplane altogether. Nor did the FAA distin-guish the P-Navajo in its hours-flown estimates, so were unable to come up with a separate number for the P-model.

Twin Comanche

The PA-30 and PA-39, still adored for their speed, efficiency and quiet, show up poorly in the accident statistics. The Twin Comanche's 2.1 fatal rate and 10.7 total rates rank 14th and 16th out of the 17 airplanes. The Twin-C is known for two safety problems: stall/spins and botched landings. The stall/spin accidents began occurring in the mid-60s when the Twin Comanche became popular for multi-engine training. Numerous fatal stall/spins occurred during Vmc and engine-out maneuvers. It turns out that Piper's Vmc number was hopelessly optimistic, and the FAA later raised it from 80 mph to 90. Piper also came out with an anti-spin retrofit mod, but few have been put into service.

The Twin Comanche's landing problems are well-known to anyone who flies the plane. A NASA team that evaluated the PA-30B (among other aircraft) in 1966 noted the Twin Comanche's nose-high attitude (with all three gear planted on the ground) caused pilots to land nosewheel first and to porpoise excessively. Takeoffs were also criticized for the same wheelbarrow tendency unless the aircraft was horsed off below Vmc. An old CAB report also noted that the Twin Comanche had a landing

Twin Comanche has superb reputation for speed and efficiency, but its accident record is discouraging.

The Cessna 411 has by far the worst accident rate of any twin. The main reason is extremely poor single-engine handling coupled with fairly unreliable engines.

overshoot rate triple that of the Bonanza, and suggested that the Piper's hopelessly optimistic handbook landing distances might have been to blame for giving Twin Comanche pilots a false sense of confidence.

Combine these factors with the Twin Comanche's rather crotchety landing gear system, and we have the formula for lots of non-fatal gear-up landings, hard landings and overshoots. This may account for this twin's unusually high number of non-fatal accidents —worse than any other airplane except the notorious Cessna 411.

Piper PA-23 Apache/Aztec

Piper's most popular twin ranks 15th out of 17 in fatal accident rates, but is only marginally worse than its historical rivals, the 310 and Baron. In total accidents, the PA-23 ranks 13th, just behind the Baron series, but well ahead of the Cessna 310.

Unfortunately, neither the FAA nor NTSB distinguished between

the Apache and the Aztec versions of the PA-23. (The difference is considerable; early Apaches had 150 hp, while late Aztecs were equipped with turbocharged 250s.) The previously mentioned NASA study of handling qualities had harsh criticism for the Apache it tested. At aft c.g., the Apache was determined by NASA to have neutral stability in the approach configuration—a very dangerous state of affairs, particularly in IFR conditions. NASA called the trait "unacceptable."

An NTSB study a few years ago of engine-failure accidents in twins showed that the Apache had an engine-failure accident rate about twice as high as the other aircraft studied. (The 411, incidentally, was not individually analyzed in that study.) Since the Apache is known for benign engine-out handling qualities and marginal (if not negative) single-engine climb rates, the NTSB concluded that power loading was perhaps more important in avoiding engine-failure accidents than good handling qualities.

PA-44 Seminole

As in the case of the Duchess, the Seminole has flown too few hours to reach any grand conclusions about its safety record, but it's interesting to note that the Seminole's numbers are virtually identical to those of the Duchess. The little Piper ranks eighth out of 17 in fatal accident rates, and fifth in total accidents.

The Cessna Skymaster, touted as an easy-to-fly step-up twin, nevertheless has a high accident rate. Most surprising is poor record of landing safely with an engine out.

Aerostar

We were particularly curious about the accident rate of the sleek, unorthodox Ted Smith design that was taken over by Piper a few years back. The Aerostar has had more than its share of safety problems, most of them well-documented in these pages. Fuel system idiosyncracies caused nearly a dozen crashes before the FAA issued a series of ADs in 1978. Since then, the fuel-related accidents have died out. But we had noticed what seemed like an unusually high number of Aerostar accidents over the years, particularly engine-out stall/spins and engine fires. But we had nothing more to go on than a gut feel that the Aerostar was having a lot of accidents; without a full NTSB accident count combined with an FAA hours-flown esti-

Best fatal and total accident rates were chalked up by the Cessna 414.

mate, no assessment of the Aerostar's overall safety was possible.

Unfortunately, it looks like that assessment will have to wait. The FAA, for some reason, made hours-flown estimates only for the Aerostar 600 series, the original non-turbocharged version that appeared in 1969. The turbocharged 601 and the pressurized 601P and 602P, however, account for most of the Aerostar hours flown.

And, frankly, the FAA hours-flown numbers for the 600 look a little suspicious. For example, in 1977, the FAA estimates the Aerostar 600 flew 137,000 hours. The next year, the figure plummeted to 64,000. That doesn't make any sense. In 1978, the FAA had listings for both the "Smith 600" and the "Piper 600, with no explanation of the difference, if any, between the two.

Faced with these uncertainties, and with the prospect of energetic controversey between Aerostar critics and supporters, we decided it was simply impossible to give the Aerostar a fair shake with currently available data. However, we hope to pursue the Aerostar's mysterious hours-flown numbers through the bowels of the FAA bureacracy. If that doesn't work, we'll try to come up with an hours-flown estimate of our own, based on the number of Aerostars in service and FAA estimates of the average number of hours flown each year by each aircraft.

SINGLE-ENGINE
FIXED GEAR
TWO-PLACE

Piper Tomahawk

Piper's PA-38 Tomahawk trainer is one of the very few "clean sheet of paper" designs of the last decade. Most Tomahawks are of course operated by flight schools, but the Tomahawk fleet is now beginning to age, and more and more of them are coming onto the used-plane market.

The 1981 model had some minor refinements, including larger tires.

It's an economical little two-place sport and traveling machine with a lot of good features and a distinct personality, but questions about quality control and stall/spin characteristics deserve close study by any potential buyer.

History

The Tomahawk first appeared in 1978, amid a great burst of Piper hoopla and carefully orchestrated "surprise." It was intended to be a replacement for the venerable Cherokee 140, which was a fine trainer, but too big, powerful and inefficient to do the job economically for Piper flight schools, who found their rental rates undercut several dollars per hour by the smaller, cheaper Cessna 150. Piper made much of the fact that it had surveyed hundreds of flight instructors to find out what they really wanted in a trainer. The Tomahawk was supposedly the answer to their prayers.

There have been very few major design changes over the years. Paint job aside, only an expert could tell a 1977 Tomahawk from a 1982 model. But there have been many important mechanical changes, virtually all of them the result of early problems. Because of this, a Tomahawk shopper should try to get the latest serial number he can.

The 1981 model year got the "Tomahawk II" name, as if to suggest a whole new generation of airplanes, but the improvements

were mostly cosmetic and convenience changes. Perhaps the only significant change came in 1979, when a second set of stall strips was added to the wing in an attempt to tame the airplane's rather squirrelly stall. But the stall strips may be retrofitted, so there is no particular reason not to buy a two-strip airplane.

Resale Market

The Tomahawk had an unusual pattern of production. Because of pent-up demand by Piper dealers, a torrent of Tomahawks flowed out of Piper's Lock Haven plant during the 1978 and 1979 model years—nearly 2,000 aircraft in all. Then, in 1980, the torrent suddenly slowed to a trickle, and only a few hundred were built after 1979. So most Tomahawks on the used market will be '78 or '79 models.

Because of certain problems that we'll get into later—and of course because of the terrible market for single-engine planes in general—now is a buyer's market for the PA-38. "The Tomahawk market is lousy," according to one broker we talked to. "They're very difficult to sell." "Bluebook" retail value of a 1978-79 Tomahawk in 1985 is $9,000 with average equipment—about $2,000 less than a comparable Cessna 152. But a buyer should be able to do better than that.

Because the Tomahawk is a flight school airplane, some good deals

may be had. A school may be renewing its fleet and put up half a dozen used Tomahawks for sale at once. Or you may find a flight school in financial distress that would be happy to unload a Tomahawk or two for some quick cash. But on the other hand, there are few things harder on an airplane than long-term flight-school duty. Thousands of student pilot landings and repeated pattern work take their toll on both airframe and engine.

Performance

The Tomahawk's performance is typical of most two-seaters. It'll cruise along at a modest 90 knots or so, burning about six gallons of fuel per hour. That's close to 17 nmpg, and about as good as the vaunted Mooney 201. Fuel capacity is 30 gallons, good for about four hours at moderate power, with reserves, so a range of up to 350 nm is possible. While this may seem piddling to pilots of bigger, faster airplanes, it is not bad for a production two-seater.

The Tomahawk has a good rate of climb, thanks to its efficient high-aspect-ratio wing. In side-by-side tests, *The Aviation Consumer* found that the Tomahawk smartly out-climbed both the Cessna 152 and Beech Skipper. Since two-place airplanes quite often take off at or near gross weight, climb perform-

ance can be critical. In this respect, the Tomahawk stacks up well—although on hot days at high altitudes, climb performance will be marginal.

Cockpit and Cabin

The Tomahawk is quite roomy for a two-seater. The cockpit is 42 inches wide, just as wide as the four-place Arrow series and five inches wider than the notoriously cramped Cessna 152.

Getting in and out of the Tomahawk is somewhat awkward, but still better than most two-placers. One must step over a rather high door sill. Each door has two latches, like the Cherokee. Because of poor quality control, door closing and sealing has been a problem.

The Tomahawk panel is excellent, although utilitarian. A huge three-position fuel selector lever dominates the panel, with the selector lever pointing directly to the gauge of the tank selected. This is a fine safety feature. Some pilots may find the throttle and mixture controls awkward because of the odd angle of travel.

Visibility is one of the best features of the airplane. The view is superb in all directions, but particularly over the nose. The cowling sits just on the horizon during a normal climbout, allowing full forward vision.

The interior appointments are in our opinion a bit chintzy, particularly in older aircraft. Compared to, say, the Beech Skipper, the Tomahawk seems crude and Spartan indeed.

Tomahawk (left) is virtually indistinguishable from its rival, the Beech Skipper.

Handling Qualities

We previously alluded to the Tomahawk's handling qualities by saying it had a "distinct personality." Either you like the way it flies or you don't. The Tomahawk's T-tail, a styling gimmick designed to fit Piper's grand plan for a full line of flashy T-tail airplanes, has some effect on the Tomahawk's handling qualities.

On the takeoff roll, the elevator is useless until about 30 knots because it is up out of the propeller blast. When the tail does take hold, it does so suddenly, and it's possible to overrotate on takeoff. Because the tail had to be big enough to rotate the plane at a reasonable speed without prop blast, it is very powerful—perhaps too powerful—at flying speed. Pitch control is very sensitive, and it's easy to overcontrol, particularly in the landing flare. However, most Tomahawk pilots like the powerful pitch control once they get used to it.

Rudder control is also very powerful and sensitive. On takeoff, very sure feet are required to roll absolutely true down the runway. In the air, the yaw stability is not very good. A bump of turbulence sets the tail wagging much like a V-tail Bonanza.

In contrast to the strong, sensitive pitch and roll control, the ailerons are rather slow and stiff. In this respect, the Tomahawk is not a well-harmonized airplane. (Compare the Grumman American

AA-1 series, which is light and sensitive in all three axes.)

Trim stability of the Tomahawk is excellent. If you trim it to 70 knots, and take your hands off, it will stay at 70 knots through all manner of power and flap adjustments. The trim system in the 1978 and 1979 models, however, is poorly set up. One pilot told us his Tomahawk could not be trimmed to approach speed—a rather startling drawback. Others complain that too much trim-wheel rolling is needed once the Tomahawk levels out in cruise flight. Another reported the trim system springs wore out, and that "even with the trim rolled all the way back, you couldn't fly hands off for even a moment without going into a nose dive."

The Tomahawk's flaps are not the big "barn-door" altitude-killers of

Read 'Em and Weep: Tomahawk ADs

The Piper Tomahawk has compiled an atrocious AD record. At one time or another, virtually all of the airplane's major systems and/or subassemblies have been targeted by Airworthiness Directives (some sweeping, some affecting only a limited run of serial numbers). In considering any prospective purchase, a Tomahawk buyer would do well to check the effectivity of the following ADs:

A.D.	Subject
78-22-1	rudder beefup
78-23-4	wing spar
78-23-9	control wheels
78-25-1	Slick mag coils
78-26-6	vertical fin spar
79-3-2	rudder hinge
79-8-2	stabilizer bolts
79-13-8	Airborne vacuum pumps
79-17-5	ground wire to instruments
79-18-5	ELT
80-06-5	mag impulse coupling
80-11-9	landing gear attach bolts
80-22-13	rudder hinge bracket
80-25-2	valve pushrods
80-25-7	Stewart-Warner oil cooler
81-16-5	mag coil
81-18-4	oil pump
81-23-7	engine mounts
82-2-1	aileron balance weights

the Cessna 150, but they allow a pretty good sink rate and lower approach speed by about eight knots. The flaps are manual, which allows quick, positive control and promises low maintenance costs. Maximum flap extension speed is only 80 knots, however.

The Tomahawk's rather sensitive "twitchy" handling springs partly from Piper's philosophy that a trainer should not be *too* forgiving and easy to fly, lest the student never learn from his mistakes. Later on, goes the teaching theory, the student will be more prepared to handle heavy high-performance aircraft that are not so forgiving as trainers like the Cessna 150 or Cherokee 140.

That philosophy may be fine for student pilots, but it makes little sense for the owner/pilot who simply wants to fly his Tomahawk as comfortably and smoothly as possible. Sensitivity to torque effect or adverse yaw has no saving graces for the non-student pilot.

Stall Spin

One of the Tomahawk's "distinct" traits is its stall and spin characteristics. The airplane has a sharp-breaking stall that can easily develop into a spin. Recovery from the spin demands quick, decisive and forceful pilot action. Once again, there are two schools of thought on the subject: one says a trainer *should* "bite" the student when he makes a mistake so that he will not make the same mistake in the future; the other camp says training airplanes should be forgiving and gentle because neophyte pilots are more likely to get into unintentional stalls and/or spins. But once again, the "let 'em learn the hard way" philosophy has no

Tomahawk panel is well laid out and features an easy-to-use fuel selector.

merit for the owner-pilot who wants to fly safely, not learn lessons for the future.

The Tomahawk stall/spin question took on new urgency after a rash of fatal stall/spin accidents, three in the state of Alabama alone during one four-month period several years ago.

We believe the Tomahawk's stall and spin characteristics are too unpredictable to justify the "scare the pants off the students so they'll make the mistake only once" philosophy. Instructors as well as students have been killed in Tomahawk stall/spin crashes.

The 1978 and 1979 models, which had a single stall strip on the outboard section of the wing, seem to have especially unpredictable stall traits. A former Piper engineering test pilot who flew Tomahawks to check their landing characteristics said he found no two that stalled alike. Some dropped the left wing sharply, others the right. Some dropped 30 degrees, some 60, some 90. (The maximum allowed

by certification regulations is 15 degrees.) Some rolled inverted.

After serial number 1400, a second set of stall strips was added in an attempt to moderate the Tomahawk stall. (This action by Piper reportedly came after a big Florida flight school refused to accept delivery of the fleet of Tomahawks it had ordered because the stall was too violent.) The new stall strips increased stall speed by about four knots and lengthened takeoff and landing distances. The new strips may be retrofitted to older Tomahawks at a cost of about $25, plus an additional $100 or so for a new airspeed indicator to reflect the higher stall speed. However, even the four-strip airplane is not exactly docile in the stall. We're aware of one flight school that will not teach stalls in the Tomahawk—even the four-strip models.

Spins

If a Tomahawk does accidentally get into a spin after a stall, the pilot is in for an interesting ride, to put it mildly. Piper made a big point of the fact that the Tomahawk was certified for spins, and flight instructors cheered when they first heard the news. But the Toma-

Cost/Performance/Specifications

Model	Year	Number Built	Average Retail Price*	Cruise Speed (kts)	Rate of Climb (fpm)	Gross Weight (lbs)	Useful Load (lbs)	Fuel (gals)	Engine	TBO (hrs)	Overhaul Cost
PA-38-112	1978	821	$ 8,500	108	718	1,670	540	30	112-hp Lyc. O-235-L2C	2,000	$5,500
PA-38-112	1979	1,179	$ 9,000	108	718	1,670	540	30	112-hp Lyc. O-235-L2C	2,000	$5,500
PA-38-112	1980	189	$12,000	108	718	1,670	540	30	112-hp Lyc. O-235-L2C	2,000	$5,500
PA-38-112	1981	173	$15,500	108	718	1,670	540	30	112-hp Lyc. O-235-L2C	2,000	$5,500
PA-38-112	1982	NA	$19,000	108	718	1,670	540	30	112-hp Lyc. O-235-L2C	2,000	$5,500

* Includes navcom, VOR, marker, transponder, gyros, lights, 900 hours on engine, all ADs complied. Wholesale prices approximately 20 percent less.

hawk is no Cub in a spin. It winds up quickly in a steep nose-down attitude. More importantly, quick and correct pilot action is required to recover from the spin. Full forward movement of the yoke—not just release of back pressure—and full anti-spin rudder is required for recovery. (Some other aircraft must be held *into* a spin, and will come out quickly if the controls are released. Not so with the PA-38.)

Once the pilot has reacted quickly and correctly to the spin, the Tomahawk will continue for one to two turns before it recovers. Altitude loss in a one-turn spin can be 1,000-1,500 feet, according to the Tomahawk manual. There is also what Piper calls a "very steep, fast spin mode." If recovery procedure is incorrect or delayed, the spin winds up tighter. This can disorient the pilot, according to Piper. (Incidentally, the expanded handbook description of spins, including the info about the steep, fast spin mode, did not appear until April, 1981. Handbooks issued before that contained a much more cursory discussion of spins. We'd advise any potential Tomahawk buyer to get a copy of the updated manual.)

Production Problems

We could write a book about the Tomahawk's AD history and quality control problems, but we'll try to be mercifully brief. Several factors bear on the problem. Among them:

• Piper apparently believed price was a big factor in its sales battle with the Cessna 152. As a result, the Tomahawk was designed to be as economical to build as possible. (Uncharitable types might prefer the word "cheap" or "chintzy.")

• The Tomahawk prototype had been built and certified at Piper's Vero Beach, Fla. plant. But Piper decided to manufacture the plane in Lock Haven, Pa. Tools, jigs, and paperwork were transferred to Pennsylvania, but a good deal of Tomahawk expertise stayed in Florida. Also, the Southern Region FAA people who shepherded the airplane through certification couldn't afford to send anyone

Aircraft Resale Value Chart

Piper Tomahawk

'80 Tomahawk

'78 Tomahawk

$/M: $25,000 — $20,000 — $15,000 — $10,000 — $ 5,000 — 0

Year: '78 '79 '80 '81 '82 '83 '84 '85

north to watch over the Tomahawk production startup. In Lock Haven, both the Piper and FAA people charged with building the Tomahawk had to learn a lot very quickly.

• Piper built a whole bunch of Tomahawks very fast those first two years—about 2,000 aircraft in all. That's the most airplanes of one type Piper has built in such a short time since the great Cub-building spree of 1946. There was little time to work out the inevitable production-line bugs and get the production people on the front side of the learning curve.

• Piper had to hire hundreds of new production workers all at once, and in the great rush to churn out Tomahawks, we believe it's very likely that many of the rookie

In many early model Tomahawks, the doors are poorly sealed. The result can be difficult latching and a noisy cabin.

plane-builders did a lot of on-the-job learning.

• Piper's internal system of engineering-audit flight testing apparently broke down, and many Tomahawks went out the door without being checked carefully. (In some cases, horizontal tail bolts were found loose on brand-new aircraft.) The plan was for the engineering test pilots to fly the first five Tomahawks off the line, and a random sampling of aircraft thereafter. But the production people didn't deliver a Tomahawk to the engineering department for an audit flight until more than 100 airplanes had been shipped out, and only sparsely thereafter.

The Tomahawk seems to have been a classic case of an airplane that was designed to be cheap, rushed into production too fast, and not checked carefully enough before delivery. The results were predictable: a rash of ADs, service bulletins and quality control problems that have tainted the Tomahawk's reputation to this day.

The AD Parade

The first Tomahawks came off the line in February, 1978, and it didn't take long for the AD notes to start piling up. In four years, the PA-38 accumulated 19 ADs, a very high number. And 12 of the 19 concerned airframe problems resulting directly from poor design or quality control. (The other seven were engine and accessory ADs—oil pump, ELT, vacuum pump, oil cooler, etc.—that applied to many other airplanes as well.) Virtually every major piece of the airframe—fuselage, wing, ailerons, fin, rudder, stabilizer, landing gear and engine mount—were hit by ADs.

The fall of 1978 was a particularly bad time for Tomahawks (and their owners). Five major ADs came in a two-month period, including one that grounded the fleet for a month. At about the same time Piper issued a massive 20-page service letter (euphemistically labeled "Tomahawk Product Refinement Program") that listed 16 different service problems. Among them: loose carpeting in the cockpit and baggage compartment, backwards seatbelt bolts, leaky doors, loose spinner rivets, reversed oil cooler shroud clamps, cracked landing gear fairings, leaky fuselage, balky heater, etc. You get the picture. Obviously, before buying a PA-38, one should have a knowledgeable mechanic carefully check compliance with all ADs.

One AD in particular deserves mention. Directive 81-23-7 requires 50-hour inspections of the engine mount for cracks. (The mounts had begun cracking back in '78 and a

Piper service letter recommended reinforcing them. That didn't work.) But the mount must be replaced at 1,000 hours in any case. Flight schools have found the engine mount AD to be an expensive nuisance. "You'd be surprised how many Tomahawks get put on the market with around 950 hours on them," one flight school operator told us.

Another potentially expensive service problem is the trim system. Updated trim wheel assemblies cost about $200 plus labor, according to Piper service letter 865. Other Tomahawk service bulletins that have not been turned into ADs deal with binding rudder fairings and jamming control wheels (S.B. 661).

If you get a Tomahawk with all ADs and service bulletins complied, maintenance costs should be reasonable. The plane is very simple, with excellent engine access and many interchangeable parts.

Like the rest of the late-model two-seat training fleet that uses the Lycoming O-235-L2C engine, the Tomahawk is very susceptible to lead fouling of the spark plugs. In extreme cases, this can cause engine failures; at best it will increase maintenance costs. Operat-

Low light in this photograph shows uneven wing skin—a possible contributor to the airplane's unpredictable stall characteristics.

ors should be careful to lean at all times below 75 percent power, particularly on the ground. The use of TCP anti-fouling additive also helps.

Safety

Overall, the Tomahawk seems to have a good safety record. According to statistics compiled by our sister publication, *Aviation Safety*, the Tomahawk had a lower accident rate than the Cessna 152 during the 28 months after the introduction of each airplane. The Tomahawk's fatal accident rate was about 16 percent lower than the Cessna 152, and its total accident rate about 38 percent lower.

One Owner's Maintenance Summary 1981 Tomahawk

Date	Descriptiion	A/C Time (hrs)	Labor Cost	Parts Cost	Amount Covered by Warranty	Running Total Cost
8/31/81	50 hr. #1 ignition lead	54	$ 36.92	$ 25.34	$ 86.95	$ 62.26
8/24/81	548-097 clock	73			$ 66.98	$ 62.26
8/26/81	77781-03 housing	77			$440.19	$ 62.26
9/8/81	100 hr.	105	$207.00	$ 38.67	$307.93	
9/28/81	50 hr.	148	$ 45.00	$ 25.60		$ 378.53
10/7/81	548-581 turn cord	160			$246.20	$ 378.53
10/14/81	61906-002 Ind.	164			$142.09	$ 378.53
11/4/81	100 hr.	200	$300.60	$ 71.16		$ 750.29
11/17/81	77519-02 guide	220	$ 18.00	$ 45.48		$ 813.77
1/14/82	100 hr.	299	$140.40	$ 32.52		$ 986.69
2/15/82	50 hr. linings	353	$ 54.00	$ 35.71		$1,076.40
3/8/82	100 hr.	405	$126.00	$ 47.14		$1,249.54
3/23/82	L&R tires	432	$ 48.60	$ 80.24		$1,378.38
4/5/82	50 hr.	450	$ 54.00	$ 21.75		$1,454.13
4/14/82	misc.	466	$ 48.60	$ 12.10		$1,514.83
4/23/82	492-022 valves	473	$ 9.00	$ 5.60		$1,529.43
5/10/82	100 hr.	493	$229.50	$ 30.95		$1,789.88
5/28/82	clean plugs	533	$ 25.20	$ 5.60		$1,820.68
6/11/82	landing light	550	$ 9.14			$1,829.82
6/28/82	annual	595	$107.92	$162.00		$2,099.74

Piper Tomahawk

As we mentioned, however, the Tomahawk has a special problem with stall/spin accidents. By mid-1982, the Tomahawk had a total of 19 fatal accidents, nine of which were stall/spins. That is an extraordinarily high percentage of fatal stall/spins. Mechanical problems have triggered several fatal Tomahawk crashes. Both the magneto coil and engine pushrod ADs were spurred by accidents, not by inspections or mechanics' reports.

Owner Comments

Concerning your Tomahawk survey, we have operated five PA-38s in our flight academy since they were first introduced. In fact, I believe we had the first "fleet" order of four aircraft placed with Piper Aircraft. Outside of the initial mag problems, the little machine has performed like a champ! Visibility, particularly in the pattern, is absolutely outstanding—a major flight safety issue when you fly thousands of hours a month as we do. The airplane is a fine "teaching aid," i.e., you must learn to use rudder, ailerons, and elevators to fly the machine well—you *cannot* flop around and get the job done as one can in some other trainers. It develops a better pilot.

Maintenance-wise, the PA-38 performs well, particularly the engine, gear and tires, and electronics. We can run a 100-hour inspection in about eight man-hours at an average cost of $250-$300.

There are a few glitches: the original carpeting was cheap and came unsecured rather quickly, the door latches were a bit "Mickey Mouse" and required replacing—otherwise, no problems.

All in all, I consider the airplane to be a major improvement over our previous trainers; i.e., the Cherokee 140 and Cessna 150/152. In fact, the Tomahawk blew the Cessnas right off our line. Once our students got a little PA-38 time, they would not fly the 150s, which soon departed. It is a comfortable, fun-to-fly machine, and certainly the safest trainer in our experience.

Jack Doub
H&D Aviation
Terre Haute, Ind.

The biggest problem I've found is the lack of a genuine trim tab system. They have a cheap, and less effective spring-load assist, and after a year or two the springs apparently weaken so that even with full aft trim one can't fly hands-off for even a moment without doing a nose dive. The plane isn't very stable in the lateral axis, either—perhaps a good thing for a student.

The noise level is awfully high, especially in view of the low performance level. It is so light and the elevator so responsive that one can delay a flare until the last moment; thus a student may not develop a proper respect for a high sink rate that might be more characteristic of a higher performance plane, such as the earlier Cherokees.

The abrupt pitch-down in stall-spin is a great "gut" test of a student's cool; however, for serious spin training perhaps it would have to be supplemented by a "flatter" type reaction plane. The nose steering is awfully sensitive.

On the positive side, first is the marvelous Piper mechanical flaps. The handle is right there beside either pilot, one can feel the clicks and never has to look down at an indicator. And you can control the rate up or down as desired, unlike electric flaps. I assume they are even more service-free than electrics. I love my '77 Mooney 201, but would pay extra to have the Piper flap system in it.

The visibility is great—much better than in the wider Cherokee, and better than in the 172, where the wing blocks the view everywhere except down and forward. The panel layout and fuel controls are excellent. I like the throttle quadrant; however a student transitioning to a more complex plane like my Mooney Ranger or an early Bonanza would have to discipline himself to look harder for items, especially in fuel management. Having full access to the engine with the removable cowling is excellent.

I'm a private pilot, 360 hours, and took my first lesson in a Tomahawk at San Diego Montgomery Field. I did most of my training in a Cherokee 140 since it was a bit more like a heavier "real" plane. I returned to the Tomahawk for spin training and have about 15 hours in it. While doing instrument training at Vero Beach (Flight Safety), I found most of the students liked the Tomahawk well enough, and the instructors felt it was a good teacher, though the older instructors preferred to ride in the 140s.

Bill Greenwood
Aspen, Colo.

I just finished training as a student pilot using a Tomahawk.

Pros: 1) It forced me to fly since it was very sensitive to changes in attitude.

2) Comfortable seating.

3) Good visibility.

Cons: 1) Sometimes the plane would not start even though the engine was well maintained. On two occasions, I had to cancel my lesson and once (for a X-C) we used a Warrior, because the Tomahawk would not start. The mechanic kept the plugs clean and checked and re-checked the engine. They never could figure out the cause of the starting failure.

2) The T-tail makes pre-flight check of the elevator very difficult.

3) Not very stable in up/down drafts.

Curt J. Firestone
Ukiah, Calif.

28

Cessna 152

Sleek and shiny, with good manners aloft, and designed to digest 100LL with ease, the Cessna 152 was to have been Cessna's ultimate improvement on the ultimate trainer—the venerable 150. But alas, a panoply of mechanical gremlins, plus high parts prices and high acquisition cost (not to mention one of the worst recessions ever to hit the U.S. aviation industry) sent new-152 sales into a screaming spiral dive just three years after the model's introduction. The used market, as a result, now draws from a vast reservoir of late-vintage Cessna 152s—many available at fire-sale prices.

Whether a used 152 represents a true bargain is another question. For the owner willing to live with 100-knot cruise speeds, frequent bouts with lead fouling, and relatively expensive (for a trainer) annual inspections, a several-year-old Cessna 152 can provide a reasonable modicum of performance and utility in the $7,000-$17,000 "sport plane" category. But the prospective 152 purchaser who thinks he's merely getting a modernized, "improved" Cessna 150 may need to think again. A fancy 150, the 152 is not.

History

"Operators of the 150 told us they wanted a training airplane that would burn 100-octane fuel, while producing lower noise levels, better fuel consumption and more payload," Cessna's Bob Lair remarked at the time of the 152's debut in spring of 1977. What operators got was an airplane that was—and is—subject to severe lead fouling, while delivering performance about equal to that of the Cessna 150—at a cost that made

some operators wince. The original 1978 Cessna 152 (introduced in May 1977) listed at $20,635 with Nav Pac.

In changing from the 150 to the 152, Cessna gave its trainer a 110-hp Lycoming engine (with 2,000-hr. TBO) to replace the previous 100-hp Continental (1,800-hr. TBO); a McCauley "gull wing" propeller; an oil cooler as standard equipment; a 28-volt electrical system; and flaps limited to 30 degrees (instead of the previous 40). For all these changes, the 152 owner got 40 pounds more useful load than was available in the original 1958 Cessna 150 (and about 60 pounds *less* than a 1948 Cessna 140 could carry).

After 1978, relatively few important model changes were made to the basic 152. Those that *were* made point to the original airplane's mechanical shortcomings, some of which were quite notable.

In the 1979 model year, for example, Cessna incorporated impulse couplings on both magnetos—rather than just the left one, as before—to improve the 152's conspicuously lousy starting characteristics. (Likewise, direct priming to all four cylinders was made standard.) In addition, a split cowl nose piece was conjured up (retrofittable under a service bulletin), to

Darling of the flight-school circuit, the 152 sold in prodigious numbers on its initial introduction in 1978. (A 1978 model is shown here.) Subsequent models have seen few outward changes, but many internal ones. The fleet now numbers in excess of 6,300. Production was halted for a while in 1985.

enable shops to remove the whole cowling without first taking off the plane's propeller. (If you intend to buy a '78 model, be sure it has this feature.) An improved brake master cylinder, with fewer parts, first made its appearance on 1979 models.

In 1980, again addressing the airplane's poor startability, Cessna went to a slower-turning starter (the applicable armature is retrofittable under Service Letter SE79-43), which allowed the impulse couplings to do their job better; and the plane's float carburetor got an accelerator pump as standard equipment. (Before, apparently, owners had been pumping the throttle to prime the engine, not realizing that without an accelerator pump, no fuel was coming from the carb.) Dual windshield defrosters were offered, and an even-more-expensive type of 24-volt battery (a "manifold" type) was made standard, eliminating the battery box.

In 1981, Cessna made the enlightened move of putting a spin-on oil filter on all 152s as standard—not optional—equipment. Larger battery contactors, with appropriate current capacity to eliminate contact welding, were instituted (to keep owners from having to replace so many $230 batteries after contactor fry-ups); and an avionics cooling fan became part of every avionics installation. Also in 1981, the 152's list price took a 25-percent jump, the largest single jump ever, to $30,175 equipped.

For 1982, Cessna added a quick-drain to the standpipe below the fuel selector (at the belly of the airplane), to allow drainage of sediment and water from the fuel system's true low point. This modification can be—and should be—retrofitted to all 150s and 152s (an STC'd kit is available for only $12.50 from Middle Tennessee Aircraft Components, P.O. Box 472, Smithville, TN 37166; Cessna wants $82.20 for its version of the kit), but has as yet been incorporated in relatively few applicable aircraft.

Finally, for 1983-model 152s, Cessna has gone to a 108-hp O-235-N2C engine that better tolerates the lead in 100-octane avgas; the avionics cooling fan is improved; a panel vacuum warning light is standard; and the gyro panel is redesigned to allow removal of gyro instruments from the front of the panel.

Investment Value

It generally takes four years for a new plane to bottom out on the depreciation curve—and that point was only recently reached in 1982 for the oldest 152s. However, trainers have been known to continue depreciating much longer than "normal" aircraft. Nonetheless, it is interesting to note that the 1978 models, after losing some 55 percent of their value in the first four years, had recouped six percent of their original value, or about $1,000 per airplane by mid-1984. As it turns out, this upswing in prices is not limited to 152s, but affects even 10- and 15-year-old 150s, which are also now commanding $1,000 more per

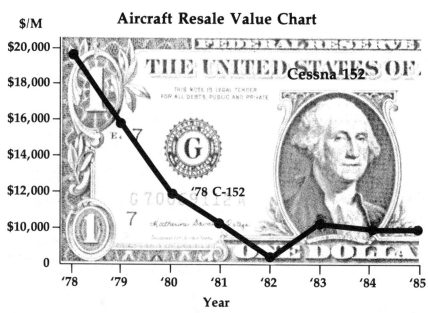

Aircraft Resale Value Chart

plane than they did a few years ago. (Piper Tomahawks have not done as well.) Evidently, buyer resistance to Cessna's latest new-152 prices has begun to put pressure on the used market. Several FBOs we talked to agreed. "I haven't got $36,000 to spend on a new 152 this year—or any year," one disgruntled flight school operator told us in 1983.

Sales of new 152s generally go to flight schools and/or school customers, who put the planes on leaseback. (In rental service, the plane becomes a source of revenue for lessor and lessee, while the owner realizes huge tax benefits. Or so the theory goes.) But leasebacks have been hard hit by the recession, and FBOs are struggling to maintain cash flow. Buyers for new 152s have suddenly disappeared. Recent sales figures confirm this: Cessna shipped 25 trainers in the first seven months of 1984 (compared to nearly 200 a month in 1978).

Still, training activity remains strong in many of the nation's flight schools, and replacement training aircraft have to come from somewhere. It will be interesting to see whether demand for used 152s at the FBO level will continue to increase, driving resale prices higher—or whether cost-conscious rental operators, realizing the potential of autogas, will opt for a return to the Continental-powered Cessna 150 (which can legally use

unleaded motor fuel, even in training use).

Performance and Handling

In terms of cruise performance and payload, the 152 enjoys no significant advantage over its Beech and Piper peers (the Skipper and Tomahawk), nor over the 150, for that matter. Top speed for the 152 is listed by Cessna as 109 knots, the same as for the Tomahawk and 150M (two knots more than the Skipper); likewise, the 152 Trainer's standard useful load of 528 pounds very nearly matches that of the Skipper (572 lbs.) and Tomahawk (542 lbs.). Some of the earlier 150s (E/F/G models) topped 600 pounds in load-carrying ability. But the useful-load issue is made moot by the 152's optional fuel capacity of 39 gallons—33 percent greater than the Skipper's 29 gallons or the Tomahawk's 30. In range and payload flexibility, the 152 thus enjoys a slight edge over its competitors—although you may well have to sacrifice a passenger (and/or baggage) to take full benefit of the 152's longer range.

Runway performance for the 152 is good. The Cessna simply gets off quicker—and stops shorter—than Brand B or Brand P trainers (a reflection of the 152's fortunate lack of a T tail). If short- or rough-field operations are being contemplated, the 152 wins hands down over its T-tail peers. Figure on an unstick distance of 725 feet for a fully grossed 152 at sea level (versus 780 and 820 feet for the Skipper and Tomahawk); and set aside a mere 475 feet for landing roll (vs. 670 or 707 ft. for the T-trainers). The 152, incidentally, lands about 10 percent longer than the 150—apparently due to the 152's 30-degree flap-travel restriction.

So where does the 152 really shine? Its confidence-inspiring slow-flight characteristics and straightforward Cessna-like handling provide the key. The plane stalls well and with plenty of warning. (Power on, you can get zero-knots indicated before approaching the burble.) Stability in all axes is outstanding. The barn-door flaps—electric, alas—are monstrously effective (but watch out for the pitch up on initial deployment). The 152's light wing loading makes it a bit uncomfortable in more than very light turbulence; otherwise, however, it flies very much like a miniature Skyhawk. Which is just what Cessna wanted, of course.

The 152, like the 150, also comes in an Aerobat version—which the Skipper and Tomahawk don't. (Only about one in 20 152s is an 'A' model, however.) If loops and hammerheads are your cup of pekoe, the A152 will grudgingly comply. But don't expect Pitts-like—or even Citabria-like—performance, and forget about sustained inverted flight (the engine dies).

Comfort

Although significantly better than, say, a Luscombe or Taylorcraft, the 152's cabin comfort is nothing to brag about (and in fact takes a back seat to that of either the Skipper or Tomahawk). Visibility is poor, noise level is high, and shoulder room is almost nonexistent. Thicker seat padding became standard with the 1979 models (the previous cushions taxed the endurance of even the most hardened CFIs), but even so, pillows are highly recommended for cross-country work.

Ventilation (via the wing-root pull tubes, and air leaks around the doors) has always been good in 150s and 152s, even, unfortunately, in the dead of winter. To add insult to misery, Cessna located cabin-heat and carb-heat pickoffs next to each other on the muffler shroud. (Even with carb heat turned off, the carb-heat plumbing provides a sizable plenum for the escape of desperately needed cabin BTUs.) In 1979, Cessna released a service letter, SE79-12, describing a kit to relocate the carb-heat source to the number-four exhaust riser. This allowed the muffler's total heat output to be utilized for cabin heat, resulting in a 30-percent increase in cabin heat flow. All 1980 and later 152s were delivered with this cabin-heat mod. The first 4,100 airplanes off the line, however, did not get the deluxe heater kit, and most remain unmodified. Check for compliance with Cessna Service Letter SEW79-12 before buying a '78 or '79 airplane.

Engine

In going from the 150 to the 152, Cessna switched from the venerable 80-octane Continental O-200-A to the somewhat more expensive (and powerful) Lycoming O-235-L2C. The rationale behind the engine change was threefold. First, with 80-octane avgas in increasingly short supply, more and more flight schools were reporting problems with lead buildup in their 150s' O-200 engines; Cessna wanted to give its dealers a trainer that could digest the higher-leaded 100-octane fuels. Second, the 150—which had seen empty-weight increases totalling nearly 150 pounds (or 15 percent) since 1958—was overdue for a horse-power boost. And third, Cessna—in accordance with proposed FAA and ICAO noise standards—wanted to see a reduction in the 150's internal and external sound levels. The high-compression Lycoming O-235-L2C, delivering 110 horsepower at 2,550 rpm instead of the O-200's 2,750, seemed a natural answer to all three requirements.

Many operators say that the switch to the Lycoming engine has been a mistake. Although it did rid the Cessna trainer of the O-200's starter-clutch woes (the small Continental uses a $600 starter adapter that can fail frequently and without warning), the Lycoming O-235 brought its own constellation of mechanical quirks. Parts prices were, in some cases, astoundingly high: The O-235-L2C's sodium-filled exhaust valves, for instance, listed for $213.08 each—versus only $64 for the O-200's solid-stemmed valves. (Likewise, a piston for the Lycoming engine cost about twice what the corresponding Continental piston cost.) What's more, the O-235's cylinders may not be ground over-size during a top overhaul (since it

Shoulder room is not great in a 152, and while the baggage area may look ample, useful load is not; Payload with full fuel (39 gals.) is 280 pounds—one pilot, plus enough left over to fill the copilot's seat or baggage area, but not both.

removes the nitride layer), whereas the O-200's jugs can be ground over. And if an owner elects to salvage run-out cylinders by chroming, extreme difficulty may be had in finding piston rings for final buildup. Unchromed rings must be used in chromed jugs—and no one, at present, supplies unchromed rings for 0-235s.

Other service quirks that have not endeared schools or their shops to the 152's powerplant:

• As originally delivered, the Cessna 152 came with Slick 4000-series "sealed" (i.e., unrepairable in the field) magnetos. A rash of unexplained capacitor problems led to engine failures in Tomahawks using the same engine/magneto combo, but the 152 was mysteriously unaffected. Nonetheless, operators soon tired of spending hundreds of dollars on new mags every time their "throw-away Slicks" needed points or bearings. A black market in bogus 152-mag "repair kits" sprang up, and Slick finally introduced a field-repairable version of the mags.

• The O-235 is one of few aircraft engines in current production that uses solid (not hydraulic) tappets. Valve lash in the O-235 thus varies with engine temperature, and O-235 valve-train clearances must be checked scrupulously every 100 hours, not unlike a motorcycle.

Lycoming, in an attempt to minimize lash problems, devised hollow-aluminum pushrods with steel ball ends (the idea being that the aluminum, which expands more than twice as much as steel on heating, would tend automatically to readjust lash at higher temperatures). Such construction calls for very critical ball-end fit tolerances, however, and—unfortunately—Lycoming's pushrod vendor failed, initially, to meet the necessary specs. As a result, pushrod "mushrooming" (pounding of the steel ball ends down into the pushrod) became common. After a fatal accident related to pushrod shortening in November 1980, FAA issued an AD on this subject. All defective rods should

Can you spot the maintenance design faux pas in this picture? Notice the one-piece nose cap, which presents total cowl removal with the propeller in place. (Late-model 152s have two-piece nose caps—a definite maintenance plus.)

by now have been taken out of circulation, but it bears mentioning that valve train clearances are critical and subject to frequent rechecking in the O-235.

• The O-235-L2C did not escape the inspection requirements of a 1981 AD (81-18-04) that called for replacement of iron oil pump impellers with late-configuration steel and aluminum ones. This caused many 2,000-hour engines to be summarily grounded.

Miscellaneous reports of low static rpm and uneven operation led Lycoming to issue a special bulletin for the O-235 (S.I. 1388C) outlining trouble-shooting procedures to restore full power. This service letter is now in its third revision.

Lead Fouling

Lead buildup—not only in spark plugs but in nooks and crannies in the combustion chamber, and on valves—has been a persistent problem in O-235 engines. So much so, in fact, that Champion designed a special spark plug just for this engine—the extended-electrode 'Y' series (e.g., REM37BY). The long-prong plugs do not scavenge lead any better than standard plugs; they merely have electrodes that sit far enough away from lead encrustations to constantly "burn clean." Once filled with lead, the 'Y' plugs continue to fire. (But they still must be replaced often.)

Most operators find that even with judicious leaning, spark plugs must be cleaned every 25 hours in a 152. "Otherwise," remarks one A&P, "at 100 hours, you can throw the plug away—it won't even be cleanable." Lead buildup on the inside of the cylinder affects spark plug life: Lycoming found that lead can be redeposited from the combustion chamber to clean spark plugs in as little as 25 hours. Accordingly, in Service Instruction 1418, Lycoming outlines a procedure whereby O-235 cylinders can be blast-cleaned with walnut shells without removal for top overhaul. (Prior to this, some operators were finding that early top overhauls were needed to prevent lead from reaching excessive levels in O-235 jugs.)

Safety

Safety statistics for the 150 and 152 are quite good. (In this regard, at least, trainers have come a long way since Piper Cub days.) An NTSB study found the Cessna 150 series with the lowest fatal accident rate—at 1.35 per 100,000 flight hours—of any two-seater, and one of the lowest fatal crash rates of *any* single-engine aircraft, period. The total accident rate, at 10.3 per 100,000 hours, is also quite respectable, again bettering most trainers *and* four-place aircraft.

If there's one fly in the safety ointment, it's the 152's relatively weak showing against the Piper Tomahawk. A special study by *Aviation Safety* (covering the period January 1978 through April 1980) found the 152 with a 38-percent higher total accident rate than the Tomahawk. (Fatal accident rates were about equal.) As a percentage of total accidents, the Cessna 152 is involved in disproportionately more groundloops, overshoots, undershoots, and fuel mismanagement accidents than the Tomahawk. The 152, on the other hand, fares much better than its Piper counterpart in the proportion of hard landing accidents and stall-spins.

Overall, the 152 has a sterling safety record, bolstered by the fact that there has never been an in-flight breakup of the airplane (despite a fair number of IFR-weather encounters by low-time pilots).

Maintenance

Many of the 152's early maintenance foibles (the most serious of which have been touched on above) have now been laid to rest and should not pose recurrent problems for used-trainer buyers. The 152's most serious ongoing maintenance problem involves lead fouling, which (according to some owners) can be severe even with proper leaning, the use of low-lead fuel, addition of TCP concentrate (a lead remover marketed by Alcor) to 100LL, correct adjustment of idle mixture, and switching to Champion long-prong plugs. All of these measures are unnecessary, of course, in a Cessna 150 operating on grade-80 avgas or unleaded automotive gasoline. But unfortunately, the 152's engine is restricted to 100-octane avgas for the foreseeable future. (In all fairness, private owners should experience fewer bouts of lead fouling than flight schools, since much of the 152's lead fouling is due to chronic overrich operation in the pattern.)

Prospective 152 buyers should check to see whether these important service bulletins have been complied with:
• E82-23 required a one-time inspection of 152 starter and battery contactors.
• SE81-38 outlined brake master cylinder modifications for 1979 through mid-'82 Cessna 152s (and post-1966 150s).
• SE81-24 puts a fuel quick-drain in the belly of pre-'82 Cessna 152 (and post-1966 150s).
• SE80-96 (Revision 1) calls for recurrent inspections of certain

The standard 152 panel features ARC radios, limited instrument space, and a generous amount of Royalite.

Stewart-Warner oil coolers on a variety of Cessnas, including the 152. This was also the subject of an AD.

• SE79-7 modifies the nose cap to allow removal of the cowl without first taking the prop off.
• SE79-11 and -43 concerned mods to improve the starting characteristics of pre-1980 152s.
• SE79-12 reroutes carb heat plumbing to improve cabin heat.
• SE79-16 outlines flap cable clamp mods that must be accomplished prior to 1,000 hours in service. This was also the subject of an AD (80-6-3); so make sure it has been complied with on any airplane you intend to buy.
• SE79-46 describes periodic inspection requirements for 152 carburetor airboxes. In 1982, Cessna came out with a service bulletin (SE82-12) describing an airscoop mod for the 152, compliance with which is also recommended.
• SE79-49 mandates vertical fin hardware attachment inspections every 100 hours. This now carries the force of law, under an AD (No. 80-11-04).
• SE79-57 describes a much-improved flap actuator mechanical stop for 1979 and earlier 152s.
• SE80-2: Another cabin heat mod.
• SE80-10 requires use of Loctite on certain starter screws, which have shown a tendency to back out.

We mentioned before the 152's bout with self-shortening pushrods (the subject of a late-1980 AD, and Lycoming S.B. 453). What we didn't mention is that compliance with this AD doesn't guarantee that you'll *never* see pushrod mushrooming in your 152's engine. There have been reports (not many, but a few), subsequent to the AD, of engines with the improved pushrods experiencing ball-hammering or mushrooming. Hence, along with a compression check, we'd recommend a check of valve clearances (or pushrod length) in any pre-purchase inspection of a 152.

Modifications

There are relatively few approved mods for the 152. Brackett Aircraft offers conversion kits for installation of wet-foam air filters on the 152 (replacement elements are only a few dollars for this type of filter, whereas Cessna gets about $25 for a new paper element). Brackett filters are available through any large FBO.

Avcon Industries holds STC No. SA1384CE for installation of a Lycoming O-320-E2D 150-hp engine in the A152 only. However, J&S Engineering, Inc., of San Antonio has an STC to install the 180-hp Lycoming O-360 in 150s as well as 152s, allowing a gross

Cost/Performance/Specifications

Model	Year	Number Built	Average Retail Price*	Cruise Speed (kts)	Engine	TBO (hrs)	Overhaul Cost
152	1978	2,625	$10,000	107	110-hp Lyc. O-235-L2C	2,000	$5,500
152	1979	1,559	$11,000	107	110-hp Lyc. O-235-L2C	2,000	$5,500
152	1980	949	$12,250	107	110-hp Lyc. O-235-L2C	2,000	$5,500
152	1981	619	$16,500	107	110-hp Lyc. O-235-L2C	2,000	$5,500
152	1982	432	$23,500	107	110-hp Lyc. O-235-L2C	2,000	$5,500
152	1983	245	$39,500**	106	108-hp Lyc. O-235-N2C	2,000	$5,500

Based on no damage history, six-month annual, all ADs complied, large tanks (39 vs. 26 gals.), 850 hours SMOH, full gyro panel, transponder with blind encoder, and 720-channel navcom. Add $500 if Aerobat.   ** *Deduct $47 per hour for every hour past 50 TTSN.*

weight increase of nearly 100 pounds to boot. Also, nose-wheel amputation is available through Custom Aircraft Conversions of San Antonio. The tailwheel conversion is claimed to boost speed by ''8 to 10 mph,'' by eliminating drag and substituting prop thrust that would otherwise be blanked out by the nose gear. Details of the 180-hp engine conversion and the so-called Texas Taildragger mod can be obtained by calling Custom at 512-349-6347.

Organizations

The Cessna 150-152 Club has been around for several years and claims upwards of 1,000 members. The group's monthly newsletter (The Cessna 150-152 News), edited by Skip Carden, is an excellent clearinghouse of service-related information and info on new mods, discount parts sources, etc. Membership is $15/yr. domestic and Canada, $25/yr. foreign. Contact the club at 3557 Roxboro Rd., P.O. Box 15388, Durham, N.C. 27704, or phone 919-471-9492.

Owner Comments

We have operated four Cessna 152s for the past three and one half years here in our flight school. Our most popular one (a 1980 model) is doing about 700 hours per year. Hourly maintenance cost is about five dollars per hour. They burn six gallons per hour if properly leaned, lots more if run hard or full rich. All have had lousy compression since new, and even after tops or overhauls. 65/80 is typical throughout the 2,000 TBO span. Valve clearances must be checked each 100 hours. We go 100 hours without cleaning the plugs or changing the oil providing they are religiously leaned and run up to 1800 rpm for a minute before shut down. The 24-volt electrical system is a pain in the neck requiring $239 batteries at least once a year. The RT-385A radios are also expensive to repair when the lights (digits) burn out or they quit cold.

All in all it is a good trainer and rental but a few pet gripes of mine are:

Skylights on top provide a bit of extra visibility inside steep turns.

1) Who the hell needs a cruise prop (and therefore a 104 knot cruise speed) on a primary trainer used to build hours of training and proficiency? 2) It's a gas hog. 3) Cabin is four inches too narrow. 4) I miss the 40 degrees flap setting. 5) Too noisy (I *always* wear ear plugs). 6) Cessna Aircraft Co. overprices CPC supplies, parts, etc. 7) It's too damned expensive. In 1979 I bought two for $30,000. Now I can't get *one* for that price (new).

Despite the shortcomings, it is the best *new* airplane around for my purpose but honestly, I'd rather have a C-150 if I could find lots of clean low-time late models. Our answer to the problem is an Aeronca Champ. We have *one* but I hope it continues in popularity so we can buy another. In that Aeronca we can teach students how to really *fly* the airplane.

David B. O'Brien, Pres.
FBO Lakewood Airport
Bay Head, N.J.

My 1978 Cessna 152 is leased to a flying club, so perhaps all of my comments and data may not be comparable to aircraft operated by private owners. In addition, I am an A&P mechanic and do almost all of the maintenance myself, so labor cost is not included in maintenance cost, except for the annual inspection. But I am a pilot, so general comments are relevant.

Handling and performance are good, and the aircraft is certainly satisfactory for training purposes. However, on cross-country flights comfort is average to poor because

of lack of leg room for the taller pilot and skimpy seat padding. Seating width is poor for large people when both seats are in use. Power is adequate under all conditions (home field elevation is only 469 feet though).

Most complaints center around the rapid lead-fouling of the lower spark plugs which causes many flights to be cancelled after ground runup with a 200-300 rpm mag drop. Even using TCP and the newer Champion REM37BY plugs, the lower ones must be cleaned every 20-25 hours. Fuel availability is limited to 100 octane at the home field—no 100LL is available—so perhaps the plugs would stay clean longer with 100LL.

Nose wheel shimmy is a problem from time to time due to linkage wear and the pounding the nose gear takes from students and operation primarily from an unpaved runway.

I am not too happy with the 24-volt electrical system when it comes time to replace the battery. Last year the starter shorted internally and the parts cost for starter (rebuilt) and a Gill battery was $500. Parts availability is not a problem.

Cost of the last two annual inspections was $211 and $245. Annual maintenance cost (wthout annual inspection or reserve) was $658 in 1981 (largely due to replacement of entire ignition system due to intermittent ''misses'') and $636 in 1982 (due mostly to the starter/battery failure).

The way the aircraft is used in flight training makes it difficult to accurately check fuel consumption (takeoffs and landings, forgetting to lean the mixture, etc.) but it appears to be close to the numbers published in Cessna's Pilot's Operating Handbook.

I hope your other readers will benefit from this information, and perhaps someone has a solution for the plug-fouling problem.

Norman J. Makowski
Fairport, N.Y.

Rutan VariEze, Long-EZ

The Rutan VariEze and Long-EZ are neat-looking, fast, efficient and dirt-cheap to fly. But because they are homebuilt kit planes, they have remained fond dreams for the majority of pilots, who can't muster up the skill and dogged determination it takes to build an airplane in the basement. As the number of Rutan canard pushers climbs past the 800 mark, however, a reasonable number of already built Ezes and EZs has come onto the used-plane market. It's now possible to own and fly one of these Star Wars sportplanes without having to build it.

But buying a used homebuilt is a whole new ballgame, fraught with risks. To buy a good, safe home-built aircraft requires a lot more homework than it takes to pick up a used Skylane. (More on this subject later.)

The VariEze, when it first appeared in 1975, turned the homebuilt in-dustry on its ear. Before it, the typical homebuilt plane was an antediluvian wood or steel-tube design whose construction (usual-ly from bare-bones plans) required the skills of a carpenter, welder, aircraft mechanic and scrounger. In most cases, these old-generation homebuilts, the result of thou-sands of hours of painstaking labor, performed no better than comparable production aircraft. Homebuilders were dedicated ex-pert hobbyists who typically got more fun from the building than the flying.

The New Generation

But the VariEze was refreshingly different: a futuristic design with a canard foreplane, swept wings and wingtip rudders, made of foam and fiberglass. It succeeded where the BD-5 before it had failed: it of-fered performance superior to pro-duction planes, and construction was easy enough to bring it within reach of the merely persistent rather than the totally fanatical. The VariEze spawned a whole new generation of slick-looking com-posite kits like the Quickie, Q-2 and Glasair. All of a sudden, regular folks were interested in building their own airplanes.

Long-EZ, with bigger wing, more power and 52-gallon fuel capacity, is worth two or three times as much as the smaller, older VariEze.

The VariEze is now the world's most popular homebuilt airplane. An estimated 600-plus are now flying. The Long-EZ, which essen-tially replaced the VariEze in 1981, now numbers about 200 in the air and 1,300 in some stage of construction.

History

The first prototype VariEze flew in 1975, powered by a Volkswagen engine. But designer Burt Rutan was unhappy with the reliability of the VW and decided to redesign the plane to take the small four-cylinder Continental engines from 65 to 100 hp. The first set of plans for the enlarged Continental-powered VariEze was sold in 1976, and the first customer-built airplane flew in 1977.

Although VariEze pilots loved the efficiency and the eye-catching look of the airplane, it had a number of problems. Baggage room was nil. Landing and takeoff distances were high. And the VariEze had some very odd handl-ing characteristics. Also, most builders were unable to match the light weight of the factory pro-totype, and many added things like starters and generators that Rutan hadn't counted on. As a result, useful load and center-of-gravity envelopes were very limited in some Vari-Ezes. And then, in 1977, Continental halted production of the Continental O-200, the prime VariEze engine. Prices for used O-200s shot up as hundreds of VariEze builders started bidding against each other.

To correct these problems, Rutan began working on a bigger version of the airplane designed to use the Lycoming O-235 with full electrical system. Called the Long-EZ, it made its debut in 1980. Essentially,

the VariEze was obsolete the day the Long-EZ plans went up for sale. Virtually all plans sales since have been Long-EZs.

But because of the long lead time between plans sale and first flight, freshly built VariEzes are still taking to the air at the rate of a couple a month.

Used-Plane Market

You won't find a VariEze on the ramp out at the local used-plane dealer's. Best sources are *Trade-A-Plane*, the EAA magazine *Sport Aviation* and the Rutan Aircraft Factory newsletter.

The used-plane marketplace has clearly decided in favor of the Long-EZ. While good VariEzes can be bought for sums in the $12,000-to-$16,000 range, a flyable Long-EZ goes for at least $25,000 in most cases. A creampuff Long, built with fanatical devotion to detail and IFR-equipped, will command as much as $40,000. One fellow claims he turned down $60,000 cash for his immaculate Long-EZ.

Performance

The Rutan canards are known for excellent performance and efficiency. By comparison, they put factory-built aircraft with the same engines to shame. This fact is usually credited to the canard design, which is said to cut drag by eliminating the download of a conventional tail. More likely, the Ezes are faster than production airplanes of the same power because they are much smaller (less frontal area) and have high aspect ratio wings. The smooth fiberglass skin and the careful attention to detail of

some builders is also a factor. The Ezes seem to be no more efficient than other small smooth-skinned homebuilts of conventional design, such as the Glasair.

Cruise efficiency of the VariEze is better than that of the Long-EZ, since it has less frontal area, less wing area and less weight. Owners report typical cruising speeds for both aircraft in the 150-170 mph range. (The Long-EZ does it on about five gph, the VariEze on four gph.) Speeds vary significantly according to the skills of the builder, of course. Probably the most efficient Rutan canard in the air is an 80-hp VariEze that can fly 156 mph on 3.2 gph and can achieve a max cruise speed of 186 mph. More typical is the 155 mph on five gph reported by the owner of a 100-hp VariEze.

Realistic Cruise Speeds

A word about max cruise speeds in Ezes: almost nobody ever revs them up that fast. Rutan's "book" cruise figure for the Long-EZ is 185 mph, but because of the fixed-pitch prop, the only way to achieve such high cruise speeds is to rev the engine well beyond Lycoming's 2700-rpm red-line. Rutan claims this is okay because the low-inertia prop puts less strain on the crankshaft. But in any case, revving an O-235 to 3100 rpm is very noisy, and it certainly does nothing to help engine reliability. Virtually every Eze owner who wrote us listed a typical cruise speed well below the maximum available.

(This is a common problem among small, fast homebuilts, and there's probably a fortune awaiting the fellow who comes up with a light,

cheap, reliable two-position variable-pitch propeller that can be controlled from the cockpit. A pilot could take off and climb—with vastly improved efficiency—in low pitch, and then "shift gears" to high pitch for cruise, where full throttle would be available without exceeding redline.)

The Ezes' rate of climb, because of the high-aspect-ratio wings, is excellent, about double that of O-235-powered production trainers. Book climb for the Long-EZ is 1,200 fpm at gross weight; owners report climb rates as high as 2,000 fpm for a Long-EZ at very light weight to 400 fpm for an 85-hp VariEze at 5,000 feet.

Payload/Range

The VariEze is not bad in this respect if the plane is built light, but many planes have payload problems. Rutan has set gross weight at 1,050 lbs. for the O-200-powered VariEze (less for the 65-85-hp models), and average empty weight is about 650. That leaves about 400 pounds for people and gas. Fill the 25-gallon tanks, and there's only 250 pounds left. An overweight, sloppily built plane with extra equipment might top 700 pounds empty; consider such a plane a single-seater.

It's tempting to bust gross weight limitations in homebuilts, simply because they are arbitrary and have no legal force. (Theoretically, the individual builder sets the gross weight at any number he likes.) But the Rutan-recommended figures should be taken as Gospel, since the structure of the plane was designed to those numbers. For payload-hungry VariEze pilots, Rutan does allow a takeoff weight up to 1,110 pounds (on long, smooth runways only), but you'll have to burn off 10 gallons of fuel—that's more than two hours of flying—before you can land. Moral: carefully check the empty weight, as equipped, of any Eze considered for purchase.

Range of the VariEze is good. With 25 gallons, five hours of moderate cruising is available at 150-160 mph, for a range of around 750 miles at nearly 40 miles per gallon.

The bigger, more powerful Long-EZ is a better cruising machine, but payload/range is still a bit limited. Gross weight is 1,325 pounds, and empty weights average around 850 pounds, for a useful load of 475 pounds. With two standard people and 50 pounds of baggage, there's room for about 12 gallons of gas, enough for a couple of hundred miles and a decent reserve. Using the long-smooth-runway takeoff weight of 1,425 pounds authorized by Rutan, allowable fuel increases to about 28 gallons, good for about 800 miles.

With reduced cabin loads, the Long-EZ's 52-gallon fuel tank makes it a mile-eater *par excellence*. With full fuel, a Long-EZ can fly nearly 2,000 miles at about 40 percent power (140 mph or so). Dick Rutan, brother of designer Burt Rutan, has set a closed-course distance record of 4,800 miles in a special Long-Eze with 130-gallon fuel tanks.

Flying Qualities

In this respect, the VariEze and Long-EZ are worlds apart. The Vari is a hot, quirky handling little plane, while the Long is, by all reports, a delight to fly.

The first VariEzes had very poor roll control. Rutan, in his quest for lightness and simplicity, originally designed the plane without ailerons. Roll control was to come from differential movement of the canard elevators. It didn't work; roll control was virtually nil below 100 mph and actually reversed at very low speeds. The original VariEze had to be banked almost

Original prototype VariEze weighed under 400 pounds empty with a 65-hp Volkswagen engine.

entirely with the rudders. To solve this problem, spoilers were added on the top of the inboard wing strakes. That didn't help much. Finally, ailerons were added, but even they have rather limited authority. The key to banking a VariEze is to help out with the rudder.

On the other hand, the VariEze's pitch control is hair-trigger. A delicate touch is needed on the small side-stick controller to avoid porpoising on takeoff. This trait is more pronounced if the aircraft is tail-heavy, as many Ezes are.

Before tackling a VariEze, the average pilot should get some dual instruction in a plane with sensitive pitch controls, such as an AA-1 Yankee or Trainer.

The Long-EZ, on the other hand, is well-harmonized. Roll authority is much better, and pitch is not quite so sensitive. By all reports, the average pilot can handle a Long-EZ pretty well, once he gets used to the tight cockpit, sidestick controller and semi-reclining seat position.

Both airplanes are virtually stall-proof if built precisely according to

the plans. The canard is designed to stall before the main wing, dropping the nose slightly before the main wing can reach the stall angle of attack. With the stick held full back, both planes merely bob their noses gently, descending or climbing according to power.

However, things like center of gravity, canard incidence and wing shape can change stall behavior. A couple of VariEze accidents have looked suspiciously like stall/ spins, and a few builders report real stalls. Moral: test-fly any Eze considered for purchase to make sure the individual airplane is stall-proof, and check the factors mentioned above to ensure the airplane conforms to the plans.

Both aircraft are quite stable, particularly in the roll axis. Owners report that the Long-EZ will fly level hands-off almost indefinitely, even righting itself in turbulence. This makes it one of the few homebuilts that might be suitable for some limited IFR flying.

Long Runways

But watch the runways. The major flaw of both VariEze and Long-EZ is the inordinate amount of real estate required for takeoff and landing. This stems from a number of traits. First, takeoff and landing speeds are fairly high for a light two-seater. "The VariEze is a hot little airplane," says Rutan's Mike Melville. "The rear wing doesn't work as well as it does in the Long-EZ." Owners report landing speeds in the 75-80 mph range, which requires approach speeds of at least 85 mph. (The Long-EZ, with its lower wing loading, has a slightly lower approach speed.)

The dark side of the Ezes' aerodynamic efficiency is a very flat glide angle, which makes it

Cost/Performance/Specifications

Model	Year	Number Built	Average Retail Price	Cruise Speed (mph)	Rate of Climb (fpm)	Useful Load (lbs)	Fuel Std/Opt (gals)	Engine	TBO (hrs)	Overhaul Cost
VariEze	1977-84	600	$12,000-16,000	170	1,500	400	25	100-hp Cont. O-200	1,800	$5,000
				160	1,100	375	25	85-hp Cont. C-85	1,800	$4,000
Long-EZ	1981-84	200	$25,000-40,000	180	1,200	475	52	115-hp Lyc. O-235	2,000	$5,000

Rutan VariEze, Long-EZ

tougher to land the airplane on a spot. Bring it in a bit too fast, and it'll float forever, much like a Mooney. Some Ezes have speed brakes, which help a bit, but still don't solve the problem.

On takeoff, there's not enough elevator power to lift the nose below about 65 mph. This is partly due to the tail-in-front, engine-in-back layout, which means there's no prop blast to help the elevator do its job. Secondly, the elevator itself is, by design, limited in authority to make the plane stall-proof.

Rutan sets the minimum runway at 2,500 feet unless the pilot is very skilled and confident. (One pilot of an 85-hp Eze reports his takeoff rolls average 2,000 feet.) Some VariEze pilots use 1,500-foot strips if they have to, but others make 3,000 feet their minimum runway, and we would agree. For a low-time VariEze jockey, a 5,000-foot runway is a good idea. (Incidentally, grass runways severely degrade takeoff performance. Because the plane can't rotate early to take some of the load off the wheels, drag on the small, high-pressure tires is significant. Rutan recommends the airplanes for hard surfaces only, or on turf runways where the grass is no longer than two inches.)

Creature Comforts

For the pilot accustomed to Skylanes and Bonanzas, the Eze cockpit takes some getting used to. It is very tight. The pilot sits in a semi-reclining position, with the canopy an inch or two above his head, and his legs encased in two small tunnels that lead eventually to the rudder pedals. Once the pilot adjusts psychologically to being virtually wrapped in the airplane, however, the pilot's seat is very comfortable indeed. Owners report making four- or five-hour flights without fatigue or discomfort. The back-seater doesn't get as much legroom, but comfort there is still not too bad.

The Ezes are noisy, however, particularly for the passenger, who sits with his or her ears only a foot

or so from the engine. Cabin heat can also be a problem, although on sunny days the fuselage and canopy act like a big solar collector to keep things reasonably warm, except for the pilot's toes.

Poor Baggage Space

A glaring drawback of the VariEze is the total lack of baggage space. (Rutan occasionally lets his mania for light weight and aerodynamic efficiency overwhelm human factors.) Basically, you can carry in a VariEze whatever you can get on your lap or under your knees. The Long-EZ is better in this respect; it has small baggage areas, accessible from the rear seat, in the wing-root strakes. But still, don't plan on any golf bags.

Visibility is superb, with one major exception. During landing approach and on takeoff, in the VariEze particularly, the canard surface greatly impairs the pilot's view of the runway. The Long-EZ is somewhat better in this respect.

Maintenance and Operating Costs

By the standards of most other high-performance airplanes, the cost of running a VariEze or Long-EZ is startlingly low. Fuel consumption is about that of a small trainer, averaging four to five gallons per hour. Since they are homebuilts, auto gas can be used, and by all reports works just fine. So total fuel costs should run around $5 to $6 per hour.

Maintenance is virtually nil, since in most cases the owner can do it himself. The planes are disarmingly simple to inspect, since there is virtually no internal structure that can be inspected. The wing, for example, is simply a piece of solid foam sheathed in fiberglass and epoxy. What's to check?

Owners report that tires and brakes wear out very quickly because of the high landing and takeoff speeds. Wheel alignment is critical. Others report problems with nosewheel shimmy and advise careful adjustment of the shimmy damper. One VariEze

owner calls the entire nosewheel assembly "relatively weak," and says he's had to replace the fork, spring strut rod ends pivot bearings and wheel, assembly. Other than that, the engine is about the only thing that will eat up maintenance dollars.

Buying A Homebuilt

Checking out a homebuilt airplane can be a mystifying exercise. The big sign in the cockpit that says "Experimental" is no joke—you are truly buying somebody's experiment. If the experimenter was diligent and competent, you'll have a fine airplane—probably better built than a Wichita product—but no FAA man looked over the builder's shoulder to make sure that he followed the plans precisely, that he did all his fiberglass layups properly, or that the weight-and-balance calculations are correct.

Unfortunately, the Ezes' construction method traps the used-plane buyer in a pincer of uncertainty. First of all, seemingly minor errors in construction (a layer of fiberglass with the fibers running the wrong way, for example) can seriously weaken the airplane. Secondly, the internal structure can't really be inspected. "It's very hard to analyze," comments Mike Melville. "There's no way to verify that the structure is good."

Fortunately, Rutan took these uncertainties into account during the design of the plane, and a properly built plane has huge structural margins—up to 12 Gs in some areas. Even if a builder screws it up and the plane is only half as strong as it's supposed to be, the result is just as strong as a production airplane. There has been only one accident caused by a structural failure in an Eze. A winglet separated during a high-speed pass. It turns out that the builder had completely left out several key layers of fiberglass in the winglet attach structure, in gross violation of the plans and common sense. Nevertheless, there would have been no way to discover this serious flaw beforehand.

Long-EZ with long, slender wings, is more efficient than its distant ancestor, the pioneering delta Vari-Viggen.

Buyer's Checklist

Here's a list of things to look for when buying a VariEze or Long-EZ. While they can't absolutely guarantee a properly built airplane, they can make the odds very good:

• Check the weight. Construction technique plays a big role in the empty weight of the finished product. A slapdash builder tends to slop on the epoxy to save time, and he'll cover up imperfections with filler. Both add weight. A properly built VariEze should weigh between 620 and 650 pounds (with an O-200 engine, equipped for day VFR), according to Rutan's Mike Melville. "If it weighs 700 pounds, the guy was sloppy with the epoxy. He may have been sloppy on the other stuff, too." A Long-Eze should weigh in at about 820 to 860 pounds. If it's much heavier than that, be suspicious.

• Check the plans and the construction logbook. Did the builder keep meticulous records? That's a good sign. Are the plans complete? Are all the plans changes up to date? (A builder is supposed to have all copies of the Rutan newsletter, which contains these changes.) Are the maintenance logbooks up to date and complete? In general, you are looking for signs of a meticulous, methodical, conscientious attitude on the part of the guy who built the plane.

• Check general detail work. As one VariEze owner put it, "Look at the details, fillets, hinges, general surface smoothness and trueness of contour, fit of cowling and canard

. . . If it looks good, the owner probably followed the construction instructions faithfully."

• Check the paint for cracks or peeling. Oddly, paint can play a role in the structural integrity of the Ezes. The epoxy used in construction begins to break down under heat, so all airplanes must be painted white to reflect sunlight. If the paint has come off, you may have a weak spot. If the paint is cracked, sand it off to see whether the crack extends into the epoxy and fiberglass itself. If it does, there might be a problem. (One cheery note: if you do find a structural problem, it's usually very easy to repair.)

• Check the integrity of the fiberglass in critical areas by tapping the surface with a quarter. A dull "thud" instead of the usual sharp tap may signal a delamination.

• Check the attach points of the wing and canard for cracks. Structural integrity here is vital.

• Check the landing gear legs and attach points. These were notorious weak spots in the VariEze; the bolt holes tend to elongate, and the bolts get loose. Many Varis have been retrofitted with Long-EZ gear.

• Check the quality of the engine baffling. Cooling efficiency apparently varies dramatically from airplane to airplane, and a flight test on a hot day is a good idea. Give the engine compartment a thorough once-over. "There's some awful-looking work out there," comments Melville.

• Finally, make sure you test-fly the plane, or hire someone to do it for you. One reader who bought a used VariEze reports he found one for sale with badly misrigged wing cuffs. As a result, it tended to roll strongly to the left in cruise, and stalled with a sharp wing drop.

Modifications

Rutan has come up with several major improvements over the years, some of them labeled "mandatory." But it's a fact of Experimental life that Rutan's "Airworthiness Directives" have no legal force, and a builder may choose not to adopt them. We would not advise buying an Eze lacking a Rutan-mandated mod. Among the mods to look for:

• VariEze wing leading-edge cuffs. These improve stall behavior and are considered mandatory. As this is written, Rutan has just approved so-called "vortilons," a sort of protruding stall fence, to replace the cuffs for better climb performance.

• Revised canopy latch and warning system. This is another "must-have" item; there have been several accidents caused by in-flight canopy openings, which render the plane virtually uncontrollable.

• High-performance rudders on the Long-EZ give better ground handling in a crosswind. With the original rudders, one owner comments, "Crosswind takeoffs are a disaster."

• Long-EZ landing gear retrofit for the VariEze.

• Improved nose gear. Mods include an easier crank-up system and a redesign for improved crashworthiness.

• Cleveland brakes instead of the originally specified Rosehans models.

• Belly-mounted speed brake. This steepens the glide angle and makes spot landings easier.

• Flush cowl scoop reportedly improves engine cooling.

• Improved canard. This major modification is still under development, but it promises to lower the high rotation speed, reduce or eliminate the nose-down effect in rain, and perhaps improve performance in the bargain. Look for the new canard to be available this spring.

Safety

The safety record of homebuilts is not particularly good. The Ezes were designed with safety in mind, but they don't seem to have lived up to their promise in this regard. There have been 11 fatal VariEze accidents and three Long-EZ fatals.

Because there are no good estimates of hours flown for homebuilts, it's hard to figure per-hour accident rates. But assuming an average of 400 airplanes in the air over the last eight years, each flying an average of 100 hours per year, we arrive at a rough guesstimate of about 320,000 flight hours.

The total of 14 fatal accidents works out to about four fatal accidents per 100,000 flight hours, a moderately high figure compared to the typical single-engine production airplane. The Cessna 150, for example, has a fatal accident rate of about 1.3, while the Piper Cherokee scores a 2.0 The worst of the modern single-engine planes is the hot, sporty little Grumman/American AA-1 series, which rates a 4.8.

If our guesstimate is correct, The Ezes' fatal accident rate is roughly comparable to those of older two-seat taildragger sportplanes like the Cub, Swift, Luscombe and Er-

coupe, which all have rates in the four-to-five range. For all the Ezes' advanced aerodynamics, they seem to represent little safety improvement over the two-seat sportplanes of four decades ago.

However, we must compliment RAF for its frank, safety-minded attitude. Safety is constantly emphasized in the plans and newsletters, and the company is quick to make safety-related changes. RAF sends an investigator to inspect most fatal Eze accidents, and writes them up in detail in the newsletter. Few homebuilt plans sellers—not to mention the Wichita manufacturers of ''real'' airplanes—take this much trouble in safety matters.

''Factory'' Support

Rutan Aircraft, by all reports, does an excellent job of supporting its airplanes. Unlike some other kit sellers, Rutan always answers the phone and patiently answers questions. Rutan Aircraft Factory, Building 13, Mojave Airport, Mojave, Calif. 93501; 805-824-2645.

Primary sources of parts and materials (Rutan dispenses only plans and advice) are Aircraft Spruce and Specialty, Box 424, Fullerton, Calif. 92632, 714-870-7551; Ken Brock Aircraft, 11852 Western Ave., Stanton, Ca. 90680, 714-898-4366; Wicks Aircraft Supply, 410 Pine St., Highland, Ill. 62249, 618-654-7447; and Task Research, 848 E. Santa Maria, Santa Paula, Ca. 93060; 805-528-4445.

Owner Comments

I have a VariEze powered by a Lycoming O-235-C. The airplane is relatively light in weight at 650 pounds (it doesn't have lights, starter, gyros or any extras), so performance is very good with this engine. Cruise at 75 percent is 200 mph, but I usually fly at reduced power at about 175 mph on 4.3 to 4.5 gph.

It's a hot little aircraft and not for everyone. The controls are very

sensitive, but easy to get accustomed to. The high runway speeds —80 mph for liftoff and touchdown —wear out the little tires in a hurry, so they last only about 200 landings. The airplane has been trouble-free with almost no maintenance required. My major costs are hangar and insurance. With everything included, flying about 150 hours per year, my cost is $20 per hour.

I would rank the Eze above all other planes I've flown except for baggage space.

W. Butters
Florissant, Mo.

I do the annual inspections on my VariEze myself. It takes about six hours. It's a low-maintenance airplane, except for tires and brakes. The small tires and high landing speeds (80 mph) result in high tire wear. Al steering is done by brakes, which results in high brake wear.

The VariEze is very responsive, the closest thing to a jet fighter most people will ever fly. The side stick is very nice. The small amount of stick travel takes some getting used to. To land, the plane is flown onto the runway at 75-80 mph, not flared and held off in the usual manner. Once these points are understood, flying the plane is EZ. Noise levels are similar to other small planes, but an intercom is a must due to the tandem seating arrangement. My cruise speed is 175 mph, 185 with wheel pants, burning five gph. Useful load is 400 pounds, or 500 pounds at the maximum takeoff weight.

Will Thorn
Canton, Mass.

I purchased a used VariEze in January 1984. I based my selection on visual appearance and workmanship, consultation with the FAA men who inspected the airplanes during construction, review of airframe mods and updates; and flight characteristics of each airplane.

I selected six airplanes as candidates for evaluation. Four were located from *Sport Aviation*, one from *Trade-A-Plane* and one was for sale in my local EAA chapter. Two were eliminated for price and logistical reasons (too far away), and I looked at four airplanes. Time on the planes ranged from 400 to 600 hours. All had the Continental O-200, and all cruised 150-170 mph at 3,000 feet. My strategy for evaluating airframe integrity came down to looking at the details, fillets, hinges, general surface smoothness and trueness of contours, and the fit of the cowling and canard. Since there is no true way to determine structural integrity, the best you can do is assume that if it looks good, the builder probably followed the construction instructions faithfully.

The airplane I bought rotates at 60 mph indicated, lifts off at 80, climbs at 90 at 1800 fpm solo, 700 fpm dual. Full throttle (2550 rpm, I can't seem to get more) is 160 mph at 3,000 feet. Final approach is 80-90 mph, touchdown at 80. Stall (mine does in fact stall, dropping the left wing smartly, due to an improperly built wing) is at 62 mph power-on and 64 mph power-off.

I love the bird for all its quirks, and wouldn't trade it for anything but a Christen Eagle or a Long-EZ.

Dan Morris
Dana Point, Calif.

I built a Long-EZ in 1981-82, with a new Lycoming O-235-L2C. It has 150 hours on it. It is full IFR with all pre-fabricated parts. I expect it would sell for about $45,000.

My advice to Long-EZ buyers: remember that each one is built by an individual, and there is no way of inspecting the internal structure of the craft. One must beware of poor workmanship. The canard and wings should not show any fiberglass weave and have straight leading and trailing edges. Tapping with a quarter will reveal any delaminations with a dull thud instead of a sharp tap.

Check the dimensions with the owner's manual; the weight-and-balance should not show a c.g. too

far from the center of the envelope. Basic empty weight of an IFR-equipped EZ with upholstery, generator and starter should not exceed 925-950 pounds. If so, suspect excess epoxy (not a structural defect) or lots of filler to cover bumpy layups.

The engine should be well-baffled in a professinal way. All the metal parts for the Long-EZ are available ready-made, and unless the builder is a professional metalworker, I wouldn't touch a plane without the pre-made metal parts. The plans call for a canopy safety catch and a gear-up canopy-unlocked warning system that should be installed during construction.

The flying qualities are superb—it is fast, responsive and a joy to the pilot. It is sensitive in pitch, and the rudders are not coupled to the ailerons, so it may take some getting used to, perhaps an hour or two.

Speed and fuel consumption are right up to Rutan's book figures. However, it is not really a two-seat airplane—more like one-and-a-half. The tandem seating can be unpleasant at times, especially if the rear-seat person gets weary in turbulence.

Ground handling, with the differential-brake steering, is not the best feature of the plane. I am on my third set of brake linings. One learns to use more runway on landing to save the brakes. I did lose a nosewheel to a very rough runway in Albuquerque (Alameda). It shimmied off in seconds, even though I had just checked the damper. Now I have it adjusted even tighter.

Backup from Rutan has always been super. The owner's manual is better and more candid than that of most production aircraft. A quarterly newsletter is mandatory for updates and ''ADs.''

Robert Forest
Santa Barbara, Calif.

I built a Long-EZ and have been flying it for a year and a half. In that time I've put 162 hours on it, with 263 landings. Performance is with-

High-aspect-ratio wing plays a big role in the EZ's excellent climb and cruise performance.

in one or two knots of the RAF predictions.

Handling on the ground is very maneuverable and nimble. In flight, it is very stable, but the controls are quite sensitive. It must be flown with a light touch. Does not stall. There is a slight pitch-down in rain, but I have made many wet takeoffs, and they are no problem.

Maintenance: I've replaced one set of brake pads. The Lycoming O-235-L2C does not foul plugs like it does in the Tomahawk and 152. No lead-fouling detected to date.

Parts availability from Brock, Aviation Spruce and Wicks is very good. Props are a bit slow coming through, but my B&T is of excellent quality. RAF support is outstanding; Mike and Sally Melville do a very good job.

Cost of operation is low; it's the cheapest way to fly. Overall fuel burn is about 5.6 gph, which yields 140 knots. Liability insurance is $450 per year. Annual cost is the $50 hangar rent while I do the inspection myself. Overall, the Long-EZ is a very addictive flying machine. I cannot go to the airport without flying it.

David Domeier
Fall Village, Ct.

Piper Super Cub

The Piper PA-18 Super Cub is the original bushplane, and plenty of pilots still swear its the best STOL (Short Take Off and Landing) aircraft flying today. Super Cubs abound in Alaska, where the loads are heavy and the landing strips are short and rough, but they are also a favorite of sport pilots who want a cheap, strong-flying craft just for fun. More than 10,000 of the fabric-covered anachronisms have been built over the years, and the Super Cub continued in production until 1983, when hard times at Piper forced shutdown of the ancestral Lock Haven plant in Pennsylvania.

History

The Super Cub is, of course, a direct descendant of the hallowed Piper J-3 Cub, which first appeared back in 1940. The J-3 was spruced up into the PA-11 in 1948, and the first PA-18 Super Cub, which appeared in 1950, was very similar to the PA-11. Called the Super Cub PA-18-95, it had a 90-hp engine, no flaps and the old Cub-style elevator. That first year, a 115-hp Lycoming-powered version (the PA-18-105) was also available, and it had the flaps, counter-balanced elevator and other features that were to distinguish Super Cubs from their forebears. (In fact, some purists don't really consider the 90-hp version to be a "real" Super Cub, even though it was produced in small numbers until 1961.)

In 1951, power of the Lycoming version was boosted to 125, then to 135 the next year, and finally to 150

A high-lift wing, light weight and a big engine combine to make the Super Cub a super STOL.

in 1955. The Super Cub remained virtually unchanged after 1955, probably the longest career of any airplane without major modifications.

Performance

Quite simply, for heavy loads and short fields, the Super Cub has no peer. Only the big, expensive Helio Courier can approach the Super Cub's STOL performance, and some Super Cub users insist it will outperform the Helio when both are heavily loaded. One Alaskan operator reports, "I've been full circle from PA-12s to 170s, 180s, 185s and a Helio Courier, and when you get right down to the dirty work, the Super Cub fits our needs better than anything built." Another Alaskan says, "Up here, the Super Cub is pretty much considered the ultimate airplane for bush flying and performance."

According to the book, a Super Cub's takeoff ground roll is 200 feet at max gross weight. Pilots tell us of 300-foot takeoff rolls under heavy overload conditions. One Super Cub owner wrote to tell us the results of a short takeoff contest he witnessed. With a 20-mph wind down the runway, a PA-18 got off the ground in exactly 19 feet. The Super Cub has won the annual takeoff competition every year it's been held.

Standard useful load is about 800 pounds, but overloads are com-

mon, particularly with the float-equipped version, which has more room to lash on excess cargo. We've heard of Super Cubs carrying five people with aplomb (pilot, one passenger sitting on another's lap in the back seat, and one hanging on each float). One bush pilot reports hauling a whole dressed-out moose, plus the hunter, in a Super Cub.

The Super Cub's performance formula is simple: a big, high-lift wing and a monster engine. The Cessna Skyhawk used the same basic engine, but had a gross weight 550 pounds higher, and a smaller wing. It's easy to see why huge overloads are almost the rule with the Super Cub, and why gross-weight performance is so spectacular. "With just the pilot and a little bit of gas, the climbout angle approaches vertical," reports one owner.

Unfortunately, the Super Cub's horizontal performance is not so spectacular. In fact, it's downright awful. Max cruise is only 115 mph. Drag is so high that it's almost pointless to use max cruise power, so many operators choose to fly at very low power settings at perhaps 90-100 mph.

Fuel capacity of the Super Cub is 36 gallons in all versions except the 90-hp model, which had only one 18-gallon tank in the left wing. (The others have another in the right

wing.) The 36-gallon supply providew perhaps four hours endurance, for a maximum range a shade over 400 miles. It's definitely not a cross-country airplane, although it can match most of the two-seat trainers in that regard — at a much higher fuel consumption.

Because of its odd mix of performance capabilities, the Super Cub is primarily a working airplane, occasionally a "fun" STOL sportplane or trainer and virtually never a practical family transportation machine. For that sort of duty, a Cessna 150, Cherokee 140 or other two-seater will fill the bill just as well for far less money.

The Super Cub is approved for limited aerobatics. It loops and spins nicely, but rolls are a real chore because of the ponderous aileron response.

Safety

Like most of the old taildragger aircraft, the Super Cub has a poor safety record. In fact, it had the highest accident rate (overall and fatal) of any aircraft still in production, according to NTSB statistics for the period 1972-76. The Super Cub's fatality rate is three times higher than that of the Cessna 150, for example.

This may be partly due to the type of flying Super Cubs do. Bush flying, fish-spotting, coyote hunting and such are rather dangerous activities for which the Super Cub is widely used.

The Super Cub rates particularly poorly in stall accidents, "uncontrolled collisions with the ground" (as the NTSB calls them) and mid-air collisions. A study of stall/spin accidents covering the years 1965-73 shows the Super Cub with a fatal stall/spin rate of 2.36 per 100,000 hours, poorest of any recent production airplane except for the Bellanca Citabria. (The Citabria's statistics include its Aeronca predecessors, long out of production.) By comparison, the Cessna 150 has a rate of 0.55 and the top-rated Cessna 182, 0.17 — nearly 15 times better than the Super Cub. The NTSB's "collision

Bluebook Prices

Model	No. Built	Retail Price	Model	No. Built	Retail Price
90-hp			1963	173	$15,000
1950-55	4,617	$7,500	1964	153	$15,000
	(Incl. 125-135-hp)		1965	138	$16,000
1956-61	2,914	$8,000	1966	125	$16,000
	(Incl. 150-hp)		1967	136	$16,500
115-hp			1968	170	$17,000
1950	522	$9,000	1969	106	$17,500
125-hp			1970	64	$18,000
1951-52	1,420	$12,000	1971	54	$18,500
			1972	47	$19,000
135-hp			1973	9	$19,500
1952-54	2,565	$13,000	1974	124	$20,000
150-hp			1975	142	$21,000
1955-57	2,334	$13,500	1976	156	$22,000
1958-60	1,404	$14,000	1977	198	$23,500
1961	225	$14,000	1978	188	$22,500
1962	124	$14,000	1979	200	$27,500
			1980	61	$30,000
			1981	86	$32,000
			1982	25	$35,000
			1983	25	$39,000

*For 1950-60 airplanes, price includes com radio. For 1961-79 airplanes, price includes nav-com, full panel, vacuum system, lights, electric starter. In all cases, price assumes mid-time engine, good fabric and paint, no major damage history. Dealer wholesale prices are about 30 percent below retail.

with ground" category is too vague a category upon which to draw conclusions, but the Super Cub's poor showing in the mid-air collision category is probably the result of its poor visibility and use in low-level maneuvering activities such as fish-spotting, etc.

On the other side of the coin, the Super Cub has a very low rate of engine failure accidents, hard landings and overshoots.

Creature "Comforts"

By modern standards, the Super Cub is a cramped airplane. Although a bit roomier than the old J-3, the PA-18 is still far from comfortable. The fuselage dimensions of the J-3 and the PA-18 are actually identical, but the Super Cub wing spar does not protrude into the cabin, allowing the seats to be raised and moved back a bit, which gives a roomier feeling and eases the contortions the pilot must endure. With two people aboard, baggage space is severely limited; the Super Cub is a reasonable cargo hauler only with the rear seat removed.

The PA-18 can safely be flown solo from either front or rear seat. Although the Super Cub is more nose-heavy than the J-3, the Super is generally soloed from the front, while the J-3 is soloed only from the rear. These restrictions are the result of differing regulations only; both aircraft have an extremely wide c.g. tolerance.

As in most high-wing airplanes, visibility is very poor, particularly in the landing pattern. The Super Cub has a skylight-type window in the top of the cabin, but this provides little relief. (There are a few 135-hp L-21 military observation versions of the Super Cub still around; they have much better visibility down and to the rear through greenhouse-type rear windows.) Like most taildraggers, the Super Cub has poor visibility over the nose during taxi, and a back-and-forth weaving is necessary for safe taxiing.

Owners report the airplane to be fearsomely noisy. One *Aviation Consumer* staffer recalls that his ears rang for three days after a 1,000-mile trip in a 1952 Super Cub.

Handling Qualities

The Super Cub flies like a . . . well, like a Cub. It's stable, not very responsive, and generally tolerant of less-than-expert piloting technique in the air — although it will stall with a sharp break, a trait that may surprise Cherokee-trained pilots.

The Super Cub is a taildragger, of course, and has all the handling liabilities of that breed: inherent instability on the ground, terrible visibility during landing and take-off, and severe bouncing tendencies upon landing. Within the framework of taildraggers, however, the Super Cub is relatively easy to handle, with none of the crow-hopping tendencies of the Cessna 180 or ground-loop love of the Luscombe. The standard model, however, comes with heel brakes, which are an abomination for anyone used to conventional toe brakes. For pilots not clever at heel-and-toe shifting, these can provide a hasty introduction to a groundloop in gusty, crosswind conditions.

Resale Value

The Super Cub holds its value well, particularly the later models. This is not surprising, since there have been so few changes to the line. A well-cared-for 1975 model with 400 hours on it has more intrinsic value than a 1978 model with 1,000 hours, and could probably be bought for the same price. Late-model Super Cubs, in fact, don't seem to follow the standard aircraft depreciation pattern, which is a decline of about four years, followed by a leveling off or (in the case of a sought-after aircraft like the A36 Bonanza) steady appreciation. A 1975 Super Cub, for example, sold new for $19,700 but dropped in value only to $16,500 the next year (about 15 percent depreciation, compared to the usual 20 percent first-year loss of value for the average aircraft). After just two years, the value of a 1975 Super Cub climbed up to $17,250, and has climbed steadily since. It now has a "bluebook" value of $22,000 — 12 percent more than when it was new. Not even the blue-chip Bonanza can match that claim.

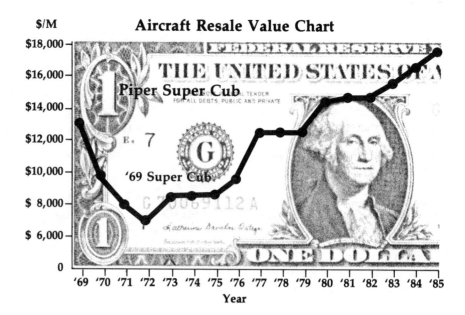

Aircraft Resale Value Chart

Piper Super Cub / '69 Super Cub

Even a 1969 Super Cub is today worth 10 percent *more* than its original price, an astonishing display of value.

It's not likely that late-model production Super Cubs will do as well, however; the last price of $45,000-plus (for a 1983 model) was highly inflated, and it's doubtful that a 1983 Super Cub purchased today will ever fetch $45,000 again (assuming reasonable inflation rates). On the other hand, surging prices for new Super Cubs help keep the value of used ones high.

Shopping Checklist

Even though the Super Cub has remained virtually unchanged over its lifetime, there are a few optional features that any used-plane shopper should look for. Among the appraisal points of the Super Cub:

• *Metallization.* Some Super Cubs have been "metallized," which means the steel tubing in the fuselage and tail feathers has been coated with zinc (aluminum in the early models). This is a very desirable feature, for corrosion of the metal tubing is a common problem in older Super Cubs. The airplane's paperwork should indicate if it has been metallized, and there is also a stamp on the firewall attesting to it. You should also visually inspect the tubing, of course.

• *Metal belly skin.* This is another big plus, although in some cases the blessing may be mixed. The metal skin is obviously more resistant to damage and aging than fabric, and the mod includes extra beefy tubes in the rear fuselage. Unfortunately, the metal belly also may be a signal that the aircraft was once a cropduster, and therefore subject to the ravages of chemical corrosion, in addition to having the hell flown out of it. The agplane version with metal belly was available from 1952 through 1960. Since then, the metal belly skin has been an option on non-duster Super Cubs, so check this out carefully.

• *Fabric.* The 1971 and later model Super Cubs have Ceconite Dacron covering, a fairly long-lived fabric. The 1970 and earlier models were covered with Grade A cotton, which has a lifespan of three to 10 years, depending on care and conditions. (Some cold-weather operators prefer the cotton because it doesn't shrink as much as Ceconite in frigid temperatures, but most people prefer the synthetic fabric.) If the bird you're looking at has cotton, count on replacement at a cost of $3,000 to $4,000 within a few years.

• *Cleveland brakes.* These were fitted to the 1978 and later models, and can be retrofitted to older aircraft. They are a desirable feature.

• *Tailwheel.* Several different tailwheels have been available over the years; the eight-inch double-fork Scott is the best.

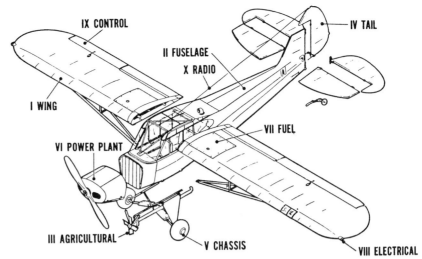

• *Strobe light.* A tail-mounted strobe was made an option on 1973 and later models.

• *Fuel gauges.* Electric gauges replaced the old visual gauges in the 1976 and later models. Although neater looking, they are less accurate, and many pilots prefer the old-style gauges.

• *Alternator.* A 60-amp Alcor alternator kit was made standard equipment in 1977. A standard generator was used from 1950-76, but the Alcor kit is retrofittable to older models, and is a desirable feature if the airplane is equipped with radios, strobe lights or landing light.

• *Vacuum pump.* A wet-type vacuum pump was available on 1954-62 models, and a dry pump on 1963-83 versions. The wet pumps, although more expensive and messier (they tend to vent a fine spray of oil overboard), are more reliable, have a longer lifespan and may be overhauled fairly inexpensively. (Dry pumps can only be replaced.)

• *Wing corrosion-proofing.* About 1965 (even Piper couldn't tell us exactly) zince chromate corrosion-proofing was applied to all wing parts. If the aircraft you're looking at is of mid-60s vintage, remove an inspection panel and check for yourself. (Greenish yellow is good; silver is bad.) At about the same time, more hard 4130 steel and heli-arc welding were incorporated in Super Cub fuselages.

• *Flaps and ailerons.* After 1977, flaps and ailerons were covered with metal instead of fabric, mostly for ease of construction. They are retrofittable to older aircraft. Although cheaper to build, they are not as repairable if damaged, a disadvantage for remote operators.

More important than all the niggling mechanical changes over the years is the individual history of the aircraft you are buying. Try to avoid aircraft used for glider or banner-towing, crop-dusting or heavy bush work. Pipeline patrol aircraft, on the other hand, are usually desirable despite the high airframe times, because they area flown long distances at low power settings, which puts very little strain on the engine, landing gear and structure. As with any used aircraft, have a knowledgeable mechanic go over the airplane with a fine-tooth comb. This is critical for aircraft such as the Super Cub, which are more likely to have suffered abuse or damage sometime in their history.

Although the Super Cub has long since been put out to pasture by the manufacturer, most every last screw, hinge and grommet is still available through part suppliers like Univair Aircraft Corp.

Maintenance Checks

Have your mechanic check these common Super Cub trouble spots with special care:

• Fatigue cracks in wing strut threaded clevis bolts.

• Worn out landing gear hinge and shock strut bolts and bushings.

• Corrosion in fuselage steel tubing, particularly in lower rear.

• Internal rusting of wing struts. This is not widespread, but has occurred on some aircraft and is the subject of an AD.

• Top rudder hinge bushing, especially on those aircraft equipped with rudder-mounted Grimes beacon.

• Loose or worn out elevator trim jackscrew, particularly in aircraft used for glider or banner towing.

Generally, the Super Cub is a rugged and robust aircraft that is extremely easy to fix in the field. The only trouble spot may be the fabric covering and steel tube structure, which are unfamiliar to many mechanics accustomed to all-metal aircraft. The engine is very reliable, has a 2,000-hour TBO.

Naturally, compliance with all ADs should be checked. Actually, the Super Cub has been subject to

Cost/Performance/Specifications

Engine	Cruise Speed (Kts)	Rate of Climb (fpm)	Useful Load (lbs)	Fuel Capacity (gals)	TBO (hrs)	Overhaul Cost
150-hp Lyc. O-320-A2A	100	960	804	36	2,000*	$6,300
135-hp Lyc. O-290-D2	95	870	872	36	1,500	$5,800
125-hp Lyc. O-290-D	97	940	655	36	2,000	$5,800
90-hp Cont. C-90-F	87	710	700	18	1,800	$4,500

Pre-1968 models may be equipped with 7/16-inch valves. In that case, TBO is 1,200 hours.

relatively few ADs; a 1964 model, for example, has just eight directives, about half the number of a Cherokee of similar vintage.

Parts and Customer Support

Piper has recently bailed out of the Super Cub parts business. A better alternative may be Univair Aircraft Corp., Rte. 3, Box 59, Aurora, Colo. 80011. Univair also supplies virtually any Super Cub part — at prices often far less than Piper's former charges. The company also publishes a complete parts catalog for the PA-18 series.

Some Super Cub parts are also available from Wag-Aero, Inc., in Lyons, Wisc.

Owner Comments

I have owned a 1952 '125' Super Cub, a 1963 '150' Super Cub, and a 1960 '95' Super Cub. The 125 was a good airplane; however, I consistently had problems with engine temperature. The oil temperature would get so hot sometimes, the engine smelled like it was burning. I had it approximately eight months and had this problem on and off the whole time. The Piper distributor never could find the trouble. (I might add that I purchased this airplane used.) When the engine would get hot, the only solution was to close the throttle and dive the airplane, which would cool the engine down. Usually, the problem didn't recur on that particular flight.

Takeoff roll was in the neighborhood of 200-300 feet with flaps. Cruise was in the 90- to 95-mph range with standard metal prop, and fuel consumption at cruise six to seven gph. Other than engine overheating, the airplane gave me no problems.

The 150 was my favorite. This airplane would do anything you asked of it. The 150 Lycoming always purred along with absolutely no problems whatsoever. Takeoff, with light fuel and solo, was almost vertical. My technique for shortest

Inherent instability on the ground combined with poor visibility, a severe bouncing tendency and heel brakes make it a challenge.

possible takeoff was stick full back, add full throttle, reach down and pull full flaps, and you were immediately airborne. Immediately upon breaking ground, forward stick was applied to keep from getting a stall as you got out of the ground effect. Takeoff roll at gross *plus* probably averaged in the 200-to 300-foot range. I equipped this airplane with Alaskan "tundra" tires. With these, I flew off sand beaches along south Louisiana, where I would go fishing. The brakes, although adequate with standard 800x4 tires, were useless with the big tires. They carried only four psi pressure, and when you taxied across dry sand, they made a track on the sand that looked like you had rolled a ball on it.

When I purchased this aircraft from a fish-spotting outfit, the airframe had approximately 4,300 hours on it, and the engine had about 700 hours since new. The fuselage had been metallized, and I had no rust problems while I owned it. When I bought it, it had a 61-inch pitch prop on it and it would give a good, honest 120 IAS with this prop. When I changed to the standard 56-inch prop, the IAS dropped to about 105 or 110 IAS at 2,000 feet.

You could see the look of surprise on Cessna 172 pilots as I would pass them in level flight with the 61 prop that was on the airplane when I first bought it. I really don't think that takeoff performance suffered much with this prop and the loads I normally carried.

I thought fuel consumption was high, probably averaging nine to 10 gph at the low altitudes, full rich. Leaned out it would burn 8 to 8-1/2

gph at 5,000 feet. Stalls were always gentle, with the airspeed indicator reading ground 40-45 mph.

This airplane would haul anything you could put in it, and it still is the only airplane I have ever flown that I felt had more than enough power to do anything I wanted to do.

The 95 is another story. I purchased it used, also. It had the 'plane booster' wing tips on it and all these did was add weight and block visibility to the sides. I had flown a 95 previously without these tips, and it was a sweet-flying airplane. My airplane performed about like a 65-horse J-3 or 7AC, with a cruise of 80-85 mph at about 5-1/2 gph. I flew it out of a 1,100-foot strip, and on a warm day with a heavy load, it was close. I really feel the booster tips hurt this particular airplane more than they helped and would never put them on any airplane I owned.

I picked up my 1976 Super Cub at the factory in Lock Haven and have since amassed 210 hours on the plane. I bought it with the metal belly pan, because I feel it is a necessity for the type of in-and-out flying I do — into nurseries for the commercial purchasing of plants and shrubs for our business.

I installed 8.50x6 tires for better floatation on rough, furrowed fields. They're a heck of a lot cheaper than the tundra ties, which go for something like $800 a piece, I'm told.

The stainless steel control cables were prematurely replaced at 200 hours, apparently wearing flat where they pass through the eyelets on the struts. Vibration of the engine has necessitated repeated welding of the muffler cover, and has loosened paint on the wheel strut cover. Nothing big, though.

I have had a definite problem with a recurring mold or fungus, a black film that forms on the painted surfaces throughout the plane. A good scrubbing will eliminate it for a while, but it always comes back. The airplane has always been hangared.

Piper Cherokee 140

Thanks to a quirk of fate, Piper's Cherokee 140 at this stage in history has achieved a mildly special status. It's about as cheap and basic a knockabout flying machine as can be found this side of the old tail-dragger crowd that won't leave you feeling like a leaf pressed in a dictionary. That's because of its hybrid status—as a roomier-than-average two-placer that can carry four.

As for availability—there are zillions of them around at fields everywhere—6,300 is a ballpark figure from a recent census—and a great nesting ground of them in *Trade-A-Plane*. Furthermore it's an airplane every A&P can work on in his sleep—it's a known commodity in the maintenance shop. And it won't bite; it's as easy to fly as an airplane can be, and it has an excellent safety record, as well.

It's not, by the way, the cheapest transportation available. Among its contemporaries, the two-place Cessna 150 is a full $5,000 cheaper on the average for the same model year (1977, the last year the Cherokee 140 was built), and believe it or not a Piper Tomahawk of a year's later vintage can be had for even less than that ($8,500 or so). See the chart nearby.

History of the Line

It is perhaps fitting that the Cherokee 140, later to be given more genteel names like Flite Liner and Cruiser, began life as an improvisation. First came a four-place 160-hp Cherokee as a replacement to the rag-wing Tri-Pacer. For some unfathomable reason, a 150-hp version was brought out shortly after that.

Then it occurred to Piper to retrogress a bit further and make

the 150-horse version a 140-horse aircraft, throw out the two rear seats and make it an ad hoc trainer and a competitor to the Cessna 150, which was selling like hotcakes. Some convoluted marketing reasoning compelled the company to actually "derate" the engine to put out only 140 horses by using a restricted 2450 rpm on a climb prop.

When the silliness of this concept became apparent, in 1965 another prop was installed allowing the normal 2700 rpm, restoring the 10 horses temporarily lost. In the process the aircraft was given a 200-pound boost in gross weight (to 2,150 pounds) to restore it to full respectability. And the two-plus-two concept was introduced by slapping a couple of snap-on seats on top of the plywood plank that up till then had served as a luggage bin.

Following are other modest changes that came along through the years:

● In 1969 the B model came on the scene with a new instrument panel incorporating the famous "multi" throttle quadrant, introducing circuit breakers instead of fuses, and rocker switches for toggles. And it finally provided a decent, standard instrument layout in place of the scattergun arrangement used on Cherokees up till that point. The so-called deluxe Cruiser option

Starting in 1971 Piper brought out a stripped economy model of the 140 called the Flite Liner. This was a '73 version.

had wheel fairings and rear seats installed.

● With the 1970 C model came larger dynafocal (rubber) engine mounts to dampen engine vibration, along with overhead air vents and highly adjustable seats.

● The D model in 1971 brought a redesigned dorsal fin and inertial reel seat harnesses, with autopilots as an option. A stripped-down model was called the Flite Liner that year.

● In 1972 with the E model came the miracle of air conditioning—a great novelty in small aircraft, and a boon of no small dimensions for flight training in the blazing heat of the southlands in summer.

● In 1973 an entrance step was made standard.

● And in 1974 Piper put bungees on the rudders and increased the turn angle of the nosewheel for easier ground handling, and toe brakes became standard on the copilot's side.

● The last Cherokee 140 rolled off the line in 1977, eclipsed by the Tomahawk and overshadowed by the genuinely four-place Warrior.

Handling and Performance

The Cherokee 140 has come through the years with a deserved reputation as a benign trainer. In fact, its stall is so hard to induce that some instructors believe it insufficient to show the student a good, clean break. By the same token, some instructors say it's almost too easy to land.

Nevertheless, quite a few owners say it takes a bit of concentration to get a really nice greaser landing. Come in too fast and it floats; too slow, and it hits hard. One answer: come in slow with a little power in the flare.

The three-position manual flaps are quick and effective—so much so that many pilots say they rarely use over two notches. Watch that overhead trim—does it crank left or right? At least the nose pitches *down* with lowered flaps—a logical reaction if there has to be any. Some owners also complain of a high rate of sink at idle. The Hershey Bar wing is no sailplane airfoil.

When it comes to maneuverability, the 140 is no Pitts. Owners rate the control forces a bit heavy. The Warrior, by comparison, shows the beneficial effect of that plane's new wing geometry with lighter, more pleasant ailerons. The other side of the coin is stability, and instrument pilots characterize the 140 as a good, stable IFR platform.

As for performance, owners talk about cruise speeds of only 110 to 117 mph/96 to 102 knots TAS, though the book calls for 132 mph/115 knots at 75 percent power. Pilots count on burning about nine gph at 75 percent and seven to eight gph at 65 percent.

The 140 has 50-gallon capacity fuel tanks, with tab markings in the filler neck showing 36 gallons. In fact, the standard fuel was normally listed as 36 gallons, with 50 optional—presumably to discourage fliers from viewing the airplane as a true four-placer and overloading it.

Indeed, owners caution against ex-

The lowly 140 can really put on airs with air conditioning. Flight instructors and students need not "sweat it out" in southern summer climes.

pecting rocketship performance on takeoff and climbout in high-density altitude situations. Naturally, the temptation to load the aircraft too heavily when the rear seats are installed can lead to trouble.

Cabin Comfort

Since the 140 shares the same ample cabin width as other Cherokees, not counting the Lance, of course, it's a comfortable aircraft for two riders—much more so than the Cessna 150. This naturally makes the 140 a more sensible aircraft for cross-country flying. And if the rear compartment is used for baggage as originally intended, it's more than adequate. But there's no separate baggage bay when two passengers are in the back. Owners complain, incidentally, that there's no separate baggage door.

Comparison Buys

Except for its rather higher price, the Piper Warrior would be a much more sensible buy, since it has the same basic simplicity and durability of the 140, but nicer handling and standard seating for four plus space for baggage through a rear access door. On top of that it has another 90 pounds or so of useful load and better climb performance.

Unfortunately, the average price of the oldest, cheapest Warrior with

the 160-hp engine (the '77 model) is about $18,000, compared with $14,000 for the Cherokee 140. And older 140s can be bought for as low as $8,000.

Comparable Cessna 150s can be found for $6,000 to $9,000, and they'll yield better fuel economy; but this comes at the cost of shorter range, slightly lower cruise speed, a more cramped cockpit and lower payload. Cherokee 140 owners claim their aircraft gives a quieter cockpit as well.

Another even cheaper option is the Piper Tomahawk. Ironically, originally intended as a replacement for the 140, the T'hawk is selling for even less than the Cessna 150. Count on maybe $8,500 for a '78 model. Figure that one out. The used-plane market evidently has rated the Tomahawk a rather poor commodity.

Perhaps a dark horse in the two-place used-plane niche is the Beech Skipper, an "ultramodern" aircraft compared with the 140. The '79 model Skipper is going for an average of $12,000, though there aren't many of them out there, since only 312 were built.

Pilots with a fetish for aircraft with an abundance of *lebensraum* in their aircraft might also take a glance at the Beech Sport—which like the 140 is a kind of two-plus-two bird, but has an even more cavernous interior. The $12,500 average price tag (for a '77 model) afforded this aircraft, however, presumably reflects its even doggier performance.

Resale Value

Like most trainers, the Cherokee 140 does not exhibit the handsome rise in resale value of highly regarded aircraft with inflation—though that has now subsided. Instead, the typical resale value curve of a 140 is a dip to the bottom in three or four years, followed by a plateau for the rest of its history, perhaps with a modest rise in worth.

Tracking the history of a 1969 model, for example, we see that it dropped from an equipped list price of slightly over $15,000 to about $8,000 three years later. It then began an almost imperceptible rise in paper value through the years (hardly compensating for inflation) to where this year it has peaked at a bit over $10,000. A 140 produced in the last model year, 1977, started out at over $24,000 equipped and proceeded to plummet to a low of $11,300 or so six years later. This was less than half its original cost and close to the resale value of its much more ancient '69 hangarmate. In the last couple of years, however, the aircraft has taken a turn upward, perhaps reflecting the ever more exorbitant cost of new aircraft, and the drop in production of all the two-placers.

Maintenance

Owners describe the Cherokee 140 as a fairly easy, inexpensive aircraft to maintain, with widespread familiarity by mechanics in the field. However, they say parts are expensive out of proportion to the value of the aircraft. And during 1985 most Piper parts were extremely slow in coming for all classes of aircraft because of drastic company reorganization and relocation. The cost of an annual inspection ranged from $300 to $600 in reports from users to *The Aviation Consumer*.

Since the aircraft are often used as trainers, they've been put through the mill and experienced the toughest handling by students. Indeed, we noted a fair share of landing gear problems in the Service Difficulty Reports, suggesting lots of pounding on landings.

The right-side passenger door is the only access to the cabin. There is no separate baggage door—a distinct handicap when loading baggage.

Feedback by Cherokee 140 owners in 1981 warned of a series of problems we did not note in our current survey. These concerned matters like malfunctioning rotating beacon lamps and landing lights, landing gear struts sticking and shimmy dampers going on the fritz (though there were a few Service Difficulty Reports on this last item). Also, although in '81 we received complaints about fuel tank leakage, that pattern was not repeated this time around.

ADs and Service Bulletins

The Cherokee 140 has had a fairly demure AD history down through the years. Control balance weights came in for their share of attention in 1967 and 1970 as ADs called for inspections for possible corrosion or cracks in aileron balance weights, rudder horn assemblies and stabilator balance weight tubes.

In '69 mechanics were cautioned to peer beneath the Piper medallion on the control wheels to check for cracks to prevent possible failure of the wheel. This was to be a repetitive inspection unless the wheels were replaced by metal ram's horn types.

Other noteworthy ADs zeroed in on replacing the fuel selector valve cover to prevent possible binding of the handle, and installation of new oil hose assemblies to prevent possible rupture.

Fuel gauges on the Cherokee 140s have also come in for their share of attention, once for erratic indications, because of possible internal wire failures; and in 1977 for possibly showing as much as two and a half gallons of fuel remained when the tanks were actually empty. A placard warning pilots of this situation was mandated, until the gauges were correctly calibrated.

Nonmandatory Piper Service Bulletins worthy of note included ones calling for: baggage floor brace (in case none had been originally installed), replacement of the carburetor heat cable and rerouting away from the exhaust stack, inspection of stabilator hinge attach bolts, aft spar wing attach bolts and tailpipe replacement to

Cost/Performance/Specifications

Model	Year	Number Built	Average Retail Price	Cruise Speed (mph)	Rate of Climb (fpm)	Useful Load (lbs)	Fuel Std/Opt (gals)	Engine	TBO (hrs)	Overhaul Cost
PA-28-140	1964-65	1,386	$8,700	115	660	770	50	150-hp Lyc. O-320-E2A	2,000	$6,300
PA-28-140	1966-67	2,725	$9,400	115	660	970	50	150-hp Lyc. O-320-E2A	2,000	$6,300
PA-28-140B	1968-69	2,287	$10,300	115	660	970	50	150-hp Lyc. O-320-E2A	2,000	$6,300
PA-28-140C, D	1970-71	1,186	$11,100	115	660	970	50	150-hp Lyc. O-320-E2A	2,000	$6,300
PA-28-140E	1972-73	1,276	$11,700	115	660	970	50	150-hp Lyc. O-320-E3D	2,000	$6,300
PA-28-140	1974-75	784	$12,400	115	660	970	50	150-hp Lyc. O-320-E3D	2,000	$6,300
PA-28-140	1976-77	565	$13,500	115	660	970	50	150-hp Lyc. O-320-E3D	2,000	$6,300

prevent the restriction that could be caused from separation of the muffler inner baffle.

In December 1982 Piper also issued a SB (No. 753) giving elaborate instructions on how to spin the aircraft safely. Spinning is permitted when the aircraft is loaded in the utility category, which imposes certain gross weight and cg limitations. In this context the SB notes that even seat positions should be carefully calculated to prevent exceeding the aft limits. Placards were issued with the SBs.

The latest significant Service Bulletin, issued in May 1985 urged Cherokee 140 owners to install a special access panel to permit inspection of the aft wing spar. This was done because of reports from the field that the aft wing spars were inaccessible for corrosion inspection. If corrosion is found, Piper provides a spar modification kit. As we mentioned in our SDR survey, several reports described serious wing spar corrosion problems.

Service Difficulties

A survey of Service Difficulty Reports filed on the Cherokee 140 showed a broad range of airframe and engine problems that a buyer might be on the lookout for. One area that received more notice than others involved cracked aileron bellcrank brackets. Some users reported they suspected wind damage. There were 12 cases in this category.

Perhaps testimony to hard training use of the aircraft and extra strain on the landing gear system was a clutch of reports of broken or loose main landing gear attach bolts. There were cases of main landing gear torque link cracks, as well. In addition, some users reported cracks in the rudder pedal assembly, bar and support brackets, while there were half a dozen reports of loose attach bracket bolts for the vertical stabilizer.

A handful of pilots reported cracks in the control wheel, with a couple breaking off, one in flight. Luckily

The Hershey Bar wings hold 50 gallons of fuel, which gives the aircraft a generous five hours-plus of range.

the aircraft usually has another wheel to grab onto.

Pilots looking at older 140s might pay close attention to the integrity of the wing spars. There were several reports of heavy corrosion and delamination of spars, requiring wing replacement. As we mentioned earlier, Piper has brought out a kit to provide access to aft wing spars at the attach fittings to aid in inspecting for corrosion.

When it comes to engine longevity, broken exhaust valves apparently represent a big problem. There were 22 reports in this category. In eight instances there were problems with cracked or broken cylinders. Magneto failures took their toll in Cherokee 140s, as well, with no less than 39 reports, almost evenly divided between Slick and Bendix mags. Problems were reported with bearings, coils and gear teeth on the magnetos.

Worried about vacuum pump failure? Only five cases were reported for the 140—three EdoAire and two Airborne with driveshafts shearing.

There also was a handful of exhaust stack failures—something common to many aircraft, and muffler baffle problems. We noted seven cases of oil cooler hoses failing, deteriorating or chafing, and see that in 1977 Piper issued a Service Bulletin calling for replacement of engine oil hoses.

Incidentally, these trouble areas pretty well jibed with the results of an SDR search we performed in

1981, so things haven't changed much.

Modifications

There is a sizable catalog of Supplemental Type Certificate mods on the Cherokee 140—most designed, naturally, to coax greater performance from it. There are upgraded engines of both 160- and 180-hp. Among those offering 180-hp conversions are Avcon Conversions, Udall, Kans. One of those offering 160-hp upgrades is RAM Aircraft Corp. in Waco Tex.

R/STOL Systems, Inc., which took over Robertson's full dossier of mods, can equip the Cherokee 140 with everything from aileron gap seals to leading edge cuffs, stall fences and drooping flaperons. The full treatment goes for $7,995. They're at Snohomish County Airport, Bldg. C-72, Everett, Wash. 98204, (206) 355-2736.

Jim Bradshaw's Knots 2 U can provide speed mods for Cherokee 140s, including aileron and flap seals that are supposed to boost the cruise speed by about four to seven knots and lower the stall speed some and give crisper aileron control. The address is 1941 Highland Ave., Wilmette, Ill. 60091, (312) 256-4807.

Laminar Flow Systems has devoted a lot of its attention to sprucing up the Cherokee 140. With streamlined wheelpants, flap and aileron gap seals along flap track fairings, this company claims to coax as much as another 17 knots from the old bird. They're located in St. Thomas, the U.S. Virgin Islands, Box 8557, zip 00801, (809) 775-5515.

Met-Co-Aire in Fullerton, Calif. provides new wingtips, and Bob Fields Aerocessories in Santa Paula, Calif. will give you door seal.

A Lakeland, Fla. outfit, Globe Aero, will put a one-piece windshield on your Cherokee 140 for $775. Tinted glass is only slightly extra.

Safety Record

A survey of two years of Cherokee

140 accidents suggests the aircraft is no killer. Out of 451 accidents in 1980 and 1981 there were only 14 fatals, and five of those, or nearly 36 percent, involved pilots flying under the influence of alcohol. The others show a bizarre mix of causes that had little bearing on the inherent safety of the aircraft—such as flying inadvertently into IFR conditions, making low passes, a suicide. There was, however, one fatal when a 140 was climbing out and hit some trees. This may represent the tip of an iceberg, however, since there were quite a few similar nonfatal accidents of this category.

There were no instances in the two-year period of Cherokee 140s breaking up in flight. Since all the PA-28s are generally lumped together in breakup surveys, it is hard to isolate the 140, but the two- and four-place Cherokees in general are about in the middle of the pack, or average, in this category, statistically.

Among the nonfatal accidents, engine failure accidents took the heaviest toll—as is commonly the case with other aircraft. There were 24 of these. About half are shrouded in mystery, with no cause for the engine failure determined. The greatest number of engine stoppages—six—involved some kind of fuel interruption not of the pilot's doing. In one case it was noted that the engine-driven fuel pump failed. In three other cases there were cylinder problems and in one instance an oil problem. On two occasions carburetor ice was blamed.

Despite its reputation as a "starter" aircraft often used by low-time pilots and in flight instruction, there was only one instance of a pilot inadvertently shutting off the fuel—or fuel mismanagement. But on nine other occasions Cherokee 140 pilots simply ran out of fuel, which suggests inattention to the gauges, or pushing to make the last few miles—or perhaps poor-reading fuel instruments.

Although pilots like to rave about the wide-gear stance of the aircraft

The deluxe, so-called 2 + 2 Cruiser had full rear seats rather than snap-on pads. A split flexible cowling—the snaps may be barely visible in the photo—makes the engine eminently accessible from either side.

and, therefore, its adept handling in tricky crosswind situations, the 140 logged a hefty share of ground-loops and swerve accidents —19 in all. A total of 12 of these were on the landing; the other seven occurred during takeoff.

Since the number of undershoots (18) and overshoots (13) is so close, this appears to be evidence more of the inexperience of pilots rather than to some intrinsic shortcoming of the aircraft.

There were quite a few accidents (15) from Cherokee 140 pilots hitting obstacles on climbout after takeoff. And we mentioned there was one fatal. The aircraft is obviously no rocketship in climb, and it might be a temptation to overload what is basically a two-place aircraft.

Among the so-called miscellaneous accidents were quite a few involving reckless pilots making low passes.

The Association

Cherokee 140 owners can get in touch with the Cherokee Pilot's Assn., P.O. Box 20817, St. Petersburg, Fla. 33742, (813) 576-4992. Terry Lee Rogers is editor of the newsletter.

Owner Comments

I bought my Cherokee 140 in 1984 for $8,500, then sunk another $2,000 upgrading the avionics for IFR flight. Since then I've put over 200 hours on the plane, which I use primarily in my book packaging business. I make primarily short hops under an hour. Many planes aren't practical or economical for this sort of puddle-jumping, but this one does just fine.

The Cherokee 140 is a slow plane. I average about 100 knots ground-speed on my trips. But it's simple and easy to fly. A thorough pre-flight takes just 15 minutes. She handles well in turbulence and crosswinds, although there are times when I feel the response to the controls is a little sluggish.

Landings are sometimes a bit tricky. My Cherokee has the old constant-chord Hershey Bar wing. If you let the airspeed drop below 74 knots on approach, the plane loses altitude quickly, and you find yourself jockeying the throttle to make it to the runway. She also gets wing-heavy as she flies. As you use the gas from one wing tank, the other wing gets heavy. The handbook says to switch tanks every hour, but I find if I let it go much past a half hour, it gets hard to hold the heavy wing up, and the plane wants to wander off course. A crossfeed fuel system would have been a nice addition.

Still, I have very few complaints with the overall design. The cabin is roomy, and not as loud as many lightplanes I've been in. The engine compartment is easily accessible, since both sides of the cowling lift up. Brake shoes can be checked without removing the wheel pants.

The plane has an O-320 low-compression Lycoming, and I've got an STC for autogas from Petersen Aviation. I find there's absolutely no difference in performance from avgas. You have to change throttle settings a little more slowly to avoid backfiring, but this is no problem. The handbook advertises 7.2 gph, but with all the short hops I make, I find the plane drinks about eight gph. That's still plenty economical for me.

Maintenance has also been economical. The plane sat for almost eight years without being flown before I bought it. In that time, a lot of hoses, seals and gaskets dried up. For the first few months after I bought it, I was constantly cleaning or replacing some minor part. I began to think that I had a real lemon on my hands. But after a while, the plane straightened up and flew right.

For the last 150 hours, I've missed only one flight because of mechanical problems, and that was nothing more than a burned-out landing light.

Even with the host of minor mechanical problems in the first months, maintenance has run me about $1,200 since I bought the plane, and that includes a thorough annual. So far, it's costing me about $27 an hour in the air, including maintenance, gas, oil, insurance, loan payments and hangar fees. Mile for mile, that's about the same as it would cost to drive a new mid-size car.

Nick Engler
West Milton, Ohio

I purchased my '74 140 in 1984 from an owner that claimed to be an A&P mechanic. It had 1,600 hours on the tach and about 60 hours

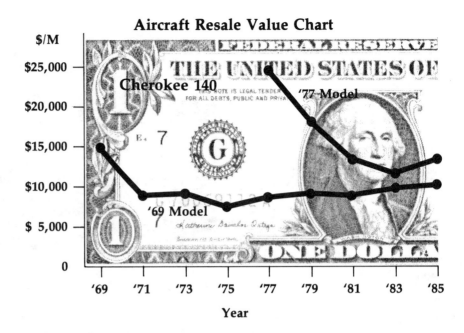

Aircraft Resale Value Chart

since a total engine overhaul, according to the log. I thought I was getting a great deal. Only later did I wish I never purchased the aircraft.

On my first annual my mechanic found No. 2 cylinder with only 40 pounds of compression. He pulled the jug and found the cylinder was blued from overheating, the rocker arms were reversed so the oil holes did not line up, the rings were the wrong size and type, the exhaust valve was severely pitted. I had a bad feeling about the other cylinders so had them pulled. Sure enough, the others had the wrong rings and were severely worn and had other problems.

I ended up with a complete top overhaul. Now, everything on the engine is right.

As far as operating costs, my annual cost is $280. Cost per hour averages $25 to $30. A complete top overhaul cost $1,090. I replaced the right wheel fairing for $90 from Windy's. Piper wanted $350 for one.

Parts availability is poor. Ask the local Piper dealer for a part and you end up waiting three to six weeks for it. Some parts can't be had from Piper.

James L. Carl
Pikesville, Ind.

Among the Cherokee 140's good points is the low wing. It makes anybody's landings look good. The manual flaps are nice. There's less to go wrong. On long flights the plane is fairly comfortable and has ample legroom in front. The back seat is cramped for adults. The handling qualities are good, as is visibility.

There are only a couple of bad points. First, it's a dog climbing above 5,000 feet. Second, it has just one door, making loading of cargo very inconvenient.

We have found Piper parts extremely expensive for this price-class of airplane. Ours did not come with the hatshelf/baggage compartment bulkhead. Piper wanted an arm and a leg for a fiberglass factory model. We found a company in Kirkland, Wash. making a more attractive design out of a molded ABS material for half the price of Piper's. The company is Pegasus Northwest, (206) 822-0217. Another superb source of information is the Cherokee Pilots Assn.

Overall, we have enjoyed the Cherokee. I wish it had a bit more room in the back seat, and a bit more horsepower. But as it is, it's good, cheap, reliable flying.

Randall Schatz
Bothell, Wash.

Airknocker Roundup

The anticipated new recreational flying license may unleash upon the world a flood of interest in cheap, old airplanes in which basic stick-and-rudder skills can be taught for a pittance. These nice elderly airknockers might be the answer for many who don't really savor the rustic flying qualities of the ultralights, yet can't afford anything more exotic. Advocates envision these elderly, sometimes primitive aircraft as a possible new avenue toward inexpensive flying—pegged to a license requiring only rudimentary skills unencumbered by radio communication.

The following represents an attempt to sort out the advantages and deficiencies of a special group of six aircraft that seem to be most likely candidates for this new class of flying.

Airknocker Availability

How many of these old birds are still around and flying? The Census of U.S. Civil Aircraft in 1981 gave the following totals, ranked in descending order:

    Cessna 150s: 14,902.
    Piper/Taylor J-3s: 3,829.
    Cessna 120/140s: 3,345.
    Aeronca 7s: 2,101.
    Ercoupes: 1,631.
    Taylorcrafts: 1,405.

Going Prices

The dollar queen of our study group of possible recreational license trainers has to be the Piper J-3 Cub. Since it has evolved into something of a classic, it goes for the handsome price of around $10,000, according to the *Aircraft Bluebook Price Digest*. This may well put it out of reach for sensible consideration as an economy flivver.

Why mess with a fussy-handling taildragger when you can get a nice-flying Cessna 152 with excellent parts availability?

The cheapest aircraft in our group are the Ercoupe, Taylorcraft and the Cessna 150 (asssuming we're talking about the older C-150s built between 1959 and 1963 and the older Taylorcraft manufactured from 1939 to 1950). All of these can be bought for between $5,000 and $6,000.

As it turns out, the Cessna 120/140s seem to be climbing in the class heirarchy, and pulling down rather bigger prices for old aircraft. Hence, the *Aircraft Bluebook Price Digest* quotes the C-120s as going for about $6,500, with the C-140s pegged right up around $7,500, on the average. And these prices are for oldies built between 1946 and 1950.

Appropriate for Training?

Granted that all the aircraft in our little group of airknockers are pretty cheap to acquire and operate and maintain. But how desirable are they for training new pilots? This brings up the ancient debate on taildraggers vs. tricycle-gear aircraft. One argument is that you learn a special and beneficial finesse (or maybe raw agility) with a tailwheel aircraft that stays with you throughout your flying career. The other point of view is that whatever extra adroitness might be afforded by dealing with the trickier art of taildragger flying is in a broad sense completely wiped out by the much higher accident rate—usually involving groundlooping.

Can You Get Parts?

When it comes to parts availability, surprisingly none of these old birds is really an orphan. The two most common suppliers for Aeronca 7, Ercoupe and J-3 parts are Univair Aircraft Corp. in Aurora, Colo., 303-364-7661; and Wag-Aero in Lyons, Wisc., 414-763-9586.

Since the Taylorcraft Aviation Corp. has been building newer versions of this model since 1974, it still supplies most of the parts for the older models like the BC-12D, over 1,400 of which still survive. However, a few parts are hard to get even from the parent company.

As for the Cessna 120/140 series, even though the manufacturer is still around, not many parts are available from the big Wichita plane-maker. In fact, the overall parts situation for these aircraft has been pretty dismal, but now is improving slowly, thanks mainly to increasing work by Univair with these aircraft.

And finally, since the Cessna 152 is still in manufacture, its close sibling C-150 has pretty good parts availability.

Maintenance

Most of these aircraft are quite simple and straightforward and therefore fairly easy to work on and maintain. But buyers should not be lulled into thinking ownership will necessarily be a picnic, from a maintenance point of view. The problem is that many of the younger, newer mechanics are not familiar with them, and it may take quite a bit of poking and peering and learning from them to catch on. And naturally, the owner will be paying for the extra time and effort.

Also, the rag-and-tube construction on half the aircraft will present problems rarely encountered by quite a few contemporary repair stations. And the likelihood of

Though parts availability is good for the Ercoupe, the accident rate is poor, and early models have no rudder pedals—a training oddity.

finding a service manual at the local shop for rigging or complicated tasks is less than good.

We advocate the view that the taildragger is an anachronism better consigned to bygone days, except for special uses like rough-field work, or just fun in "personality" aircraft. In a training situation, we submit that tailgear operations represent a needless burden on the student that will more often generate grief than inculcate better skills, even though we don't regard any of this particular airknocker group as specially wicked examples of the genre.

Also, the old taildraggers have a less than savory record in stall/spin accidents. The Aeronca 7, Taylorcraft and J-3, in fact, came out first, third and fourth worst among the 33 single-engine aircraft compared by the FAA in stall accidents in a special study which we discuss in detail in the safety section.

Safety

Most of the six aircraft in the group have a pretty dismal accident record. The one exception is the Cessna 150, which has to be one of the safest aircraft flying, despite its traditional role as a knockabout trainer. All the other six have an accident rate that puts them in the worst half of 33 aircraft whose safety records were compared in a monumental 1979 FAA study.

The poorest accident rate of the group (tallied during the years 1972 through 1976) was garnered by the Cessna 120/140 with a figure that made it sixth worst of all 33 aircraft.

The Ercoupe, Aeronca 7, Piper J-3 and Taylorcraft followed quickly behind, in that order.

In terms of fatal accidents, the Piper J-3 Cub had the dubious distinction of being the most dangerous of the group, coming out sixth worst of all 33 aircraft compared. Right behind was the Aeronca 7, followed by the Ercoupe, Taylorcraft (a bit farther beyond), with the Cessna 120/140 switching roles and coming out sixth best of all 33 aircraft.

In both categories, overall accident rate and fatal accident rate, the Cessna 150 was among the safest two or three airplanes on the roster.

In-flight Breakups

What kind of accidents plagued the various airknockers we are studying, and were any trends noticeable? Perhaps the scariest kind of accident is the in-flight airframe failure. In the FAA study, the Ercoupe had the third worst record after the Bellanca 14-19 and the Globe GC-1 Swift, with the others in our group spaced out pretty well down the list.

This is not to suggest that Ercoupes are constantly fluttering out of the skies, because the rates reflected a total of six in-flight breakups. But correlated with hours flown, the rate is high. This is corroborated by a separate study by Brent Silver, our contributing editor, over a much larger period of time, from 1964 through 1977, comparing 20 fixed-gear aircraft, including our six.

This time the Ercoupe came out with the most devastating record as worst of the 20, with a break-up rate twice that of the next most failure-prone fixed-gear aircraft, the Luscombe 8 Silvair. This reflected a total of nine accidents.

Ercoupe Miseries

Following up on the Ercoupe, we find that the FAA study discloses it was worst of the group in engine failures (third worst among the 33) and undershoots (worst of all 33).

On top of that, it was credited with having the highest rate of hard landings of our study group (and third worst among all 33).

Since all but two of the airknocker group have tricycle gear, the groundlooping tendency of the others is a matter of some concern. Here we find out that the Cessna 120/140 class is the worst (and fifth worst among the 33 studied overall). Just two counts later comes the Aeronca 7. Fairly far down the list is the J-3 Cub, in 19th place overall.

When it comes to stall-related accidents, the Aeronca 7 is a disaster, relatively speaking. It ranked at the very top of the list among all 33 aircraft, with 136 accidents. By comparison, the next-ranked airplane in our airknocker group, the Taylorcraft, showed a stall-related accident rate less than a third as high, even though it was third worst overall among the 33 airplanes.

There's little doubt, therefore, that the Cessna 150 comes out the winner hands-down in the safety comparison ranking of airknocker aircraft that might be used for a recreational license.

Salient Facts for Buyers

Here is a thumbnail sketch of each of the six aircraft under consideration with highlights and caveats:

AERONCA CHAMP 7AC—a pleasant, docile old clunker with tandem seating, good visibility and a stick control. Owners talk about cruising at 75 to 85 mph with two aboard, burning four to five gph. As with most of the other aircraft, cockpit noise is horrible. Owners characterize the Champs as durable, and parts are quite accessible. The airplane has a terrible stall accident record.

PIPER J-3 CUB—now a classic with stratospheric prices, for this category, near $10,000 on the average. Slowest of these oldies, the J-3 can be expected to yield no more than about 70 mph and grind out only 175 miles in range. It does have marvelous short-field performance, though, and benign handling. Since it has no electrical

Comparative Accident Records

(According to the FAA's 1979 study of 33 aircraft.
Rates based on each 100,000 flying hours.)

Overall Accident Rate (and rank among the 33)		Hard Landing		Groundloop	
Cessna 120/140	28.69 (6th worst)	Ercoupe	2.90 (3rd worst)	Cessna 120/140	8.99 (5th worst)
Ercoupe	28.51 (7th)	Cessna 150	1.37 (10th)	Aeronca 7	7.48 (7th)
Aeronca 7	28.26 (8th)	Cessna 120/140	1.35 (11th)	Taylorcraft	3.58 (12th)
J-3	26.97 (11th)	Aeronca 7	1.2 (14th)	Ercoupe	2.74 (16th)
Taylorcraft	24.80 (13th)	J-3	1.04 (15th)	J-3	2.07 (19th)
Cessna 150	10.28 (31st)	Taylorcraft	0.48 (23rd)	Cessna 150	1.37 (24th)

Fatal Accident Rate		Overshoot		Engine Failure	
J-3	4.73 (6th worst)	Cessna 120/140	0.71 (23rd worst)	Ercoupe	9.5 (3rd worst)
Aeronca 7	4.58 (7th)	Ercoupe	0.64 (24th)	J-3	7.61 (6th)
Ercoupe	3.87 (9th)	Aeronca 7	0.48 (28th)	Cessna 120/140	6.73 (8th)
Taylorcraft	2.62 (19th)	Cessna 150	0.35 (29th)	Aeronca 7	4.23 (15th)
Cessna 120/140	1.7 (28th)	J-3	0.34 (30th)	Taylorcraft	3.81 (17th)
Cessna 150	1.34 (32nd)	(Taylorcraft N/A)		Cessna 150	2.48 (28th)

In-Flight Airframe Failure		Undershoot		Stall	
Ercoupe	0.97 (3rd worst)	Ercoupe	2.41 (1st)	Aeronca 7	22.47 (1st)
Aeronca 7	0.27 (14th)	Taylorcraft	0.95 (7th)	Taylorcraft	6.44 (3rd)
Cessna 120/140	0.27 (16th)	Aeronca 7	0.59 (13th)	J-3	5.88 (4th)
Taylorcraft	0.24 (18th)	J-3	0.57 (15th)	Cessna 120/140	2.51 (12th)
J-3	0.23 (19th)	Cessna 120/140	0.53 (17th)	Cessna 150	1.42 (19th)
Cessna 150	0.02 (27th)	Cessna 140	0.35 (26th)	Ercoupe	1.08 (21st)

system, it must be hand propped—an additional negative safety factor to be wary of. There are still nearly 4,000 of these aircraft around, and parts availability is little short of outstanding.

TAYLORCRAFT—and here we're talking about the old BC-12Ds built before 1951, not the newer Model F19 with 100-hp engines that till recently was in production. This is probably the speed-demon of the group, getting around 95 mph on the 65-hp engine and maybe over 100 with the 95-hp version. Efficiency is high, too, since the 65-horse plane can fly on just four gph for a mildly sensational 24 mpg. Pilots say it is sluggish-handling in the air and a real floater on a landing unless you keep an approach speed around 50 to 55 mph. Parts situation is good, thanks to a factory still in operation. The cockpit is perhaps even more cramped than the others of this category. With only about 1,400 of the BC12-Ds still around,

this airplane is probably the least plentiful of the old birds in our sextet.

CESSNA 120/140—Probably as fast as the Taylorcraft, but with twice the fuel capacity for a range of some 400 miles. Prices are a bit higher for this class of aircraft, ranging from $6,500 for the C-120 to around $7,500 for the C-140. Probably the lightest aileron control forces of the group. The aircraft has the worst accident rate of the bunch, presumably thanks to its ignoble groundlooping record—again worst of the six. However, the airplane had a very low fatal accident rate, so most of the problems are most painful economically. Although there are over 3,000 of these aircraft still flying, parts availability is poor.

ERCOUPE—Probably ill-suited for training because the early models do not have rudder controls. Handling is pleasant and visibility good; the rate of climb is unremarkable, but this bird can really

descend with a healthy mush. With no rudders, the aircraft must be landed in a crosswind with a crab all the way to touchdown. The aircraft has a rather poor accident rate in several categories. Parts availability from Univair is quite good.

CESSNA 150—There are nearly 15,000 of them still around, at prices that range between $5,000 and $6,000 for models built before 1964. Parts availability: excellent. Maintenance situation: the same; mechanics all over the country are familiar with them. Safety record: outstanding—best of the group by far. Although the relatively big engine can draw six gph, in return the aircraft yields a cruise of up to 115 mph or better, the best of the bunch. Handling is delightful; rate of descent can be spectacular. Stalls are honest, and the bird can spin like a top. There's even an aerobatic version. It's even approved for autogas with the EAA STC.

The Taylorcraft is probably the speediest of the group, if you call 95-100 mph fast. Gas mileage is sensational.

Our Choice

Our out-and-out favorite is the Cessna 150. From where we sit it's got the others beat by a mile in every category except fuel consumption and, of course, antique appeal. But the autogas approval will bring fuel prices way down (even though quite a few owners of other airknockers said they were burning autogas, illegally, in the 65- and 85-horse engines with no problems).

Our second choice would be the Aeronca Champ 7AC, though we'd be wary of its stall record. It's cheap to buy and operate, and parts appear to be no real problem. And our personal experience corroborates the generally held impression it is a pleasant-flying machine with not too many vices.

Helpful Associations

Here is a list of clubs and groups that share information on the airplanes:

Aeronca Lovers Club; Contact Buzz Wagner at Clark, South Dakota; 605-532-3862.

Taylorcraft Owners Club, Bruce Bixler at Alliance, Ohio; 216-823-9748.

West Coast Cessna 120/140 Club; Rick Paige at San Mateo, Calif.; 415-574-0920. And the Cessna 120/140 Assn., Box 92, Richardson, Tex. 75080.

Ercoupe Owners Club; P.O. Box 15058, Durham, N.C. 27704; and International Ercoup Assn., Rte. 1, Box 151, Stilwell, Kans. 66085.

Owner Comments

Ercoupe

The Ercoupe is a sleeper in safe, cheap transportation. At the risk of appearing over-enthusiastic, I'll say, after owning three of them, and putting in many hours of operation since 1941, that it is in the top three two-place planes ever designed. The 85-hp model will carry two people and 21 gallons of gas on hot days with ease. The fabric wing will climb better than the all-metal wing, although the metal wing is also excellent. The maintenance costs are low compared to the two-place planes I've owned.

Crosswind takeoffs and landings are simple because of the unique landing gear engineering. All that is required is a crab to hold centerline, and on touchdown the plane straightens itself for the rollout. On takeoff, just hold the nose down till it flies. A high approach is corrected by rocking the wings, which results in altitude loss without speed increase. This allows good control at all times unlike using cross-control for a slip. As any aeronautical engineer who has studied its construction will tell you, the airframe is a marvel of engineering design.

All this for about $6,000 has to be a best buy in the low-price market. Parts are readily available from Univair, which owns the design rights. A strong Ercoupe Owners Club distributes information and helps maintain a good market value. And, like Marlene Dietrich, it doesn't look its age.

Jim Van Dyke
Stockton, Calif.

J-3 Cub

I think the J-3 Cub is the best primary trainer I have ever seen,

whether one intends to stop after a recreational license or even continue on up to more complex aircraft. It's easy to fly so that five or 10 hours is enough to be comfortable in it, and one can move up—as long as you avoid strong winds. Despite what some say about tailwheel planes, I found it wasy to land, but fast taxi and runouts do require quick responses.

Bill Greenwood
Aspen, Colo.

Taylorcraft

I purchased a somewhat tattered though charming 1946 Taylorcraft BC-12D about a year ago [in 1982] for $3,500. The annual was good for another six months, and I spent many happy hours last summer boring holes through much of the air over northwest Washington State. This was my first real experience with taildraggers, and I found the plane forgiving if not downright understanding. We even tried out a few gentle loops, rolls and spins (strictly amateur) and there was never a complaint from either one of us (although if you don't keep positive Gs when inverted, the old style cork and wire gas gauge might spill fuel all over your windshield).

The 65-hp Continental burns only four gph while scooting us along at 95 mph. Use regular auto gas (as I've been doing all along) and your hourly flying costs may be less than $5 (not counting annuals and maintenance).

The fabric was pretty tired and needed a bit of silver duct ("hundred-mile-an-hour") tape now and then to keep loose ends down. I took her home four months ago when the annual finally ran out to re-fabric and ended up virtually restoring her. The restoration has been educational, fun, and not all that expensive. I might add that the Taylorcraft factory until recently was still in operation thanks to a handful of dedicated folks in Alliance, Ohio and made parts acquistion a snap. I estimate I'll be spending about $2,000 to put her back in "like new" condition, including Stits fabric, new cowls, windshield, cables and all new woodwork. That will add up to around $5,500 for an essentially new airplane. With a little luck and help from my friends I hope to have her back in the air by this summer.

I've never met a pilot who didn't take an instant liking to the little plane or who didn't reminisce longingly of his very own flights in one "back when." In short, I've never regretted the purchase and would do it all over again in a minute.

Name withheld
Washington

Cessna 150
Speaking of book figures, our C-150 cruises roughly eight knots less than book figures at 75 percent power. Her nine antennas explain much airspeed loss. Wheel pants add a whopping one knot to cruise speed; however, they make the plane look so much better the 12.5 pounds of wheel pants are often mounted during the summer.

Many pilots talk of the Cessna 150's reliability and low accident rate. Ours has one reliability problem. Its engine gets vapor lock in density altitudes between 12,000 feet at 75° Fahrenheit and 14,500 feet at 0°. Other than that, it indicates the great reliability in the 150 breed.

Unlike many of the $5,000 to $6,000 aircraft, most 150s have full gyro panels, putting small IFR capabilities within reach. Since it is slow, I practice a two-hour IFR fuel reserve rather than 45 minutes. The 150 is really at the mercy of the winds. Flight through showers of light to moderate intensity are somewhat safe. I feel good about the fact that the 150 is in the utility category, and it cruises slower than maneuvering speed. I feel less good about the way this light bird gets thrown around. A 360-degree attitude gyro could come in handy (a true joke).

Operating costs will run you $15 to $20 per hour, of which over $10 is attributed to fuel. You can choose $100 annuals and operate at $15 per hour or $500 one hundred-hour in-

The Piper J-3 Cub has become a classic, and prices have soared accordingly. It has no starter, so must be hand propped.

spections with operating costs of $20 per hour. Don't think that the 150's safety record will carry you through poor maintenance. Unless you thoroughly and consistently check all systems, an aging "safety" plane will finally hit its limits.

For a purely recreational airplane, the Cessna 150 lacks the antique charm that is at the heart of the Champ, Luscombe, and Cessna 120/140. These aircraft can take you back in time to a beautiful, healthy, fantasy dream. Instead, the Cessna 150 contains qualities that allow it to accomplish flight in both an uncontrolled atmosphere and modern controlled airspace. Flight performance into large airports is not exceptional, but with a 110-knot 75 percent power glide down a three degree glideslope, it makes it. Acceptable performance on a variety of tasks.

In summary, if you're looking for simple enjoyment, it is my opinion that the Cessna 150 is inferior to the old taildraggers. I would much rather fly a Champ with the window open, sectional chart out, tent and sleeping bag in the rear, and the earth below frozen in time. The Cessna 150 has superior performance and safety; however, it has no personality and can be quite boring to fly.

Stu Moment
Chairman, Sublogic Corp.
Champaign, Ill.

Aeronca Champ
Having owned and operated several Aeronca Champs, and also given dual instruction in Cubs, Taylorcrafts, Luscombes and several other old taildraggers, let me visit my prejudices upon you. The only airplane in this category which can still function and compete with modern aircraft is the Champ. It has more room than a Cub, is more durable than a Taylorcraft or a Luscombe, but it has one virtue which puts it completely beyond comparison with everything else in this class but the Ercoupe: You can see out of it! More on that later.

Continental 65s and 85s are the most common engine in Champs, and they are completely reliable. They start easily when cold, even without preheat. They will run forever, it seems, and cost very little to overhaul. If the engine has a serious flaw, it is that it runs well even when it's in terrible condition. Common problems are the usual ones for any machine this age: cracks, especially around the upper flange of the air box at the carburetor, and exhaust stacks.

Expect four to five gph fuel flow, slightly less when executing takeoffs and landings. About one quart of oil per seven to eight hours of operation is normal. Expect cruise speeds of 75-80 mph.

Instructing in the airplane is a joy, except that I am rather hoarse after a day of it. A decent intercom is an excellent addition, and makes the Champ a superb trainer. Students must learn pitch control, since the airspeed indicators fluctuate wildly and are nearly useless. Full-stall landings are easy, and the directional control problems of taildraggers are vastly exaggerated (takeoff usually presents more problems). The ailerons are supposed to be heavy but after flying Pipers, Cessnas and similar toys, no one seems to notice. Everyone likes the stick control.

A few items are worth mentioning about operating Champs. In cold weather the engine will flat quit if the throttle is opened abruptly. Carb heat helps this considerably.

The Cessna 120/140s have the worst accident history of the group and a terrible ground-looping record.

The brakes are ineffective and trouble-prone unless they are adjusted frequently and carefully. It is best to use them only when:
1. You are going very slowly, and
2. You are all out of other ideas.

The only good thing about them is that I doubt they could ever cause a "nose-over."

"Fear of Fabric" puts some people off, but it needn't. Many Champs are flying with Dacron cover, which will last indefinitely with good painting and reasonable care. Recovering any airplane is a big job, but not insurmountable. Material costs for that will range from $2,500 to $4,000 depending on the covering material and finish desired. On synthetic-covered Champs, be sure that adequate inspection holes are included so that thorough checks for rust or rot can be made. Dacron may last forever, but wet steel and wood won't.

Structurally, a Champ is extremely strong as long as airspeeds are kept reasonable. The only part I've heard give any problem is the diagonal tube running from the lower to the upper longeron immediately aft of the firewall. There are lots of bent ones around, but they can be safely straightened while cold (I think it's 1025 steel rather than 4130).

Overall, the cost to operate Champs is as low as can be—$13-$15 per hour is very possible in a 200-hour year. I've never insured one for "in-flight" hull coverage, but liability and "not-in-motion" hull coverage should range from

$300-$400 per year for a 300-hour private pilot with 25 hours in type.

I mentioned the visibility, and that is a decisive factor in using the Champ as a primary trainer or personal puddle-jumper. The view is quite good every way but straight back. Compared to the cave-like qualities of the other airplanes of this genre, the Champ is infinitely superior. If our Cessna 150s were as reliable and durable as our Champs, we'd actually make money running a flight school.

In summary, the Aeronca can only be described as a Champ. The clear star in the under 100-hp taildragger category.

William T. McSwain
Columbus, Ohio

About three-and-a-half years ago, I purchased an old 1946 Aeronca Champ 7AC for $3,600. I found it long forgotten in an old dilapidated log hangar 35 miles east of Great Falls, Mont.

It had been almost five years since its last visit to the maintenance shop for an annual, so I decided that was the first order of business. Since I was an A&P and AI myself, that presented no major problem.

The big shock came when I was shopping through *Trade-A-Plane* for engine parts! A complete set of +.015-inch piston rings, main and connecting rod bearings, gaskets, pushrod housing seals, induction hoses and an overhaul manual mounted to about $96! (An incredible value in anybody's book.) The parts were purchased from Fresno Air Parts in Fresno, Calif.

Most of the 65-hp Continental parts available today (at what I call reasonable prices) are surplus 1940s vintage and of extremely good quality and in my opinion superior to parts manufactured later.

Since the overhaul I have flown the aircraft approximately 350 hours, with 300 or so hours running *regular* auto gasoline, the remainder of 80/87 avgas. For the past three annuals the compres-

sion has remained good, oil consumption decreasing to about one quart in five hours, no spark plug fouling problems or any other problems related to the use of auto gas. The only change I have made is replacing the old Stromberg carburetor with a Marvel Schebler which has the benefit of an accelerator pump. The old Stromberg carburetor was notorious for extremely poor acceleration in cold weather—the engine was almost impossible to keep running while advancing the throttle during an attempted go-around. According to the Type Certificate this change in carburetion ups the minimum octane rating from 73 to 80/87 for the engine. (I guess I'm not old enough to have even ever heard of 73 octane avgas.)

I have been using AeroShell straight weight oil in the engine since the major overhaul (straight mineral for the first 50 hours then the ashless dispersant since).

In my opinion, the Champ/Chief, are an extremely cost effective means of either learning to fly, recreational flying or even cross country (as compared to an ultralight). My theory is: why buy an ultralight when you can buy a "real" airplane for the same green, or less? The Champ cruises with two at a respectable 85 mph, on four gph, can get off or on in less than 600 feet (standard day at 3,500 ft. msl), stalls at about 35 mph, has excellent visibility (at least from the front seat), and you never have to worry about the cabin heater burning you out.

Prior to purchasing a Champ or Chief, I would bribe a knowledgeable A&P (a six pack would probably do it) to take a look at the wood spars, test the fabric, inspect lower aft fuselage tubing for corrosion, and check the logbooks for an idea of what kind of maintenance it has been getting. There have only been about three or four ADs issued on the 7AC since 1946, all of which are of more or less minor difficulty and expense to comply with.

David R. Kissner
Precision Flightcraft
Great Falls, Mont.

Boeing Stearman

For pilots who consider the modern lightplane yawn-provoking, there is a robust, swaggering alternative guaranteed to blast away boredom and represent a spanking-good investment in fun, sport and aeronautical assets. Searchers who reach beyond the more humdrum realm of the Luscombes, Navions and J-3 Cubs will stumble upon a treasure lode of classics known as the Boeing Stearman Model 75s.

The great charm of these lusty biplane warriors is that they were built like the classic brick biffy and cranked out in vast armadas. And the parts that aren't still legion can be made by a competent mechanic with a small outlay in fuss and bother. Even the old radial engines have been guaranteed a kind of immortality since the same basic type (220-hp Continental) used in many Stearmans was built in great numbers as powerplants for military tanks. And this has left a serendipitous legacy of still-unused engine cylinders.

Combine these practical considerations with the aircraft's intrinsic panache and machismo, and the appeal is obvious.

History

About 8,500 Boeing Stearman Model 75s were built over a nine-year span from 1936 to 1945 as military trainers. The FAA reports it still had 2,237 of the aircraft on the books at last count. For the Army, the airplanes were designated PT (primary trainer) -13s, -17s and 18s. The Navy designated them N2S. The nickname for both services was the Kaydet. The Royal Canadian Air Force received 300 winterized PT-17s labeled PT-27s. The PT-17s, and the Navy counter-

part, the N2S-1, -3 and -4, all with the 220-hp Continental engine, were built in the greatest numbers—about 6,000 during the 1940s. About half as many PT-13s (and Navy N2S-5s) were built with the 225-hp Lycoming radial for which parts now seem to be in very short supply.

The third powerplant supplied for the aircraft was the 225-hp Jacobs, with about 150 PT-18s built carrying this engine.

Presaging the future role for some Stearmans in civilian life, a batch of PT-17Bs was actually built for the military as mosquito control dusters.

After the war, hundreds of Stearmans were dumped on the market as surplus, available for a song—$200 to $500, some say, in crates. Many of these were snapped up and converted to cropdusting, often with 300-hp or 450-hp engines and a hopper installed in place of the front cockpit.

Buying Tips

According to Tom Lowe, president of the Stearman Restorers Assn., an average flyable Stearman in reasonable condition can be found these days for from $25,000 to $28,000. A battered one with a

For cross-country flying, goggles and helmet are de rigueur. A 60-pound baggage sack is located behind the rear cockpit.

high-time engine might go for around $20,000. And one that has been recently restored might be available for $30,000 to $40,000. Owners of prime freshly rebuilt models at the top are asking $40,000 and up.

For the *creme de la creme* in custom-conversions, Mid Continent Aircraft Corp. in Hayti, Mo., will totally reconstruct one to like-new condition for around $45,000 to $80,000, depending on the powerplant (220 hp up to 450 hp).

As for ex-cropdusters, some Stearman aficionados say they've found examples in good condition with extra corrosion protection, but most Stearman critics believe a lot of extra travail and money will probably be needed to bring a tired, old workhorse duster around to top condition because of the hard use and chemical corrosion. Also, the wings may have been clipped.

Word is also that front cockpit hardware is in short supply as restorers seek to convert dusters to the standard tandem cockpit configuration. Furthermore, extra fuselage structural work has to b done to finish the conversion.

The 220-hp Continental powerplant is probably the preferred one mainly because parts are more readily available than for the 220-hp Lycoming or the 225-hp Jacobs. The nine-cylinder Lycoming may be a bit smoother in operation than the seven-cylinder Continental, but some pilots feel the Continental has "more guts" and a better throttle response. Also, they characterize the Lycoming as a bit greasier and oilier, and the "shaky Jake" Jacobs as the worst in this respect.

The McCauley propeller might deter some buyers, since there is an Airworthiness Directive that requires removal for inspection and magnafluxing every 100 hours. A Hamilton-Standard metal prop does not have this limitation. Then again, some of the birds have wooden props.

Potential buyers might also keep an eye out for the tailwheel configuration. Originally, the Navy Stearmans had a tailwheel that (1) would swivel freely or (2) lock for takeoff and landing, while the Army models were steerable with the rudder pedals. Obviously, the Army system is more manageable, and lots of Navy models have been converted.

The brake system is a source of constant debate among Stearman owners. Most have long since converted to automotive master cylinders for better durability, though other diehards maintain that the original ones were just fine if you knew how to maintain them. One expert, Lary Kampel, says Cleveland brakes are the best of all, with new-type linings. At any rate, Stearman pilots say you want good brakes since you'll need all the help you can get for proper ground handling with the tailwheel configuration, especially with a nonsteerable tailwheel.

Handling and Performance

Pilots characterize the Boeing Stearman as a pretty honest, straightforward aircraft that was,

Single wing tank in the center section dangles its cork-in-a-tube fuel gauge. The round mirror aids in inter-cockpit communications. (top photo).
For basic flying, basic instruments and never a vacuum pump failure.

after all, designed as a trainer. It will do all the basic aerobatic maneuvers—loops, spins, hammerheads, snap rolls. The engine is not designed for continuous inverted operation, however, and it will quit if you hold it upside down for long.

Also, aerobatic devotees should be aware that it's no Pitts Special—the controls are heavy—heavier than a T-6's, and a protracted spate of aerobatics will leave you arm-weary.

The original models had only one set of ailerons, on the lower wings. Some fancy aerobatic mods add another pair of ailerons on the top wings for more maneuverability.

Stearman cognoscenti say you shouldn't worry too much about the wings or tail coming off if the aircraft is in proper condition, since it is supposed to be able to take

about 12 Gs positive and seven to nine negative.

"Built like a truck" is the favorite description by owners.

No speed demon, though, the 220-hp Stearman will climb out at about 70 mph, cruise at about 95 mph behind a nice slow-ticking 1900 rpm max, burning about 12 gph, and come down final at about 70 mph.

A newcomer will be struck by the airplane's general docility. It's like a big kite. It doesn't have or need flaps. "It glides like a brick," said one owner in the time-honored expression. Pull the power off on final, and she'll come down sharply. In a stall, she'll buffet nicely and drop off on a wing.

The toughest maneuver in the Stearman's repertoire is probably a gusty crosswind landing. Cockpit visibility of the runway on the flare is nearly nonexistent, and the pilot has to use a sixth sense and great powers of peripheral vision. And he's got to have dancing feet.

The landing gear stick out like a pair of giant tree trunks, and they're about as unyielding when you hit the ground if you haven't eased it on—there's very little give to the oleos; the monster tires probably provide as much cushion as a hard landing will allow. But the tailwheel has the luxury of its own oleo, for what that's worth.

Instrumentation will range from crude original to elaborate custom fittings. Most of the original aircraft came without electrical systems— that meant starting by the old-fashioned inertial crank, or by propping. The high prop intimidates some for hand propping, however. But some models have been updated with batteries and electric starters and navigation lights.

Systems on the airplane are rock-bottom basic. The fuel gauge consists of a graduated plastic tube with a float marker about six inches long dangling from the bottom surface of the upper wing, in the breeze, right in front of the pilot's

Used Aircraft Guide

nose. The fuel tank is located in the center section right above the fuselage. You can switch it on or off—period.

Other system controls are a throttle, mixture and mag switch. The pitch trim control is a simple swiveling knob on the left side of the cockpit—a joy to use, and an object lesson to modern aircraft designers. Naturally, this airplane has a control stick, not a wheel.

Get Parts and Maintenance

Dusters & Sprayers Supply in Chickasha, Oklahoma (405-224-1201), is the big name in Stearman parts. President Bob Chambers says they can supply just about any Stearman part needed, and those they don't have they can make under PMA authority in their machine shop. Chambers claims to have about 3,000 customers in this country as well as in Mexico and Argentina, where they apparently still use the aircraft as trainers.

Dusters & Sprayers even has parts for the Lycoming, Continental and Jacobs engines, and makes all the hardware for the front cockpits except the seats, according to Chambers.

Scroungers can also get help locating parts from members of the Stearman Restorers Assn. (more about that later) and from *Trade-A-Plane*. One of the Stearman gurus, Chris Stoltzfus in Coatesville, Pa., has a good selection of parts, too (215-384-1145).

Although there are quite a few capable mechanics around the country who can work on the aircraft with no great problem due to its straightforward design and construction, the older hands with experience in wood and fabric are preferred, naturally. And a few are known as Stearman specialists. Among them are Larry Kampel of Kampel Enterprises in Wellsville, Pa.; and Tom Cawley of Cawley's Aviation Service at Kobelt Airport in Wallkill, N.Y. For engine overhaul, Gulf Coast Dusting in Houston, Tex., is one of the better known shops (713-991-3520). Owners say the Stearmans are

Cost/Performance/Specifications

Model	Year	Number Built	Gross Weight (lbs)	Fuel (gals)	Engine	TBO (hrs)	Overhaul Cost
PT-13	1936-41	2,141	2,950	46	225-hp Lyc. R-680-B4B, -E	650	$6,000 with 2 engines*
N2S-5	1943-45						
PT-17	1940-45	5,923	2,950	46	220-hp Cont. W-670-6A, N	1,000	$3,950 with exchange $4,450 outright
PT-27							
N2S-1, 3, 4							
PT-18	1940-41	150	2,950	46	225-hp Jacobs R-755-7	1,000	
Modifications		N/A	3,200-3,520		300-hp Lyc. R680-E3, -A, -B	1,500	$6,200 with 2 engines*
					450-hp P&W R-985-AN-1, 3	1,400	

Overhauler demands two engines, one for parts.

quite reasonable to maintain. Big front fuselage panels open on hinges and are held up by metal hooks for beautiful access to accessories and the master brake cylinder.

Construction is straightforward and simple, consisting of a massive, welded tube fuselage with longerons, covered by fabric. The tail is metal with fabric covering; the wings have wooden spars and ribs, and fabric covering, once again.

Originally, the fuel tank in the top wing had no fabric covering, but

Two giant hinged panels open in seconds for access to engine accessories and the famous master brake cylinder, parallel with the flying wires on the right side.

unless it now does, the tank must be pulled every year to allow an inspection of the center section, to meet the requirements of an AD.

And talk about nice touches, the flying wires that fasten to the horizontal stabilizer go through little plastic viewports, allowing easy walk-around inspection for security—another object lesson for modern designers.

Since the wing ribs are wooden, great care must be taken to ensure against rotting from moisture, especially along the aileron bay. An AD calls for drilling drain holes to prevent moisture accumulation.

A Boeing service bulletin (available from the Stearman Restorers Assn.) outlines the modifications necessary for conversion from the

original military to civilian status. By now, most of these have presumably been complied with, but buyers should confirm. The service bulletin requires items like: no spin strips on the upper wing only, replace the aluminum firewall with a stainless steel one, installation of a battery cutoff switch and CAA-approved position lights on ships with electrical systems, etc.

Modifications

Most of the Supplemental Type Certificates on the aircraft are aimed at converting to ag configuration, but a bunch allow use of Seconite or fiberglass covering. And one even installs metal wing ribs with the wooden spars—by Vincent Aeronautical, Covington, La.

Books and Manuals

A nice history of the entire Stearman line comes in the *Stearman Guidebook*, by Mitch Mayborn and Peter M. Bowers, published by Flying Enterprise Publications in Dallas, Tex.

Air Service Caravan Co. in New Bedford, Mass. (617-992-1655), can provide Stearman pilot manuals along with maintenance and parts handbooks.

Organizations to Join

As we've already mentioned, the Stearman Restorers Assn. is the one. They publish a nice-looking newsletter and can provide everything from moral support to a clearing house for parts and services. President of the Association is Thomas E. Lowe, 823 Kingston Lane, Crystal Lake, Ill. 60014 (815-459-6873). They hold an annual fly-in at Galesburg, Ill., the week after Labor Day.

Owner Comments

I first soloed a Stearman in 1948 as a new private pilot. The checkout consisted of three or four landings and seemed easy at the time, but I had flown nothing but tailwheel

planes prior to this. I flew the Stearman only a few hours but concluded that if I could ever afford one I would buy one.

I bought one with a 300 Lycoming and constant-speed prop in 1967 and am still flying it. The airplane has been very serviceable. It is a fine trainer both for landings and takeoffs and for aerobatics. These skills, well developed and practiced in a Stearman, transfer to adept handling of much more modern and sophisticated airplanes.

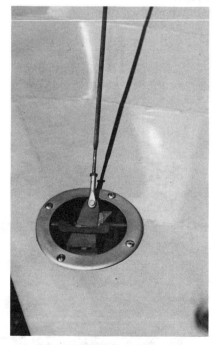

Security at a glance: a plastic panel allows hands-off inspection of the flying-wire attachment point on the horizontal stabilizer.

Much has been written and said about Stearmans being hard to land. They are not, but need to be kept straight, and even a strong crosswind on a paved runway can be handled with the control available. The aircraft is heavy on the controls, and one needs considerable muscle to do aerobatics. Maneuvers develop relatively slowly and must be properly flown through for good execution. This doesn't make it easy but is a training virtue.

I have flown some indifferently maintained stock Stearmans and also some highly modified working dusters, and they have all flown and handled fine, which says a lot for the underlying strength and design, which are superior to most planes of that vintage.

Fuel consumption on the 300 is about 11.5 gph cross-country and 14 for aerobatics, and roughly one quart of oil per hour. Stearmans seem to be almost universally greeted with affection, but in the last year or so more than one line boy has said, "Gee mister, what kind of airplane is that?"

●

I've got a pristine PT-27, which was the only Boeing Stearman produced with an electrical system and starter as standard.

No other biplane has such delightfully smooth control feel. The input is through torque tubes and bell

The Model A of airplanes, Stearman power controls, above, consist of mag, throttle and mixture. At bottom left of photo is pitch trim knob.

Bob Fritt's Stearman, page 62, climbs at 70 mph, lands at 70 and cruises at 95 with a 220-hp Continental.

It may look good from the outside, but check for 40-year-old wood behind the compression members. (Above, right)

Page from an aircraft manual shows the basic components: tubular fuselage with longerons, four separate wing sections.

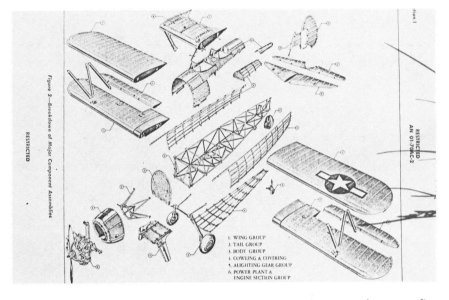

cranks, so the slack and binding of the ordinary cable setup is absent.

The Stearman is very roomy and solid. Its cowlings are like armor plate and look as if they belong on a DC-4. The tubular framework is truly massive. All this gives you a secure feeling, but with its standard engines, the 225 Lycoming and the 220 Continental, it is unimpressive in climb rate and cruise speed. I'm never in a hurry when I fly my Stearman, so it doesn't bother me. If you want speed or sustained performance in vertical maneuvers, the P&W 450 would be the answer.

Certainly this is the safest biplane around. Besides being overbuilt, it has the most predictable low-speed handling characteristics. The stall is a long time in coming, with all kinds of signals; and with its huge wings you generally can fly out of

any problems by releasing back pressure.

Once you get used to the limited forward visibility, the landings are a cinch, though you've got to stay tuned to the rudder on the rollout, particularly in a crosswind since the gear legs are so close together. It is crucially important to keep airflow over that rudder as long as possible. For this reason newcomers to the Stearman should probably avoid days when the wind is shifting around rapidly. A nice steady 10 knots within 30 degrees of the nose is fine. Always use grass when available.

Parts for some old airplanes are impossible to find. You need a tool and die maker for a close friend. The Stearman is a notable exception. Apparently during the war spares were produced in amazing quantities. Any part you want is

available right away from outfits like Dusters & Sprayers.

All these old airplanes have wooden wings. A lot of supposedly "rebuilt" Stearmans have 40-year-old wood behind compression members and other out-of-the-way spots. The only way to be sure is to insist on brand-new wings built up from scratch. We dismantled an airplane completely a few years ago after a crackup. It had a beautiful cover and finish. The wood you could see with the cover off was excellent, but in the inaccessible spots behind permanent fittings dry rot and corrosion were severe.

I've got close to $40,000 in my Stearman. If a man didn't have at least thirty to spend on a completely remanufactured airplane, he'd be better off with a good clip-wing Cub or T-craft.

SINGLE-ENGINE
FIXED GEAR
TWO-PLACE

Cessna 172

Even today the Cessna 172 continues to be the airplane most commonly associated with general aviation. It's been built in such numbers that the word ubiquitous seems hardly sufficient when describing this commonest of commonplace singles. The 172's characteristic high-wing shape, docile, dependable performance and and pleasant handling have introduced thousands to flying.

History

The 172 and its little brother, the 150, both appeared on the market in 1956. The new 172 spelled the end of the line for its taildragging older cousin, the venerable Cessna 170. It did this by outselling the 170 by a 10-to-one (1,170 to 174) margin in that first production year. Flightline planespotters can easily identify those first-edition 172s by the straight tail and "fastback" cabin. A peek under the cowl will reveal a 145-hp Continental engine, standard on the 172 line until 1968.

Changes in the 172 line have been slow in coming. The year 1960 saw the introduction of a sweptback tail in the "A" model; the 1963 "D" model featured "Omni-vision" rear windows. The 172E boasted electric flaps, to the chagrin of many pilots who considered them more a handicap than an improvement. Since that year, the 172 airframe has been virtually cut in stone with no changes to speak of.

What is probably the most important single improvement made to the 172 line came in 1968, when the 150-hp Lycoming replaced the old Continental engine as standard equipment. The following year's model was available with a 52-gallon fuel tank option, and by

1973 Cessna had re-designed the wing leading edge for supposedly better stall characteristics.

By 1974, Grumman American's Traveler was cutting deeply into the 172's market. Cessna countered with modifications to the wheelpants and cooling airflow, picking up some seven miles per hour in cruise speed.

As the ancient adage says, "If it ain't broke, don't fix it." Cessna ignored that advice in 1977 when the company shot itself in the foot by introducing the infamous 160-hp Lycoming O-320-H camshaft-and-valve-train-eating engine to the 172. The O-320-H episode lasted four years, and is remembered by both Cessna and Lycoming as a major embarrassment. (More on that in the "Engines" section to follow.)

Again, not content to leave well enough alone, Cessna opted for a 28-volt electrical system in the 172, a change that has meant problems for landing lights and rotating beacons.

Even these troubles have not done much to damage the 172s "generic airplane" image, although aircraft from the troubled '76-'81 period

Benign handling characteristics go with a superb safety record.

must be viewed with a jaundiced eye.

Used Skyhawks

With over 24,000 172s out there, the used market in Skyhawks is one of the busiest. A recent issue of *Trade-a-Plane* contained 220 ads for more than that number of 172s, since some ads offered more than one aircraft. With this much give-and-take in the market, prices tend to be rather steady, without much variation. An aircraft that's a true "steal" is unlikely because demand is so high. On the other hand, the supply is so great that no seller can get away with an exorbitant asking price.

However, used Skyhawk shoppers shouldn't waste too much time trying pinch the penultimate penny; their time would be better spent thoroughly checking out the mechanical condition of the aircraft, hopefully with the help of an experienced A&P.

Resale Value

In 1981, when *The Aviation Consumer* last reviewed the Cessna 172

line, we predicted that the older pre-1968, O-300-powered C-172s would not be able to hold onto their value due to the fact that replacement engines and parts would become more and more expensive and harder to find. According to the *Aircraft Price Digest*, this is just what happened.

A C-172D Skyhawk sold for $14,751 new in 1963, and is listed in the 1985 spring *Digest* at $10,750, a decrease of $4,001. This doesn't seem at first glance like that much of a decline after 22 years, but when the effects of inflation (the Consumer Price Index has more than tripled since then) are figured in, the weakness of this investment becomes readily apparent. The fact that prices are as high as they are reflects the relatively scarce supply of good condition 1963-model 172Ds, of which 1,027 were built.

While the cost of buying a 172D hasn't risen, the cost of overhauling its O-300-D powerplant has, rising to an average of $7,500 (TBO 1,800 hours), $1,500 more than the 150-hp O-320-E2D. While unusually low resale values for post-1977 model 172s have yet to appear, the listing in the *Aircraft Price Digest* bears an ominous asterisk, followed by the words, "Price assume engine fixed—see notes below." The notes continue to say the stated price is for a 172 in compliance with ADs 77-20-7 (tappets) 78-12-9 (replace crankshaft) and 78-12-9 (replace oil pump impellers). More about pertinent ADs later.

Performance

The Skyhawk's performance is not exactly spectacular. Loaded up to

The 1983 Skyhawks placed landing lights up in the left wing leading edge, where they are less prey to vibration problems than in the nose.

gross weight, the 172 is lethargic, and we wouldn't want to try any hot-day, high-field takeoffs in a heavy airplane. The 1977 and later models, with their 160-hp engines, are, however, noticeably more energetic, with a book-climb rate about 20 percent higher than the 145- and 150-hp versions.

Cruise speed at 75 percent power is a modest 104 to 113 knots under most conditions, with a fuel burn of about eight gph. The post-'73 models are faster by four knots or so because of generally cleaner aero-dynamics. The 38-gallon standard usable fuel supply provides about four hours of flying with a small reserve, enough for about 435 nm or so if you really want to stretch it.

Optional 52-gallon tanks (48 usable) extend endurance to over five hours, enough for 522 nm or so. Of course, payload is reduced when 52 gallons of fuel are hoisted aloft; count on three medium-sized adults and no baggage, at best.

Handling Characteristics

In a word, the Skyhawk's handling is stable, even positively benign. Rather heavy controls inhibit pilots with Luke Skywalker fantasies, but these same steady controls make instrument work a pleasure. Elevator forces are very heavy, meaning that stalling is extremely difficult. The Skyhawk's handling characteristics are spectacularly average—for the simple reason that the airplane's universal popularity

has helped make it the standard against which other aircraft are judged. Almost by definition, the Skyhawk is the average airplane.

If all this makes the 'hawk seem a little lackluster, there is one flight regime in which the 172 positively excels: short-field performance. A skillful pilot can plunk a Skyhawk down in not much more runway than a so-called STOL specialty machine like a Rallye or Maule. At light weights, takeoffs can be nearly as short. The Skyhawk's huge flaps allow it to make steep, Space Shuttle-style approaches, and we wouldn't hesitate to pit a 'hawk against either a Rallye or Maule in a slow-flying contest.

Safety

A big part of the Skyhawk story is its superb safety record, pure and simple. In an NTSB study of accidents involving 48 different aircraft types between the years 1972 and 1976, the C-172 posted the best overall accident record of any four-place fixed-gear single. Its fatal accident rate also was excellent. In fact, out of the 32 most popular single-engine airplanes, the C-172 ranked in the top, or safest, 10 in eight out of 10 accident categories. It had the lowest engine failure rate and in-flight airframe failure rate of any lightplane.

The areas in which the Skyhawk is only average are mid-air collisions, presumably a result of the aircraft's poor visibility, and overshoot accidents.

A search of NTSB accident reports involving 172s in 1982, the latest year available, turned up total of 98, of which nine resulted in fatalities, with 20 deaths. Six of these deaths occurred in five VFR flights that continued into IFR conditions. A total 177 people came away with minor injuries or none at all. Seven people were killed in two midair collisions (there were five people in one of the airplanes involved).

The 172's good safety record is likely due to a variety of factors shared by all Cessna high-wing aircraft. High elevator forces and low stall speeds discourage killer stalls. Stalls accounted for just six of the 1982 mishaps and one of the fatalities.

The Skyhawk's fuel system is simplicity itself, with a well-placed selector that has only left, right, off and both positions. It takes a perverse form of determination to foul up the 172 fuel system, especially if pilots simply leave the selector on "both," as most do. Even more simply, the high-wing gravity-feed system requires no fuel pumps.

Debates have raged for years among high-wing vs. low-wing fans, with claims made on both sides for visibility, handling qualities, aesthetics, and the like. And while the 'hawk's big, strut-braced wing may look old-fashioned, a fatal in-flight airframe failure in a Skyhawk is a great rarity.

The durability of that wing was evidenced by a June 1982 mishap in which a 172 struck and severed a number of powerlines, each a half inch in diameter. Afterwards, the airplane managed to return to its home field. Damage inspection revealed that three of the four left wing strut attach rivets were

sheared, the entire engine cowling torn loose from the firewall attach points, and prop tips bent *forward* about three inches.

Engines

While the basic 172 airframe has changed little over the years, the 'hawk has been powered by three basic powerplant designs. Which one of these three engines lurks under the cowl of the used 172 you buy will play a starring role in how happy you'll be with the airplane. Our advice on engine choice can be summed up as follows: 1968-76 'hawks, terrific; 1956-67 models, fair; 1977-80 models, awful; 1981 through present models, again, fair.

The Lycoming O-320-D2J engine which replaced the troubled H2AD has had a fairly ordinary maintenance history, marred only by a service letter dealing with stuck valves. The problem seems to center on a buildup of gunk in the valve guides. This gunk inhibits valve movement when the engine is cold, causing rough running on startup. As the engine heats up, it smooths out. This so-called "morning sickness" in the D2J is a symptom that valve guides need to be checked.

For 12 years, new 172s trundled down runways and into the skies propelled by six-cylinder 145-hp Continental O-300s, an engine little more than a four-banger O-200 (used in the C-150) with an extra pair of cylinders tacked on. The O-300 has an adequate reliability record, but the combination of comparatively low 1,800-hour TBO and $7,500 overhaul cost make it a costly antique. "The problem is you've got six of everything to replace instead of four," one overhauler told us. "An old engine like this can be a real can of worms."

Parts for the O-300 are available factory-direct, although their price adds to a total upkeep cost for the engine that is, in the words of one overhaul firm, "not commensurate with the cost of the aircraft. It's just not worth it to put $7,500 worth of work into an aircraft with a value of only $11,000, which is about what one of those early '60s Skyhawks costs today."

The Lycoming O-320-E2D engine climbed aboard the 172 in 1968, giving the airplane an extra five horsepower. That same engine costs $6,000 at its 2,000-hour TBO time, $1,500 less than the O-300 with a TBO that's 200 hours longer.

Cost/Performance/Specifications

Model	Year	Number Built	Average Retail Price	Cruise Speed (Kts)	Rate of Climb (fpm)	Useful Load (lbs)	Fuel Std/Opt (gals)	Engine	TBO (hrs)	Overhaul Cost
172	1956-59	4,022	$8,500	108	660	940	37	Cont. O-300A	1,800	$7,500
172A	1960	991	$9,500	108	660	940	37	Cont. O-300C	1,800	$7,500
172B	1961	987	$10,250	114	730	875	42	Cont. O-300D	1,800	$7,500
172C	1962	809	$10,500	114	675	920	42	Cont. O-300D	1,800	$7,500
172D	1963	1,027	$10,750	114	645	970	42	Cont. O-300D	1,800	$7,500
172E	1964	1,249	$11,000	114	645	970	42	Cont. O-300D	1,800	$7,500
172F	1965	1,569	$11,250	114	645	970	42	Cont. O-300D	1,800	$7,500
172G	1966	1,499	$11,500	114	645	970	42	Cont. O-300D	1,800	$7,500
172H	1967	1,619	$11,750	114	645	970	42	Cont. O-300D	1,800	$7,500
172I	1968	630	$12,500	115	645	1,000	42	Lyc. O-320-E2D	2,000	$6,000
172K	1969-70	2,420	$13,250	115	645	985	42/52	Lyc. O-320-E2D	2,000	$6,000
172L	1971-72	1,533	$14,250	115	645	985	42/52	Lyc. O-320-E2D	2,000	$6,000
172M	1973	1,139	$15,000	115	645	965	42/52	Lyc. O-320-E2D	2,000	$6,000
172M	1974	1,559	$15,500	120	645	965	42/52	Lyc. O-320-E2D	2,000	$6,000
172M	1975	2,225	$17,000	120	645	965	42/52	Lyc. O-320-E2D	2,000	$6,000
172M	1976	1,899	$17,500	120	645	965	42/52	Lyc. O-320-E2D	2,000	$6,000
172N	1977	1,724	$17,000	120	770	876	43/54	Lyc. O-320-H2AD	2,000	$6,500
172N	1978	1,724	$18,500	122	770	876	43/54	Lyc. O-320-H2AD	2,000	$6,500
172N	1979	1,849	$19,500	122	770	876	43/54	Lyc. O-320-H2AD	2,000	$6,500
172	1980	1,124	$23,250	122	770	876	43/54	Lyc. O-320-H2AD	2,000	$6,500
172P	1981	1,024	$29,500	122	770	876	43/54	Lyc. O-320-D2J	2,000	$6,500
172P	1982	724	$35,000	122	770	876	43/54	Lyc. O-320-D2J	2,000	$6,500
172P	1983	319	$45,000	120	680	1,078	54/68	Lyc. O-320-A4N	2,000	$6,500
172P	1984	N/A	$64,940	120	680	1,078	54/68	Lyc. O-320-A4N	2,000	$6,500

This four-cylinder engine carries a reputation for going well beyond TBO with careful maintenance. Flight schools who put 100 hours a month on their airplanes and pay attention to maintenance regularly get 3,000 hours. "There's no better engine," one mechanic told us. The O-320 seems to handle 100LL with ease, as well as autogas, although careful leaning is recommended.

Messing with Perfection

As 80-octane avgas went the way of the nickel newspaper, Cessna ordered a redesigned O-320 from Lycoming. Dubbed the O-320-H2AD, it was a hard-luck powerplant, a disaster and major embarrassment for both Cessna and Lycoming and the first major engineering blunder to mar the 'hawk's record. Hundreds of 1977 Skyhawks suffered serious camshaft and valve train damage, at a cost of thousands of dollars borne by their owners. What's more, there were a dozen or so abrupt engine failures caused by sheared oil pumps and accessory drive gears. Admitting its error in April of 1978, Cessna recalled all 1977 and 1978 Skyhawks for major engine repairs.

Oil pump and drive gear problems were fixed at that time, but camshaft/tappet problems continued unsolved through the 1980 model. Lycoming tried three different camshaft/tappet mods. None of them worked. Cessna finally admitted defeat in 1981 and changed to the O-320-D2J.

After Cessna switched engines, Lycoming belatedly came up with a fourth major mod, featuring an enlarged crankcase, which it hoped would solve the problem once and for all. The modified engines have slowly worked their way into the fleet through attrition, replacing the original faulty equipment. This mod will be found on engines with serial numbers 7976 and above. Barring evidence to the contrary, it seems that this fix, while not cheap, has held. Trouble is, if a 172 owner is willing to spend the roughly $1,500 extra at TBO time for the so-called O-320-

H2ADT mod, opting for one of the extra-horsepower engine conversions may prove more cost-effective over the long run. More on them in the STC section of this article.

Our Opinion

We would not advise the purchase of a Skyhawk with an O-320 engine serial number below 7976, except at an extremely low price, low enough to allow for possible premature engine replacement. After 7976, the odds improve, but the engine is still far from a sure thing, in our opinion.

In 1981 Cessna had a special 2,000-hour, pro-rata warranty period. Under this, if a Skyhawk was purchased with 900 hours and the engine failed 100 hours later, Cessna would provide a new or remanufactured engine at half price. Four years after this offer, however, most 'hawks have flown enough to make the pro-rata discount percentage insignificant.

There is a Way Out

For 172 owners who would prefer to avoid the maintenance headaches of both the O-300 and -320-H, there are alternatives. Unfortunately, they're quite expensive, with costs approaching the value of the airplane itself in

Skyhawks with the Lycoming O-320-H engines suffered serious valve train problems of a sort that tested the patience of the most ardent C-172 fans.

many cases. RAM Aircraft Modifications, Inc., based at Madison Cooper Airport, Waco. Tex. 76708, (817) 752-8381 can put in a 160-hp O-320-D2G for between $10,000-12,000, depending on the model. That's 100 percent of the book value of a 172 built from 1956 to 1968.

A couple of firms offer upgrades that would make for a peppy Skyhawk with the addition of a 180-hp Lycoming O-360 engine, but again, it's an expensive improvement. Cost for an Avcon Industries installation complete with constant-speed prop comes to $17,260 for C-172s built before 1967, with the mod on 'hawks built after that date amounting to $16,935. If owners prefer to cut their own deal on a O-360 engine, installation kits (less prop governor and engine) for pre- and post-1967 'hawks are available for $2,875 and $2,750 respectively. Avcon Industries is at 1006 West 53rd North, Wichita, Kan. 67204. Phone: (316) 782-3317.

Mike Kelley Aircraft is marketing its own O-360 installation, this time with a fixed-pitch prop the company touts as lighter and cheaper. The Kelley mod used to be the property of Horton STOLcraft. Although the exact price varies by aircraft model year, the Kelley kit costs between $1,500 to $1,600. Add to that the approximately $7,500 cost for a used overhauled O-360, and cushion the shock of what this will cost with Kelley's claims of cruise speeds 13 knots over book. Mike Kelley Aircraft is at Wellington Municipal Airport; Wellington, Kan., (316) 326-8581.

If you want rocket-propelled performance and have a very large wad of cash burning a hole in your pocket, go for the 250-hp six-cylinder turbocharged Franklin 6AFAS350A conversion offered by Seaplane Flying Inc., Box 21586, Vancouver, Wash. 98666. Phone: (206) 694-6287. The engine transforms a stock 172 into "a little hot rod," in the words of a woman we know who has flown one. It should, considering the cost is $6,595 for the kit, with the engine itself another $11,995. The company also markets a 220-hp

Franklin conversion costing $4,695 for the kit, another $10,495 for the 6A350C Franklin.

A Very Special Problem

Thousands of 172s built between 1977 and 1982 have a good chance of developing an insidious illness that in extreme cases could lead to making the airplane unairworthy. We're talking about filiform corrosion, and it may affect the majority of the 25,000 airplanes built at Cessna's Pawnee Division plant in the years 1977-1982, including over 8,000 Skyhawks.

Filiform corrosion is almost impossible to spot in its early stages. It occurs principally on airplanes covered with polyurethane paint, since polyurethane is flexible and semipermeable and can allow water and contaminants to get next to the metal. The best defense against filiform is careful preparation of the bare metal surface prior to painting. DuPont, makers of Imron, a popular polyurethane paint, recommended a combination of Alodyne and epoxy primer surface treatment to Cessna, which evidently disregarded this advice, perhaps because Alodyne treatments require a 16- to 24- hour drying time. By opting for wash primer, a cheap surface prep requiring just a few hours' drying time, Cessna saved many man-hours of labor and plant space.

Careful inspection of any used 172 is therefore important before the decision is made to buy. Look around rivets and seams, where corrosion usually begins. Unfortunately, inspection won't always reveal filiform corrosion. It spreads subtly under the aircraft's finish, often without producing surface blistering and peeling, like ordinary corrosion. Like cancer, treatment often takes desperate forms. As a DuPont pamphlet says, ''If any trace of corrosion is found, it is quite likely to be widespread... as drastic as it sounds, the only reasonable action is to strip all the finish from the airplane and remove every spot of corrosion.''

So far the filiform problem is a localized one, cropping up in areas

of warm, humid coastal areas, such as Florida and the Gulf states. That is no guarantee that it won't happen in other areas as the 172 fleet ages. The best advice we can offer is to carefully check the history of any 1977-82 Cessna considered for purchase. If it was ever based in Florida, or any other hot, humid, seaside area, we suggest you be cautious about buying it. Perform a meticulous inspection (use a magnifying glass) in search of corrosion traces. Be suspicious if the 172 was recently painted. Even with a fresh paint job, filiform corrosion will likely return in a few months.

Today, new 172s come off the Wichita line wearing Alodyne underwear, but inexplicably Cessna still refuses to use epoxy primer.

ADs, SDRs

The 172 line has enjoyed a comparatively quiet AD history, aside from the O-320-H2AD episode. Some of the more recent Directives cover the 172M, N, and P models, requiring modification of the right-hand control yoke to prevent possible elevator control jamming (AD #83-10-3). The two most recent ADs (83-17-6 and 84-26-2, respectively) applied to 172 equipped with Robertson STOL mods, some of which had reported problems with aileron flutter, and with elderly induction air filters shedding bits of filter material into the intakes they're supposed to keep clean. Since the filter is an inexpensive

Fuel gauges are on the pilot's side for better visibility than on some other Cessnas. Electric flap lever has pre-set notches for convenience.

component, why not make it SOP to replace it at the annual?

A look at Service Difficulty Reports compiled from 1984 through April 15, 1985 (omitting engine SDRs) revealed the old familiar problems with stuck valves, including 19 reports on bent pushrods and bad guides on the older O-320-E2D powerplants. Other reports covered problems with brakes, chiefly cracked wheel hubs and brake housings; leaking, chafing and worn fuel lines on M,N, and P models; and the infamous Slick magnetos.

Maintenance

Economy and low maintenance costs have always been the Skyhawk's strong suits. With the post-1968 four-cylinder engine, fixed-pitch prop, fixed gear and no cowl flaps, the average Skyhawk owner should survive an annual for $400 or so.

Not that the 'hawks are without their weak points. Late model '77 and '78 Skyhawks with 28-volt electrical systems burn out their landing lights at a fantastic rate. Comments from one owner claimed an expenditure of $323 for landing light bulbs over the last 212 hours of flight, working out to $1.52 per flight hour, just for landing lights.

Aircraft Resale Value Chart

$/M

- $35,000
- $30,000
- $25,000
- $20,000
- $15,000
- $10,000
- $ 0,000
- 0

'70 '71 '72 '73 '74 '75 '76 '77 '78 '79 '80 '81 '82 '83 '84 '85

Year

Cessna has a "landing light improvement kit."

Cessna owners have reported similar problems with beacon bulbs, claiming they last a mere 100 hours and cost $40 a pop to replace. A remedy to this costly bother is offered by Aeroflash Signal Corp., 3900 West Palmer St., Chicago, Ill. 60647 Phone: (312) 342-4815. Aeroflash sells beacon bulbs carrying a 750-hour warranty.

Older Skyhawks tend towards problems with the nosewheel, particularly those flown by students and novice pilots who land fast and hard. Nosewheel problems can produce damage to the firewall where the nosewheel strut joins it. This should be checked before purchase. Mechanics tell us that Cessna nosewheels are notoriously chintzy and soon succumb to minor punishment. Nose gear shimmy can also be troublesome. Flap actuator jack screws have a dicey history, and are subject to an AD in pre-1973 models.

Operating Costs

Operating costs can vary widely depending on the aircraft's age, how much it is flown and what it is used for. Readers have reported average annual bills ranging from $100 to as high as $600. One meticulous reader reported operating costs of $29.75 per hour, including reserves, insurance, debt

service, and taxes based on some hard flying: 1,240 hours in 15 months (the aircraft is used for IFR training).

Avionics

We usually don't talk about avionics in a used-plane article but in Cessna's case, we really must make an exception. The reason is the poor reliability of the ARC avionics inflicted on virtually all 172s since 1974. ARC had serious management, production, and quality control problems in the late 70s, and the result was a plethora of customer problems. The years 1977 and 1978 seemed to be especially bad.

If your search for a used 172 turns up a '74 or later model with Collins, Narco, or Kind equipment, you may save yourself future avionics headaches by buying it instead of an ARC-equipped airplane. If you must accept ARC avionics with your 'hawk, demand documentation of repairs and past problems. Particularly check the synthesizers in series 300 navcoms. If the Skyhawk you're looking at has a long history of avionics squawks, don't buy it. There are plenty more Skyhawks where that one came from, and you owe it to yourself to find one with reliable avionics.

Modifications

Everybody and his brother have come up with a mod for the 172 at

one time or another. Many of the more popular STCs have changed hands repeatedly over the years, and tracking down some of the more esoteric can be frustrating. If you get stuck, we suggest contacting the Cessna Pilots Association at P.O. Box 12948, Wichita, Kan. 67277. Phone: (316) 721-4313. Executive Director John Frank edits the CPA newsletter and can be quite helpful.

Among the more popular mods:

- Robertson STOL has been bought out and reborn as RSTOL Systems, Inc, though the new company still resides in the same building at Everett, Wash.'s Snohomish County Airport. Cessna 172 STOL mods for the pre-1973 'hawks come with a recontoured leading edge and full-span flaps as well as drooped ailerons. Newer post-1973 Skyhawks already come with a leading edge cuff, so their STOL mods cost less. At a price of $6,200 for 1973-79 models and $7,200 (both factory-installed prices) for 1956-72 airplanes, we wonder if they're worth the money.

The Skyhawk already had very good short-field performance, and the aircraft's limited power means that, barring the use of JATO bottles, takeoffs will never be spectacular, no matter what is done to the wing. RSTOL Systems, Inc., Snohomish County Airport, Building C-72, Everett, Wash. 98274. Phone: (206) 355-2736

- Horton STOLcraft offers a much less expensive STOL kit in the $400 neighborhood. Horton will install the kit at their Wellington, Kan. plant for another $1,000. Owners report a 20-mph reduction in stall speed with resultant reduction in takeoff and landing rolls. A more "solid" feel in Vmc flight was also reported. Phone: (316) 326-2241.

- Flint long-range fuel tanks add 24 gallons capacity for $2,450 plus installation. The tanks are mounted internally and do not change the contour or size of the wing. Flint Aero, 8665 Mission Gorge, Building D-1, Santee, Calif. 92071. Phone: (619) 448-1551.

Owner Comments

I'd have to say the Skyhawk is the greatest of the all-time greats and is already a legend in its own time. In time to come it will be in the same league as the DC-3 and other bigger-than-life aircraft.

I'm a part owner of a C-172 in a club where we also have a C-152 and a Comanche 260B. All three are popular, but the 'hawk outshines them all and not only pays for itself, but sometimes has to support the other two.

Pilots love it, and it's a joy to instruct in. You can park it alongside any other comparable aircraft and pilots will fly it two to one. It's easy to fly, is not a greenhouse in the summertime, and its high wings act as a shelter in the rain. The high wing eliminates problems getting in and out.

The aircraft is so stable you don't need automatic pilots, and since most students train in a C-150/152, a C-172 is a natural step-up. It's no wonder it's the world's most popular airplane.

As for performance, handling, maintenance, comfort and part availability, I would have to rate it excellent in every category. One fly in the ointment is that ordering a small part, like a knob or something similar, from Cessna is impossible. And trying to get a dealer (if you can find one) to order it is an even bigger impossibility.

Just how Cessna can build the world's greatest airplane, then do such a sorry job on small parts is unforgivable.

E. R. Ritch
Huntsville, Ala.

The plane (a 1981 model 172 P II) has, in general, been good to us. It now has 1,800 hours on it with no major engine problems or work to date. We've gone through more Slick mags than seems reasonable, including one that died shortly

The wing struts may look draggy, but they contribute to a nearly flawless record of avoiding in-flight airframe failures.

after being installed. I was so mad about that (it happened over mountainous terrain) that I demanded an explanation. Slick wrote back saying they don't normally explain themselves, but it was a quality control problem and they were upping their vigilance.

We were very fortunate to have purchased an '81, the year they went back to the O-320-D2J engine. My partners and I were unlicensed, unititiated, blind, dumb, and lucky when we bought the plane. It could just as easily been the valve-eater engine.

The radios are, of course, ARC. Never again. We had more than a bit of trouble with them at first, though they've been stable in the last two years. We installed a used 400 series DME. Two visits to the factory and about $1,500 in repairs later, it began working right. It should. They replaced every circuit board in it. Not exactly a bargain by the time we got done.

What can you say about Skyhawks? Reliable, easy to deal with, dependable, friendly, gentle. Not fast, not great load haulers. Ours has taken us to the tip of Baja, to Santa Fe, New Mexico, and to lots of places great and small. It has done so without causing missed heartbeats, and without the need to fly 50 hours a month in order to stay competent to cope.

The Skyhawk is a good, honest three-person airplane if you're really traveling somewhere far enough away to require baggage. As equipped, ours will haul 620 pounds, and full fuel. Four at 150

pounds plus the pilot's flight case just about gets you there. Three of us plus baggage sufficient for a one-week journey through Baja almost read tilt.

It's disappointing to see that on a $50,000 piece of equipment, the best we can get for air vents is two tubes that push in and out about the pilot and co-pilot's head and can never be tightly closed. This contributes a continuous source of both noise and cold air. The noise is never welcome, and cold air may or may not be, depending on the season. This arrangement makes the description "Mickey Mouse" seem like an improvement.

We're suffering filiform corrosion, for which I do not expect Cessna to run forward and claim responsibility. I'm certain they'll tell us it's absurd to expect to have an airplane parked within five miles of the ocean and not have it convert to aluminim dust by corrosion. I just wonder why they don't mention that possibility (necessity? inevitability?) *before* you buy?

I took my private and instrument instruction in the plane, and am glad I did. Life was a lot more comfortable there than it would have been in a 152, and I think it made getting through a lot easier and a lot more fun.

The plane isn't perfect, but it performs pretty much as advertised. For a first plane, I don't see how anyone can go too wrong with a Skyhawk, though I'm also not too certain how anyone can afford one anymore. I can only afford the payments on an '81 with the help of two partners and a leaseback, and then just barely.

Brian Weiss
Santa Monica, Calif.

Cessna 172

Grumman American Tiger

The Grumman American Tiger has won wide acclaim as a speedy, economical and nice-flying airplane that can deliver more performance per dollar than any fixed-gear airplane. The Tiger has a few off-beat features—a sliding canopy, all-bonded construction and a free-castering nosewheel, for example—that make it seem odd to first-time pilots, but once converted, a Tiger aficionado is usually vociferous in his enthusiasm for the aircraft.

History

The AA-5B Tiger was introduced in 1975 as an outgrowth of the AA-5 Traveler. Developed by speed demon Roy Lopresti (formerly with Mooney and the man responsible for the Mooney 201), the Tiger got a 180-hp Lycoming engine to replace the Traveler's 150-hp, a bigger horizontal tail, and cooling drag plus aerodynamic improvements that raised cruise speed to a blistering 139 knots—faster than most 200-hp retractables. The airplane was an immediate hit, and soon became the second best-selling 180-hp airplane, behind the Piper Archer. About 1,300 Tigers were built, and there were no major changes during the airplane's five-year career.

Unfortunately, the Tiger production line shut down in 1979 shortly after Grumman American was purchased by Allen Paulson and renamed Gulfstream American. Paulson apparently felt he could put the factory space to more profitable use building multi-million-dollar Gulfstream bizjets. Several groups have negotiated to take over production of the Tigers (and perhaps the other Grumman light-planes as well), but so far nothing has come of it.

So fast it will out-drag some retractables, the Tiger has delightful handling qualities, but deficient flaps for steep approaches.

Used Tiger Market

Surprisingly, the Tiger does not have a particularly high value on the used-plane market—perhaps because of the halt in production. A Tiger holds its value about as well as the Cessna Cardinal and Beech Sundowner, (according to the *Aircraft Price Digest*) and not as well as the Piper Archer. A 1977 Archer, for example, commands $27,000 today, while a 1977 Tiger is worth about $20,500. Both cost roughly the same when new.

Performance

The Tiger's performance is, in a word, stunning. Cruise speed is a sizzling 139 knots. In fact, our editors have flown the Tiger side-by-side with a Piper Arrow and pulled away from it by a knot or two. In a side-by-side test with the 180-hp fixed-gear Piper Archer, the Tiger zoomed by the Archer by a good 15 knots, and was able to keep up with a flat-out Archer while turning a leisurely 59 percent power and burning 20 percent less fuel. Readers report that the 139-knot book figure is easily reached in the real world (and we have gotten as high as 144 knots

out of a lightly loaded Tiger). Typical owner reports show: 142 knots on a fuel burn of 9.7 gph; 137 knots at 7.8 gph; 130 knots at 8.2 gph. (Variations are mostly due to altitude.)

Climb rate is also strong; owners report it will deliver about 1,000 fpm at sea level with all but the heaviest loads. Listed gross-weight climb is 850 fpm, superior to any of the 180-hp competition. Climb rate tends to decay quickly at heavy weights under high/hot conditions, however, and the Tiger's service ceiling is only 12,800 feet, quite a bit less than the Archer's and the Cardinal's.

Handling

It's a toss-up whether Tiger owners rave more about speed or handling qualities. Its light controls and responsiveness in the air win praise from pilots, and the Tiger seems to achieve this sprightly handling without the twitchiness, pitch instability and high sink rate that plagues the smaller two-seat AA-1s, which enjoy a similar reputation for "sports car handling." The Tiger's controls are all nicely harmonized; landings are relatively simple, with no sudden drop or excessive sink rate, and owners report the Tiger tracks reasonably well in IFR conditions or in turbulence—though perhaps not in the rock-solid manner of a

Skylane. With no retractable landing gear to worry about, and no prop lever, the pilot has little to do during takeoffs and landings except fly the airplane.

One drawback is the flaps, which don't have much effect. As a result, steep descents aren't possible, and it's easy to overshoot the landing, particularly if approach speed is too fast.

On the ground, the Tiger is unusual. There is no steerable nosewheel; one steers by differential braking while the nosewheel swivels freely. Although ground maneuverability in tight places is superb, crosswinds can make taxiing a real chore—not to mention hastening brake wear from constant pressure to keep the plane from weathercocking. But such idiosyncrasies are easily adjusted to, and most Tiger pilots come to prefer the free-castoring nosewheel because of the quick, light response and extraordinary agility on the ground.

Loading

The Tiger carries an average load for this class of aircraft. Gross weight is 2,400 pounds, while typical IFR empty weights run a bit over 1,400 pounds, for a useful load of about 950 pounds. That's good for full fuel and four people, but no baggage. The baggage compartment is adequate, but the baggage door is not. (One owner referred to it as a "mail slot.") With four people and 100 pounds of luggage, fuel is limited to perhaps 35 gallons—enough to fly comfortably 435 miles with a small reserve, or 348 miles with IFR reserves. Competitive aircraft like the Archer and Sundowner offer slightly better useful loads, but this advantage is partially offset by the Tiger's extra speed, which allows it to fly the same distance on less fuel—and thus carry a little more payload for the same useful load on the same trip.

Creature Comforts

Here is where the Tiger departs from the norm. The first thing a Tiger passenger notices is that he

or she must slide back the canopy and step down and in, rather than enter by the usual open-the-door method. This is generally no problem, but if you are fat and/or wearing a dress, it may be a bit awkward. Rain also makes entrance a bit messy, since sliding open the canopy drenches the entire cabin. Take an umbrella.

Once you're inside, the Tiger is comfortable, if not sumptuous. Room is adequate front and rear, but the seats seem a bit chintzy, and have neither height nor recline adjustments. One feature of the Tiger is unique: the rear seats fold down into a six-foot cargo area that will hold skis, a couple of ten-speed bikes or whatever. A pair of short people can even sleep back there.

One caveat for boarding passengers: If you've got two heavy people to go in the back, board one of them after a front-seater is already in the plane. With two big people in back and nobody in front, the Tiger will tip back on its tail, a gyration that may disturb a first-time passenger.

The Tiger is noted for its superb visibility, which makes both pilots and passengers happy. For pilots, it's easy to watch for other aircraft and see the runway on landing; for passengers, the rather tight seat

The next best thing to having both fuel tanks feed together automatically is to have the fuel tank selector point to it respective gauge, right below the throttle quadrant.

room is less noticeable because of the airy, open feeling provided by the canopy and broad side windows.

Safety

The one black mark against the Tiger is its accident record. According to NTSB accident statistics for the period 1972-76, the AA-5 series (which includes the 150-hp Traveler as well as the Tiger) had the worst fatal accident rate of any popular fixed-gear four- or six-place airplane, with 3.9 fatal accidents per 100,000 flight hours. By comparison, the Cessna 172 had a fatal accident rate of 1.5. In overall accidents, the AA-5 series also ranked poorly, trailing all the comparable four/six-placers except the taildragger Cessna 170 and 180 and the Piper Tri-Pacer.

A major cause of AA-5 accidents seems to be landing overshoots. In fact, the AA-5 led all 33 aircraft studied by the NTSB in landing overshoot accidents. The Tiger's flaps are not very effective, and the plane tends to float if speed is too high. Another trend in AA-5 accidents is the overload takeoff on high/hot conditions. (Most of these crashes presumably occurred in the 150-hp Traveler, which performs poorly under those conditions, and not so often in the more robust Tiger.)

NTSB figures show no other obvious pattern in AA-5 accidents, and frankly we are mystified by the high accident rate. Wing loading is a bit higher than for competitive Cessnas and Pipers, but approach speeds are a reasonable 65-70 knots under most conditions, and sink rate is not excessive.

Operating, Maintenance Costs

For a 140-knot airplane, Tiger operating and maintenance costs are extraordinarily low; for a 180-hp fixed-gear airplane, they're average or a little better. Fuel costs generally run around $20 per hour, and owners report the typical annual costs around $300-$500. The Tiger has no standout maintenance problems that we're aware of.

Grumman American Tiger

The Lycoming O-360-A4K engine generally has an 2,000-hour TBO, and the O-360 series in general has a superb reputation for reliability. But for some reason—perhaps a tendency to run hot—the Tiger seems to suffer more engine problems than other 180-Lycoming-powered aircraft. Top overhauls and/or cylinder and valve problems are not unusual at the 1,000-hour mark, and we have no reports of the Methuselah-like 3,000-hour engine lifetimes reported for the small Lycomings in other aircraft.

One maintenance kicker on the Tiger: in case of an accident, few mechanics will have any experience fixing the bonded wing and tail surfaces or the honeycomb fuselage skins. Instead of getting a quick-fix repair job, an owner may find it necessary to order a whole new component.

Airworthiness Directives

The Tiger has had its share of ADs, but none have been crippling. In addition to the ELT, vacuum pump and oil pump ADs that it shares with many aircraft, the Tiger has had ADs on the rudder control bar, cowl hinge, carb mixture control, bonded skin joints, oil cooler, alternate static source, and seat belts. A ludicrous AD (apparently triggered by a slight roll oscillation in a few airplanes) would have required a complete rework of the aileron system, but this was amended after a storm of protest; now only an inspection is required. All of these directives should have long since been complied with, of course. Two ADs deserve close checking though: a repetitive 100-hour inspection of the propeller hub once it reaches the 800-hour mark, and an inspection/replacement of the Slick magneto impulse coupling.

Maintenance Checkpoints

The Tiger, with its fixed gear, fixed prop and simple design philosophy, has been a fairly trouble-free aircraft. (''The most trouble-free machine of any kind I've ever owned,'' reports one owner.) But the Tiger does have its problems, of

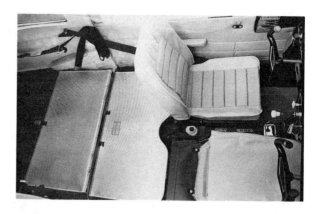

If the ''mail-slot'' baggage compartment door leaves a lot to be desired, the fold-down rear seat baggage bay makes up for it.

course. In addition to the previously mentioned ADs, which should be complied with on any airplane considered for purchase, check the following maintenance points:

• Cracking prop spinner. Pre-1979 Tigers (serial numbers before 1048) had a poorly designed spinner. Check to see that any Tiger you're looking at to buy has the improved spinner used on the later models. According to Gulfstream, virtually all of the Tigers in the field have the new spinner.

• Nosewheel shimmy. The Tiger's nosewheel not only looks like a supermarket shopping cart wheel; it sometimes acts like one. Properly rigged and maintained, it should not shimmy, but adjustment and maintenance are critical. A competent Tiger mechanic should be able to eliminate any shimmy; if not, check whether the nosewheel strut may be slightly bent.

• Air induction box problems. Although this is not an AD item, it should be. Tigers built before about mid-1977 (serial numbers 1-550) had the ''banjo-style'' air box, which tended to crack and come loose. We have received several reports of gaskets and air filter material breaking loose and blocking the carburetor, causing power interruption. Some Tigers have been updated with the later-style air box; check this carefully. The 1978 and later Tigers (serial numbers 551 and up) had the improved air box to begin with.

• Magneto replacement. According to reader reports, the Slick magneto may not last the engine TBO. Many seem to malfunction

after 600-700 hours, and one reader reports the left (impulse) mag is more trouble-prone.

• High brake wear. Because of the Tiger's steer-by-brakes setup and the need to ride one brake at the start of a crosswind takeoff, brake wear can be higher than on comparable aircraft. Although pads are cheap, the brakes should be inspected regularly, for brake failure leaves a Tiger owner helpless to steer or maneuver on the ground.

• Sticking canopy. Canopy rails need to be kept lubricated, with either graphite or Teflon lubricant.

Grumman American had won praise from Tiger owners for its product support. The company has often paid for defects that showed up after the warranty period (a bad batch of interior fabric that faded severely, for example). The company also came through with flying colors in fixing bond-line separations in many 1975-76 Tigers. In a couple of cases of severe delamination, customers had their airplanes virtually rebuilt at no charge.

Help & Support

Tiger owners can get information and support from The American Yankee Assn, P.O. Box 3052, Everett, Wash. 98203. They publish a newsletter six times a year. Ken G. Blackman is the editor.

Cylinder Problems

The most expensive maintenance surprise a Tiger owner is likely to discover is a bad cylinder or valve well before overhaul. We have received several reports of cylinder and valve problems at the 800-1,000-hour mark, and Tiger mechanics say that such problems are quite common. "The cylinder barrels run very hot," one mechanic told us, "and the walls get glazed and they really start to pump oil." As a result, plug fouling is common in Tigers.

The villain is heat. The Tiger's designers, in an attempt to achieve maximum speed by reducing cooling drag to the bare minimum, may have cut the cooling margin too thin. Tiger owners tell us they've seen cylinder head temperatures as high as 450 in normal cruise conditions. Cooling suffers particularly when the engine baffling is not perfectly aligned and sealed. Because of thinner-than-usual baffles and what we'd characterize as chintzy sealing and fitting, many Tigers run hotter than they are supposed to. The almost inevitable result is premature cylinder problems.

Any used-Tiger shopper should carefully check cylinder compression and the condition of the cooling baffles. A borescope inspection of the cylinder walls would also be a good idea. Check cylinder head temperature during flight. (One reader reports that using probe-type CHT pickups instead of the standard sparkplug style type caused his CHT readings to shoot up. So it's possible that standard Tiger CHT gauges are too optimistic.)

One way to lessen the heat buildup and decrease the possibility of cylinder problems is to avoid full-power climbs at low airspeeds.

(Climb rate at 95 knots is only slightly less than at the Tiger's best rate-of-climb speed, which ranges from 78 to 90 knots, depending on altitude.) Also, use restraint in leaning on hot days.

A better solution is offered by Gunnell Aviation at Santa Monica Airport in Calif., 213-391-6355. Gunnell's Bill Heard has developed a cooling outlet modification which, combined with baffle improvements, has dropped CHTs by 50 to 75 degrees on first eight Tigers modified. The mod is basically an enlarged cooling air outlet with a small fixed flap. According to Heard, there is no noticeable performance loss. We'd recommend the mod for any Tiger. We'd also suggest that Tiger owners purchase a four-probe CHT gauge to more carefully monitor engine temperatures. At the very least, keep the baffles and seals in tip-top shape.

Bond Separations in 1975 Models

The Tiger's innovative bonded construction technique backfired in the mid-70s when a spate of bond-line separations started showing up, often on the trailing edges of control surfaces. Aircraft in hot, humid, salt-air environments seemed to have the worst problems. Some minor separations had occurred in all the Grumman American airplanes for several years, but the problem grew to near epidemic proportions in 1976 and 1977, the result of an improper bonding sealant, American Cyanimide FM-123, known as "purple passion" among production employees. The FM-123 adhesive was

used in all Grumman American aircraft built from April 1974 until December 1975—some 760 airplanes. All 1975 Tigers and perhaps a few early 1976 models, up through serial number 125 or so, were glued together with the purple stuff.

At least one severe delamination occurred in flight on a 1975 Tiger, but no crashes resulted. Two Tigers, serial numbers 15 and 19, were virtually rebuilt from scratch because of severe delaminations in major structures. A former Grumman American employee told us that some 30 or 40 honeycomb fuselage test panels bonded with FM-123 mistakenly found their way into production aircraft during late 1974, possibly affecting Tigers with serial numbers below about 30.

In any case, have an experienced Tiger mechanic closely inspect any 1975 Tiger considered for purchase, with special emphasis on the fuselage panels of the first couple of dozen aircraft built. Also find out if the aircraft was based in a tropical, salt-air environment. Tigers built in 1976 and 1977 should also be scrutinized for bonding delamination, since a few problems were reported in those models, too. The 1978 and later models had a completely new primer/sealant system that has apparently solved the problem completely.

Mods 'n' Ends

The only STC on the Tiger we're aware of is held by Ameromod Corp. in Everett, Wash., 206-353-3559. Ameromod's Manard Crosby

Cost/Performance/Specifications

Model	Year Built	Number Built	Average Retail Price	Cruise Speed (kts)	Rate of Climb (fpm)	Useful Load (lbs)	Fuel Std/Opt (gals)	Engine	TBO (hrs)	Overhaul Cost
AA-5B Tiger	1975	111	$17,750	139	850	950	51	180-hp Lyc. O-360-A4K	2,000	$6,750
AA-5B Tiger	1976	288	$19,000	139	850	950	51	180-hp Lyc. O-360-A4K	2,000	$6,750
AA-5B Tiger	1977	292	$20,500	139	850	950	51	180-hp Lyc. O-360-A4K	2,000	$6,750
AA-5B Tiger	1978	212	$22,000	139	850	950	51	180-hp Lyc. O-360-A4K	2,000	$6,750
AA-5B Tiger	1979	417	$25,000	139	850	950	51	180-hp Lyc. O-360-A4K	2,000	$6,750

in fact, is something of a Grumman American guru, and offers several modifications for the two-place AA-1 series as well as the AA-5. The only current Tiger STC is a very useful one: a Sensenich propeller in place of the standard McCauley. Not only does the Sensenich prop increase speed by several knots and climb rate by about 100 fpm, according to Crosby, but it also removes the ''yellow arc'' rpm restriction that applies to all Tigers. This rpm restriction, which prohibits engine operation between 1850 and 2250 rpm in descending flight because of vibration of the engine/prop combination, is extremely annoying during the landing approach, particularly ILS approaches. According to Crosby, ILS approaches must be made either below 100 knots or above 140 knots to avoid the critical rpm band.

The new prop also eliminates a recent AD on the McCauley calling for dye-penetrant inspection of the prop spacer every 100 hours, at a labor cost of $50-$100. Price of the new prop and STC paperwork is $1,680 if the aircraft is already equipped with an updated spinner; $1,413 if a new spinner is necessary. By eliminating the AD, the new prop would pay for itself eventually.

Ameromod is also working on an STC to increase the Tiger's fuel capacity to either 60 or 70 gallons, but that approval isn't expected until the end of the year.

Contact Maynard Crosby at Ameromod Corp. in Everett (206) 353-3559 for parts, service and a series of upcoming engine mods including a 180-hp turbo and a 250-hp installation that is expected to push the aircraft to 165 knots.

Owner Comments

The following comments come from Ken Blackman, an expert on Grumman American airplanes and their maintenance.

Many accidents chalked up to the Tiger are a result of overshooting.

Aircraft Resale Value Chart

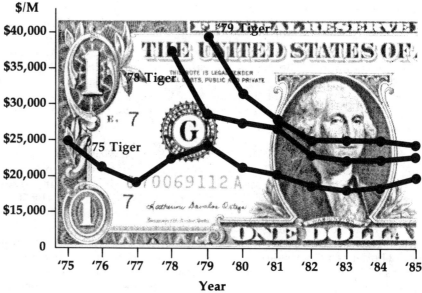

This is because the Tiger has one of the best glide ratios in the industry, especially for fixed-gear airplanes, and a too-fast approach speed can cause a long float. The two-place version is the opposite and gives birth to the falsehood that all Grummans will drop like a rock if you are slow. The sad result is that many pilots go through life trying to land a Tiger at 80 knots and will porpoise if they try to force it onto the runway. When the Tiger sets up a porpoise, chances are good it will get the prop, or nosegear, or worse. The proper approach speed is 65 to 70 knots over the fence for a normal landing. However, short-field approaches may safely be made at the ragged edge of stall, yet still leave a margin for safety.

The Tiger has many other safety attributes, such as the ability to recover from a stall, yoke full back, flaps full down. The super strength of the airplane gives it the ability to ''take a licking and keep on ticking'' in hard landings. Another unique feature is its ability to float, almost indefinitely, if ditched in water. If the Tiger remains upright, *it will float*, simple as that. Several cases are on record of the planes being towed to shore, dried out, and returned to service with only minor repairs required. If you compare the Tiger with a Cessna or Piper, you measure the time afloat in hours rather than minutes, or even seconds. A very important feature for those who spend a lot of time over water.

Short-field capability is another grossly misconceived area that has never been publicized. The Tiger is a great short-field performer, if flown properly. The manual recommends using zero degrees of flaps, which is okay, but one-third to one-half flaps will make all the difference in the world.

The grass takeoff procedure is as follows:
1. one-half flaps down
2. hold brakes
3. full power
4. right rudder as required
5. yoke back two-thirds
6. nose will lift at about 20 knots and the airplane will lift off at about 45 knots (in ground effect) then settle slightly before making like an elevator at about 55 knots. Note: *Do not* lower the nose until the airplane is positively climbing or it will settle back onto the ground.

During this procedure, the stall warning horn will be on steady until about 65 knots, so for all practical purposes, ignore it.

The same procedure should be followed for short hard-surface takeoffs, except leave the nose flat and flaps up until 45 knots IAS, then pull back and hit one-third flaps at the same time.

Takeoff roll, standard day, gross weight will be between 500 and 600 feet, and 50 feet AGL will come in less than 1,000 feet using the above technique.

There were no major changes in the Tiger during its five-year career. The only way to tell them apart is by the paint job. This is a 1977 model, worth about $20,000 on the used-plane market.

As far as maintenance, there are several unique things to look for with the Tiger. The infamous "Purple Passion" or "Blue Glue" was limited to some 1975 and 1976 models. Just because an airplane was built with this bonding agent doesn't mean it will have separation problems, as I have seen many cases of trouble-free specimens. However, the buyer should be beware of the fact that problems are prone to happen. Most cases will be evident by logbook entries of bond line repair history or replacement of parts, such as wing panels or controls surfaces, not associated with damage. Such an airplane should be avoided, unless inspected by an experienced G.A. mechanic or shop.

The best way to identify these airplanes is to pull a wing tip and look. If there is a blue or purple line around all the bonded seams at the spar-to-rib, rib-to-wing-skin area, it has it. This can also be seen by removing the ELT cover and looking inside the tail cone.

Gulfstream American will, in most cases, still furnish replacement parts and some labor credit for repairing delaminated airplanes, so don't pass up a good deal on a Tiger because of this potential alone.

The next most common maintenance item is nosewheel shimmy. This can be caused by a variety of things: improper tension or worn spring washers, too-loose adjustment of the axle nuts, out-of-balance or out-of-round nose tire, or a loose strut in the torque tube. Only the latter is costly, unless it can be shimmed. Many shops don't follow the checklist, on annuals, allowing the nosegear to go without proper treatment. The strut should be removed from the torque tube, all rust and corrosion cleaned, coated with zinc chromate and lubricant and reinstalled. The 1977 and later models with the

shocks on the nosegear are very difficult to remove, especially after a couple of years of neglect. This can take several hours and requires the knowledge of how to do it without damaging the strut or fork.

The fork has a stack of spring washers which may be shot. The tension required is 18 to 22 pounds of side pull, at the axle point, to cause the fork to turn left or right. Most shops think the book means "torque," thus causing a too-loose adjustment.

The axle should be tightened to allow the nosewheel to spin only a couple of turns after lift off.

Another nosegear item is the torque tube. It has bonded "shear joints" at each end which can be broken loose on hard landings. If you hear a metallic "clicking" when the nose is bobbed up and down, check these points inside the cabin. If the joint is working, the torque tube assembly *must* be replaced at a cost of around $1,000 parts and labor. Also check the attaching points for honeycomb damage and worn bolts.

I own a 1978 Tiger with 980 hours. I would choose a Tiger over *any* other single-engine aircraft costing $75,000 or less.

Ground handling—superb. The Tiger can turn virtually in its own circle. I've even seen a Tiger taxiied into a hangar, shut down, then turned around in the hangar and ready to taxi out. The castering nosewheel and differential braking are just excellent for ground handl-

ing, in almost all situations. Three minor disadvantages: (a) you have to start moving at least a little bit to start a turn; (b) the plane tends to weathercock in a good stiff crosswind, but continuing to move at least five mph and use of brake covers this problem; (c) backing the plane (especially without a towbar) is a real terror because that nosewheel wants to turn sideways.

Takeoff—Very good to excellent. Again, there is a tendency to weathercock on strong crosswind, but I've never even come close to losing control or ground-looping. It's much better than high-wings, and as good (and generally better) than other aircraft.

It has a rather long takeoff roll, partially because of its high-speed (as opposed to high-lift) wing, and partially because of that fixed-pitch propeller. At 55 knots, I lift the nose two or three inches off the runway, and it flies itself off about 70-75 knots.

Climb—excellent under the circumstances (fixed gear, fixed prop, no turbo). Best rate at our field elevation (5,000 feet) is about 85 knots, with very good visibility. Best angle is about 65-67 knots, but poor visibility, and in the summer, it might overheat an engine (I have not had it happen, but with no cowl flaps or CHT/EGT, and small cowl opening near the prop, *I would not recommend frequent maximum angle climbs, especially in heat of summer*). I find that climb performance degrades very little at 90-95 knots (about 100 feet per minute), and even 100-110 knots is good, to say nothing of improved cooling and visibility.

Cruise—fantastic. This is the Tiger's major element, where the fixed-pitch prop is most effective. I consistently obtained 139 knots true (I've measured it), at 7,500-8,500 feet. Now that gas prices are way up, I pull back on the throttle and get 130 knots, and about 9.0-9.5 gph. With the engine at 980 hours, my top cruise speeds at 7,500-8,500 (full throttle) is about 137 knots, and 2650 rpm—both down somewhat from the speeds when new. I haven't seen a Tiger yet in its first 500 hours that can't at least meet the "book" claims on speed.

At cruise, handling is sheer delight, with even faster response—of course—than the very good response at slow speeds.

With 51.5 gallons usable fuel, you have an easy 550-nm range, especially if you lean properly. However, I consistently get much better than the book by pulling back to 2500 or even 2400 rpm (depending on altitude), leaning until the engine just begins to run rough, pushing mixture in until the engine runs smoothly, and pushing in one more "notch." With that technique, I've made a nonstop flight of 677 nm (with 10 gallons left).

Landings—I think, are superb—if you keep the airspeed in hand. A Tiger is "clean," especially without flaps. If you keep it at 65 knots, or about 70 in crosswinds, you'll be fine. But above 70 knots (especially below gross weight), you'll have a long "float," and a temptation to "force" the plane to land. If you try that above 75 knots, you'll get a nosewheel landing and a possible porpoise that tends to aggravate itself.

Crosswind landings—the equal or best of any other single-engine I've flown, and much better than any high-wing (Cessna), especially better than tail-draggers.

Comfort—good, but not superb. The seats are not orthopedic (but are decently comfortable), and do not recline or adjust the backs. On a five-hour flight, I am not as comfortable as in seats in a Bonanza, or good cars. Seats aren't bad, but definitely are not the highlight of a flight.

Baggage area is fair—120 pounds maximum behind the rear seat. The baggage door is small ... a little too small ... and you have to press on it quite hard to lock it (or unlock it).

With back seat down, baggage capacity is great. I've carried bicycles back there. It's like a station wagon, and takes only a few seconds to unlatch the seat backs and lay them down.

Maintenance—I've found it very low—lower than any other good-performing or high-speed airplane. The fixed gear and fixed-pitch prop are great for minimal maintenance. The landing gear is incredibly strong, and has no oleo struts or seals or places to leak (except brake lines, and I haven't had a leak there yet). The nosewheel can shimmy (mine has been free of this, but I've had other Grummans that are rather fierce on shimmy), requiring sensitive adjustment. The rubber at the nosewheel fairing where the nose downtube enters routinely deteriorates and needs replacement each year.

The nose spinner commonly cracks and requires replacement with a new-model spinner that eliminates that problem.

Annual inspections have cost me $350-$500, and I'm about to have another one. Sparkplugs tend to foul at times, especially if you run rich or use a lot of carb heat without leaning mixture.

Disadvantages—the problems in the Tiger are so few that to list them is a real compliment. Here are all I can think of:
1. The yellow arc on the tachometer (1800-2250 rpms)—cured with a Sensenich propeller.
2. Wind noise/rain leak in the forward seal of the canopy, and ungluing of the canopy seal. (Easily cured with the several strips/seals available.)

3. Castering nosewheel cocks when pushing the plane back, unless you use the towbar, or are really careful.
4. "Float" on landings if airspeed is too high. Of course, this is true for most planes, but float is longer on the Tiger than others.
5. Weather-cocking tendency in crosswinds—a little more than other planes, but easily controlled with a little extra taxi speed and use of the good brakes.
6. Cracking spinner. On the other hand, the new spinner—furnished on 1979 planes and easily available on others from parts suppliers and the factory—has no problems and fits right on. Indeed, it fits on a Sensenich prop (which avoids the yellow arc).
7. Small baggage door. (Fortunately, items can be loaded through passenger compartment, especially if rear seat is temporarily or permanently folded forward for the trip.)
8. A tendency to be a bit of a "cork" in moderate turbulence. It takes more attention and being "on top" of the plane in turbulence, especially in an instrument approach, than in some of the other planes like big Cessnas—which in turn trade good stability for "station wagon" handling.
9. Seats that do not recline. They are comfortable as far as they go, but do not have the comfort of (heavier) seats in Bonanzas or good sportscars.
10. Engine instruments too far to the right. They're easy to read, but they are out of sight of peripheral vision, and you have to make a deliberate effort—better yet, a habit every 20 minutes—to look at them.
11. Muffler/exhaust pipe. Mine lost its innards at 400 hours, and I've heard they do the same about every 500 hours (at 980 hours, I haven't had it happen again).
12. The seat adjustment lock can slip and the seat slide back. I've never had this happen or seen it happen, but I've heard of it happening on a friend's Cheetah. I always make sure my seat is carefully and securely locked. This probably is the most significant complaint I can think of about the plane.

Cessna 182

Even if the Cessna 182 hasn't been around as long as the Old Testament, it sometimes seems like it has. The third most popular lightplane in history, the Cessna 182 has long been the keystone of Cessna's step-up marketing philosophy, bridging the gulf between Cessna's low-profit 150/172 entry-level airplanes and the higher-profit, higher-performance 210 and light twin aircraft.

Today, almost 30 years after the 182's introduction in 1956, the aircraft is still *the* basic medium-performance aircraft, an economical flying machine capable of hauling four people, bag and baggage, a reasonable distance, in comfort, and at a reasonable speed.

The first Skylanes rolled off the production line the same year as the first 172s. Together, the duo marked the beginning of Cessna's 20-year dominance of the single-engine market.

The basic 182 design was cut in stone in those days and both airframe and powerplant have remained fundamentally unchanged ever since. The overall effect is generous, with a fuselage of ample size, topped by a big slab of a wing.

In 1958, Cessna introduced the "Skylane," a 182 fitted with enough amenities and creature comforts to raise the empty weight approximately 100 pounds, and therefore decrease useful load by roughly the same amount. Those 1958 Skylanes included rudder trim and a ratchet click elevator trim device, along with optional autopilot. Later Cessna bestowed the Skylane name on the 182, and made the marginally upscale version of the same plane the "Skylane II."

The 230-hp Continental O-470 has proved a dependable performer through the years, despite some break-in problems reported in the later O-470-S model. Those first 182s used the O-470-L engine, which featured larger cast shell cylinder heads, thinner and more numerous cooling fins, and an engine mount improved over the early O-470-K installation in the Cessna 180 design.

Cars with enormous swept tail "fins" were all the rage in the late 1950's. Eventually this vogue found its way into airplane styling, with Cessna sweeping back the tail on the 180 in 1960. Basic fuel capacity was increased in 1960, from 55 gallons to 65, with long-range 84-gallon tanks introduced as an option. Later Skylanes would boast a 92-gallon capacity.

Two years later the airplane got a rear window and electric flaps. The year 1971 witnessed an alteration to the 182 in the form of its so-called camber lift wing. The wing was given a constant radius droop—a downward curl. The aim of the droop was to provide better low speed handling and stall reaction. Combined with the aircraft's washout, the result is good lateral control even while deep in the stall zone.

Gross weight has grown steadily over the years, from the original 2,550 pounds to 2,650 in 1957 to 3,100 today. Empty weight has also increased, although not quite as

Back in the days of JFK and the New Frontier, the 182 got a cleaned-up look. Performance, however, remained basically the same.

fast as gross, so that useful load numbers for the 182 have not increased dramatically, starting at 1,010 pounds in '57, and topping off at 1,377 today.

Overall, however, the 182 design has gone through remarkably few changes over the years.

Built for Comfort, Not for Speed

Book speeds have remained in the 139- to 143-knot range through the years with evolutionary aerodynamic refinements making up for the speed penalty of higher gross weights. Most owners report such speeds are possible in the 182, but prefer to drone along at lower power settings to save fuel, with 130 knots a commonly mentioned figure. One owner reported burning 12.5 gph to get 140 knots at 75 percent power. Another said his 182, burdened with a "full load" cruised at 135 knots at 75 percent between 6,500 and 8,500 feet, while consuming a quart of oil every four hours. Performance like this may seem pokey for an airplane driven by a 230-hp engine, and it is. The Mooney 201, albeit a retractable, slips through the air 30 knots faster than a 182, while using less horsepower.

Cessna has traditionally promoted the 182 as the businessman's airplane through publicity shots such as this one, showing the Skylane on the job.

While no one ever said the 182 was a racer, the airplane does climb, with 1,000 fpm easily obtainable at heavy weights, and 1,500 fpm at lighter weights (both from sea level, of course).

If the 182 doesn't get you there particularly fast, it treats you kindly along the way, thanks to a spacious interior. It's a real four-seater, the kind that allows the back seat mob to abandon the fetal position and stretch out. Two wide doors ease entry and exit. On the negative side, cabin noise levels approach brain-damage thresholds, and can make long flights fatiguing without a good pair of earplugs.

Handling

In a word, the 182 is stable. Most pilots praise it both as an IFR platform and as a reasonably comfortable aircraft in turbulence. Nonetheless, in the air, as on the ground, there ain't no free lunch, and this stability is paid for with rather heavy control forces.

To use another word, the 182 is ponderous, especially in pitch. With full flaps and two people aboard, flaring to land takes maximum muscle and maximum back trim. This heaviness of control is the price paid for the 182's vast CG envelope.

Trying to stall the 182 with power on is probably the nearest anyone will come to aerobatic maneuvering in this staid aircraft. It will buck and shake like a bronco until the pilot either relaxes back pressure to lower the nose or settles for a pronounced wing drop.

Such performance will never come as a surprise, however, because the 182's humungous elevator forces

make the airplane virtually impossible to stall by accident. Slow-speed maneuvering in a Skylane builds confidence; there's no feeling of flying right on the edge. On the other hand, aileron control at low speeds is relatively clumsy, and gusty crosswinds can prove challenging.

Loading

Unless you're transporting ingots of solid neutronium, the 182's load limits are pretty tough to bust. It's acknowledged as one of the few airplanes you can almost always fill all the seats, all the tanks, stuff the baggage compartment to capacity, and still be legal (and safe). Admittedly a well-equipped 182 with long-range tanks might require a degree of fuel/passenger tradeoff, but on the whole, Skylane pilots don't fuss much with weight and balance. If it fits, it's probably legal.

CG balance is also generous. One Skylane owner reports he can put himself up front, load a pair of 200-pounders in the back, fill the baggage compartment to the max, and still be within CG limits.

Safety

The Skylane has a good safety record—well above average as measured against the GA fleet overall. Both accident and fatality rates come in below the norm. FAA records from 1980-81 list 41 fatal accidents for the 182 fleet, with over 3 million hours flown during that period.

The Skylane has among the best stall/spin accident rates of any aircraft. In both a 1972 stall/spin study from the NTSB, and a 1984 study conducted by our sister publication *Aviation Safety*, the 182 scored

among the lowest in both accidents and fatalities attributed to stalls or spins.

Thanks in part to the airplane's megalithic pitch performance, in-flight structural failures are virtually unheard of. It's nearly impossible to pull hard enough on a 182 to overstress the airplane. That high-drag fuselage and fixed gear also limit speed buildup in an unintentional dive. When measured overall, Cessna designs featuring wing strut braces have an excellent record of holding together when the going gets tough.

The Skylane also excels in the area of fuel management. Its no-frills fuel system consists of a high-wing, gravity-feed system, and an idiot-proof left-right-both fuel selector.

Deadly Fuel Cells

One of the more disturbing ADs to emerge from the FAA's regulatory woods, AD 84-10-1 has caused thousands of Cessna owners to delve deep into the innards of their fuel-bladder equipped wings for potentially deadly water-trapping wrinkles. For years the problem eluded detection during the traditional sump-draining preflight because the water trapped by wrinkles could also be kept isolated from the quick-drain openings. Such a tank could be sumped and no water would show in the sample.

A simple attitude change, such as that encountered in takeoff, would spill the water out of its wrinkle containment area, through the intake, and into the engine. Too often, this water was more than the three ounces that can be stopped by the gascolator. Result: engine stoppage at the worst possible time, just seconds after takeoff. AD 84-10-1 affected all 182 models built between 1956 to 1978, the year Cessna changed over to a wet-wing design.

A worthwhile discussion of this AD requires some background. In an *Aviation Safety* examination of accidents from 1975 through 1981, 396 accidents in various types of aircraft were found in which water-contaminated fuel was cited as a cause or factor. A total of 155 (about 39 percent) of these accidents involved Cessna aircraft and 39 of those mishaps involved Cessna 182s.

What's more, 25 of the 39 C-182 accidents involved the P-model, the 182 model in production from 1972 through 1974. In those days, the rubber fuel bladders installed at the plant were made of Goodyear BTC-39. The passage of time revealed that BTC-39 bladders deteriorated rapidly, becoming brittle, "cheesy," and eventually leaking copiously. An AD mandated their replacement with bladders made of stiffer BTC-67, a urethane material.

The extra stiffness of BTC-67 seems to be the contributing factor to the wrinkle problems that were to be discovered later. As Bob Stevens, then FAA manager of Standards and Evaluations, put it, "There's two ways to install a tank like this. If the tank is put in on the assembly line as the airplane is built, that's fairly easy. The tank just fits in before the butt rib. It's installing the tank in the field as a replacement where the trouble starts. As delivered in the field, these tanks aren't too wrinkled. The procedure to install is to soften the BTC-67 tanks in warm water, and then wad

Skylane engines seem to suffer less from 100 LL than other 80-octane airplanes. They also can use autogas.

them up and stuff them into the wing. That's where I think the wrinkles come from."

"Smoothing and Blending"

The AD required an inspection of the bladders, "smoothing and blending" of any wrinkles found, and installation of new quick drains on aircraft in which the "smoothing and blending" process requirement involved movement of the drains. The chief target of the inspection is a water-trapping wrinkle that commonly extended at a 45-degree angle across the inboard rear corner of the fuel tank floor. Such a large wrinkle can trap quite a bit of water. More than a few 182 owners reported discovering their tanks harbored as much as a quart, sometimes more.

The entire "smoothing and blending" process is something akin to

eliminating the wrinkles in a carpet. Stomping on one wrinkle can make it vanish, only to reappear somewhere else on the carpet. Often what's needed is to take up the whole carpet and lay it again. In the fuel bladder case, this move required relocation of the drains. Cessna has provided a quick-drain kit for $89 (part number SK-206-24 and 25).

Rock n' Roll!

Another move mandated by AD 84-10-1 is the famed "rock n' roll preflight." The aircraft is sumped normally, on level ground. Then the tail is lowered to within five inches of the ground while rocking the wings 10 inches up and down at least 12 times. Then the sumps are drained again, checking for any water that may have been shaken out.

After the main wrinkle has been eliminated, the AD specifies that the amount of fluid trapped by any other wrinkles must be determined. If this trapped fluid measures more than three ounces, the aircraft is placarded with the "rock n' roll preflight" procedure, making those moves mandatory before flight.

The wording of AD 84-10-1 has been criticized as vague. For example, it's unclear whether these "rocking and rolling" moves have to be done simultaneously, something clearly beyond the ability of just one person. Plus, pilots of petite stature would probably find

Cost/Performance/Specifications

Model	Year	Number Built	Average Retail Price	Cruise Speed (Kts)	Rate of Climb (fpm)	Useful Load (lbs)	Fuel Std/Opt (gals)	Engine	TBO (hrs)	Overhaul Cost
182-A	1956-57	1,753	$12,250	117	1,210	1,010	55	230-hp Cont. O-470-L	1,500	$7,250
182-A&	1958-59	1,648	$13,500	120	1,030	1,090	55	230-hp Cont. O-470-L	1,500	$7,250
182-C&D	1960-61	1,239	$14,750	123	1,030	1,090	65/84	230-hp Cont. O-470-L	1,500	$7,250
182-E&F	1962-63	1,459	$16,250	123	980	1,190	65/84	230-hp Cont. O-470-R	1,500	$7,250
182-G&H	1964-65	1,175	$17,250	123	980	1,190	65/84	230-hp Cont. O-470-R	1,500	$7,250
182-J&K	1966-67	1,820	$18,250	123	980	1,175	65/84	230-hp Cont. O-470-R	1,500	$7,250
182-L&M	1968-69	1,549	$19,750	123	980	1,175	65/84	230-hp Cont. O-470-R	1,500	$7,250
182-N	1970-71	769	$21,000	121	850	1,310	65/84	230-hp Cont. O-470-R	1,500	$7,250
182-P	1972-74	1,009	$23,750	125	1,010	1,169	61/80	230-hp Cont. O-470-R	1,500	$7,250
182-P II	1975-76	1,699	$28,000	125	1,010	1,169	61/80	230-hp Cont. O-470-S	1,500	$7,250
182-Q II	1977-80	2,559	$36,000	121	1,010	1,169	61/80	230-hp Cont. O-470-U	1,500	$7,250
182-R II	1981	339	$48,000	124	865	1,390	92	230-hp Cont. O-470-U	1,500	$7,250
182-R II	1982	237	$56,000	124	865	1,373	92	230-hp Cont. O-470-U	1,500	$7,250
182R II	1983	74	$70,000	124	865	1,373	92	230-hp Cont. O-470-U	2,000	$7,250
182R II	1984	65	$93,625	124	865	1,373	92	230-hp Cont. O-470-U	2,000	$7,250

the tail-lowering maneuver impossible. And it's unclear as to just how owners of float-equipped aircraft are supposed to perform these moves.

As more and more 182s come into compliance with this AD, some evidence is emerging that it has been effective. Life-threatening wrinkles have been detected and corrected. However, there have also been reports of heavy labor costs for airplanes with particularly convoluted wrinkles.

What Else Can You Do About Water?

Two devices intended to prevent undrainable water from reaching the engine seem to us worthwhile. The Silver-Wells water separator is a well-known product by now. Basically an enlarged gascolator, the separator is so commodious it increases the maximum permissible amount of water trapped by wrinkles from three ounces to a full quart under provisions of the AD. As of this writing, it is the only approved alternate form of compliance for this portion of the AD.

The Silver-Wells separator costs $500. When added to the cost of compliance with the rest of the AD, the total tab can run upwards of $1,000. The separator is available from TurboPlus, 1520 26th Avenue NW, Gig Harbor, Wash. 98335, (800) 742-4202.

Another device, quite similar to the separator, fits under the 182's cabin floorboards. Designed by Skylane pilot Rodney Gross, who himself experienced a water-contaminated engine failure on takeoff in a 182, the system consists of two small reservoir tanks located near the fuel system low point in the aircraft's belly. These tanks allow water which was not drained during pre-flight sumping to settle, and are equipped with quick drains of their own, so that water can be eliminated from the system.

Gross's system has received a revised STC, and cannot be installed until the rest of the AD has been complied with. "These tanks are just an insurance policy," Gross

said. "They don't solve the problem."

Priced at $330, the system is available from Saturn Components Corporation, 15268 Earlham Street, Pacific Palisades, Calif. 90272, (213) 454-6714.

Speaking of water contamination, leaking and deteriorating fuel caps and seals are also likely avenues for aqueous invasion. Check them thoroughly for a tight fit.

Carb Ice

In figures released by the NTSB in 1977, an alarming number of accidents involving carb ice and 182s emerged. While the 182 isn't as prone to carb ice problems as some other designs (notably the C-150), anyone who regularly flies a Skylane in heavy weather should invest in a carb ice detector.

Crunch

When shopping for a used 182, examine the firewall carefully. The nose-heaviness of the 182, coupled with the airplane's heavy elevator forces, makes for frequent hard landings with a potential for gear-bending nose-low landings. The firewall is usually the first to suffer.

Another casualty of the 182's nose-heavy handling is the nosewheel assembly, with buckling and shimmies the usual result.

Overall...

Plenty of power, a big wing, heavy pitch forces, solid handling and a simple, safe fuel system (providing AD 84-10-1 has been complied with) make the Skylane one of the safest buys around.

Big, bulbous, and beefy describes the Cessna 182, shown here in its 1983 version.

Maintenance

The 182 is a simple, robust aircraft, with a healthy, but normal appetite for maintenance as the fleet ages. When we evaluated this airplane in 1979, readers reported annuals in the $250-$300 range. Today's readers have cited annuals in the $1,000 to $2,000 neighborhood. Looking at those numbers, it seems to us that the 182 line hasn't become any less reliable mechanically, but that maintenance and parts costs have gone through the roof. One reader calculated his hourly operating cost for labor alone at $25.

The Skylane shares the same Mc-Cauley/Hartzell prop AD that encumbers many aircraft designs, Cessna and otherwise, equipped with constant-speed propellers. With the exception of this and the fuel bladder problem, the AD scene for the 182 is relatively clear.

Powerplant

The Continental O-470 engine has a good record, although it doesn't seem to be as reliable as the four-cylinder carbureted Lycomings. TBO for the O-470 was 1,500 hours until 1983, when it was boosted to 2,000 for the O-470-U model.

A well-maintained engine should meet or exceed the TBO. The key to longevity on this engine appears to be a rigorous break-in period. "Firewall that sucker," is how one O-470 operator put it. The theory is that the heat of heavy initial operation seats the piston rings and valve seats firmly in place, cutting oil consumption and smoothing operation.

Some 1975 and 1976 Skylanes had special engine problems that used airplane buyers should be aware of. Aircraft built in those years bore the 182P designation, and featured the O-470-S engine, which had a new ring design. Some of these engines had break-in problems, in some cases using as much as a quart of oil per hour. Despite its efforts, Continental apparently never really figured out what was wrong, and instead switched to higher-compression O-470-U in 1977. The most plausible theory offered to date is that the S-series engines were babied in break-in by well-meaning owners. Check for tell-tale high oil consumption on these engines.

Valve Problems

Earlier this year, Continental issued a mandatory service bulletin covering some 75 new and rebuilt O-470 engines evidently shipped with the wrong exhaust valves. It seems that soft, stainless steel valves were installed in the engines by mistake. This engine has hardened Nitralloy valve guides, which promptly chewed up the soft valves, a process resulting in stuck valves and metal particles wreaking havoc throughout the oil system. Proper valves for the O-470 engine carry part number 637781.

At roughly the same time, Continental sent out about 40 O-470 cylinder assemblies (P/N 646680) fitted with the wrong valves. By the time the problem was discovered, Continental had been sending these faulty assemblies out for almost a full year.

As of April, 1985, about 15 engines had been replaced due to extensive metal contamination of the oil. The rest were being reworked with the correct valves. During the valve replacement, valve guides must be reamed out to remove any metal build-ups.

The Skylane seems to have suffered less from 100LL problems than other 80-octane airplanes.

Nevertheless, the proven process of careful leaning, plug rotation, and 50-hour oil changes is the best policy, along with use of TCP should lead fouling be suspected.

Skylanes have paper induction air filter elements that can swell up in the presence of moisture and restrict airflow. Even worse, old paper filters can decompose to the point where they can be ingested by the engine. Such an ingestion was blamed as cause of a fatal Skylane crash leading to AD 84-26-02, which put a life limit of 500 hours on paper filters. The filter on the downed Skylane reportedly was more than 10 years old, and had accumulated 1,100 hours in the time of the crash.

This AD did not include foam induction air filters such as those made by Brackett Aircraft Co., which recommends their filters be replaced every 12 months or 100 hours if one inch thick, and every 200 hours if two inches thick. Since paper filters range in price from about $20 to over $100, the Bracketts might actually be cheaper to use. They are priced from $10 to a little under $60, and replacement filters cost even less. Brackett claims its filters stop potentially damaging particles down to 15 microns for a longer period than paper filters.

Aside from water and dirt, another factor that can cause great distress to paper, and maybe even foam

The first edition 182, a 1956 model with squared-off tail and rear-view window but no wheel pants. A workaday airplane destined to become the third-best selling lightplane in history.

filters is a ''backfire'' in the manifold system that belches flame out into the filter. This flame can burn portions of the filter into ashes and cinders that do no good for the engine. Suggestion: next time a backfire is encountered on startup, shut down, get out, and check the condition of the induction air filter.

Modifications

The marriage between airframe and powerplant has been such a happy one in the case of the 182, that there have been relatively few STC'd mods. EAA and Petersen Aviation both hold the autogas STCs for the 182 series, with Petersen's usable for both leaded and unleaded fuels (see Owner Comments for more on the difference in fuels). Robertson Aircraft, 839 West Perimeter Road, Renton, Wash. 98055, offers an extensive and expensive STOL mod. Less elaborate systems featuring new leading edge cuffs, sealed ailerons and stall fences are marketed by Horton STOL-craft, Inc., Wellington Municipal Airport, Wellington, Kan. 67152.

The major slick-up mods offered for the 182 line come from Charlie Siebel's Flight Bonus, Inc., located at Box 120773, Arlington, Tex. 76012, (817) 265-1650. Depending on the year of manufacture, Siebel's slick-ups promise to boost a 182's cruise speed from 12 to 20 mph and range in price from $2,485 to $3,425.

Skylane Club

There is a combination Skylane/Centurion Club headed by Bob Green, Box 75068, Birmingham,

Ala. 95253, (205) 879-7414. Annual dues are $20. Owners of 182s preferring more polyglot company might also join the Cessna Pilot's Assn., located at Wichita's Mid-Continent Airport at 2120 Airport Road, Box 12948, Wichita, Kan. 67277, (316) 946-4777. CPA also charges $20 a year.

Owner Comments

I own a 1981 Cessna Skylane 182R, and have put over 800 hours on it since new. There is a lot of good news about the plane, and a little bad.

First the good news: Performance.

The Skylane is a terrific instrument platform, both stable and forgiving yet able to fly fast approaches when mixing it up with the big planes at major airports. Its outstanding range adds flexibility for hard IFR.

Its short-field performance is exemplary, as are its load-carrying capability and, more important, its wide center-of-gravity tolerance. I can truly haul four people, full fuel, a panel full of avionics, and a little luggage, and be within both payload and CG limits.

Its controls, while not light, are balanced and authoritative, so that it handles crosswinds and turbulence very well. In fact, its smooth ride, coupled with generous inside space, make it a comfortable cross-country machine.

The Skylane's speed is consistently better than book, flying at over 140 knots at most altitudes and weights. Fuel burn is as advertised—12.5 gph at 75 percent.

There's plenty of room on the panel and in the payload for a full complement of avionics (King, Stormscope) and other options (standby vacuum pumps, carb ice detector). It's noisy; headphones and intercom are a must.

Now the bad news: Cost.

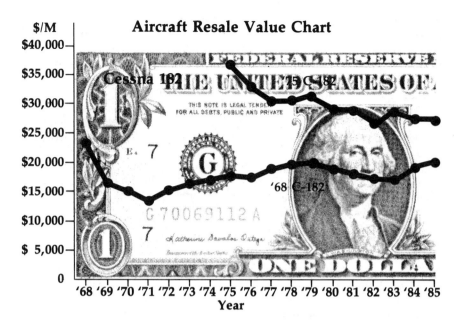

Aircraft Resale Value Chart

While parts availability and backup have presented no problems, I've had too many opportunities to find out. Annuals have cost from $500 to $1,800, even though painstaking maintenance is performed at every 50-hour oil change. Operating cost, exclusive of hangaring, insurance, and allowance for overhaul, exceeds $40 per hour. All three left-side cylinders needed rings and valves at 600 hours, although the subsequent reduction in oil use (from 4.5 hours per quart to nine) indicates there may have been a problem from the beginning.

Now the worst news: Reliability.

I'm on my seventh alternator control unit. It's no fun while IFR suddenly to be reduced to battery power, but it has happened so often that I carry a spare ACU so that at least when (and if) I land, I can get an immediate repair. Neither Cessna not my repair shop have a found solution.

In summary, the Skylane offers balanced performance, with a cost penalty. Buy a clean used one, but if the alternator control unit is over 10 months old, replace it immediately before venturing into a cloud.

Dr. Stephen J. Browne
Cambridge, Mass.

With Charlie Seibel's full-speed equipment I cruise 160-165 mph at 10,000 feet on 2,250 rpm and 18.5 inches at about 12 or 11.5 gph and use a quart of 50-weight Shell every three to four hours.

With RSTOL strips, 1,500-foot takeoffs are easily manageable.

Granted, it is a little ponderous compared to my Bonanza, but it's a wheels down grandpappy airplane and rock solid on VFR—very predictable when flying the numbers for climb, descent, approaches, etc.

Maintenance has been very predictable—no surprises, but then I'm meticulous. Nothing's too small for attention; therefore my $2,000 annuals are high. The 25-hour checkup and oil change is around $250 with no problems with either parts availability or backup.

My wife and I spent three weeks plus in the airplane last summer going to British Columbia, Alaska and the west, having plenty of room throughout—though packed stem to stern with camping, living and survival gear.

Henry G. Wischmeyer
Dallas, Tex.

We have owned a 1979 Skylane since 1981. This aircraft was purchased with 700 hours on it. It has an all ARC panel with the exception of a King 62A DME and a Sigtronics four-station intercom. In four years we have had minor nav-com trouble four times—trouble that takes about $100 and three days to be corrected each time. No trouble at all with the 300 A/P or KN62A. We average 100 hours of pleasure flying per year. Annuals average about $350. One went to $600 because a jug had to be reworked at 1,000 hours. Seems Continental used a hammer to seat an exhaust valve guide. Other than that, the cylinders always hang in there at 72 to 76.

Our useful load is 1,146 as equipped. With a full load and 75 percent power at 6,500 to 8,500 feet we true at 135 knots. A light weights we reach 145 knots. It burns 12 gph and a quart of oil every four hours. For local flying we can get the burn down to nine gph.

Generally speaking, we like the overall performance and big plane feel it has over, say, a 172 or Cherokee. On the downside, we might wish for a little better fit and finish All of the door-to-airframe fits are atrocious, with very bad air leaks. We had a bad spell of water leaks which we finally stopped on our own through judicious use of silicon sealant.

I can say that after four years the paint and interior have held up real good. We keep it hangared.

There is one mod we were really interested in: the Seibel speed mod. But another Skylane owner at our airport did it, and the only good thing he had to say about it was that it didn't slow his plane down, which was kind of disappointing because we just know that the ol' 182 could be Mooney-ized a la 201.

Bob Billa, Jr.
San Antonio, Tex.

I purchased my 1979 Skylane II in the summer of 1983. The airplane has reportedly been hangared since new. The two navcoms, ADF, and encoding transponder are ARC equipment. Last February I installed an Rnav R20.

The ARC radios have naturally given me some difficulty, but a nearby shop knows them well and repairs them at what I think is a

reasonable cost. I had a sticking VOR needle, a problem left over from the previous owner who had installed three different VOR heads before I purchased the aircraft (repair cost $62). I had a comm transmitter go out (repair cost $125.00). I have also replaced a fuel gauge and sender unit. I have replaced the EGT gauge and have had the clock/timer rebuilt. The ADF antenna spontaneously snapped last week and is being replaced. I've also noticed that the static eliminators ''spontaneously'' break, and naturally I wonder. I've also noticed areas where the paint is peeling along with areas where filiform corrosion is appearing under the paint.

There was a problem with the control-mounted microphone switch wire, and I've replaced some panel lights which are outrageously priced by Cessna.

My annuals cost from $375 to $450. The first one uncovered some problems while last year's found nothing significant. I also have 100-hour inspections done, and I have oil analysis done when the mechanic remembers to submit the sample.

Although the 182 leaks like a sieve, I don't plan on leaving it outdoors or flying it in the rain anyway. I burn about a quart of oil every two hours. I get a lot of oil under the fuselage. I was told not to fill it to the nine-quart level unless I am going on a long trip. I do this and I have never seen the oil level go below eight quarts. I've wondered if the engine would quit using oil altogether if there were only eight quarts in the crank case; however, I'm not going to try that out.

It may seem strange that there appear to be so many faults with this aircraft; I've not named them all, yet I like it so much. I'm very picky.

John S. Ford, M.D.
Texarkana, Tex.

I bought my 1981 C-182 new for $58,500 complete with the Skylane II package and Narco DME. I wanted a full four-passenger fixed-gear that I could move into im-

mediately after getting my license, as well as one that would be a stable IFR trainer. I got my instrument ticket in the plane and my wife (she's also a pilot) and I have owned it for four years.

Total time is 450 hours and we have perceived no engine problems. I knew that huge oil consumption was a possibility, and true to form I use a quart every four hours —always have. I change the oil and filter every 50 hours and have an oil analysis done at every change. It shows normal.

Fuel economy has not been outstanding at 12-13 gph but it is outweighed by the 1,300 pound payload and 92-gallon tanks. My bladder is out well before the six-hour range. The comfort level is quite good, and coupled with headsets for all four seats, a four-hour trip to Mexico is quite pleasant at 142 knots true.

Besides the usual ARC radio glitches, squawks have included a broken carb heat control cable (my wife's heavy hand!) at 400 hours, a turn coordinator out at 410 hours, a new battery at 375 hours, three new tires at 390 hours, as well as new landing lights every 30 hours. Other than these items, we have been trouble free.

An annual inspection without any major problems runs a very healthy $1,500+. I've been told that late-model 182s normally run half this amount, but I've never seen it. As a result, my hourly maintenance costs clock in at $25 per hour.

My wife and I are happy with our airplane and have no plans for upgrading. We have a neighbor who has owned his 1962 Skylane since new and loves it still. We fly to our mountain home, where the airport elevation is 6,000 feet, a dozen times each summer, and have never had a problem taking off from the 3,000-foot strip even at gross. For us, the Skylane has lived up to our expectations beautifully. I'd buy another one!

Dr. Tom Bales
Novato, Calif.

Piper Dakota 235

The big dream of most pilots is to have an airplane that will go fast, haul a big load, fly forever without refueling and cost peanuts to maintain in the process. Subtract the one element—speed—and you have the formula for success of the Piper Dakota and its predecessors, the Cherokee 235, the Charger and the Pathfinder.

With the Dakota came semi-tapered wings and better climb performance. Fuel capacity went down as two of the 235's four tanks were dropped.

Together they form a singular class of aircraft in which you often can top off the fuel tanks to the point of spilling, load four good-sized adults along with a bunch of baggage and take off with a legal load. Since the gear is fixed, you won't break the sound barrier—so count on no better than 125 to 140 knots, depending on the model and the kind of wheel fairings. But with 82 gallons to burn over the course of six hours or so (or 72 gallons in the Dakotas), you can often beat faster, shorter-legged aircraft to your destination.

And since the gear if fixed, the electro-hydraulic engineering foibles of many retractables is eliminated, meaning generally cheaper maintenance costs. The 235-hp Lycoming O-540 engine, derated from 250 as used on the Aztecs and Comanches, is generally regarded as a relatively solid, free of glitches and quirks. Contributing further to repair economy, if maybe not fuel economy, are carburetors, rather than fuel injection.

History

The line began two decades ago, in 1964, as the Cherokee 235—a bigger-engined clone of the Cherokee 180. It was even certificated in the utility category at gross—which meant greater strength limits—and Piper salesmen liked to boast that it could carry its own weight in useful load. And, by gosh, it could.

The early models were really low-maintenance aircraft since not only was the the landing gear fixed, but even the prop was fixed pitch as standard equipment. A further cost-saving factor (back then, at least) was the ability of the powerplant to burn cheaper 80-octane fuel. The early B models had only 50 gallons of fuel in two wing tanks, standard, or 84 optional.

The 84-gallon standard configuration, using four tanks (two in the main wings and two in the tips), came in 1968 with the C model. The first significant change in the line came in 1973, however, with the Charger, thanks to a lengthened fuselage (like the Arrow's), which gave rear-seat passengers another welcome five inches of leg room. At the same time the useful load went up a paltry few pounds along with a 100-pound boost in the gross, reflecting the bigger cabin. Piper also widened the stabilator for better controllability with the extra fuselage length and longer loading envelope.

In 1974 the Pathfinder introduced mostly window dressing. Appropriately, part of this consisted of heavier, new one-quarter-inch-thick windshields in an attempt to lower the cabin sound level. (Earlier models had one-eighth-inch-thick windshields.) A few other fillips were vertically adjustable front seats—by pushbutton, thank you—"cushioned nosewheel steering" (thanks to bungees) standard toebrakes on the right side and a supposedly more crashworthy seat design.

The Dakota

In 1979 the next "epic" change came to the line with the semi-tapered wings brought out by the Warrior a couple of years earlier, along with an engine variant designed to burn 100 octane. Since 80 octane was getting scarce, this was intended as a boon to eliminate lead fouling. But as the move to autogas for 80-octane engines gains momentum, it may in retrospect have been a mixed blessing. The good-looking new wings were not, however, outfitted with tip-tanks, so the fuel load dropped by 10 gallons' useful to a total of 74 in two main wing tanks.

Unfortunately, though the racy-looking new low-drag plastic wheel fairings offered as an option on the Dakotas (and other Pipers) raised the cruise speed by a healthy six to nine knots, in the beginning they were plagued with cracking and breaking problems. Piper replaced them with fiberglass ones intended to be better wearing.

There's no doubt that the higher-aspect-ratio wing on the Dakota gives the aircraft better climb performance than the Hershey-bar forebears. And pilots believe lateral control is nicer.

Even Turbocharging

Unafraid of mixing performance metaphors—i.e., a low-performance aircraft with a high-performance engine—Piper provided the ultimate option to the fixed-gear Dakota: turbocharging. In hindsight it took a gamble on reliability, however, by switching from the good-old trusty Lycoming to a lower-horsepower blown Continental—the 200-hp TSIO-360 that turned out to have more than its share of problems.

Performance and Handling

At equal weights, the 235, etc. will get 55 horses more performance than the Cherokee 180/Archer from which it is cloned—all of which translates into better climb and shorter runway demands (especially in high density altitude situations), along with more load and more speed. Its only natural competitor is the Cessna Skylane, with similar power and load-carrying ability. Our side-by-side tests conducted in 1979 suggested cruise speeds of these two aircraft were nearly identical; the Cessna could get in and out of shorter runways and had lower stall speeds, but the Piper could climb faster.

Aficionados of low wings like the extra stability during ground

handling in high winds, but the accident reports are far from devoid of pilots going awry landing or taking off in gusty crosswinds.

Nevertheless, the 235/Dakotas in most modes are benign aircraft that will shake themselves apart rather than stall precipitously, that have somewhat sluggish controls and that exhibit all the handling personality of a Chevy sedan. Like most Cherokees, they tend to wander during cruise, with a wing dipping on one side or the other, no matter how attentive the pilot is to balancing the fuel burn in the tanks.

Cockpit Design, Cabin Comfort

Three pleasant aspects to the 235 cockpit, to our mind, are the old-fashioned Cherokee hand-brake parking lever, which is the most secure in the business; the equally old-fashioned but delightful-to-use Johnson-bar flap lever (who needs electric flaps?); and the location of the fuel selector under the throttle quadrant where everybody can see it, rather than hidden behind the pilot's knee on the left wall. The Dakota, however, is the exception

The Pathfinder version of the Cherokee 235 has a thicker windshield for better soundproofing.

and has the fuel selector—guess where?

Our theory about the safety factor of having the fuel selector under the quadrant may be wishful thinking in the real world, however, since the 235s experience a goodly portion of accidents because of fuel mismanagement.

Location of the mp and tach near the pilot's knee is a bit less than ideal, but logical in one sense—that it's near the throttle and prop levers.

Naturally, choose the stretched models—Charger and later—for the extra leg room in the back. Owners also tend to rave about the comfort of the seats in these aircraft. "The well-designed bucket seats in the Dakota nicely fit my 'bucket,'" said one. "My nonpilot 200-pound husband has mentioned taking his right seat home for his den," she added. "Piper seats are very comfortable," said another. "I can fly for five hours without getting a backache."

Cost/Performance/Specifications

Model	Year	Number Built	Average Retail Price	Cruise Speed (kts)	Rate of Climb (fpm)	Useful Load (lbs)	Fuel Std/Opt (gals)	Engine	TBO (hrs)	Overhaul Cost
PA-28 235	1964-65	719	$16,300	136	825	1,404	50/84	235-hp Lyc. O-540-B4B5	2,000	$10,000
PA-28 235B	1966-67	320	$17,300	136	825	1,404	50/84	235-hp Lyc. O-540-B4B5	2,000	$10,000
PA-28 235B,C	1968-69	301	$18,600	136	825	1,404	84	235-hp Lyc. O-540-B4B5	2,000	$10,000
PA-28 235D,E	1970-71	106	$20,500	136	825	1,404	84	235-hp Lyc. O-540-B4B5	2,000	$10,000
PA-28 235F	1972	23	$22,000	136	825	1,404	84	235-hp Lyc. O-540-B4B5	2,000	$10,000
Charger	1973-74	285	$23,500	132	800	1,450	84	235-hp Lyc. O-540-B4B5	2,000	$10,000
Pathfinder	1975-76	316	$27,500	132	800	1,450	84	235-hp Lyc. O-540-B4B5	2,000	$10,000
Pathfinder	1977	89	$32,000	132	800	1,450	84	235-hp Lyc. O-540-B4B5	2,000	$10,000
PA-28 236 Dak.	1979-80	466	$41,500	143	965	1,366	77	235-hp Lyc. O-540-J3A5D	2,000	$10,200
PA-28 201T	1979	89	$37,000	154	902	1,321	77	200-hp Cont. TSIO-360-FB	1,800	$10,700
Dakota	1981-82	141	$58,000	143	965	1,366	77	235-hp Lyc. O-540-J3A5D	2,000	$10,200
Dakota	1983-84	25	$99,400	143	965	1,366	77	235-hp Lyc. O-540-J3A5D	2,000	$10,200

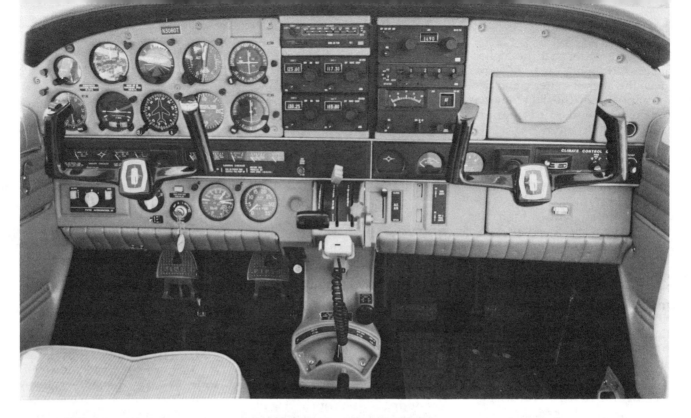

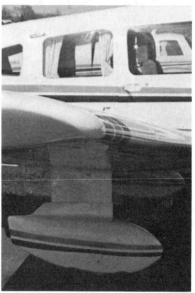

Safety Record

Although the NTSB was unable to sort out the Cherokee 235s and Dakotas from the great mass of PA-28s of all classes for us, we did examine five and a half years of accidents (146 in all) by Cherokee 235/Dakotas reported by the FAA from 1979 through mid-August 1984. Of course, they do not have the Safety Board's probable causes listed.

Among the Cherokee 235s (including Chargers and Pathfinders) the greatest two accident generators were engine failure and fuel

mismanagement, with 14 and 11 cases respectively. Next came groundloops or swerves—nine, followed by hard landings—six.

Among the Dakotas and Turbo Dakotas groundloop/swerves were blamed for the most damage along with various mechanical problems, with five cases each.

The 235's engine problems presented a fairly mixed bag, with no specific trend. Examples: fuel valve clogged with tank sealant, broken pin on drive shaft gear, broken exhaust valve, blown gasket, loose oil screen ("secured [?]by pilot"),

Though the fuel selector is under the throttle quadrant for easy viewing, the need to switch among four separate tanks may heighten the possibility for fuel management error, a common problem in this model.

Structural capacity of the baggage compartment is a hefty 200 pounds.

Tiny door allows access to the tire of Dakotas with snug modern speed fairings. Early plastic ones had cracking, breakage. Some owners of later fiberglass wheel pants claim similar problems.

even a field mouse nest in the carburetor air duct. There was one failed magneto impulse coupling, failing the drive gear. A series of engine stoppages on the 235 could not be explained when the powerplants were later inspected.

On the Dakotas, engine failures were attributed to such causes as a fuel leak at the wing root, and subsequent fuel exhaustion; loss of oil pressure from an oil leak at the base of the vacuum pump, connecting rod failure, a broken oil line and a mixture arm that came loose from the carburetor. In one case a Dakota experienced an engine fire on runup when the engine backfired and blew out the muffler. Exhaust gases were reported ignited by a leaky boost pump.

On the Turbo Dakotas engine stoppages were blamed on broken connecting rods in two instances, a cracked cylinder, loss of engine oil from an oil cooler leak, and loss of oil pressure because of a turbine seal failure.

Among the 235s, time and again the reports cited pilots going dry on one fuel tank while there remained fuel in others—and apparently neglecting to switch. The existence of four tanks to juggle in the 235s as opposed to just two in the Dakotas may explain the black mark on the former, even though the fuel selector is located right under the throttle quadrant where both pilots in front can see it.

The groundloop/swerve category that claimed so many victims among both the 235s and the Dakotas is a broadly mixed bag that encompasses everything from losing control because of "improper, inadequate braking" to losing directional control on the landing roll "when hit by gusty crosswind, veered off runway into a ditch." The lesson is that even with a marvelously "wide gear stance" and tricycle gear, the 235/Dakotas are not immune to mishandling, by a long shot.

Maintenance

In general, owners describe the 235/Dakota as presenting a modest maintenance burden. There are problems, however. Some criticize the brakes as "too light for the weight of the aircraft." One owner said he had to change them every year (or 100 hours). Also, alternator mounting brackets seem prey to an unusual degree of cracking and strain. This was the largest single problem area we noted in Service Difficulty Reports on the aircraft—and mostly on the Dakotas. Second worst: problems with the carburetor air boxes —separations, breaks, vibration.

To a lesser degree we noted reports of Bendix distributor blocks cracking and engine mounts cracking and breaking. A few complained of fuel vent hoses leaking and tank sealant in the fuel, causing blockages. As we noted above, at least one engine stoppage accident was blamed on a fuel valve clogged with sealant. Also, the "improved" fiberglass wheel fairings that replaced the original troubleprone thermoplastic ones (not always—check for them) still are prey to cracking according to some owners, and are expensive to replace.

On the Turbo Dakotas high cylinder head temperature was the bane of at least one respondent. "The gauge almost reaches the red on climb, even with full rich mixture," he noted. SDRs showed some cracking of turbo housings.

Airworthiness Directives

No big, devastating ADs have struck 235/Dakota owners over the past few years, except for one on the turbos. Most of the other ADs of any note and consequence appear related to fuel leakage prob-

lems. A 1979 AD called for removing the fuel tanks and modifying the vent system, for example, on both 235s and Dakotas. The Dakotas also were hit with an AD calling for a check and torquing of fuel fittings and unions to eliminate a fire hazard from fuel leakage. In 1978 Cherokee 235 owners were required to replace the fuel drain cover so it would not inadvertently drain fuel from the valve. And a year earlier another AD called for a check and possible replacement of fuel valves to prevent engine stoppage on 235s.

Mods & Improvements

Among the more useful STCs available to Cherokee 235 and Dakota owners are efficiency kits offered by Knots 2U and Laminar Flow Systems, providing gap seals on the ailerons and flaps, hinge covers, etc. Said one Laminar Flow installer, "We are making better time on our trips at 65 percent cruise (after the mod) than we did at 75 percent cruise before, and saving on gas." He added: "I have not given up the idea of a trade-in for a faster plane...Makes you wonder why Piper doesn't clean up the wings and do the same..."

Want better visibility at night? Devore Aviation in Albuquerque, N.M. will install vertical tail floodlights. Need better door sealing on a Dakota? Bob Fields Aerocessories in Ventura, Calif. has an STC on an inflatable door seal. Norton Co. of Akron, Ohio,

The Charger received a five-inch cabin stretch and a wider entry door, improving legroom and access for rear-seat passengers.

even has a radome kit for earnest weather busters.

Turbo Dakota owners might consider installation of Turboplus intercoolers and cowl flaps to cool down their powerplants (they are located at Gig Harbor, Wash.). S.G.H. Inc. of Auburn, Wash. has an STC for pressurized magnetos, as well.

Resale Value

As an investment, the Cherokee 235s and Dakotas are nothing to brag about. The typical resale value curve on the 235 and Dakota is a constant sag through the years, with no turnaround to account for inflation. Buyers should turn to the retractable singles for a more advantageous kind of curve. However, as a basic heavy hauler, the aircraft is matched only by the Skylane in its class, and anyone wishing more speed and equivalent useful load would have to lay out a fair amount more for a big retractable.

Owner Comments

I have been pleased with my '79 Dakota. It will take off in our average 90 degree weather in about 1,000 feet with four adults, full tanks and filled with baggage. Maintenance, apart from two ADs on fuel lines and mags, has been minimal. The greatest problem has been the brakes. They must be changed yearly. They are apparently too light for the weight of the aircraft. The aircraft is flown about 200 hours yearly.

The engine has proved flawless. It always starts instantly. We change oil every 25 hours. The interior finish is very well done and has held up very well in view of the fact that the Dakota is parked outside in our hot and humid Puerto Rican weather and constantly exposed to the broiling sun. The aircraft is now in need of painting. The paint is disintegrating and corrosion is starting on the left side of the aircraft only and the cabin top. The

Aircraft Resale Value Chart

$/M — $60,000, $50,000, $40,000, $30,000, $20,000, $10,000, 0

'79 Turbo Dakota
'79 236 Dakota
'75 235 Pathfinder
'72 235

Year: '72 '73 '74 '75 '76 '77 '78 '79 '80 '81 '82 '83 '84 '85

right side shows little corrosion problem.

The plane was bought from Red Aircraft in Florida. They have been excellent in back-up. I have purchased several additions since new and simply by calling Red, they responded by sending parts and billing me later. I've written twice to Piper and they've never answered. Once I wrote regarding the possibility of installing a small children's seat in the baggage department, once regarding new gas tank screws. Never a response.

I was considering changing to a slightly faster plane last year, until I heard about Laminar Flow Systems in St. Thomas. Since it's only a short hop from San Juan, I flew over to speak to Robin Thomas. I was convinced. In short order they installed the system on the wings, gap seals on the ailerons, covers on the hinges, and Wow! It is like another airplane. The cruise has increased to about 150 knots or better. Drop the nose for a power glide and the airspeed drops into the yellow arc. It never did that before. We are making better time on our trips at 65 percent cruise than we did at 75 percent cruise before and saving on gas.

The takeoff has become almost unbelievable. With light loads—two and gas—it's lifted off in 500 to 600 feet. It will fly itself off the ground at 70 knots, which it never did before. It simply won't stay on the

ground. We increased our rate of climb about 200 feet a minute, and with a lower nose angle. The stall speed is somewhere down to about 50 knots as opposed to 59 knots before.

I have now given up the idea of a trade-in for a faster plane. By the way, we now pass every single flying in our area with the exception of Mooneys. The change to the plane with the laminar flow system has been startling. It's given us retractable performance with the simplicity of fixed gear. Makes you wonder why Piper doesn't clean up the wings and do the same as the Laminar Flow people.

In summation the product is great, the company that produces it seems uninterested in client relations. By the way, our averge yearly maintenance including the annual, has run between 800 to $1,000. I consider this reasonable.

Ronald Sobin
Guaynabo, Puerto Rico

My 1979 Dakota is turbocharged. It has a total 550 hours since new. It is pleasant to fly, and it is forgiving.

The major problem I have faced through the years is high cylinder head temperature. The gauge almost reaches the red on climb, even with full rich mixture. Sometimes I have to put the auxiliary fuel pump on. On 75 percent power cruise, gas flow is about 13.5

gallons per hour, speed about 140 knots.

Maintenance cost me $2,000 to change the turbo in compliance with the AD note last year. Annual inspection is between $500 and $700 if everything checked right.

I would appreciate your giving me any suggestion regarding the head cylinder temperature.

Nabil Koudsi, M.D.
Upland, Calif.

I have owned a 1979 Piper Turbo Dakota since September 1981 when it was a corporate aircraft with only 120 hours on it. At present, it has about 363 hours total time. Most of the time I cruise at altitudes between 9,500 and 13,500 feet.

As for performance, I climb at 105 knots indicated (for better cooling in warm weather) and set about 140 knots true in cruise at 65 percent power. Fuel consumption varies between 12 gph at low altitudes to about 13.5 gph at high altitudes on a warm day. The extra fuel is required to keep the cylinder temperature a few needle widths below the red line.

I have no real complaints about handling or comfort. But for long trips an autopilot is very desirable. Without it, the airplane will for sure wander off one way or the other, but not really more than most other similar airplanes. I have also flown the Saratoga, and it is more stable. Piper seats are very comfortable, for me anyway. I can fly for five hours without getting a backache. One minor complaint: the towbar is too short, and the little hooks do not provide a secure attachment to the nosewheel.

The Dakota's forte is its load-carrying ability. Mine is well equipped, including DME, but I can legally carry four FAA-sized people (including myself), 5½ hours of fuel and about 10 pounds of junk and not exceed gross weight or so out of CG.

During the 242 hours I've flown the plane, fuel has cost me an average

of $22 per hour of tach time, and out-of-pocket maintenance costs have cost me an average of about $28 per hour of tach time. The last annual cost me $1,800, including the cost of an overhaul on the turbocharger and calibrating the transponder, encoder, altimeter and static systems.

Within a year or so, I plan to upgrade to either a Saratoga SP or a Bonanza A36. But after having flown a turbocharged plane for almost three years, I have concluded that for the type of flying I do (VFR only), the benefits of turbocharging are outweighed by the penalties of increased fuel consumption and increased maintenance costs. My next airplane will be non-turbos, but I will opt for better low-level performance and retractable gear. And big double doors on the side, for all the junk I tend to carry.

Charles Pack
Los Altos Hills, Calif.

About two and a half years ago, I acquired a one-owner, well-equipped, well-maintained, clean 1979 Dakota, my first venture into ownership. It is one fine airplane, and I couldn't be more pleased. When I began to think seriously about buying, my analysis of my flying needs pointed me toward either a Skylane or a Dakota. Both possessed two critical characteristics: good reserve power and load carrying capability. Rereading the "Fly-off" comparison article in *Aviation Consumer* (June 1, 1979) was helpful and confirmed most of my own impressions.

The Dakota won out for the following reasons: 1) I had always felt more comfortable in low-wing airplanes (the "wing-under-me" and visibility in the pattern factors); 2) being 5'3" tall and non-gymnastic, I felt the skylane presented two problems: visibility over the high panel and climb-on-top visual fuel checks; 3) the excellent reputation of the 2,000-hour Lycoming O-540 engine; 4) repeated experiences with minor glitches in ARC avionics becomes annoying—I wanted Kings; 5) I align with those who believe low-

wing, wide-stance planes are easier to land in gusty conditions and crosswinds; 6) the well-designed bucket seats in the Dakota nicely fit my "bucket"; and 7) an emotional reason—I just plain liked the Dakota's good looks.

I've logged over 500 hours in my PA28-236, in all conditions. The Lycoming has never missed a beat and at 1,150 hours shows no leaks, good compression, and clean oil analysis checks. Over the last 200 hours, fuel burn has ranged from 11 to 14 gph, with an average of 11.8. Note that most of my flying is done out of our 5,000 feet MSL airport, at 6,000 feet to 9,000 feet MSL. I currently have to add only two quarts of Aeroshell 15W-50 oil between changes every 40-50 hours.

Speed and climb? As advertised. Once, at 17,000 feet in quiet and cold morning mountain air, I was able to coax it into a 200 fpm climb with three people aboard and nearly full fuel. Even our oxygen masks smiled!

It is docile and easily handled in both cruise and slow flight, with slightly heavy (which I prefer) but smooth and positive aileron control. It will slowly drop a wing during cruise if you stop paying attention, and you cannot fly totally hands-off. Pitch control is easy with the electric trim. An unsolved rigging quirk in my Dakota is intermittent refusal to hold left rudder trim, and I have to spend a little more time than I would like twisting the somewhat inconveniently located rudder trimknob. Turbulence—and we get plenty of that out here—presents no significant problems.

A most comforting pleasure is to plan on loading up another couple and luggage and find that, after weight/balance and takeoff distance calculations, I can say to the lineman, "Top it off," before we head for wherever.

The Dakota fits my flying needs perfectly.

Bonnie Titley
Ft. Collins, Colo.

Cessna 185

From the North Slope of Alaska to the desert badlands of Australia, the Cessna 185 Skywagon reigns ubiquitous as the Marlboro Man of workhorse airplanes . . . tackling short bush strips, jungle rivers, or high-mountain snowfields with equal ease. As a potent taildragger, this plane has long been the "utility pickup" in Cessna's product line.

Like many of its automotive counterparts, however, the C-185 Skywagon has a lavish options list and suave enough manners in the air to appeal as well to the more hairy-chested end of the "family airplane" market.

History

The Cessna 185 first appeared in 1961 as a big brother to the 180, which the company had introduced back in 1953. Motivated by a 230-hp Continental, the 180 was limited in useful load with full fuel, so the 185 arrived sporting a 260-hp fuel injected Continental IO-470-F, toting 84 gallons of fuel, and offering 1,680 pounds of useful load . . . nearly 200 pounds higher than its basic empty weight.

Since the 180 and 185 were virtually identical in fuselage dimensions

Here's the typical 185 environment: mountains, grass strips, and snow.

(the 185 had a larger strake up front of the horizontal stabilizer), the 185's more sprightly performance was due entirely to his larger engine. In its workhorse role, this first 185 also offered optional Edo floats, skis, and a Sorenson spray rig. The next year a belly-mounted cargo pod with a 300-pound useful load was offered as a further utility option. All of these items are still available 22 years later on Cessna's current model.

With few exceptions, the development of the C-185 line has been evolutionary rather than revolutionary, so would-be purchasers have only a couple of major changes to bear in mind. Most of the cosmetic or functional improvements like the articulating pilot seats, standard "T" instrument configuration, better panel lighting, split electrical bus, Omniflash rotating beacon, and Stabili-Tip conical cambered wingtips are retrofittable.

The first major change occurred in 1966 when Cessna offered the larger fuel-injected Continental IO-520-D engine as an option. This gave the 185 300 hp for takeoff (285 hp continuous), allowing a 100-pound increase in gross to 3,300 with only 10 pounds added to the empty weight. This switch also im-

proved cruise speed by about five knots, reduced the gross weight takeoff roll by about 200 feet, and raised the service ceiling to 17,300 feet. The 260-hp version was called the C-185E while its "big-bore" brother was the C-A185E. (The 1966 serial numbers from 185-0968 through 185-1149 don't give any clue to this engine swap.)

Customer response to this larger engine must have been favorable because Cessna made it standard the very next year, so all the '67s are C-A185E models, and this designation prevailed until 1973 when a major wing improvement was added. One other useful addition to the '67 bird, by the way, was a new aft baggage compartment. Along with this new storage space, an optional elongated cargo "stretcher" door was offered; this greatly facilitates loading long objects like bicycles or skis (not to mention stretchers) and is worthy of consideration as a retrofit to any of the 185's.

The 1973 model received a new Camber-Lift wing featuring the vaunted "fat leading edge" cuff originally developed by Robertson for their STOL kits. This change reduced the stall speeds in all configurations by about two knots, but it also improved the low-speed roll control, and rumor has it that this fatter leading edge is safer in icing conditions, though neither wing is approved for flight in known icing. This later wing can be added to earlier models by Robertson (see the information under Modifications) for purchasers who are otherwise enthralled by a pre-1973 skywagon.

The 1974 model year ushered in three options for the 185 that could be of interest to prospective users with special requirements for improved visibility: a pair of "bubble" side windows, extra windows built into the lower door panels, and a pair of amber-tinted skylight windows built into the ceiling above the cockpit.

Several changes were made in 1976, along with one seemingly regressive step. The first notch (10 degrees) flap extension speed was raised from 96 knots to 120, and a new three-position (Left/Both/Right) fuel selector switch was installed to replace the inherently more dangerous Left/Right/Off arrangement. Optional tailcone lift handles became available to ease manhandling the beast around on the ground. For the first time, primary airspeed readout was displayed in knots rather than miles per hour. But a puzzling change was made to the fuel system. The capacity of the fuel bladders in the long-range tanks was reduced from 81 to 74 gallons usable, which cut the plane's economy-cruise time aloft by 45 minutes.)

Over the next three years, several other notable changes were made to the C-185. In 1978, a new 80-inch three-blade McCauley prop became available as an option. It became standard in 1980 along with beefier engine mounts to damp its different vibration patterns. The former two-blade Skywagon props were very noisy at high rpm, emitting an awesome and unmistakable snarling howl at takeoff revs when the prop tips went supersonic. The wide-chord three-blade prop has a noise emission rating of only 77 db, which also helps to quiet things down inside the cabin.

The other major change was the switch, in 1979, to a new "wet" wing holding a total of 88 gallons . . . 84 of which is usable. Interestingly, Cessna still offers the old-style 40-gallon "twin-cap" bladder tanks as an option; while somewhat prone to water-trapping wrinkles, especially if sloppily installed, these bladders over the long run may prove to be less leaky than the wet wing in really rugged environments, and there is some evidence to suggest that bladder tanks will retain fuel more reliably in a wing-deforming crash.

Since 1981, Cessna has made only token changes to the 185 line, (apart from raising the price by $18,110, seemingly an act of near-suicidal bravado that flies in the face of all recent market supply and demand figures). External cosmetics, to be sure, have been changed, and the ARC radios (always a hot item if not a hot seller) got two more revisions to their oh-so-necessary cooling fan. A new-design single-piece flex shaft connects the fuel selector to the main fuel valve, providing greater reliability and more positive detents (this in 1982), and for '83 a change (actually made by Continental) to the engine crankcase allows the use of the new short-cannister spin-on oil filter while eliminating the old two-pound filter adapter. A low-vacuum warning light was added to the instrument panel in 1983, and considering the notorious unreliability of Cessna's Airborne vacuum pumps in the past, we can only wonder why this particular gizmo didn't make an appearance sooner.

Performance

This is where the Cessna 185 shines. Other aircraft can fly faster, and a few smaller, lighter ones like the Maule or the Super Cub can levitate in a shorter distance, but no other single-engine piston-powered taildragger can take off in 825 feet carrying four 220-pound adults, full fuel, and 170 pounds of baggage, show an initial rate-of-climb of 1,075 fpm and then cruise 800-plus nautical miles averaging 140 knots.

Maximum cruise speed at 75 percent and 7,000 feet is a very respectable 147 knots. The rpm "green arc" on the C-185 goes from 2200 rpm for cruising at 6,500 feet or below. This setting yields about 145 knots at average aircraft weights, and, depending on outside air temps, will burn anywhere from 14.3 to 14.7 gallons per hour of 100 or 100LL fuel.

Climb performance is robust. The 185 will still show upward mobility of at least 500 fpm at 10,000 feet at average weights, and the gross weight service ceiling for the current model is listed as 17,900 feet.

At higher altitudes (and consequent lower manifold pressures) the 185 becomes progressively less thirsty. Also, Continental allows leaning the IO-520 to peak EGT at 65 percent power or below, a condition reached naturally at about 8,000 feet at settings of 2400 rpm and (max available) 22 inches of manifold pressure. As in any airplane, the permutations and combinations of fuel flow versus power settings are many, but for example, at 12,000 feet/2400 rpm/18 inches, the C-185 will have a true airspeed of about 130 knots while burning only 10.3 gallons per hour. This is

Cost/Performance/Specifications

Model	Years Built	Number Built	Average Retail Price	Cruise Speed (kts)	Useful Load (lbs)	Rate of Climb (fpm)	Fuel Std/Opt (gals)	Engine	TBO (hrs)	Overhaul Cost
Cessna 185, A	1961-62	512	$16,300	145	1,680	1,000	81	260-hp Cont. IO-470-F	1,500	$8,750
Cessna 185B, C	1963-64	263	$17,300	145	1,680	1,000	81	260-hp Cont. IO-470-F	1,500	$8,750
Cessna 185D, E	1965-66	372	$18,700	145	1,680	1,000	81	260-hp Cont. IO-470-F	1,500	$8,750
Cessna A185E	1966-67	332	$20,500	146	1,785	1,040	81	300-hp Cont. IO-520-D	1,700	$9,250
Cessna A185E	1968-69	298	$22,500	146	1,785	1,040	81	300-hp Cont. IO-520-D	1,700	$9,250
Cessna A185E	1970-71	334	$24,700	146	1,785	1,040	81	300-hp Cont. IO-520-D	1,700	$9,250
Cessna A185E, F	1972-73	375	$26,500	145	1,785	1,040	81	300-hp Cont. IO-520-D	1,700	$9,250
Cessna A185F	1974-75	527	$28,000	145	1,785	1,040	81	300-hp Cont. IO-520-D	1,700	$9,250
Cessna A185F	1976-77	619	$36,500	145	1,785	1,040	74	300-hp Cont. IO-520-D	1,700	$9,250
Cessna A185FII	1978-79	479	$39,500	145	1,600	1,075	74	300-hp Cont. IO-520-D	1,700	$9,250
Cessna A185FII	1980-81	389	$48,000	145	1,600	1,075	84	300-hp Cont. IO-520-D	1,700	$9,250
Cessna A185FII	1982-83	NA	$70,000	145	1,600	1,075	84	300-hp Cont. IO-520-D	1,700	$9,250

Cessna 185

respectable efficiency, especially considering that up to 1,100 pounds can go along for the ride in the cabin.

While Cessna does not formally tout the stock 185 as a STOL aircraft like the Helio Courier, the Skywagon sports four notches of manually-operated flaps (10-40 degrees in equal increments) which, along with the big engine and fat wing, contribute to splendid short-field performance. With full flaps and power off, the 185 stalls at an indicated airspeed of only 41 knots; with partial power and at lighter weights, this figure will be even lower, although somewhat academic because it would fall below the scale on the airspeed indicator.

The "book" landing distance for the 185 is just 585 feet, but this figure is relatively meaningless because in real life, planes rarely land at full gross or in dead calm air. Even more to the point, experienced 185 pilots regularly make true "bathmat" landings within 300 feet by dragging the plane in under partial power with full flaps at a nose-high altitude and 53 knots, then dumping flaps and braking assiduously right after the three-point full-stall touchdown. As with any aircraft, this technique is not recommended in gusty wind conditions when errant downdrafts could be lurking off the end of the runway.

Cabin Space and Comfort

The Cessna 185 is advertised and certified as a "six-passenger" airplane, but only the Marquis de Sade would commit even a small child to this airplane's third-row "seat," which hugs the floor of the standard baggage bay area (an area limited to 120 pounds) and offers only a vertical pad snapped to the aft bulkhead as a seat backrest. Unless they have very small and unusually pliant children, most 185 owners immediately chuck the worthless rear "seat," thereby assuring themselves of a comfortable four-place bird with a reasonably spacious baggage area in the normal location. This also allows insuring the plane as only a four-seater, which saves considerable money these days, especially in Alaska.

Seating in the 185 is quite comfortable for four adults. Both front seats can be purchased with hand-cranked articulating height and back-tilt adjustments, and the split rear bench seat, while lower-backed than the front seats, also has individual provision for reclining when the aft baggage load permits. Both legroom and headroom are ample up front, even for pilots up to 6'6" and legroom is adequate in the rear as well. Although the cabin is just under 41 inches wide, broad-shouldered crews up front can increase the comfort level in this dimension by staggering the seat positions.

Even with the three-blade prop, cabin noise in the Skywagon is fairly high, but much of it is high-pitched and seems to come, especially in the well-worn older birds, from air leaks around the doors, windows, and main upper air vent tubes (whose felt seals are notoriously flimsy).

Loading

In view of the "back-country pick-up truck" primary role for this airplane, we remain mystified why Cessna hasn't done more engineering work to improve the loading access on the C-185. The two main doors on either side of the cockpit are adequate for loading people, but attempting to load anything large like a crate, trunk, or 55-gallon oil drum requires the removal of both the backseat and the copilot's seat along with the right front door. Unfortunately, the wing struts prevent the front doors from opening a full 90 degrees like those huge lovely doors on the old C-177 Cardinal, but at least the right-hand door on the 185 has "quick-pull" pins to expedite its removal, and the back (bench) seat also releases quickly from the floor.

The Skywagon's lone standard baggage door is only 18 inches x 20 inches . . . barely large enough for a case of Coors or a fat watermelon. Larger backpacks or hefty suitcases must routinely be manhandled back over the seats from the front doors with occasional scuffs to the headliner plus lots of sweat and swearing. A few years ago, Piper ran a nice ad showing a piano being loaded into a Cherokee Six; the only way a Cessna 185 could ever carry a piano would be strapped outside on the roof . . . and there might even be an Alaskan bush pilot somewhere crazy enough to try it. When we queried the factory on the subject of loading limitations, a marketing spokesman said, "If they want to carry oil drums or pianos, they should buy a 206." This corporate philosophy bodes ill for any major airframe improvements to the 185 in future.

Cessna does offer an optional external cargo pod that fastens to the belly of the 185 with myriad screws. This fiberglas pod is just over nine feet long and 14 inches deep with an 11x23 door in its left flank and another at the rear. While obviously not deep enough for bulky cargo, this unit is ideal for boards, skis, packs, or suitcases, and it is approved for retrofit installation on any of the 185 models. However, a brand new one costs over $5,000, plus installation, and cuts about four knots off cruise speed.

Handling Quirks

Once off the ground, the 185 is every bit as mild-mannered and pleasant to fly as any of its high-wing Cessna siblings. Aileron response is quite similar to that of the 182 and definitely much lighter in feel than the ponderous C-206. Pilots almost universally praise the manual flaps system for its quick and trouble-free operation. Float plane operators, in particular, often choose the 185 over the 206 just to get these speedy flaps which, when used adroitly, allow heavily loaded seaplanes to hop off the water faster. The controls in the Skywagon are well harmonized, so that very little rudder is required for turns. Rudder trim makes keeping the ball centered a cinch during the climb.

The 185 is quite sensitive to longitudinal trim changes, but the stabilator trim wheel is geared very low. This means that about 15 backward swipes of hand-to-wheel are required to alter trim from normal cruise position to full aft for a three-point landing. Novitiates to the C-185 universally bemoan the lack of electric trim, but Cessna chose the present manual system for its low-maintenance reliability.

The Cessna 185 is not an easy plane to land. Like all other taildraggers, its c.g. is well aft of the main wheels, so the plane is ever ready to swap ends while in motion along the runway, especially in crosswinds. However, forward visibility is reasonably good (taller pilots can see directly over the nose while taxiing), and the 185 is not nearly as short-coupled as smaller planes like the Pitts. The secret to staying out of trouble in the C-185 (or any taildragger, for that matter) is constant attention and fast feet. C-185 pilots savor an extra bit of macho quotient for having mastered their mounts after an inevitable stint of bronc-busting work during the early flights.

Wheel landings are particularly difficult, partly because the C-185 has very springy steel gear legs. In gus-

ty conditions or when the pilot makes just a slight miscalculation of the proper instant for the "pin-on" forward stick pressure, a substantial bounce is almost certain. This can easily and rapidly develop into a disastrous series of phugoid kangaroo hops if not caught immediately with smooth steady backpressure on the yoke to salvage a gentle three-point landing at the end of that first inadvertent balloon off the runway. There is also a critical period right after a successful two-wheel touchdown. If a crosswind gust hits the tail of the 185 during this crucial period of transition, only a quick and skillful application of downwind braking can save the plane from an expensive groundloop.

Most 185 pilots concur that a full-stall three-point landing (with the tailwheel locked for any bad crosswind or really rough field conditions) is the safest form of arrival because the airplane's speed is lower, stability is greater, and steering control is easier.

One final caveat . . . be very careful when attempting a go-around in a Skywagon. Once the flaps and full aft trim have been set for a three-point landing, the sudden application of full takeoff power will try to pull the nose straight up. It takes at least eight seconds to hand-crank the trim back to neutral, and you will feel like the proverbial one-arm paperhanger trying to dump a couple notches of

The 185 is a popular floatplane. Because its manual flaps allow more precise control, some bush pilots prefer it to a 206 for float flying.

flaps while slapping the trim wheel with the same hand. The best trick for coping with a last-minute go-around surprise is to add only partial power, which will arrest the descent without initiating an inadvertent Cape Canaveral climb profile.

Maintenance

Since the Cessna 185 is a derivative of the 180 (which, itself, evolved from the 170), it is no surprise that most major maintenance trouble spots or potential AD areas have been bred out of the bird. We have counted up ten AD notes that seem most significant, but of these, only three pertain to the airframe: 73-23-07 is a general call to check for defective spar attach fittings, 78-05-06 mandates a check for leakage of the Goodyear fuel cells installed between 1961 and 1971, and 79-10-14 requires a check on fuel tank venting with a possible need to switch fuel caps. Three more ADs have to do with the cylinder attach screws, activating pins, and possible blade shank failures on various of the McCauley props. One AD (72-20-02) specifies checking the older 470 series engines for H (heavy) cylinders, then the final three all refer to the IO-520 engines: 70-14-07 on fuel injection-by-pass needles, 77-05-04 for possible crankshaft failure due to scoring from oil pick-up hole in prop governor, and finally the ubiquitous 77-13-22 warning of possible crankcase cracks (which hit many other aircraft hard but never became much pf a problem in the 185 line).

Annual inspection base prices for the C-185 seem to run around $495

and bare minimum repairs on an average year with no major problems will add another $500. However, there are a number of airframe and engine spots that require vigilance. The Cessna exhaust mufflers and internal cones seem to crack or wear out at around 400 hours. The tailwheel bolt holding the fork assembly to the tailspring wears out or elongates its seating holes, which contributes to tailwheel shimmy. The McCauley wheels during sharp pivot turns, and quite a few pilots have reported the brake mechanisms pulling loose, rotating around, and cutting the brake line. The switch to Clevelands costs about $800 but is well worth the price in the long run.

The manual elevator trim is another potential trouble spot. At cruise speed, the elevator jackscrew can require 300 foot-pounds of torque, which puts a heavy strain on the roll pins that connect the trim wheel to the chain drive sprocket. They are very prone to shear, which leaves the trim jammed wherever it was set. While this is rarely lethal because it usually happens at a near-cruise setting, Cessna finally came up with a fix in 1981 that simply does away with the pins altogether and rivets the wheel to the sprocket . . . a worthwhile retrofit in our opinion.

Overall, the Continental IO-520-D engine has been quite reliable in the 185 (with the usual smattering of horror stories, to be sure). With large cowl flaps, spacious cowling, and no turbocharging, the engine rarely has any overheating problem, even while taxiing on a hot day. In fact, the greater danger is likely to be overcooling the powerplant during a power-off descent. Continental and Cessna blithely promise a 1,700-hour TBO for the IO-520 in the Skywagon, but most experienced owners consider this a joke. With frequent oil changes and some general pampering, the bottom end of the motor can usually make TBO, but the exhaust valves are the weakest link, and these cannot be expected to work properly much past 1,200 hours. Most conscientious owners end up doing a top overhaul at about this

time. Prospective 185 buyers should keep this in mind while shopping high-time planes and budget accordingly.

Modifications

Four companies (Bush, Horton, Met-Co-Aire, and R/STOL Systems) offer a variety of drooped tips, stall fences, fatter leading edges, and other related mods designed to increase the low-speed performance of the 185 wings. Owners of pre-1973 Skywagons would do well to consider updating to the "fat cuff" wing and the newer-style drooped wingtips, plus a set of aileron/flap gap seals, which make a noticeable difference in low speed roll control and add a bit to rate of climb. For normal (wheel) operations the C-185 does just fine without any esoteric STOL kits; however, when operating on floats or skis (where touching down at the lowest possible speed can mean a lot less wear and tear), these kits are a worthwhile addition.

The PeeKay division of DeVore offers a three-blade McCauley prop STC for all the pre-1979 Skywagons. PeeKay just sells the STC, and buyers must go direct to McCauley for the prop (which is part number D3A32C90/82NC-2).

Recently, an outfit up in Washington called Seaplanes, Inc., has started offering two interesting engine conversions: a swap to the

turbocharged TSIO-520 Continental (at 300 hp) or the very reliable 350-hp Lycoming TIO-540. In theory, either engine would give a performance boost to the 185, especially at higher altitudes, but the kits are so new that no reliable user reports or service data is yet available.

Since the 185 is still being produced, obtaining parts is no more difficult or expensive than for any other Cessna (which is not to say that the company's parts are either cheap or quick to arrive). Many non-structural replacement parts can be obtained from outside vendors: the Wall-Comnolloy exhaust muffler is a good case in point; it costs only half as much as the stock Cessna one and has proven to last more than twice as long.

A careful pre-purchase inspection by a disinterested mechanic with 185 maintenance experience is highly advisable. Many of these planes have done long years of yeoman toil out in rural operations where maintenance is sometimes skimpy. Obviously, if the plane has ever seen service on floats, corrosion is almost certain to exist somewhere in the airframe, and even a plane that has merely been tied down on a seaside airport for extended periods can have insidious corrosion problems. Most reputable shops will do a pre-purchase inspection just like an annual (and at the same price) without actually fixing any of the squawks.

Since the C-185 is mostly "standard Cessna," service is widely available, although mechanics in back-country areas tend to see more Skywagons and thus have more experience with the few unique maintenance problem areas, such as tailwheel shimmy-spring adjustment or cable tension on the manual trim system. If your mechanic at Teterboro or Long Beach has never laid hands on a Skywagon, you will pay extra for his experimental learning curve. On the other hand, up in Anchorage, where the C-185 is the unofficial state bird, half the people walking down the street could probably do a Skywagon oil change blindfolded.

Owners Association

The official International 180/185 Club is run by the President, C. E. ("Bomber") Bombardier, 4539 N. 49th Avenue, Phoenix, Ariz. 85031. The 180/185 Club currently boasts nearly 1,000 members, which is a respectable percentage of the nearly 4,500 C-185s that have been built to date.

Safety Record

While the overall accident rate of the Cessna 185 is about average, the fatal accident rate is quite a bit better than average. In fact, according to a special NTSB study of single-engine aircraft accidents between 1972 and 1976, the Cessna 185 was fourth best in fatal accidents of 33 aircraft compared.

Also, the Cessna 185 almost never has an in-flight airframe failure. A special study by Brent Silver of the 14-year period between 1964 and 1977 showed that the C-185 shared the best record with two other aircraft—the Cessna 172 and 175. During that period, the C-185 experienced not one airframe failure.

A computer run of C-185 accident briefs for the years 1979 through 1981 provided by the National Transportation Safety Board showed that by far the greatest portion of accidents stemmed from groundloops and swerves on land and water. There were no less than 40 of these. Since these aircraft,

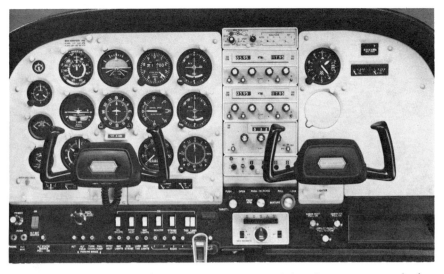

Control wheels, not sticks, are standard equipment on this tail-dragger, of course. Don't look for an electric flap switch; flaps are manual. Watch out for ARC radios.

many of them outfitted with floats, often are used for bush operations, quite a few accidents occurred in rough terrain or on wilderness lakes and rivers with hidden sandbars, logs, etc. There was a sizable number of nose-over accidents as well: 13 of them.

The C-185 had its share of engine failure problems, as well, with 21 of those noted during the period studied. There seemed to be a mixed bag of causes, however, with no single obvious trend. There were a couple of cases of water in the fuel and of fuel mismanagement.

Aircraft Resale Value

The old 260-hp Cessna 185s seem to have fared better over the years in investment value than the new 300-hp models. We tracked a '65 D model as it climbed in value from 1969 to 1984—gaining about $5,000.

In 1969 the average resale price was about $12,900. Then in 1977 it suddenly jumped to about $18,300, where it has remained.

A 1975 F model we tracked showed rather lackluster investment performance, however, starting out at an equipped price of $40,200 and steadily sagging to its 1984 value of about $28,000. This aircraft did not

even exhibit the turn-around after four years or so that most popular models do.

Owner Comments

The 185 is an excellent and well-designed aircraft that is highly refined. I don't think it is appropriate for one to learn about taildraggers in, however. I had about 500 hours in a Citabria before I acquired the 185. While not vicious by any means, it requires constant attention and prompt correction, sometimes with a little muscle. It is often compared to the 206 in Alaska, but I prefer the 185 for personal transportation and aesthetics. There is no comparison on skis. Performance on the 206 is comparable and it offers better cargo carrying, but at 300 pounds more weight. Also, manual flaps on the 185 are infinitely preferable to electric, particularly on floats. Edo 2960 floats, which I have, are quite long and will dig their heels in if too much stick pressure is applied to achieve liftoff. An extra tug on the flaps accomplishes much the same as far as the wing is concerned without altering the planing angle of the floats. This maneuver requires feel and would be impossible with electric flaps.

Realistic flight plan block speed on wheels is 140 knots at 8,000 feet. Edo 2960's are relatively fast floats

With this 1979 model, the 185 got a wet wing with 84 gallons usable.

in the air but will still take 20 knots off at the same altitude. At normal float operation altitude 115 knots is more realistic at 24/24.

I always lean 50° rich of peak on the EGT at either 23 to 24 inches of manifold pressure and 2400 rpm for cruise. I plan for 15 gph with 14 as a good actual overall average at altitude. Some operators do not feel the IO-520 should ever be leaned below 14 gph.

At 450 hours total time on the engine I switched to AeroShell 15/50 and within 20 hours thereafter noticed vibration. Inspection of the oil filter revealed metal that was diagnosed by Continental as bearing material. The engine was replaced.

The choice of floats depends somewhat on fresh water or salt. I prefer Edo floats myself although PeeKay makes a good float which doesn't get off smooth water quite as well but is more suited for ocean operation. The 1960 floats are listed on the Cessna equipment list and provide the best combination of speed in the air and performance on the water. Most commercial operators seem to prefer the Edo 3430s where airspeed is not a factor and overloading is. Aqua floats are noted for their leaking and do not have a particularly good reputation. CAP floats are not seen very much any more and have a reputation for porpoising in a step turn, a not really necessary maneuver.

I use Landes wheel penetration skis, which are a good compromise ski and half the price of retractable skis, which are superior, however. The penetrating tire gives a surprising amount of drag. I do not like straight skis myself as it limits the aircraft's utility, particularly in areas around sea level. The 185 is simply too heavy to manhandle on the ground like a Super Cub.

I found that the best way to land a 185 in most circumstances is with an approach speed of 65 knots, three or four notches of flaps, trimming full aft when ground effect is felt, and timing the full retarding of the throttle with touchdown in the three-point altitude. Wheel landings have more style and are unquestionably the way to go in gusty winds. In the last several years my landings have been evenly divided between wheel and three-point.

I have owned a 180 and not groundlooped either plane, or any taildragger for that matter, yet. I don't feel that a groundloop is inevitable as it can be avoided in most cases. I have abandoned several landing attempts, however, where I felt that there was a definite possibility of losing control. In gusty crosswind conditions it is not unusual to use full rudder, and a pilot should be ready with a touch of brake, which is usually quite effective. Twenty to 25 knots is the most direct crosswind that I would care to attempt. Also be careful of a left crosswind on takeoff as, when the tail comes up, full rudder will probably be needed. If I had to land in conditions with the wind stronger I would land into the wind across the runway.

Robert H. Wagstaff
Anchorage, Alas.

I had my doubts about the IO-520 engine before we bought our 185. It is amazing how actually owning an airplane changes your point of view. I have really grown to resent Continental's attitude, both to their customers and as exemplified in the poor engineering and a pinch-penny attitude in assembling their products.

We recently lost a cylinder on our 400-hour IO-520. Continental's comment was, ''Oh Gee, you must be doing something wrong, that's not a problem anybody else has.'' Now that we were feeling properly guilty and had resolved to run the engine three points rich of peak lean instead of the recommended two, we removed the cylinder and took it to the machine shop. The machinist was not at all surprised to hear that the cylinder was from a 400-hour engine. He told me from which position (#) it had to come, and said that this was quite normal. Starting at about 500 hours, I could expect to replace at least three cylinders before a major would be necessary at 1,200 hours!

The problem with this particular cylinder (in addition to its location at the right rear of the engine) was bad seating in the exhaust valve, caused by excess guide clearance and lack of seating at the factory. Continental assembles all heads at the maximum allowable clearance, so the TSIO heads can be interchanged with the IO heads. The result is excess clearance for IO heads when they are new. Continental's somewhat unique views on seating valves and balancing engines are too well known to be worth any long comment.

In addition to sloppy assembly there is a design problem with the engine (in addition to the weak crankcases), in the area of top cylinder cooling. There are not nearly enough cooling fins in this area, and (it must be assumed) for reasons of cost Continental refuses to use sodium cooled valves, a combination that ensures overheating and rapid wear in the upper-cylinder and valve area.

Name Withheld

Cessna 195

From out of the past rumbles one of aviation's all-time classic beauties. A vision in metal modeling with livingroom comfort and a reputation as a groundlooping-Lena, the Cessna 190-195 sets up great internal stresses among potential buyers seeking a satisfying balance between practicality and a touch of class and mystique.

History

Cessna cranked out some 1,200 of the 190s, 195s and military LC-126s between 1946 and 1954. The main distinction among the four different models built is the engine configuration. The C-190 came with a Continental radial putting out 240 hp. The C-195 had a 300-hp Jacobs, while the A and B models had 245-hp and 275-hp Jacobs respectively. There were plenty to choose from that first year since all but the 275 were offered concurrently.

The C-195B came out rather late in the production cycle, but its R755-B2 engine is generally considered to be the most reliable of the group, even though all three of the Jacobses have the same displacement. The 300 received a deeper intake manifold to get its

Called the Cessna Businessliner in its day, the C-195 with its giant cantilever wing is still an awesome sight.
(Howard Levy photo)

extra 25 horses, but this seems to make it more susceptible to case cracking.

The other significant changes were slightly larger flaps along with a modified horizontal tail at serial number 16084. And in 1953 the Goodyear crosswind gear was offered as standard, along with a lighter, springier set of main gear struts.

Performance and Handling

Owners report they get from 117 to 140 knots on the various models with a fuel burn of 12 to 19 gph. With 76 gallons of usable fuel on board, that means a range of from 520 to 780 nm. With the 275-hp Jacobs, count on a cruise of a bit over 130 knots, burning about 13½ gph, with a comfortable no-reserve range of about 600 nm.

The aircraft is described as having "authoritative" pitch and rudder control, but ailerons that are a bit on the heavy side. One owner characterized handling as similar to a Cessna 210's, except for the "more ponderous" aileron control. Stalls are gentlemanly.

Although the aircraft is commonly described as an excellent, stable instrument platform and cruise ship, it possesses an annoying tendency to wander in pitch in a mild never-ending phugoid. One pilot bemoaned the lack of a more capable autopilot to counter this characteristic than the "old, heavy Lear L2," which he said was the only one approved.

Another comment shed some doubt on the "stable instrument platform" characterization. Said one flier, "Since it has no dihedral, it is impossible to trim the airplane to fly hands off."

Suggested ways to land the C-195 without groundlooping it are, naturally, legion. The Cessna owner's manual suggests doing it three-point, and many owners subscribe to this philosophy. Others swear by the wheel landing technique, if only in crosswinds or gusty wind conditions.

But everybody agrees that the pilot must keep highly alert throughout the entire landing process. Said one reader: "Airspeed control on final is the key to good three-point landings (70 knots or less), and the pilot *must* remember to look straight down the runway until the airplane has slowed to a walking speed. Taking your eye off the runway to glance in the cockpit is inviting a groundloop. It must be remembered that this is a relatively heavy taildragger with the CG located well behind the main gear. Allow a swerve of more than 10 or 15 degrees to develop, and you don't have enough brake to stop it. A groundloop in this airplane will usually cause major damage to the gearbox, fuselage and wing."

Cabin Load and Comfort

Roominess is the aircraft's strong suit, with space for four comfortably, or five cozily. The useful load on an IFR-equipped 195 goes around 1,200 pounds, which allows full fuel and four 170-pound adults plus about 29 pounds of baggage.

The view out the cabin is really nothing to brag about, since the windows are long, but not terribly deep, except for a monster skylight right above the pilots' heads. Many 195 pilots say visibility is quite good in cruise (though abominable in taxi and on the landing flare), while others say they live constantly in fear of a midair because the pilot's head is lodged just about in the wing root.

In cold weather the 195 offers instant cabin heat thanks to a Southwind gas heater located right under the rear seat. One pilot had an interesting adventure thanks to this configuration when a spare can (a cardboard can, actually) of oil he'd tossed in the back rolled around and made contact with the heater, generating a bit of cockpit IFR.

Investment Value

With the passage of years—inflation, and perhaps the plane's reputation as a classic—have slowly brought the resale value of the 195s up close to their price when new. Tracking a 1952 B model, we noted a big trough in the l960s and early 1970s when the aircraft was selling for only about $6,000. Then in 1973 the price took a jog upward to about $9,000, and in 1976 commenced a steady climb until in 1979 it peaked out at $20,000. Since then it has sagged only slightly to about $19,000 according to the *Aircraft Bluebook Price Digest*. The various models range in average Bluebook price from about $16,000 to $19,000.

Safety Record

According to the National

Electrically operated split flaps project down ahead of the trailing edge of the wing.

Transportation Safety Board's special study of single-engine aircraft accidents between 1972 and 1976, the Cessna 195 enjoys the unhappy distinction of being the worst groundlooper of all 33 aircraft compared. It was worse than even the Luscombe 8.

The aircraft also came away in that report with the stigma of having the second highest overall accident rate—just behind the Luscombe 8, incidentally. Things improved somewhat in the fatal accident rate, with the C-195 coming out 11th worst.

And although the aircraft experienced only two in-flight airframe failures during the period studied, that brought the rate up to fourth worst among the 33, based on flying hours.

We understand that during the period 1964-1977 there were five fatal in-flight airframe failures. One of these seemed to involve pilot incapacitation due to carbon monoxide, another was a spin in the clouds, one a wingtip failure, another an empennage separation.

Cessna 195 owners are justifiably proud of the fact that so few Air-

worthiness Directives have been issued against the aircraft through the years since it was introduced. But one of them requires an inspection of the wing spar and addition of a steel reinforcement kit. It was issued following a fatal accident involving fatigue failure of the front wing spar fuselage carry-through lower cap.

Misdirectional Control

As we mentioned earlier, by far the greatest number of accidents and incidents tallied by the NTSB and the FAA on the Cessna 190-195s concern groundlooping this taildragger. We counted 43 of these in a recent six-year period on printouts made for us. Damage was to pride, airframe and pocketbook in each case; no injuries were reported.

Fatal accidents in this period were caused by engine failures in three cases. In one, the aircraft had lost oil from a fractured rubber hose from the oil sump to the main screen, with the pilot making an emergency descent in bad weather. In the second, water was found in the fuel after the crash. Two other nonfatal accidents were also caused by water in the fuel. The third fatal accident occurred after the number one piston disintegrated. The aircraft was reported to have an oil leak from the vicinity of the oil cooler prior to departure.

Another nonfatal engine failure and forced landing was blamed on carburetor ice, and quite a few C-195 pilots report great care has to be taken to avoid this problem, because the engine is quite prone to build carb ice. Yet another engine failure, this one in the traffic pattern, resulted from fuel starvation because engine vibration caused the fuel selector valve to move to the off position.

Cost/Performance/Specifications

Model	Year	Average Retail Price	Gross Weight (lbs)	Useful Load (lbs)	Cruise Speed (kts)	Fuel (gals)	Engine	TBO (hrs)	Overhaul Cost
C-190	1947-53	$15,500	3,350	1,335	139	80	240-hp Cont. W-670-23	1,000	$7,000
C-195	1947-53	$18,500	3,350	1,300	148	80	300-hp Jacobs R-755-A2	1,000	$8,000
C-195A	1947-53	$17,500	3,350	1,320	139	80	245-hp Jacobs R-755-9	1,000	$8,000
C-195B	1952-54	$19,000	3,350	1,300	143	80	275-hp Jacobs R-755-B2	1,000	$8,000

Another pair of fatal accidents stemmed from problems on climb-out or go-around. One took place in high density altitude conditions in the Grand Canyon when the pilot made a steep turn and stalled. In the other, the pilot attempted a go-around late but neglected to move the prop pitch to the takeoff range.

A final fatal accident involved a float-equipped C-195 which the pilot attempted to take off in wind gusting to 35 knots with an un-balanced fuel load. The wing tip dug into the water, and a passenger drowned.

Many of the groundlooping accidents were caused simply by pilot inability to keep the aircraft going straight down the runway during the landing, sometimes in gusty crosswind conditions. However, a fair number were blamed on faulty brakes. Even though some pilots said it was impossible to nose over the big bird by hard braking on the landing roll, even after a wheel landing, in several instances pilots did just that, and even flipped the aircraft over on its back.

The Goodyear brakes the aircraft came with are often described as inadequate, with Cleveland brake conversions making a big difference.

At least one pilot claims that groundlooping problems can be corrected by the use of the proper tailwheel tire: i.e., a channel tread.

Landing Gear Struts

In some groundloops involving Cessna 190 and 195 aircraft, more than embarrassment results because one of the landing gear struts is torn off. Reader Larry Bartlett has some information on that topic:

"Two types of spring steel gear legs were installed. The later type, on the '53 and '54 models, was thinner and weighed about 20 pounds less. It is often referred to as the 'Wasp' or 'Spider' gear, or sometimes as the 'light' gear. The earlier 'heavy' gear is much stiffer, and I think causes more damage in

Tail strut leakage is a chronic problem but Granville Strut Seal seems to be an effective antidote.

a groundloop since it generally tears out of the fuselage, whereas the 'light' gear will spring or spread out and remain intact. I have no empirical data to support this, but all totaled 195s that I've seen that were groundlooped (and I've seen a few) had the 'heavy' gear.''

A never-ending debate rages on the use of crosswind wheels for the taildragging Cessnas. Some old, experienced pilots maintain that only fools fly without them; others maintain that with a little care and experience, a pilot will have no problems.

The Goodyear castering gear was installed as standard equipment in 1953, and about 75 percent of the aircraft currently flying have them. Bartlett, for one, dislikes them. "I guess they do reduce the possibility of a groundloop and cover up for sloppy pilot technique, but I hate the looks of them," he says. "Aesthetically, the airplane needs

wheel fairings, and they will not fit over the crosswind gear.''

Another C-195 pilot said the narrow nine-foot track of the main gear adds to the problem of landing the 28-foot-long aircraft. "Once you let the tail wheel swing outside the track of the mainwheels on roll-out, even with full differential braking, you will probably ground-loop,'' he reported.

Short-field Performance

In the six-year accident listing, only four patently obvious cases were reported of C-195s getting into trouble with short fields. In one instance already mentioned, the pilot attempted to land on a short private field, overshot, then attempted a go-around too late and stalled (with coarse prop pitch). In the other, the pilot stalled on takeoff in a high-density altitude situation. In two other cases the pilots landed long while attempting to cope with strong crosswinds.

For a Cessna the aircraft has un-characteristically modest flap "power." The aircraft has a strange-looking set of split flaps that project down from the bottom of the wing, not from the trailing edge, but several inches forward. Naturally, they provide no lift, just drag.

Said one pilot, "Slow-flight is a dream, and as a result you can make very short landings with it. Unfortunately, the lack of a Fowler type flap keeps it from being a true short-field airplane. The split flaps are good speedbrakes, but provide no lift.''

The Shaky Jake with the cowling off. The entire engine can be swung out on its mount. Oil filler aft of the engine takes five gals.

Judging from the NTSB's big study of single-engine accidents, however, the C-195 has a comparatively rotten record in overshoots. Its accident rate in this category was second only to the Grumman Traveler's. Note that because of the number of hours flown by C-195s, there were only five overhoot accidents.

A set of slightly larger flaps was added with the B model along with a shorter-chord horizontal stabilizer and modified trimtabs. But some pilots say the bigger flaps don't really affect performance in a beneficial sense that much. In fact, they seem to make it more difficult for a solo pilot to land three-point, according to Dwight Ewing, president of the International 195 Club.

Maintenance

Naturally, maintenance on these old birds is something of a chore because they're rather rare, and not too many mechanics nowadays are familiar with the old radial engines. Owners say, however, that the parts situation is really not too bad these days. But a glance at the 195 Club's newsletters shows that scrounging, upgrading and trading of parts is a matter of continuing concern.

The engines go about 1,000 to 1,200 hours on the TBO, with frequent oil changes recommended (at around 25 to 30 hours). An overhaul or an exchange will cost $7,000, $7,450, or $7,950 from the Jacobs Service Co., depending on the engine. Working on the old radials is made easier by an engine mount design that allows the powerplant to be swung out from one side, as on a hinge.

One common problem with the 195s is leaking tail struts. Owners through the years have resorted to various cures, including installing Chevy valve springs. But some believe Granville Strut Seal might be the answer.

Old heads advise potential buyers to feel the fuselage skin in front of the main landing gear struts for smoothness, because it's hard to disguise rupturing of the gearbox,

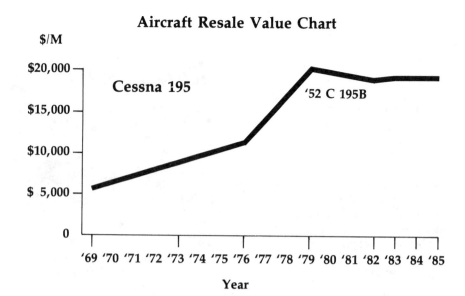

Aircraft Resale Value Chart

as it's called, by groundlooping.

Owners are wont to extoll the grand old birds by claiming that only one solitary Airworthiness Directive has been issued during the entire history of the bird. And of course that was the big one concerning the wing truss. But the records show three others on the 190 and two others on the 195.

One required inspection of the rudder cables to detect premature fraying at the forward pulley. Another called for inspection for cracking and failures of the cowl mounting ring channels, until new channels and stiffening angles were installed. A third required inspection for fatigue cracks in the elevator spar webs at the outboard hinges until reinforcing doublers were installed. A final one, shared with many other Cessnas, involved checking the electrical system to prevent in-flight fires.

Parts and Service

Despite the fact that these days Cessna provides little more than moral support to the some 720 Cessna 190s and 195s still registered, owners report the parts situation is not too bad. In fact, it should even improve, thanks to a whole new enterprise devoted to building and overhauling the Jacobs engines.

The Jacobs Service Co. in Chandler, Ariz. acquired the type certificates, tooling, drawings and parts inventory from Page Industries. It also received PMA approval, and does overhauls as well as providing exchange engines. Check with shop foreman Jim McCracken at 602-961-9641.

A couple of West Coast maintenance and repair facilities that are characterized as "excellent" by the International 195 Club are Ray's Aircraft (run by Ray Woodmansee) at Porterville, Calif. and Roy McLain, Colton, Calif.

Andy Brennan of Brennan Formed Sheet Metal Parts, Torrance, Calif. manufactures sheet metal parts for the C-195.

Out in the East, the late John Van Sant's family is carrying on in providing parts for the aircraft at Erwinna, Pa. And according to lifetime 195 Club member George Jackowski of Dayton, Ohio, Air Ads of Dayton at the Moraine Air Park is well known for its repair and service work on 195s.

Down south in the Florida panhandle, John Hambleton of Gulf Coast Air Service in Fort Walton Beach provides service for the aircraft.

Operating Characteristics

Along with the panache of the big radial-engine Cessna comes a healthy dose of fussing—even before you can start the grand old bird. Since oil collects in the bottom cylinders if the aircraft has been sitting more than a few hours, the pilot must pull it through five to 12 blades, depending on whom you talk to. This will allow the start to generate less of a smokescreen.

The pilot is not home free once he gets taxiing, either, since many of the old radials begin to heat up with prolonged ground operation. This is one reason C-195 pilots like to avoid big, busy airports with long rides to and from the active, and much sitting in line waiting for takeoff. Some owners even install double oil coolers to diminish the problem.

And the type of spinner installed has an effect on the cooling efficiency of the aircraft—though presumably only after the aircraft is airborne. The so-called Cessna "floating" bullet spinner is generally regarded as the most efficient. But some owners have used BT-13 spinners because they were more easily available.

Though the engines are designed for 80-octane avgas, quite a few C-195 owners report they have used autogas with success.

Modifications

Although owners say only one autopilot, the Lear L2, is approved for the 190-195s, we note that Brittain has an STC for its B2C system.

Judging from the comments of owners, one of the most useful conversions is from the troublesome old Goodyear brakes to Cleveland brakes, which are many times more effective. Some say they're almost too effective and take a cautious touch or they can get the pilot into trouble. Also, of course, the airplane can be equipped with floats and is regarded as a marvelous seaplane whose squirrelly groundlooping tendencies have been purged.

We understand also that a number of 195s have 330-hp Jacobs L6MB engines that came from surplus World War II stocks in Canada and were installed with a modified cowl to accept the larger engine.

Some 195s also received 450-hp Pratt & Whitney powerplants. And a 350-hp turbocharged version of the Jacobs was developed by Page, using an AiResearch turbo.

Also, the Jacobs Service Co. is developing a 325-hp fuel injection mod for the 275-hp engine that not only should reduce fuel consumption and even out fuel flow to the cylinders but eliminate the specter of carb ice.

Organization to Join

The International 195 Club takes good care of members and publishes a slick-looking bulletin. Contact Dwight Ewing at the club address of P.O. Box 737, Merced, Calif. 95340, 209-722-6284.

Rationale

The airplane obviously oozes aesthetic appeal. It has to be one of the all-time sculptured beauties. And at $16,000 to $20,000 or so, can it really be matched in a broad-shouldered contemporary ship of similar performance? As one owner comments: "In summary, the Cessna 195 is a five-place all-metal airplane which will produce an honest 140 knots on 15 gph. No AD hassle, easy maintenance, easy to fly. Have we really made any progress in 30 years?"

Answer: maybe not in looks and classic aura, but in safer, easier ground handling, certainly anything with tricycle gear excells. And for a similar investment, something on the order of the 1964 to 1974 Skylane will offer fairly similar cruise speeds and load-carrying ability with better parts availability, and a pretty decent cabin size. But as they say, love is blind.

Owner Comments

The Jacobs engine is a very reliable unit and does not have any unusual maintenance problems, but it does have some quirks. Smokey starts are common, more so than

most radials, and it must be pulled through 10 or 12 blades to clear oil from the bottom cylinders if it has been sitting more than several hours. The engine will produce carburetor ice faster than an ice maker, and in cool, moist air it should be flown with partial carb heat, using the installed carburetor air temperature gauge.

Many times in flight in clear air the engine will cough or sputter momentarily, leading many to believe the mixture is too lean. But the "Shakey Jake" is merely swallowing some ice.

A major difference between the Jake and other engines is that instead of two magnetos, it has one mag and a battery distributor just like a car. You might say it has a one-and-a-half ignition system instead of a dual system because the loss of the generator will soon have you operating on one mag.

The airframe is solid; you might say it was built like a tank. Parts can usually be found for most anything. The hardest parts to find have been cowling sections and the gearbox.

Good brakes are essential on this airplane. A Cleveland conversion is available and it does a great job. It is expensive, but well worth it. The only problem with the Clevelands is that they provide more braking action than the gearbox

Cleveland brakes much better than the original Goodyears.

was designed to handle. I've seen two cases of popped rivets in the gearbox due to hard braking with Clevelands installed. You have to really bear down on the Goodyears, but a light touch will do the job with the Clevelands.

Larry Bartlett
Aviation Seminars
El Paso, Tex.

The best feature is the large internal volume. In the front you sit up in chairs off the floor, as at your kitchen table, and in the back you can stretch your legs out as in a Cadillac Limo.

The worst feature to me was the visibility to the sides in level flight. The pilot's head is located in the wing root; hence, to scan, one must duck down in an uncomfortable position, or lean forward.

Paul Taipale
Bellevue, Wash.

The biggest problem with the plane is the air-filled tail shock unit, and I found few who flew the plane who had not had a large spring installed inside the shock and used that to [reduce] the vibration. I tried for a long time to keep the darn shock filled, and most of those you see are sitting down low on the wheel, indicative of the fact that their tail shock doesn't work either.

It is a smooth-flying machine—easy to fly, wonderful and stable platform, big and comfortable. I can't remember having difficult landings, and always made wheel landings to keep pressure off the tail and its poor shock.

The flaps don't do anything for all practical purposes as far as slowing you down; but they do pitch you forward so you can see to land.

Art Brothers
Salt Lake City, Utah

It has been a most satisfying aircraft. It is as rock steady in all types of weather as you can expect a single-engine civilian craft to be. In the air, it feels much like a Cessna 210, except it is more ponderous in aileron control.

Its one big drawback initially is its ground handling. Visibility over the nose in three-point attitude is nil, the slow-turning prop (2200 rpm at takeoff while delivering 300 hp) provides plenty of torque to contend with. All of which adds up to what is probably one of the most difficult civilian aircraft to handle on the runway. On landing, it is worse.

For the first few months of ownership, the local airport wags will sell tickets to your landings. However, once you master the aircraft, the feeling of accomplishment is tremendous, and more of a thrill than you will ever get with any modern tricycle-gear plane.

Annuals are now running about $450 to $500. The only real annoyance is the tendency to overheat on the ground. Despite twin oil coolers, the tightly cowled Jake will run near the top of the green arc at cruise in the summer, and takeoffs and landings are out. If you buy a 195, buy it in the winter, when you can get your 100 takeoffs and landings for your checkout at a rate of more than one per day. On normal operations, the handbook even suggests you do part of the runup while taxiing as "fast as safely possible" to the runway. You can live with it, but crowded airports need careful planning.

You can find modern aircraft that go faster on less fuel . . . but if you are willing to pay for your enjoyment, for sheer classic elegance, panache, *joi de vivre*, return to the challenge and romance of flying . . . you can't beat the 195.

Carlos R. Diaz
Clinton, Md.

My 195 receives more attention from lookers, gawkers, askers, admirers than any aircraft I have seen. And the roomy, solid comfort will impress you. The best 195 combination is a 275-hp Jacobs engine, Cleveland wheels (no cross-wind gear), IFR radios and nice paint and interior. You'll love it. It is the Cadillac of all Cessna singles.

Thomas J. Schmid
Roseburg, Ore.

The engine was susceptible to carburetor ice, the fuel system had a tendency to collect water, and flight in icing conditions was hazardous because the fuel tank vents had a tendency to ice up.

Twice during flight in turbulence my rear door opened in flight. This unnerved my rear-seat passengers, but didn't seem to affect the flight characteristics adversely. I was able to close the door after I cranked down the left front window.

I found that wheel landings were consistently better than three-point landings. You can brake a 195 as soon as the main gear is planted on the ground, so wheel landings require no more distance than three-pointers.

David M. Baker
Huntington, W. Va.

The horror stories about ground-loops can be corrected by the simple use of the proper tailwheel tire —a channel tread.

Reports of engine oil overheating can in all cases be traced to improper type of spinner and elimination of cowling cooling rings. Many owners use a blunt bullet spinner, then wonder why they have to add oil coolers. The bullet spinner deflects the airstream outside the cowling while the original Cessna Spinner directs the airflow to the cylinders.

Several propeller seal modifications are STC'd and are available at a reasonable price to eliminate prop oil leakage permanently. Cylinder head bolts should be tightened every 250-300 hours. And exhaust valve clearance should be checked at that time. If the engine is equipped with valve rotators, no adjustment of valves will normally be necessary.

I feel my aircraft is now worth $24,500. And I could not get the comfort, speed and safety at double that amount with any other airplane.

Harry E. Reed
Baldwinsville, N.Y.

SINGLE-ENGINE RETRACTABLES

Cessna Cardinal RG

By many accounts, Cessna's 177 RG Cardinal has survived the ravages of time and a defunct production line quite well. It perhaps now can even be considered the queen of the used economy retractables, at least in terms of near tag sale prices.

It is less doggy in performance than similar aircraft like the Piper Arrow and Beech Sierra, and though still 10 knots or more slower than the Mooney 201, costs a small fortune less. For example, where a 1978 Mooney 201 is going for a handsome price of around $49,000 these days, a '78 Cardinal RG can be fetched for a relatively paltry $29,000 or less, according to *Aircraft Bluebook Price Digest* figures.

Cardinal RG owners don't seem to complain too much about parts availability, though the line was closed down in 1978 after only eight years of production. And they rave about its looks and novel design features. They even seem rather inured to the aircraft's Achilles heel—its trouble-plagued landing gear system. Owners who reported to us this time sounded off lot less bitterly on the gear problem they did for our last call for

The rearward location of the wing provides the pilot with a rare high-wing glimpse of sky and traffic inside the turn. The notch in the fuselage for the main landing gear can be seen on the belly in the wing's shadow.

user feedback on the 177 RG in 1980.

Peer Pressure

In comparison with the Piper Arrows, Mooneys and Beech Sierras that have the same 200-hp powerplant, the Cardinal RG is fastest, except for the Mooney, of course. It is roomiest, except for the Sierra. And it can carry the best useful load of all of them, by a small margin. In terms of price, it is $5,000 cheaper on the average than the Arrow on today's used market (for a '78 model), and even about $1,000 cheaper than the Sierra.

In General

Although the 75-percent book cruise speed for the Cardinal RG is supposed to be a sizzling 148 knots/170 mph, in the real world most owners talk about speeds closer to 140-145 knots/161-167 mph. But on the other hand, they boast of economy gas burns of eight to nine and a half gph. And

with a generous 60-gallon fuel capacity on all but the '71 RGs, range is superb.

Owners report the Cardinal RGs ride well in turbulence, have nice-handling controls, provide a "stable instrument platform" and behave well in slow flight. "It is like driving a sports car compared to the cumbersome Skylane," said one owner. "Handling is superb."

Cabin Load and Comfort

As a safety-enhancing corollary to the spacious cabin, owners say the aircraft is almost impossible to load out of the cg envelope. But the baggage compartment is a strange one, since it is bisected by the hump that accommodates the retracted landing gear. This means suitcases that fit through the horizontally mounted baggage door then must be finessed into one of the two vertical slots on either side of the wheel well hump.

Said one owner, however, "The much maligned baggage compartment swallows an enormous amount of luggage, despite the hump. A useful load of 1,025 pounds works out to four adults, 120 pounds of baggage and enough fuel to fly four hours with IFR

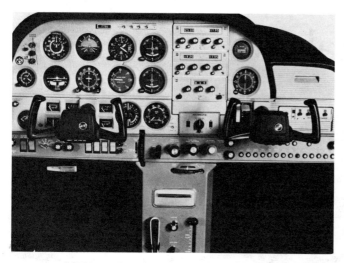

From the '71 through '75 models, the aircraft had a "left-handed" panel (photo on left) that was more notable for styling than for instrument space. The '76 model corrected this with an enlarged panel. In a rare bit of human engineering, the suction gauge is placed on the top left corner of the panel, where the pilot can see it, rather than way over on the right, as is common practice.

reserves. It is a true four-place single."

Whistling in the Wind

The four-foot wide cabin doors are everybody's pride and joy for ease of access, and they can catch the wind like sails to open a full 90 degrees to the fuselage. (Watch out.) Along with the benefits come some drawbacks, however, since owners still complain about door sealing problems. One said he solved the problem by simply removing the "hardened original seals" and replacing them with new ones.

But we remain skeptical in the light of comments by Bob Fields (of Bob Fields Aerocessories in Santa Paula, Calif.). Instead of providing inflatable seals for what we figured would be the ultimate solution to the problem, Fields told us he threw up his hands in frustration at getting any seals to work on the Cardinal RG, even though numerous owners came to him for help. "The variation in space between the doors and the fuselage is terrible," he said. "Some portions of the doors fit too tightly, others too

loosely, so when you get one part of the seal to inflate properly, another is pinched off." Fields attributed the awful fit to poor quality control.

Wet and Wild

If the doors can leak air, it stands to reason they can leak water. And so owners testify. The windshields tend to leak as well. But then Cessnas as a class seem prey to leakage problems. One Cardinal RG owner said he solved his leaky windshield problem simply by applying a bead of clear RTV around the outside of the windshield. As a final line of defense for the pilot, however, he suggested covering the pilot's left leg with a plastic chart.

Many aircraft also are noted for poor heating of rear seats in winter. The Cardinal RG tackled that problem by running heating ducts in back through the big doors. Alas, owners report little hot air makes it as far as the rear seats.

History of Model Changes

The aircraft has experienced a few modest changes through its eight-year production life. Though none is terribly significant alone, perhaps the collective improvements through the years to the landing gear system and its many idiosyncracies amounts to something. The 1972 model gained a few knots in cruise and a slightly better climb rate thanks to a new prop. Also, the fixed cabin steps were dropped. They tended to expose the bottom of the fuselage to even

more grief when the aircraft landed gear-up (as they did with some regularity). Instead, small foot pads were placed on the main gear struts. In addition, landing and taxi lights were mounted in the nose instead of the wing.

The '73 model received a slightly redesigned nose cowl and an extra 10 gallons in usable fuel—up to 60 gallons. The fuel selector system was changed from one limited to "off" and "both," to one that also provided "left" and "right" positions. The problem on the earlier model was that one tank could be depleted more rapidly than the other, since the pilot could not select either a right or a left wing tank. This often meant unbalancing the aircraft.

In 1976 the instrument panel was redesigned and enlarged, and a simplified landing gear hydraulic system was offered, along with a stronger nose gear trunion.

For the '77 model, the aircraft received a fuel selector that gave it commonality with other Cessna singles, had a more positive detent and was supposed to be more easily maintainable.

And finally in 1978 the aircraft received a 28-volt electrical system and an improved gear retraction power pack that cut retraction time in half to six seconds.

Resale Value

Despite inflation, the Cardinal RGs on the whole exhibited rather mundane resale curves, never soaring up as highly valued aircraft do. Instead, they merely sagged to a certain level in the standard four years after new, then remained pretty much on a plateau through the years. Thus, the original '71 model dropped from about $31,000 to around $20,000 and remained within a couple thousand dollars of that through the years. The last model, the '78 ship, dropped from about $54,000 to $29,000 in the classic four-year span, and remained in that vicinity to the present.

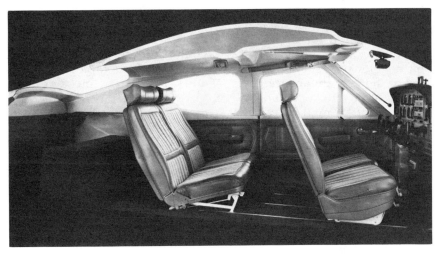

Safety Record

A study of accident rates in the decade 1972 to 1981 by *The Aviation Consumer* gave the Cardinal RG an excellent ranking in terms of fatal accidents and a slightly better-than-average rate in total accidents. In fatal accidents, the Cardinal RG came out third best after the Cessna Skylane RG and the Beech 33 Bonanza/Debonair and tied with the Beech 36 Bonanza with 1.5 fatal accidents per 100,000 hours. In total accidents it was seventh out of seventeen with 7.8 accidents per 100,000 hours. (See the May 1, 1984 issue.) The study compared single-engine retractables.

What kind of accidents predominate among Cardinal RGs? A study of NTSB accident records for the years 1979-1980 by our sister magazine *Aviation Safety* showed the most—slightly over 37 per cent —involved engine failures. But there seemed to be no particular pattern. Of those in which the problem could be determined, the most—three—occurred after breaks in oil hoses, but all different hoses going to different parts of the aircraft. One engine failure occurred when the oil pump impeller gear broke. This was later the sub-

ject of an Airworthiness Directive, but we noted in a three-year runout of the FAA's Service Difficulty Reports (up through September 1981) at least a dozen problems involving broken oil pump gear teeth.

Landing accidents accounted for the next highest category, with nearly 12 percent, with hard landings and groundloops leading the way in unpleasantness.

Gear Nemesis

As for the traditional nemesis of the Cardinal RG—landing gear problems—the two-year study showed it only third in the rankings along with a host of other problems like fuel management, takeoff accidents and weather-related problems. Nevertheless, failure of the gear to extend or actuator failure brought three RGs to grief.

Our earlier detailed study of 78 Cardinal RG accidents covering the five-year period from 1973 to 1977 showed once again that engine failures predominated, with about 34 percent of the accidents. These

That big carpet-covered hump squarely in the middle of the baggage compartment is not a picnic box, but a receptacle for the retractable main gear. Otherwise, the cabin is gorgeous and roomy.

were seldom fatal. That time, though, gear-up landings and gear collapses and retractions accounted for second place or about 20 percent—or a total of 16 accidents. Some of these were pilot error, however.

Stall/spin/mush accidents in the Cardinal RG were fairly infrequent. In the five-year period there were two in-flight airframe failures. One occurred in weather and was fatal. In the second the pilot overstressed the aircraft and bent the wings, but actually managed to land safely. In general, despite the lack of wing-strengthening struts, the aircraft has a good record of in-flight airframe failures.

Maintenance

Powerplant accessories and brakes were the main problem areas reported on our most recent feedback from Cardinal RG owners.

Cost/Performance/Specifications

Model	Year	Number Built	Average Retail Price	Cruise Speed (mph)	Rate of Climb (fpm)	Useful Load (lbs)	Fuel Std/Opt (gals)	Engine	TBO (hrs)	Overhaul Cost
Cessna 177 RG	1971	213	$18,600	144	860	1,170	50	200-hp Lyc. IO-360-A1B6D	1,800	$8,600
Cessna 177 RG	1972	70	$19,600	148	925	1,155	50	200-hp Lyc. IO-360-A1B6D	1,800	$8,600
Cessna 177 RG	1973	150	$20,600	148	925	1,140	60	200-hp Lyc. IO-360-A1B6D	1,800	$8,600
Cessna 177 RG	1974	160	$22,400	148	925	1,140	60	200-hp Lyc. IO-360-A1B6D	1,800	$8,600
Cessna 177 RG	1975	195	$23,300	148	925	1,120	60	200-hp Lyc. IO-360-A1B6D	1,800	$8,600
Cessna 177 RG	1976	264	$25,400	148	925	1,093	60	200-hp Lyc. IO-360-A1B6D	1,800	$8,600
Cessna 177 RG	1977	215	$27,000	148	925	1,093	60	200-hp Lyc. IO-360-A1B6D	1,800	$8,600
Cessna 177 RG	1978	100	$29,000	148	925	1,106	60	200-hp Lyc. IO-360-A1B6D	1,800	$8,600

Cessna Cardinal RG

But most seemed to feel that maintenance required for the aircraft was reasonable, in general. A recent maintenance survey yielded average hour maintenance costs for the Cardinal RG of around $17 an hour and annual inspection costs averaging a bit under $800. Unscheduled yearly airframe and engine costs together averaged about $600.

We received nowhere near the litany of complaints we did on our last survey several years ago, when owners railed about chronic maintenance problems. Biggest problem areas then were alternator failures, Bendix magneto breakdowns, cracking exhaust pipes, malfunctioning fuel quantity gauges, breaking alternate air induction doors, leaking fuel caps, hot-running engines, landing gear horn malfunctions and malfunctioning landing gear mechanisms, especially hung-up nosegear.

A check of Service Difficulty Reports from 1979 through most of 1981, however, suggests some troublesome areas. A few were: stabilator problems such as loose bolts, worn bushings and cracked brackets; cracked and broken prop spinners; cracked crankcases; broken engine oil pump gear teeth (mentioned before); Bendix magneto failures; and throttle cable malfunctions.

Focus on Landing Gear

Though some owners this time around reported problems with the notoriously quirky landing gear system, the complaints were by no means legion as before. It would appear that the constant focus of attention on the problem by pilots and maintenance shops, and by Cessna's own progressive series of fixes, have diminished its impact significantly. And this comes in the face of the '81 SDR breakdown showing page after page of gear problems. (One must temper this finding, however, with appreciation for the fact that so many of Cessna's *other* retractable-gear aircraft through the years have experienced more than their share of gear problems.)

Through the eight years of its production, the Cardinal had four different landing gear systems, as Cessna strived to correct all its quirks. The first, most problem plagued one on the '71 and '72 Cardinal RGs, was a Rube Goldberg combination of electrical and hydraulic components whose weakest link was its electrically actuated main gear downlocks. The '73 Cardinals got hydraulic downlock actuators that improved reliability. Then on the '74 aircraft the gear selector handle itself was turned into a hydraulic valve and hydraulic pressure was routed not directly but through a panel-mounted valve controlled by the handle. This system also eliminated the remote electrical control unit.

Finally, with the '78 models the 12-volt Prestolite hydraulic power packs were eliminated in favor of a 24-volt power pack of Cessna's design. This has proved to be the most satisfactory of all the systems and, of course, would be the one to choose if cost considerations permit. At any rate, potential buyers should check to see which, if any, of Cessna's recommended service instructions have been applied to whichever model they are looking at. There are at least eight of them, including numbers 71-41, 72-26, 73-28, 74-26, 75-25, 76-4, 76-7 and 77-20.

The aircraft has a rather brief Airworthiness Directive history, with only six ADs against it from 1972 through 1979. And we already mentioned the Lycoming AD (81-18-04) affecting IO-360 engines and calling for replacement of the oil pump impeller and shaft to prevent oil pump failure.

Modifications

Among the STCs published for the Cardinal RG are the following: Wing leading edge cuffs and vortex generators on the vertical stabilizer, by Horton STOL Craft, Wellington, Kans.; chrome-plated brake disc installation, by Engineering Plating & Processing, Kansas City, Kans.; installation of an air/oil separator, by Walker Engineering Co., Los Angeles,

Calif.; and recognition lights on the horizontal stabilizer, by Devore Aviation, Albuquerque, N.M. Also, Silver Instruments and Shadin have STCs for fuel computers.

What to Join

The Cessna Cardinal Club is located at 1701 Saint Andrew's Drive, Lawrence, Kan. 66044 and its president is Beth Harrison. Also, Cardinal owners can contact the Cessna Pilots Assn., P.O. Box 12948, Wichita, Kans. 67277, (316) 721-4313.

Owner Comments

The average cost over the life of my '74 Cardinal RG (purchased when it was one year old) is about $40 to $45 an hour. (That includes direct operating and and fixed costs, flying about 175 hours a year.) This may be higher than average, but I spare no expense on maintenance. The aircraft is maintained by Howard Aircraft Service, at Craig Field in Jacksonville, Fla., and Bob Howard is a real nitpicker. My annuals run from $1,500 to $2,000. My hourly maintenance cost for 1984, the highest ever, worked out to $28.06.

Mechanically, the aircraft has presented only one major problem. Following a fast, no-flap landing, the nose gear collapsed as the aircraft turned off the runway. An improperly adjusted nose gear linkage was found to be at fault. Apparently the aircraft left the factory in that condition and flew for two years before the accident. At normal landing speeds, the hydraulic system apparently could overcome the air pressure on the nose gear. At high speeds this was not the case. Result: a new prop.

Brake pads also were a constant problem. I should have installed chrome disks years ago. Parts, however, are no problem.

I flight plan for 140 knots at about eight to nine gph. It is a fine cross-

Aircraft Resale Value Chart

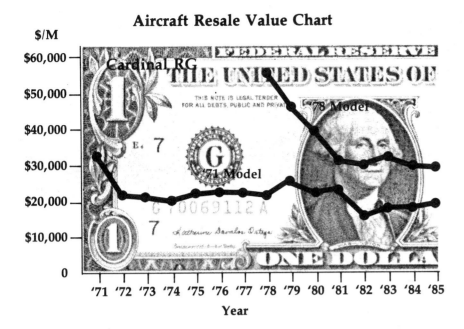

$/M

- $60,000
- $50,000
- $40,000
- $30,000
- $20,000
- $10,000
- 0

Cardinal RG

'78 Model

'71 Model

'71 '72 '73 '74 '75 '76 '77 '78 '79 '80 '81 '82 '83 '84 '85

Year

country machine for my purposes. I usually fly the aircraft with an average of two people aboard. The handling characteristics are outstanding. The controls are firm, crisp and effective. The aircraft has the feel of a much heavier machine, more like a 182 than a 172. The stalls are mild with prompt recovery. The placement of the wing is one of the characteristics of the aircraft that I dearly love, since you are forward of the leading edge, which gives you outstanding visibility.

The avionics are ARC. What more can I say! One of the avionics people that worked on the radios said, "You really have to be wealthy to fly with ARC equipment," and I believe her. I had two problems: finding someone who would work on them, then finding someone whose repairs would hold up until I got back to my home base. I am going to install new avionics following completion of the new paint job.

All in all, I am very fond of the aircraft. Frankly, I don't find any of the aircraft of the same class being marketed today comparable to a Cardinal RG.

John D. Shea, Jr.
St. Augustine, Fla.

Early in 1980 I read *The Aviation Consumer's* Used Airplane Guide

on the Cardinal RG, and decided the aircraft had the performance and range I was looking for. Later that year I bought a 1973 model which had been operated by a flying club in Wisconsin. I selected this particular craft, which had about 2,300 hours on the airframe, because someone had the good sense to install a complete Collins Microline avionics package. This has proven to be a reliable set of equipment during many hours of IFR cross-country flying.

After purchasing the airplane, I gave it new paint, new interior and a zero-time engine and prop. Also, I replaced the horrible plastic instrument panel cover and glove box door with a hardwood panel. The cheap plastic panel does make a good template for laying out its replacement.

The airplane pretty much meets book speeds and delivers 165 mph cruise at 70 percent power. I always plan nine gph from takeoff to touchdown. Sixty gallons works out to six and a half hours of fuel on board. I was surprised that with two on board, it is relatively easy to get to 14,000 feet if you just increase the rpm to 2700 during the climb after leaving 8,000 feet. The book permits this power setting from sea level.

There seems to be a lot of additional power in the last 200 rpm, which is also nice when the bird

starts to collect a little ice. It sees a lot of IFR and is a good IFR aircraft.

On two occasions, the gear down-and-locked indicator would not illuminate without a few cycles of the landing gear. After spending hundreds of dollars at repair stations where they found nothing, I was looking at the connections to the microswitches in the end of the main gear struts during an annual, and found the inline connectors to be loose on the wires. After five minutes with a soldering iron, there have been no more gear indicator problems. I suggest examining these little connectors whenever you have a chance.

I've spent some time trying to reduce the noise level in the airplane even though it is fairly quiet for a single-engine machine. I found that some thin cork with adhesive backing made by Sound Coat of Santa Ana, Calif. applied on top of the glareshield running to the windshield was more effective than other sound absorbent material on the floor or in the ceiling panels, etc.

I had a Walker Engineering Air/Oil Separator added to the engine breather, and this has helped tremendously in keeping the bottom of the airplane clean.

Maintenance on the airplane is not too far out of line. The aircraft has settled into about an $800 annual, with no big surprises during the year except maybe an alternator—due, I feel, to the vibration of the IO-360. Small inspections throughout the year and a hangar have done a lot to keep maintenance costs down.

I was considering moving to a T210 for more speed and the ability to climb up through the clouds here in western Oregon, but the Cardinal RG is much more economical, very comfortable, and has been pretty darn reliable—in five years only two delayed trips—so I plan to keep it for some time.

John Desmond
Vice-president, Engineering
Flight Dynamics, Inc.
Hillsboro, Ore.

Mooney M20

Mooney's M20 series is one of the most enduring elderly aircraft on the used-plane market. More than 4,000 M20s were built between 1955 and 1977, and they are beloved by their owners for their speed and efficiency, if not cabin room. (This article will discuss only the M20s built until 1977, when the M20J and M20K versions—popularly known as the 201 and 231—were introduced.)

History

The M20's history is a complex one, and only fanatical Mooney buffs seem to know all the changes of nomenclature and corporate parentage. We will refer mainly to the type certificate nomenclature (M20A, M20B, etc.) rather than the various labels affixed by succeeding marketing departments.

The first M20 appeared in 1955. It had a 150-hp Lycoming engine and wooden wing and tail, a throwback to the M18 Mite, the all-wood single-placer from which the M20 was derived. In 1958, the M20A was introduced with a 180-hp Lycoming.

The first all-metal Mooney was the 1961 M20B, called the Mark 21. It retained the popular 180-hp engine. The next year, in 1962, gross weight was raised from 2,450 pounds to 2,575, and the designation changed to M20C. The M20C also had electric flaps (M20B's were manual) with 11 degrees more travel, and it had more rudder power. This general configuration (known variously as the Mark 21 and Ranger) was continued until the late 1970s. It is the most economical of the four basic Mooney models.

In 1964, Mooney added a souped-up 200-hp version called the M20E.

It lasted until 1975, and was known as the Super 21 or Chaparral. It is the fastest of the pre-201 Mooneys.

In 1967, Mooney bowed to the wishes of the marketplace and offered a version with a 10-inch stretch in the cabin. This, at last, turned the Mooney into a true four-place airplane. This long-cabin fuselage was offered with the 200-hp engine (M20F Executive) in 1967, and with the 180-hp engine (M20G Statesman) in 1968. The M20G lasted only three years, but the M20F was an immediate hit, selling more than 500 the first year and prompting Mooney to drop the Super 21 for 1968. (It returned as the Chaparral in 1969.) It survived until 1977, providing the starting point for the aero-dynamically refined M20J—the current production 201.

Mooney also made a little-known fixed-gear model, the M20D Master, in 1963 and 1964. It was simply a fixed-gear version of the 180-hp M20C. Nearly all Masters have been converted to retractable gear, however. The economic argument is compelling; a Master is worth about $13,000, and it costs about $3,000 to convert it to retractable gear. The result, virtually an M20C, is worth about $18,000. Now you know why there are so few original Masters. In any case, if you are shopping for a 1963-64 so-called Mark 21, check the serial

The Executive has a longer cabin and an extra window. This is a 1975 model built by Republic, and today worth about $26,000.

number plate to assure that it is not in fact a converted Master.

Adding to the confusion of all the model changes were several changes of ownership. The original Mooney Aircraft Corp. was eventually taken over by Butler Aviation in 1969—just in time for a big recession that severely depressed aircraft sales. Butler didn't help itself much; among other things, it attempted to jazz up the Mooney's looks by grafting a bizarre-looking appendage to the top of the tail. This triggered widespread derision and immediately became known as the "Butler buttonhook." Few, if any, survive. After selling less than 50 planes in 1971, Butler folded its tent, and it wasn't until three years later that Republic Steel came to the rescue and bought the line. Production resumed in 1974, setting the stage for the introduction of the 201 in 1977 and the company's ascent to the dominance of the four-place retractable market that it holds today. Then, in 1984, the firm was purchased by a partnership led by, Alexandre Couvelaire, head of Euralair of Paris, along with Armand Rivard, president of Lake Aircraft. Production of the Mooneys continues at Kerrville.

Best and Worst

Mooney connoisseurs tell us the best Mooneys ever built were the 1966-67 models. These had most of the airplane's desirable features—the square windows, flush-riveted wing, retractable step, optional manual landing gear (preferred for its simplicity by many Mooney nuts), good corrosion-proofing and the "wide-deck" engines. "The 1966 E models seem to have the smoothest wings I ever saw," comments long-time Mooney mechanic Charlie Dugosh. The long-cabin Executive also became available for the first time in 1967.

Around 1968, the company started running into financial problems, partly due to the disastrous M-22 Mustang program, and partly due to some financial chicanery that eventually landed the company president and secretary/treasurer in prison for 13 counts of fraud. The company was sold to American Electronics Laboratory in 1968, and to Butler Aviation a year later. Both companies naturally tried to cut down on expenses, and the 1968-1971 Mooneys showed signs of economizing: fixed steps, round-head rivets on the under side of the wing leading edge, exposed inspection plates, reduced corrosion-proofing, etc. As a result, Butler-built Mooneys were consistently two to four knots slower than the earlier models. And reliable sources tell us that some Butler-built airplanes had improperly shaped wing curvature, due to lack of attention to detail in the jigging/building process. This had no structural effect, but could disrupt laminar airflow and increase drag noticeably. Mooney modifier Coy Jacob says he's seen one Butler-built airplane that flew 13 knots slower than an otherwise identical earlier model. If you're considering a 1968-1971 model, flight test it carefully to make sure performance is up to snuff.

Beware of Wood

If the 1966-67 models were the cream of the crop, the dregs were certainly the early wooden Mooneys. We can sum up our view on the wooden-tailed airplanes very succinctly: don't buy one. One Mooney expert we consulted took a slightly softer position: "Well, I suppose if you wanted a unique-looking flower planter for your front yard, it would be all right."

The M20 and M20A have the worst record of in-flight breakups of any airplane, almost entirely the result of failures of the wing and tail. A prohibitively expensive AD requires a pull-test of the vertical fin every six months, at a cost of $500 or more. (To put that cost in perspective, the whole airplane is only worth about $9,000.)

Some mechanics doubt the AD's effectiveness. Mooney guru Charles Dugosh says, "I won't do the pull test. You could break a glue joint without even knowing it, and later you'd have a catastrophe. I won't do any work at all on a wood-tail airplane. I don't want my signature anywhere in the logbook."

As a result of the AD, most M20s and M20As have been retrofitted with metal tails, at a cost of about $5,000. This still leaves the question of wooden wings, however. The wood-wingers are the cheapest of the old Mooneys, and very likely have been left outside in the weather by an owner who couldn't afford hangar rent. An AD on the wooden wing requires a yearly inspection (about five hours of labor). Dugosh believes that a *properly inspected* wooden wing will not fail prematurely. But finding a mechanic who's intimately familiar with wooden Mooney wings and knows where to look for the tell-tale signs of wood rot could be a problem. We'd advise buying a wood-wing Mooney only with extreme caution, and only if it passes the careful scrutiny of a mechanic with long experience looking at wooden Mooney wings.

Appraisal Points

• Windows: Curved side windows are the hallmark of a truly elderly Mooney. In 1965, they were replaced by square ones. That was fine for the rear seat passengers, who got more visibility to help cure the claustrophobia of the rear seats, but the pilot's visibility actually declined out both the side front window and the windshield. Nevertheless, the square windows are the most obvious way to tell very old Mooneys from merely old ones.

• Landing Gear: Early Mooneys had manually operated landing gear. Electric gear became available in 1966, and standard in 1969. Surprisingly, most owners of manual-gear Mooneys seem to prefer them that way. "I love the simplicity and reliability of the manual gear," one Super 21 owner wrote. Maintenance and inspection costs on the gear should also be less. A manual-to-electric conversion kit is available, but not many are sold. According to one Mooney dealer we talked to, the manual-gear airplanes sell for just as much—if not more—than comparable electric-gear airplanes. Nevertheless, the

Performance/Specifications

Model	Gross Weight (lbs)	Cruise Speed (kts)*	Fuel (gals)	Engine	TBO** (hrs)	Overhaul Cost
M20	2,450	143	35/52	150-hp Lyc. O-320	2,000	$6,000
M20A	2,450	157	35/52	180-hp Lyc. O-360-A1A	2,000	$7,000
M20B	2,450	158	52	180-hp Lyc. O-360-A1A	2,000	$7,000
M20C	2,575	143-158	52	180-hp Lyc. O-360-A1D	2,000	$7,000
M20E	2,575	160-163	52	200-hp Lyc. O-360-A1A	1,800	$9,000
M20F	2,740	156	64	200-hp Lyc. IO-360-A1A	1,800	$9,000

* *Book cruise speeds are considered optimistic in early models.*
** *TBO assumes half-inch valves in 180-hp engines (1,200 hours if not); and large dowel pins and updated camshaft in 200-hp engines (1,200 and 1,400 hours if not).*

manual gear does take a hefty heave, and is not recommended for small or weak pilots. "It's a barrel of laughs to watch even a contortionist try to raise the gear the first few times," one owner writes. "A veteran manual-gear Mooney pilot could probably scratch his right elbow with his deformed and scarred right hand."

• Instrument Panel: Through 1968, Mooney panels were awful, from 1969-71 merely mediocre; and from 1975-77, pretty good. Several companies refit instrument panels, however, and many older aircraft have improved panels. Try to find one.

• Engine: Early 180-hp Mooneys used the O-360-A1A; in 1962, the switch was made to the -A1D version, which had the "shower of sparks" magneto. Until about 1965, that engine had a 1,200-hour TBO, but larger valves extended TBO to 2,000 hours. Make sure the engine has been updated with the larger half-inch valves.

The 200-hp engine has been the IO-360-A1A since the beginning, but early versions proved troublesome. Check that any M20E or -F considered for purchase has been overhauled with improved connecting rods (Service Bulletin 439) and large main bearing dowel pins (S.B. 326). Lycoming also recommends that the camshafts in early IO-360s be replaced (Service Instruction 1263), but one big overhaul shop told us they've seen no difference in service life between the two camshafts. The updated part, however, does allow a 200-hour TBO extension.

Generally speaking, the 180-hp Lycoming engine is one of the two or three most reliable aircraft engines currently in production. The IO-360, although uprated somewhat, also has a pretty good record, assuming that the aforementioned updates have been made.

• PC: A unique feature called Positive control (or PC) was standard on Mooneys for a while in the 1960s. PC was simply a full-time wing-leveler autopilot linked to the electric turn coordinator. A button on the yoke allowed it to be disengaged for maneuvering. But unless the button is depressed, the airplane will fly more or less straight with its wings level.

Theoretically, this is a fine safety feature, and may well play a role in the Mooney's extraordinarily low rate of in-flight airframe failure. (Most breakups are triggered by the pilot's losing control of the aircraft and diving into a high-speed spiral.) But some Mooney pilots dislike PC intensely, and go to great lengths to defeat it. (A rubber band to hold down the button is a popular ploy.) Our advice: stifle your macho pilot tendencies and look for an airplane with PC installed and operating.

Performance

Here is the big selling point of the old M20 line. The hot performer of the group is the 200-hp short-cabin M20E, whose owners report cruise speeds of around 140-150 knots on a fuel burn of about 10 gph. The 180-hp M20Cs are generally about four to nine knots slower, as are the long-cabin M20F and M20G.

Several owners commented that the 180-hp Mooneys are underpowered near gross weight. "It doesn't exactly snap your neck on takeoff," comments one owner. Perhaps recognizing this, Mooney lowered the gross weight of the 180-hp long-cabin M20G by 50 pounds, perhaps assuming that since there was finally room to put a couple of big people back there, overloading would be more likely.

Listed climb rate ranges from a rather mediocre 800 fpm for some M20C models to 1,125 for the M20E. Book cruise speeds range from 143 to 163 knots, but these are hopelessly optimistic. We're told that in those days Mooney fudged its speed figures by measuring them at very light weights. Airspeed calibration was also questionable.

Mooney owners prize the airplane's efficiency, with fuel burns of only about 8-9 gph for the 180-hp models and 9-10 gph for the 200-hp versions. Fuel capacity is 52 gallons in most models. (Exceptions are the M20 and M20A, which had 35 gallons standard and 52 optional, and the M20F Executive, which carries 64 gallons.) The M20C with full tanks is good for about five hours cruising with a small reserve, or about 750 miles. The 200-hp Mooneys can fly about the same distance in a little less time.

Safety

The M20 has a good—but not excellent—safety record. According to an *Aviation Consumer* study covering the years 1972-76, the Mooney ranked fifth among the 13 most popular single-engine retractables. Its fatal accident rate was 2.4 per 100,000 flight hours. (The range among the other 12 aircraft was 1.0 to 4.2.) Total accident rate was 11.3, in a range of 4.6 to 16.8.

According to an NTSB report covering the same period, the M20 ranked about average in engine failures, overshoots and undershoots, and good or excellent in stalls, in-flight airframe failures, ground loops and hard landings. In no category listed by the NTSB did the Mooney rank poorly.

For owners concerned about airframe integrity, the Mooney is virtually in a class by itself. We're aware of only two fatal in-flight airframe failures in the past two decades. Legend has it that Republic Steel, before it bought the line in the early 1970s, decided to test a wing to destruction just to see how strong it was. What they ended up doing was testing the test rig to destruction; the hydraulic jacks finally broke at 11 Gs, with the wing doing just fine. The fuselage is also practically bulletproof; a steel roll cage surrounds the cabin, in addition to the normal aluminum airframe. Such quaint conservatism of design would be considered too expensive and heavy these days, but we don't hear too many Mooney owners complaining.

The Mooney's great structural strength is no surprise; one of the structural designers who converted the original wooden Mooney to the all-metal configuration was Ralph Harmon. (Harmon was also president of the company for a time.) Harmon had also played a major role in the structural design of the Beech V-tail Bonanza, whose old models have the highest fatal in-flight break-up rate of any metal airplane, and none come under fire for alleged structural shortcomings in the wings (early 1947-48 models) and tail. Apparently Harmon learned his lesson, and an "overbuilt" Mooney is the result.

Creature Comforts

In a word, they're lousy. Only the M20F Executive and M20G Statesman are what we'd call real four-adult airplanes—and large folks might even argue with that. The short cabin airplanes (M20, M20A, M20B, M20C, M20E) are horribly cramped in back. "The plane is excellent for one or two people, but when long-legged front occupants slide the seats all the way back, it gives the impression the rear seats were designed for double amputees," comments one Ranger owner. Cabin noise is very high, as it is in virtually any old plane. (Or new one, for that matter.) Wear your E-A-R plugs.

Handling Qualities

While generally a decent-flying machine, the Mooneys do have some odd qualities. Pilots generally describe the aileron controls as stiff (perhaps the result of the pushrod linkage). Response is quick, however, despite the high forces. The airplane is reasonably stable and makes a decent instrument ship, particularly with the PC feature. Without the PC, though, "You really gotta fly it IFR," reports one owner.

The long-body M20F Executive and M20G Statesman should theoretically be more stable because of their extra length. (If the tail is moved farther away from the wing, stability generally improves.) Stall characteristics can be abrupt, and you certainly wouldn't want to spin one, either accidentally or on purpose. Compared to an Arrow, Skylane or Cardinal, a Mooney is not a good staller.

Landings can be tricky if the pilot doesn't use the right technique. (This is complicated by the rather mediocre flaps, which make steep approaches impossible.) Owners tell us that 65 knots is about the right approach speed, never any faster than 70. At light weights, even 60 knots leaves plenty of energy for the flare. Some pilots pop the flaps up during the flare, but this is unnecessary if approach speed is on target.

Landing gear and flap extension speeds are very low, which limits the pilot's flexibility during descent, particularly with the manual gear. One owner reports it's virtually impossible to operate the manual gear much above 80 knots. Because of the Mooney's relatively clean airframe and high-aspect-ratio wing, rapid descents are difficult without overcooling the engine.

Crosswind capability is only fair. Very early models (M20, -A and -B) had more limited rudder travel and even less crosswind ability—only about 12 knots, according to one owner.

The Mooneys are rather awkward on the ground. "It takes about 40 acres to turn one around," comments one owner. Mooneys are also somewhat skittery on takeoff, although any competent pilot will adjust quickly.

Maintenance

The average mechanic will groan

Mooney cowling is a mechanic's—and an aerodynamicist's—nightmare.

when an old Mooney rolls into the hangar door for maintenance. The planes were not designed to be easy to work on. The cowling, for example, is attached with hundreds of screws; unfastening them all takes a lot of mechanic's time (and owner's money). Engine access is difficult because of the tight cowling, and working behind the instrument panel can be a nightmare.

Mooneys are not as common as Cessnas and Pipers, and the average mechanic may not be familiar with them. Advises one owner, "Find a good Mooney mechanic—otherwise, you'll be paying for a lot of on-the-job training." We echo that advice: the Mooney is one airplane that should not be taken to any old mechanic. If there's a Mooney specialist in your area, seek him out. In the case of a wooden M20 or M20A, our advice would be even stronger: Entrusting your airplane to a mechanic who doesn't have long years of experience with wooden Mooneys could be fatal.

The premier Mooney maintenance center in the country is Charles Dugosh Aviation in Kerrville, Tex. Dugosh has worked on Mooneys for decades, and is based right on the same airport as Mooney headquarters, and so has a very close working relationship with the factory. If the factory learns something about maintenance, it's likely that Dugosh will know it a day later.

We've also received good reports on Wittenbrook Flying Service, Barnsville, Ohio; Coast Aircraft in San Diego; Aero Venture, Robbinsville, N.J. and Wilmar Aviation, Wilmar, Minn. Mooney service centers in the Northeast are Conn Mooney, Danbury, Conn. and Weber Aircraft in Lancaster, Pa.

Service Problems

Letters from Mooney owners and FAA service difficulty reports highlight several areas of concern for the used-Mooney shopper. Among them:

• Leaky fuel tanks. The fuel sealant in the tanks of older Mooneys, designed for 91- and 100-octane fuel, apparently breaks down after long contact with 100LL fuel, which is high in aromatics. This has created a real problem for Mooney owners, many of whom have had to reseal their tanks. ("And those that haven't, will," comments one Mooney expert.) Any Mooney shopper should check very carefully for leaks. A reseal job can cost anywhere from $500 to $3,000, and it's difficult to do the job right.

• Dented or broken nose gear struts. The Mooney nose gear design allows very limited nosewheel steering travel before something bends or breaks. Unfortunately, the nation's linemen don't seem to have gotten the message yet, and towing limits are routinely exceeded.

• Corroded fuselage tubes. Although not widespread, some cases of tube corrosion have been reported, primarily in the lower longerons. Replacement can be hideously expensive; one owner reports he spent over $6,000 replacing corroded tubes. Moral: check carefully before buying.

• Hartzell prop AD. This hated directive is not limited to Mooneys, of course, but is nevertheless a major expense. The AD requires a complete prop overhaul every four years. Initial date of the AD was 1977, and the first wave of repeat overhauls is already past, with the next one due in 1985 on many aircraft. Incidentally, the M20B model has a McCauley prop and is not subject to the AD.

Modifications

The "modifications" section of most of our used-plane reports merits only a paragraph or two, but the Mooney is different. M20 loyalists have developed a vast array of mechanical and cosmetic modifications that can turn virtually any old Mooney into a very good approximation of a 201. The mods include

This 1964 Super 21 sports the round windows that are the tipoff to the truly ancient Mooneys.

a bewildering array of fairings, seals, covers, windows, windshields, and cowlings that can boost speed by up to 17 knots and make the plane look virtually brand-new. You can drop $15,000 so fast it'll make your head spin.

There are two main purveyors of Mooney mods. Summa Sales, Inc., 4551 Commerce, High Ridge, Mo. 63049, 800-325-9445, offers a 201-style cowling ($7,200), a 201-style windshield ($2,097), 201-style instrument panel ($4,375), a speed fairing and gap seal kit ($1,975) and other smaller mods. Coy Jacobs, head of the self-proclaimed "Mooney Mod Squad" has a gorgeous 1967 M20E that is virtually indistinguishable from a new Mooney 201—and flies even faster, according to Jacobs. Reports we've received describe the workmanship on these mods as excellent.

Another modifier is Paul Loewen of Lake Aero Styling and Repair, Box 545, Lakeport, Calif. 95453, 707-263-0412. Lake likewise has a 201-style cowling and windshield, but no instrument panel. Lake also offers a dozen different aerodynamic mods that, in combination with the cowling and windshield, provide 201-like performance. The third firm offering Mooney mods is Miller Air Sports, San Marcos, Tex. 78666, 512-353-7422. Miller offers a 201-type cowling and a 201-style windshield. Summa- and Lake-modified 201s earned awards at the

national Mooney fly-in in 1981 and 1982.

McCauley Aviation, Pine Bluff, Ark., sells a speed fairing kit and chrome brake discs.

Owner Club

The Mooney Aircraft Pilots' Association is one of the best of the owner group/fan clubs. They publish a monthly (rather primitive) newsletter, hold regional and annual conventions, and, most importantly, can provide sound advice on service problems. Any owner should know as much as possible about his airplane; even if you disdain the rah-rah Mooney boosterism and down-home good fellowship, we'd recommend joining the MAPA simply for its pool of knowledge about maintenance problems. Mooney aircraft Pilots Association, 314 Stardust Dr., San Antonio, Tex. 78228; 512-434-5959.

Owner Comments

In deciding to purchase our 1965 "C" model Mooney, I rejected all earlier models because they used machine screws rather than quick-release Dzus fasteners to attach the cowling and they had "old-style" windows. I also liked the smaller cooling-air inlet used in 1965 compared with the later models. The '65-'67 models also have superior flush riveting and fasteners, a vacuum-retract step, cowl flaps, and smooth elevator and rudder skins. The manual gear and hydraulic flaps are elegantly simple.

The older short-fuselage Mooneys respond beautifully to the same aerodynamic clean-up and attention to detail that the 210s and 231s received. Modifications to N1PF include Mooney 201 flap gap fairings, flap hinge fairings, horizontal stabilizer root fairing, and a plexiglass landing light fairing that were installed in accordance with John Porter's STC. Aileron lower gap seals, brake rotation, a 231 style dorsal fin, and hinge covers for the rudder and elevator were also installed in accordance with Paul Lowen's STC. Other modifications included cleaning up the antennas, removing the belly strobe and replacing it with wingtip strobes, removing the OAT gauge, installing a 201 tail skid, and re-rigging the flaps and ailerons. These modifications netted a speed increase of at least 10 knots.

As much as I like our Mooney, I do curse some during maintenance procedures such as replacing a starter motor, resealing fuel tanks, adjusting the trim stops on the horizontal stabilizer, or removing the hundreds of screws that fasten access panels. Lubricated stainless steel screws help somewhat, but a power assisted screwdriver is essential.

Expert advice regarding Mooney maintenance is readily available. At the Mooney factory, Ed Penney is very knowledgeable and helpful. Mooney Service Centers such as Charlie Dugosh, on the Kerrville airport, and Paul Lowen's "Lake Aero Styling and Repair," at Lakeport, Calif., are outstanding.

Many Mooney fuel tanks do leak avgas. I attribute this problem primarily to 100LL avgas and I avoid it like the plague. Our right wing tank leaked like a sieve when we bought our plane. I resealed it several years ago using the methods and materials specified in the Mooney maintenance manual and it has sealed perfectly since then. Resealing the fuel tanks is not particularly difficult but it is very tedious and time consuming. I found it too depressing to keep

track of the time I spent, but it was about 100 hours for one wing. There is no substitute for removing *all* the old sealant. This means physically scraping around all rivets and fasteners. Solvents, such as MEK, are not useful, and they could cause problems later if they seep into the cracks and attack the new sealant from the underside. My main sustaining thought while resealing the tank was that the only thing worse than resealing it the first time would be redoing the job if it were not done properly.

One of my highest priority maintenance items is periodically checking and adjusting the preload that holds the landing gear linkage in its "over-center" position that maintains the landing gear in the down-and-locked position. The Service and Maintenance Manual (section S.F. 2&3) and Service Bulletin M20-35A describe how to measure and adjust the preload.

Our records show that we have spent $5,942.60 maintaining our aircraft during the last 602.7 hours of flight for a cost of $9.86/hr.

Pilots of carbureted Mooneys should pay careful attention to Mooney's Service Bulletin M20-64 and Service Instruction M20-14. They detail inspection and maintenance procedures for the carburetor heat box. We had owned our airplane less than one

year when our butterfly broke loose and blocked the carburetor air inlet. The engine was running at cruise power and sucked up the loose valve, and it blocked the air inlet. The engine would lose about 500 rpm before the valve would drop, and the cycle would repeat.

The ground-handling qualities of the aircraft are definitely inferior to the flight-handling qualities. The neoprene rubber discs that Mooney uses to absorb the shock of normal taxiing and landing are undamped and require some pilot adaptation. The turning radius of a Mooney is large. Mooney pilots seem to accept the inferior ground handling qualities presumably because of the many good features of the airplane.

I would particularly recommend pre-201 Mooneys to pilots who are both mechanically inclined and who value the speed and efficiency benefits enough to outweigh the annoyance of maintaining items inside the compact airframe.

Maurice McEvoy
Berkeley, Calif.

Our Statesman Flying Club has operated a 1968 Mooney M20G Statesman for five years and finds it the ideal aircraft for our use. It travels at 140 knots and burns 8.3 gph, the perfect combination for economical trips or training and

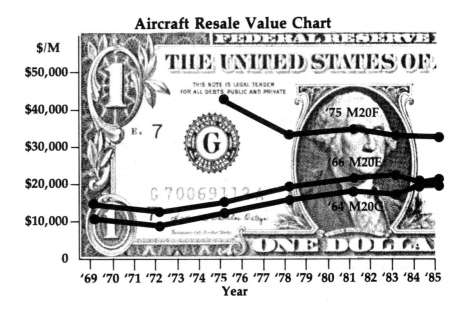

Aircraft Resale Value Chart

practice. What's more, it has the long body (10 inches more in the rear seat than the C&E models), the supremely reliable carbureted O-360 engine, the ease and assurance of the "PC" wing leveler and, best of all, the failure-proof manual gear. It is exquisitely designed and crafted, although mechanics often curse the cramped engine compartment.

Our plane flies 300 hours per year and has cost 8, 6, 9, 7, and 10 dollars per hour for maintenance in each of the respective years we've run it, for an average of $8 per hour. This includes minimal avionics repair (about $0.75 per hour) as well as semi-annual inspections. The inspection labor runs about $400 and the associated repairs typically lift the cost to $800. Thus, the other $800 per year in maintenance is unscheduled. The engine was overhauled last spring by Lycon in Mesa, Ariz. for less than $5,000 using Superior parts and has performed admirably in its first 75 hours, using one quart of oil each 12 hours after ring seating on the chrome cylinders.

Periodically we think of replacement, but there is no competition. The Tiger is extinct, the Arrow is not as efficient, the Archer slow and the Cessna RGs lack quality. Even the Mooney 201 is not as economical as our '68, and it only completes a one-bladder trip a half-hour quicker. I only hope our Statesman can fly on as long as there's avgas.

R.B. Sherwood
Torrance, Calif.

I have owned a 1965 Mooney M20C for the past three years. It is a

Tubular construction is used in the front half of the Mooneys, semi-monocoque in the rear. Check for corrosion in the lower longerons.

strong, comfortable IFR airplane that turns out 145 knots TAS at nine gallons an hour and gives a nominal range of 550 nm with IFR reserves. The useful load with full fuel (52 gallons) is 682 pounds, even though it is well equipped for IFR.

For a 180-hp airplane, the Mooney M20C exceeds or matches the real-world performance of all the current 200-hp retractables except for the Mooney 201. I chose it, in large part, based on articles in *The Aviation Consumer* over the years and because of the Lycoming O-360-A1D engine, which is well characterized as very reliable.

My first annual cost $982 plus two days of my own work. However, this included several overdue repairs: new main gear shock discs, air box rebuild, brake pads, new tail pivot bolts, oil return line, strobe toggle switch and shimmy dampener rebuild.

The next two annuals averaged $283 plus two days of my own labor. I have managed to keep the inspection costs in line by promptly correcting problems as they arise. Fortunately I have an A&P friend who has been willing to supervise and sign off my work when it has been within my own capabilities.

The manual gear is great. A little learning is required, but once mastered it seems very natural. At the annual inspection it is neces-

Cost Comparison

Model	Year	Average Number Built	Retail Price*
M20	1955-58	200	$ 9,000**
M20A	1958-60	500	$11,000**
M20B	1961	222	$16,000
M20C	1962	336	$17,000
(Mark 21,	1963	328	$18,000
Ranger)	1964	183	$18,000
	1965	379	$19,000
	1966	280	$19,000
	1967	147	$20,000
	1968	196	$20,000
	1969	97	$21,000
	1970	88	$22,000
	1971	9	$23,000
	1974	37	$25,000
	1975	39	$26,000
	1976	33	$27,000
	1977	25	$29,000
	1978	15	$30,000
M20E	1964	368	$19,000
(Super 21,	1965	361	$20,000
Chaparral)	1966	474	$19,000
	1967	62	$20,000
	1969	73	$23,000
	1970	54	$25,000
	1971	23	$26,000
	1974	36	$28,000
	1975	19	$29,000
M20F	1967	539	$24,000
(Executive)	1968	206	$25,000
	1969	92	$26,000
	1970	72	$27,000
	1971	12	$28,000
	1974	65	$30,000
	1975	126	$32,000
	1976	126	$33,000
	1977	6	$35,000
M20G	1968	164	$21,000
(Statesman)	1969	20	$22,000
	1970	6	$23,000

* Price assumes dual navcom, VOR, glide slope, marker beacon, transponder, ADF single-axis autopilot, mid-time engine, good paint and interior, no damage history. Subtract 15-20 percent for wholesale prices.
** Price assumes aircraft has been converted to metal tail.

sary to check the over-center gear lock torque during the retract test. This requires only a few minutes.

The scheduled maintenance works out to $516 per year and unscheduled to $491 per year. Total maintenance works out to $12.58 per hour, not counting avionics.

Tim Jensen
Minneapolis, Minn.

Used Aircraft Guide

Cessna Skylane RG

Cessna's Skylane RG—a retractable-gear version of the old standby Skylane—is one of Cessna's success stories. The RG was introduced in 1978, with a turbocharged version coming on the scene in 1979. The RG had a rousing initial sales success, with nearly 2,000 sold by mid-1981, and a goodly number of Skylane RGs turn up on the used-plane market.

It is a good all-around airplane that wins praise from its owners for the big things—performance, comfort and engine reliability—but draws fire for myriad mechanical and quality control problems. A used-plane buyer who manages to avoid a lemon will probably be very satisfied with his Skylane RG.

History

The Skylane RG's history is without major changes. The fixed-gear Skylane has been around since the mid-50s, of course, and the retractable six-place 210 Centurion almost as long. But Cessna didn't fill the gap with the Skylane RG until 1978. Visually, the RG looked exactly like a Skylane from the belly up, but Cessna made a major change under the cowling: instead of the six-cylinder 230-hp Continental O-470 that had powered the Skylane for two decades, Cessna installed a brand-new engine, the Lycoming O-540-J3C5P, a de-rated powerplant that delivered 235 hp at just 2400 rpm. That turned out to be an excellent decision by Cessna; the big Lycoming has turned in a fine record so far, without the cylinder problems that have plagued the O-470 over the years (particularly the -S model in '75-'77 Skylanes). The Skylane RG uses basically the same "wounded-grasshopper" landing gear as in the 210 and the old Cardinal RG, without gear doors.

Save for the addition of the Turbo model in 1979, there have been few major changes in the RG. Perhaps the biggest is a 12-gal. boost in fuel capacity, from 76 to 88 usable, in 1979. But minor changes abound, for the RG has had more than its share of mechanical problems. In addition to correcting these defects, Cessna has in most cases offered retrofit kits to update older aircraft. How completely a used Skylane RG has been updated and modified may well be the single most important factor in how pleased a used-RG buyer is with his purchase. Year-to-year changes are thus not very important, and a buyer might be better off buying an older airplane that is near the "trough" of its depreciation curve (assuming, of course, the older plane is updated with all available service kits).

Resale Market

Despite the current soft market for single-engine aircraft, demand for Skylane RGs is high. "Resale is very good on those planes," one big broker told us. "A '79 RG is worth almost as much right now as it was three years ago." The typical depreciation pattern for most aircraft shows a bottoming out after four or five years, with a leveling off or slight increase thereafter. The Skylane RG bottomed out after only two to three years.

Incidentally, the RGs "real" depreciation is probably not as great

Skylane RG is Cessna's most successful new single in years, and they are now showing up on the used-plane market.

as indicated in our charts nearby. The listed "new" price is Cessna's factory list price, which virtually nobody pays. Older RGs were similarly discounted when they were new, so the '78 RG listed in our charts at $64,000 actually had a real value of only about $54,000 new.

Performance

The Skylane RG offers a fine combination of speed, range and payload. While it's no Mooney, the RG turns in respectable speed numbers: about 150-155 knots for the standard RG and 5 to 10 knots faster for the Turbo RG, depending on altitude. One Turbo owner reports 178 knots on only 66 percent power, at 19,000 feet and light weights. Owners typically report the airplane delivers book cruise speeds or better, even at gross weights. (The book calls for a max cruise of 156 knots for the RG, 173 knots for the Turbo at high altitudes.)

The Skylane RG has one odd characteristic noticed by *Aviation Consumer* pilots and confirmed by several owners: at light weights, the RG flies noticeably faster, with speed increases up to eight knots reported. One RG owner has studied this phenomenon carefully and reports a predictable increase of two knots for every 100 pounds below gross weight. No one is sure why this is so, but our guess is those gaping wheel wells. At higher angles of attack, air may spill into them, causing a lot of drag, but at the flatter angles for light-weight cruising, the slipstream may slide over the wells undisturbed.

With 235 hp up front, the RG climbs well, about 1,140 fpm at sea level, according to the book. The turbo version can maintain full power all the way to 20,000 feet, and is therefore an energetic climber at all altitudes. Reports one owner, "I have climbed through 14,000 feet with an inch of ice at 900 fpm, and I'm here to tell you this is the true value of a strong turbocharged engine." The great reserves of power in the big-displacement detuned RG engine were praised by several owners.

Range is also good; the big 88-gal. tanks hold enough fuel for at least six hours flying at high cruise speeds. One owner reports he can fly 7½ hours at 145 knots, with a very conservative IFR range of 800 nautical miles.

Loading

One of the best selling points about the RGs is their ability to fly a long way with the cabin full. "It's a true four-place-and-baggage aircraft," one owner reports. Typical useful load of an IFR-equipped Skylane RG is about 1,200 pounds, which allows four standard people and full tanks and still leaves room enough for 50-100 pounds of baggage. "The loading flexibility is superb," reports one '79 RG owner. "Mine will take 340 pounds in the front seats, 400 pounds in the rear seats, 200 pounds in the baggage area and a little over four hours worth of fuel, and still be within gross weight and c.g. limits."

Handling

Owners report the RG's in-flight handling is pretty much standard Skylane: rock solid, with fairly heavy control forces in all axes. This is of course fine for IFR flying but does little for a pilot's fighter-

Up front is one of the airplane's strong points: the sturdy, reliable Lycoming O-540 engine.

jock fantasies and can present problems during gusty crosswind landings. The huge flaps allow steep descents and short landings without excessive float. One owner writes, "The RG is a bit stiffer at cruise than the straight-leg 182 because of the higher indicated airspeed, and 182s tend to feel heavy in general. My RG is no exception, although a good lube job on the hinges and other moving parts helped greatly at the last annual."

The RG's takeoff and landing characteristics are somewhat different than the standard Skylane's, according to some owners. The RG, with its different landing gear, sits on the ground with its nose at a slightly higher angle than the old Skylanes. This increases the tendency to "wheelbarrow" on the nosewheel on landing and takeoff, particularly in crosswinds. (Perhaps it's no coincidence that RGs have had terrible shimmy damper problems with the nosewheel. More on that later.)

Creature Comforts

The Skylanes have always been known for big, roomy cabins, and the RGs carry on the tradition. Rear-seat legroom is especially good. Unfortunately, the little amenities that make the cabin so much nicer are either missing altogether or rarely work. Owners complain that the rear air vents fall out in their hands, and windshield leaks allow cold drafts, rain and annoying slipstream noise. "The heater is a joke," sneers one owner of a Turbo RG who flies high in the

wintertime. "It's ski-parka time for the passengers." Several owners also complained about noise, although this is a shortcoming of virtually all light aircraft. (The Turbo RG, with its muffled exhaust, is somewhat quieter than the standard RG.) Overall, however, the RGs are more comfortable than most. One owner comments, "With the articulating seats in front, I have found four- and five-hour legs to be okay, and have spent several days with eight to 10 hours in the airplane that left me none the worse for wear."

Operating Costs

The Skylane RG's speed, room and load-carrying abilities come at no small price: rather high fuel consumption and the extra maintenance headache of retractable gear. Owners report fuel consumption ranging from 11 to 14 gph, depending on power setting and leaning procedures. A typical setting is about 12 gph at 65 percent power. (The turbo model will burn about half a gallon more per hour at equivalent power settings.) At today's fuel prices, we're talking at least $20 per hour for fuel alone—no small sum.

Maintenance costs of course vary all over the lot, depending on luck and aircraft usage. Flat-rate annual inspections for the RGs run about $400-$600 (assuming no discrepancies) with actual total costs running typically $200 to $500 more for needed repairs. Four owners who kept careful track of maintenance costs reported hourly figures of $5.00, $6.29, $8.12 and $8.75. We should caution that these figures took into account warranty help from Cessna. Used-plane buyers, out from under the warranty umbrella, might count on higher hourly costs. On the other hand, once past the initial de-bugging period (and the RGs seem to have a lot of bugs), maintenance costs may well be less.

Predictable engine costs are fairly reasonable. The 235-hp Lycoming has a 2,000-hour TBO and a typical field overhaul cost of about $10,250, for an hourly engine reserve of $5.13.

Maintenance Checkpoints

The Skylane RGs have a large number of chronic problems that every RG buyer should be aware of. Here is a list of the more critical ones, as gleaned from owner reports and FAA service difficulty files:

• Balky throttles. This has been a notorious problem that defied a complete solution for a long time. A grand total of five different service bulletins and modifications kits were issued to combat the problem (SE-79-18, 79-38, 80-13, 80-36 and 81-7), and any used RG should have all those applicable mod kits installed. If you have to do all these mods after you buy the airplane, it can run into big money; one kit alone costs $120 for parts and is described by an owner as a "first class bitch to install," requiring 12 hours of shop labor.

• Shimmy dampeners. Many owners reported problems. "The shimmy can ferocious," commented one RG owner, "and caused a failure of the shimmy mounting bracket on the strut assembly." Cessna Service Bulletin 80-67 offers a modification kit ($170 plus labor); make sure any RG you buy has the kit installed. And still check carefully for nosewheel shimmy.

• Turn coordinator. Virtually every RG owner who responded to our survey mentioned premature turn coordinator failures. Most said they'd replaced theirs several times. (We're not aware of any Cessna service bulletins on this

Smaller tires make the RG less suitable for rough strips than the standard Skylane.

matter.) Check the service history of any RG you buy; it appears the turn coordinator is simply a defective design that is doomed to fail in a few hours—not a comforting thought, considering the abysmal reliability of dry vacuum pumps, to which the coordinators are supposed to serve as backup.

• Cabin air leaks. Several owners reported gaping leaks around the windshield and wing roots, resulting in frigid cabins and water-logged carpets. Two service bulletins address this subject (80-58 and 80-15), calling for a new improved sealant to be applied in certain critical areas.

• Erratic manifold pressure and fuel pressure gauges. Owners often wrote of their exasperation with these instruments, which failed repeatedly. In late 1980, Cessna finally came out with an im-

proved gauge; check to see if it is installed (Service Bulletins SE-80-77 and SE-80-92). Be prepared for an expensive retrofit if not already installed; the new gauge is a $200-plus item.

• Failure-prone instrument panel "eyebrow" lights. Numerous owners reported lifetimes of five to 10 hours at best. Multiple replacements seem to be the rule rather than the exception. No improved lights from Cessna that we're aware of. Moral: carry a flashlight.

• Sticking nose gear strut. Several owners report that the nose gear strut sticks in the maximum extended position after landing. That locks the nosewheel, making steering impossible. One owner says he occasionally has to hop out while still on the runway and rock the nose to release the strut.

• Avionics problems. Owners sing the usual song of woe about the factory-installed ARC avionics, although the horror stories don't seem to be as bad as they were some years ago. Worst offender appears to be the ARC 300 autopilot, which got few words of praise and many words of excoriation. The VOR tracking mode was particularly criticized. Although Cessna worked hard to improve the ARC line before they sold out, we still consider a panel full of ARC equipment to be a major liability on any Skylane RG. A fair percentage of new RG buyers, however, ordered their aircraft "green" (no radios) and installed King or Col-

Cost/Performance/Specifications

Model	Year	Number Built	Average Retail Price	Max Cruise Speed (kts)	Usable Fuel Std/Opt (gals)	Useful Load (lbs)	Engine	TBO (hrs)	Overhaul Cost
R182	1978	583	$ 39,000	157	56/75	1,200	235-hp Lyc. O-540-J3C5D	2,000	$10,250
R182	1979	729	$ 43,000	157	88	1,200	235-hp Lyc. O-540-J3C5D	2,000	$10,250
TR182 (turbo)	1979		$ 48,000	173	88	1,150	235-hp Lyc. O-540-L3C5D	2,000	$10,250
R182	1980	314	$ 47,500	157	88	1,200	235-hp Lyc. O-540-J3C5D	2,000	$10,250
TR182	1980		$ 56,000	173	88	1,150	235-hp Lyc. O-540-L3C5D	2,000	$10,250
R182	1981	NA	$ 62,500	157	88	1,200	235-hp Lyc. O-540-J3C5D	2,000	$10,250
TR182	1981	NA	$ 70,000	173	88	1,150	235-hp Lyc. O-540-L3C5D	2,000	$10,250
R182	1982	NA	$ 75,000	157	88	1,200	235-hp Lyc. O-540-J3C5D	2,000	$10,250
TR182	1982	NA	$ 87,500	173	88	1,150	235-hp Lyc. O-540-L3C5D	2,000	$10,250
R182	1983	NA	$108,150*	157	88	1,200	235-hp Lyc. O-540-J3C5D	2,000	$10,250
TR182	1983	NA	$119,505*	173	88	1,150	235-hp Lyc. O-540-L3C5D	2,000	$10,250

Deduct $104 (R182) or $116 (TR182) per hour for every hour after 50 TTSN.

lins gear on their own, so it's possible to find non-ARC RGs in the used-plane market. Look for them.

• Sticking landing gear motor switches. Several owners reported their motors run continuously even after the gear cycle is complete (they may be shut off in this event by popping the circuit breaker). The problem is apparently a bad solenoid, a problem shared with the 210. The history of the Cessna landing gear has not been a particularly happy one (listen to the cries of anguish of older 210 owners about cracked saddles and bad power packs, or look at the gear-up statistics of the Cardinal RG). Those particular problems have been licked, but landing gear malfunctions have been known to make up nearly half the malfunction and defect reports submitted to the FAA by mechanics working on Skylane RGs.

• Other reported glitches and service bulletins apply to carburetors, waste gate springs, magneto coils, prop governor brackets and gear motor brushes.

The Skylane RG's AD history is nearly flawless. However, the standard RG is subject to the ubiquitous Airborne vacuum pump, ELT and Stewart-Warner oil cooler directives that apply to literally scores of aircraft models of various manufacturers, and the Turbo RG has an AD on the carburetor.

Owner Organization

Since the Skylane Sociey of America appears to have taken a very low profile, Skylane RG

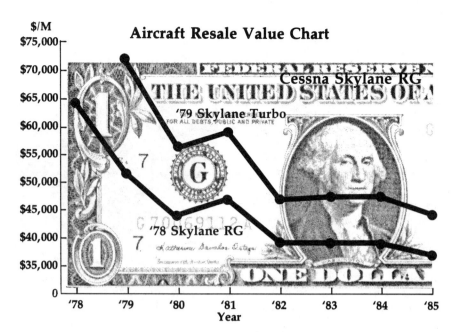

Aircraft Resale Value Chart

owners can look toward the Cessna Pilots Assn. for support and information. Their address is Wichita Mid-Continent Airport, P.O. Box 12948, Wichita, Kans. 67277, (316) 946-4777.

Owner Comments

Performance, handling and comfort on my Turbo RG are typical Skylane. Performance is pretty much right "on the book." The plane is quite comfortable, and the cabin is reasonably quiet except for air leaks around the doors. Based upon the way the doors fit both inside and out, it is apparent that Cessna still hasn't figured out how to make a well-fitting trouble-free door for the Skylane. As for idiosyncrasies, the Lycoming O-540, which has performed flawlessly for over 500 hours now, is somewhat prone to lead fouling of the plugs.

Panel is standard Cessna—but avoid the ARC radios if you can.

The Lycoming engine in this plane is a real gem. It is responsive, runs smoothly, burns little or no oil between 25-hour changes, and has given me no problem whatever. The turbocharger has likewise been trouble-free. The airplane was delivered to me with what I consider an above-normal number of quality control problems, and has continued to show signs of poor quality control to the present time. A couple of design problems which come to mind are rear-seat vents and avionics cooling. The rear-seat vents are made of plastic and fall apart any time you try to adjust or re-direct air flow. Avionics cooling is a real problem here in the southwest. In this airplane you cannot sit on the ground with the radios on for more than about 10 minutes if the temperature is above 85° or so, or you will be without radios. Once you are flying, they do come back on and I have never had them go out in the air.

Parts availability and backup: now the bad news. My experience with Cessna dealers has been good, and the warranty coverage was generally good as well. Even in cases where the dealer felt that a problem was not covered under warranty, an appeal to the factory usually resulted in a decision favorable to me (although the time consumed was substantial).

Here in California we are blessed with a "Zone" distributor who is supposed to stock much more inventory than the dealer. The zone concept seems to be an anachronistic hand-me-down from years past, and of limited utility now that overnight package delivery services have spread. My experience is that the zone stocks almost nothing for these airplanes that the dealer doesn't already stock. Consequently the zone has to order everything from the factory.

The zone situation is even more maddening when you realize that Cessna will not ship direct if there is a zone distributor operating in your area. Cessna has published several stiffly written directives to dealers to ''knock off the direct drop shipment stuff'' and use the zone instead. All the dealers can do is grit their teeth, and when relations between the dealer and the zone deteriorate because of poor service, the customer invariably gets caught AOG (aircraft on the ground).

Idiosyncrasies: (1) I have had problems with the nose-gear strut sticking in the extended position, and after adjustment of fluid level, strut pressure, and general fussing with the thing, it still persists. It is annoying to apply the brakes in a jerky fashion to get the strut down so you can turn the thing to get off the runway.

(2) The nose gear shimmy problem led to a service letter for a stronger attach fitting between the shaft of the shimmy damper and the strut assembly. I never had a problem, but put the stronger fitting on anyway (factory paid). I did experience a failure of the bracket encircling the strut assembly that supports the barrel of the shimmy damper.

(3) The windshield leaked a long time until I learned that the time to apply the clear silicone was on a cold morning when the Plexiglas shrinks from the aluminum and you can fill the resulting gaps better.

(4) The Turbo Skylane throttle linkage is a complex slotted and roller affair that permits the throttle butterfly to be opened with the first

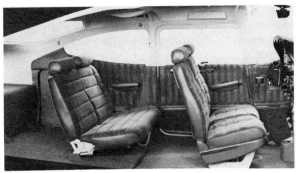

Skylane is renowned for room, and the retractable gear doesn't encroach on the baggage area, as it did in the Cardinal RG.

half of travel, and the wastegate to be closed with the second half of throttle travel. I found that the throttle was increasingly difficult to move past the detent where the wastegate begins to close, and during one trip, over the mountains IFR, I couldn't move it at all when I began to get some ice. The airplane became a normally aspirated airplane with not much poop at 11,000, and I iced up and came out the bottom after about half an hour (fortunately over low terrain). At the end of the trip I arrived home to find a service letter for a kit to ease the sticking problem with the throttle. I put the airplane in for an annual, and naturally the factory did not have stock on the kit (it wasn't even in their computer, so they spit out the order twice). The kit was $120 plus some extra parts, and it was a first-class bitch to install, consuming 12 hours of mechanic's time of which I was charged 8.5. The dealer ate the difference. There was no factory support for this item even though in my opinion the old throttle linkage has major problems, and I feel was poorly designed.

(5) The big Lycoming runs a lot smoother at higher rpm than lower. I installed an electronic fuel flow monitor and confirmed that running ''over square'' is more efficient for a given power setting, but the vibration at 25 inches and 2200 rpm makes me think that things would shake loose, so I have reverted to 23/2300 settings for cruise.

(6) The pressure switch on the gear hydraulic pump sticks occasionally. It used to stick in the low-pressure position, which caused the pump to continue running, and the pump had to be shut off by pulling the breaker before it

burned up. Then for a year no problems. Recently the switch stuck several times in the high-pressure position, and I couldn't get the gear up. (The gear can be pumped manually only to the down position.) Now that problem has gone away. Might be tiny bits of dirt getting into the switch, and then moving on.

(7) The heater is marginal in cold weather during climbout. The situation improves greatly when the cowl flaps are closed and the cowl pressurized.

I am in the process of adding the Flight Bonus Inc. drag reduction kits for the strut fairings and the flap/aileron gap seals. These should add about three to four knots. I am corresponding with Charlie Seibel of Flight Bonus Inc. about adapting their exhaust stack closure, spinner brush, and prop root/spinner gap closure kits to the RG aircraft. I am also exploring ways of reducing the drag of the open gear wells. If experiment supports theory, a 195-knot Skylane (FL 200, light weight, 75 percent power) should be attainable.

I have to close with a favorite story. I was cruising one day at 65 percent and 11,500 when Center reported that a Bonanza had just leveled at six o'clock and three miles. The Bonanza driver was warned of a 182 at 12 o'clock and three miles. ''Keep us posted, Center,'' he said. ''We should be passing him soon.'' After a minute Center reported that ''The 182 is still at three miles, and seems to have about a five-knot speed advantage.'' ''So long Bonanza,'' I crooned into my mike, and proceeded to push the throttle up to 75 percent. After a couple of minutes the Bonanza called again and wanted to know where we were. "The 182 is still at 12 o'clock, and still seems to have a speed advantage." The Bonanza subsequently made a 20-degree turn to the left, and began descending. We never heard from him again.

•

Performance: My 1979 turbo model makes all its book performance at the weight, temperature and altitude conditions given. Operated at light weights, however, cruise performance is substantially in excess of book figures. Two plus baggage and half fuel can cruise at FL 180-190 at 175-180 knots TAS and 65-70 percent power. My highest sustained TAS was on a flight from Palo Alto to Los Angeles, alone. With full fuel (about 400 pounds below gross) it showed 184 knots at 17,500. At non-oxygen altitudes, 450 pounds in the cabin, full fuel, 11,500 and 75 percent, I went from Merced, Calif., to Coeur d'Alene, Idaho, starting at 165 knots, with speed rising to 175 knots near the end as we burned off fuel. The weight sensitivity seems to average about two knots per 100 pounds.

Short-field performance is excellent, typically 182, although the heavier RG is a little more sluggish than the straight-leg 182. With the cuffed leading edges and Hoerner type wing tips, I find that stall and low-speed handling are a bit better than my 1965 Skylane. The RG is a bit stiffer at cruise because of the higher indicated airspeed, and 182s tend to feel heavy in general. My RG is no exception, although a good lube job on the hinges and other moving parts helped greatly at the last annual. The aircraft makes an excellent instrument platform, and the higher cruise speed seems to make it more stable than the straight-leg 182.

Comfort is very good. Passengers have been enthusiastic about the back-seat legroom and space, finding the accommodations superior to airline tourist class legroom. With the articulating seats in the front, I have found four- and five-

Bizarre landing gear contortions are the price Cessna pays for a high wing.

hour legs to be okay, and I have spent several days with eight to 10 hours in the airplane and emerged none the worse for wear.

There is one area where the RG is decidedly inferior to the straight-leg: in crosswinds. The main gear of the RG don't extend down as far from the fuselage as on the fixed-gear versions with the result that the aircraft sits a bit nose-high. Consequently the aircraft tends to get "light" earlier in the takeoff roll, and if the aircraft is lightly loaded, it is easy to ride up on the nosewheel and start "wheelbarrowing" just before you are ready to rotate the airplane. This is sometimes accompanied with nosewheel shimmy. The same problem occurs on landing, when shimmy can occur more easily. The shimmy can be ferocious and caused a failure of the shimmy mounting bracket on the strut assembly of my aircraft.

I feel that the strongest feature of the airplane is its flexibility. I can fly four adults into 1,500 feet of dirt (comfortably), depart, fly over mountains IFR, and then maneuver easily with high approach speed while blending into the jet traffic into LAX. I can also depart Palo Alto (near San Jose) and fly three people to Denver nonstop with good reserves. And I have no problem with four six-footers in the cabin as long as I don't top the tanks. The flip side is fuel consumption, which tends to be on the high side of today's standards. I tend to fly at 65 percent and leak to peak, and block fuel consumption is around 13 gallons per hour, in-

cluding ground and air operations. It's no Mooney on fuel consumption, but then I don't feel that the 231 can fulfill the same set of mission profiles that the TR182 can.

Maintenance costs for 500 hours have averaged $8.12 per hour. This includes annual and 100-hour inspections which are $375 if there are no problems, and have averaged a little over $460 out the door. Consider too that a good share of the work was done under warranty. Fuel burn has averaged about 12.7 gph overall.

•

Over the last 16 months, these are the breakdowns. Since new, 400 hours flown. Average fuel consumption 12.6 gph. Fuel $20.64, maintenance (including 50 and 100 hr) $6.29, warranty work (no cost to me, but perhaps of interest) $3.53 and tiedown and insurance $8.18 for a total of $35.11 per hr. Allowance for engine overhaul would add another $5-$6 per hour.

I have had an average 100-hour cost of $709. ADs or Service Information Letters have been few. The oil cooler was replaced, and a shimmy dampener was attached on the front strut.

Warranty work has consisted of replacing the battery (twice), the digital clock and the fuel pressure gauge. The pilot's door also needed re-hanging and a new electric turn coordinator was installed. Most of this was done within the first few months and done quickly and professionally by my local Cessna dealer.

Mooney 201/231

The Mooney 201 has been on the market since 1977, the Mooney 231 since 1979. Both aircraft have established excellent reputations and inspired tenacious owner loyalty, judging from the reader reports we received. In fact, we can think of no other aircraft in the Used Airplane Guide series that has won such acclaim from owners. Typical comments: ''Finest plane imaginable,'' ''superb,'' ''greatest airplane I've ever owned,'' '' a sweetheart.'' The 201 and 231 are prized mainly for sterling performance and economy, along with first-rate quality control.

The other side of the coin for used-plane buyers, of course, is the high prices commanded by used 201s and 231s. A 1977 201 has a *Bluebook* price of $42,500. Compare that with the $32,000 value of a 1977 Piper Arrow. (Both aircraft sold new for about $47,000 with normal equipment.)

History

The M-20J (201) was first introduced in 1977 as a modification of the stalwart M-20F Executive, which had been in production since the 1960s. Aerodynamic and cooling refinements increased cruising speed by an astonishing 15 knots. The 201 has continued in production since then with no major changes. Among the minor improvements were a repositioned fuel selector and an improved instrument panel in 1978. Generally, though, the model year of a 201 is virtually no factor for the used-201 shopper; the condition and history of each individual aircraft is what counts, depreciation patterns aside. Likewise, the 231 has had virtually no changes during its two-year production run. The ma-

Identical except for the engine and a few details, the 231 (left) and 201 are highly prized by their owners. As a result, used-plane prices are quite high.

jor difference between the 201 and 231 is the engine: the 231 has more power and is turbocharged. The 200-hp Lycoming four-banger in the 201 is replaced by a six-cylinder 210-hp turbo Continental TSIO-360 in the 231. The 231 also has some aerodynamic refinements that the 201 originally lacked, along with changes in the control system to accommodate the new engine and a prop shaft extension designed to give the 231 a racy shark-nose look. The performance of the two airplanes is very similar at low altitudes, but the turbocharged 231 is of course superior above 10,000 feet or so. (Its maximum ceiling is 24,000 feet.)

In 1984, the firm was purchased by Mooney European distributor Alexandre Couvelaire and Armand Rivard, who owns Lake Aircraft. Both the 201 and 231 continue to be produced in Kerrville, Tex.

Resale Value

The 201 is definitely blue-chip; its resale value rivals that of the hallowed Beech Bonanza. A 1977 201 is today worth 78 percent of its new price, a proportion only slightly less than a 1977 V35B. Normal aircraft depreciation patterns show a ''valley'' after about four years; after that, most aircraft hold their value or increase slightly (in

inflated dollars, of course). A 1977 201 reached its maximum depreciation in just two years.

Performance

The 201 and 231 are truly superior performers, far better than competitive aircraft. The 201, for example, outpaces its 200-hp four-place competition by more than 20 knots, using the same amount of fuel. (It may be no coincidence that the Rockwell 112B and Cessna Cardinal RG were dropped after falling far behind Mooney in the 200-hp sales race.) The 201, in fact, can nip at the heels of a Beech Bonanza or Cessna 210 while using only two-thirds of the fuel.

Owners consistently report that the 201 meets or exceeds its book performance figures. (This doesn't surprise us; Mooney's performance testing and measuring procedures put the rest of the industry to shame.) At 75 percent power, 201 owners report speeds approaching 170 knots. At a more conservative 65 percent power, cruise speed is 160 knots or so, according to owners. Fuel consumption ranges from 9 to 12 gph, depending on power and mixture settings. *Aviation Consumer* pilots have confirmed these astoundingly good numbers on their cross-country trips.

Range is also excellent; the high speed of the 201 combined with a generous 64-gal. fuel supply allow trips of up to 1,000 miles with a small reserve. Practical IFR range

for the 201 is about 900 miles at 75 percent power.

The 231 is no faster than the 201 up to about 10,000 feet, and burns about two gph more fuel. At extremely high altitudes, however, the 231 can rack up airspeeds exceeding 190 knots at light weights. At the more normal 12,000-18,000-foot cruising altitudes preferred by most 231 pilots, 180 knots is about right.

In the real world, however, the performance of the 231 is not all that much better than the 201's, except for high-altitude climb. The 231's impressive 190-knot speeds are often theoretical. In warm weather at very high altitudes, the engine tends to run hot. That requires either the use of cowl flaps, which reduces speed by about five knots, or running an ultra-rich mixture, which burns excessive fuel. The 231 engine also tended to "miss" or "stumble" at high altitudes until pressurized mags were retrofitted by the factory free of charge. Turboplus, Inc. offers an intercooler designed to keep engine temperature lower, however.

Although the 231 is faster and carries more fuel than the 201, range is about the same. The 231 burns more fuel and must climb very high to achieve its maximum speeds, which decreases range.

Takeoff and landing performance of the 201 is about average for this class of aircraft. It requires precise speed control to achieve the short landings promised by the book. Pilot technique is also critical to achieve the published density altitude takeoff performance; a difference of a couple of knots in lift-off and climb speed can lengthen takeoff by 1,500 feet at 10,000 feet in the 201, for example.

The 231, because of its higher gross weight, higher stall speed and huge cowl flaps, has a rather long takeoff roll—nearly 50 percent longer than the 201's. The turbo-

charging naturally closes this gap at higher field elevations.

Handling Qualities

The 201 and 231 don't have the innate grace of control of aircraft such as the Bonanza. Aileron control is rather stiff, although better than in the older Mooneys. The only other major handling quirk of the 201 and 231 stems from their low drag: it's hard to get slowed down during descent. As one owner puts it, "Because the 201 is aerodynamically slick, it is absolutely the wrong plane to be in when you're cleared to land, close to the end of the runway and 3,000 feet above the ground. There is no sane way of losing altitude and slowing at the same time."

On the ground the 201 and 231 are rather awkward. Turning radius is large, and the nosewheel steering rather heavy.

By the standards of other nosewheel aircraft, the 201 is rather squirrelly on takeoff, particularly in those last few seconds when the airplane is deciding whether it wants to fly or not. The 231, because of its different weight distribution and pitch control system, seems more stable on the takeoff roll.

Both aircraft are "floaters" on landing if approach speed is a bit too fast. This fact, combined with the landing gear geometry and pitch response, cause a tendency to "porpoise" or "wheelbarrow" on

the nosewheel if the pilot is not sharp. The knack of landing smoothly comes quickly in most cases, however.

Loading

Both aircraft have useful loads of 950-1,000 pounds with the usual IFR equipment. Thus, as with most aircraft, it's impossible to carry full fuel, full seats and a good load of baggage. But the 201 will carry three 170-pound adults in most cases. Because the 231 needs more fuel to go the same distance, cabin payload will be less for a given trip, but not by much. The aircraft are not particularly sensitive to balance; any reasonable load will be within the c.g. envelope.

Accommodation

The 201 and 231 have a reputation for snugness that is not totally justified. The cabin is 44 inches wide, about the same as the Piper Arrow's. However, the seats are much lower to the floor and the instrument panel closer to the pilot; this no doubt creates the impression of snugness, as it does in a sports car. As one reader puts it, "You don't get into a Mooney, you put it on." This is somewhat of an exaggeration; another 201 owner writes, "Many people fault the Mooney on room, but I am 6'2" and 200 pounds, and I do not have any problem ..." Another writes, "We fly frequently with another couple on cross-continent flights in full comfort. The leg room, shoulder room and rear seat room are quite comfortable for the usual four-hour legs we fly.'' Although certainly less spacious than, say, the Bonanza, the 201/231 does not suffer by comparison to most other 180- to 200-hp four-placers.

Safety

Unfortunately, both the 201 and 231 are too new to have amassed enough flight time and accidents to establish a strong pattern. However, the older Mooneys (the Rangers, Executives, Super 21s and so forth) have a fairly good overall safety record. Fatal accident rate for the period 1972-76, according to NTSB figures, was 2.4, which ranks fifth best among 13 retractables in a recent *Aviation Consumer* study. The older Mooneys rank exceptionally high in structural integrity (only two documented in-flight airframe failures in the aircraft's history). In stall/spin accidents, the older Mooneys rank 16th best out of 31 aircraft studied between 1965 to 1973.

Naturally, the 201 and 231 are different aircraft from the earlier M-20 models, but the family resemblance is strong enough to suggest the 201 and 231 accident rates may be comparable.

One safety point: do not spin a Mooney. It loses altitude by something like 1,000 feet per turn.

Maintenance

Generally, the 231 and 201 are reliable, low-maintenance air-planes. One owner reports his last annual inspection turned up absolutely no discrepancies and cost a grand total of $230. Typical comment: ''Super airplane. What problems I've had to date are very minimal ...''

No airplane is perfect, of course, and there are certain trouble spots a potential 201 or 231 buyer should check closely:

• Landing lights. The 1977 model 201 in particular had landing light problems, due mostly to vibration. The 1978 model had an improved light mount, and a retrofit mod is available for 1977 models. Check to see if this mod has been installed.

• Cowl flap hinges. The 1977 and 1978 models have a poor design that causes trouble. In 1979 a stronger hinge, larger bolt and bushings were added. This may not have solved the problem, however; we got one report of loose cowl flaps on a 1979 model as well. A retrofit mod kit is available to beef up the flap hinge on 1977 and '78 models.

• Landing gear motor. The 1977 had an unreliable Dukes motor. Later models have a much superior one.

• Nosewheel and strut. It's easy to ''porpoise'' a 201 on landing, and that's hard on nosewheels. Replacement is quite expensive, so have a mechanic check it carefully. Also check the logbook for prop repairs; ground strikes caused by the same porpoising tendency are fairly common.

• Fuel tanks. The fuel tank sealant used in the 201 and 231 is apparently vulnerable to the aromatic compounds in 100LL fuel, and there have been several reports of tank leaks.

All of the above, of course, are in addition to Airworthiness Directives, which should be complied with in any aircraft you consider buying. Major airframe ADs required replacement or rework of the static system and oil cooler (77 model only), landing gear brace bolts and the Bendix fuel injector (1977-78 models); and auxiliary fuel pump and oil pressure transducer (1977-80 models). (The listed year models are approximate; check serial numbers in the ADs against the particular aircraft you're looking at.) There are also other ADs common to many aircraft, such as the Bendix dual magneto, Airborne vacuum pump and lithium-battery ELT directives. Any well-maintained 201 or 231 should have these ADs complied with.

The 231 has a special maintenance problem that can be annoying: a high-altitude ''miss'' in the Continental TSIO-360 engine. The thinner air at high altitude has less electrical resistance, which can result in ignition system arcing that momentarily cuts out the spark plug. More than half the 231 owners we queried for this article reported the problem. Careful maintenance of the ignition system and massive-electrode spark plugs

Cost/Performance/Specifications

Model	Year	Number Built	Average Retail Price	Cruise Speed (kts)	Rate of Climb (fpm)	Gross Weight (lbs)	Useful Load (lbs)	Usable Fuel (gals)	Engine	TBO (hrs)	Overhaul Cost
M-20J (201)	1977	377	$ 42,000	170	1,030	2,740	1,100	64	200-hp Lyc. IO-360-A1B6D	1,800	$ 9,250
M-20J	1978	385	$ 48,000	170	1,030	2,740	1,100	64	200-hp Lyc. IO-360-A3B6D	1,800	$ 9,250
M-20J	1979	136	$ 52,000	170	1,030	2,740	1,100	64	200-hp Lyc. IO-360-A3B6D	1,800	$ 9,250
M-20J	1980	136	$ 57,000	170	1,030	2,740	1,100	64	200-hp Lyc. IO-360-A3B6D	1,800	$ 9,250
M-20J	1981	175	$ 70,000	170	1,030	2,740	1,100	64	200-hp Lyc. IO-360-A3B6D	1,800	$ 9,250
M-20J	1982	112	$ 80,000	170	1,030	2,740	1,100	64	200-hp Lyc. IO-360-A3B6D	1,800	$ 9,250
M-20J	1983	90	$113,000	170	1,030	2,740	1,100	64	200-hp Lyc. IO-360-A3B6D	1,800	$ 9,250
M-20K (231)	1979	246	$ 62,000	192	1,080	2,900	1,100	73	210-hp Cont. TSIO-360-GB	1,800	$10,750
M-20K	1980	199	$ 68,000	192	1,080	2,900	1,100	73	210-hp Cont. TSIO-360-GB	1,800	$10,750
M-20K	1981	165	$ 79,000	192	1,080	2,900	1,100	73	210-hp Cont. TSIO-360-GB	1,800	$10,750
M-20K	1982	104	$ 95,000	192	1,080	2,900	1,100	73	210-hp Cont. TSIO-360-GB	1,800	$10,750
M-20K	1983	62	$127,000	192	1,080	2,900	1,100	73	210-hp Cont. TSIO-360-GB	1,800	$10,750

are some help, but Mooney has decided to use a different magneto and harness for the 1981 model 231. The new ignition setup has been available free for retrofit to older 231s.

We have also received reports of induction icing problems in the 231. One owner reported a complete stoppage and lost 5,000 feet before restarting.

One concerned 201 owner reported a vexing maintenance problem. "I may be dreaming," he wrote, "but it seems that birds have a strange attraction for my airplane. They love to sit on the tail and leave droppings all over it. My 201 is parked in a row of perhaps 50 aircraft, from an MU-2 to a Cub, and mine is consistently the only airplane to suffer this disfigurement. I was talking to another 201 owner recently, and he described precisely the same problem. Something is going on here."

Perhaps the solution to the bird problem is an AD requiring a large doo-doo shield to be permanently affixed to the 201 tail. This would certainly discourage the birds, and shouldn't cause a speed loss of more than 20 knots or so, although further flight tests might be necessary to ensure no adverse effect on stability and handling qualities.

Service

Although the 201 and 231 seem to be reliable, well-built aircraft, if you do have a problem, you'd better find the right mechanic to work on it. Average Joe Mechanic may never have worked on a 201 or 231 before, and financing his learning curve could be expensive. As one owner writes, "Phone calls to non-Mooney shops have left me with nightmares ..."

By almost universal acclaim, the top Mooney service center in the country is Dugosh Aviation in Kerrville, Tex. (the same field as the Mooney factory). According to the Mooney Pilots Association, four other top Mooney shops are Willmar Air Service, Willmar, Minn.; McCauley Aviation, Pine

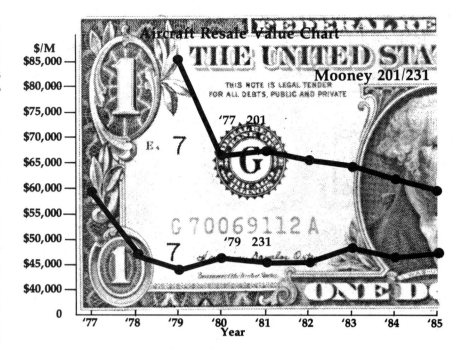

Bluff, Ark.; Performance Aircraft in Long Beach, Calif.; and Daytona Beach Aviation in Daytona Beach, Fla.

Unfortunately, the Mooney dealer network is one of the weak links in the system. They are few and far between, and some are rather small-time operators. (A couple of years ago, one Mooney Marketing Center accepted full payment from a customer for a brand-new 201, but never sent the money on to Mooney, and then went out of business. When the buyer showed up at the factory to pick up his plane, he got a sad surprise.) One 201 owner wrote, "Very happy with the plane, very unhappy with the dealer." Another complained that his mechanic (not a Mooney dealer) encountered delays ordering parts from the factory because the nearest dealer, through whom the parts had to be channeled, was hundreds of miles away.

We were not exactly showered with compliments about Mooney factory support. The company rarely pays for ADs or service bulletins beyond the warranty period, even in cases of obvious design defects, such as the cowl flaps and landing lights. In this respect, Mooney lags behind the rest of the industry, which has gradually begun to pay for certain ADs on late-model aircraft even

beyond the warranty period.

Owner Club

The Mooney Aircraft Pilots Association is closely allied with the Mooney company, and we would recommend membership to any 201/231 owner. Address is 314 Stardust Drive, San Antonio, Tex. 78228; phone: 512-434-5959.

Owner Comments

The 201 does everything the book says. It is common to get cruise speeds of 155-160 knots at 4,000-8,000 feet using 63-68 percent power. The 64 gallons usable fuel gives great IFR range and flexibility.

The ADs on the magneto, boost pump, cowl flaps, and spinner are a source of irritation. The greater irritation is that the cowl flaps are not a permanent fix, and I've had to have the tanks on my '77 201 completely resealed due to aromatics in fuels. Ouch!

Four people and any baggage can compromise some fuel. With full fuel I am limited to 595 pounds. Two 850-mile trips to Florida used

10.2 gallons per hour at 160 knots. Like an albatross, it is cumbersome at other than high-speed flight. On the ground it has a large turning radius, and when trying to ''grease it on'' it floats forever until *it* wants to land.

I've had my maintenance performed by Byerly Aviation in Peoria, a Mooney dealer, and had excellent service. Phone calls to non-Mooney shops have left me with nightmares of what would happen at other than a Mooney dealer or someone very familiar with Mooneys.

•

The speed for the 201 is about as advertised but the 231 will exceed Mooney's claims. I've confirmed this with other 231 owners. Up to 8,000 feet I see no difference between the 201 and 231. Over 8,000, the 231 really begins to shine! Most of my flying is in the 10,000-14,000-foot range. It's good to have a plane that doesn't feel ''slushy'' at those altitudes. I used to think 6,000-8,000 feet was plenty high. But when you get used to being above much weather, getting better reception and selecting favorable winds, higher altitude becomes second nature.

I have 200 hours on my 231 and have had little maintenance. However, there is a slight ''miss'' problem somewhat common to 231s. This is attributed to the fine wire plugs. Both Mooney and the dealers state that going to the massive electrode plugs corrects this, and I hear Mooney is considering switching to massive electrodes. I had this miss but had the plugs cleaned and rotated, and it appears to have stopped.

I bought a new 201 in 1978. It is a superb flying machine. Aside from the fact that several days after delivery it was down with an AD on the mags, it has been healthy and working well. The 201 is economical and handles like a dream. It is a great instrument platform and very comfortable. Maintenance and parts have been good.

However, I am disappointed with the aircraft industry's lack of

responsibility on ADs. If they make a mistake in the manufacturing of a product, I certainly don't feel I should be responsible for their blunder.

I'm extremely well satisfied with my 201's performance, handling, roominess and low repair and operating costs. My only complaint is the fuel tank valve between my legs on the floor. The newer 201s corrected that problem.

The 231 is a quality airplane, well put together and gives every impression of durability and strength. There have been a few minor problems so far, two which I consider to be serious.

The first and most difficult to cure is induction ice. If the temperature is below freezing and there is visible moisture, you will very shortly suffer a loss of manifold pressure, the turbine inlet temperature will drop, and you will start trimming the nose up to maintain altitude. You could open the alternate air door, but there will be a marked loss of power.

•

I have over 500 hours in my 1978 201. Couldn't be more pleased. It is an excellent instrument airplane. Cruise speeds and fuel burn are by the book. I often load full fuel, two couples and baggage and am within weight and balance limits. Workmanship is excellent. Had trouble with fuel pressure gauge several times. Other than that, no serious problems. With today's fuel prices, this is the airplane to own if you plan on doing a lot of flying and don't own your own refinery.

The 231 has a propeller shaft extension to give it a sleeker look.

Maintenance has been reasonable and minimal. I have only had to cancel one trip in two years due to mechanical problems. Of course I have the services of the best Mooney mechanic in the country (Charlie Mathews, Mathews Aircraft, Riverside Airport, Tulsa, Okla).

•

My 231 is the greatest airplane I've ever owned. That includes seven airplanes, Piper and Cessna.

I purchased my airplane last September with 350 hours TT. Since then I've flown the plane 45 hours. Nothing has needed fixing. The 100-hour was an inspection and oil change only. Cost: $480.

The performance of the plane meets or exceeds the book figures. The quality of the Mooney workmanship far exceeds Piper and more so Cessna. The paint job is far superior. It will carry a good load of ice and is a superb IFR platform. When it rains, the Mooney does not leak. The plane can be hot on landings, and persons without Mooney experience must adjust.

Over 15,000 feet the plane has a miss in the engine. The local Mooney dealer is experimenting with different spark plugs.

Another problem inexperienced Mooney pilots have is porpoising when a hard landing is made if power is not added. If the nose is forced over after a bounce, you will surely end up with a prop strike.

Piper Comanche

The luster of the Piper Comanche, with its superb roominess, great old Lycoming engine and modest price tag, has dimmed slightly with the passage of time. Though parts availability is generally reported as good despite the production halt of the entire line in 1972, some airframe parts take longer and longer to get, and two decades' accumulation of Airworthiness Directives adds to the psychological and fiscal burden of ownership.

Countering these deficiencies is a superb owners' association—The International Comanche Society—along with an energetic mod shop—Knots-2U—with an intriguing roster of update revisions that keep the old birds' performance and looks up with the times.

History

Piper manufactured five different single-engine models between 1958 and 1972. The arrival of the cheaper-to-build Arrow and a great flood that swamped the Lock Haven plant ended the Comanche line, however. The various models were built in these time spans:

- Comanche 180, from 1958 to 1964.
- Comanche 250, from 1958 to 1964
- Comanche 260, in 1965.
- Comanche 260B, from 1966 to 1968.
- Comanche 260C, from 1969 to 1972.
- Comanche 260C turbo, from 1970 to 1972.
- Comanche 400, from 1964 to 1965.

General Value Points

The powerplants of all the different models are characterized by owners almost universally as outstandingly troublefree. With optional fuel of 86 gallons usable translating into around seven to nine hours' flying time, the Comanches have unbeatable range. All the Comanches have fine roomy cabins that are several inches wider than those in the later Arrows. The 260B and C models actually have six-place seating, with two rather cozy seats in the baggage compartment.

The aircraft will climb at a good rate, and most pilots praise its short-field characteristics. Control reaction is crisp and pleasant, with a generous slam-bang warning stall buffet. There is good parts availability for accessories and engines. And prices for this kind of high-performance aircraft are quite decent in this day and age. Figure on from $20,000 to $40,000 for the later models.

On the debit side, all the Comanches are bears to land with finesse, the doors fit poorly, the instrument panel is archaic and nonstandard, and acquisition of airframe parts may require a good wait. Also, the Comanches have suffered a string of ADs—a good number of them repetitive ones—over the years—11

The barrel-chested Comanche 400 has demonstrated phenomenal climbing ability both in the air and in resale value over the years. This relatively rare bird evidently has already become a collector's item.

in the last decade alone. The 250 model by itself has accrued over 25 ADs since it was first built.

Comanche 180

The Comanche 180 is highly regarded for its economy, but naturally cannot haul great loads or operate effectively at high density altitudes heavily loaded. Max useful, nevertheless, is around 1,000 pounds, which should allow a full 60 gallons of fuel and three or four passengers. Owners report speeds of 135 to 140 knots, burning 8.5 to 9.5 gph. Rate of climb is 700 to 900 fpm at gross weight.

The 180 came with just a hand brake until 1960; after that, most were built with optional toe brakes. We noted at least one accident related to the use of hand brakes during the checkout of a pilot unfamiliar with this system. The optional 90-gallon fuel tanks became available in 1961 (60 gallons were standard). A full load of 90 gallons yields a phenomenal nine-hour endurance but limits payload to a couple of people and baggage.

Electric flaps were introduced in 1962, but some pilots consider this a step backward over the simple, quick-acting manual flaps. The 1960 and 1961 models are best for conversion to the 250-hp engine.

Our choice of 180s: a 1961 model with 90 gallons, toe brakes, manual flaps—approximate cost is $18,000.

Comanche 250

The 250 is the classic Comanche, probably one of the best airplanes available today for under $25,000. Even the 1962 Beech Debonairs (225-hp) are going for about $28,000, as are 1960 Bonanzas with the 250-hp engine.

Preferable models are 1961 and later, which had 100 pounds more gross (up to 2,900 lbs.) and useful load, 90-gallon fuel tanks and optional toe brakes.

Owners report cruise speeds in the 154-160-knot area on 12 to 14 gph. Climb rate is strong: about 1,000 to 1,400 fpm, according to owners.

The carbureted 250-hp Lycoming engine is a good one, presuming it has the half-inch valves. TBO is then a healthy 2,000 hours, and users report engine times several hundred hours longer.

Comanche 260

The 260-hp model was introduced in 1965, but the big change didn't occur until 1966. The '65 model is thus unique—the only four-seat carbureted 260-hp model. Because of its smaller gross weight, it has the highest book rate of climb of any Comanche except the 400: a robust 1,500 fpm.

In 1966 with the B model the fuselage was stretched slightly to allow for two extra (little, padded) seats that were actually in the baggage compartment, along with extra windows. In addition, fuel injection was provided and the gross weight raised 200 pounds to 3,100 pounds. Because of the extra gross weight, book speed is only slightly higher than that of the older 250s; but with the same load, the Comanche B is about four knots faster than the 250, according to reader reports.

The B is also presumably a bit quieter than the plain 260 because of a thicker windshield and side glass. And the 260's slightly longer fuselage is reported to give it better longitudinal stability than the 250 has—an advantage for autopilotless cruising and IFR flight, of course.

The 260C model, the ultimate refinement of the breed, was introduced in 1969. Recognizable by its shark-nose cowl, it had another 100

pounds' gross, which raised the standard useful load to a whopping 1,427 pounds. In order to avoid aft c.g. problems, however, the prop was moved forward several inches, resulting in the nice-looking streamlined nose. The C model also introduced cowl flaps and an aileron-rudder interconnect. The latter has the unfortunate side effect of making the ailerons heavier.

Turbo Comanche C

The turbo model was introduced in 1970 and built for three years until the Comanche line expired in 1972. The "second throttle" dual Rajay turbo system boosted high-altitude (25,000 feet) speeds to 198 knots at 75 percent and 182 knots at 55 percent. At more reasonable altitudes of 12,000-15,000 feet, the Turbo Comanche will true about 174-183 knots on some 16 gph.

The Turbo's modified exhaust system results in a noticeably quieter cabin, especially at altitude. The engine itself is beefed up to take the higher turbo temperatures, though the Rajays did not ground boost manifold pressure, but merely "normalized" to deliver a full 29 inches up to 25,000 feet. The pilot has to crank in the extra turbo boost manually.

Comanche 400

The Comanche 400 appeared in

Cost/Performance/Specifications

Model	Year	Number Built	Average Retail Price	Cruise Speed (kts)	Rate of Climb (fpm)	Fuel (gals)	Engine	TBO (hrs)	Overhaul Cost
PA-24-180	1958-59	1,176	$15,500	139	910	60	180-hp Lyc. O-360-A1A	2,000	$ 6,500
	1960-61	1,366	$17,500	139	910	60/90	180-hp Lyc. O-360-A1A	2,000	$ 6,500
	1962-63	713	$19,200	139	910	60/90	180-hp Lyc. O-360-A1A	2,000	$ 6,500
	1964	129	$20,000	139	910	60/90	180-hp Lyc. O-360-A1A	2,000	$ 6,500
PA-24-250	1958-59	1,476	$18,000	157	1,350	60/90	250-hp Lyc. O-540-A1A5	2,000	$ 9,100
	1960-61	1,366	$19,500	157	1,350	60/90	250-hp Lyc. O-540-A1A5	2,000	$ 9,100
	1962-63	713	$22,500	157	1,350	60/90	250-hp Lyc. O-540-A1A5	2,000	$ 9,100
	1964	129	$24,000	157	1,350	60/90	250-hp Lyc. O-540-A1A5	2,000	$ 9,000
PA-24-260	1965	299	$25,500	158	1,370	60/90	260-hp Lyc. O-540-E4A5	2,000	$ 9,000
PA-24-260B	1966-67	451	$27,500	161	1,370	60/90	260-hp Lyc. IO-540-D4A5	2,000	$ 9,500
	1968	51	$30,000	161	1,370	60/90	260-hp Lyc. IO-540-D4A5	2,000	$ 9,500
PA-24-260C	1969-70	147	$33,000	161	1,320	60/90	260-hp Lyc. IO-540-D4A5	2,000	$ 9,500
	1971-72	50	$38,000	161	1,320	60/90	260-hp Lyc. IO-540-D4A5	2,000	$ 9,500
PA-24-260TC	1970-71	50	$39,500	198	1,320	60/90	260-hp Lyc. IO-540-N1A5	2,000	$10,500
	1972	28	$41,000	198	1,320	60/90	260-hp Lyc. IO-540-N1A5	2,000	$10,500
PA-24-400	1964-65	145	$39,000	185	1,600	100/130	400-hp Lyc. IO-720-A1A	1,800	$17,000

1964 and disappeared after only a year on the market, for some good reasons. A total of 145 were built, and they have become something of a collector's item. The 400 has the basic four-seat Comanche airframe, but the engine is a monster 400-hp eight-cylinder Lycoming IO-720.

The engine and airframe marriage was not a happy one, however, for the Comanche 400 is a nose-heavy gas guzzler with performance only a little better than the Comanche 260's. Cruise speed is listed at 185 knots, and owners report an honest 174-183 knots at 75 percent cruise—but at an excessive fuel flow of about 20-22 gph. At 10,000 feet and 65 percent power, speed drops below 174 knots and fuel consumption is about 18 gph, according to owner reports.

Compared to a 1969 Comanche C (260 hp), which sells for $7,000 less, the $39,000 (the recent average going price) Comanche 400 rates poorly except for its specialty value. Gross weight of the 400 is 400 pounds higher than the 260's, but since the 400 weighs 337 pounds more empty, the useful load advantage is only 63 pounds.

Because of the 400's voracious appetite for fuel, the cabin payload is actually less than the 260C's for any flight of more than about 300 miles. With the optional 130-gallon tanks full, in fact, an IFR Comanche 400, for all its brute power, is a three-passenger airplane.

The original Comanche 400 gained a reputation for being notoriously hard to start, especially when hot. The problem was the Bendix 700 magneto used on early versions of the IO-720 (it tended to slip out of proper timing). Lycoming solved the problem on later engines by going to 1200 mags, but all Comanche 400s originally had the troublesome 700 ones. Presumably most or all have been converted to the 1200 series. Naturally, we

The Comanche 180. Note the short main gear legs and nose-high attitude. Owners advocate pumping up the main struts to simplify landing.

wouldn't advise buying one without the conversion.

Other points to bear in mind: an average IO-720 overhaul will cost about $18,000, compared to about $10,000 for the 260-hp model.

Despite its hefty operating costs, the 400 has a loyal cadre of owners, most of whom see the plane as a classic collector's ship. The plane is a delightfully stable IFR platform, exceptionally smooth, and its rate of climb is matched by few conventional single-engine aircraft.

Handling Qualities

The most notorious handling idiosyncrasy of the Comanches is the way they land. It's extremely difficult to make greasers consistently without some special magic. The aircraft tend to float during the flare, then pay off jarringly.

Special techniques for landing Comanches could fill a book. Some pilots use half flaps until committed to the landing, then lower them all. Other pilots counsel never using flaps at all. One pilot advises he makes golden landings by approaching at 104 knots and coming over the lights at 90 and flaring at 74 knots. Another asserts, "70 knots is just right." Years ago we used to make a normal approach with full flaps and then, when smoothly into the flare inches above the runway, retract the flaps and settle in. To each his own.

An almost universally condoned practice to improve landings is to pump up the main gear oleos and

bleed off the nose strut to change the landing attitude. The Piper Arapaho that was designed to replace the Twin Comanche (but never did) had whopping large main struts to counter the problem.

Along with landing problems come takeoff problems when pilots attempt to hold the aircraft on the ground in gusty conditions. The reason is the aircraft has a tendency to wheelbarrow in this kind of situation. Once in the air, however, the Comanches have a good reputation for handling, with light ailerons and a docile stall.

One operating quirk to watch for: When the Comanche landing gear is raised, the emergency gear handle between the seats pivots from a vertical position to a horizontal one against the floor. If a chart case or other object gets in the way, the gear will jam, the circuit breaker will blow, and serious gear problems may arise later.

Safety Record

According to a special NTSB study of accident rates of single-engine aircraft (over the years 1972-1976), the Piper Comanche PA-24 line came out quite a bit worse than average in only one category: overshoots. The Comanche was fourth worst in all 32 aircraft compared, after the Grumman Traveler, Cessna 195 and the Beech 23. This might suggest that either Comanche pilots are coming in too hot, or that the flaps are deficient in allowing a good angle of descent.

Despite the Comanche's notoriously poor cockpit visibility, the Comanches had only a slightly

higher than average record of midair collisions and ranked ninth out of 25 aircraft.

On the other hand, in a separate study by Contributing Editor Brent Silver of fatal in-flight airframe failure accidents, the Comanche showed up very poorly. In the span of 14 years between 1964 and 1977 the Comanche had the fifth worst breakup record of 29 fixed-gear and retractable-gear aircraft. In fact, it trailed just behind the V-tailed Bonanza. The other four worst records went to the wooden Mooney, Bellanca 14-19, 17-30, 17-31 and the Navion.

A study by *The Aviation Consumer* of Piper Comanche accidents briefs provided by the National Transportation Safety Board (for the years 1979 through 1981) showed the biggest problem was engine failures because of some mechanical breakdown.

There were 22 such accidents (out of a total of 147), plus another two engine stoppages attributed to carburetor ice. In three other instances engine failure was caused by water in the fuel. Hence, although Comanche owners characterize their powerplants as troublefree, there appears to be a problem with poor or inadequate maintenance on these older aircraft.

Second biggest accident generator was fuel mismanagement, with 19 cases where pilots either exhausted the fuel totally or ran a tank dry and crashed or made forced landings.

Third biggest accident problem with Comanches was gear-up landings caused by the pilot's either inadvertently retracting the gear on landing or failing to make sure it was down and locked. There were 13 of these. In several instances, however, the problem was compounded by some kind of electrical failure, a low battery or popped circuit breaker; and the pilot didn't notice the electrically operated gear wasn't down and locked. Another eight cases of gear collapse were attributed to maintenance problems.

Fourth biggest problem area concerned stalls, stall/mushes or spins. There were 10 of these, with at least half related to pilots expecting better short-field performance than they got or tackling high density altitude situations.

As for the problems disclosed by the other studies we mentioned above—in-flight airframe failure and overshoots—we tallied six Comanche breakups. Five of them occurred in thunderstorm areas, one with a gyro failure in IFR conditions. And we counted eight cases of overshooting.

Despite the Comanche's reputation as a tricky lander, there were only three accidents blamed on hard landings, and in one of those the aircraft had a load of ice. And poor cockpit visibility or not, there was only one midair among the roster.

Maintenance Considerations

Since the Comanche is not exactly a vanished species, there are quite a few mechanics around the country who were weaned on them. But it is imperative to find knowledgeable ones, or pay the Piper(!). There are reportedly quite a few capable shops around the country, and lots of inexpert ones. For a good one in your local area, we suggest you get in touch with the International Comanche Society.

As for gurus, we suggest Maurice F. Taylor, the Society's technical advisor, at either 704-963-5529 summers, or 813-439-2792 winters. He, in turn, suggests that one of the most knowledgeable Comanche people is Robert Gift of Lock Haven Airmotive in Lock Haven, Pa., 717-748-5582.

As for maintenance costs, another Pennsylvania shop that says it has been working on Comanches since way back (Penn-Air, Inc. at Altoona—Blair County Airport in Martinsburg, Pa., 814-793-2164) provided the following average costs for annual inspections, including parts, labor, fluids and state sales tax in 1983:
- PA-24-180—$795.
- PA-24-250—$835.

When the Rockwell 114 came out, the "old" Comanche C outraced and outclimbed it despite powerplants of similar size.

- PA-24-250, -260 fuel injected—$885.

Service Manager Danny R. Claycomb also said that a 50-hour oil change, lower plug cleaning, tire service along with a check of lights, brakes, and clean up would amount to from $225 to $250. However, if an aircraft came in without the records summarized and up to date, this could take the IA another eight to 10 hours to accomplish.

Parts Availability

Almost all the Comanche owners who provided us with feedback staunchly maintained that parts were no problem whatever. Even the International Comanche Society said Piper was doing a "superb job" for an aircraft out of production as long as the Comanche. Owners said if the dealers can't get the parts from Piper, then the Society can help scrounge them up.

We did get a few contrary signals from some Piper dealers, however. These said service was quite poor, and the delay in actually getting parts delivery could be months long. One old-timer in the business suggested that actually right now the parts situation was at its nadir, and that the time was ripe for an outside supplier like Univair or Wag-Aero, perhaps, to pick up the rights to make parts.

Maurice Taylor of the Society said that the hard-to-get parts are not the kind that ground the airplane, but are more likely to be items like inside moldings for windows or perhaps parts that local shops can fashion with a Form 337.

Service Difficulties

A survey of five years of SDRs for Comanches showed the landing gear system to have caused by far the greatest number of problems, often resulting in belly landings or gear collapsing. Typical callouts involved lower drag links binding; bungee arms cracked, broken or bent; and circuit breakers popping a "chronic problem with PA-24s." Mention was made of installing 30-amp circuit breakers in place of 25-amp ones according to Piper instructions, to alleviate the problem.

Next biggest problem area concerned the powerplant, with a varied assortment of problems involving everything from bearings and valves and cylinders to crankshafts and crankcases.

Third worst problem involved exhaust stacks and muffler components cracking and breaking.

Lesser problems involved magnetos, cracked aileron nose ribs (per AD inspections) cracking and rusting engine mounts and cracked wing skin around rivets where the stringer crosses the ribs. Still other problem areas were cracking control wheels and fuel cells that had collapsed, deteriorated or were leaking.

Airworthiness Directives

The AD that caused most consternation among Comanche owners recently was 82-19-01, which called for inspection of the main wing spar for cracks. This was issued after a Comanche in Canada lost its right wing when the pilot pulled

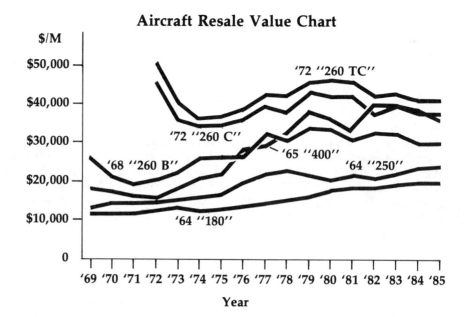

Aircraft Resale Value Chart

up in a climbing left turn after flying over a friend's house. Transport Canada found the failure had been caused by a fatigue crack in the spar, and it found similar fatigue cracks in the other wing. The aircraft had experienced minor damage previously, but nothing significant that would have affected the wing's integrity, we were told. This runs counter to rumors that the aircraft had sustained serious wing damage earlier.

The AD called for the mechanic to cut out a small piece of metal skin to allow access for the inspection. What rankled owners is that some shops apparently charged four to 11 hours for what should have been no more than a one-hour $80 to $100 job.

The FAA reports that so far no cracks have been discovered as a result of the AD-mandated inspections. However, during the inspections another potential problem was discovered in the form of chafing of the wing spar lower cap where the spar enters the fuselage.

As a result, Piper issued a Service Bulletin (No. 751) in May 1983, calling for inspection to detect any chafing that might have occurred. This, Piper maintained, might in turn affect the structural integrity of the spar cap. At last word, the FAA was considering issuing an AD making the SB mandatory.

To further burden Comanche owners, the spar crack inspection AD was made a repetitive one, to be performed each 100 hours. We counted eight other repetitive ADs on the Comanche airframes (there may be more on accessories, engines, etc.), some of which can be terminated with installation of a corrective Piper kit.

Modifications

One of the notorious problems on the Comanches is poor door sealing. Owners who wish to add another latch (overhead, as on the Cherokees) to enhance door closing and security should contact the International Comanche Society for details of a mod for which they received one-time approval via a Form 337. Another possible solution to the problem is an inflatable door seal, provided by Bob Fields Aerocessories in Santa Paula, Calif.

Knots-2U can provide several performance boosters such as aileron and flap lower (and now upper) seals for $1,450 installed or $1,050 in kit form; wing root fairings for $425 installed or $355 kit; and a removable fiberglass dorsal fin to allow access to antennas for $1,080 installed or $895 kit; plus installation of the cabin air vent in the dorsal fin for $400. Contact Jim Bradshaw (312) 256-4807.

One-piece windshields have been

STC'd by several different organizations. Among them are Beryl D'Shannon Aviation Specialties, Atlanta, Ga.; Wayne Airframe, Inc., Van Nuys, Calif., Cee Bailey's Aircraft Plastics, Long Beach, Calif.'; Great Lakes Aero Products, Flint, Mich. Users say they do a marvelous job of eliminating some of the tunnel-like qualities of the cockpit. Knots-2U also has one.

To help diminish the coat of oil on the underbelly, an air-oil separator is available from Walker Engineering Co., Los Angeles, Calif.

If extra range is desired, 15-gallon tip tanks are available from H.S. Osborne, Oro Grande, Calif.

In addition, R/STOL Systems, Bellevue, Wash. can provide STOL equipment in the form of recontoured wing leading edge, stall fences, drooped ailerons and new wing tips.

Since the older Comanches have generators that poop out at low rpms, owners might wish to upgrade to an alternator. InterAv in San Antonio, Tex., 512-344-2785 sells a kit for about $500.

Organization to Join

As we've mentioned above, the International Comanche Society, Inc., is highly touted by Comanche owners for its support, expertise and its *Comanche Flyer* newsletter. Their latest address is Box 468, Lyons, Kans. 67554-0468, 316-257-5138. The Society also publishes a special booklet of maintenance tips that owners say is extremely useful.

Investment Value

We plotted the resale value of each of the lines, and interestingly enough, the Comanche 400 showed the most dramatic climb in equity. After bottoming out at about $15,000 in 1971, it took off to where it has more than doubled in 1984, to $39,000, according the *Aircraft Bluebook Price Digest*. The 260B model showed the next best climb in value over the years, with all the others plodding slowly upward, driven by the pressures of infla-

tion, except for a brief plunge in 1980 and 1981.

Owner Comments

Comanches have accrued in value. Some things to look for are one-piece windshields, center stack radios, brake drums on wheels turned around so that they retract up *into the wheel well*. Other neat things are gap seals, wing root fairings, and others. I've replaced the 1955 vintage airscoops with 'NASA' scoops for improved cooling.

Although I enjoy and use my Comanche, I have a definite problem: lack of certain critical parts. Lack due to an "out of production" airplane. Piper helps where they can—but it is usually "sorry—out of production."

The mere mention of certain AD notes makes me mad. The gear AD at about $500 was bad enough. The prop AD at about $600 was understandable. The aileron nose rib AD was ridiculous. I personally requested the FAA for a variance on this one. All the supporting data, documents, letters, etc. FAA said no. And now it's every 100 hours inspect the aileron nose rib.

In September 1982, another AD. In the next 20 hours, said the AD, cut a hole in the wings and inspect for cracks.

C. Lamar Carlton
Sebring, Fla.

I have gone on many long trips in this plane and I really don't think there is a better-performing plane for load carrying, speed, density altitude, or ecconomy on the used-plane market. Compare the numbers with say a new RG-182, then the price and you'll get what I am driving at.

My 250 has the Brittain tip tanks, 15 gallons each, and 30 gallons in each wing tank. The end-plate effect of the tips allowed an increase of 200 pounds in gross weight. The nice thing is that the 200 pounds does not have to be in fuel. Keep the tips

empty, and you get the 200 pounds in the cabin. Gross weight is now 3,000 pounds with tips.

Density altitude is always a concern out west and the Comanche gives excellent D/A performance. The owner's manual is the pits on figuring out D/A, and some other things, so each pilot ought to be conservative on his first trials. However, with 60 gallons, four real-size passengers, I can get out of a 2,200-foot paved strip, D/A of 4,000 feet with no real problems.

With just pilot and full fuel, you are right up at the very front of the c.g. envelope—nothing dangerous, but gives you a decided nose-down feeling at cruise. Might just be an illusion, but you are right up at the front of the envelope.

Comfort can't be beat. I am a big person and I still have plenty of room. Noise level is a bit high, mainly due to poor door sealing—a generic fault in Comanches, unless fixed, and this is usually expensive. I usually use 143 knots for flight planning.

Carlton S. Yee
Eureka, Calif.

The Comanche 250 will fly an honest 160 knots, and I have had mine to 20,000 feet to get over weather. I generally burn 13 to 14 gallons per hour at 2400 rpm, full throttle, leaned, at altitudes between 12,000 and 15,000 feet.

Handling is generally very straightforward, and control pressures are average, in my opinion. The airplane does have two idiosyncrasies: first, it can be a difficult airplane to trim, and in rough air the airplane will not stay easily at a given altitude. Second, when the airplane is landed, a pilot must be very alert to his airspeed for touchdown. The airplane will make perfect landings time after time if flareout is done at the correct airspeed. Alternatively, the airplane will jar your teeth if you are three knots too fast or three knots too slow.

Jeffrey Bowen
Denver, Colo.

Lake Amphibian

If you're looking for a reasonably-priced land-or-water personal plane, the Lake LA-4 amphibian is virtually your only choice. For 40 percent less money, the Lake offers much better payload and similar performance to a hulking Cessna 185 on amphibious floats.

A Lake won't haul a moose or a 55-gallon oil drum, but that doesn't matter much to the typical individual buyer looking for a used amphibian for pleasure and/or business. Rather than, "Which amphibian should I buy?" the question becomes "Which model Lake?"

History

The Lake first appeared in the early 1950s as the Colonial C-1 Skimmer, a 150-hp three-placer developed by a couple of ex-Grumman engineers named Dave Thurston and Herb Lindblad. In 1958, power was increased to 180 hp, seating capacity increased to four, and the result was called the C-2. In 1960, the Skimmer got a major facelift, including a longer bow, a stretched wing, and a new name, the Lake LA-4. About 250 Skimmers and LA-4s had been built when production shut down in 1962.

The Lake was revived in 1963 under a new marketing arrangement whereby the aircraft were built by one company, Aerofab, and sold and serviced by another, Lake Aircraft. (That basic arrangement continues today.) In 1970, the 180-hp engine was replaced with a 200-hp fuel-injected Lycoming and the aircraft was renamed the Buccaneer. A small number of turbocharged models have been built over the years, and there was even one straight seaplane version built. The marketing company changed hands in 1979, and two new

When all the cold, rational analysis is finished, this is what hooks pilots on the amphibian: the idyllic summer lakeside setting.

models have been introduced since. The Buccaneer got an extended propeller shaft and other modifications in 1983 and was rechristened the EP, and an enlarged 250-hp five-place version called the Renegade has been certified. This report will not deal with the EP or Renegade.

Used-Plane Market

A first-time Lake buyer should be cautious. The market is fairly small (a recent issue of *Trade-A-Plane* lists fewer than a dozen for sale), and prices can vary all over the place because watercraft are much more susceptible to such value deflaters as corrosion or damage history. The Lake factory has also gotten into the refurbishing business in a big way, and now sells a dozen or so spruced-up used Lakes every year.

Because the Lake is rare and unusual, we'd strongly recommend a thorough prepurchase inspection by a knowledgable Lake mechanic—not just the guy down at the airport who has maintained your Cherokee for years. A good Lake man, for example, would know to check the hull bulkhead at station 97 for hard-landing damage. Not many Cessna wrenches would know that, we'd wager.

Performance

The price of doing land-water double duty is rather anemic performance by landplane standards. A 200-hp Buccaneer performs about on par with a typical 150-hp landplane. Lake used to advertise a max cruise speed of 130 knots but this was notoriously optimistic, as the present company admits. Most owners report cruise speeds in the 105-115-knot range. Unfortunately, fuel consumption matches that of other 200-hp planes at about 10 gph, so fuel mileage is a very poor 10 nmpg or so. A Mooney will fly 40 or 50 knots faster than a Lake on the same fuel. (On the other hand, you don't see many Mooneys landing in the water; those that do certainly don't take off again.)

Performance of the 180-hp Lakes is less by about 4-8 knots.

The Lake has a big wing that helps make up for the high drag, so book climb rate is a respectable 1,200 fpm. Several Lake pilots report, however, that at heavy weights it is rather sluggish getting "on the step" and in climb. The 180-hp airplanes should be considered two-place airplanes off the water, unless the takeoff area is huge.

At light weights, the Lake could almost be called a STOL plane. Owners report ground rolls of under 400 feet on land, and approach speed is a Cessna-150-like 57 knots.

Useful loads average about 800 pounds for a VFR 180-hp airplane to about 950 pounds for the 200-hp models—quite comparable to 200-hp landplanes. One loading quirk to look out for: as more passengers are added, c.g. moves forward. The Lake tends to be nose-heavy anyway (that's why the heater is on the ceiling instead of in the nose), and we read one Lake accident report in which the craft was loaded more than an inch ahead of the forward c.g. limit.

Fuel capacity is one shortcoming of the Lakes. Standard tanks hold 40 gallons, good for about three hours with a small reserve. At slow Lake speeds, that's just over 250 nm range. Auxiliary tanks in the wing sponsons can increase fuel capacity to a reasonable 54 gallons. Try to find a Lake with the extra tanks.

Creature Comforts

Inside room is adequate in the front seats, but rather tight in back. Two large adults will be very cozy in back. (L.L. Bean types tell us, however, that it's entirely possible to sleep two people in a Lake with the seats folded down.) The rear baggage compartment is small and accessible only through the two front clamshell doors—a "class A pain in the butt," according to one owner. The Lake's cargo/baggage limitations and docking problems are the main reasons it is rarely used by bush pilots.

Despite the location of the engine up and away from the fuselage, the interior is very noisy, according to owners. "I really need my David Clark headphones," commented one owner. The Lake factory now offers an interior soundproofing kit that is claimed to reduce the roar to some extent. Cosmetically, most Lake interiors are reminiscent of 1956 Nash Ramblers.

Handling

One of the Lake's worst features is ground handling. There's no nose-wheel steering, so the pilot must steer by differential braking. While

this approach works reasonably well in some planes, like the Grumman Americans, in the Lake it's lousy. Comments one owner, "It will quickly, and without warning, swerve to either side and become a monster to get straight again...I consider it dangerous for the novice."

On the water, the Lake is slow to get on the step with a heavy load. (One owner describes how rear seat passengers have to hike forward even at sea level in smooth water.) But once skimming along the surface, the Lake is exceptionally agile by seaplane standards, prancing through spray-soaked gyrations that would leave the typical floatplane pilot scared to death, if not upside down six feet under water.

In the air, the Lake has rather mediocre handling. The ailerons are nice and light, owners tell us, but the rudder is a thigh-crusher. Stalls are gentle, with good control from the huge rudder, and come at about 43 knots indicated. A maneuver favored by Lake demo pilots is the free-falling anvil descent: power off, gear and flaps down, and push over the nose. Thanks to the aforementioned Peterbilt aerodynamics, astounding descent rates can be achieved without building up excessive airspeed—and a good thing it is, since red line airspeed is only 127 knots.

One handling quirk of the Lake is its pitch response to power. Push the throttle sharply forward, and the nose goes down for a moment. Pull it back and the nose rises. (This, of course, is due to the high engine position, which generates

big pitching moments with power changes.) Also, takeoff requires a definite rotation by the pilot to overcome the high-power low-speed noseover tendency. Such unairplanelike traits might shock the Lake novice at first, but owners tell us they adjust quickly and find them no problem.

Overhead Engine

New Lake owners will have to adjust to the overhead engine controls. (Four levers in the turbo models.) Another oddity: because of the engine location, exhaust heat can't be used to heat the cabin. Heavy, expensive maintenance-hog gasoline heaters are unfortunately the only alternative. Up through 1973, Lakes had the troublesome Janitrols, which are subject to an AD requiring complete overhaul every two years. After 1974, Lake switched to Southwind heaters that were more reliable, but had only two positions, on or off. "You either cook or you freeze," is the way one owner put it. The 1983 models have an improved Janitrol that is supposed to be fantastic.

Maintenance

The Lake is a rather complicated airplane, with more than the usual number of systems. Gear, flaps and trim, for example, are all hydraulic. When the great bugaboo of all water airplanes—corrosion—enters the picture, the possibility arises for truly nightmarish maintenance prob-

On the water, Lakes take a surprising amount of abuse. Brake steering makes for awkward ground handling, however.

Early models had negligible corrosion proofing—a critical matter on these aircraft. Bulge at base of engine pylon is a gas heater.

lems in old or poorly kept-up Lakes, particularly those operated in salt water. Many used Lakes will be advertised as "never flown in salt water," but they should nevertheless be meticulously inspected for corrosion.

Corrosion-proofing deserves special attention. The 180-hp airplanes built during the '60s had no zinc chromate treatment, and some didn't have Alodine, either. "As far as we can tell, there was no pattern on the Alodining," says Bruce Rivard of Lake, who was part of the new regime that took over Lake marketing in 1979. "Some of them had it, some didn't." Alodine treatment has a faint gold tint; look for it in the interior structure on any pre-1970 airplane. Even with the Alodine treatment, the lack of the green zinc chromate primer makes those airplanes susceptible to corrosion. "A 180-hp Lake that's been in salt water is bad news," comments Rivard.

Starting in 1970, all Buccaneers were Alodined and zinc chromated. Starting with the 1983 models, an additional poly-chromate primer was used.

One mechanic described to us a $10,000 repair job on a corroded 1969 LA-4. (*Bluebook* price of a 1969 LA-4 is about $19,000 or so.) A bad case of corrosion in an old airplane can make it virtually worthless.

Water operations can also be hard on the hull structure. Hard landings on the water are fairly common because of unpredictable wind and waves, not to mention submerged sandbars and logs.

Carefully check the fuselage/hull structure for internal damage, especially the bulkhead at station 97. (This was strengthened in 1982 models.)

Once again, we recommend Lake specialist for this inspection. One owner reports sadly that the two mechanics he hired to do a prepurchase inspection of a used Lake missed $2,000 worth of internal damage, along with some leaky hydraulic lines.

Our check of FAA service difficulty reports revealed no major problem areas. We did notice several reports of nose gear malfunctions, and an odd reoccurrence of exhaust cracks at the number two cylinder, however. And one report caught our eye: "During taxi, engine fell over on wing."

Maintaining a Lake will probably be more expensive than taking care of a comparable 200-hp landplane—after all, you are keeping it both airworthy and seaworthy. At the right shop, however, the bill shouldn't be too high. One owner reports a $450 flat fee for the inspection alone, with additional repairs bringing the total bill to $850. The Lake factory has an unusual service for owners: they'll do an annual right at company headquarters (Laconia, N.H. in the summertime, Kissimmee, Fla. in

the winter). Flat rate is $400, with repairs extra, of course. "We'll give the owner a detailed list of problems so he'll know what he's getting into," comments a Lake spokesman.

Unfortunately, the factory doesn't like to do prepurchase inspections.

Here is a list of recommended Lake shops. (Just because a shop doesn't make our list is no cause for alarm. These just happened to have been recommended; other equally good, or better, shops may not have come to our attention.)

Ed Nelson, E&H Aircraft, Seattle, Wash. (206) 762-9285.

Mark McKinney, Midwest Airmotive, Plainfield, Ill. (312) 759-3988.

Elton Townsend, Gravenhurst, Ontario, Canada (705) 687-4343.

Alexander Aircraft Sales, Peoria, Ariz.

Frank Persson, Frank's Aircraft Service, Tulsa, Okla. (816) 836-3396.

Engines

The 180-hp Lycoming O-360 generally has a better service record than the fuel-injected 200-hp version. The IO-360 had some problems in the early 1970s, and Buccaneers of that vintage should be checked to make sure they have updated valves, camshafts and piston pins. TBO of unmodified early engines is only 1,200 hours, although this was increased to 1,400, then 1,600, and finally 1,800 hours if the improved parts were retrofitted.

Lake claims that the IO-360 runs cooler in its pylon installation than in any other aircraft, and that as a result engine life is longer. Lycoming has not officially endorsed this claim with a longer TBO specifically for the Lake, however.

Service Support

We get reports of uneven service support. One owner told us it was excellent; another described a four-month wait for a flap. A mechanic reported, "Some days it's good, some days it's bad, you can never tell." One buyer of a new 1983 airplane reports he had to replace a nose gear strut, a main gear strut, and a battery, and has had problems with a cracked cowling, magneto housings and the encoding altimeter. The plane was down for six months during its first year. He reports that Lake seemed unenthusiastic about providing service info or financial aid.

Other owners report good reliability, however, and our impression is that the small Lake sales/service organization can be responsive at the top levels. (The disgruntled 1983 Lake owner reports things improved after he called Lake president Armand Rivard.)

Safety

Our scan of NTSB records shows a total of 51 accidents during the period 1978 through 1981. Ten were fatal. About 43 percent of the accidents involved water operations. (This number is a bit uncertain, since the exquisitely vague language in the NTSB accident briefs sometimes didn't make it clear whether the accident occurred on the water or a land runway. The NTSB computer cleverly covered its butt by referring to "ground/water loop/swerves" on several occasions.)

The FAA has no hours-flown data on the Lake, so we are unable to calculate a precise accident rate. However, figuring that there are about 600 or so Lakes flying, and assuming an average of 150 hours per year for each airplane, we can make a rough guesstimate of 2.8

fatal accidents per 100,000 flight hours, and about 14 total accidents per 100,000 hours.

Both of these guesstimated numbers are fairly high in comparison to other single-engine retractables, which have fatal rates ranging from 0.8 to 3.3. Total accident rates of other retractables range from 4.6 to 15.0. The Lake seems to rank near the bottom of the safety standings among its peers. (Some may argue that the Lake's only peers are other amphibians. We don't have numbers for other amphibs, but our impression—an impression backed up by insurance rate numbers—is that amphibs as a class have far more accidents than comparable landplanes.)

The Lake's poor accident statistics are no big surprise, considering the unpredictability of water operations and the limited water experience of most Lake pilots. Of the 24 pilot-related water accidents in Lakes during the four-year period, just one involved a pilot with more than 200 hours time in type. Half the pilots had less than 50 hours in Lakes. "An amazingly high percentage of Lake accidents occur to new pilots in their first few hours of water flying," one insurance adjuster told us.

The message is clear: If you can get through the first couple of hundred hours in your Lake, the chances of a water accident go way down.

The water accidents we surveyed covered the predictable gamut— bounced landings, noseunders,

swerves and spinouts. Although splashily embarrassing and spectacular, Lake water accidents rarely hurt anybody. Only three were fatal—about 13 percent of the total. But water accidents did bend a lot of metal; every water accident listed by NTSB resulted in either destruction of the airplane or "substantial" damage.

Total flying experience seems almost irrelevant when it comes to flying a Lake safely. One fellow, for example, had nearly 9,000 hours total time, but only 10 hours in Lakes. He misjudged the distance required for a glassy water takeoff (apparently forgetting that the hull tends to "stick" longer to glassy-smooth water) and hit trees.

Lake pilots seemed to have their share of troubles taking off and landing on *terra firma* as well. More than half (16 out of 27) of the non-water crunches occurred on takeoff or landing. We also counted two engine failures, and two Lake pilots ran out of gas.

The secret to flying a Lake safely is to get a thorough checkout from an experienced Lake instructor. We're not talking an hour of touch-and-goes here; the factory usually spends 10 to 15 hours checking out purchasers of new Lakes. The factory also offers a check-out program for used-Lake buyers or owners, and we would strongly recommend it.

Insurance

Besides common sense and self-preservation, there's an economic

Cost/Performance/Specifications

Model	Year	Number Built	Average Retail Price	Cruise Speed (kts)	Rate of Climb (fpm)	Useful Load (lbs)	Fuel Std/Opt (gals)	Engine	TBO (hrs)	Overhaul Cost
C-1	1957	23	$ 10,250	97	700	790	30/39	150-hp Lyc. O-320-A2A	2,000	$6,000
C-2 IV	1958-59	128	$ 14,000	117	800	830	30/39	180-hp Lyc. O-360-A2A	2,000	$7,000
LA-4	1960-65	82	$ 16,000	114	800	850	40	180-hp Lyc. O-360-A2A	2,000	$7,000
LA-4	1966-69	102	$ 18,000	114	800	850	40	180-hp Lyc. O-360-A2A	2,000	$7,000
LA-4	1970-71	26	$ 20,500	114	800	850	40	180-hp Lyc. O-360-A2A	2,000	$7,000
LA-4-200	1970-71	53	$ 25,000	130	1,200	1,065	40/55	200-hp Lyc. O-360-A1B	1,800	$9,000
LA-4-200	1972-75	232	$ 29,500	130	1,200	1,065	40/55	200-hp Lyc. O-360-A1B	1,800	$9,000
LA-4-200	1976-77	150	$ 34,000	130	1,200	1,135	40/54	200-hp Lyc. O-360-A1B	1,800	$9,000
LA-4-200	1978	70	$ 36,000	130	1,200	1,135	40/54	200-hp Lyc. O-360-A1B	1,800	$9,000
LA-4-200	1979	52	$ 38,000	130	1,200	1,135	40/54	200-hp Lyc. O-360-A1B	1,800	$9,000
LA-4-200	1980	24	$ 42,500	130	1,200	1,135	40/54	200-hp Lyc. O-360-A1B	1,800	$9,000
LA-4-200	1981	49	$ 58,000	130	1,200	1,135	40/54	200-hp Lyc. O-360-A1B	1,800	$9,000
LA-4-200	1982	8	$ 82,500	130	1,200	1,135	40/54	200-hp Lyc. O-360-A1B	1,800	$9,000
LA-4-200EP	1983	N/A	$106,600*	130	1,200	1,135	40/54	200-hp Lyc. O-360-A1B6	1,800	$9,000

Lake Amphibian

incentive to get a factory checkout: lower insurance rates. Amphibious airplanes are notorious for high insurance rates. In Alaska, hull rates are so outlandish that most bush pilots do without. In the lower 48, a floatplane pilot may pay over 10 percent per year for hull coverage.

Luckily for Lake pilots, one insurance company has taken a special interest in Lakes. Alpha Aviation (800-526-0415) insures more than 200 Lakes, nearly half the fleet. The company gives an 18 percent discount to any pilot who has completed the factory training. And it generally charges lower rates than for comparable amphibious-float-equipped aircraft.

For example, the cost to insure a 1980 Lake Buccaneer flown by a pilot with 750 hours, 100 hours of Lake time and a factory checkout might be four to five percent annually. This would be about 30 percent higher than a comparable Mooney or Piper Arrow, but only about half that of a Cessna 185 on amphibious floats.

A low-time pilot with a fresh seaplane writing and a late-model airplane would pay about eight percent for hull coverage, perhaps $6,000. Thus the 18 percent discount for a factory checkout would amount to a savings of $1,000-plus the first year—enough to pay for the checkout.

"Our loss experience with the Lake has been excellent in liability and about average for hull," comments Frank Brown of Alpha. "Virtually every loss is water-related."

Turbochargers

Several dozen Lakes have been delivered with turbochargers. We'd advise buying one only if you plan to operate regularly out of high-altitude lakes. The airplanes are so slow that it's hardly worthwhile to climb high for speed. And the normal reasons people use to justify a turbo—the ability to climb above weather, maintain altitude over mountainous terrain, and to maintain altitude with a load of ice—just don't apply, since a Lake really has no business in such con-

Aircraft Resale Value Chart

ditions in the first place.

Balanced against the improved takeoff performance at altitude is the price of higher maintenance. The add-on Rajay turbos don't have a very good reliability history; 500 to 800 hours is considered to be a normal turbo life span. And of course the turbo makes the engine itself run hotter.

The turbo Lakes use manual wastegates. While this adds a fourth lever to the power quadrant and requires more pilot workload, it is more efficient and easier on the engine than the fixed-wastegates used in other Rajay installations like the Turbo Arrow, Seneca and Mooney 231. The Lake turbo is only a normalizer; that is, it may be used only to restore normal manifold pressures at high altitude. Max manifold pressure is still the normal 30 inches.

The turbo installation weighs about 40 pounds, and high-altitude flight requires a heavy-duty heater. Useful load is reduced to the point that an IFR Turbo 180 is a two-place airplane, and a Turbo Buccaneer not much better. And the small fuel supply limits the turbo's utility even more. Face it, the Lake is basically a low-altitude fun machine, and not even a turbocharger will turn it into a cross-country cruiser.

The original C-1 Skimmer built from 1956 through 1960 had a bow

two feet shorter and a wing four feet shorter than later Buccaneers. Consequently, the Skimmer tended to porpoise a lot, and climb rate was rather sickly. Only a handful of the 150-hp C-1 Skimmers are still flying, and perhaps a few dozen 180-hp C-2 Skimmers. They rarely come up for sale; the few that are left tend to be prized as antiques by doting owners. Value can range from $7,000 to $15,000, depending on condition.

The LA-4-180 can be a good bargain. There simply is no cheaper way to carry four people in an amphibian, although performance with four full-size adults is marginal. LA-4s generally run in the $15,000-20,000 range, although a factory-refurbished airplane with all the latest updates could go for as much as $27,000.

Most Lakes on the used-plane market are Buccaneers. There were no major changes in the Buccaneer until the 1983 EP model, but minor evolutionary changes over the years are worth looking for. Examples: the 1981 model has more grease fittings, polychromate primer, an improved canopy and better, more rust-resistant cabin vents. The 1975 model has improved grease fittings in the landing gear.

STC Mods

The only STC mod we're aware of is the Causley Super Lake, which appeared in 1982. But the company is apparently now out of business (the phone was disconnected when we called). The mod consisted of wing root fairings, float fairings, wheel well fairings, sculptured wingtips, trailing edge fillets called "batwings," a dorsal fin and new prop spinner. The aerodynamic improvements were claimed to add nine knots of cruise speed and "drastically" increase climb rate.

The Lake company itself is now the main purveyor of retrofit mods. It has taken over the "batwing" mod of the Causley STC, which Lake says helps improve flow around the pylon and propeller and provides more lift, particularly in ground (or water) effect. Cost: about $3,000.

Lake also offers the "Hydrobooster" hull mod, which consists of four external strakes. In addition to reinforcing the structure, the strakes are claimed to reduce water drag and make the craft more stable in turns. At a price of $1,580, the mod is "worth 10 times its price in what it does for the airplane," according to Bruce Rivard. The Lake factory can also retrofit improved canopies, instrument panels, interiors, soundproofing kits, wingtip foam flotation kits, and seven-gallon sponson fuel tanks.

The float tanks can be easily retrofitted to 1972 and later models, which already have the internal fuel lines in place. Cost is $4,032, or $3,537 if the old floats are in good shape and can be traded in. (Note, however, that full sponson tanks affect water handling and reduce buoyancy.)

Lake also can retrofit the cargo door it designed for the Renegade. Cost: $2,015.

Owner Comments

I have operated a Lake LA4-200EP about 300 hours since December of 1982. I have been more than pleased by my experience with this

Lake Amphibian

aircraft. The performance is truly phenomenal, and the aircraft is straightforward and easy to fly. I have found the performance claims of the manufacturer to be conservative.

In 300 hours the only parts replacement that was not part of the scheduled annual inspection was a trim actuator which the manufacturer cheerfully replaced under warranty.

The annual inspection was $580 with a standard labor cost for the inspection of $450.

Handling on both land and water is better than any other aircraft that I know.

Other new aircraft I have operated required constant attention for up to two years before all the "bugs" were removed.

John G. Kehlar
McLean, Va.

This is my second Lake Amphibian, which has to say something about my feeling for it. I have well over 1,000 hours in the aircraft. One sort of needs it. It is a difficult airplane to fly. It is a demanding aircraft. Very heavy rudder, for example.

The engine has performed flawlessly. And, as a matter of fact, there have been no real problems with the structure of the aircraft (except one real lousy water landing I once made).

It is sort of junky: It should be cleaned up for higher speeds. I

Extra cabin door, as on the Renegade here, can be retrofitted on older Lakes.

have the Q-tip propeller and it seems to help with the high noise level. I also use the David Clark headsets, which I think are vital against the noise.

Gerald R. Dillon
Minneapolis, Minn.

We purchased a 1981 demo approximately one year ago.

The aircraft was flown over 200 hours between April and October of 1983. Its performance was as expected: true airspeed at cruise (5,000-7,000 ft.) is 123-126 knots. climb rate 750 fpm; functional ceiling 8,000-9,000 ft. (where it runs out of strength). In almost all configurations we generally burned under 10 gph.

There is no question, however, that the Lake is the best thing going for water work. Once you have experienced the "greased swish" of a Lake landing, dry-land landings are of little further interest. As a watercraft, it excels. The only real drawback is docking; that is definitely easier on floats. The payload also lives up to expectations; with full fuel (54 gals.) we can still handle three good-sized souls (180 pounds) and 100 pounds of luggage within gross and c.g. limits.

All of this good commentary must be tempered, however, by serious servicing problems on this aircraft. From the day we purchased the Lake, we have experienced continuing problems with the nose strut, electrical systems and other items detailed in our correspondence to Lake Aircraft Co. While the staff at Lake was generally helpful, the fact remains that the aircraft underwent a factory annual at the time of purchase, a 100-hr. inspection during the month of July (1983) and a recommended second annual in November (1983) that was only just completed last month because of the aforementioned problem areas. We realize that an airplane is a big hole in the sky in which you pour money, but this has been ludicrous.

J. A. Germ
Naperville, Ill.

Piper Turbo Arrow

Although it occupies a marketing niche as a bargain-basement turbo single, the Piper Turbo Arrow is the ultimate refinement of the classic four-place Cherokee series—certainly the most popular low-wing airplane class ever. The turbocharged, retractable member of the Cherokee line was introduced in 1977 as a companion to the best-selling Arrow III, and it has proven very popular. In 1982, for instance, the Turbo outsold the standard Arrow by nearly five to one, proving once more that sophistication and performance are bigger selling points than reliability and low maintenance.

While the Turbo Arrow does have some reasonable performance numbers, and can be picked up on the used market for as little as $35,000, potential trouble spots under the cowling deserve serious consideration by any used-plane shopper.

History

The Turbo Arrow's genealogy so far has been fairly brief and not very eventful. When it first appeared in 1977, there were some eyebrows raised at the 200-hp six-cylinder Continental TSIO-360 engine. The standard Arrow had received good service from the four-cylinder 200-hp Lycoming, and the logical progression would have been to turbocharge that power-plant. But Rockwell had already taken that approach with its 112TC, with very poor results. And Piper had already used the Continental TSIO-360 for several years in its Seneca II, so it chose virtually the same powerplant for the Turbo Arrow.

Turbo Arrow is distinguishable from its non-turbo brother (rear) by sharp spinner and landing light pod below the cowl. These are 1978 models.

After two years on the market-place, the Turbo Arrow III underwent a facelift—or rather tail-lift—to become the Turbo Arrow IV. The standard, boring, quiche-eating tail was discarded in favor of a bold new T-tail. It was strictly a cosmetic move, designed to fit Piper's new T-tail motif (already established by the Tomahawk, Lance II and Cheyenne III). The 1979 Turbo Arrow IV also got a new version of the TSIO-360 with a beefier crankshaft, denoted by the suffix '-FB' instead of the previous '-F.' That change increased TBO from 1,400 hours to 1,800. Other than engine and tail, changes have been minor.

Used-Plane Market

The market for Turbo Arrows is fairly active. "They're a popular plane," one big broker told us. Real-world prices generally start at about $30,000 for a 1977 model with a high-time engine, and climb to upwards of $75,000 for a cream-puff loaded 1983 model. A typical 1980 Turbo Arrow with a few IFR goodies would go in the low forties. The T-tail version suffers a bit in today's rather depressed market compared to the "old-fashioned" low-tail models. "I wouldn't pay one scratch more for a '79 T-tail than a '78 low-tail," the broker commented. "That's because my customers won't pay any more, either." The T-tail penalty on the Turbo Arrow, however, is nowhere near as heavy as that on the T-tail Lance, which is a real dog on the market because of its poor handling qualities compared to the standard Lance (and subsequent Saratogas).

One reason Turbo Arrows are so popular is that prices are comparatively low. Compare the Turbo Arrow to the Mooney 231, for example. Both are four-place retractables powered by identical engines. Yet the Mooney commands a far higher price on the used-plane market, a measure of the relative esteem in which the two airplanes are held by the flying public. While a 1980 Turbo Arrow IV can be had for just over $40,000, you'll need better than 60 grand to take home a 1980 231. The Turbo Arrow is worth $5,000-$10,000 less than even the non-turbocharged Mooney 201, which has similar performance. Compared to the standard Arrow, the Turbo version commands from $3,000 to $8,000 more, depending on the year.

Performance

The Turbo Arrow has reasonably good, although by no means sizzling, performance. Most Turbo Arrow owners fly in the 10,000-13,000-foot altitude range, just below the point where oxygen becomes necessary. At these altitudes, the airplane turns in cruising speeds ranging from about 165 knots at 75 percent power and about 14 gph to 150 knots at 65 percent power and 11 gph. Several owners report speeds well in excess of book figures, although Piper airspeed indicators are often optimistic.

The maximum book cruise figure is 172 knots at 19,000 feet. The only owner we heard from who's flown that high reported achieving 167 knots at 65 percent power—right on the book number.

Owner-reported power settings are not very reliable, however, because of the primitive and incorrect power charts Piper supplies with the airplane. The Turbo Arrow book says that at a given rpm, the same manifold pressure will give the same power output at any altitude from sea level to 20,000 feet. This is nonsense, of course; exhaust back pressure and compressor discharge temperature vary with altitude, and both of these factors affect power output. (Mooney's power chart for the same basic engine shows up to three inches variation in manifold pressure for constant power at various altitudes. Even Piper notes such variations in the power charts for its Seneca III, which uses essentially the same engine as the Turbo Arrow.) The Turbo Arrow owner is thus very poorly equipped to set power precisely. At 14,000 feet, what he believes to be 75 percent power "by the book" is in reality closer to 83 percent power.

Turbo Arrow cruise speeds are about 20 knots below those of the Mooney 231. It's slower than even the non-turbocharged Mooney 201 at any non-oxygen altitude. But the Mooneys are unusually fast; compared to other competitive airplanes, like the Rockwells and Cessnas, the Turbo Arrow stacks up pretty well.

Climb rate is a creditable 950 fpm at sea level and gross weight. As with any turbo aircraft, rate of climb is maintained constant (or nearly so) at altitude, and owners report climb rates of 1,000 fpm with typical loads (below gross) all the way up to 10,000 feet. At moderate weights, ROC is still 500 fpm at 20,000 feet. While this is quite good by non-turbocharged standards, it again falls well short of the Mooney 231, the only directly competitive airplane. Under the same conditions, the 231 will climb 840 fpm.

Range of the Turbo Arrow is good. It has big 72-gallon tanks, enough for about five hours normal cruising with a small reserve. At an average cruise speed of 160 knots, that's nearly 800 nm. (Max cruise at rich mixtures reduces this range appreciably.) Throttled back to 55 percent power at 10,000 feet and 9.2 gph, the Turbo Arrow is good for seven hours at 135 knots—better than 900 nautical. Basically, the Turbo Arrow will take you about as far as you'd want to go in one hop. (Unfortunately, that nasty ol' 231 is still there to embarrass the Turbo Arrow; the Mooney will fly about 100 miles farther.)

Loading

The Turbo Arrow has a gross weight of 2,900 pounds. Real-world empty weights of IFR-equipped airplanes typically run around 1,900-1,950 pounds, leaving a useful load of about 950-1,000 pounds. With full fuel, that's 550 pounds for payload—three people and 10 pounds of carry-on. A cabin full of people and luggage will cut fuel capacity to 30 gallons, enough for perhaps 200 nm with IFR reserves. Such loading numbers are typical of four-place retractables.

Piper makes a big deal out of the

Cost/Performance/Specifications

Model	Year	Number Built	Average Retail Price*	Gross Weight (lbs)	Useful Load (lbs)	Cruise Speed (kts)	Fuel (gals)	Engine	TBO (hrs)	Overhaul Cost
PA-28R-201T (III)	1977	427	$ 35,000	2,900	1,200	172	72	200-hp Cont. TSIO-360-F	1,400	$11,000
PA-28R-201T (III)	1978	427	$ 40,000	2,900	1,200	172	72	200-hp Cont. TSIO-360-F	1,400	$11,000
PA-28RT-201T (IV)	1979	310	$ 41,500	2,900	1,200	172	72	200-hp Cont. TSIO-360-FB	1,800	$10,750
PA-28RT-201T (IV)	1980	178	$ 51,000	2,900	1,200	172	72	200-hp Cont. TSIO-360-FB	1,800	$10.750
PA-28RT-201T (IV)	1981	167	$ 61,500	2,900	1,200	172	72	200-hp Cont. TSIO-360-FB	1,800	$10,750
PA-28RT-201T (IV)	1982	68	$ 77,500	2,900	1,200	172	72	200-hp Cont. TSIO-360-FB	1,800	$10,750
PA-28RT-201T (IV)	1983	48	$114,440**	2,900	1,200	172	72	200-hp Cont. TSIO-360-FB	1,800	$10,750

*Price assumes dual navcom and VOR, localizer, glideslope, markers, transponder, encoder, ADF, two-axis autopilot, oxygen, 750 hours on engine. Wholesale prices about 20 percent less.
** Deduct $112/hr. for every hour after 50 TTSN.

Turbo Arrow's load-carrying abilities, claiming in magazine ads that it is superior to that of the nemesis Mooney 231. This is hogwash. The 231 has useful load numbers very similar to the Turbo Arrow's.

Loading balance is no problem in a Turbo Arrow unless it is equipped with air conditioning. The heavy (60-lb.) rear compressor limits rear-seat and baggage loading, according to two different Turbo Arrow owners who responded to our survey. The air-conditioning option moves the c.g. back by nearly an inch, or about seven percent of the envelope. Without air conditioning, however, a typical IFR-equipped Arrow demands only normal everyday attention to c.g. matters.

Handbook figures for the 1978 T-Arrow III and 1979 IV version suggest that the IV has dramatically better takeoff performance. At 7,000 feet and 20° C., for example, the book says a Turbo Arrow III will clear the obstacle in about 5,700 feet at gross weight. For the T-Arrow IV, the figure is 3,400 feet.

Why the astounding difference? Should a mountain dweller insist upon only a T-Arrow IV? Not necessarily. Piper engineers admit that there is no actual performance difference between the two airplanes, side-by-side on the same day. Apparently Piper simply changed its procedures for measuring (and extrapolating) takeoff data. So which figure reflects reality? We have no idea. The lesson for Turbo Arrow shoppers: Don't take the handbook numbers very seriously.

Creature Comforts

The Turbo Arrow rates about average in cabin roominess. The Cherokee was originally designed not to be *too* wide, in order not to make the top-of-the-line Comanche look bad. So the Turbo Arrow gets stuck with a fairly narrow 42-inch cabin. Headroom is pretty good, with a floor-to-ceiling distance of 48 inches, very typical of single-engine airplanes and four inches more than the low-slung Mooneys. Legroom in the rear is

good, the result of a fuselage stretch given the whole Cherokee line back in 1972.

Flying Qualities

Turbo Arrow owners praise their craft for its benign and solid handling, particularly in IFR conditions. It has no unusual vices that we're aware of. There are some differences between the later T-tail models and the earlier low-tail versions, however. According to one owner who has flown both extensively, the primary difference is in the planes' reactions to gear and flap lowering. Putting down the wheels causes no pitch change in the T-tail and a nose-down pitch in the low-tail. Flaps trigger a sharp nose-up surge in the low-tail, and nose-down action in the T.

Runway traits are also different. The T-tail airplane does not rotate as quickly on takeoff, and does not have as good pitch authority at low speeds. (The low tail sits in the prop blast and is therefore more responsive.)

Engine

The heart of any airplane is its engine, and beneath the cowling of the Turbo Arrow beats a heart of . . . well, it's not gold by any stretch of the imagination. The TSIO-360-F and -FB are hot-running, high-vibration engines that have had a host of problems. (For details, see the March 1, 1983 issue of *Aviation Consumer*.) And we're not just talking maintenance headaches. The fixed-wastegate TSIO-360 series as installed in the Turbo Arrow, Turbo Dakota, Seneca III and Mooney 231 has an engine-failure accident rate eight times

higher than the Bonanza's, for example. FAA data shows 26 Turbo Arrow accidents or incidents stemming from powerplant failures in a recent five-years period. (The Turbo Dakota, essentially a Turbo Arrow with fixed gear, is even worse; seven percent of the fleet had engine failures in only three years.)

Here's a laundry list of major Turbo Arrow engine problems:

• Broken connecting rods. Apparently a batch of improperly heat-treated rods found their way into some engines built around 1979. Failures in Turbo Arrows have resulted.

• High-altitude "missing." Above about 12,000-15,000 feet, the thin air has markedly less insulating effect. Therefore, magneto current is more likely to leak out and "arc," causing possibly severe misfiring. Keeping the ignition system in perfect shape and plug gaps tight can help, but the real solution is to pressurize the magnetos. Mooney fixed the same problem on its 231 a couple of years ago (offering free retrofit kits to owners), but Piper so far has ignored it.

• Cylinder, piston and valve problems. Generally caused by running too hot at too high boost. The fixed-wastegate design means that the turbocharger is always running,

This aircraft with good IFR equipment was able to carry full fuel, 200 pounds in the baggage compartment, plus two 170-pounders in front and a 123-pounder in the rear seat and remain within limits.

whether it's needed or not. This increases stress on the engine and raises inlet air temperatures. That, combined with poor cooling, causes all sorts of upper-end distress.

• Turbocharge cracking. This has been the subject of a recent (and very expensive) AD. Turbos must be inspected every 200 hours and replaced if cracked (many have been found that way). Cost to replace a housing: about $1,000.

• Poorly designed breather tubes. They can freeze up, causing all the oil to be vented overboard. At least one accident has resulted. Check Service Bulletins M80-18 and M79-19. Applied to 1977-78 airplanes only.

• Oil pump tach drive. Improperly torqued bolts cause oil pumps to break. Major AD in 1981.

In addition, there have been literally dozens of service bulletins on the engine.

All this is not to say that the TSIO-360-F or -FB cannot be a safe, reliable powerplant. Several Turbo Arrow owners reported no problems at all over hundreds of hours. The secret seems to be to keep the engine cool and to avoid high-boost conditions.

Cooling Problems

The Turbo Arrow's engine reliability woes are partly a result of poor engine cooling. Many owners report that cylinder head temperatures run right at the redline in warm weather, and find they must use special procedures—climbing flat and fast, running rich mixtures, and foregoing high altitudes—to avoid overheating the engine. Piper designed the Turbo Arrow without cowl flaps, apparently in a misguided effort to save money and keep the price down. As a result, the Turbo Arrow runs very hot in climb, yet during cruise on cold days the engine can actually be overcooled. This wastes several knots of cruising speed.

The cooling problem also wastes a lot of money, since pilots must

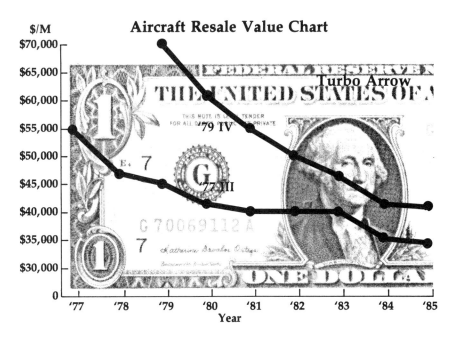

Aircraft Resale Value Chart

often run extra-rich fuel mixtures just to cool the engine. An extra gallon an hour can easily add up to over $500 in fuel per year (assuming 300 hours annually). Some Turbo Arrow pilots find that even full rich mixture is not enough during climb, and have taken to turning the fuel boost pump on to force even more excess fuel through the overheated cylinders.

The integrity of the cooling baffles is absolutely critical to Turbo Arrow engine health. Check them carefully, particularly the rubber seals. We'd also recommend installation of an optional Piper cooling kit. It consists of new baffles and extra louvers in the bottom of the cowling. (It's kit number 764-152V, listing at $458.36.) Installation is estimated at eight hours. Piper for some reason seems almost to keep the kit a secret, describing it only in an obscure ''Service Spares Letter'' (No. 388) rather than the normal service bulletin/service letter network to which most mechanics and some owners routinely subscribe. (The kit is available for 1977-79 models, but not, as best we could discern, for 1980s or 1981s. The cooling mod was a factory option in 1982, and was made standard equipment for 1983.)

There is a flip side to the cooling kit, however. Because more air is flowing over the cylinders at all times, the airplane will be more prone to overcooling during descent, which can cause engine

damage due to thermal shock. (At least one engine expert dismisses thermal shock as an old wives' tale, however.) In any case, pilots of Turbo Arrows with cooling kits installed should resign themselves to the loss of a couple of knots of cruise speed and be very careful on descent.

Operating Quirks

To assess the Turbo Arrow's role as an economy turbo—it is in fact the cheapest turbocharged airplane currently in production—Piper decided on a fixed wastegate. The gate is stuck part way open at all times. Sure, it's cheaper to build that way, but such a primitive system has some disadvantages. First, the turbo works all the time, even when it's not needed. Second, minor changes in speed, altitude or rpm cause big swings in manifold pressure, even with the throttle fixed.

As a result, takeoff procedures are weird; the pilot advances the throttle only to about 35 inches to start the takeoff roll. As the plane accelerates, mp shoots up to the redline of 41 inches all by itself. During climb, mp drops off with increasing altitude. And any rpm change results in huge mp variations. In fact, we once flew a Turbo Arrow in which power was increased for climb by *reducing* the throttle. The previous rpm adjustment had already caused the mp to zoom up above the redline by itself.

Starting the TSIO-360 can be a problem on cold mornings. Try to buy an airplane with the optional priming system. We once had to leave an airplane (not equipped with the primer) sitting for several days when it absolutely failed to start in 30° weather. One owner describes the priming system as "worth its weight in gold."

Safety

We have no overall fatal accident figures for the Turbo Arrow alone. However, the Arrow series in general had a fatal accident rate of 11.3 per 100,000 flight hours for the period 1972-76. (This acocunts for fatal accidents from all causes.) The 11.3 figure is about average, ninth among 13 retractable singles sampled by *Aviation Consumer*. (The rates ranges from 4.6 to 16.8.) Considering that the Arrow is often a "step-up" retractable flown by less experienced pilots, that is not a bad record.

The Turbo Arrow differs only in the engine, and as we have already said, the engine failure accident rate is very high. Fortunately none of those engine failures have yet resulted in fatalities.

The T-Arrow has one good feature that reduces embarassing runway crunches: the famous automatic landing gear. The autogear works, there's no doubt about it; the Arrow series has a gear-up accident rate less than a third of the Cessna Cardinal's. Some pilots dislike the auto-gear intensely, however, mostly because it can stay down too long on takeoff, or possibly extend inadvertently in a steep climb situation if improperly calibrated or adjusted. The system can be overridden, however, and some pilots choose to do that. Nevertheless, we feel the Arrow automatic gear system is a praiseworthy safety feature.

Maintenance

A Turbo Arrow is almost certain to be far more expensive than a standard Arrow to maintain. A factory remanufactured TSIO-360-FB costs about $14,000. Pro-rated over the 1,800-hour TBO, that's nearly nine

Turbo Arrow is a bargain basement turbo, but a combination that can sometimes spell trouble.

dollars per hour. For the 1,400-hour -F engine on 1977-79 T-Arrows, the number is a formidable $11 per hour plus. (Incidentally, according to one owner, Continental will not accept an older -F engine in exchange for an -FB reman. He was forced to either buy a reman engine with a crankshaft of questionable strength, or spend $6,400 extra to buy an -FB engine outright, with no trade-in.)

Annual inspection costs for the Turbo Arrow can be high. Typical costs reported by owners ranged from $1,100 to $3,400, although one fellow reported $500. (He apparently didn't bother with any AD notes.) Hourly maintenance costs seem to run in the $15-$25 range.

The only major relatively recent AD is that on the Rajay turbo housing. Try to buy an airplane with a late-model, ductile ni-resist housing that does not need repetitive 200-hour inspections and is less likely to crack. Naturally, all ADs should be complied with on any airplane considered for purchase.

A recent service bulletin recommends an inspection for cracked nosegear link and brace assem-

blies. Determine whether this has been accomplished on any plane under consideration.

Modifications

Knots 2U Inc., (312) 256-4807, offers aileron and flap gap seals for about $1,000 plus installation. These are said to increase cruise speed by about five knots; reduce stall, takeoff and approach speeds by about four knots; and provide crisper aileron control. "It makes a whole new airplane out it," one Turbo Arrow owner told us.

Turboplus Inc. (800) 742-4202, has developed an extensive engine mod for the Turbo Arrow that should go a long way toward solving the overheating and reliability problems. It consists of an improved induction system, a turbocharger intercooler, pressurized magnetoes, cowl flaps and improved engine instrumentation. Cost of the mod kit is $4,995 plus installation by your local mechanic. Or Turboplus will install it for you at a cost of $6,495.

Frankly, Turboplus appears to be doing what Piper should have been doing all along. Currently, The Turbo Arrow can be characterized as an excellent airframe with a poor engine installation. The Turboplus mod promises to make the Turbo Arrow an all-around good airplane.

Owner Comments

I have owned my Arrow for 20 months and have flown 225 hours during that time. My aircraft now has a total of 660 hours. I fly out of Colorado Springs at an altitude of 6,175 feet and find the turbo a necessity. I average 10.4 gph block to block cruising at 65 percent power at usual altitudes between 10,000 and 15,000 feet. I file for a TAS of 155 knots and believe this aircraft offers an excellent balance between speed, efficiency, and payload. The plane is a stable instrument platform and has a generous center of gravity envelope. The optional electric primer makes starting even in cold weather a snap, and I consider this feature a must. The cabin is average for this class of aircraft, but even with my wife and two children under three, we get along comfortably on long trips.

The fixed-gate turbo means constant throttle adjustments are necessary while climbing and descending. This does not create a problem for a regular user, but I would not recommend this aircraft for rental pilots without a *thorough* checkout.

My maintenance has been expensive. My first annual cost $1,721. This did include a complete review of all the maintenance history and a costly fuel tank inspection. My last annual cost $3,401. However this included a recurring propeller overhaul (a real aggravation since the AD is irrespective of hours flown) and the recent Rajay AD compliance, which fortunately for me was published while my aircraft was down for the annual.

Thanks to a great maintenance facility (West Aire, Inc., Colorado Springs, Colo., Verlin Schauer, chief of maintenance) I was able to have one of the few improved "04" housings available installed, which relieves me of repetitive inspections. This alone accounted for approximately $1,200 of my annual costs, and the prop overhaul cost approximately $700. My direct operating costs have been $57 per

Piper Turbo Arrow

hour. This does not include insurance, tie down, new radio equipment (Stormscope or heat shields), or overhaul reserve.

The two other items: I used to have a problem with cylinder head temperatures rising into the red, but I have found that using continuous LO fuel boost pump during climbout and a slightly higher or richer mixture has practically eliminated this problem. I figure the slight increase in fuel consumption will offset the possibile earlier overhaul.

Also, I have been spoiled by the turbo capabilities, and if I ever move from the Rockies, I believe I will still want a turbocharged aircraft for its tremendous performance and reserve power. Also I feel a turbocharged aircraft is one of the best defenses against unexpected icing. I love my plane.

David S. Lennon
Colorado Springs, Colo.

I have owned a 1978 Turbo Arrow III for the past 18 months. It is simply the best four-place aircraft that I have flown. While not as fast as the Mooney 231, it does offer the following:

• Comfort. The cabin is large enough for six-footers without cramping.

• Cruise performance of 165 to 170 knots at 12,500 feet.

• A good useful load (1,090 pounds on mine), leaving a payload of 670 pounds with full fuel.

• An honest 1,000-fpm climb at gross weight below 10,000 feet.

Since buying this aircraft, I have had no turbo-related problems. The engine does run hot, and the leaning can put the CHT into the red if one is not careful. In the summer additional fuel is burned (1-1½ gph) to cool the engine. Pulling 75 percent power on a hot day will

Interior space is adequate, if not sensational. "Luxury" velour interior was an extra-cost option on this 1978 model.

burn about 15 gph. Starting is easy. The manifold pressure must be monitored on takeoff and minor prop variations in speed can change the boost by two to three inches.

Would I buy another Turbo Arrow? Yes, if it was not a T-tail. It beats the tacky interior and complicated landing gear of the Turbo Skylane and provides room for large people, unlike the Mooney.

Michael G. Salish
Lakeside, Calif.

I have owned a 1977 Turbo Arrow for the past two years. I have also flown extensively a 1980 T-tail Turbo Arrow. In regard to flying characteristics, I have found that the major difference between the two is the trim control. In the low-tail version, lowering the gear causes a nose-up attitude that can be only partially compensated for with 10 degrees of flaps. The T-tail model shows no sudden trim changes with gear extension. It does require, though, full back trim with full flaps on landing. Both planes are extremely easy to fly and do very well in IFR conditions and crosswind landings.

Cost of owning the airplane has been quite dear. Two ADs have alone cost $1,600 over the past year. One was for a nose gear overhaul and the second for the oil pump torque adjustment. The other major cost has been leaking fuel-sending devices, requiring gasket replacement and 16 hours of labor. The last annual cost $2,200, which does include the above men-

tioned torque adjustment AD, but not the nose gear. The plane has cost $60 an hour, dry, to fly. There is currently an AD against the turbocharger. If ours has a crack, I am looking at another $1,400 for a replacement.

The engine now needs a major overhaul at 1,500 hours. Will I do it? Perhaps. I am also looking at a Mooney.

Gerald R. Moress
Salt Lake City, Utah

I recently purchased a 1979 Turbo Arrow and am very pleased with it. It is a very stable, good-handling airplane. My T-Arrow trues at 146 knots at lower altitudes and 156 knots at higher altitudes at 65 percent power, and burns 11 gph. The annual inspection cost $497.

All in all, the T-Arrow is a pretty good airplane, it is faster than some and slower than others, but it does a pretty good job for me. Outside of cosmetic purposes, I don't see much of an advantage of the T-tail over the low tail. I like Piper's soundproofing package. The quiet ride is the first comment that Cessna drivers make.

Mike Casey
Lewis, Iowa

To date I have logged 60 hours in my 1977 Turbo Arrow, bought used in October 1982. I am very satisfied with the stability, handling and overall performance, with the following observations:

One of the first modifications was to pressurize the Bendix mags. At 17,500 feet the engine was smooth as silk, no roughness. But I could not operate above 55 percent power at this altitude due to CHT overheating. Perhaps a richer mixture would have helped, but economy would suffer. Perhaps an intercooler. Turboplus, maybe?

At 15,500, no problems. About 165 knots TAS at 65 percent power gave about 11 gph (30 inches at 2400 rpm).

Only mechanical problem so far was the gear retraction hydraulic

pump. An "O" ring failed and the gear would not retract. Repair cost was $202.

Robert Doenges
Rancho Palos Verdes, Calif.

The recent AD on Rajay turbos turned up an interesting situation. If your repair station orders the casting from Continental, you'll be charged about $650 for the part. However, if the part is ordered from Rotomaster for a turbocharger that fits a Lycoming engine (same part number), the price is $477. Combs Gates at Arapahoe Airport has replaced more than a dozen castings at the $477 price, while nobody else around here has caught on.

The speed and fuel consumption is acceptable to us—we figure on 11.5 gph and plan for 155 knots. Our maintenance reserve is high because of our experience with Continental's optimistic estimate of TBO. Annuals are in the $500 range, and we fly about 150 hours per year.

Philip Williamson
Aurora, Colo.

My plane is a 1978 model I bought new and by fixing and modifying as needed. I have a very satisfactory plane. We took delivery and had to argue with the dealer that the loose horizontal stabilizer was not designed that way—he wanted to charge me to tighten the hinges.

Most cooling problems have involved careless assembly of the rubber baffles, which I got hardnosed about. I finally added the optional cooling kit, which now gives me a very normal operating temperature.

I had a high-altitude missing problem from day one, and it would *almost* go away with a very careful tune-up, but gets worse very quickly. In desperation, I started to completely replace the magnetos, and lo-and-behold, guess what! The mag shop discovered a hairline crack in the distributor cap. After replacing the cap, no more high altitude missing. I wonder how

many misfiring Turbo Arrows have cracked caps?

Vibration and shaking from the two-blade prop on that six-cylinder Continental had always bothered me. Three power pulses for two prop blades are impossible to balance. So six months ago I had a new full-size 76-inch three-blade prop put on. What a difference! I should have done it sooner. It changed the character of the plane completely, but for the better. Very smooth, super acceleration on takeoff, much quieter, faster cruise at low rpm and much steeper closed-throttle approaches for obstacle clearance.

Merrill D. Martin
Emeryville, Calif.

As an owner of a 1978 T-Arrow, I have been very happy with its performance. I have not kept specific records of maintenance and hourly costs, but I consider mine to be about average. I have replaced my attitude indicator two times and DG once, however.

I have not experienced the heating problems that have been mentioned, but I did experience the engine roughness at high altitude. The roughness was corrected by my FBO. It was found to be a faulty mag condenser. I generally fly 10,000-13,000 feet on long trips, and it has been fine so far.

My only real complaint has to be the numerous ADs on the airplane and a 100 percent lack of support from factory and/or parts manufacturers. I have very strong feelings that the ADs are due to faulty manufacturing and installation and should be borne by the companies, as the ADs are not due to lack of maintenance and performance of my part. These have been very costly: 1) gas line replacements and gas valve problems, 2) heat shield, 3) mags, 4) Rajay turbo cracks, 5) nose wheel, and more. I have been told by my FBO that Piper will not do any repairs or accept responsibility on out-of-warranty items. *This is wrong.*

David A. Gray, Jr.
Sacramento, Calif.

Rockwell 114

The Rockwell 114 is a sad story—a fine-looking, well-built aircraft that survived only four years in the marketplace. The 114 doesn't fly very fast and guzzles a lot of gas, but perhaps its most damaging liability is the fact that it was marketed by Rockwell, which never was successful in the single-engine plane business and finally packed it in for good in 1979, taking the 114 with it, of course. Fewer than 500 Model 114s were built. "They're hard to sell," one big used-plane broker told us, "but there's still a following for the airplane."

History

The 114 is an outgrowth of the 112, introduced in 1972. The 112 was developed after marketing studies showed that customers wanted zippy styling and comfort above all. The 112 had all that, but was so underpowered with its 200-hp Lycoming that it could barely get out of its own way. As a result, the 112 is a slug on the used-plane market (we heard of one changing hands for $12,000 back in 1982). In 1976, Rockwell introduced the 114, which was simply a 112 with a 260-hp engine. The 114 is commonly characterized as "the plane the 112 should have been in the first place."

The 114 was in production only four years, with no model changes of consequence. The 1977 model had aerodynamic improvements resulting in slghtly improved performance, plus better soundproofing and fixes for earlier compass interference and trim-tab freeze-up problems. In 1979, the "Gran Turismo" version was offered, with a three-bladed prop, new cowl flaps, a fancy interior—and an outrageous price. The $95,000 price

tag (more than the bigger, faster, more powerful Cessna 210) was apparently a desperate attempt by Rockwell to recoup some of its losses, but the strategy backfired, and 114 sales declined sharply in 1979. Shortly thereafter the entire Rockwell single-engine line was aborted.

Used-Plane Market

The 114 is not exactly a gem on the used-plane market. In the current depressed single-engine market, a 114 can be had for anywhere from about $30,000 for a 1976 model to about $40,000 for a 1979 Gran Turismo.

Currently, 114s of almost any vintage are worth only a little better than half their new-plane price tags—a very low figure. Used blue-chippers like the Mooney 201 and Bonanza are worth 75-85 percent of their new prices. (We should point out that the 114's new price tags were ridiculously inflated, and that most new 114s were sold at heavily discounted prices, so the picture is not quite as bad as the numbers portray.)

Performance

The 114 is a mediocre performer, considering its power. Owners report cruise speeds in the 150-knot range, not very fast for 260 hp. The Mooney 201, and Cessna Skylane RG both fly faster on

One of the few low-wingers with two doors, the 114 is noted for its creature comforts.

less power (the Mooney dramatically so). When the 114 was introduced, *Aviation Consumer* pilots flew the aircraft in a side-by-side test with a 1972 Piper Comanche, which had the same 260-hp engine. Results: the Comanche was not only faster, but climbed better and stalled slower to boot. Book max. cruise figure is 156 knots for the 1976 model 114, and 161 knots for later versions.

Fuel efficiency is directly related to speed, and again the 114 looks bad compared to its main competition, the Mooney and Skylane RG. Owners report fuel flows of 12-14 gph at moderate cruise speeds, for an mpg rating of about 12-13. In these days of $2 per gallon avgas, it is rather hard to justify such poor fuel efficiency (particularly in a retractable). At the prevailing $1 a gallon price when the 114 was first introduced, fuel efficiency was not so critical, but every fuel price increase particularly hurts the 114. (In the last few years, of course, there has been talk of oil gluts, and crude prices have actually fallen, and many soothsayers predict fuel prices will hold steady or decline for several years to come. That is good news for 114 owners, who can almost watch their plane's resale value curve mirror the spot-market crude price zigzags.)

Climb performance and range are both adequate. Listed rate of climb is just over 1,000 fpm for the 1976 model, and 1,160 fpm thereafter, comparable to performance by the Mooney and Skylane RG's, and superior to that of the economy 200-hp retractables such as the Arrow, Sierra, Cardinal RG and, of course, the sickly 112. Range is 600 nm or so, well short of the Mooney's and Skylane RG. The 68-gallon fuel supply is enough for four hours or so at high cruise and five-plus hours at low cruise, but the 114 lacks the huge reserves of endurance of the Mooney and RG, both of which carry more fuel and burn it at a slower rate.

Creature Comforts

If Rockwell salesmen didn't like to dwell on performance, they positively glowed when talking about the 114's cabin. It is 47 inches wide, wider than that of any other single and a lot of twins. Owners invariably cite the roomy cabin as a prime reason for buying the airplane and, particularly in the later models, the 114's interior trim complemented the roominess. The rear seats, however, are a bit short on legroom. Linebackers should love the 114; power forwards maybe not.

Early 114s were quite noisy, but Rockwell has offered a sound-proofing kit to cut a few decibels from the cockpit din. Later models are quieter, but still typical of the horribly noisy (90-95 dBA) cockpits of virtually all light aircraft.

Loading

While the 114's useful load is rather low for a 260-hp airplane (it's about 350 pounds less than the Cherokee Six 260, for example, and less than a 260-hp Bonanza or Comanche), the fact that the 114 is limited to four seats and 68 gallons of fuel makes it one of the very few full-seats-plus-tanks-plus-baggage airplanes flying today. This is a fine safety factor. A 114 owner virtually never needs to think about gross weight limits, unless he is hauling cement blocks or circus fat ladies. "I have been comfortably able to travel with four adults, baggage,

The Commander 114 is one of the few low-wing aircraft to have a "both tanks" position on the fuel selector—a good safety feature.

skis, ski boots and full fuel for five and a half hours' flying time," reports one owner. Another reports a cabin payload of 773 pounds with a well-equipped IFR airplane with full fuel.

There is one flaw in the 114's rosy loading picture: a zero fuel weight limit of 2,732 pounds. This limits cabin payload to about 750 pounds in typical aircraft. That's ample for most flights, but doesn't allow for extreme situations like four 200-pounders. The zero-fuel weight limit is unusual among single-engine aircraft, and makes you wonder about the supposed structural superiority of the 114 due to its highly touted certification under Amendment 7 regulations. A zero-fuel limit means that the wing spar's bending load limit may be exceeded when the gross weight is safely below limits. We wonder how many 114 owners are even aware of the zero-fuel weight limit and its significance.

Resale Value

Resale value for both the 1976 and 1979 Model 114 are down, down, down. Normally, an aircraft will bottom out after three or four years, and then either hold its value or appreciate slightly (in inflated dollars, of course). The 1976 Model 114 has declined in value every year since 1976, with no sign of leveling off. In 1982, it was worth $36,000; two years later the value was down to $33,000. The 1979 model, meanwhile, lost nearly half its value in three years, to com-

mand only $62,000 in 1982; it brought around $45,000 in 1984.

Handling

The 114 is a fine-flying airplane in most respects. The controls are well-harmonized and the aircraft has a nice "feel." The 114 shows remarkable speed stability with gear and flap extension; virtually no trimming is necessary even if flaps and gear are thrown out at the highest permissible speed. This is a very nice feature during IFR letdowns and approaches. The only black mark is a tendency to wallow in turbulence.

The 114 is universally praised for being easy to land. The plane's pleasing controllability and ultra-forgiving trailing-link landing gear make greasers routine, a fact that no doubt sold a lot of 114s, since pilots like to impress passengers (and themselves) with smooth landings. Crosswinds are a problem, however; the 114 has insufficient rudder to handle crosswinds much above 15 knots. The same rudder insufficiency can make crosswind takeoffs a bit dodgy, particularly when the wind is from the left.

The 114's panel is well arranged. The fuel system also deserves praise: it is one of the few low-wing aircraft to have a "both" position on the fuel selector, an important safety feature.

Styling

Normally, we don't comment on an aircraft's styling, but in the case of the 114, we'll make an exception. It's a nifty-looking airplane, with a gracefully tapered wing, pleasing fuselage lines and a nicely-proportioned tail. The good looks of the 114 will certainly help its resale value in the years to come. "I've sold a couple of them on looks alone," one used-plane salesman told us. More than most pilots care to admit, styling plays a big role in the choice of an aircraft. A man's personal aircraft is a statement, an ego extension and a status symbol; Rockwell played on the 114's good looks by marketing it as a "class" item—expensive, but worth the price for those who could afford it.

Maintenance

The 114 has no outstanding maintenance problems that we're aware of. The engine is the very reliable 260-hp Lycoming IO-540, which has an excellent track record in the Comanche 260 and a 2,000-hour TBO. There have been only a few airframe ADs on the 114, but it shares with dozens of other aircraft the across-the-board ADs on the Hartzell prop, Bendix fuel injectors and magnetos, Lycoming fuel diaphragms, Airborne vacuum pumps, Aerosonic fuel flow transducers, plus the ubiquitous lithium battery ELT directive.

Nevertheless, as with any aircraft, there have been a number of maintenance glitches on the 114. Here is a list of some 114 service bulletins:

• 114-1: Rerouting of aileron control chain to prevent possible binding/interference and/or excessive wear. This applies only to very early 1976 model aircraft.

• 114-2: (September 1976; applies to approximately first 100 aircraft): Inspection and/or modification of the throttle control cable to prevent throttle malfunction.

• 114-3: (October 1976; approximately first 100 aircraft): Inspection of main landing gear retract cylinder bearing. Came as a result of landing gear problems in early aircraft, a not unusual occurrence in a new design.

• 114-4A (March 1978; serial number 1-134): Replacement of fuel selector valve. Although not an AD, this is one service bulletin that should be complied with.

• 114-5B (December 1977; approximately first 150 aircraft): Modification of seat and seat belt. The seats and shoulder harnesses were a bit of a trouble spot on the 114, and it took three bulletins to get it right. This one eventually became an AD. Incidentally, the 114 shoulder harness is a very poor design from the crashworthiness standpoint. The harness is anchored to the seat back itself rather than a hard point on the cabin framework. This makes a neat, cosmetic installation, but is virtually useless in a crash, since the crash forces are transmitted through the harness and seat back to the seat mounting brackets, which, like virtually all aircraft seats, are prone to rip loose from the floor.

• 114-6 (November 1976; s/n 1-158): Modification of cabin air vent system to prevent carbon monoxide gas from entering the cabin. This also became an AD.

• 114-7 (January, 1977; s/n 1-155): Inspection of the main landing gear orifice assembly. Through poor quality control, some of these were installed improperly at the factory, resulting in possible gear problems.

• 114-8 (February, 1977; s/n 1-214): Modification of the engine breather tube to prevent ice buildup.

• 114-9 (March, 1977; s/n 150-199): Installation of placard on seat headrest.

• 114-10 (August, 1977; s/n 1-282): Replacement of clamp on parking brake valve. Designed to prevent slippage of cable and inadvertent release of parking brake.

• 114-11 (November, 1977; s/n 1-319): Replace main gear rod assembly pin retaining screw. This is the third service bulletin dealing with potential landing gear problems.

• 114-12 (November, 1977; s/n 1-318): Modification of vertical fin rib to prevent cracking.

• 114-13 (December, 1977; s/n 1-149): Another modification of the seat/harness, this one to correct a problem in the first series of bulletins.

• 114-14A (May, 1978; s/n 1-376): Inspection and replacement (if necessary) of aileron hinge supports.

• 114-15 (March, 1978; s/n 1-367): Modification of passenger seat locking pin. Designed to assure the locking pin locks into the seat track properly, thus preventing seat slippage at a critical moment. Another crashworthiness item.

• 114-16 (May, 1979; s/n 1-513): Replace prop governor. Leaky governors were a common problem; although not an AD item, it should have been done to any 114 considered for purchase. Cost is listed at $390 in the service bulletin, but take inflation into account

Cost/Performance/Specifications

Model	Year	Number Built	Average Retail Price*	Cruise Speed (kts)	Rate of Climb (fpm)	Gross Weight (lbs)	Useful Load (lbs)	Fuel (gals)	Engine	TBO (hrs)	Overhaul Cost
114	1976	134	$33,000	157	1,050	3,140	1,235	68	260-hp Lyc. IO-540-T4B5D	2,000	$11,000
114	1977	169	$35,000	162	1,160	3,140	1,235	68	260-hp Lyc. IO-540-T4B5D	2,000	$11,000
114	1978	98	$39,000	162	1,160	3,140	1,235	68	260-hp Lyc. IO-540-T4B5D	2,000	$11,000
114A Gran Turismo	1979	40	$45,000	162	1,160	3,140	1,235	68	260-hp Lyc. IO-540-T4B5D	2,000	$11,000

Price includes dual navcom with VOR, LOC, glideslope, transponder, encoder, ADF, Century III autopilot, soundproofing mod, strobes, all ADs complied, 700 hours SMOH. Wholesale prices are 15-20 percent lower.

when figuring current costs.

• 114-17 (July 1979; s/n 1-511): Modify aileron bellcrank doubler to prevent cracks. This is third bulletin dealing with aileron system; check it carefully before purchase.

There were only two service bulletins issued from May 1979 to April 1982, about the time production was suspended and Rockwell got out of the single-engine business. We presume this is not because 114s have become suddenly trouble-free, but rather that the Rockwell service department no longer had time to issue service bulletins unless they were really critical.

Backup Support

We've received mixed reports on Rockwell's product support for the defunct single-engine line. Several 114 owners say they have had no problems at all getting parts, but one fellow said that Rockwell support was "zero" and that he was forced to scrounge parts up himself. In any case, Rockwell service dealers are few and far between. The secret seems to be to find a mechanic experienced with the airplane; it's rare enough that not every A&P has even seen one.

Service responsibility for the 114 has been taken over by Gulfstream American. "We're trying our best to continue supporting the airplane," said a spokesman of the Commander single-service department. He concedes that some parts now have to be built to order, presumably at very high costs and after a long wait. There are only 13 service centers for the Model 114 around the country, so a prospective owner might do well to establish a good rapport with the factory's main main. The phone number in Bethany, Okla. is 405-789-5000. For extra help and advice, contact the 112/114 owners association at Box 406, Woodbury, Conn. 06798, (203) 266-4554.

Safety

Because so few 114s were built,

Aircraft Resale Value Chart

there is not enough of a statistical base for a valid safety analysis of that particular model. However, the 112 and 114 series combined, of which about 1,500 were delivered, had a fairly mediocre fatal accident rate of 3.1 per 100,000 flight hours during the period 1972-1976. This is about average for the single-engine retractables as a group; fatality rates ranged from 1.0 for the Beech 33 Bonanza to 4.2 for the Bellanca Viking.

The 112 and 114 accidents show no particular pattern; there were a total of 12 fatal accidents in the 112/114 up through 1978. But just two of these involved the 114; one was the result of the pilot running out of fuel. The other occurred when the aircraft hit trees off the end of the runway after a downwind takeoff on a soggy grass runway. (The pilot hadn't bothered to taxi all the way to the end of the runway for takeoff.)

One problem involving seat harnesses was revealed early in 1985. The Rockwell singles came from the factory with front seats featuring an unusual shoulder harness installation. Rather than attach the harness to the fuselage structure, Rockwell designers chose the seat backs themselves as the attach points. In what is undeniably a convenient, if unorthodox location, the harness retracted into the seat backs when released.

Perhaps Rockwell designers were attempting to encourage shoulder

harness use by making the harness easy to find and stow. The attempt unfortunately didn't work. An AD issued in March, 1985 called for relocation of the shoulder harness attach point from the seat back to the cabin wall just aft of the door.

This AD was in response to a pair of accidents involving a 112A and 114 in which two people died and another was severely injured due to failures of the front seat rollers which caused the seats to release. With the shoulder harnesses integral to the seats themselves, there was no secondary system that would hold the seats in place.

However, after howls of protest arose from owners over the $1,500 mod, AOPA took up up the cause and filed a petition urging the FAA to reconsider the AD. The petition was successful, and the AD, which would have required relocation of the harness attach points and modification of the front seat base, was suspended.

Owner Comments

We own a 1976 114 and couldn't be happier. More than enough cabin room for four big people and the reclining seats make even all-day flying comfortable. It is the most forgiving airplane I have ever flown. You can load it *full* with baggage, fuel, and people and not worry whether it will fly or land. The trailing beam gear allows you to dive into the ground when landing and cut down on the flare.

Also, landing this way allows you plenty of control, because (as everyone knows) the rudder isn't all that great.

The noise level is probably excessive to passengers, but a good headset almost puts the pilot to sleep in cruise. At 55 percent power and optimum altitude (8,000 feet) we get an honest 13 gph fuel flow including takeoff and climb. We changed to Shell 15W-50 about two years ago and now average a quart every 5-6 hours.

We are fortunate to live in a town that has a twin Commander dealership, and so parts and labor have never been a problem. They know the airplane well and handled the in-warranty problems as well as any manufacturer. Our last annual was $500.

C.L.M.
Indianapolis, Ind.

We bought our Rockwell 114 Commander in November of 1979. I have put an average of 400 hours per year on it, and we have been extremely pleased with the overall characteristics of the airplane.

Performance—We found the 114 highly superior to the 112 due to the larger engine. We are able to carry approximately 950 pounds of useful load with full fuel and have approximately five and a half hours fuel and cruise at 140 knots, making the airplane very useful.

Handling—The 114 handles far better than any other high-performance plane in its class. The cruciform tail configuration makes it a very stable plane to fly in any weather condition. The trailing-arm landing gear makes even the most novice an expert during landing.

Maintenance—The maintenance expense has been in line with Cessna or Piper products. The only thing I found out of line is that there have been three muffler replacements within the 1,000 hours that we have flown the airplane.

Comfort—The plane is touted as

being the "cabin-class single," and it lives up to the claim. I like the two large doors, one on either side, for easy access and the spacious interior as well as large luggage compartment. The seats are comparable only to something in the cabin-class category.

Parts Availability—So far, parts availability has been no problem.

Backup—My selling dealer in Shelby County, Ala. has maintained excellent backup support for all the single-engine Rockwell line. Mechanics at Beechcraft, Piper and Cessna dealers have been anxious to do any repairs needed on the 114, saying everything is well laid out and accessible.

During 1981 maintenance costs amounted to about $3,900 for 387 hours, just about $10 per hour. Insurance was $1,230. We figure about 12 gallons per hour for fuel, totalling about $24 per hour. Depreciation in 1981 was $9,000, hangar and tiedown $4.12. Total operating cost came to $62 per hour, including depreciation (but not including overhaul reserve, which would add about $4 per hour).

W.E. Ogburn, Jr.
Gulf Breeze, Fla.

I have a 1979 114A. The aircraft is identical to the 114 except for a three-blade prop, cowl flaps, door-locking mechanism and sound insulation.

Performance: at 5,000 feet, 152 knots, burning close to 15 gph. Rate of climb at sea level in excess of 1,200 fpm. At 8,000 to 10,000

Though the 114 is one of the few aircraft that normally can hold full fuel, four riders and baggage, some owners describe baggage space as minimal.

feet, 142 to 144 knots at 12 gph. Range a comfortable five hours.

Handling: Strong crosswind take-offs can be hairy unless no flaps are used. Airplane will not take crosswind landings in excess of 20 knots. Apart from that, superb handling on the ground and in flight, the Commander is a very stable instrument platform and with its good climb rate can also climb through moderate icing. There is absolutely no trim change when flaps or gear are lowered, which makes the Commander very easy to handle in busy airports.

Maintenance: No problems except nose gear shimmy damper and trim controls, which have a tendency to freeze.

Comfort: Very comfortable for two or four. Our plane was flown to Puerto Rico and back to New York with four people and bags. The only incovenience was the slow cruising speed and the heat on the ground.

Parts availability and backup: Poor at the beginning, presently zero. The dealer network is non-existent in the Northeast.

Average cost of annual: $500 to $600.

We are very pleased with the comfort and the loading capabilities of this very strong, well-built airplane, but not too happy with the speed and fuel consumption. We are now considering trading her for a Mooney 231 or a Baron 55.

Erik Larsen
New York, N.Y.

Beech Debonair/F33

Beech's Model 33, called both Debonair and Bonanza in its various versions, has emerged in the past few years as perhaps the most prestigious blue chip on the used-aircraft market. While the value of most used planes has fallen precipitously during general aviation's recent hard times, the Bonanza and Debonair have held virtually all their value. Ironically, the increasing demand for the 33 has come about mostly because of the slumping value of its V-tailed stablemate, the 35 Bonanza, due to worries about its high in-flight breakup rate. The 33, along with the larger A36 model, has become known as "the Bonanza that doesn't break up."

Used-Plane Market

The turnaround in the relative value of the V-tail and straight-tail Bonanzas has been startling. In 1979, before the V-tail's breakup record was widely known, the 35 reigned supreme. In those days, a two-year old 1977 V35B was valued at $84,000, while a 1977 F33A —identical in every way except for

the tail—commanded only $77,500. By 1982, the tide had started to turn; that same 1977 V35B had dropped $15,000 to $69,000, while the F33A had lost only $10,000 and was still worth $67,500. By 1985, the V35B had declined another $4,000, to $65,000, while the F33A had *increased* in value to $73,000. That's a $14,500 turnaround.

Over the entire six-year period, the 1977 V-tail lost 22 percent of its value, while the straight-tail F33A declined just six percent. The premium price pilots used to pay for the looks and "prestige" of a V-tail now goes for the better safety of the straight-tail airplane. That sounds like a step in the right direction to us.

The 33 still looks good compared to other aircraft, too. We're aware of only one late-model single or light twin that's held its resale value better than the F33A over the past five years: its big brother the A36 Bonanza. Not even the Mooney 201, a darling of the used-plane market since its introduction in 1977, can match the F33A's resale record.

Geneology

The straight-tail 33 was an outgrowth, of course, of the original V-tail Bonanza. The V-tail was introduced back in 1947, and

had the high-performance single-engine market sewed up until the late 1950's, when Piper brought out the Comanche, and Cessna introduced the 210—both at prices way below the Bonanza's.

Rather than lower the price of its cherished prestige flagship, Beech fought back against the 210 and Comanche with the model 33—an "economy" Bonanza without the distinctive V-tail and with a 225-hp engine instead of the Bonanza's then-250-hp. To avoid sullying the Bonanza's regal moniker by association with a less expensive airplane, Beech named the new economy model the Debonair. It debuted in 1960. List price of that first Model 33 was $19,995, about the same as the Comanche and a bit less than the 210. (The "real" Bonanza listed at $25,300.)

Beech lost little time refining the Debonair. The A33, introduced in 1961, featured a small third cabin window in the rear, and a hat shelf behind the baggage compartment. Gross weight was increased 100 pounds, from 2,900 to 3,000 pounds. In 1962, the B33 was fitted with the standard 74-gallon Bonanza fuel tanks, a big advantage over the previous four-tank system, which had less capacity (63 gallons) and required dangerously arcane fuel management procedures. (More on this in the Safety section.) The B33 also had a much-improved instrument panel, along with a fillet in the vertical fin to give it a more flowing look. Since the B33 is the oldest model with the big tanks, higher gross weight and the new panel, some owners consider the 1962-64 models the best bargain of all the 225-hp Debonairs.

With the C33 in 1965 came a couple of cosmetic changes: a larger third window and a still sleeker dorsal fin. Gross weight was bumped up another 50 pounds to 3,050 while convenience features like rear bucket seats (no more bench), a new ram's-horn control wheel, a bigger hatshelf and an improved heater were added. The E33 and F33 (vintage 1968 and 1970) had no significant changes, except the dropping of the name "Debonair." At last, the 225-hp straight-tail airplane was officially welcomed into the "Bonanza" brotherhood.

In 1966, Beech decided to add another Debonair to the line. In addition to the 225-hp C33, it introduced the 285-hp C33A—essentially a full-fledged "big" Bonanza with a straight tail instead of a V-tail. (For psychological and marketing reasons, however, the straight-tail airplane carried a slightly lower price tag.)

To add to the nomenclature confusion, Beech also called the C33A a Debonair until 1968, when it changed the name of the 285-hp airplane to Bonanza as well. Also in 1968, it introduced a short-lived aerobatic 285-hp version called the E33C. Both the aerobat and the 225-hp airplane were phased out in 1970. By 1971, there was only one standard-body straight-tail Bonanza: the 285-hp F33A. (The stretched 36 Bonanza had been introduced in 1968, but that's another story.)

The "economy" Bonanza made a brief comeback in 1972-73, however, with the 260-hp G33, but from 1974 on, only the F33A remained. By this time, Beech had abandoned the pretense that the V-tail was somehow more desirable, and it set the prices of the V-tail V35B and straight-tail F33A exactly the same. Throughout the 1970's, the V-tail outsold the straight-tail by about a two-to-one margin, but in 1980, shortly after the V-tail breakup controversy became public, the F33A pulled even in the sales race, and in 1981 and 1982, the F33A outsold the V35B by two-to-one. The V-tail, soundly repudiated in the market-

place, was laid to rest in 1983, while the F33A continues in production.

Performance

The 33 series, in the Bonanza tradition, has excellent performance. The 225-hp airplanes will cruise at 148-156 knots on 11.5 to 12 gph, while the more powerful 285-hp models will top 165 knots on about 15 gph. (If the plane has been modified with the Smith Speed conversion, an aerodynamic slick-up mod, these speeds will increase by 13-17 knots.)

Rate of climb is listed at about 900 fpm for the various 225-hp models and about 1,200 fpm for the 285-hp versions. Not surprisingly, the 260-hp G33s fall in the middle, at 1,060 fpm. As with most aircraft, in the real world, these figures are rarely matched, but pilots and owners report strong climbing abilities under most conditions. The 225-hp airplanes, however, are sometimes judged wanting in high-altitude climb and high-density-altitude takeoffs.

Again, climb performance is substantially improved with the Smith Speed Conversion.

Payload-Range

Standard useful load of the 225-hp Debonairs is about 1,200 pounds, but a well-equipped IFR airplane would have about 1,000 pounds available for payload and fuel. With the 74-gallon tanks full, payload is only about 550 pounds —three average people and not much baggage. Because of the limited loading, says one Debonair pilot, "All Deb owners habitually overload their aircraft, especially those planes with the large tanks."

The small-tank (50-gallon) A33 has an extra 120 pounds' payload with full fuel, but the straight 33, with its lower gross weight, is comparable to the B33 and later airplanes in full-fuel payload (with less fuel, of course).

The 285-hp Debonairs have enough extra load-carrying ability to make them four-pax-plus-luggage airplanes from the poundage standpoint. But watch the center of gravity! The entire Bonanza series is notorious for its limited c.g. envelope, and the stretched A36 model was developed primarily to solve this problem. The 33 series has a wider c.g. envelope than the otherwise-identical V-tails (the straight tail does a better job of stabilizing and therefore permits more aft loading), but the 33s are still somewhat limited. In most cases, it's simply not legally possible to put two adults in the rear seats and a bunch of bags in back.

The balance situation is complicated by the fact that all fuel is carried in front of the c.g. As fuel burns off, c.g. shifts aft. That means that for takeoff on a long flight, a Debonair must be well forward of the rear limit to account for the aft shift as fuel burns off.

Handling Qualities

The Bonanza series has always been a pilot's favorite. The handling is delightfully quick and smooth in the air, with controls well harmonized in all three axes. "My Debonair is the best-flying airplane I've ever flown," crows one typical owner.

But the other side of the "light and responsive" coin is poor stability in IFR conditions. As one Debonair

owner put it, "The model 33 is not a particularly good instrument airplane. The same qualities that make it such a pleasure to fly turn it into a handful on instruments. It has almost neutral stability, and one must devote a great deal of attention to just controlling the aircraft. If any serious instrument flying is anticipated, a reliable autopilot should be a high priority."

The 33 is not particularly stable in the yaw mode, although it does not have the stomach-wrenching Dutch roll in turbulence that the V-tail has.

Landings are particularly easy in the Debonairs; most pilots agree that the Deb has an excellent combination of handling qualities and landing-gear geometry. However, a 1966 NASA "secret" report on the handling qualities of various general aviation aircraft criticized the A33 Debonair it tested for poor lateral stability in the landing configuration. NASA test pilots also criticized the A33 for awkward crosswind takeoffs because of the rudder-aileron interconnect.

The 33s, like the 35s, stall rather sharply, particularly with gear and flaps down and power on. Watch the go-arounds and base-to-final turns. However, the 33 is apparently not so violent as the 35; the NASA test pilots criticized the V-tail stall traits in the 1966 report but found no fault with the A33's.

Cabin and Cockpit

Bonanzas have won fame for their roomy, airy cabins, and the 33 model is no exception. There's so much headroom that a pilot of average height looks like a midget from the outside. Forward visibility is excellent out the panoramic windshield, and, in the later models with the three large cabin windows, out the sides as well. Noise is about average for this class of aircraft—that is to say terribly noisy.

The 285-hp Debonair is listed as a six-seater, but this is an optimistic delusion of the Beech sales department. The optional fifth and sixth seats are tiny and claustrophobic,

and are virtually impossible to use because of c.g. restrictions anyway. Unless you have four little kids to haul around, consider all the 33s to be strictly four-place airplanes.

The B33 and earlier 225-hp models have old-fashioned bench-type rear seats, but they are surprisingly roomy and not really a liability from the practical standpoint.

From the pilot's point of view, the 33 line has the traditional Bonanza ergonomic quirks. A single throw-over control wheel was standard equipment on the Debonairs, although many have been fitted with optional dual controls. The massive control bar connecting the yoke or yokes to the center control column can block the pilot's view of parts of the panel and get in the way of the engine controls.

In the older models, the mixture knob is located below the throttle instead of to the right of the prop control, as in most airplanes. And the landing gear and flap switches are reversed from their normal positions in most aircraft, a quirk that has caused many embarrassing (and expensive) gear retractions on the ground. (During the years 1974-78, in fact, inadvertent gear retractions were the leading cause of non-fatal accidents in 225-hp Debonairs.) These quirks aside, however, the post-1963 Debonairs have generally good instrument panel layouts.

The fuel selector is less than ideal, located low on the cockpit side wall by the pilot's left knee. Thus, to

The bigger rear window first appeared in 1965 on the C33 model. It can be easily retrofitted to older aircraft.

switch tanks, a pilot must crane his neck and reach down in a rather awkward cross-hand manner. Also, there is no "both" position on the selector, which assures that the pilot will be switching tanks at least once during a long trip. (From the safety point of view, the less tank-switching a pilot has to do, the better.)

Operating Costs

Fuel efficiency of the Debonairs is good, with fuel costs running from $25 to $30 per hour. (That's figuring gas at $2 per gallon.) Owners of 225-hp Debonairs can cut their fuel costs dramatically, however, by using auto fuel. With the proper STC paperwork (available for $112.50 from Petersen Aviation, Rte. 1, Box 18, Minden, Nebraska 68959, (308) 832-2200) it's entirely legal to use either lead-free or leaded regular autogas in the 225-hp airplanes, which normally burn 80-octane avgas.

Typically, liability insurance coverage runs $400 to $500 a year, with hull insurance ranging from perhaps $1,000 a year for an old 225-hp B33 to $2,000 for a late-model F33A.

Engine overhaul reserve amounts to about $6 per hour for both the 225-hp and 285-hp models. (Oddly, the smaller IO-470 costs very nearly as much to overhaul as the bigger IO-520.) Count on about

$9,000 to overhaul either engine; the 285-hp powerplants have 1,700-hour TBOs, compared to 1,500 hours for the 470s.

Adding it all up, assuming 200 hours per year, operating costs—excluding maintenance—should run from $40 to $50 per hour. Whether *total* operating costs end up at $50 or $100 per hour depends, of course, on the unpredictable and potentially disastrous maintenance bills.

Maintenance

According to owner reports and conversation with mechanics, Debonair maintenance costs can run from pretty low to pretty outrageous, depending on hourly utilization, the owner's mechanical aptitude and blind luck. While the well-proven, solidly built airframe has stood up well over time, three potential bugaboos haunt the Debonair owner: cracking crank-

cases, leaking fuel bladders, and Beech's high parts prices.

Assuming nothing major goes wrong—and in many cases it doesn't—Debonair annuals are reasonable. "Annual inspections run around $400 unless additional parts and labor are required," said one owner. To date (I've owned it three years) there have been no surprises at annual time." The owner put his total maintenance cost at an extraordinarily low $2 per hour. Others disagree. "Maintenance costs are very high, if not exorbitant," writes one. "We try to keep everything working, and that costs a lot." Echoes another, "The Debonair is not a high-maintenance airplane, but it *is* expensive to maintain. This is because...anything purchased from Beech is outrageously expensive."

Cracking crankcases have been a continuing problem in the 285-hp

Debonairs (along with many other aircraft). The so-called "heavy" cases introduced in the mid-1970's didn't help much, and cracks continue to crop up despite all manner of design and material changes over the years. Case cracks usually aren't immediately dangerous, and small ones can be lived with until overhaul, at which time the crack can be welded up and the case heat-treated. (Cost: typically, $500-$700.) If the crack is bad enough to ground the plane (an AD sets out the guidelines), an owner faces two expensive options: overhaul the engine prematurely (about $9,000, plus the cost of case repair) or completely disassemble the engine and repair the case ($4,000 or so, mostly for assembly/disassembly labor and the extra new parts required when the engine is put back together again).

Moral for F33A shoppers: check with microscopic care for crankcase cracks.

Cost/Performance/Specifications

Model	Year	Number Built	Average Retail Price	Cruise Speed (Kts)	Rate of Climb (fpm)	Useful Load (lbs)	Fuel Std/Opt (gals)	Engine	TBO (hrs)	Overhaul Cost
33	1960	233	$24,000	156	1,010	1,170	44/63	225-hp Cont. IO-470-K	1,500	$8,750
A33	1961	152	$25,000	161	960	1,250	44/63	225-hp Cont. IO-470-K	1,500	$8,750
B33	1962	200	$27,000	161	960	1,250	44/74	225-hp Cont. IO-470-K	1,500	$8,750
B33	1963	137	$28,000	161	960	1,250	44/74	225-hp Cont. IO-470-K	1,500	$8,750
B33	1964	89	$29,000	161	960	1,250	44/74	225-hp Cont. IO-470-K	1,500	$8,750
C33	1965	157	$32,000	161	980	1,200	44/74	225-hp Cont. IO-470-K	1,500	$8,750
C33	1966	86	$33,000	161	980	1,200	44/74	225-hp Cont. IO-470-K	1,500	$8,750
C33	1967	62	$34,000	161	980	1,200	44/74	225-hp Cont. IO-470-K	1,500	$8,750
C33A	1966	102	$41,000	174	1,200	1,525	44/74	285-hp Cont. IO-520-B	1,700	$9,250
C33A	1967	77	$41,500	174	1,200	1,525	44/74	285-hp Cont. IO-520-B	1,700	$9,250
E33	1968	81	$38,000	161	930	1,200	44/74	225-hp Cont. IO-470-K	1,500	$8,750
E33	1969	34	$39,000	161	930	1,200	44/74	225-hp Cont. IO-470-K	1,500	$8,750
E33A	1968	69	$43,000	174	1,200	1,375	44/74	285-hp Cont. IO-520-B	1,700	$9,250
E33A	1969	41	$45,000	174	1,200	1,375	44/74	285-hp Cont. IO-520-B	1,700	$9,250
E33C	1968	13	$41,500	174	1,200	1,380	44/74	285-hp Cont. IO-520-B	1,700	$9,250
E33C	1969	12	$43,500	174	1,200	1,380	44/74	285-hp Cont. IO-520-B	1,700	$9,250
F33	1970	20	$40,500	161	930	1,375	44/74	225-hp Cont. IO-470-K	1,500	$8,750
F33C	1970	5	$47,500	174	1,200	1,380	44/74	285-hp Cont. IO-520-B	1,500	$8,750
G33	1972	45	$46,500	168	1,060	1,365	44/74	260-hp Cont. IO-470-N	1,500	$8,750
G33	1973	5	$46,500	168	1,060	1,365	44/74	260-hp Cont. IO-470-N	1,500	$8,750
F33A	1970	20	$50,000	172	1,200	1,300	44/74	285-hp Cont. IO-520-B	1,700	$9,250
F33A	1971	34	$52,000	172	1,200	1,300	44/74	285-hp Cont. IO-520-B	1,700	$9,250
F33A	1972	52	$54,000	172	1,200	1,300	44/74	285-hp Cont. IO-520-B	1,700	$9,250
F33A	1973	63	$56,000	172	1,200	1,300	44/74	285-hp Cont. IO-520-B	1,700	$9,250
F33A	1974	71	$60,000	172	1,200	1,300	44/74	285-hp Cont. IO-520-B	1,700	$9,250
F33A	1975	75	$64,000	172	1,200	1,300	44/74	285-hp Cont. IO-520-B	1,700	$9,250
F33A	1976	62	$68,000	172	1,200	1,300	44/74	285-hp Cont. IO-520-B	1,700	$9,250
F33A	1977	69	$73,000	172	1,200	1,300	44/74	285-hp Cont. IO-520-B	1,700	$9,250
F33A	1978	82	$80,000	172	1,200	1,300	44/74	285-hp Cont. IO-520-B	1,700	$9,250
F33A	1979	68	$86,000	172	1,200	1,300	44/74	285-hp Cont. IO-520-B	1,700	$9,250
F33A	1980	45	$92,500	172	1,200	1,300	44/74	285-hp Cont. IO-520-B	1,700	$9,250
F33A	1981	49	$107,500	172	1,200	1,300	44/74	285-hp Cont. IO-520-B	1,700	$9,250
F33A	1982	36	$127,500	172	1,200	1,300	44/74	285-hp Cont. IO-520-B	1,700	$9,250
F33A	1983	10	$147,500	172	1,200	1,300	44/74	285-hp Cont. IO-520-B	1,700	$9,250
F33A	1984	32	$175,000	172	1,200	1,300	44/74	285-hp Cont. IO-520-B	1,700	$9,250

Fuel bladders are another weak spot in the Debonairs. The Goodyear tanks in older airplanes are particularly prone to cracking; Uniroyal bladders are a better bet, experience has shown. If the bladders do develop leaks, the tab can be $2,000 or more for replacement, according to owners. The 33 and A33 with the four-tank systems have an even bigger potential for disaster.

Another Goodyear product—the brakes on early models—are also short-lived and trouble-prone. Many Debonair owners have replaced them with Cleveland brakes, which have proven superior. Look for Clevelands on any Debonair you buy, or anticipate putting them on soon.

The 225-hp models are susceptible to lead-fouling of the spark plugs if 100-octane fuel is used instead of the 80-octane the engine was designed for. (Even "low-lead" 100 has four times the lead of 80 octane.) If 80 is unavailable, try unleaded auto fuel.

Beech parts prices are the demon that haunts any Debonair owner. The buyer of a new $200,000 A36 may not balk at a $2,000-plus price tag for a control wheel yoke assembly, but that amounts to nearly 10 percent of the value of a 1961 A33. That's the problem with new replacement parts—they cost the same whether the plane is old or new, cheap or expensive.

Safety

Here's the best news: the 33 series has the lowest fatal accident rate of any single-engine retractable, according to *The Aviation Consumer* statistics for the period 1972-81. The 33's fatal rate was only 1.4 per 100,000 flight hours, compared to an average of 2.3 for 16 other single engine retractables. (The Cessna 210, for example, had a fatal rate of 2.3; the Mooney M20J 2.4. The Piper Comanche had a rather high 2.9.)

By comparison, the late-model V-tail Bonanzas (1964 and later) had a fatal rate of 1.7, and the older

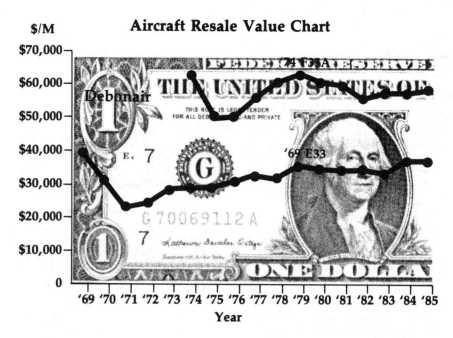

Aircraft Resale Value Chart

Debonair

'69 E33

$/M: $70,000 — $60,000 — $50,000 — $40,000 — $30,000 — $20,000 — $10,000 — 0

Year: '69 '70 '71 '72 '73 '74 '75 '76 '77 '78 '79 '80 '81 '82 '83 '84 '85

V-tails (1947-63) a rather terrible 3.3.

Where the straight-tail 33 really shines is in-flight breakups. An *Aviation Consumer* study for the years 1977-83 shows that the 33 (and 36) have a break-up rate just one-tenth of the V-tail's. We're aware of only three in-flight breakups of 33 series Beeches, compared to more than 200 for the V-tails.

The reasons for this big difference aren't entirely clear. The 33 has slightly better pitch stability and heavier pitch forces than the 35, and so may be less prone to pilot loss of control and overstress. The straight tail also provides slightly better lateral stability, reducing the tendency to enter a "graveyard spiral" in instrument conditions. The straight tail also gives better yaw stability, reducing Dutch roll gyrations in turbulence.

Another possibility: the straight tail is simply stronger and stays intact through all manner of high-speed dives, pullouts and turbulence that may break a V-tail. The V-tail has been criticized for the excessive "overhang" of the stabilizer ahead of the front spar, and at least three companies offer kits to beef up V-tails structurally.

Beech Aircraft's official position is that there's really little difference between the 33 and 35. Pilots of both aircraft occasionally lose con-

trol in IFR conditions or severe turbulence, says Beech, pushing the aircraft beyond its airspeed and/or g-load limits. It doesn't matter much, according to the Beech theory, whether the plane breaks up before it hits the ground (35) or hits the ground in one piece (33). Either way, the occupants are dead.

We disagree with Beech's interpretation. When we examined NTSB records of both in-flight breakups and "uncontrolled impact with ground" crashes for the 33 and 35, it turned out that the 35 still had a rate of fatal loss-of-control accidents—either breakups or uncontrolled impacts—nearly three times higher than the 33.

Although they have an excellent overall record, the early Debonairs have a quirk or two to watch out for. Pre-1970 models had no baffles in the fuel tanks, which allowed fuel to slosh away from the fuel line pickup in slips, skids or during fast turns on the ground (such as those preceding a hurried takeoff). Beech was aware of the fuel unporting syndrome (which affected Debonairs, Bonanzas and Barons) as far back as 1961. It issued a service letter warning that a turning-type takeoff could result in a "momentary power interruption" at "about the same time the airplane becomes airborne." The letter assured owners that "...this does not create a hazard."

Used Aircraft Guide

But the FAA identified 16 fuel-unporting accidents by 1971, and issued an AD prohibiting takeoffs with tanks less than a quarter full. Beech installed baffles in 1971 and later models and retrofit kits for the older airplanes, but few have been retrofitted. We'd consider the fuel tank baffles a must in any Debonair considered for purchase.

The early Bonanzas had a bad record of fuel mismanagement accidents, and the early 33 and A33 Debonairs have similar fuel systems, with multiple tanks that require lots of switching, an out-of-the-way fuel selector that's hard to see and a gauging system that makes it easy to read the wrong tank.

Modifications

When it comes to airframe and cosmetic mods, Debonair owners are in hog heaven. Literally dozens of mods are available to make an old Debbie look new: windows, windshields, panels, spinners, interiors, etc. Chief purveyor of Debonair cosmetic mods is Beryl D'Shannon Aviation Specialties, P.O. Box 840, Lakeville, Minn. (612) 469-4783.

The aforementioned Smith Speed Conversion includes a series of detail aerodynamic improvements that typically improve cruise speed by 13-17 knots. Smith also offers a modified cowling that is claimed to improve cooling, cut drag and allow better engine breathing for more power at high altitudes. Mike Smith Aero, Stanton County Airport, Box 430, Johnson City, Kans. (316) 492-6840.

Bonanza Society

Perhaps the most active of the owner groups is the American Bonanza Society, P.O. Box 12888, Wichita, Kans. (316) 945-6913. The ABS publishes a monthly newsletter with technical info and how-to tips, along with the usual rah-rah stuff about members' creampuff planes. While the ABS is sometimes timid about confronting safety problems head-on (it likes to maintain good rapport with Beech), the club is still a good

source of info and a good bet for any 33 owner. (Yes, the Bonanza boys do allow straight-tail owners to join their ranks.)

Owner Comments

I have had a Model 33 for six years. I usually fly it at 60 percent power using 2300 rpm. It uses 10.8 to 11.2 gph and trues out about 135 knots. As you can see, it doesn't come up to the handbook data, but it is a sturdy, comfortable but noisy bird. Annuals run $600 to $900. The original 600 x 6 tires were replaced with 700 x 6, and their life is considerably longer, with no clearance problems. The tail does waggle like the V-tail, but by holding the rudder so it doesn't move, you can stop the waggle. (The same technique worked on the V-tail I had before the Debonair.)

Of the light aircraft I've flown, the 33 has the best visibility, and as far as I'm concerned is the safest and best-built of the lot

Newton Kerr
Olmstead, Ohio

A year and a half ago, I purchased a 1962 B33 with 1,600 hours total time and 350 hours on a chrome major. The Deb is one of the smoothest planes I've ever flown. It's a good instrument ship as long as you're wide awake, stay ahead of the airplane and maintain proficiency. Load-carrying and range

(over 1,000 nm) are good as long as you realize that the c.g. moves aft as fuel burns off.

My Deb has the speed-slope windshield and aileron gap seals, and I have removed the step. I climb and cruise better than book numbers, 180 mph cruise on 12 gph or less. Stall speed with everything hanging out is 50 mph indicated. I wonder what's being built this year that will match it in speed, range, comfort and safety record?

Cost of operation runs about $25 per hour for gas, a quart of oil every six hours, $1,000 a year for insurance, $400 for annuals. In 200 hours and 19 months, the only problems have been with the prop control and propeller lubrication. My only complaint is a universal one: the high cost of Beech parts.

Raymond McDonald
Ferndale, Wash.

My partner and I have owned a 1964 B33 Debonair since October 1981. It's been a pleasure to own and fly, providing us with 200 to 300 hours a year of safe, reliable transportation.

Because of the quick and smooth roll characteristics, an autopilot is recommended for serious IFR flying. The Deb can be a handful in turbulence. We can carry four

Double control bar arrangement can be used on the Model 33 instead of the throwover wheel, but this makes control access more awkward.

The B33, circa 1962-64 is recognizable by the small rear window. Though the cabin is short, it is high, beamy and quite comfortable for four.

passengers and baggage for as long as we're able and still have a reserve. Rear c.g. is the only thing to watch carefully, as the c.g. shifts to the rear as fuel burns off. We count on burning 12 gph while averaging 165 mph.

In 1984 we flew 318 hours with maintenance costs of $13 per hour for mechanical and only $1.00 per hour for radios. Our annual ran an additional $500, which is typical unless we let some things go until the annual. The 1968 Cherokee 180D I owned previously cost about the same amount per mile to operate. Our insurance runs $1,018 per year for $30,000 hull and $2 million liability.

As far as the IO-470-K engine goes, it has been all routine so far. We have 1,200 hours on it and expect to get TBO without a problem. We run platinum plugs to avoid the lead-fouling problems we have with 100 LL gas. We are now considering the autogas STC. Leaky exhaust gaskets have always been a problem. We recently had all the studs removed and the cylinder seats resurfaced, and that has solved the problem so far. Oil consumption is about a quart every two or three hours because of improper break-in.

Like most Beech owners, we have many mods, including one-piece windshield, Beryl side windows, Beryl rear air exhaust, Cleveland brakes, three-inch gyros, alternator and instrument post lighting.

Gary Otto
Duluth, Ga.

Three partners and I own a 1966 C33. We spent $10,000 on it in 1982 for a complete firewall-forward overhaul, including propeller.

Performance has been by the book in all phases of operation. We consistently get 158-160-knot cruise speeds at 6,000 to 8,000 feet with fuel burn of 13.5-14.0 gph. I try to

lean the mixture to about 25-50 degrees on the rich side of peak EGT.

I find the Deb very enjoyable to fly, with light, harmonized controls. Longitudinal stability is adequate, whereas lateral/directional stability is somewhat weak. The cabin is as comfortable as anything in its class. The only problem I've found is that the landing gear geometry leaves a very lightly loaded nosewheel if the plane is near the aft end of the c.g. envelope. There have been times when I thought the tail would hit the ground. (It hasn't actually happened yet.)

After 19 years and 3,100 hours on my aircraft, Beech quality is apparent. Other than spark plugs, batteries, tires and brakes, we've had very few mechanical expenses. Checking the numbers for the past 300 hours of operation, the average hourly cost works out to about $41 (not including avionics or reserve for overhaul). Maintenance accounts for about $2 of this figure. Annual inspections run around $400, plus whatever parts and extra labor are required beyond the inspection.

Jerry Jordan
Leawood, Kans.

As an airline pilot with extensive general aviation background, I believe the Beech 33 is the most satisfying cross-country single-engine airplane I've ever flown. The early Debonair provides an outstanding combination of economy and performance. The

Continental IO-470 engine at 65 percent power will burn 11.5 gph at 10,000 feet and give an honest 150 knots. I flight-plan one gallon of fuel for every five minutes of flight time, and can usually tell the line person how much fuel the tanks will hold to within half a gallon.

The Debonair is a real four-place airplane. My full-IFR airplane will *legally* carry four 170-pound adults, 100 pounds of luggage and 50 gallons of fuel (full tanks in my plane), enough for three hours plus a reserve. That's as long as I can stand to sit in a light airplane cabin, anyway. VFR, I plan 500-mile legs. IFR, I would like to have more fuel capacity. Factory-installed aux tanks on the early 1960-61 models are of limited value because they only added about 20 gallons but increased weight substantially. The Flight Extender tip tanks made by Beryl are a better choice.

Cabin comfort improves with each year up to about 1967. In my plane, ventilation is better than a Comanche, but not nearly as good as a 210. Visibility is excellent. Noise level is average (high).

The Model 33 is not a particularly good instrument airplane. The same qualities that make it such a pleasure to fly visually make it a handful on instruments. It has almost neutral stability, and one must devote a great deal of attention to just controlling the aircraft. If any serious instrument flying is anticipated, a reliable autopilot should be a high priority.

Bellanca Viking

Riding on the wooden wings of yesteryear, the Bellanca Viking is an airplane Howard Hughes would have approved of. The spruce-and-mahogany wings, the Dacron-coated fuselage, and quaintly bestrutted empennage, combine to give the Viking a charm all its own (not to mention the drag coefficient of a flying boat).

But persistent concerns about wood rot, and a general perception of the airplane as an orphaned design (production was suspended in 1980), have kept resale values extraordinarily low: A 1976 Super Viking with good avionics can be had for $33,000, while an F33A Bonanza of the same year commands $66,000. And in most cases, used Vikings come with low total airframe time. Apparently, few enter any kind of commercial service.

As with most oddball (er, distinctive) aircraft, the Bellanca Viking has its own loyal cadre of boosters and supplicants, who literally praise it to the skies as "the best all-around high-performance single." Owners mention easy handling, simple systems, and cruise speeds in the 160-knot ballpark as reasons for continued ownership; and routine maintenance seems to require no special connections with the International Monetary Fund. Owners consistently report annuals in the $350 to $700 range, although some said parts—while easy to get—were "high." (Non-routine maintenance is another matter: Several operators cited wing repair bills that were, in their words, "sufficient to cause heart attack" and "impressive.")

Group Characteristics

When Viking owners talk of their planes' family "tree," they're not just speaking figuratively. The

Bellanca mahogany wing dates to before World War Two; and the last of the Super Viking wings, produced in 1980, differs little from the original. The same glass-smooth, curvacious wing that marked the Cruisaire (the Viking's forerunner) as a "hot ship" in the Forties still draws praise from owners today as "the most perfect wing of any modern light aircraft." Nary a rivet-head protrudes to ruin the airfoil's perfect contour.

Unfortunately, the rest of the Bellanca is not so slick aerodynamically. The bottoms of the wings sprout ugly, drag-producing wheel bumps; the horizontal stabilizer has struts (a la Curtiss Robin), and the fuselage is a bit slab-sided, for a "high-performance" plane. As a result, the plane turns in no better than Mooney Executive performance on 300 horsepower (even though the Bellanca's fuselage is no wider than the Mooney's). An efficiency queen, the Viking definitely is not.

Efficiency isn't everything, of course, and there are other reasons for buying an "old-fashioned" airplane like the Bellanca. Its methods of construction demand a high level of craftsmanship, and in this area, Bellancas excell: Owners report unusually fastidious workmanship throughout the aircraft, especially inside the typically well-appointed cabin. The fit-and-finish is far above industry standards for this size aircraft.

Exposed nosewheel and bulbous main-wheel bumps under wings contribute to draggy performance. The 300-hp Viking delivers real-world cruise speeds of 150 to 160 knots.

How do the various year models differ? For the most part, they don't. Since the first Viking's appearance in 1967 (which marked the end of the triple-tailed, 260-hp Cruisaires), subsequent models have differed externally only in paint scheme. A variety of power-plants can be found under the hood, however. The original staple engine was the 300-hp Continental IO-520-D (TBO 1,700 hours), which could be supplanted (at customer request) by a 290-hp Lycoming IO-540-B (TBO 1,200 hours, normally aspirated) or IO-540-G (TBO 1,400 hours, turbocharged). Post-1970 models sported either the 300-hp Continental IO-520-K or the 300-hp Lycoming IO-540-K (TBO 2,000 hours), which—for $8,000 extra—could be fitted with dual Rajay turbochargers. Most Vikings have the Continental engine.

Performance and Handling

"Performance," according to one owner, "is adequate but not outstanding." Except for the Super Turbo models, which one owner says trues out at 186 knots at 12,000 feet, the Vikings are sluggish cruisers compared to Bonanzas and 210s. One operator reported 170 knots at 10,000 feet; another said he flight-plans 140 knots, based on 60-percent power and block-to-block fuel burns of 15 gallons per hour. Apparently, there is considerable variation among individual airplanes, due to rigging and vagaries of construction over the years.

Owners are less than enthusiastic about the airplane's short legs: Standard fuel tankage is a mere 60 gallons (three hours plus reserves), all in the wings. The 15-gallon fuselage aux tank is a common option; but even with 75 gallons, it's difficult to fly a 700-nm trip without stopping for gas.

On the plus side, owners offer nothing but euphoric praise for the Viking's handling, one (typical) owner describing it as "an absolute joy to fly." Ailerons are said to be light and creamy-smooth; rudders heavy but responsive; pitch forces, moderate to challenging, depending on c.g. location. Flaps do not betray any rude behavior, nor does gear deployment (at the manageably high speed of 124 knots). Gobs of drag and a 3,000-lb.-plus gross weight combine to give very steep descents for the unwary, however.

Useful loads for well-equipped Vikings (which most are) run around 900 pounds—a bit less than you'd expect for a 300-hp low-wing retractable (and far short of the Cessna 210's 1,500 pounds). Given the poor payload, it's perhaps a blessing that the airplane was not given larger fuel tanks, or a more capacious interior.

Speaking of interiors, owners are generally complimentary of seats, fabrics, etc. (which is good, since it diverts passengers' attention from the lack of shoulder and leg room), but the noise level is almost universally regarded as too high—no doubt a consequence of the large engine and fabric-skinned fuselage construction. "The airplane has got to have the highest noise level of any modern production aircraft," one owner observes, adding: "Headset, ear plugs, and intercom should be go/no-go items." Factory engineers surely must have considered additional sound-proofing at some point; we can

The Viking panel is sensibly laid out, which is something you can't say for most used planes. View is obstructed by steel tubes (as in the Piper Aztec, which, like the Viking, has a tube-truss fuselage).

only wonder if they didn't rule it out on the basis of weight, since payload is already critical. We'll never know for sure.

If stealth is a consideration, one owner reports that the Viking exhibits an extraordinarily poor primary radar return—no doubt the result of mahogany's elusive X-band signature.

Systems

Like many older designs, the Viking betrays a number of idiosyncrasies which a new pilot would do well to study. The absence of cowl flaps on most models is a plus point, at least in terms of pilot workload (although it may compromise cylinder and accessory life). The prop, throttle, and mixture controls are all vernier types—with the prop knob directly above the mixture knob—which may cause some vertigo for all but Bonanza pilots, who wouldn't be caught dead in a Bellanca anyway.

Then there's the fuel system. On some early models, there were two fuel selectors with eight possible combinations of selector settings;

later models have just one selector (between the front seats, at knee level) with four positions, of which one can be used in level flight only. Fuel quantity is read on vertical-readout gauges which owners say are highly non-linear—i.e., accurate only in the "full" and "empty" extremes. The three-position boost pump rocker switch is also a source of confusion, as reflected in pilot's statements in accident reports. Many pilots are not aware that the Viking's boost pump is so powerful that it can flood the engine, preventing easy restart. What's more, pump usage varies according to the type of engine installed. Obviously, it behooves the pilot to get a thorough checkout, and study the handbook.

Until May 1968, Vikings had an unusual combination flap-and-gear actuation system that worked off the engine-driven hydraulic system and was located between the pilots' seats. In 1968, electric flaps were substituted for hydraulic, and control levers mounted on the front lower panel, in convention arrangement (gear left, flaps right).

Panel layout is good, with flight instruments where they should be, nav heads in midpanel, radios in a stack on the right, and autopilot-cum-miscellany to the far right, above the flap switch and circuit breakers. (Visibility through the one-piece windshield, however, is compromised by the presence of two steel tubes at ten and two o'clock, a la Aztec.) Reclining seats are optional.

A pneumatic switch in the landing gear circuit forms the basis of something called "Auto-Axion," which automatically lowers the landing gear at an airspeed of 83 knots (which is about what you'll indicate in cruise going over the Rockies). To our knowledge, it has caused owners no grief, and may actually be preventing gear-up accidents: in a recent three-year period, we could find in NTSB files only four gear-up landings involving Bellancas—two of which were pilot-induced, not mechanical.

The fuel drain knob is under the cowling, but it only drains the tank you've selected, so count on lots of walking between cabin and cowl to get all points drained.

One owner reports that his alternator belt always slips in heavy rain.

Maintenance

Although miscellaneous airframe parts are expensive (e.g., $80 for flap cables), and repair costs for replacement of the Viking's "lifetime fabric" or wings can rival the Polish national debt, routine upkeep is said by owners to be quite reasonable. Extensive annuals can run upwards of $2,500, but the average inspection seems to come in at $700—about the same as the tab for a Bonanza, 210, etc.

Several important repetitive Airworthiness Directives apply to the Bellanca Viking. The most important (and notorious) of these is AD 76-08-04, the 1976 directive on wood rot. Under the terms of this AD, the Viking wing must be inspected for moisture content in accordance with Part I of Bellanca Service Letter 82A at each annual inspection. Since not all shops are familiar with Bellancas, it pays to seek out expert counsel for this type of work. Owners recommend Tom Witmer at Cap Aviation in Reading, Pa.; Miller Flying Service in Plainview, Tex., and Dave Poole at Dennis Martin Aircraft at Ft. Lauderdale Executive Airport. (Miller is also a good source of Viking info, in general.)

The wing moisture check should be a starting point for any pre-purchase inspection. Don't take the word of the previous owner nor a logbook entry; actually have a qualified shop check the wings prior to delivery. Special tools are required for this; it requires more than "an eyeball and a screwdriver" (as one man states)—unless, of course, you open the inspection covers and find, as one owner did, "mushrooms growing in right wing."

Other important ADs are 76-23-03 on exhaust failure (an inspection is required each 100 hours); 77-22-02 on nose landing gear engine mount sections; and 75-20-06 on vertical side fuselage tube cracking in the tail section (repetitive inspection each 100 hours until Service Kit

SK1234789-0004 is installed). Additional ADs may apply to individual accessories installed on various airplanes (certain magnetos, Lycoming oil pump impellers, etc.); make sure to have an A&P do a complete AD listing for the particular plane you intend to buy.

In 1983, the Viking line went back into production, with first deliveries to Miller Flying Service. This should, of course, have a positive effect not only on parts availability, but aircraft resale value as well. The new manufacturer is Bellanca Inc., P.O. Box 964, Alexandria, Minn. 56308 (phone 612/762-1501). Their distributor: Miller Flying Service, P.O. Box 190, Plainview, Tex. 79072 (phone 806/293-4121).

Accident Record

The Bellanca Viking was one of several aircraft spotlighted as having a particularly poor safety record in the National Transportation Safety Board's 1979 study of accident rates by aircraft type. (Other poor-showing airplanes included the Grumman AA-1 series and the Cessna Skymaster.) Shortly after the NTSB released its report, Bellanca Aircraft Corp. sent a cheer-up letter to aviation editors, defending the Viking's safety record. As it turns out, the Safety Board did lump Viking data together with Cruisaire (i.e., early-Bellanca) data to arrive at its findings. And this did produce a skewed result, at least for non-fatal accidents—the Crusaire series

Cost/Performance/Specifications

Model	Years Built	Number Built	Average Retail Price	Cruise Speed (kts)	Useful Load (lbs)	Rate of Climb (fpm)	Fuel Std/Opt (gals)	Engine	TBO (hrs)	Overhaul Cost
Viking 17-30	1967-70	290	$18,000-$20,000	163	1,300	1,840	58/92	300-hp Cont. IO-520-D	1,700	$ 9,800
Viking 17-30A	1971-74	419	$22,000-$27,000	163	1,108	1,085	60/75	300-hp Cont. IO-520-K	1,700	$ 9,800
Viking 17-30A	1975-77	129	$29,000-$39,000	163	1,108	1,085	60/75	300-hp Cont. IO-520-K	1,700	$ 9,800
Viking 17-30A	1978-80	106	$45,000-$57,000	163	1,108	1,085	60/75	300-hp Cont. IO-520-K	1,700	$ 9,800
Super Viking 17-31A	1969-70	34	$18,000-$21,000	164	1,375	1,800	60/75	290-hp Lyc. IO-540-G1B5	1,400	$12,000
Super Viking 17-31A	1971-74	104	$21,000-$26,000	164	1,190	1,800	60/75	300-hp Lyc. IO-540-K1E5	2,000	$12,000
Super Viking 17-31A	1975-77	23	$28,000-$38,000	164	1,100	1,170	60/75	300-hp Lyc. IO-540-K1E5	2,000	$12,000
Super Turbo Vik. 17-31ATC	1969-70	11	$23,000-$24,000	204	1,305	1,800	72/92	250-hp Lyc. IO-540-G1E5	1,400	$12,000
Super Turbo Vik. 17-31ATC	1971-72	23	$26,000-$29,000	294	1,190	1,800	72/92	300-hp Lyc. IO-540-K1E5	2,000	$12,000
Turbo Viking 17-31ATC	1973-75	75	$30,000-$34,000	193	1,053	1,170	60/75	300-hp Lyc. IO-540-K1E5	2,000	$12,000
Turbo Viking 17-31ATC	1976-77	17	$38,000-$44,000	193	1,053	1,170	60/75	300-hp Lyc. IO-540-K1E5	2,000	$12,000
Turbo Viking 17-31ATC	1978-80	16	$50,000-$57,000	193	1,053	1,170	60/75	300-hp Lyc. IO-540-K1E5	2,000	$12,000

(mostly taildraggers) had many more non-fatal accidents than the Viking, on an apples-to-apples exposure basis. However, the *fatal* accident rate for the Viking and Cruisaire is the same: 4.5 fatal accidents per 100,000 flight hours)— about twice the rate of the Mooney M20 series (2.4 per 100,000 hours), and quite a bit worse than the Beech Bonanza (at 2.6). In a nutshell, the Viking does not compare well with its peers for safety.

The Viking's non-fatal accidents seem to be lumpable into three categories: a broad category subsuming all the more-or-less ''expected'' bad-luck events that befall all planes more or less equally (hard landings, crankshaft failure, water in the fuel, and so on) . . . engine failure for undetermined reasons . . . and fuel mismanagement. In a review of data covering the years 1979 through 1981, we find that out of 37 total Viking accidents, 32 were non-fatal; and of those, six involved unexplained powerplant failure, while ten involved fuel mismanagement, and the rest fall into the grab-bag category. It's clear that fuel mismanagement and engine problems loom large in the Viking's accident picture. A possible reason seems to be that Viking pilots—once they encounter water contamination, vapor lock, or fuel starvation (from not switching tanks) in the air—are not able to restart the engine easily. Simple restart procedures that work in other airplanes don't always work in the Bellanca, apparently (a problem compounded by a too-effective boost pump, as explained earlier).

In the fatal-accident category, we find that about half of the accidents are attributable to VFR pilots who blunder into IFR weather. More ominously, looking at the 56 fatal Viking accidents that have occurred through 1981, we find that *one out of eight* fatal Viking crashes involves in-flight airframe failure. On an equal-exposure basis, this makes the Viking's in-flight breakup rate not much different from that of the Beech Bonanza. (Remember that there are only 1,000 Vikings on the civil registry, compared to 10,000 Bonanzas; and the

Aircraft Resale Value Chart

Viking's flying history starts in 1967, whereas the Bonanza's starts in 1947. Thus there is greater statistical significance to the Bonanza's breakup data.)

The Viking is a strong airplane. But contrary to the bold rhetoric of the factory a few years ago (when Bellanca claimed that there had *never* been an in-flight structural failure of a Viking), there *have* been breakups—eight fatals, in fact. Most have been weather-related. But it is interesting to note that of the eight fatal Viking breakups on record, six happened in 1969-70 model airplanes. (There has been only one breakup of any Bellanca made after 1970.) This strongly suggests structural problems in a small batch of airplanes. Former Bellanca factory personnel say, however, that there were absolutely no changes in materials or methods of construction in the Viking line over the period in question.

In sum, it appears that the Bellanca Viking—while not gifted with a particularly superb safety record—need not be a particularly hazardous plane to own if pilots will simply avoid aerobatics, invest in good maintenance (particularly of the wing and fabric), take time to understand the fuel system (including in-flight restart techniques), and stay clear of thunderstorms and/or weather for which the pilot is not prepared.

Owner Comments

I have owned three Bellanca Vikings since 1973 and have found them to be an exceptional value and one of the last vestiges of craftsmanship in American manufacturing. In particular, the last two new Bellancas were very well built. Everything was working and tight when I picked the airplanes up from Miller Flying Service in Plainview, Tex. The interior and exterior finishes are particularly nice. The crush velour with leather (or vinyl, I'm not sure which) has held up well. The Imron paint has stayed new-looking with very little attention. No unscheduled maintenance was required in the first 200 hours on either airplane.

My direct operating cost including gas, oil, maintenance, insurance and hangar have run about $40 per hour. In 1,500 hours of flight time spanning seven years, other than routine maintenance, I have required replacement of a propeller govenor, an overvoltage relay, and a nose gear strut seal.

The aircraft is an absolute joy to fly. The handling is very responsive. It is especially nice in the banked maneuvers such as steep turns and chandelles. With very little effort one can imagine he is at the controls of a WWII fighter instead of a good stable cross-country airplane. In any large, powerful aircraft proper attention to speed management is important, and this aircraft is no exception. Speed and power must be controlled on approach in order to prevent excessive sink rates. Power off, C-150-type landings require considerable pilot technique, but power-on landings are very easily one. The aircraft is especially good in a crosswind. The low wing, large flaps, and wide gear make it very stable at touchdown.

The cross-country profile is good. I generally plan 500 nautical mile legs in 3.25 hours and have a 100-mile reserve. My airplane will carry two couples, overnight baggage and four hours of fuel and be well within its weight limit. The airplane is very stable in instrument conditions and has no tendency to fall off into a spiral. The panel layout is good and the radio options are quite varied. I have a two-axis autopilot but seldom use it because the airplane is so stable.

In general, I am quite pleased with my Bellanca. I was delighted to hear that the aircraft is back in production. I plan to buy another one if the present one ever wears out.

Bill Bass, Jr. M.D.

I purchased my 1975 17-30A Continental Super Viking in June 1976, as a dealer's demo with about 200 hours on it. I have put about 1,000 hours on it since then. My use is 100 percent business, traveling from Ohio to Montana and south as far as Missouri and Kansas. The plane has done all that was asked of it and some that wasn't, such as carrying a whale of a load of ice into South Bend one winter day.

It is a good solid airplane, steady instrument platform, and reasonably fast. I flight plan 140 knots. Fuel consumption leaned at 22/23 is 12.5 gph. Try as I may, block to block, it works out to 15 gph.

Handling is superb; it is very responsive but will hold a course, hands-off without use of autopilot, with tinkering. Trim changes on

Fabric covering can cost several thousand dollars to replace.

gear/flap extension/retraction are noticeable but easily controlled with the electric trim button on the yoke. I have managed significant wind shear and crosswind situations that even caused tower personnel at a large (DTW) airport to comment on doing a better job than the large commercial jets. The Viking responds to being flown like a light twin—carry a little power right down to the flare.

I don't take my plane into unapproved fields—the fiberglass main wheel doors don't take kindly to abuse. Full-flap slips are permitted and you can really get down in a hurry but need power to stop the sink. Overall, it does a fine job, but I would caution against low-time or occasional-use pilots trying anything unusual. This is a heavy, powerful, high-performance airplane that takes time and experience to get the most out of.

The cabin is tight for four, but so well done that you really don't notice. Workmanship is just what you would expect from an almost custom hand built plane; i.e., it is terrific!

Maintenance between annuals is minimal if plane is properly ccared for. I change the oil every 25 hours, Philips X/C 20W-50W, capacity is 12 qts.; however I run one new quart through it and add 11 qts. since the 12th quart always seemed to end up on the belly anyway. Between changes I'll add two qts. and be a quart low (10 qts.) when the next change comes up. I've replaced one vacuum pump (about

700 hrs.) and one exhaust valve. Compression is 70 to 75 over 80.

Needless to say I am very pleased with the plane, and since Continental raised the TBO from 1,500 to 1,700 hours, I feel it is better to keep it than to sell and then try to replace it. I understand they are starting to build them again which should help the resale value. In the meantime, I think a properly maintained, well kept Viking is the best buy on the market.

Dean I. Grauer, Jr.
Allen Park, Mich.

My latest Bellanca is a 1976 Super Viking. I have owned this plane for four years and have never had any difficulty. The annuals are done by Miller Flying Service, and the cost runs from a low of $590 to a high of just around $700.

I did Microlon the engine when I first got it at a little over 300 hours. It now has approximately 1,000. There have been no problems in starting the Lycoming engine. I true out at about 186 knots at 12,000 feet.

If there is anything to complain about concerning the Bellanca, in my opinion it would be the room on the inside. I am 5'9" and weigh approximately 210 pounds and make a number of trips cross-country.

I am probably prejudiced, but I sincerely believe this to be the best-flying and best-handling of any plane this size.

Ellis B. Qualls
Show Low, Ariz.

Beech Bonanza 35, 36

The word "legend" is tossed around rather freely when people talk about airplanes, but the Beechcraft Bonanza probably has a better claim to legendary status than any other modern lightplane. The Bonanza was the first high-performance post-war design (it was introduced in 1947). Its various models have been in continuous production since then, and are still considered by many to be the best single-engine airplanes flying.

The most innovative postwar aircraft to emerge on the civilian market, the early Bonanza 35 is inspected by Walter H. Beech and Olive Ann Beech.

The Bonanza's astonishing success is the result of excellent performance, sleek good looks, responsive handling and a "Mercedes of the air" image. The loading limitations, high parts prices and cracking crankcases are not part of that legend, however.

For many years, the Bonanza enjoyed a blue-chip reputation on the used-plane market. Because of high demand and huge inflationary price increases of new Bonanzas during the 1970s, it was routine for a decade-old Bonanza to be worth more than its new selling price. Owners reported paying top dollar for a used Bonanza, then selling it a few years later at a profit.

But the V-tail version of the airplane has in recent years suffered a sharp decline in value because of its bad record of in-flight breakups. (More on that later.) A V-tail is now worth about 10 percent less than an equivalent straight-tail 33 Bonanza; a few years ago the reverse was true. The generally bearish used-plane market of the mid-80s has hurt resale value of virtually all other aircraft, but the 33 series has taken over from the 35 the role as the best resale investment among light aircraft.

A prospective Bonanza buyer should carefully examine his motivation for buying. On a coldly rational cost-effective basis, a used Cessna 210 or Piper Comanche will generally provide more airplane per dollar. But pilots seem to be more impressed by macho appeal, plush interiors and the "feel" of the airplane. In this realm the Bonanza is supreme. We wonder how many used-aircraft buyers choose to buy Bonanzas after objective comparisons with other makes. Most, we suspect, simply decide to buy a Bonanza and don't even look seriously at other types. For those buyers, the question is merely which used Bonanza is the best buy?

Models

There is a bewildering variety of Bonanza models. There are three basic types: the Model 35, the classic V-tail form of the aircraft that was in continuous production from 1947 until 1982, with power ranging from 185 to 285 hp; the Model 33, introduced in 1960 with a conventional tail and engines ranging from 225 to 285 hp; and the Model 36, a "stretched" six-seat conventional-tail version introduced in 1968 with a 285-hp engine. (Adding to the confusion is the fact that the 33 model was called the Debonair for seven years.)

Engines

Early Bonanzas up through the G35 in 1956 had Continental "E" series engines. Although the powerplants are reasonably reliable, the supply of parts and knowledgeable mechanics for these engines is rapidly dwindling. Continental no longer makes remanufactured E series engines, and there are no more crankcases or crankshafts being made. Other parts are generally available, but rapidly becoming more expensive as production dwindles. Cost of an overhaul for an old Bonanza is about $8,000, hefty fee considering that the airplane itself may be worth only $15,000, even with a fresh overhaul.

Later Bonanzas have either the IO-470 or IO-520 Continental engines. Prior to 1970, both these engines were rated at 1,200 hours TBO. In 1970, the valves were improved, and TBO went up to 1,500 hours. Older engines overhauled with the better valves also have the 1,500-hour TBO. This should be a major checkpoint for buyers.

Cracking Cases

Literally thousands of Bonanza owners have suffered the "Curse of the Cracking Crankcases," either directly or indirectly because of overhaul considerations.

IO-520-B and -BA engines built prior to mid-1976 have a severe problem with crankcase cracking. The overhauling of those engines has virtually ceased because no reputable overhauler will sign off without a new post-1976 "heavy" case. The cost of case replacement added to normal overhaul cost is about the same as the cost of a re-manufactured engine from the factory, which now includes the heavy case. The result has been a bonanza (sic) of reman IO-520 bus-iness for Continental, and the elimination of the option of a lower-cost standard overhaul. The factory does offer some credit for cracked cases on trade-ins for reman-ufactured engines, but in most cases, "light case" Bonanza buyers will find themselves paying a couple of thousand dollars more than the usual overhaul cost when their engines are due for rebuilding.

Incidentally, beware of the phrase "heavy case" in advertisements for used Bonanzas. There have been at least three "heavy" case versions designed to combat the cracking problem. The first two didn't work. Only those engines manufactured or remanufactured after July 1976 have the true "heavy" case.

However, even the "heavy" cases aren't immune to cracking. A 1983 *Aviation Consumer* study showed that heavy-case engines had a record nearly as bad as the "light" cases. Crankcase cracks continue to be a problem in Bonanzas.

Maintenance Problems

The other two major Bonanza maintenance checkpoints are shared with various other aircraft: the Hartzell prop AD and the leaking Goodyear rubber fuel tanks. The prop AD — which applies only to IO-520-powered Bonanzas — generally costs $1,000.

The fuel tank AD is not as expensive in most cases, since only an inspection is required. However, if a leak is discovered, replacement can be costly. There is no consistent pattern, but most Bonanzas built between 1961 and 1975 are subject to the Goodyear AD. All Bonanzas have rubber bladder tanks of some sort, and their life expectancy is six to eight years. Replacement cost

Cost/Performance/Specifications

Model	Year Built	Number Built	Cruise Speed (kts)	Rate Climb (fpm)	Useful Load (lbs)	Fuel Std/Opt (gals)	Engine	TBO (hrs)	Overhaul Cost	Average Price
Bonanza 35	1947-48	1,500	150	950	1,092	39/60	185-hp Cont. E-185-1	1,500	$ 8,000	$ 14,250
A35	1949	699	148	890	1,075	39/60	185-hp Cont. E-185-1	1,500	$ 8,000	$ 15,250
B35	1950	479	148	890	1,075	39/60	196-hp Cont. E-185-8	1,500	$ 8,000	$ 16,250
C35	1951-52	719	152	1,100	1,050	39/60	205-hp Cont. E-185-11	1,500	$ 8,000	$ 17,250
D35	1953	297	152	1,100	1,050	39/60	205-hp Cont. E-185-11	1,500	$ 8,000	$ 17,750
E35	1954	705	160	1,300	953	39/60	225-hp Cont. E-225-8	1,500	$ 8,000	$ 18,500
F35	1955	392	160	1,300	978	39/60	225-hp Cont. E-225-8	1,500	$ 8,000	$ 19,000
G35	1956	489	160	1,300	1,003	39/60	225-hp Cont. E-225-8	1,500	$ 8,000	$ 19,500
H35	1957	464	165	1,225	1,080	39/60	240-hp Cont. O-470-G	1,500	$ 8,000	$ 22,750
J35	1958	663	174	1,250	1,080	39/60	250-hp Cont. IO-470-C	1,500	$ 8,750	$ 24,500
K35	1959	435	169	1,170	1,118	49/70	250-hp Cont. IO-470-C	1,500	$ 8,750	$ 26,000
M35	1960	399	169	1,170	1,118	49/70	250-hp Cont. IO-470-C	1,500	$ 8,750	$ 27,500
N35	1961	279	169	1,150	1,270	50/80	260-hp Cont. IO-470-N	1,500	$ 8,750	$ 29,500
P35	1962-63	467	169	1,150	1,270	50/80	260-hp Cont. IO-470-N	1,200	$ 8,750	$ 32,000
S35	1964-65	665	178	1,200	1,385	50/80	285-hp Cont. IO-520-BA	1,200	$ 9,300	$ 36,000
V35	1966-67	625	178	1,135	1,485	50/120	285-hp Cont. IO-520-BA	1,200	$ 9,300	$ 37,500
V35TC	1966-67	555	195	1,225	1,450	50/120	285-hp Cont. IO-520-BA	1,400	$11,000	$ 41,500
V35A	1968-69	468	177	1,136	1,440	44/74	285-hp Cont. IO-520-BA	1,200	$ 9,250	$ 42,000
V35A-TC	1968-69	252	200	1,225	1,373	50/120	285-hp Cont. IO-520-BA	1,400	$11,000	$ 47,000
V35B	1970	142	172	1,167	1,313	44/74	285-hp Cont. IO-520-BA	1,500	$ 9,250	$ 44,000
V35B-TC	1970	110	200	1,225	1,373	50/120	285-hp Cont. IO-520-BA	1,400	$11,000	$ 50,000
V35B	1971-72	185	172	1,167	1,313	44/74	285-hp Cont. IO-520-BA	1,500	$ 9,250	$ 47,000
V35B	1973-74	285	172	1,167	1,313	44/74	285-hp Cont. IO-520-BA	1,500	$ 9,250	$ 50,000
V35B	1975	128	172	1,167	1,313	44/74	285-hp Cont. IO-520-BA	1,500	$ 9,250	$ 55,000
V35B	1976	131	172	1,167	1,313	44/74	285-hp Cont. IO-520-BA	1,500	$ 9,250	$ 60,000
V35B	1977	120	172	1,167	1,313	44/74	285-hp Cont. IO-520-BA	1,500	$ 9,250	$ 65,000
V35B	1978	109	172	1,167	1,313	44/74	285-hp Cont. IO-520-BA	1,500	$ 9,250	$ 70,000
V35B	1979	123	172	1,167	1,313	44/74	285-hp Cont. IO-520-BB	1,500	$ 9,250	$ 75,000
V35B	1980	50	172	1,167	1,313	44/74	285-hp Cont. IO-520-BB	1,500	$ 9,250	$ 82,500
V35B	1981	28	172	1,167	1,313	44/74	285-hp Cont. IO-520-BB	1,500	$ 9,250	$ 97,500
V35B	1982	20	172	1,167	1,313	44/74	285-hp Cont. IO-520-BB	1,500	$ 9,250	$112,500

can run between $1,500 and $2,500, depending on the model.

Several *Aviation Consumer* readers mentioned vacuum pump failures, and the Airborne pumps used in many Bonanzas have a poor record. Failure of the vacuum pump in IFR conditions, of course, can be fatal.

Safety

The Bonanza's safety record is generally good — with a couple of important exceptions. According to *Aviation Consumer* studies of NTSB and FAA statistics for the period 1972-76, the 33 and 36 models have excellent records (see the list of single-engine retractable accident rate at the beginning of the book). The 33, in fact, has the lowest fatal accident rate of any single-engine airplane, and the 36 is not far behind.

The V-tail 35 model is another story. Newer V-tails, including the 1964 S model and later models, all with 285-hp engines, have a reasonably good fatal accident rate, but the older models rank very poorly, with a fatal accident rate nearly twice as high as the later V-tails and nearly quadruple that of the 33 series.

In-Flight Breakups

A major reason for the poor fatal accident rate of the older V-tails is the relatively very high rate of fatal in-flight airframe failures in those models. Over the years, there have been more than 230 Bonanza in-flight breakups, in which we estimate some 500 people have died. We have reprinted here a chart of the in-flight breakup rates of the various Bonanza models. As you can see, the old ones are the worst, with the 1947-48 "straight 35" having an especially high breakup rate. (The lower percentages for late-model V-tails are a bit misleading, however, since they haven't had enough time to build up a high number of accidents.)

What makes the V-tail's high record of in-flight breakups all the more ironic is the very low breakup

How well will this 1975 V35B hold its value? Until the V-tail breakup record became widely known, used Bonanzas appreciated in value. However, a 1975 model has lost $20,000 in value over the past four years.

rate of the straight-tail 33 and 36 models, which are essentially identical to the 35 except for the tail. The V-tail's breakup rate, according to one study, is 24 times higher than the straight-tail's.

The typical scenarios of a V-tail breakup is this: the pilot gets into bad weather and/or heavy turbulence, the airplane gets away from him, and comes apart in the ensuing high-speed dive and/or pull-out, which exceed the structural limits of the plane. The reasons for the high breakup rates of V-tail Bonanzas are not crystal clear, but

Bonanza 35 Fatal Inflight Airframe Failure Accidents*

Model	Number FIFAFAs	Number Produced	Percent FIFAFA
35	71	1500	4.8
35R	0	13	0.0
A35	17	701	2.4
B35	11	480	2.3
C35	20	719	2.8
D35	14	298	4.7
E35	10	301	3.3
F35	6	392	1.5
G35	7	476	1.5
H35	2	426	0.4
J35	5	396	1.3
K35	4	436	0.9
M35	10	400	2.5
N35	4	280	1.4
P35	7	467	1.5
S35	7	667	1.1
V35	5	622	0.8
V35A	5	470	1.1
V35B	3	n.a.	n.a.
Total	208		

Through 1979.

we believe the problem has two major facets: structural weak points and handling qualities.

Structural problems most likely play a big role in the high break-up rate of the 1947-48 model 35. Those years, the Bonanza had unusually thin wing skins and no shear web in the outboard leading edge —structural shortcuts designed to save weight. Although the break-up problem abated somewhat after Beech beefed up the wings in 1949, it did not go away, particularly in the A through E models. The problem seemed to move back to the tail; while the majority of "straight 35" breakup involved wing failures, the majority of failures in later models occurred in the tail. Some critics have faulted Beech for the front spar design in the stabilizers, particularly after the "overhang" in front of the spar was increased with the C model. Accident investigators report a pattern of tail failures in which the stabilizer skin fails and folds over the spar.

Any airplane will fall apart in the air if pushed far enough past its airspeed or g-load limits, and Bonanzas usually don't break up unless pushed past their limits. The question is, why do the pilots of older V-tails allow their craft to exceed speed and load limits so much more often than pilots of other airplanes?

The answer, we believe, may lie in the handling qualities of the V-tail Bonanzas.

The V-tail airplane has very light ailerons and low lateral stability — what the test pilots call high spiral divergence. Once a wing drops a little, it tends to keep going. In instrument weather and turbulence, this low rolling stability can put the pilot into the ''graveyard spiral'' quickly.

The V-tail airplane is also very light on the controls in the pitch axis. This low longitudinal stability means turbulence or pilot inattention will cause larger, quicker airspeed and altitude excursions. The light controls also mean that just a moderate pull on the wheel results in a sharp pullup and high g-forces.

The V-tail Bonanza's low longitudinal stability is exacerbated by the rather narrow center-of-gravity envelope. (Some models even have 30 pounds of lead in the nose to counter the balance problem.) With any passengers in the back seat, a Bonanza can be very close to its aft c.g. limit, and it's not uncommon for V-tails to be flown illegally beyond their aft limit. An aft c.g. further reduces the V-tail's already low longitudinal stability, making the airplane even more sensitive in pitch and making wheel forces even lighter.

The low stability in the roll and pitch axes can team up against the pilot. A typical scenario: pilot looks down at chart while gust drops right wing. Airplane begins rolling to the right, simultaneously dropping the nose and picking up speed. Pilot looks up from chart, notes very high airspeed, and pulls back on the wheel abruptly. Airplane pulls six g's and breaks off the wings or tail.

The famous ''Bonanza waggle'' may also play a role. The V-tail has very poor Dutch roll (yaw) characteristics in turbulence. In extreme cases, severe turbulence may yaw the plane to such high angles that the tail could literally be blown off, particularly at high speeds, according to some engineers.

The poor stability in all three axes is due mainly to the design of the V-tail itself. The straight-tail 33 and 36 Bonanzas have much better stability, and an almost perfect record of in-flight breakups (only two that we're aware of).

Another factor may be the sensitivity of the V-tail ruddervators to flutter. The V-tail Bonanza's margin of flutter is fairly small, and tests have shown that as little as two ounces at the trailing edge of the ruddervator — a piece of ice, or even a repaint job — can cause flutter under some conditions.

Stall/Spin

Older Bonanzas also show up poorly in stall/spin and fuel mismanagement accidents. According to NTSB accident statistics for the period 1965-73, the Bonanza had a fatal stall/spin accident rate of 0.68 (per 100,000 flight hours) — second only to the Beech 23 series (Sierra, Sundowner, etc.) among modern aircraft. By comparison, the Cessna 210 had a fatal stall/spin rate of only 0.24 — only about a third as high.

The Bonanza does have a sharp stall, often accompanied by a wing drop. There is little aerodynamic buffeting as warning of an impending stall. Some pilots have reported severe wing drops, even to the point of ending up on their backs in certain situations. We asked a former Beech engineer about the Bonanza's stall, and he said that no two Bonanzas stall alike. ''Even at the factory, some of them were very straightforward in the stall, while others dropped off rather abruptly.''

Another major cause of design-induced accidents is fuel mismanagement. Again, the older Bonanzas are near the top of the list in fuel mismanagement accidents. Ac-

Beech Bonanza 35,36

cording to a 1964 CAB report on fuel mismanagement, the Bonanza ranked second worst (to the Piper Tri-Pacer) in fuel mismanagement accidents that year. An NTSB study for the years 1965-69 ranks the Bonanza as having the highest incidence of fuel starvation accidents of any light aircraft. And a study of fuel starvation accidents during 1970-72 puts the Bonanza in the "higher than average" group along with three other aircraft.

The reason for the Bonanza's high incidence of fuel mismanagement accidents is presumably due to the placement of the fuel selector and the rather odd fuel pump operation in older models. The selector valve is on the floor under the pilot's left leg, which forces the pilot to crane his neck and divert his attention from the windshield and instrument panel to change tanks. Consequently, Bonanza pilots may switch tanks by feel, a riskier procedure. Also, the selector detents are poorly defined in some models, and it's possible to hang up the selector between tanks, which shuts off the fuel.

If an engine does quit from fuel starvation, the Bonanza pilot faces a dilemma: turn on the boost pump or not? If he doesn't according to a CAB study, the engine may take as long as 35 seconds to restart. If he does, he may flood the engine if the pump is left on too long. The owner's manual of one model Bonanza instructs the pilot to turn on the boost pump "momentarily" when switching from a dry tank. The pilot must tread a narrow line between a fuel-starved engine on the one hand and a flooded-out engine on the other hand. Not a happy choice.

The 1957 Bonanza incorporated a major series of wing and tail strengthening features.

And then, of course, there is the notorious "fuel unporting" syndrome that has resulted in numerous Bonanza accidents and lawsuits against Beech. In extended slipping or skidding maneuvers or in fast turning type takeoffs in pre-1970 models, fuel would slosh away from the fuel pickup if the tank was less than half full. Beech issued a service letter as far back as 1961 on the fuel unporting phenomenon. It warned that fuel unporting was a possibility after a turning takeoff, and stated that in such a case the air bubble in the fuel line would "reach the engine at about the same time the airplane becomes airborne and could cause momentary power interruption." The letter went on to say, "This does not create a hazard . . ." We think a lot of people would argue with that statement.

In any case, the FAA had identified 16 accidents caused by fuel unporting by 1971, when an AD was finally issued. The AD required no modification of the fuel system, merely a yellow arc on the fuel gauge and an admonition not to take off or slip or skid excessively if the fuel was in the arc. Beech did modify the tanks in 1970, and offered a retrofit kit for older Bonanzas, but only a handful of the retrofit kits were sold. Thousands of pre-1970 Bonanzas still have the unmodified tanks and are susceptible to fuel unporting. We would strongly urge any buyer to check whether the baffle kit has been installed, and to install it himself if it has not been done.

Summing up, while the straight-tail 33 and 36 models and the more recent 285-hp V-tail airplanes have good to excellent safety records, the older V-tails rank poorly. These older less-than-$30,000 Bonanzas are an attractive buy, but they are not for the overconfident or underqualified. More than 30 percent of the fatal accidents in older V-tails are in-flight breakups, and the stall/spin and fuel mismanagement accident rates are also quite high. Clearly, the older Bonanzas demand the pilot's full attention and adequate skills.

Loading

Early 185- and 225-hp Bonanzas have useful loads of about 900 pounds with normal equipment, and equipped useful load has grown over the years as horsepower increased to about 1,200 pounds in later 285-hp models. (The all-time Bonanza lifting champ is the 1968-69 straight 36 model, which had a standard useful load of 1,620 or about 1,400 with normal equipment.) Although 1,200 pounds is a fairly creditable figure, it is well short of the later Cessna 210s. Standard useful load of the 35 model took a big jump in 1961 with the N35 and another in 1964 with the S35, paralleling horsepower increases to 260 and 285. Generally speaking, Bonanzas are not full-seats-and-full-fuel airplanes with baggage, even the 285-hp four-placers.

However, most owners find that their loading is limited by c.g. restrictions before gross weight restrictions. The 35 models have especially narrow c.g. envelopes and it is very easy to load them aft of the limit, even with the 30-pound lead weights that some Bonanzas have in the nose for ballast. In many cases, it simply isn't possible to put two adults and significant baggage in the rear of a Bonanza, no matter how much fuel is off-loaded. In fact, c.g. problems become more pronounced with less fuel because the Bonanza's leading edge fuel tanks are ahead of the c.g. As a result, c.g. moves aft as fuel is burned off. This can be quite tricky for the pilot, who may be entirely legal when he takes off, but could find himself well out of the c.g. envelope to the rear as he approaches his destination after a long flight.

One of the results of a too-far-aft c.g., of course, is decreased pitch stability and lightened stick forces. Considering the Bonanza's already light pitch control forces and its tendency to build up speed quickly, an out-of-c.g. Bonanza can really take a pilot by surprise. If you plan to buy a Bonanza for four-person weekend outings, be sure to do some same weight-and-balance computations for each particular airframe you look at.

Performance

Here is where the Bonanzas shine. The first ones totally outclassed all the competition in performance, and there's still no non-turbocharged single-engine airplane in production today that will catch a good clean V35B. All Bonanzas deliver excellent speed for their horsepower and therefore good fuel economy. Book speeds range from 148 knots for the old A and B models to 178 knots for the V35 (and a snorting 200 at altitude for the turbo-charged V35 TC). Real-world speeds may be somewhat lower than the book (and sometimes the airspeed indicators) say, but owners nevertheless report good speeds: 165 to 174 knots for the 250-, 260- and 285-hp models, and 152 to 161 knots for the Bonanzas with the 225- to 240-hp engines. Fuel consumption runs from a high of about 16 gph with the 285-hp models to 10 gph with the E-185.

Rate of climb is also energetic, with only the very oldest Bonanzas climbing less than 1,000 fpm at gross weight (by the book, at least). Bonanzas are excellent short-field aircraft, partly because of their good performance, partly because of the rugged landing gear. The gear, incidentally, is so beefy that virtually the same gear is used for the Baron, which weighs a ton more.

Creature Comforts

Again, the Bonanza is strong in this respect. The cabin is quite large, especially in terms of headroom. (In fact, most pilots look like midgets while flying Bonanzas because of the high roof and window line.) Back-seaters aren't quite as well off because of the fuselage taper, but room is still adequate. Excellent visibility from broad windows accentuates the feeling of roominess of the airplane.

Interior appointments are traditionally excellent in Bonanzas. Beech apparently believes that a man who pays five or ten times the price of a Cadillac expects to have a quality interior — a philosophy apparently shared by few other manufacturers. Interior plushness is an important part of the Bonanza mystique.

Rear passengers in V-tail Bonanzas are usually miserable in turbulence, however. The V-tail looks neat and is the shining symbol the Bonanza line, but it does a lousy job as a tail. In turbulence, the V-tail models fishtail excessively, usually requiring several oscillations to recover from a good jolt. (See the "Modifications" section for a report on the Airskeg yaw damper, which apparently works decently.)

The 36 and A36 Bonanzas have a "club car" seating arrangement, with two pairs of rear seats facing each other. With three or four people aboard, this is a wonderfully roomy compartment, but a fifth and sixth person makes things chummy indeed. Virtually no one ever flew six full-sized people in an A36 (until the '79 models) because there was no room at all — literally none — for baggage. A small baggage compartment was added in 1979.

Many models of the 33 and 35 Bonanzas are called five- or six-seaters, but this is an optimistic delusion. A fifth or sixth seat, if installed, fits in the luggage compartment and is sutable only for very young children. In most cases, c.g. and/or baggage loading considerations make it impossible to use the rear seats, even given a supply of willing children with cast-iron stomachs.

Handling

The Bonanza has a uniquely fortuitous blend of aerodynamics and ergonomics that results in marvelous flying characteristics. Pilots praise it for well-harmonized and responsive controls, and many owners have told *The Aviation Consumer* that the Bonanza is the easiest of all planes to land. (Our own personal experience tallies with those opinions.) The "feel" of the Bonanza is another major element of the airplane's legend.

Cost/Performance/Specifications

Model	Year Built	Number Built	Cruise Speed (kts)	Rate Climb (fpm)	Useful Load (lbs)	Fuel Std/Opt (gals)	Engine	TBO (hrs)	Overhaul Cost	Average Price
Bonanza 36	1968-69	184	168	1,015	1,620	50/80	285-hp Cont. IO-520-BA	1,200	$9,250	$ 48,000
A36	1970-73	291	168	1,030	1,443	44/74	285-hp Cont. IO-520-BA	1,500	$9,250	$ 61,000
A36	1974-75	288	168	1,030	1,443	44/74	285-hp Cont. IO-520-BA	1,500	$9,250	$ 70,000
A36	1976-77	385	168	1,030	1,443	44/74	285-hp Cont. IO-520-BA	1,500	$9,250	$ 80,000
A36	1978	228	168	1,030	1,443	44/74	285-hp Cont. IO-520-BA	1,500	$9,250	$ 88,000
A36	1979	222	168	1,030	1,443	44/74	285-hp Cont. IO-520-BB	1,500	$9,250	$100,000
A36	1980	171	168	1,030	1,443	44/74	285-hp Cont. IO-520-BB	1,500	$9,250	$115,000
A36	1981	165	168	1,030	1,443	44/74	285-hp Cont. IO-520-BB	1,500	$9,250	$126,000
A36	1982	117	168	1,030	1,443	44/74	285-hp Cont. IO-520-BB	1,500	$9,250	$140,000
A36	1983	60	168	1,030	1,443	44/74	285-hp Cont. IO-520-BB	1,500	$9,250	$157,000

Beech Bonanza 35,36

Modifications

There is a welter of airframe modifications available for Bonanzas, and many owners have modified their older aircraft to the point that they're virtually indistinguishable from brand-new '78 models. Among the more popular Bonanza mods:

• Airskeg aerodynamic yaw damper, which supposedly improves V-tail wagging in turbulence. (Walker Engineering Co., Los Angeles, Calif., 213-272-1248.)

• Maybe a better answer to the yaw problem is a $1,495 electronic damper made by S-Tec Corp., Mineral Wells, Tex., (817) 325-9406.

• Cosmetic mods include one-piece windshields, late-model side windows, baggage doors, pointed spinners and a host of other interior and exterior touch-ups. Biggest of the specialists in this field is Beryl D'Shannon Aviation Specialties, Inc., in Lakeville, Minn., (800) 328-4629.

• The Smith Speed Conversion is a wide-ranging aerodynamic cleanup that increases speed by 13-17 knots. Smith resets the wing incidence, installs flap gap seals and performs a myriad of other small aerodynamic cleanups. But taken altogether, their effect is large. A modified cowling is also available that cuts drag, improves cooling and allows better engine breathing. The mods aren't cheap, however; the full speed treatment is $13,000, with the cowling an additional $5,250. Smith Speed Conversions, Box 430, Johnson, Kans., 67855, 316-492-6840.

• Smith also developed an internal beefup kit to strengthen the V-tail. It costs $1,975 installed by Smith; the kit costs only $825. For cost-conscious Bonanza owners not so concerned about appearance, Smith also offers an external cuff to support the leading edge of the V-tail stabilizer. It's $595 installed, or $395 for the kit alone. A second external cuff-type V-tail beefup is offered by Knots 2 U, Inc., 1941 Highland Ave., Wilmette, Ill.

60091, 312-256-4807. Cost of the kit is $575, plus three to four hours installation time. A third kit is offered by B & N Cameron Park Airport, 3280 Cameron Park Dr., Shingle Springs, Calif. 95682, 916-933-1367.

• Numerous engine conversions are available to upgrade older Bonanzas to 240-, 250-, 260- or 285-hp engines. Also, an STC allows conversion to a 300-hp Lycoming, which has the uncracking crankcase and a 2,000-TBO. Continental conversions are done by D'Shannon (address above); Lycoming mod is by Machen, Inc., Spokane, Wash., 509-838-5326.

Here's a quick rundown of the "milestone" Bonanza models with which major changes occurred:

35	Original airplane, 185-hp engine, 2,550-pound gross weight.
A35	Thicker wing skin, heavier spar carry-through.
C35	205-hp, 2,700-pound gross weight, larger tail with wider-angle V.
E35	225-hp.
F35	Third side window, stronger tail.
H35	First of "second generation" Bonanzas with O-series engine. 240-hp, gross weight 2,900 pounds, major structural beefup.
J35	Fuel injection, 250-hp.
N35	260-hp, third side window enlarged, fuel capacity increased to 74 gallons.
P35	New instrument panel.
S35	First of "third generation" Bonanzas, 285-hp, extended cabin. Very close to current configuration.
V35TC	Turbo-charged model, 132 built 1966-70.
V35B	Last production V-tail model.
33	First straight-tail model, 225-hp, named "Debonair."
C33A	285-hp.
E33	Renamed Bonanza.
E33C	Aerobatic model.
36	Straight tail, lengthened fuselage, cargo door, 3,600-pound gross weight.

American Bonanza Society

Perhaps the best of all the owner groups is the American Bonanza Society. Membership is nearly 7,000, and accounts for more than half of all Bonanza owners. The Society's newsletter is relatively sober and technically oriented, without so much of the gushy effusiveness of other aircraft owner association newsletters. Anybody shopping for a used Bonanza should get in touch with the American Bonanza Society, Box 12888, Wichita, Ks. 67277.

Owner Comments

The Bonanza is excellent for cross-county flight in smooth air. In turbulence you quickly find that yaw stability leaves much to be desired. Rear-seat paseners find the well-known Bonanza tail wag to be particularly objectionable.

Weight-carrying capability of the Bonanza is good, but it is nearly impossible to load it to gross weight without exceeding the aft c.g. limit.

The Bonanza is fun to fly. It handles nicely and offers ample performance. All of us had previous experience in high-performance singles, and little trouble was encountered in learning to fly and land the Bonanza smoothly. Some undesirable characteristics deserve mention, though. Low-speed aileron control becomes sluggish, making for interesting encounters with gusts on short final. Stalls call for an alert pilot, since the plane tends to drop its left wing abruptly at the break. In this circumstance the pilot finds himself looking for more rudder control, as he does during landings in strong crosswinds. Also, in the transition from landing approach to go-around, the pilot finds himself straining to keep the nose down while he takes out the high degree of nose-up trim used in the approach. The bungee interconnect in the controls gets criticized from time to time, particularly after

Aircraft Resale Value Chart

crosswind landing and other maneuvers performed using cross-controlling.

Hot starts of the fuel-injected Continental engine can be exasperating. When cold, it generally starts after the first few blades.

Parts are extremely expensive. The Beech dual control yoke costs $1,800. The new fuel cell costs $1,252, but by the time it was installed we were out $1,600. We found this out after discovering that one cell leaked and could not be repaired. The cell was replaced, but the replacement also leaked and it was, in turn, replaced. The FBO applied for reimbursement credit from Beech, and was finally applied four months later. The reimbursement covered the parts and installation but did not cover some $40 in freight charges. The FBO said we were fortunate since Beech generally does not make reimbursements that complete. We did not consider ourselves fortunate at all.

After the fuel cell, the second most expensive of these maintenance items was replacement of the vacuum pump. This makes the fifth vacuum pump on the plane since new, indicating a history of problems in the pressure system. We recently replaced the pressure regulator as well.

Beech Bonanza 35,36

As with most older aircraft, performance is somewhat less than published figures after antennas, rigging and engine age impose their penalties. Our F model (225-hp) trued out at 163 mph while our M model (250-hp) gives an honest 182 mph. Twenty-five additional horsepower gives 19 more miles per hour. We have often wondered whether Beech did more than just increase power. The additional power, speed and perhaps a bit of redesign also provided a firmer IFR platform.

●

We asked Bill Guinther, former president of the Bonanza Society, to offer a few tips for buyers of used Bonanzas. Keeping in mind that Bill is both very knowledgeable about these airplanes and at the same time a professional Bonanza booster, we offer his comments:

When Beech engineers started to make plans for a civilian single-engine high-performance airplane after World War II, they asked military pilots what should be included in a civilian airplane. The answer that came back was 'very light control forces.' Most of the fighter pilots cited the Spitfire's balanced controls as most desirable, stating that the newer P-51 Mustang, with its bigger engine, had very heavy stick forces. Therefore, the engi-

neers at Beech decided that the airplane they planned would have balanced surfaces with very little force changes through the whole range of airspeed.

The 1947 'straight' 35 is still one of the finest-flying, best-feeling airplanes ever designed. Of course, in those days most of the pilots had military background flying high-performance airplanes, so the light control pressures were not a detriment.

The first Bonanza, having a gross weight of 2,550 pounds, had a very low stall speed (46 mph) which meant it had outstanding short-field performance. Today's Bonanza, with an increase of more than 100 hp and 1,000 pounds gross weight, requires more takeoff and more landing space.

The first engine on our 1968 V35A went to 1,750 hours and was showing good compression. Oil had been changed every 25 hours since new, but we got nervous about paying the core charge if the crankshaft or case went bad. The engines have needed a cylinder or two topped because of valve guide and exhaust wear, but we count on 1,600 per engine.

An S or V model Bonanza is an excellent buy because the style hasn't changed in 19 years — the performance stays the same and they can be updated to look like new.

In terms of performance, my 1973 F33A delivers book or above speeds and climb rate; that is to say, 175-177 knots true at 75 percent power and 172-174 knots true at 65 percent. Timed rates of climb average 900 fpm at altitudes below 3,000 feet. The quality and workmanship are second to none and suggest an attention to detail that is simply not available in any similar aircraft.

As in every airplane, there are areas for improvement. Of primary importance to me are the Continental crankcase AD, the Hartzell prop AD, and the fuel cell AD. (My fuel cells turned out to be Uniroyal, so I'm okay for now.) The engine burned or spilled an inordinate amount of oil, but the installation of a Walker Airsep has cured that. My pet peeves are two: the price of parts is astronomical; i.e., $165 for an ammeter.

Beech loves to issue service letters. I have received no less than 10 in the year I have owned the airplane. While I admire their concern for safety, the cost of the various retrofits and inspections has amounted to a considerable sum.

Having flown both models, I feel the F33A is more stable in yaw response in turbulence than the V-tail, but still displays some fish-tailing.

Overall, other expenses have been reasonable, with annuals going for about $600. While a Bonanza is a more expensive aircraft to own in terms of initial cost and parts, it offers superior performance and a quality of construction second to none. It is a rugged, dependable machine which holds its value very well.

●

Takeoffs and landings require no special effort or techniques. Good landings are relatively simple to achieve. Short-field takeoffs and landings equal, or even better than what we have been able to get from a Cessna 182.

The well-known yaw is there occasionally, in certain air conditions. Riding the pedals eliminates most. The Airskeg is also an aid toward reducing yaw.

When modifying a Bonanza, don't expect to get all of your money back. Windows, panels, cabin interiors, wing lights and paint can be changed but you will still be flying an older Bonanza that looks pretty with essentially the same performance as before. If you do modify, our recommendation is to use only Beech parts. When turning a plane over to a modifier, insist on a written completion time. We had our F-35 tied up for four months on one accasion and seven weeks on another. My number one recommendation is to save the money you would put into a major modification and trade up.

The original Model 35 has had a much worse than average record of in-flight airframe failures.

In order to more fully understand the cost, performance and specification difference between the various models we made an analysis of true value based on weighted age, speed, range, useful load and cost. The results were fascinating: In the $20,000-$30,000 bracket the K and M models were outstanding. The J model was dragged down by range limitations.

Why own a Bonanza? The answer is simple. For $30,000, a 19-year-old aircraft will outperform the new Skylane RG and Rockwell 114 costing twice the Bonanza investment. The performance differences are even greater when comapred to the Skylane or Dakota costing approximately one and one-half times more. Justifying an aforementioned new aircraft with its high initial depreciation is difficult in the face of Bonanza performance, dependability, resale value and flexibility for modification.

The performance of the S35 Bonanza is excellent, but not quite as advertised. Although my partner and I are used to cruising at 75 percent power on Lycoming-engined aircraft we have owned before, we have chosen to fly our Bonanza at 65 percent power for greater engine smoothness and reduced noise level. This consistently produces block-to-block speed to 160 knots, and the altitude chosen seldom changes this.

The Bonanza handles more smoothly than any Piper or Cessna product I have flown. I find no other characteristics to be unusual

except for the tail-waggle in turbulence. The Bonanza is the easiest airplane to land smoothly consistently of any aircraft I have flown. This feature alone is probably reason enough to buy the airplane.

Maintenance for us has been no big problem since we have owned the airplane only 600 hours and many problems have yet to arise. The big maintenance problems are the two AD notes out on engine crankcase cracking and Goodyear fuel tank bladders. Our aircraft did have one crack problem, but in several hundred hours since the crankcase was replaced we have had no additional problems. Any pilot contemplating purchase of a Bonanza absolutely must insure that the engine has the new heavier crankcase, and has had new fuel bladders installed. The only maintenance problem which has not been resolved is the large amount of oil thrown off by the wet vacuum pump. The pump works adequately, although vacuum is almost always on the low side, but there is always oil along the firewall and belly of the airplane. So far, we have not been willing the bear the expense of converting to a dry-type vacuum pump. It has had no effect upon the operation of the aircraft but it is bothersome.

We found that the best insurance coverage was available through Don Flower and Assoc. in their group insurance policy available for members of the American Bonanza Society. They indicated to us that time in type was more important that obtaining an instrument rating in order to reduce premiums. But how do you accumulate 25 hours of Bonanza time when none are available for rent?

Cessna 210

They laughed at Cessna's fetish for high-winged airplanes way back in 1959 when the company took a Cessna 1980 airframe and, in a most unconventional manner, retracted the landing gear into the fuselage. Later, the evolution of that airplane, the Cessna 210 Centurion, became the world's best-selling large single by far. But is also has been one of the most problem-plagued.

History

Though not able to trace its ancestry back as far as the Beech Bonanza of the post-World War II epoch, the 210 has a 25-year history that encompasses three different engines and cabins and two different wings plus a host of other systems modifications.

Since the first model appeared in 1959, the gross weight has risen nearly half a ton from a modest 2,900 pounds to a hefty 4,100 pounds, making the airplane the heaviest single in production for general use. The horsepower has risen from 260 hp to 325 hp and the cruise speed peaked out just under 200 mph/174 knots.

A turbocharged model introduced in 1965 has gone on to outsell its normally aspirated sibling by nearly a two-to-one ratio.

Major Evolutionary Changes

In 1962 the cabin was enlarged slightly and given rear windows. But basically the airplane remained a four-placer. Then in 1964 a major engine change was made, going up from 260 hp to 285 hp. The first turbo model appeared in 1966. In 1967 another significant change involved replacing the strut-braced wing with a cantilever one, while boosting fuel capacity from 65 gallons to

90. The airplane cabin still could not be considered a six-placer, however; it was, at best, a four plus two (kids).

Then in 1970 a major cabin modification provided six adult seats with extra baggage spce in the rear, and the gross weight was raised by 400 pounds to 3,800 pounds. Next, in 1971 takeoff horsepower was raised to 300. And in 1972 the old engine-driven hydraulic system was replaced with an electro-hydraulic system. The pressurized P210 was introduced in 1979.

Naturally, 1970 and later models are desirable for the extra cabin space and extra load-carrying ability, and '67 and later models for the extra 25-gallon fuel capacity.

With the 1977 model, the turbo 210 finally got a boost in horsepower from 285 up to 310 hp. And in 1985 the turbo received even more power as the rating went up to 325 hp.

Earlier, in 1979, the 210 underwent a landing gear simplification operation that did away with the main gear doors. Instead, the main wheels were simply tucked into a slot in the fuselage, eliminating a lot of nuisance and complication on a gear system that had gone through its share of problems over the years. Evidently, the move sacrificed no measurable speed, either.

Also in 1979, the gross went up one more time to 4,000 pounds with the

The turbo 210s are among the few singles with approval to fly in known icing. Even though equipped with boots, nonturbos are not.

210N model, and in '85 it went up to 4,100 pounds with the 210R.

In 1982 Cessna offered optional dual alternators and vacuum pumps. Then, with the 1983 turbo models certificated for flight in icing conditions, Cessna incorporated dual vacuum pumps as standard equipment. So either vacuum system alone could provide power for deice boots along with vacuum-powered instruments. In view of the failure rate of vacuum pumps, especially when burdened with the need to power deice boots, this is an invaluable option.

Also on the '83 model, the company began installing new Slick pressurized magnetos to give more protection against misfiring at high altitudes.

In 1984 Cessna increased the engine TBO from 1,400 to 1,600 hours and made shoulder harnesses standard equipment on all seats.

Performance and Handling

Speed, useful load and range are the 210's strong suits. With a top cruising speed of 196 mph/171 knots, the later model 210s yield a range with reserve of nearly 1,000 sm — greater than any other single aside from the Mooney 201, to our knowledge.

With an IFR-equipped, full fueled payload of about 970 pounds, the late-model Cessna 210 can haul the astonishing load of five adults and about 22 pounds of baggage for each rider. No other single comes close except the Piper Lance, which is still about 70 pounds shy. To accommodate all this weight, an unusually broad center of gravity envelope tolerates loading extremes that would cause aerodynamic havoc in other airplanes.

Of course, the rear two seats are a bit cramped for long flights, and they pose entry and exit problems —but they are available if needed. Furthermore, there is a separate baggage compartment in the rear.

Left and right front-seat cabin doors provide extra flexibility for the forward four seats.

In terms of handling, as the heaviest airplane in its class at gross, the 210 must be treated with respect — something quite a few pilots neglect to do, judging from the accident reports provided later on showing overshoots and hard landings. For so large an airplane, however, the airplane should not be faulted on its aerodynamic agility, since it has very quick, light ailerons. The airplane is heavy in pitch control, however, and with its limited elevator is difficult to maneuver into a full-stall break, but naturally, it will mush with the best of them at low-power, low-

speed situations.

Despite windows all-around, visibility is limited by the high wing inside a turn; and the instrument panel is so high that when the average pilot has cranked his seat high enough to see over it, he can't see out to the left without ducking he head under the window jamb.

Cabin Comfort, Finish

A fairly common complaint among 210 owners is that the general quality of the cabin interior is not commensurate with the caliber of the airplane as a prestige top-of-the-line product. Through the Royalite material on the instrument panel is

Cost/Performance/Specifications

Model	Year Built	Number Built	Cruise Speed (kts)	Useful Load (lbs)	Rate of Climb (fpm)	Fuel Std/Opt (gals)	Engine	TBO (hrs)	Overhaul Cost	Average Retail Price
210	1960	610	165	1,160	1,300	65	260-hp Cont. IO-470-E	1,500	$ 8,800	$ 16,000
210A	1961	171	165	1,160	1,300	68	260-hp Cont. IO-470-E	1,500	$ 8,800	$ 18,000
210B	1962	281	160	1,220	1,270	65/84	260-hp Cont. IO-470-S	1,500	$ 8,800	$ 20,000
210C	1963	156	160	1,220	1,270	65/84	260-hp Cont. IO-470-S	1,500	$ 8,800	$ 21,000
210D	1964	283	166	1,260	1,210	65/84	260-hp Cont. IO-520-A	1,700	$ 9,300	$ 23,000
210E	1965	224	166	1,260	1,210	65/84	285-hp Cont. IO-520-A	1,700	$ 9,300	$ 24,000
210F	1966	101	165	1,435	1,115	65/84	285-hp Cont. IO-520-A	1,700	$ 9,300	$ 26,000
T210	1966	147	191	1,335	1,280	65/84	285-hp Cont. TSIO-520-C	1,400	$12,000	$ 28,000
210G	1967	122	167	1,440	1,000	90	285-hp Cont. IO-520-A	1,700	$ 9,300	$ 28,000
T-210G	1967	104	194	1,350	1,115	89	285-hp Cont. TSIO-520-C	1,400	$12,000	$ 29,000
210H	1968	125	167	1,440	1,000	90	285-hp Cont. IO-520-A	1,700	$ 9,300	$ 28,000
T-210H	1968	65	194	1,350	1,115	89	285-hp Cont. TSIO-520-C	1,400	$12,000	$ 32,000
210J	1969	136	167	1,440	1,000	90	285-hp Cont. IO-520-J	1,700	$ 9,000	$ 23,000
T-210J	1969	45	194	1,350	1,115	89	285-hp Cont. TSIO-520-C	1,400	$12,000	$ 33,000
210K	1970	181	164	1,552	800	90	300-hp Cont. IO-520-L	1,700	$ 9,300	$ 30,000
T-210K	1970		190	1,620	930	90	300-hp Cont. TSIO-520-H	1,400	$12,000	$ 34,000
210-KII	1971	171	164	1,552	860	90	300-hp Cont. IO-520-L	1,700	$ 9,300	$ 32,000
T-210K	1971		190	1,620	930	90	300-hp Cont. TSIO-520-H	1,400	$12,000	$ 36,000
210LII	1972	220	164	1,552	860	90	300-hp Cont. IO-520-L	1,700	$ 9,300	$ 34,000
T-210L	1972		194	1,476	1,030	90	300-hp Cont. TSIO-520-H	1,400	$12,000	$ 39,000
210LII	1973	351	164	1,552	860	90	300-hp Cont. IO-520-L	1,700	$ 9,300	$ 36,000
T-210LII	1973		194	1,476	1,030	90	300-hp Cont. TSIO-520-H	1,400	$12,000	$ 40,000
210LII	1974	474	164	1,552	860	90	300-hp Cont. IO-520-L	1,700	$ 9,300	$ 37,000
T-210L	1974		194	1,476	1,030	90	300-hp Cont. TSIO-520-H	1,400	$12,000	$ 42,000
Centurion II	1975	531	164	1,552	860	90	300-hp Cont. IO-520-L	1,700	$ 9,300	$ 42,000
T-210II	1975		194	1,476	1,030	90	300-hp Cont. TSIO-520-H	1,400	$12,000	$ 45,000
Centurion II	1976	520	171	1,552	860	90	300-hp Cont. IO-520-L	1,700	$ 9,300	$ 45,000
T-210II	1976		197	1,476	1,030	90	300-hp Cont. TSIO-520-H	1,700	$ 9,300	$ 49,000
Centurion II	1977	719	171	1,552	860	90	300-hp Cont. IO-520-L	1,700	$ 9,300	$ 48,000
T-210II	1977		197	1,476	1,030	90	310-hp Cont. TSIO-520-R	1,400	$12,000	$ 55,000
Centurion II	1978	680	171	1,552	860	90	300-hp Cont. IO-520-L	1,700	$ 9,300	$ 54,000
T-210	1978		197	1,476	1,030	90	310-hp Cont. TSIO-520-R	1,400	$12,000	$ 60,000
Centurion II	1979	685	171	1,552	860	90	300-hp Cont. IO-520-L	1,700	$ 9,300	$ 58,000
T-210N	1979		197	1,476	1,030	90	310-hp Cont. TSIO-520-R	1,400	$12,000	$ 67,000
210N II	1980	494	170	1,580	950	90	300-hp Cont. IO-520-L	1,700	$ 9,300	$ 69,000
T-210N II	1980		221	1,700	930	90	310-hp Cont. TSIO-520-R	1,400	$12,000	$ 78,000
210N II	1981	399	170	1,580	950	90	300-hp Cont. IO-520-L	1,700	$ 9,300	$ 77,000
T-210N II	1981		221	1,700	930	90	310-hp Cont. TSIO-520-R	1,400	$12,000	$ 86,000
210N II	1982	236	170	1,580	950	90	300-hp Cont. IO-520-L	1,700	$ 9,300	$105,000
T-210N II	1982		221	1,700	930	90	310-hp Cont. TSIO-520-R	1,400	$12,000	$120,000
210N II	1983	49	170	1,580	950	90	300-hp Cont. IO-520-L	1,700	$ 9,300	$127,000
T-210N II	1983		221	1,700	930	90	310-hp Cont. TSIO-520-R	1,600	$12,000	$135,000
210N II	1984		170	1,580	950	90	300-hp Cont. IO-520-L	1,700	$ 9,300	$170,000
T-210N II	1984		221	1,700	930	90	300-hp Cont. TSIO-520-R	1,700	$12,000	$182,000

Used Aircraft Guide

light and conveniently removable, it in particular often comes in for criticism as looking "cheap."

A number of owners also complain that their 210s are not weather-proof, that they leak rainwater through the cabin, pasenger doors and baggage doors. We are unable to tell whether, on this score, the 210 is any worse or better than other airplanes, since aircraft door sealing and weatherstripping has always been an occult art, with mixed success on many models.

Cabin width (44 inches in the middle) and height (47 inches) makes for sufficient passenger and pilot comfort in the front four seats, and in the cantilever-wing models the wing carry-through beams are located behind the front-seat passengers where they are out of the way.

Comparison

Stacked up against the Piper Lance and the Beech A36 Bonanza, the late model 210 is a speck faster than the A36 and about 15 knots faster than the Lance. The 210 carries a useful load about 130 pounds over that of the A36, but about 13 pounds shy of the Lance. The 210's cabin is two inches wider than the A36 at the widest, but again comes out second best to the Lance by about four inches. The 210 comes out second to the Lance in baggage space and baggage structural capacity.

Maintenance

The biggest problem reported by owners is the landing gear system, especially in the pre-1972 models with the engine-driven hydraulic system, as opposed to the later electro-hydraulic one. The task of maintaining these older ones, with accumulator, power pack, filter and hydraulic pump, was described by one mechanic as "a pain in the ass."

Owners reported long delays in getting gear system parts for the older models, too, when the gear saddle A.D. triggered a rash of repairs, though this may have eased off somewhat lately. Parts are

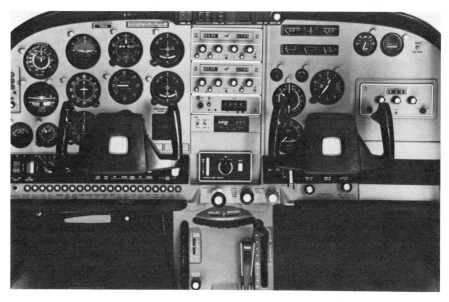

Instrument panel for a '75 turbo 210, with fuel gauges at the right of the radio rack.

also available through salvage houses. An independent IA mechanic we often consult with (John Dennis of Poughkeepsie, N.Y.) characterized the landing gear system on recent models as relatively robust and simple and requiring comparatively little maintenance.

Though some owners complained about the high cost of parts, Dennis said he felft Cessna's (and Piper's) were not high compared with other manufacturers like Beech and Rockwell.

He warned prospective purchasers of pre-1964 models 210s to have a mechanic make a thorough inspection or face the possibility of spending "big bucks" to make extensive corrections, especially in the gear system. Like all large, sophisticated airplanes, the 210 takes care and money to keep operating properly.

A.D. History

The one dark shadow lurking over the purchaser of a used 210 is the notorious landing gear saddle problem, which affects all 210s built from 1960 to 1969. Fatigue cracks began showing up in alarming numbers in the early seventies, usually after the airplane had accumulated 1,000-1,200 hours. FAA records show 181 cracked saddles from 1970-75, and there were possibly hundreds of other unreported cracks.

Typically, the cracks would be found during annual inspections. If they weren't, the saddles would eventually break altogether. The pilot then would discover his problem when one landing gear leg would hang up in the half-way position. Ten messy, expensive gear-up landings by 210s with broken saddles were reported in one 30-month period.

An AD was finally issued in 1976. Immediate saddle replacement was required for 1960 and 1961 models, but the replacement saddles themselves must be replaced every 1,000 hours — the replacement saddle is just as defective as the original. Cost of replacement is about $1,000-$1,500, so any purchaser of a 1960 or 1961 model should count on at least $1 per hour for saddle replacement. And be sure to check how soon the replacement is due — the owner may be trying to sell the plane just before his saddle replacement is due, and you could be stuck with the bill a few hours later. In all cases, inspect the saddle closely to insure that it hasn't cracked already.

The 1962-67 models had the same original defective saddles as the '60 and '61s, but differences in the retraction system allow an improved saddle to be fitted as a replacement. But there's a kicker. The "improved" saddles, it turns out, aren't much better than the originals, and we have reports of replacement saddles breaking in as few as 300 hours. According to an FAA report, "The so-called 'improved' saddles have served only to extend the life of the part, rather than eliminate the cracking/breaking problem . . . the problem has persisted and now includes airplanes with the improved saddles." The AD still requires a dye-penetrant inspection annually once the replacement saddle has accumulated 1,200 hours.

Nineteen sixty-eight and 1969 models had the "improved" saddles as original equipment, and they must be inspected at 1,200 hours and annually thereafter. Expect them to break eventually. In all cases, the saddles should be closely inspected.

In 1970, the landing gear system underwent a major redesign, and there has been no recurrence of the problem that we know of.

Potential buyers of 1960-64 210s should also be on the lookout for other gear problems. Another 1976 AD required replacement of the hydraulic landing gear actuators on those models — a $2,000 job. Make sure that AD has been accomplished. There have been no reports of recurring actuator problems, so an airplane with modified actuators should be all right.

Filiform Paint Problem

Buyers of used Cessna 210s should also be particularly careful about the paint jobs on aircraft built between 1977 and 1982 and later based in hot, humid seaside areas like Florida. Some of these appear to be subject to filiform corrosion because of Cessna's method of preparing the aluminum surface for the Dupont Imron paint.

Cessna chose to use only a wash primer, no Alodyne, and no epoxy primer barrier coat, as Dupont recommended when Cessna switched to Imron in 1977. As cases of filiform corrosion began turning up, Cessna, without publicity, began correcting some of them by paying customers for new paint

Aircraft Resale Value Chart

jobs. This program has long since expired, however. And Cessna began using Alodyne in 1982, but did not use the epoxy primer.

Safety Record

The Cessna 210 has a very poor accident rate in comparison with other single-engine retractables. In fact, it has the third worst out of 17 aircraft whose accident rates were computed for the decade 1972 through 1981. Only the old Piper Comanche and the Beech 24 Sierra had worse accident records for that period.

In terms of fatal accidents, the C-210 fares better, however, coming out only eighth worse out of the 17 aircraft, or almost in the middle of the pack. Engine stoppage is the single most common cause of accidents in the 210, accounting for 58 out of 181 accidents during the 10-year period. But only about half the stoppages were related to mechanical problems; the rest resulted from fuel exhaustion or starvation. Vapor lock problems may have contributed to the stoppages.

Among the salient facts disclosed by a study of all the Cessna 210 accidents reported by the NTSB for the two years, 1975 and 1976, out of 181 accidents reported, fully 32 percent, or 58, were related to engine stoppages. Other large tolls were related to gear-up landings (22 or 12 percent), improper IFR operations (20 or 11 percent) and

all-around poor pilot judgment (30 or 17 percent).

Since 28 engine stoppages (or 15 percent) were caused by a malfunction of some sort, pilots might give some attention to the causes reported in the NTSB listings.

The greatest number of failures — four — was caused by engine crankshaft failures. Three stoppages were caused by failure of the throttle control in some fashion (throttle control shaft broke at rod end; throttle link failed because of throttle control rod end pin; uniball rod end allowed bearing to slip off ball over washer.)

Two more stoppages resulted from mixture control failures (mixture control bolt missing, lock nut found in nacelle; mixture control assembly broke — FAA advisory circular 20-7N).

And another pair occurred when the oil quick drain opened during flight, causing the engine to lose all its oil.

Seven engine stoppages were for undetermined reasons.

Gear-up Landings

Of the 22 gear-up landings, a little over half occurred because pilots were distracted or simply forgot to lower the gear; however, in three of these instances pilots had some excuse in that the gear warning horn was not working.

There seemed to be no obvious pattern in the gear-up malfunctions, except that in two cases the gear actuator or actuating cylinder failed.

Fuel Mismanagement

The large number of fuel mismanagement problems might come as a surprise to anyone familiar with the typical "infallible" high-wing Cessna fuel system that normally allows the pilot to dispense with tank switching. However, until the 1982 model Centurions came along, a "both" tanks position was not available, and pilots had to switch from left to right tank in the conventional manner.

According to the NTSB accident reports, two engine stoppages resulted when the pilot inadvertently allowed the one tank to run dry, and then was unable to restart the engine, despite the fact there was sufficient fuel in the other tank.

In one of the instances the Safety Board said the pilot, who had low time in the 210, did not turn on the electric fuel pump when switching from the dry left tank to the right tank. Evidently, the gravity feed is not sufficient to do the job, though fuel injection engines are usually difficult to restart when starved of fuel.

What is surprising is that most pilots tagged with fuel mismanagement simply used every drop of available fuel and were obliged to make forced landings. Since there is a generous 89 usable gallons of fuel available — enough for five to six hours at high cruise speeds — it's mystifying why so many pilots apparently wanted more.

One possible contributing factor might be the poor location of the fuel gauge on the right side of the instrument panel rather far away from the pilot for easy viewing. Only starting in the '78 model 210s has this situation been altered by locating the fuel gauges down on the lower throttle pedestal directly above the fuel tank selector switch.

Pilots are warned in the operating handbook to avoid prolonged slips with fuel tanks less than one-quarter full. Since one pilot actually "flamed-out" in this condition while slipping for a crosswind landing approach, the warning should be heeded.

It also behooves 210 pilots (and all others, of course) to drain the fuel tanks for water and sediment — a fairly simple exercise on the high-wing Cessna. Six of the Cessna 210 engine stoppages resulted from water contaminents in the fuel.

Fuel Bladders

Buyers of Cessna 210s built up until the late 1970s that have bladder fuel tanks instead of integral tanks should keep an eye out for possible trapping of water in the tank wrinkles. An Airworthiness Directive was issued in 1984 mandating checking of the bladders for wrinkles that might trap water and lead to an engine stoppage.

Some aircraft in which a guarantee could not be given that the water problem was eliminated were given placards telling pilots to rock and roll the aircraft before flight to dislodge extra water trapped by the wrinkles. These aircraft must be inspected once every 12 months for wrinkle formation and overall fuel cell condition.

Although 20 crashes (all but one fatal) occurred when pilots got in over their heads in IFR weather, only two cases were reported of severe structural damage from overstressing the airplane. In one of these the airplane tumbled out of a thunderstorm in pieces; in the other the pilot brought the airplane back to base with bent wings after approaching within five miles of a thunderstorm. The 210 has a much better record than the Bonanza in this respect.

In-flight Breakups

In the past few years, the Cessna 210 has shown a marked increase in in-flight breakups. In fact, since 1976 late-model Centurions were breaking up about as often as late-model V-tails. Compared with its peers in the heavy single category, the 210 came out third worst in a comparison of breakup rates between 1977 and 1983. The Piper Lance was worst with 6.5 breakups per million hours; the Beech 35 next with 4.8 and the Cessna 210 third with 3.3. Safest of all in terms of breakups was the Beech 33/36 with a rate of only 0.5 breakups per million hours.

Vapor Lock Shock

Cessna 210s and P210s share with Cessna 206s vapor lock problems that have caused engine interruptions and engine failures. At the end of 1981, Cessna brought out kits designed to eliminate the problem, by incorporating vapor return lines. Service Bulletin SE 81-33 deals with the matter and applies to 1976-79 T-210s and P210s, which Cessna believed had the worst of the vapor problems. Make sure the aircraft you are considering has this improvement.

The new vapor line mod is similar to the fuel system in 1962-63 models, which have had few vapor lock problems.

Although prop clearance (with a three-bladed prop) is a better-than-average 10.89 inches, 210 pilots caution that the geometry of the airplace seems to make for a greater-than-average danger of striking a prop when taxiing over uneven surfaces, as from sod to ramp.

Most of the other problems in the 210 reported in the two-year NTSB rundown involved undershooting or hard landings or groundlooping, all of which suggest poor pilot judgment and inability to properly handle a big, heavy, high-performance airplane. In two cases, the airplane actually was blown over onto its nose from high winds while taxiing.

Modifications

One way to help keep the engine running cooler on the turbo model 210s is to have an intercooler installed by Turboplus in Gig Harbor, Wash., (800) 742-4202. The price is $5,995 installed. The company also can install speed brakes for $4,645. These will, conversely, help keep the engine from being overcooled on descent.

Flint Aero in Santee, Calif., (619) 448-1551, can provide wingtip tanks for the cantilever wing 210s, adding an extra 33 gallons. The price is $4,250.

R/STOL Systems, Inc. in Everett, Wash., (206) 355-2736, has taken over the Robertson mods and can install them for $7,950. One of the most elaborate STOL kits available, it includes drooped ailerons when flaps are down, recontoured wing leading edge, stall fences and gap seals.

If you fly your 210 in hot climates, Parker Hannifin Corp.'s Airborne Div. in Elyria, Ohio, (216) 871-6424, will sell you an air-conditioning kit for $6,283.

If you are concerned about oil spilling out all over the belly of your Centurion, consider contacting the Cessna Pilots Assn. for a free (for members) set of so-called Baylock drawings (named after the fellow who devised them) that reposition the crankcase breather line.

And if you don't mind spending $800 or so and another 10-15 hours of installation time, you can get rid of the gear doors and associated hydraulic paraphernalia on your 1970-78 210 with a Uvalde gear door removal kit from Mark Huffstutler in Uvalde (of course), Tex., (512) 278-4481.

To prepare for the unpleasant possibility of loss of vacuum pressure, a number of companies have STCs providing auxiliary vacuum pump systems. Parker Hannifin Corp. has one; Allison-Coffer, Azle, Tex. has an STC for an electrically-driven pump as a standby. Also, Precise Flight, Sunriver, Ore., (503) 593-1484, offers a standby vacuum system that works without any external pump.

Societies

The National 210 Owners Assn. is located at 9959 Glenoaks Blvd., Sun Valley, Calif. 91352. Contact Bill Kitchen at (213) 875-2820. They publish a quarterly newsletter. Another good source of information is the Cessna Pilots Assn., Wichita Mid-Continent Airport, 2120 Airport Rd., P.O. Box 12948, Wichita, Kans. 67277. John M. Frank, (316) 946-4777, is editor of the association's slick, four-color monthly newsletter.

Owner Comments

The performance and handling of the aircraft are very good. The only thing that has to be watched is to plan your descent since the aircraft is aerodynamically clean and needs time to descend from IFR cruising altitudes without reducing the power too much. Comfort in the cabin is very good. There is enough room to sit upright as opposed to feeling like you are sitting on the floor, and the cabin is well heated and ventilated.

Maintenance costs have been high. One problem has been the cylinders and five of the six had to be replaced for low compression; one for a stuck ring which wore the cylinder, and the other four for leaking exhaust valves. Other high maintenance items are the Cessna 300 series avionics. Parts availability from Cessna has been adequate, but a number of times Cessna has failed to get a part out as promised, leaving the aircraft stranded on the ground. Parts availability from Van Dusen has been good, when they stock the item.

The most prominent idiosyncrasy is water leakage around the baggage door. Regardless of the maintenance hours devoted to this problem, the door still leaks in heavy rain. Cold weather starting is nearly impossible below 10 degrees F unless the sun has been on the airplane during the day.

•

We purchased a new Cessna 1975 Turbo 210 II which was fully equipped with Cessna 400 avionics.

When we picked up the aircraft at Wichita, the paint was literally falling off. Flying from Cessna's field to Wichita Int'l., the autopilot 'ran wild' when switched to approach couple mode, the DME was inoperative, the number two navcom was erractic, the pilot's door and baggage door leaked, the ADF was inoperative and the approach control did not receive our transponder. We could not arrange for repairs at the Cessna factory, so decided to return to Oregon for warranty work. Unknowingly, we decided these were routine 'new car' problems.

In the ensuing 18 months and 450 hours, everything that could go wrong proceeded to do so. By then the aircraft had been painted three times; had two KN65 DMEs installed, but *never* had one operative (remember, DME is required at or above 18,000 feet and this was a turbo); had two encoding altimeters; two altimeters; two vacuum pumps; two top overhauls (including replacing two cylinders due to manufacturing defects); two baggage doors; totally new wing root seals; door seals; window seals; and a complete return trip through the factory to solve the water problem. In all the time we owned it, it leaked.

Water ran through the top shoulder harness attachments, down the shoulder harness, onto the carpet and wicked throughout the plane. At any time, you could remove the floorboards and find standing water.

While the avionics and instruments continued to deteriorate, we continued to pay. Cessna refused to pay for top overhaul number one but did pay part of number two. Most avionics repairs were paid for by us, but regardless of who paid, we *never* had a DME. The airplane was used 90 percent for business, but by the end of our first year we figured that our 200-mile average commute would have been twice as fast by car if we counted the number of missed days due to downtime.

Finally we sold the plane. Our only bright note is that some sucker paid us $1,000 less than our original cost. We will never buy another new Cessna aircraft.

•

Perhaps my best reaction to ownership of a 210 is the fact that I traded my 1969 model plus $35,000 for a new 1978 model. I feel that this is the finest single manufactured. It is is the only true six-placer.

Characteristics are: good speed, fantastic payloads, and the best instrument platform around. No weight and balance problem as with the Bonanzas.

But there are some shortcomings: the typical Cessna ten-cent-store plastic panel, noise, and less than desirable visibility.

Maintenance costs have been good. I spend more on my King Avionics than the airplane. I replaced first engine with factory reman at 1,250 hours; never had a gear or engine case crack. But I would strongly recommend three-blade prop in lieu of two-blade on older models due to noise problem.

•

I purchased a used 1961 Cessna 210A in 9175 and was advised to replace the main gear actuator shaft and gear assembly and the main gear saddles. No other problems were apparent with the aircraft, from log book studies and a current inspection.

With the exception of replacement of the gear actuators and saddles, the first year's annual inspection cost $1,074.

The second year's annual, with the exception of a fuel cell which leaked in cold weather, cost $866.

In terms of performance, I am delighted with the airplane. I frequently fly with one or two passengers at 2350/2400 rpm. Consistently, true airspeed checks out at 169/171 knots, seven or eight knots above the speeds shown in the

The 210 cabin carries an amazing load, but the rear seats are tight.

book. Numerous ground checks, combined with winds aloft, verify the accuracy of that speed.

At approximately 6,000 msl, fuel consumption is 12 to 12.5 gph. At 12,000 msl fuel consumption approximates 10 to 10.25 gpm.

The gear has been totally reliable for extension and landing, although on occasion, either on landing or after takeoff, the gear doors have failed to close because of a problem with a switch in the gear console. This switch has been adjusted once ($30) and replaced twice in 350 hours of use.

Rate of climb is excellent with one or two on board — 1,500 feet per minute near sea level in moderate weather is normal at full throttle. Rate of climb of 1,000 fpm is standard throughout most of the year, at an airspeed of approximately 130 IAS.

We consistently flight plan 160 knots, and usually find we are closer to 165 in actual practice on IFR work.

The only objection is that shoulder room in the front seat is a little less than desirable with two 200-pound men up front. Other than that, it's an ideal one-to-four person airplane, a remarkably economic plane for its speed and range.

•

Both 210s we've owned (a '68 and a '73 model) consistently performed at and above book specs in all categories, particularly speed. Gas consumption of the later model was a constant problem, with the engine burning 16 gph at 66 per-

cent, with the book calling for 14.5. Two Cessna dealers were unable to correct the problem.

The 210 is not a responsive aircraft on the controls, but can be relied upon to provide very few surprises in most flight regimes. Ground nosewheel steering is stiff, sluggish and difficult, with brakes always being needed.

Our '68 model was good. The '73 was another story. The aircraft was assembled poorly, with obviously poor workmanship and components. On one flight, I had the turn and bank fail, the vacuum pump go out, and, upon landing, the starter motor went bad. Our annual inspection was over $1,800, with very little AD work. Maintenance bills were high, even though usage was less than 250 hours per year operating two- to four-hour flights at 66 percent power. We seldom had a flight where some cheap little part didn't fail.

The landing gear on the 210 is not cheap to maintain. For a system as complex as it is, however, the gear is remarkably reliable.

Our 1971 model does not have a saddle problem, but it does have an engine-driven hydraulic pump which has given us some grief.

Proper rigging of the gear is very important, and this takes a lot of maintenance time.

The weight-carrying ability of the plane is superb. I have done many weight-and-balance calculations and have found very few realistic situations which would put the aircraft out of balance.

Beech Bonanza A36TC

The Beech A36TC Bonanza is a handsome, roomy, slick-flying machine with an eccentric fuel system some regard as its Achilles' heel. It also has the distinction of being just about the most expensive used piston single on the market. In fact, a 1979 model today demands some $27,000 more on the used-plane market than a Pressurized Cessna 210 of the same vintage, according to book figures.

And both aircraft started out life at about the same new, average-equipped price of $135,000. It might be little consolation to potential used-plane buyers, but considerable solace to owners, that the A36TC retained its value unusually well. Thus, we plotted a loss in resale value of only about 14 percent for the top-of-the-line Bonanza vs. 35 percent for the Pressurized Cessna 210.

Production Mystery

Anyone trying to assess the market attitude toward the A36TC may have a hard time simply because there are so few ships for sale out there, and many brokers have never laid hands or eyes on one. This stems from two factors, one obvious, the other theoretical. The first is that not many of the turbo Bonanzas have been built, compared with, say, Cessna T210s. The second is that presumably many owners like the birds, have learned to cope with their idiosyncrasies, and see no reason to part with them.

Since 1979, when the A36TC was introduced, through 1981, we count just 270 delivered from Beech. By contrast, almost twice as many normally aspirated A36s were shipped out to dealers—567. This is exactly the reverse of the situation with the Cessna top-of-

the-line single T210, which outsold the nonturbo 210 during the same period by 1,082 aircraft to 414, or better than two to one.

There have been no significant evolutionary changes in the A36TC since its debut in 1979. The B36TC brought out in '82 had four-foot-longer wings accommodating an extra 28 gallons of fuel, bringing the capacity up to 102 gallons—30 more than the T210 carries. This was coupled with an extra 200 pounds of gross weight.

A Matter of Popularity

Clearly, the big Cessna turbo single has been king of the roost in the marketing world for some years, and has garnered a following of sizable dimensions. It was therefore natural that Beech would try to get a bit of the action. Intriguingly, both manufacturers started out even in 1966 with turbo versions, but while Cessna went on to achieve great success with the T210, Beech simply dropped its V35TC in 1970 after only five years of production.

The big Cessna obviously has a lot going for it, including an equipped useful load some 300 pounds greater (among 1980 models) than

The turbo model has louvers instead of cowl flaps for engine cooling, so lots of fuel is used in the climb.

the turbo A36TC Bonanza's and about an hour's greater range, thanks to an additional 16 gallons of fuel capacity. On top of that, the big Bonanza costs almost one-third more than the Cessna new. (The new B36TC made up some of those differences, except price, of course.)

Handling and Performance

The aircraft has magnificent handling typical of the Bonanza line, without the tail-waggle of the V-tails. Pilots describe it as responsive, yet stable and fun to fly. Like all its clan, it is flatteringly easy to land and exhibits the kind of control response that makes flying the bird more than just a matter of driving from point A to B.

The A36TC's performance is quite similar to the T210's in cruise speed, takeoff and landing distances over an obstacle and even stalling speeds—when measured at each aircraft's gross weight. Off-load the several hundred pounds of extra useful load the T210 can carry, and when both aircraft get off at the same weight, the T210 comes away with a nice performance edge in most categories.

Comfort and Loading

The aircraft has seats for six riders, and a minuscule rear baggage compartment of only 10 cubic feet with a 70-pound capacity. Beech therefore likes to consider the rear pair of seats as part of the baggage compartment, and duly notes in its spec sheets that this offers a 400-pound capacity. We calculate that a decently equipped IFR model should be able to carry full fuel and five 170-pound riders with nothing left over for baggage.

That's about all the passenger load you'd want to carry in this aircraft, however, unless you were hauling a couple of kids or small adults in the back seat, because shoulder room there is cramped. But there's plenty of room in the front four and, like the other Bonanzas, the A36TC has marvelous big windows and a high ceiling for a good feeling of spaciousness. Naturally, the double rear entry door and club seating add a classy touch to the stretched 36 model Bonanzas.

As for staying inside the weight and balance envelope, pilots report nothing like the rear-loading problems of the V-tailed Bonanzas. But naturally they try to load from the front first. On the other hand, in a well equipped aircraft, some pilots report they can run into problems at the front of the envelope if they're flying solo, load something in the rear. Count on a useful load of about 1,250 pounds after packing the panel with avionics.

Engine Management

The one operational quirk most A36TC pilots comment on is engine management on takeoff and climbout. The aircraft has an

Turbo in this case denotes not only extra performance, but an extra degree of attention demanded to monitor the electric boost pump system on takeoff.

unusual electric boost pump system with two separate switches. One has three positions: off, low and "high/low" or "auto," depending on the serial number of the aircraft. The other is an emergency switch. On takeoff at full throttle the fuel flow rate is supposed to be between 32.5 and 34.2 gph. If the flow is not high enough, the pilot should feed in low boost pump to make up the difference. If that's not sufficient, he is instructed by the pilot's operating handbook to switch to the high/low (or auto) boost and then manually lean to the correct amount.

Some pilots characterize this as more manipulation than they care to worry about on takeoff, while others describe it as a serious safety hazard.

While the POH tells the pilot leaning is required to prevent "excessive fuel flow and possible engine roughness," it doesn't warn about the possibility of flooding and possible engine stoppage.

One pilot told us he was checking out another flier in the aircraft when they noticed the too-low flow rate on the takeoff roll, leaned over and snapped on the high/low boost, and the engine stopped pronto before they got around to leaning it.

The B36TC comes with a revised fuel system arrangement and simplified procedures that presumably are designed to reduce problems. It has enlarged fuel lines and eliminates the automatic high position in favor of a simple "high" position. (We have no indication that any of this is retrofittable to the A36 line, however.)

On the B36TC the pilot is not bothered with the need to use the auxiliary fuel pump in either the low or the high position to achieve the correct fuel flow, according to the POH. By contrast, he is specifically warned not to take off with the aux fuel pump on "HI," because, according to the manual, "Excessively high fuel flows can cause engine combustion to cease during the takeoff roll." That's a clinical way of saying the engine may stop dead.

And during the climb when encountering reduced fuel flow with high fuel temperatures, whereas the A36TC pilot is told to turn on the Hi/Low (auto) position and lean as required, the B36TC flier is counseled only to select the low position. And if the fuel flow continues to drop, instead of switching to high, he should level off and reduce power until fuel temperatures drop. Thereby the possibly risky, and at the least, bothersome, procedure of having to both add boost and lean the mixture is done away with.

Another modification in the B36TC

Cost/Performance/Specifications

Model	Year	Number Built	Average Retail Price	Cruise Speed (kts)	Rate of Climb (fpm)	Gross Weight (lbs)	Useful Load (lbs)	Fuel (gals)	Engine	TBO (hrs)	Overhaul Cost
A36TC	1979	32	$121,000	194	1,165	3,650	1,388	74	300-hp Cont. TSIO-520-UB	1,600	$14,000
A36TC	1980	125	$125,000	194	1,165	3,650	1,388	74	300-hp Cont. TSIO-520-UB	1,600	$14,000
A36TC	1981	114	$133,000	194	1,165	3,650	1,388	74	300-hp Cont. TSIO-520-UB	1,600	$14,000
B36TC	1982	50	$150,000	190	1,049	3,850	1,512	74	300-hp Cont. TSIO-520-UB	1,600	$14,000
B36TC	1983	55	$170,000	190	1,049	3,850	1,512	74	300-hp Cont. TSIO-520-UB	1,600	$14,000

Beech Bonanza A36TC

fuel boost system: the second, emergency auxiliary fuel pump is eliminated completely.

The so-called high/low automatic function of the aux pump carries with it another operational quirk that annoys some pilots. On the pretakeoff runup, the manual requires ginning up the engine to 30 inches mp and putting on the high boost. Pilots say the resulting thunder and possible squeal of brakes can be a bit too dramatic for passengers, and is better done only on occasion.

In the Climb: Fuel to Burn

There's also been a lot of discussion about how much fuel needs to be pumped to the engine on the climb to altitude in the A36TC. Aviation magazine articles evaluating the aircraft talked about fuel burns of 30 gph all the way to level-off, to keep the engine running cool at reduced forward speeds. (The A36TC has no cowl flaps; and while this lessens pilot workload, one can't help but wonder whether extra cooling fuel is needed to compensate.) But that means using up a lot of fuel in the climb to altitude in what has to be a not too long-legged bird to begin with.

Owners we talked to reported using various power settings, with fuel burns on climbout ranging from 22 gph to 28 gph. One said he uses 34 inches mp and 2,600 rpm, drawing 28 gph in a normal climb. However, he said he leans to between 25 and 26 gph fuel flow, noting that ''factory people'' said this was okay as long as the temperature levels were all kept in the green. (They asked not to be quoted.) Another pilot said he normally climbed at 29 inches mp and 2,500 rpm, and this yielded about 22 gph of fuel flow.

According to the A36TC book, cruise climb should be made at a fuel flow of 28 to 31 gph up to the critical altitude, or about 22,000 feet (the point when the turbocharger wastegate is fully closed at a given throttle setting). And then the fuel flow can be reduced according to manifold pressure setting. So the

This shows what you can load into just 10 cubic feet of baggage space, balance considerations permitting.

aircraft does gulp lots of fuel on the climbout.

Turbo Centurion pilots, by contrast, are told by the manual to keep 30 inches mp and 2500 rpm in the climb, leaning to 120 lbs/hr (20 gph), with the cowl flaps open as required, and using the auxiliary fuel pump to hold that fuel flow on hot days, if needed. The T210 engine is rated at 310 hp for takeoff and 285 hp for max continuous power. The powerplants on both aircraft are variants of the Continental TSIO-520. (Recommended fuel flow at takeoff, incidentally, in the T210 is a healthy 29 to 31 gph, though not quite as high as in the A36TC.)

Safety Record

Accident briefs provided by the National Transportation Safety Board showed a paucity of reports on the A36TC in the first two years. In fact, there were only two accidents listed, one of them involving a fatality. But in our view both accidents had significant ramifications. One other accident has come to our attention, and we'll discuss that, too.

Of the two listed by the Safety Board, one was attributed to a partial power loss, resulting in a ''stall/mush'' during a forced landing just after takeoff. The pilot, however, was accused in the NTSB's probably cause findings of

improperly set mixture and boost pump. No novice, he was an experienced test pilot with 24,750 hours of flying time and 250 hours in type. In fact, the purpose of the flight had been to start spin testing the aircraft to certify Brittain tip tanks installed on it.

The other accident also occurred during takeoff, when fire broke out in the engine compartment. The plane crashed, killing a passenger and seriously injuring the pilot. It is believed that in that accident, which occurred in March 1980, raw fuel was sprayed against the unshielded turbocharger, with the resulting flame and smoke incapacitating the pilot before he could make a controlled emergency landing.

Beech telegrammed the 146 A36TC owners on file at that time, instructing mechanics to check for a leak at the mixture adjustment screw. A drain hose was then to be installed leading from the adjustment screw out to the cowl flap, to vent overboard any future fuel leak from that area.

Airworthiness Directive 80-21-02 made the correction mandatory. The third accident came to our attention in a letter from a subscriber. He told us he was taking off in his A36TC Bonanza and had climbed about 100 feet off the ground when he noticed the fuel pressure gauge doing strange things. The needle had arced completely off its half of the gauge into the manifold pressure segment of the gauge where it was indicating 10 inches of mp. The engine quit cold from flooding, according to the pilot, and in the intervening five or so seconds before he hit the ground he tried the usual emergency moves like hitting the electric boost pumps, etc.

Ironically, as he describes it, if he'd been aware that the problem involved getting too much fuel rather than too little, he conceivably could have salvaged the situation by leaning quickly to stop the flooding. As it was, both the pilot and his passenger were seriously injured.

The pilot said the engine was a new

one, too, had only four hours on it before the crash and had been given to him by Beech and Continental because the first engine was found to have a hole in the crankcase. As a sidelight, he told us, "What got me the new engine was probably your article. I Xeroxed the article on the cracking IO-520s and gave it to them and said it was obviously a casting defect and was an ongoing thing... So for my trouble I got a new engine that nearly killed me."

On the other hand, the pilot praised both Continental and Beech for their backup in his two crises. "Beech stood 100 percent behind the product." When he had his first engine problem, Beech offered to come and pick up the airplane and to lend him a brand-new V-35 Bonanza in the interim.

Summing up, he said: "Continental and Beech have been completely nice about this thing. I had all kinds of problems with leaking fuel cells, also, and had to replace them when brand new. I think, finally, I just got a lemon."

Operational Considerations

Pilots transitioning into the A36TC from other makes of aircraft should be aware of the unorthodox positioning of the gear and flap levers (the reverse from other manufacturers) and of throttle quadrant controls (with the mixture below the throttle).

After the crash of the test pilot on takeoff, investigators found the prop positioned half-way back from takeoff pitch. The question arises: could the pilot have inadvertently pulled back the prop instead of the mixture control? Though he had a lot of time in Bonanzas, he constantly flew many different kinds of aircraft.

However, there are many circumstances that blur accurate determination of the accident cause. The pilot, Lyle Flick, was seriously injured and experienced traumatic amnesia after the crash. Also, as he made his takeoff run, another pilot on a taxiway nearby observed smoke coming from the Bonanza

The model B36TC has longer wings and additional fuel, along with a revised and simplified fuel system.

and called out this fact in the blind over the radio. Finally, rescuers at the crash scene turned off switches in the aircraft to prevent a fire, and thus altered the cockpit configuration.

Naturally, there is some interest in the pre-crash position of the auxiliary fuel pump switch in the aircraft, and whether the engine could have stopped because of flooding from an overboost.

The electric boost pump switch is located in an awkward area, hard to see, below the central control column on the Bonanza. As mentioned before, if the high position is selected, the pilot may run the risk of flooding the engine unless the mixture is leaned correctly. This arrangement has been characterized by some experienced pilots as "ridiculous, ergonomics-wise," and a safety hazard.

Maintenance

Figures we received from A36TC owners in 1982 indicated that so far they were spending about $1,000 on the average for annual inspections. The cost ranged from a low of $600, on a first annual, to $2,000, with most of them ranging between $1,100 and $1,400.

Owners characterized maintenance costs on the aircraft as high, but some seemed to feel it's part of the game. "As to parts and service," said one, "the price *is* high. But the quality is worth it, and the reliability is quite good, in my experience." Few chronic problems surfaced in the owner comments, except that one said he

had to keep replacing landing lights.

There were not a lot of service difficulty reports in the FAA roster on this aircraft at the time, either. But there were two instances of cracked crankcases, which suggests the problem on this TSIO-520 engine has not gone away.

The only other mildly repetitive problems we noted concerned a missing safety clip in the rudder cable turnbuckle, leading to excessive play in the rudder control (two cases); cracks in the vertical stabilizer skin (two instances); the fuel intake tube chafing against the turbo heat shield (two cases reported).

There was also a handful of turbo-related problems: a crack on the turbo exhaust inlet assembly (two cases noted); oil leaking past the turbo oil seal and a broken turbo inlet above the EGT probe, burning cylinder head and oil temperature wires. In addition, in one case a V-clamp failed, allowing exhaust gases to burn a hole in the cowl.

Airworthiness Directives

There have been less than a dozen ADs on the aircraft, but two early ADs were important ones relating to fire hazards. The first one (80-21-02), called for installation of a drain hose over the idle fuel adjustment screw to prevent fuel leaks in the engine compartment. The second one (81-24-06) required retorquing the through bolts of the engine-driven fuel pump to prevent fuel leakage.

Modifications

Tip tanks, gap seals and thicker windshields for extra soundproofing, and safety, are offered for the A36TC by Beryl D'Shannon Aviation Specialties, Inc., Lakeville, Minn. Kit price for the 15-gallon tips is $3,350, not including installation. Gap seals: $1,595 installed. Windshields: $1,219 to $1,419, depending on thicknesses, which go up to one-half an inch.

Smith Speed Conversions, Inc. at Johnson, Kans. provides a whole range of cleanup improvements that yield an extra 16 to 17 knots, at a price of $11,700.

Osborne Tank & Supply, at Oro Grande, Calif. has obtained as STC for its Brittain tip tanks, which will hold 20 gallons each.

For the ultimate in upgrades, the A36 owner can have an Allison turboprop installed under an STC the company was aiming for by December 1985. This gives the bird 167-knot cruise speeds at anywhere from 12,000 to 25,000 feet. Cost is about $250,000.

For the Joiners

The American Bonanza Society, now located in Wichita, Kans., publishes a handsome newsletter and provides a platform for the exchange of information among Bonanza fliers of all persuasion.

Owner Comments

I have owned an A36TC for two years. I bought the aircraft new. Since then I have logged 400 hours with no difficulties whatsoever. This is not my first Bonanza, and from previous experience I have expected and gotten extreme reliability and usefulness from each product. I have had no problems with the avionics or radar installation.

My aircraft is equipped with tip tanks, giving me 104 gallons total useful fuel. This is enough for 6½ hours of flying time. Cruise speeds

Aircraft Resale Value Chart

'79 A36TC Bonanza

(Year, $/M: $140,000, $135,000, $130,000, $125,000, $120,000, $115,000, 0 — '79, '80, '81, '82, '83, '84, '85)

between 11,000 and 13,000 feet have always been in the 190-knot range. I fly approximately 10 percent of the time at altitudes above 20,000 feet, and obtain well over 210-knot true airspeeds. The aircraft is stable, and handles turbulence rather well, and particularly handles ice rather well. I fly approximately 150 days out of the year in all kinds of weather, and have come to realize that the A36TC can handle 1½ in. of ice all over without any untoward results, other than a decrease in airspeed of approximately 15 knots, and an increased stall speed of approximately 15 knots as well.

The only unusual difficulty encountered with this airplane comes on very hot days, after a very short engine shut-down, when the engine and the fuel system are rather hot. During those times it is necessary (when taking off from airports above 4,000 to 6,000 feet above sea level) to use a high boost pump and/or emergency pump, with the engine lean for takeoff power (32 gallons fuel per hour). Unless this is done, you may find that the engine may not be able to retain the required fuel flow and manifold pressures required for takeoff.

Annual inspections have been expensive, ranging from approximately $1,100 to $1,400. There has been no extra maintenance done between annual inspections. The

Continental engine has been flawless, consuming approximately half a quart of oil (15W50) every 15 hours.

G.D. Castillo, M.D.
Champaign, Ill.

I purchased my A36 in May 1981, as a dealer demonstrator with about 60 hours on the tachometer; I have put over 200 hours on it since. My average stage is 250 nm, over 85 percent on business.

In the areas of performance, handling and comfort, all the superlatives I had read about Beech airplanes were borne out. For some reason, I have never been able to hit the book fuel consumption figures at a power setting, but the airspeed variation leads me to the conclusion that the power gauges are somewhat inaccurate. The variation is small and consistent, so I've ignored the discrepancy.

My plane is equipped with club seating with table, and I've been unable to find a procedure to reverse the middle seats without gouging the table's trim at the bottom. Perhaps someone else has solved this?

As to parts and service: the price *is* high. But the quality is worth it (I've owned all the majors, except Mooney), and the reliability is quite good, in my experience. AOG means Air Freight parts (no charge to me). Overall, it has been a great plane to own, from all standpoints.

As averages: maint./hr.—$4.50; annual $1,250.

John R. Segerstrom
Pendleton, Ore.

In July of 1981 I purchased an A36TC from Beechcraft West in Hayward, California, after having been an owner of Piper products for some 10 years. I told the sales personnel that they would have a difficult time convincing me of the justification for the cost of a Beechcraft product. After having a demonstration in June of 1981 of the A36TC, I fell in love with the handling and performance characteristic of the A36TC as well as the comfort and appearance. I have some 350 hours in the 36TC and I have participated in the round-table discussions at the Bonanza Society meetings on the A36TC.

The A36TC performs in excess of the owner's handbook specifications, and will not disappoint any owner. Handling characteristics are extremely good. On short fields in IFR conditions, and unstable and turbulent air, the A36TC performs far beyond the best of any single-engine aircraft I have flown. My experience covers almost all models of the Piper line. The aircraft I flew prior to the purchase of the A36TC was a Turbo t-tail Lance.

In comfort, the A36TC receives many compliments. All materials used in the aircraft are top quality and craftsmanlike fitted. On long trips the A36TC does very well. If it were possible, I would like to see the cabin widened just a bit to be equivalent with the PA32 models of Piper. One finds himself sharing his elbows with his co-pilot in the cockpit.

The one area that I have found to be quite expensive in a Beechcraft product is the maintenance. Since the aircraft was first delivered, we have complied with 50-hour inspections and have had a few items that have needed constant reminders to the dealer for correction.

Recognizing the fact that spark-plugs and three tires were replaced in accordance with our annual inspection and we were given a $200 credit as a promotion from Beechcraft towards maintenance, the total bill for the annual would have come to nearly $2,000.

On an aircraft with 302 hours on its tach, my partners and I found the annual cost to be excessive. We have no qualms with the quality of the Beechcraft facilities and mechanic; however, next year we will look for an equally qualified but less expensive operation for performing our annual. As an example of the expensive parts, we had a cargo passenger compartment door handle malfunction on us, and it cost $78.25, exclusive of labor. We have not run into any difficulty acquiring parts.

As for other operational idiosyncrasies, the engine requires a fuel flow of 32 to 34½ gallons for take-off. If this amount of flow is not achieved, then use of the low/high fuel boost pump is necessary, and if fuel flow is not stabilized with the use of this setting, then one turns it to the high position. An extremely crucial problem with turning it to high is that the pilot must then lean the engine back to within the 32- to 34-gallon range; otherwise over-boost of fuel or flooding could occur. Perhaps a more refined procedure on this particularly crucial item is needed.

Also, we have now gone through six landing lights and use the aircraft a limited time at night. The dealer has now informed me that a different wattage bulb should cure the problem. We are hoping this to be true as we have purchased more landing lights for this aircraft than all previously owned combined.

Overall, if I were to choose another single engine turbocharged aircraft, without any question it would be the A36TC Bonanza. Just recently I flew the B36TC and found it to be an equally fine performer. Not having the need for the large amount of fuel aboard, I

In all the 36 Bonanzas, the club seating is top drawer.

find the A36TC to meet all of our corporation needs.

Thomas A. Mantz
Oakdale, Calif.

Dale Johnson of Flightcraft, the Beech dealer in Portland, Ore., suggested I respond to your request for information on the A36TC. Our company has a 1980 A36TC which we bought new. We average a bit over 300 hours a year, with approximately 50 percent of that IFR. After working out some bugs when the plane was new, we have been well satisfied. We have 100-hour checks which at times become annuals. Average cost of an annual runs around $600.

To give you some idea of costs I've gone through our invoices including 100 hours and annuals, added them up and then divided by the hours on the plane. I have not included avionics costs, but have included strobe costs, which have been considerable. They have a problem, but can't seem to identify it. The invoices do include the cost for the oil change. Average maintenance cost runs at a bit over $14 an hour.

Our maintenance is done at a private shop which takes pride in its work, and a personal interest in our plane. Dates of all items which come up for renewal, e.g., ELT batteries, are on their computer.

I'm a corporate pilot. Of all the single-engine aircraft I've flown, the A36 is by far the best.

Charles R. Young
Portland, Ore.

Cessna P210

As a used-airplane buy, Cessna's pressurized P210 is a tantalizing paradox. The plane has one of the worst reputations of any airplane in recent years — and deservedly so, for it has plagued owners with a seemingly unending series of mechanical problems. As a result, value of the P210 on the used-plane market is relatively low.

In fact, we saw an ad not long ago placed by a P210 owner who wanted to trade his six-place pressurized P210 for a four-place non-pressurized Mooney 231 — and he was willing to trade even. However, because of the P210's depressed value, a canny buyer can get a good bargain *if* he finds the right airplane. After seven years of trial and tribulation, it appears Cessna finally made enough changes so that it's possible to get a reasonably trouble-free P210 — but only if the buyer chooses carefully.

Troubled History

The P210 is a pressurized outgrowth of the ancient 210 line. It first appeared in 1978 as the only pressurized single on the market. (It held that distinction until the Piper Malibu arrived on the scene in late 1983.) The P210 was heralded as a great, daring leap in technology, and its later problems were excused by many on the grounds that, "Well, that's the price you pay for advancing the state of the art." This is a major misconception. The P210 was indeed a daring *marketing* leap, but technologically it was nothing new. The airframe was a quarter-century old, the basic TSIO-520 engine had been around for years, and the pressurization system was lifted straight from the pressurized Skymaster. "New" features like the fixed-point controller for the turbo wastegate were in fact technical

Little windows identify the P210, which is certified for known icing. Radar pod is under the wing.

steps backward designed to cut costs.

But the marketeers certainly had done their homework; the P210 sold well from the beginning. Nearly 400 were built the first two years, and most owners seemed happy. Things looked good for the P210.

Then, during the summer of 1980, two P210s crashed after engine failures resulting from detonation. The FAA issued emergency ADs requiring ultra-rich mixtures to keep the engines cool, along with other performance-robbing anti-detonation measures. There followed a long period of technical turmoil at Cessna which has only died down in the past few years. A new turbocharger was fitted, and announced with much hoopla as the "Performance-Plus" package that would solve the detonation problems. That it did, but the "Performance-Plus" label was rather farcical; performance in fact declined dramatically, and most P210 pilots found they could not maintain manifold pressure or cabin pressurization above 16,000-18,000 feet. For six months, P210 owners screamed and fumed in frustration, while Cessna tried vainly to come up with a solution. Finally, in late 1981, Cessna announced its fix: A new air induction system, retrofitted free by Cessna, restored the lost performance. The P210s original induction system, it turned

out, had been poorly designed all along.

During all the detonation/turbocharger goings-on, P210 owners were reporting all sorts of other engineering and quality-control problems: leaky, warped exhaust systems, failed vacuum pumps, overheating avionics, engine surging due to vapor lock, and landing gear malfunctions. Many pilots also complained about poor instrumentation that left them ill-equipped to operate the complex high-performance aircraft correctly.

Choice of model year shouldn't be a major concern for the P210 shopper; most important mods have been retrofitted to the older models, making all pre-'82 airplanes essentially identical, except for the landing gear. The 1978 P210 had gear doors, whereas on later models Cessna dropped main-gear doors altogether, thereby cutting manufacturing costs (and maintenance costs for the owner). The loss of gear doors did not affect cruise speed — although gear-lowering speed did go up a whopping 25 knots in the doorless post-'79 birds, to 165 KIAS.

The 1982 and 1983 models (actually they're all 1982s; the "1983" P210 is a leftover 1982 airplane with a new paint job) did get some major nonretrofitable (for the most part) improvements that deserve attention. Among them:

• New turbo controller. The "fixed-point controller" on 1978-81 aircraft is an economy measure that maintains an upper deck presure — the pressure between the turbo compressor and the throttle butterfly — of 35 inches, even when the engine only needs 25 inches. This causes the turbo to work a lot harder than it has to, which results in more exhaust back pressure and hotter induction air. Both sap performance and reliability. The 1982-83 P210 has a "slope controller" which maintains deck pressure at a steady two inches above manifold pressure, and takes a lot of unnecessary load off the turbo.

• New fuel system. The vapor-lock-prone system of earlier P210s was discarded in favor of an excellent left-right-both system with proper vapor-return lines.

• Engine improvements. The valves, rings and valve guides were improved, and the engine designation changed from TSIO-520-P to TSIO-520-AF. In the process, TBO went up 200 hours, to 1,600 hours.

• Dual vacuum pumps and alternators were made available as options.

• Cowl flaps were improved to reduce the chances of overcooling on descent.

• A TIT (Turbine Inlet Temperature) gauge was added, along with a restriction of 1,650 degrees TIT. This serves to limit leaning and keep exhaust temperatures down.

Summing up, there are two kinds of P210s: the "Mark I" airplane built from 1978-81, and the "Mark II" that appeared in 1982. P210 buyers should make every effort

find a 1982 or 1983 model if the pocketbook allows.

Used-Plane Market

Currently, the P210 is in good supply at rather depressed prices. "It's a buyer's market," one big broker told us. "A P210 shopper shouldn't have to compromise. The well-equipped airplanes are out there."

And, as we said, prices are low. A 1979 P210 can be bought for about the same price as a comparable T210 or even a normally aspriated A36 Bonanza of the same vintage. In effect, the pressurization comes free on the used-plane market. (The current retail difference between a new P210 and a T210 is about $50,000.) The used-plane buyers thus can benefit from the huge depreciation loss suffered by the poor fellow who bought it new.

Current P210 prices run from about $70,000 for a 1978 model with ARC avionics and no de-ice equipment to $120,000 for a 1982 model. This is an improvement since 1983, when one P210 owner sadly confirmed a $100,000 ceiling price; he tried to sell his loaded 1981 model (it had even been updated with the dual vacuum and alternator systems) and the best offer he could get was $95,000 — precisely half what he paid for it new one year earlier.

Performance

The performance of the P210 can be considered from two angles. Compared to other big, turbocharged, single-engine airplanes, it has adequate performance. But compared to other pressurized aircraft such

as the Cessna 340A or Baron 58P, it falls well short.

Because of the power drain of pressurization, P210 performance is slightly less than that of the T210, which has the same airframe and power. Maximum certified ceiling of the P210 is 23,000 feet, but owners report that because of the mediocre climb performance, cruising altitudes above 20,000 feet are impractical unless the plane is very lightly loaded and the trip a long one. Time-to-climb to 23,000 feet is listed as 31 minutes at max available power, but a more reasonable figure is the 39-minute climb to 20,000 feet at normal climb power. That's a long time, and it explains why many P210 pilots prefer to stay in the 15,000-18,000-foot area.

Cruise speeds range from about 170-190 knots, depending on altitude and power setting. However, one P210 pilot reports he gets over 200 knots consistently at light weights.

The 90-gallon fuel supply is not exactly generous. By the book, it's good for a range of about 700 nm with a 45-minute reserve at 70 percent power. Throttled back to 55 percent, book range climbs to over 800 nm. However, these range figures require leaning to rather high exhaust gas temperatures, and prudent P210 pilots prefer to run richer mixtures. This results in higher fuel consumption (by about two to three gph) and range reductions of about 100 nm. A good conservative rule of thumb is 20 gallons per hour, block-to-block, at high cruise speeds. With IFR reserves, that's only about three hours cruising time.

Cost/Performance/Specifications

Model	Year	Number Built	Gross Weight (lbs)	Useful Load (lbs)	Cruise Speed (kts)	Fuel (gals)	Engine	TBO (hrs)	Overhaul Cost	Average Price
P-210N	1978	150	4,000	1,600	187	90	310-hp Cont. TSIO-520-P	1,400	$11,250	$ 75,000
P-210N	1979	235	4,000	1,600	187	90	310-hp Cont. TSIO-520-P	1,400	$11,250	$ 89,000
P-210N	1980	204	4,000	1,600	187	90	310-hp Cont. TSIO-520-P	1,400	$11,250	$ 98,000
P-210N	1981	169	4,000	1,600	187	90	310-hp Cont. TSIO-520-P	1,400	$11,250	$124,000
P-210N	1982	50	4,000	1,600	187	90	310-hp Cont. TSIO-520-AF	1,600	$11,000	$155,000
P-210N	1983	22	4,000	1,600	191	90	310-hp Cont. TSIO-520-AF	1,600	$11,000	$183,000

Takeoff and landing performance is comparable to heavier twin-engined aircraft; about 2,200 feet is necessary to take off over a 50-foot obstacle at gross weight under standard conditions. Stall speed with flaps down is 61 knots right at the FAA-imposed upper limit for single-engine airplanes.

Creature Comforts

Here, of course, is where the P210 shines. The pressurized cabin makes all the difference in the world above 12,500 feet, eliminating the need for cumbersome and uncomfortable oxygen masks. But once more, compared to pressurized twins, the P210 is rather anemic. Pressure differential is only 3.35 pounds, the lowest of any current pressurized airplane. The P210's pressure system has no rate controller; it simply starts to pressurize at the altitude selected by the pilot, maintains that cabin altitude as long as it can, and then maintains the maximum differential as the climb continues. As a result, pilot and passengers are subject to more ear-popping than they would be in, say, a Cessna 421. Such is the price of the "economy" presurized airplane.

The front four passengers have reasonable — although not lavish — room. Cabin width is a modest 42 inches, but there is lots of headroom for the pilot to sit comfortably upright. The two rear seats, however, are horribly cramped, and recommended on long trips only for children, midgets or contortionists.

Cabin quiet is one of the P210's strong points. The turbocharger muffles the exhaust roar, and the tightly sealed cabin keeps out most of the slipstream noise.

Loading

The 210 series is renowned for its big load capacity and wide c.g. envelope. The P210 generally lives up to those traditions. When it was introduced in 1978, the P210 was the heaviest 210 of them all at 4,000 pounds, 200 more than the Turbo 210. (The T210 has since been

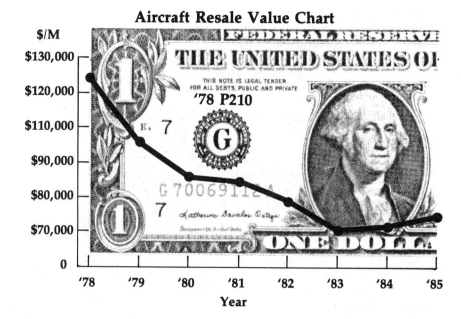

Aircraft Resale Value Chart

boosted to 4,000 also.) Typical operating weights run around 2,500-2,600 pounds for well-equipped aircraft, including de-ice equipment. That leaves a healthy 1,400-1,500 pounds of useful load. With 90-gallon tanks full, there's still about 900 pounds left for payload. That's five standard 170-pound people, or four plus baggage.

The P210 pilot is more likely to find himself loaded out the front end of the center-of-gravity envelope rather than the rear, particularly on well-equipped airplanes with full panels and dual alternator/vacuum systems.

Handling Qualities

The 210 series is known for very heavy controls, and the P210 is the most ponderous of the 210s because control cables must be routed through tight-fitting air seals where they pass through the pressure vessel. The P210 will be perceived as a stiff-handling dinosaur, both on the ground and in the air, by pilots stepping up from smaller single-engine planes. But on the other hand, the P210 is rock-solid in turbulence and IFR conditions, the environment in which it will presumably spend a lot of time.

Pitch control is particularly heavy. This makes landing with two people in front a challenge to the

biceps, but it does have the safety plus of limiting the pilot's ability to apply high G-loadings and overstress the airplane. (The 210's record of overstress-induced inflight breakups is surprisingly poor, however — 16 in the five years up to 1983. Three P210s have broken up in flight.)

Safety Record

We have no statistics on P210 accident rates, but the 210 series in general ranks about average or slightly below when compared to other single-engine retractables during the period 1972-1976. The 210's fatal accident rate was 3.1 per 100,000 flight hours, in a group that ranged from 1.0 to 4.2.

A look at P210 accidents, however, reveals some unusual trends. A surprisingly large percentage of accidents are related to mechanical malfunctions, design defects or poor human engineering of the aircraft. Of 30 accidents reported by the NTSB during the period 1978-81, only about a third were pure and simple pilot blunders. (Only one involved weather.) Thirteen of the 30 were engine failures. Of those 13, six were fuel mismanagement crashes. (These figures confirm our earlier findings of very high fuel mismanagement accident rates for the 210 series in general.) Of course the pilot must take some blame in any fuel mismanagement accident, but the design of the fuel system plays a big role, too — and the P210's fuel system apparently needed the big improvements it finally got in 1982. Several accident reports mention misleading fuel gauges.

The other seven engine failures were your basic internal crap-outs: two from detonation, with various other exhaust fires, cylinder blowoffs, and undetermined causes. The notorious vapor lock syndrome caused one crash, and another was triggered by excessive fuel from a runaway boost pump.

Another fertile ground for P210 accidents: landing gear problems. FAA accident/incident records show 19 P210 gear crunches of various sorts through 1982, more than half of them due to mechanical malfunctions. The FAA records — which appear to be more complete than NTSB data — list a total of 75 P210 accidents or incidents since 1978. That amounts to about 10 percent of the fleet.

In all, we're aware of ten fatal P210 accidents. Of those, three were in-flight breakups (one triggered by a vacuum system failure). One resulted from a cylinder blowing off the engine, another came after the pilot reported a loss of elevator control over the Gulf of Mexico.

Buyer's Checklist

We've covered the P210's myriad technical problems in detail in the past, and touched on them earlier in this article. Rather than describe the problems again, we'll concentrate on solutions. What follows is a P210 buyers' checklist which, if followed closely, will give the buyer a fighting chance at getting a safe, reliable airplane that won't drive him to the poorhouse.

• *Exhaust system.* Do not buy a P210 without the new Inconel exhaust system. (Or at least plan to retrofit it immediately after purchase.) The P210 exhaust system is, in our view, an engineering disgrace, made of unsuitable material. As a result, the P210 exhaust system has been notoriously troublesome since the beginning and carries a 50-hour AD inspection for cracks.

Slash in the side of the engine cowl exhausts air from the TurboPlus intercooler mod.

Retrofitting the Inconel system is expensive. Cessna has a "special deal": the $3,200 cost of the replacement Inconel system will be reduced by $1.17 for every hour below 1,400 hours on the aircraft. For example, the owner of a 400-hour airplane would get a $1,170 price break, and pay *only* about $2,000.

• *Fuel system.* Ideally, one should buy a 1982 airplane with the redesigned fuel system. If not, make sure that the airplane is fitted with Cessna's vapor-return line fix. (See service letter SE81-42.)

• *Vacuum system.* We'd recommend the dual vacuum system, which can be retrofitted to all P210s. It is mandated by AD for any P210 equipped with the known-icing option.

• *Dual alternator system.* 1982 aircraft were available with dual 60-amp alternators, and some 1980 and 1981 models were retrofitted at the factory. (That program was terminated in 1983, however, so it's too late to retrofit a plane after purchase.) Electrical redundancy is a must for an all-weather plane like the P210; we'd recommend the dual system. Some earlier P210s have a small emergency standby generator. This is better than nothing, but get the dual 60-amp system if you can.

• *Induction system.* Don't buy a P210 without the bigger intake scoop and improved plenum chamber introduced in 1982. Most aircraft should already be retrofitted, since Cessna paid the bill for it.

• *Avionics.* Cessna's in-house ARC line reached an all-time low in quality and reliability in 1977-78, and although things seem to be improved later, most people consider a panel full of ARC avionics to be a major liability in a P210. Look for King or Collins equipment. Also consider retrofitting the improved avionics cooling fan introduced on Cessna's single-engine line. The previous cooling fan was poorly designed and very unreliable, and when it quits, the marginal ARC radios are even more likely to malfunction.

• *Instrumentation.* Standard factory engine instrumentation on 1978-81 P210s is, in our opinion, pathetically bad. We believe every P210 should be equipped with, (1) a six-probe EGT with absolute temperature scale, (2) six-probe cylinder-head temp gauge, (3) Turbine Inlet Temperature (TIT) gauge, (4) accurate digital fuel-flow gauge. Look for a plane with this equipment (any serious pilot should already have it installed). If you can't find one, plan to install it immediately after purchase.

• *Engine.* The TSIO-520-P has a poor reliability record in the P210. Cylinder problems are common, partly a result of excessive heat. Check compression carefully, and have mechanic inspect the condition of the valves and valve guides. Check the cooling baffles with great care. Look at maintenance records closely. The engine has a nominal TBO of 1,400 hours, but few engines have reached that mark without major problems.

• *Cabin leaks.* Poor quality control at Cessna's Pawnee plant has shown up in leaky cabins, particularly the door seals. These problems manifest themselves in reduced pressure capability and loss of manifold pressure. Check the outflow valve carefully; if it's defective, a replacement valve costs more than $5,000.

Modifications

In addition to the previously listed mods, which we would consider virtually mandatory, there are other aftermarket products available for the P210. Among them:

• *R/STOL Systems kit.* Drooped ailerons decrease stall speed by about six knots, while stall strips and wing fences assure a gentle, controllable stall, according to R/STOL. A modified aileron control system with special low-friction pressure seals greatly reduces aileron control forces and increases roll rate by about 50 percent. Cost is $8,500, downtime about two weeks. R/STOL claims eye-opening takeoff performance improvements, but these are apparently based on a takeoff speed five knots below power-off stall speed — not a wise procedure, in our opinion. R/STOL, Snohomish County Airport, Everett, Wa. 98204 (206) 355-8700. R/STOL also offer wing-mounted RCA color radar for the P210.

• *Turboplus intercooler, speedbrakes.* One way to help keep the engine running cooler is to have an intercooler installed by Turboplus in Gig Harbor, Wash. for $6,695. The company also can install speed brakes on the aircraft for $4,645. These will, conversely, help keep the engine from being overcooled on descent.

• *Air American engine conversion.* This Wilkes-Barre company (717) 457-6736 will install a 350-hp Lycoming engine with a 2,000-hour TBO and an intercooled turbocharger for $73,500. Also part of the package is extra strengthening, bracing and weighting to reduce the chance of flutter, along with dual vacuum pumps and alternators. The company also sells an auxiliary fuel tank that provides an extra 20.5 gallons usable. This fits in the baggage compartment and transfers to the right main tank.

• *Flint long-range tanks.* Two tip tanks add 33 gallons' fuel capacity and a couple of feet of wing span for better climb performance. Range is increased by about 250 nm. Cost: $4,250, Flint Aero, 8665 Missouri Gorge Rd., Santee, Calif. 92071.

• *Riley Turboprop conversion.* Noted aircraft souper-upper Jack Riley has a PT6 P210 conversion. The Riley P210's cost is about $260,000, triple the value of any used P210 on the market.

Owner Comments

As a former owner of a 1968 E33A Bonanza and a 1974 F33A Bonanza, I must say that after 550 hours in a P210, it would be hard to give up the pressurization and icing capabilities. It is truly a comfort on long trips. We used to spend $10 to $20 to fill our oxygen tanks. Now I spend it for the extra fuel for the P210. But we have the extra comfort.

Beech's A36TC costs the same or more than the P210, and offers no pressurization or de-ice capability. A used P210 with all the options is a good buy today.

Howard Hermel
Mankato, Minnesota

I have experienced continuing heat-related problems and avionics malfunctions to the extent that, as of this date, I still have not had all avionics working at the same time. On the positive side, I am very impressed with the stability of the aircraft for IFR purposes and for landing. I have a Robertson STOL kit which I am very impressed with. The pressurization system makes flying much more comfortable than I had given it credit for. Overall, if I can get the avionics problem sorted out, I am certain I am going to be very satisfied.

Roger O. Weed
Anchorage, Alaska

In April 1979, I purchased a new 1978 P210 from Coronado Skyways, an authorized Cessna Dealership in Albuquerque, New Mexico. The aircraft received the full Cessna Warranty Program. I began flying the aircraft regularly (approximately 30 hours per month) and put the aircraft under a 100-hour inspection program with Sky Scenes, the new Cessna dealership.

Approximately every 25 hours, I have had an oil analysis, and from the beginning, the oil analysis revealed a high chrome and iron content in the oil. The Cessna regional manager was informed and requested Continental to look at the engine, which they did. The Continental representative examined the cylinders with a boroscope; and stated the cylinders showed evidence of corrosion, and concluded the corrosion was the cause of the high iron and chrome in the oil.

The Continental representative, the Cessna representative, and the shop foreman who maintains the aircraft, all agreed that the regular flying of the aircraft while in my possession ruled out the possibility that the corrosion developed after I purchased the aircraft.

Cessna Aircraft Company has refused to make further investigation or repairs under their warranty program. Cessna responded that the corrosion was caused from conditions beyond the control of Cessna, and declined warranty participation.

Philip J. White
Albuquerque, New Mexico

Access for all six seats is through a single door on the left. On the right an openable double-window hatch is hinged from the top for emergency exit. Baggage is loaded separately in an unpressurized rear compartment.

Piper Saratoga SP

Anyone sorting through the mixed bag of used planes for a machine that will carry six, not four, people in greater comfort and frugality than any other will probably seize upon the Piper Saratoga as the solution.

But add speed to the equation, and you have destroyed the rationale, for there is a covey of faster six-place singles and twins. However, all of the competing singles and a good number of the multis sacrifice *Lebensraum.*

Add safety as a further element to the equation, and doubts may cloud your mind, since the Saratogas have an uninspiring accident record, compared with their peers.

History

The fixed-gear Saratoga and the retractable-gear "SP" appeared upon the scene in 1980 as the third major evolution in nomenclature and, to some extent, construction and aerodynamics of the old fixed-gear Cherokee Six. The Six, which started out in 1965 with 260- and 300-hp models, was followed by its retractable clone, the Lance, in 1976.

This, in turn, was succeeded by a T-tailed version, the Lance II, in 1978. After earning an unsavory reputation for awkward handling qualities during a brief two-year sentence on the market, the T-tail was unceremoniously dumped for the Saratoga line.

As judged by all who have flown the old and the new models, the Saratogas are an improvement of real magnitude and deserve special consideration by anyone looking for a genuine six-seat used aircraft with decent handling qualities. But naturally the Saratogas—fixed and retractable, turbo and nonturbo—have not been on the market long

enough to compete with the old Sixes and Lances in price. The latter are dirt cheap, by comparison.

Peer Pressure

When classed with their slightly more cramped but speedier peers, the Beech A36 Bonanza and Cessna 210 Centurion, the Saratogas are still sometimes the cheap relatives the Lances used to be. Thus, where you can pick up a 1980 C-210 for around $78,000, the Saratoga SP of equal vintage will set you back around $67,000, on the average. Don't expect to latch onto an A36 for less than $110,000, though.

The main claim to fame of the Saratoga line is its wing, which was lengthened and tapered to give greater aspect ratio, but not burdensome extra wing area. Add to that a pair of Frise ailerons for more sprightly lateral control, and you have an aircraft that operators boast gets off more easily than the Sixes and Lances, flies faster and handles better.

As one Saratoga SP owner said, "During takeoff with the Lance, the subjective feel was that the plane just did not want to fly on lift-off and had to almost be forced into the air. The feeling of the Saratoga is completely different. The plane has the feel of almost wanting to leap off the runway, even though

The Saratogas abandoned the traditional Hershey bar wing for a tapered one with Frise ailerons and much improved control.

the power available is the same in both aircraft."

The new wing also allowed addition of extra fuel—to the tune of eight more gallons, with new bladder tanks in the outer portion. The inner wing retained its two 38.5-gal. metal leading edge tanks. Together, they provide a healthy total of 102 gallons of usable fuel.

Fuel Consumption and Performance

The extra fuel is not exactly a luxury in the Saratoga, since the airplane's big 300-horse Lycoming is a thirsty beast that will consume from 16 gph when flown conservatively in its normally aspirated version, to maybe 18 gph in the turbo version.

The high fuel consumption, which does not happen to be paired with blazing speed, is most often cited by owners as the one thorn in their side. In fact, with a typical 65-percent-power cruise of around 150 knots, the nonturbo Saratoga SP can expect to be passed by the likes of the Mooney 201, and left standing still by the A36 and C-210. Owners stress, therefore, that the

Saratogas are most sensibly used as long-range machines, to carry big cabin loads. Said one pilot, "The only drawback that I can think of is the high fuel consumption if the plane is used for local flying, such as recurrent training, touch-and-goes or local airport hopping."

Load Capacity

Not only do the Saratogas provide bountiful cabin room for six, often with club seating in the rear, they also allow plenty of room for luggage. And with a 100-pound compartment in the nose and another of equal capacity in the rear, the pilot is given an excellent opportunity to keep the aircraft balanced. With an equipped useful load of about 1,500 pounds in the retractable version, pilots can figure on carrying six adults, a full 200 pounds of baggage and still have enough fuel (47 gallons) to fly for almost three hours without reserve.

Or with full fuel, they can count on carrying five adults and some 38 pounds of baggage. The 100-pound lower useful load on the fixed-gear model will lower those figures, of course.

If the beamy Saratogas are fuel guzzlers, what's the alternative? An equally roomy twin will burn nearly twice the fuel with maintenance bills may be double or so. So there is good logic in the choice.

Handling

As mentioned above, the Saratogas are much more pleasant, facile aircraft to maneuver than the earlier Sixes and Lances, thanks to the improved wing. The stall remains vintage Cherokee, with lots of buffet and mushing, but small chance of a big wing drop and stall break. Not only is the takeoff more eager, but when landing heavily loaded, the Saratogas are less likely to come down final like lifting (or nonlifting) bodies. Pilots seem to like the manual flap system, since it is quicker than an electric one.

In turbulence, the Saratogas tend to yaw some. Therefore, passen-

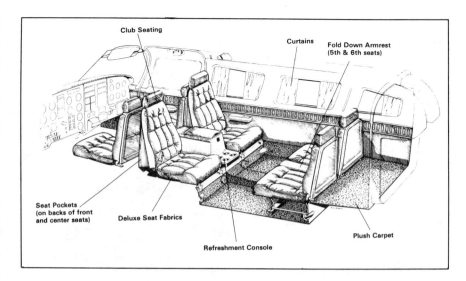

gers riding in the rearmost seats during turbulence will be subjected to an annoying amount of tail waggling, but not as badly as in the earlier T-tailed Lance.

Safety Record

The retractable-gear Lances and Saratogas collectively do not have an enviable accident history. Of 17 single-engine retractables we compared for the decade 1972 through 1981, the big Pipers shared the worst fatal accident rate with the old (35-P35) V-tail Bonanza of 3.3 fatal accidents per 100,000 hours. By comparison, the Beech A36 shared the third best fatal record with the Cessna Cardinal RG of 1.5 fatals per 100,000 hours; and the Cessna Centurion came in about half way down the list (10th) with a 2.3 rate.

In total accident rate, the Lance/Saratoga showed up somewhat better, in 12th place, actually outshining the Cessna 210 by three ranks, but being bettered once again by the A36 Bonanza, which has an excellent (low) overall accident rate.

NTSB Briefs

An accident listing provided by the Safety Board for the years 1980 and 1981, which included all fixed-gear and retractable models of the PA-32 and -32R class, disclosed that engine failures were the most common type of problem, with 28 tallied, with fuel mismanagement accounting for a large proportion of those: 11. However, the greatest

The Saratoga's main claim to fame: a beamy cabin, club seating and room for six, plus baggage.

number of fatal accidents—nine—was attributed to pilots inadvertently flying from VFR into IFR conditions.

Second highest fatal accident cause, with seven cases, involved in-flight airframe failure. Four of the breakups were in fixed-gear models; three in retractables. Most involved bad weather with thunderstorms in the area; one was in snow and ice, and another was related to spatial disorientation at night by a low-time pilot.

Third highest fatal accident cause was improper IFR operation and fourth, engine failure.

Engine Failures

As mentioned above, while engine failures claimed the biggest number of accidents among the Saratogas, Sixes and Lances, a major portion of those occurred because of fuel mismanagement. Nearly all of these were logged by pilots who had low time in that type of aircraft. The fuel selector system is quite straightforward, and located under the power quadrant where it is easy to see and reach by both pilots. However, unlike most other systems, it has a selector knob that is moved left and right rather than rotated. Although there are two tanks in each wing, there is only one position for each wing. And by the same token, there are only two fuel gauges, one for each wing.

To assist the pilot in loading fuel, there are sight gauges in each wing.

As for mechanical problems blamed for engine failures, there was no discernable trend, simply miscellaneous breakdowns involving: fuel line nut, oil exhaustion, valve failure, primer failure and resulting fire, cylinder crack, oil pump gear, valve broken, air in fuel.

A large proportion of nonfatal accidents was attributed to overshoots: 13. In many of these, pilots with low time in the aircraft simply misjudged the approach and went off the runway with unpleasant mechanical results (there was only one fatal in this category). Only half as many undershoots occurred in this type aircraft. Both types of accident are fairly common in big, heavy high-performance ships.

A fairly sizable number of accidents were blamed on ground loops and swerves—a good number of them in snow or gusty wind conditions—only two because of bounced landings and improper use of brakes.

Gear Stress

As with other big, heavy aircraft, often operated on rough strips, there are likely to be hard landings and gear failures. The big Pipers had their share of hard landings (six) and gear failures (seven). And despite the existence of an auto-

matic gear-lowering feature, the aircraft managed to land gear up on four different occasions during the two-year study period—twice because of mechanical problems. The device can nevertheless be rated a boon, though pilots must learn how to operate the override during takeoff to prevent the gear from dropping when the pilot wishes it to remain up.

Dangerous Retractables?

Can any trends be spotted from among the two years of briefs to suggest design problems among the retractables, which have such a miserable accident record? Not really, though with only a two-year run we were unable to get the big picture. In each category of accident we were able to scan, there were normally fewer accidents among the retractable Pipers, presumably because there are fewer in the fleet. The most dangerous

Oval intake scoop and cooling vents on the cowl are hallmarks of the turbo models.

category among the retractables was flying from VFR into IFR conditions, with six fatal accidents, vs. seven for the fixed-gear models.

The one area where the retractables seemed to have a worse record was in undershoots, with five accidents vs. only two among fixed-gear models. But only one of those retractable accidents was fatal, and the pilot had alcohol in his blood.

Maintenance Considerations

The nose gear on the retractable models appears to have accounted for the most trouble in a maintenance sense. The FAA's Service Difficulty Reports show several cases of the nose gear extending in flight (when it was not asked to do so) because of failed rod ends on

Cost/Performance/Specifications

Model	Year	Average Retail Price	Cruise Speed (kts)	Rate of Climb (fpm)	Service Ceiling	Useful Load (lbs)	Fuel (gals)	Engine	TBO (hrs)	Overhaul Cost
PA-32-301	1980	$ 68,000	150	990	16,000	1,667	102	300-hp Lyc. IO-540-K1G5	2,000	$12,750
PA-32-301T	1980	$ 78,000	165	1,075	20,000	1,612	102	300-hp Lyc. TIO-540-S1AD	1,800	$18,000
PA-32R-301	1980	$ 77,000	158	1,010	16,700	1,579	102	300-hp Lyc. IO-540-K1G5D	2,000	$12,750
PA-32R-301T	1980	$ 82,000	177	1,120	20,000	1,537	102	300-hp Lyc. TIO-540-S1AD	1,800	$18,000
PA-32-301	1981	$ 76,000	150	990	16,000	1,667	102	300-hp Lyc. IO-540-K1G5	2,000	$12,750
PA-32-301T	1981	$ 85,000	165	1,075	20,000	1,612	102	300-hp Lyc. TIO-540-S1AD	1,800	$18,000
PA-32R-301	1981	$ 90,000	158	1,010	16,700	1,579	102	300-hp Lyc. IO-540-K1G5D	2,000	$12,750
PA-32R-301T	1981	$ 96,000	177	1,120	20,000	1,537	102	300-hp Lyc. TIO-540-S1AD	1,800	$18,000
PA-32-301	1982	$90,000	150	990	16,000	1,667	102	300-hp Lyc. IO-540-K1G5	2,000	$12,750
PA-32-301T	1982	$100,000	165	1,075	20,000	1,612	102	300-hp Lyc. TIO-540-S1AD	1,800	$18,000
PA-32R-301	1982	$118,000	158	1,010	16,700	1,579	102	300-hp Lyc. IO-540-K1G5D	2,000	$12,750
PA-32R-301T	1982	$125,000	177	1,120	20,000	1,537	102	300-hp Lyc. TIO-540-S1AD	1,800	$18,000
PA-32-301	1983	$131,000	150	990	16,000	1,667	102	300-hp Lyc. IO-540-K1G5D	2,000	$12,750
PA-32-301T	1983	$144,000	165	1,075	20,000	1,612	102	300-hp Lyc. TIO-540-S1AD	1,800	$18,000
PA-32R-301	1983	$151,000	158	1,010	16,700	1,579	102	300-hp Lyc. IO-540-K1G5D	2,000	$12,750
PA-32R-301T	1983	$164,000	177	1,120	20,000	1,537	102	300-hp Lyc. TIO-540-S1AD	1,800	$18,000

Piper Saratoga

the hydraulic cylinder. An Airworthiness Directive was issued to correct the problem. Also, another Piper Service Bulletin was issued to replace the nose gear actuator attach bolt, which was bending and breaking.

The greatest number of complaints among SDRs dealt with problems in the Bendix magnetos. Other areas where problems developed: exhaust system, turbo system (with several instances of wastegates warping and seizing); rusted, corroded and cracked engine mounts; and cracks in the ailerons, usually at the balance weights or screws in the leading edge. We noted two instances of cracking crankcases on the Lycoming 540 engines.

One owner also reported his biggest problem was with the front door seal, which stayed deformed during cold weather and would not seal properly, despite numerous replacements. He finally solved the problem by installing an inflatable door seal sold by Bob Fields Aerocessories (Santa Paula, Calif. 805-525-6236).

Resale Value

All of the Saratogas tracked since their introduction in 1980 have showed the standard plunge in resale value, ranging from a loss of 20 percent in the fixed-gear turbo model to almost 30 percent in the retractable turbo. The curves seem to be flattening out, however, and the several models actually appears to be starting to rise in value.

Owner Comments

I have put approximately 450 hours on the plane, averaging about 150 hours per year. Prior to purchasing this 1981 SP, I owned a 1976 straight-tailed Lance.

While the Saratoga is marginally faster, there is a marked difference in how the two planes handle, especially during takeoff. The wing changes made on the Saratoga

Aircraft Resale Value Chart

markedly improve the takeoff feel of the airplane.

During takeoff with the Lance, the subjective feel was that the plane just did not want to fly on liftoff and had to almost be forced into the air. The feeling of the Saratoga is completely different. The plane has the feel of almost wanting to leap off the runway, even though the power available is the same in both aircraft.

In cruise or landing, I can find very little difference in the handling characteristics of the two aircraft.

James M. Rich, Jr.
Asheboro, N.C.

I have a 1983 Piper Turbo Saratoga SP. It was one year old as of March 15, 1984. I purchased it new and during the first 12 months of ownership I put 350 hours on the tach.

Overall, the aircraft has been absolutely superb with very few problems. It has been used for many long-distance cross-country trips. The plane has seen virtually all flying weather extremes.

On this aircraft, Piper's quality control was excellent with no squawks the first 100 hours. The interior quality, appearance and comfort with club seating and cabin size for a single is unmatched in its class.

If I could change anything on the

aircraft to make it better and/or easier to fly, I would make the following suggestions:

1. Move mp and rpm gauges up into easier pilot view.
2. Rudder trim should be more easily reached without having to bend over and reach so far forward.
3. Flap handle should have a second flaps-up position to click into after the pilot is seated so that it could be used without bending down and forward.
4. Do something with the absolutely ridiculous inside-the-cockpit fuel drain setup. It should never take two people to pre-flight an airplane, and yes, the wind is always blowing, so setting the bucket on the ground under the sump is quite a task. Finally, dumping fuel on the ramp is not nice.
5. Higher quality, larger display and more convenient positioning of EGT. It is fine in its present location if your copilot is of the opposite sex and attractive because you have to place your head in the copilot's lap to read the gauge accurately.
6. Fuel quantity, oil pressure and cylinder head gauges should be larger and with more gradations for better accuracy.
7. A small fan is needed to better push heat to passenger area of cabin.

Ralph D. Maltby
Newark, Ohio

TWIN-ENGINE PISTON

Piper Seminole

One of the few light twins still in production, the Piper Seminole is a delight to fly and serves a valuable purpose as an economical twin for multi training. But potential buyers should be aware of a flaw in its makeup: It shares the engine tappet deterioration problems that has caused so many maintenance headaches in the Cessna Skyhawk's O-320-H powerplant.

Introduced in 1979 as a multi version of the T-tailed Arrow, the Seminole was rolled out the factory doors at Vero Beach, Fla. in numbers that were never to be matched in following years. Piper delivered 142 that first year; 55 the second, and 37 in 1981, but only three were sold during the first seven months of 1984. In 1980, a turbo version was brought out; about 70 of these were built the first two years, but only seven were delivered in the first seven months of 1984.

The Multi Rationale

Except for twin-engine training, justification for a small twin like the Seminole (and the Beech Dutchess, for that matter) flunks the test of reason. With only a 161-knot cruise, the Seminole is slower than the single-engine Mooney 201, Beech Bonanza, Cessna 210 and Piper Lance, for example. Its max useful load of 1,462 pounds (51 pounds higher in the turbo version) is surpassed by that of the Beech A36 Bonanza, Cessna 210 and Stationair 6, Cherokee 6 and Lance, to name a few. And all these singles burn less fuel and are saddled with half the engine and prop maintenance and overhaul expenses.

Investment Value

Most aircraft worth their investment salt bottom out in about four years and begin to move back upward. A 1979 Seminole, which cost $105,195 (average equipped) when new, might bring $45,000 in 1985; and a 1982 turbocharged model that originally sold for $169,940, would command about $93,000.

Handling and Performance

The aircraft reacts pleasantly to the pilot's touch. The ailerons are light and the controls nicely harmonized. Pitch trim is very slow, however. Positioning the flaps either up or down induces no change in aircraft pitch. The flaps, incidentally, are set by means of Piper's traditional manual lever, which is effective, simple and sensible.

Since multi training is likely to make up a large part of the Seminole's regimen, student pilots will be happy to learn they can forget about the critical engine on this aircraft because the engines are counter-rotating. Vmc minimum control speed is a low 56 knots, though Piper provides a healthy 26-knot margin to Vsse safe single-engine speed. This is the speed below which Piper says no practice engine-out work should be initiated. Stalls give plenty of warning buffet, and that little T-tail actually has the authority to get a real stall break.

To achieve its rather sensational promotional spec numbers for takeoff performance over a 50-foot

The Seminole has nice lines and pleasant handling qualities. The fuel tanks are in the engine nacelles. The nose compartment carries a heater but no baggage and no radar.

obstacle, however, Piper employs a rather smaller margin, using a liftoff speed of only 63 knots at gross, and 25 degrees of flaps. Result: a stupendous 1,400-foot takeoff distance for obstacle clearance, vs. a much more modest 2,119-foot distance for the Seminole's big competitor, the Beech Duchess. The Duchess figures, however, are predicated on normal takeoff procedures, lifting off at 71 knots.

The Seminole's 1,400-foot landing stretch over the obstacle cannot be argued away, however, since the 75-knot approach speed calls for a very similar 76 knots on approach. And the landing figures over an obstacle for the Duchess are a much lazier 1,881 feet.

To be fair, it must be conceded that the Seminole has a good, effective set of flaps that can provide a nice, steep approach—not that this is anything special for most twins, of course. Count on a little over 700 nm range in this bird with full tanks and reserves.

Load and Comfort

The Seminole is not quite as beamy

and airy as the Duchess, and it lacks the nice triple-entry doors (one on each wing and a cargo/-cabin door on the left rear of the Beech twin). In fact, it has standard Piper Arrow dimensions. The baggage compartment also is identical, and takes 200 pounds structurally in the rear of the cabin. There is no baggage compartment in the nose.

However, our calculations showed that the aircraft would be difficult to load beyond the weight and balance envelope toward the rear. On one sample aircraft we computed that a full 200 pounds of baggage could be loaded aft, then a full load of fuel pumped in, a single pilot plumped down on the front seat, and the rear pair of seats burdened with the remaining 272 pounds of useful load—and still be within limits. That's reassuring.

Accident History

Inspection of accident and incident data from the National Transportation Safety Board and FAA files shows the greatest number of problems on the Piper Seminole stemmed from inadvertent gear-up landings. We counted 14 of these prior to 1982, with a significant proportion relating to mixed-signals during dual flight instruction. In three cases the instructor had pulled the landing gear circuit breaker as a test of emergency procedures. In another instance the gear had been left up, and forgotten, as part of a simulated single-engine landing.

Second largest number of accidents was generated by collapsing landing gear, mostly the nose gear, with seven of these noted, and attributed to mechanical problems.

Specific failures noted were: three

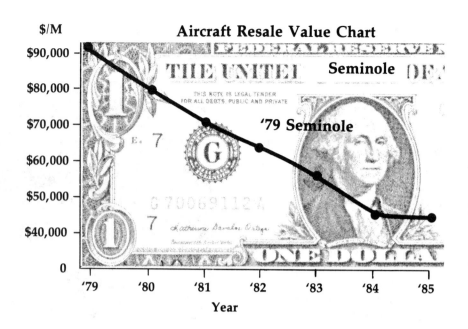

Aircraft Resale Value Chart

Seminole

'79 Seminole

cases of a broken bolt in nose gear linkage; elongated drag brace bearings, nose gear retract piston out of rig, and bolt missing from drag link assembly. On top of that there were two hard landings, one of which resulted in the wheel being broken off and props damaged.

Then came a small number of engine problems—four—with half of those not traced to any specific mechanical problem. In one instance the aircraft had made a forced landing after an oil leak was noted in the right prop. In another case a precautionary engine shutdown was made due to low oil pressure. In those crashes where no mechanical engine problem could be traced, one pilot attempting a go-around experienced a rough engine, and another detected a power loss during a maximum-performance takeoff and landed before the gear had extended.

In two cases Seminoles crashed when the instructor pulled an

engine on takeoff during an emergency test. There were also two crashes because of fuel exhaustion, one undershoot, and several taxi accidents.

We counted only three fatal accidents, altogether. One occurred when the pilot, wearing a cast on his right hand, flew into the ground on a visual approach with fog and rain in the area. Another Seminole struck some trees and crashed. It was over gross, there were thunderstorms in the area, and it had been stolen and was on an illegal drug flight. The final fatal crash occurred when the aircraft ditched into the ocean after fuel exhaustion.

Despite the fact that the aircraft is equipped with carburetors instead of fuel injection, we found no accidents related to carburetor icing.

Mechanical Problems

The predominant area of mechanical shortcomings in the Piper

Cost/Performance/Specifications

Model	Year	Number Built	Average Retail Price	Cruise Speed (kts)	Useful Load (lbs)	Rate of Climb (fpm)	SE Rate of Climb (fpm)	SE Ceiling (ft)	Fuel (gals)	Engine	TBO (hrs)	Overhaul Cost (each)
PA-44-180	1979	142	$ 45,000	161	1,462	1,340	217	4,100	110	180-hp Lyc. O-360-E1AD	2,000	$7,000
PA-44-180	1980	26	$ 56,000	161	1,462	1,340	217	4,100	110	180-hp Lyc. O-360-E1AD	2,000	$7,000
PA-44-180	1981	7	$ 65,000	161	1,462	1,340	217	4,100	110	180-hp Lyc. O-360-E1AD	2,000	$7,000
PA-44-180T	1981	59	$ 75,000	180	1,513	1,290	180	12,500	110	180-hp Lyc. TO-360-E1A6D	1,800	$9,500
PA-44-180T	1982	NA	$ 93,000	183	1,513	1,290	180	12,500	110	180-hp Lyc. TO-360-E1A6D	1,800	$9,500

Seminole appears to be one made notorious by the O-320-H engine in the Cessna Skyhawk: spalling tappets and camshafts. It turns out that the Seminole's Lycoming O-360-E engines have the same tappets used in the by now much publicized Lycoming O-320-H.

The FAA's Service Difficulty Reports for the Seminole disclosed that tappet and camshaft spalling problems formed the largest single entry block of user problems, with 43 cases, and another 11 instances of camshaft spalling, lobes flattened, etc. and discovery of metal shavings in the oil filters.

If one applies the FAA's rule of thumb suggesting that only about 10 percent of actual problems are reported, some 430 engines or 215 aircraft conceivably could be affected, statistically, at least. Of course, only some 246 Seminoles were built and delivered, by our count, when the report was issued.

Indeed, Airworthiness Directive 80-04-03 suggests that the Seminole engine may be prey to at least some of the catalog of grief that has befallen the O-320-H engines. This AD brings the Seminole's O-360-E engines under some of the same corrective orders, "to prevent excessive wear and oil system contamination associated with hydraulic lifters spalling . . ." Required are addition of Lycoming's special lubricant every 50 hours and inspection for metal contaminants in the oil every 100 hours.

Since Lycoming has brought out larger hydraulic lifters (tappets) to combat the spalling problems, along with "improved" crankcases to house them, this now confronts Seminole owners with the same unhappy decision O-320-H owners face at overhaul time: Should they risk overhauling an engine with the old tappets, or spend more on the new tappet/crankcase combination?

In terms of sheer volume, at least, the Seminole's number two problem area suggested by the Service Difficulty Reports involves cracked carburetor air boxes (37 reports)

and carburetor heat shrouds cracked (16 reports).

Number three is leaking landing gear actuator cylinders (24 reports), and four is landing gear trunions cracked, sheared and worn (23 reports). Next come 22 reports of elevator trim cables fraying, many of the problems occurring in the tail cone near the electric trim motor and windlass. In a couple of instances mechanics suggested there was too much tension on the cable and that perhaps a limit switch was needed. The next largest category involves cracked or broken engine mounts, with 18 reported.

Pilots shopping for used Seminoles might also take care to look for instances of cracking aileron spars, ribs or rib noses, since there were 15 reports of this type of problem, along with another 10 telling about loose aileron control attach fittings or the spars themselves moving at the pushrod attachments.

Other potential problem areas spotlighted by the SDRs: nose cone spar assemblies cracking (in six of the 11 cases reported this occurred at the bottom holes for the drag brace mounting plate); cracked firewalls (12 cases reported); fuel primer lines broken, cracked or chafed (eight instances); as well as the discovery of pieces of the fuel pump return spring found broken in the prop governor cavity and fuel pump cavity (10 cases). Shoppers should also be on the lookout for problems with throttle cables binding, breaking or seizing (13 reports) and finally crankcase cracks (10 of these noted).

An awkward power gauge arrangement splits the tachometers to the left of the throttle quadrant, the manifold pressure gauge to the right. The cowl flap levers below the throttle bank are well suited to the pilot's touch, however.

Airworthiness Directives

A significant portion of the problems revealed by service difficulties in the field, which we discussed above, have been dealt with by ADs. Hence, there are ADs on the following topics: binding throttle control cable fix, fuel primer mod kit (to prevent a fire hazard from leaking lines), replacement of the downlock hook and bushing to prevent nose gear retraction on landing, a fix to prevent binding of the aileron push rod and possible loss of aileron control, a mod of the nose cone spar to prevent cracks and possible malfunction of the landing gear, a mod to reduce aileron spar deflection and cracking and loss of aileron control, and reinforcement of aileron skins to prevent cracks on the outside leading edges.

In addition to the engine AD for the tappet problem we already discussed, there is another AD calling for replacement of certain types of upper exhaust valve spring seats to prevent valve failure. And one calls for replacement of the oil pump impeller and shaft to prevent pump failure.

Service Bulletins

Along with Piper SBs corresponding to the above ADs, there was

Piper Seminole

one other worth noting, calling for replacement of the carburetor air box rivets. The SB notes that if the attach rivets shear in the carb air box flapper valve bushings, the heat flapper valve could jam, putting the carb heat out of action.

In addition, a service letter was issued by Piper providing for reinforcement of engine baffles, to prevent cracks; replacement of the nose landing gear micro switch bracket to improve the reliability of the gear position indicating system by reducing the need for frequent adjustments of the up-limit micro switch. Buyers might check to see if these nonmandatory fixes were incorporated.

Owner Comments

We were probably among the first FBOs to put the Seminole on the line as a working airplane. Prior to the PA44, the alternative for a twin trainer was either an Apache, the 310, or possibly an early Seneca I. For a variety of reasons all are unacceptable. The Seminole proved to be the perfect airplane for twin training, rental, and light charter work. Our maintenance costs have been quite low, the machine is exceptionally easy to fly, and has proven to be the *safest* light twin imaginable.

Our observations: Performance: In most areas the PA44 will better the handbook specs. We have consistently flown the airplane at max gross weight with no noticeable decrease in performance. The 1,400-pound useful load is exceptional. It is not unusual to achieve 1,400-1,500 fpm climb rates at full gross weight. With two pax, cruise at 75 percent will run 172 KTAS and about 18.5 gph, using the EGT. Landing and takeoff distances can be improved by 10 percent or so with good pilot technique.

Handling: Exceptional. The smoothest flying light twin I've ever flown. The airplane is as easy

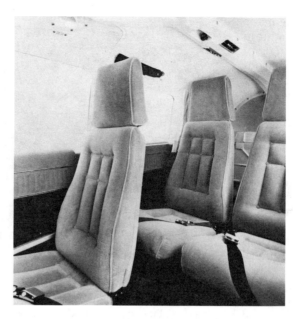

Toujour velour, the interior is posh, but the optional headrests play havoc with rearward visibility.

to land as the Warrior, which I consider to be the truest airplane to land on the market. Single-engine handling is straightforward and honest. Go-arounds are a piece of cake from any point in the approach—a considerable change from the sweaty-palm go-rounds in the Apache, etc.

Comfort: Our bird is the plush version with soundproofing, which creates about the lowest cockpit noise level I've experienced. The low sound level makes the PA44 particularly suited for instruction, also a nice touch for charter customers.

Maintenance: Our airplane has been virtually maintenance-free. The engines are now above 1,900 hours and we have not topped the first cylinder. Compression and oil consumption would indicate we'll get at least 2,200 hours or so before overhaul will be required. (Excepting our Part 135 use, of course.) Parts, since the PA44 is mostly a conglomerate of other Piper planes, have been absolutely no problem. The only unique problem we've encountered was the replacement of the left engine throttle cables, which grounded the airplane one day!

In the maintenance area the Seminole has been a most pleasant surprise. We find the cost of a 100-hour inspection to be about that of an Arrow; i.e., in the $600-$800 range.

Turbo Seminole: Although we are not operating a Turbo PA44, I think the machine worth particular mention. Through our sales work with the turbo version we were all quite impressed by its cruise speed and range. It is not uncommon in a mid-weight airplane to see cruise speeds in the 190-knot area, and at a fuel flow of approximately 19-20 gph when leaned using the EGT. And 190 knots on 19 gph definitely is not bad!

All in all, the PA44 is a fine airplane for what it is intended. It *is not* a heavy IFR airplane when icing is about. It *is not* a big, roomy airplane like the Seneca or Saratoga series. What it is is a comfortable, quiet, four-place bird, with excellent speed and outstanding range.

It is a shame that the machine did not carve out a better niche for itself with the flying public and FBO operators. For the "sophisticated single" owner who's looking for a "step-up" airplane I can't imagine a better choice.

Our bird has averaged over 55 hours/month and has, on occasion, flown over 100 hours/month with an absolute minimum of worry. It is also one of the few twins I'd feel comfortable renting—even to "qualified" customers.

Jack Doub, Pres.
H&D Aviation, Inc.
Terre Haute, Ind.

Beech Duchess

In 1974, Beech's designers — beset with the task of creating a step-up plane for the Beech Aero Centers — started laying the groundwork for a simple, yet advanced, light twin based on the Beech Sierra design. The prototype sported a T-tail, two doors (a la Sundowner), and a pair of conventional-rotating 160-hp Lycomings (which were later replaced by counter-rotating 180-hp engines). Forty-four months after its inception, the Model 76 Duchess attained FAA type certification and began rolling off the Liberal, Kansas assembly lines.

No sooner had the Duchess hit the market, of course, when the light-twin arena suddenly became quite crowded, what with the Grumman Cougar's debut in 1978 and the arrival of Piper's Seminole in 1979. (Cessna's T303 Crusader — nee Clipper — was to have been an entrant in the light-light-twin derby, but Cessna thought better of the move at the last minute and reconfigured the T303 as a Seneca-class medium hauler.) Nonetheless, Beech's Aero Centers quickly placed orders for over 200 of the bonded-construction T-twins; today, there are more than 430 Model 76s in operation, though none were sold in 1983 or 1984.

Novel Construction

Although the Duchess's lines clearly relfect its Musketeer ancestry, the Model 76 is anything but a double-breasted Sierra in actual construction. The Sierra's outward-retracting gear design was abandoned in the Duchess, for example, along with the Mooney-style rubber shock biscuits. (The Duchess displays a pair of mega-lithic oleo shocks on the main gear, while the nose strut is taken *in toto* from the A36 Bonanza.) Like the Sierra, the Duchess has bonded wet wings; but unlike the other Aero Center airplanes, the Model 76's main tanks extend to the wingtips, carrying 50 gallons usable (each). Also, the Duchess's ailerons are bigger (and travel farther) than the Sierra's.

In the fuselage, extensive use was made of honeycomb-sandwich construction techniques, to produce a light, crashworthy, and at the same time, vibration/noise-resistant cabin. A feature unique among twins is the Duchess's cabin door configuration (borrowed from the Sierra): there are doors and walkways for both pilot *and* co-pilot, plus a large baggage door on the left aft fuselage behind the wing.

T-tail Trade-offs

The Duchess's most distinctive design hallmark, however, is its T-tail. Although considered by many to be merely a stylistic (i.e., marketing) device, the T-tail actually contributes in meaningful ways to the airplane's performance. Because the horizontal surfaces are out of the propellers' slipstreams and sit far to the rear atop a *swept* tail fin, their effectiveness is enhanced; and as a result, the horizontal tail area can be reduced — with a commensurate reduction in drag — at no penalty in pitch control. (In fact, the pitch authority of the Duchess tail is so great than the

The first (and most expensive) of the new-generation light twins, the Duchess is now available on the used market at prices under $75,000 (for 1978 models) — less than half what a fully equipped 1982 Duchess costs.

original prototype experienced problems with excessively high nose angles in stalls. This problem was ameliorated, however, with the switch to heavier, 180-hp engines from the earlier 160-hp Lycomings.) As a side benefit, prop-wash buffet is also eliminated.

The real-world payoff of the T-tail for the Duchess can be measured in terms of pitch control in the flare (excellent), allowable c.g. range (10.9 inches total), versus 8.3 for the Sierra, and the amount of trim change needed after gear or flap deployment (little, if any). The T-tail's end-plate effect also contributes to rudder effectiveness, providing a low single-engine minimum control speed (Vmc) of 67 knots CAS, which is one knot below the airplane's clean stall speed (Vs) of 68 KCAS. (In a twin-engine plane, it is desirable from a safety/controllability standpoint to encounter the stall at an airspeed higher than Vmc.) Of course, these benefits do not come without a modest weight penalty for the added structure needed to carry the lofty horizontal stabilizer — estimated by Beech, in this case, at 15 pounds.

Since the Model 76's introduction, few substantive design changes have been made (although myriad minor adjustments have been incorporated in later models and published as service bulletins; see below). In early 1979, improved door locks became standard and cowl flap hinges were changed from aluminum to steel; in mid-1980, an improved engine mount was introduced; in 1981, a landing gear horn muting system (to keep the horn from sounding prematurely during high-speed power-off letdowns) was introduced. For 1982, Beech increased the number of static wicks from five to 12. Overall, the design of the Model 76 remains virtually unchanged since 1978 — a testament, perhaps, to the airplane's basic soundness.

Performance

Owners praise the Duchess as a capable medium-range cross-country machine, with 75-percent power cruise speeds typically in the 160-knot region at fuel flows of just under 10 gallons per hour per engine. To underscore the plane's economy-of-operation appeal (for a twin, at least), Beech, in 1982, appended a "super economy" cruise performance page to the Duchess handbook, claiming a 142-knot speed at 14,000 feet, with props at 2,100 rpm and manifold pressures at 18.0 inches (fuel consumption: 6.8 gph/engine). We doubt that anyone would choose to operate the plane in that fashion, but the point is well taken: this *is* a bona fide economy twin.

With a maximum takeoff weight of 3,900 pounds (100 pounds more than the normally aspirated Piper Seminole — 25 pounds *less* than the Turbo Seminole), the Duchess turns in rather mediocre takeoff numbers; to wit, a sea level ground roll of 1,017 feet and a 50-foot

obstacle clearance distance of 2,119 feet — no better than the Travel Air (Beech's original 180-hp twin) and actually quite a bit worse than the competition (Piper's Seminole gets off and over in 880 feet and 1,400 feet, respectively, assuming we can believe Piper's numbers).

On landing, the comparisons with Brand 'P' are even more striking: the Duchess rolls a full 1,000 feet after touchdown at gross weight, versus the Seminole's 590 feet. With heavy-duty brakes, the Seminole will — according to Piper — roll a mere *383 feet* after a no-wind touchdown. One wonders whether Piper's tape measures are made in the U.S.

Rotation speed in the Duchess comes at 71 knots, which corresponds with Beech's "intentional one engine inoperative speed" (Vsse) as well as with the two-engine best angle of climb speed (Vx). Upon attaining 85 knots (the best rate of climb speed for single- *or* all-engine operation), a full-throttle climbout yields a 1,248-fpm rate of ascent initially, decaying to 1,000 fpm at 4,000 feet.

The Duchess's single-engine performance specs are nothing to write home about — although, of course, the same is true for other twins in this category. On one engine, the Duchess turns in an anemic 235-fpm sea-level climb rate at gross (vs. a complexion-whitening 217 fpm for the Seminole and 180 fpm for the Turbo Seminole). The climb dwindles to 50 fpm at the single-engine service ceiling of 6,170 feet (vs. 4,100 feet for the lighter-gross-weight Seminole — again, a question of whose numbers you believe).

The usable fuel capacity of 100 gallons gives the Duchess an en-

durance, at 75-percent cruise, of around four hours with IFR reserves. The published range (with reserves) varies from 623 nautical miles to upwards of 800 nautical, depending on whether 75-percent cruise or "super-economy" power settings are used.

All in all, the Duchess's performance is on a par with — and in most cases no better than — that of the 1958 Travel Air. Which raises the obvious question: Why would Beech go to the trouble and expense of certifying a *new* 180-hp light twin when it could just as easily have revived the Travel Air, a proven (and much-loved by some) design?

When we put this question to a Beech spokesman some years ago, he answered by saying that the Travel Air was and is a complicated design, expensive to produce (as are Barons that derive from that same type certificate); the Duchess employs state-of-the-art materials and construction techniques, affording a lighter airframe (by about 200 pounds, compared to the Model 95); and in designing the Duchess, Beech had the opportunity to create a twin with truly superior slow-speed handling characteristics.

All of which is true. We can only lament the fact that Beech's efforts did not result in a twin with a lower price tag. A new 1982 Duchess sold for a whopping $171,875 (average-equipped) — two and a half times the cost of a comparably equipped new Travel Air in 1968.

Handling and Comfort

The Duchess is nothing if not comfortable. Although the cockpit tapers noticeably just forward of the pilots' thighs, the Bonanza-like

Cost/Performance/Specifications ———————

Model	Year	Number Built	Cruise Speed (kts)	Useful Load (lbs)	Rate of Climb (fpm)	SE Rate Climb (fpm)	SE Ceiling (ft)	Fuel (gals)	Engine	TBO (hrs)	Overhaul Cost	Average Price
76	1978	72	115	1,450	1,248	235	6,170	100	180-hp Lyc. O-360-A1G6D	2,000	$7,500	$ 52,500
76	1979	213	115	1,450	1,248	235	6,170	100	180-hp Lyc. O-360-A1G6D	2,000	$7,500	$ 61,000
76	1980	84	115	1,450	1,248	235	6,170	100	180-hp Lyc. O-360-A1G6D	2,000	$7,500	$ 71,000
76	1981	55	115	1,450	1,248	235	6,170	100	180-hp Lyc. O-360-A1G6D	2,000	$7,500	$ 87,000
76	1982	11	115	1,450	1,248	235	6,170	100	180-hp Lyc. O-360-A1G6D	2,000	$7,500	$120,000
76	1983	None	--	--	--	--	--	--	--	--	--	--

206

head room and 44-inch cabin width (the cabin is wider, amazingly, than that of the Baron) contribute to the feeling that one is actually flying a much larger airplane. The accommodations are strictly first-class.

Pilots transitioning to the Duchess from single-engine aircraft will appreciate the fact that the plane's panel layout (with the exception of the vertically displaced tachometers) is both logical and eye-pleasing. Gear and flap switches are where they should be — gear on the left, flaps on the right — as are the power levers (mercifully, Beech abandoned the irksome center-panel ''prop/throttle/mixture'' grouping found on the Barons and placed these controls in the standard TPM arrangement in the Duchess).

Starting the Duchess's carbureted O-360s is easy enough if you remember to press *in* on the ignition switch while cranking, to engage the primer (a solenoid-operated system which, mysteriously, feeds fuel only to cylinders one, two and four of each engine).

On the ground, the Duchess handles a bit differently from its Piper counterpart. The slow damping action of the main gear oleos — combined with the plane's large span-wise mass distribution — gives the Duchess a curiously ponderous feel while taxiing, even setting up a Dutch-roll-like oscillation as one goes around corners. Likewise, the slightest touch of the brake pedals tends to collapse the nose oleo. These idiosyncrasies are basically harmless, however.

On takeoff, the Duchess requires a positive tug on the yoke to break ground (not too much, though, or you'll overrotate). Thanks to the counter-rotating props, there is no need to correct for torque or P-factor. In the air, visibility is excellent. In fact, the nose slopes away so precipitously that it is difficult, at first, to judge the plane's angle fo attack.

Unlike the Aero Center singles upon which the Model 76 design is

Twin doors make for easy entry and egress — and twice the opportunity for in-flight door openings, although the Duchess has had no problems in this area as yet. A third door (for cargo) is located aft of the left wing.

based, the Duchess has no rudder-aileron interconnect — nor is one needed. The controls are light (as twins go) and well-harmonized, inviting comparisons with such single-engine aircraft as the Bonanza and Saratoga. Stability is excellent in the pitch and roll modes; yaw is less good, with some tendency toward short-period waggle in turbulence. Overall, however, the plane is decidedly well-behaved.

An interesting quirk of the airplane is its maximum gear-*raise* speed of 113 knots, occasioned by the design of the forward-retracting nose strut. Once the gear has been lowered (as a speed brake, say), it cannot be raised again until airspeed has been allowed to bleed off to under 113 knots.

Safety

According to NTSB records, as of 1982 there had been only six accidents involving Duchesses since the aircraft was introduced in 1978, two of them fatal. (Interestingly, only one of the six pilots involved was over the age of 33.)

• One Duchess was destroyed (and the two persons aboard killed) on a VFR flight from Long Beach to

Ramona, Calif. when the aircraft encountered zero-visibility weather and collided with the ground in a controlled descent.

• A Duchess sustained heavy damage on a training flight from Little Rock, Ark. when the flight instructor allowed his student to land gear-up.

• Confusion in the cockpit resulted in another gear-up landing (again with substantial damage) —this time in Sioux City, Iowa — when an instructor told his student to cancel a practice single-engine go-around. The CFI landed the plane wheels up.

• Inclement weather claimed a noninstrument-rated Duchess pilot with 20 hours in type on a flight from Wyoming to Salt Lake City. The aircraft crashed out of control at night, in icing conditions.

• A hard landing in icing conditions caused major damage to a Duchess on a January nighttime arrival in South Bend, Ind. Four people escaped serious injury.

• Fuel exhaustion and fuel mismanagement were mentioned in the description of "probably cause" for a double-engine-stoppage accident. The 24-year-old pilot had departed Monmouth, N.J. for West Chicago, Ill., nonstop, against undetermined headwinds; substantial damage occurred when the plane, out of fuel, made an off-airport landing near its intended destination.

Note: Perhaps it's worth mentioning that none of the 12 persons involved in the four non-fatal accidents cited above suffered serious injuries. (Perhaps it's worth observing, too, that although weather radar is available as an option on the Duchess, anti-icing equipment of the type that might have prevented two of these accidents is not.)

Slow-Speed Traits

True to the designers' original intentions, the Duchess excels at low-speed controllability — with or without both fans turning. Pitch, roll, and yaw control remain crisp at speeds near blue-line (85 KIAS), and — thanks to the presence on the center pedestal of trim knobs for ailerons, rudder, *and* elevator — the plane trims up quickly for hands-off flight after shutting down either engine. (Handling is the same with either engine out, of

course; there is no "critical" engine.)

Stalls are conventional in all respects, except that the controls remain surprisingly effective at vanishingly low airspeeds. With both engines developing power, the airplane can be flown well below 50 knots IAS, dirty, without stalling.

One of the nice aspects of the T-tail is that, since it sits high above the wing's wake, it doesn't "feel" disturbances caused by lowering/raising the gear or flaps. On deploying the landing gear (at up to 140 knots) or flaps (up to 110 knots), there is no noticeable change in pitch attitude.

Maintenance

From a reliability standpoint, the Duchess has one thing going for it that the Seminole does not: namely, the A-series Lycoming O-360 engine. Unlike the E-series O-360s installed in the Seminole, the Model 76's O-360-A1G6D engines are among Lycoming's oldest and most proven O-360 variants, utterly worthy of the 2,000-hr. TBO bestowed upon them. The Piper Seminole's O-360-E1A6D engines, on the other hand, are a more recent design with valve train components common to the infamous O-320-H "Blue Streak" engine of Skyhawk fame. As almost everyone knows by now, the O-320-H has had a history of severe tappet-spalling problems. (The spalling — which seems cold-weather related — is partially preventable by the use of Lycoming's special LW-16702 oil ad-

ditive.) What you may *not* know is that the O-360-E (and TO-360-E) engines on the Seminole are also experiencing tappet-destruction problems. The problem is so acute, in fact, that Lycoming requires regular use of the LW-16702 "mystery oil" as a prerequisite to warranty coverage for O-360-E engines. (The oil additive is *not* required for the Duchess's engines.)

This is not to say, of course, that the Duchess does not have its share of maintenance problems; seven AD notes and 45 service bulletins issued by 1982 say otherwise. For the most part, however, the Duchess's maintenance glitches are minor. Most of the ADs, for example, involve one-time inspections or fixes applicable to early-serial-number aircraft. The only important repetitive AD affecting the aircraft (other than the one targeting the plane's Janitrol combustion heater) is a 1980 AD (80-19-12) requiring 50-hr. checks

Duchess pilots need to monitor cowl flaps for overheating and carburetor heat for overcooling. There is no fuel injection.

of the engine mounts for cracks. Unfortunately, the AD names all Duchess's from S/N -1 to -415.

Space prohibits an exhaustive listing of Duchess-related Service Instructions here. Most of these bulletins involve minor product improvements or non-mandatory inspections. Some, however, are of major importance (such as S.I. 1147 — revised in March 1982 — pertaining to engine mount replacement; and S.I. 1166, regarding improved main gear doors). Prospective Duchess buyers would be well-advised to crosscheck aircraft logbooks against the Beech S.I. Master Index (publication 98-34774B, available through any Beech dealer) to see whether applicable service bulletins have been complied with.

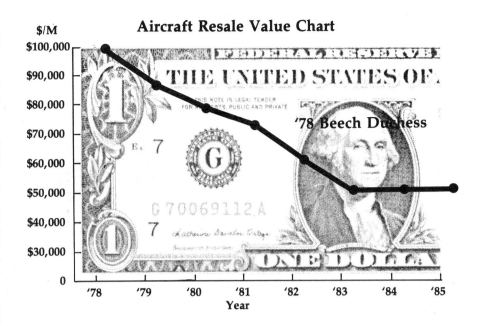

Aircraft Resale Value Chart

'78 Beech Duchess

Owner Comments

Our company presently operates two Duchess aircraft. They both have exceeded our expectations in all aspects of their operation. The handling characteristics are very good, although the elevator seems to be a bit light. True airspeeds vary between 155 and 160 knots at 65 percent power setting with a fuel flow of 19 gallons per hour. Our direct operating cost averged $53.24 per hour with no engine reserves. These figures were for a seven month period during which the aircraft flew 506 hours. We generally operate these aircraft between 650 and 700 hours a year. Their normal load is one and, occasionally, two passengers and we average about 150-mile stage lengths.

Our only major unscheduled problem was one engine overhaul at 1,400 hours, due to a lifter that disintegrated. As far as the airframe is concerned our problems have been the gear doors, which tend to develop cracks, and an engine mount inspection at 50-hour intervals. We had one cracked mount. Beech provided a fix for the gear doors and has given us very good product support.

Single-engine performance is a little better than average for this class of aircraft, and handling characteristics on one engine are very good. Our aircraft serial numbers are ME-12 and ME-31 with 1,400 hours and 2,000 hours respectively, so we are affected by virtually all the service bulletins.

I would like to add that from a pilot's point of view, these aircraft are a delight to fly, and from an accounts standpoint, easy to feed.

Marvin Pippen
Wharton, Tex.

I selected the Duchess as a moderate range business machine and feel that it will handle that task well. The visibility is good and the handling predictable. It is a little noisier than the Seminole but the visibility gain makes up for it. Also, the two entry doors are a decided convenience. Handbook figures on fuel consumption and speed appear to be accurate. I will need more time to establish *how* accurate.

The prospective purchaser will want to get the beefed up engine mounts (standard on later models) or else a repetitive AD inspection will have to be made every 50 hours. There apparently was some cracking of mounts on some of the earlier models; hence, the AD. Al-

though I had the heavy mounts installed, the AD has not officially been lifted.

The Duchess pilot will want to take special care when securing after a flight. The rudder trim should be rolled full down and the rudder locks installed. They're hard to figure out, but do it anyway. The elevator surface droops naturally at rest and will damage the rudder if the rudder is allowed to swing in the wind.

Last, but not least, have a set of "starter engaged" indicator lights installed on the panel if the airplane doesn't already have them. As I learned, extended cranking will cause the starter relay to hang up, keeping the relay engaged. The result of all this is that the starter will be damaged (probably destroyed) and the battery run down, the trouble being that you don't know it. A volt-meter would be handly at times like this. (The lesson here is to get familiar with the electrical system.) Incidentally, I have to give high marks for the position of the circuit breakers and engine instruments in the Duchess. All handy and well laid out.

Garwood Burwell
Madison, N.J.

Mine is a 1980 aircraft which has proved to be fairly satisfactory.

If the beholder equates newness with beauty, then the Duchess is handsomer than the old Travel Air, but no better a performer.

There were considerable problems with the gear actuators which required replacement six times. They continually leaked and blew seals. Also, the passenger windows are now showing stress cracks where they are riveted. Beech is supposed to be looking into this.

Handling qualities are very satisfactory and landings and takeoffs are to the book. Speed on the average is 165 knots at 75 percent power. Fuel burn is 7 gallons/hour per side. The carbureted system is easy to start. The interior is very roomy and comfortable. There is easy access through the plane's twin cabin doors and large rear cabin door.

The annuals run around $1,200 with approximately $125 per month for general maintenance. The avionics panel is small, limiting equipment choice and the yoke doesn't accommodate sufficient space for wiring of push-to-talk buttons or remote ident switches, etc. Sound in the cabin could be better and a prop synch would be nice. Visibility is excellent and loading is adequate.

In summary, I would like to see more horsepower to obtain a cruise of 185 to 190 knots. Range is good, but with larger engines or turbocharging this could be increased. In all, a good economical twin with fine handling characteristics — a high-quality aircraft.

Nathan Goldenthal
Peoria, Ariz.

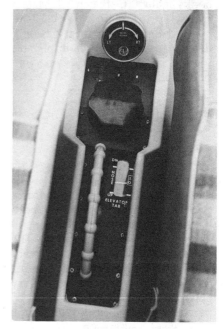

The Beech twin offers fliers the luxury of not only a pitch and rudder trim, but an aileron trim as well.

The elevated elevator may be out of reach for a walk-around inspection, but it also is out of the way of propwash buffet.

Piper Apache

"With the introduction of the Piper Apache into the utility airplane field," said the opening lines of the PA-23 Owner's Manual, **"a new era in the development of personal and business aviation is presaged."** And indeed it was so. In an 11-year production run beginning in 1954, Piper unleashed more than 2,100 Apaches on the world, demonstrating for the first time the viability of a type of plane that had never before been produced in quantity: the light twin.

Cursed by many for its poor single-engine rate of climb and generally unhurried performance, the Piper Apache is nonetheless revered by flight schools and owners alike for its easy flying qualities, spacious interior (the cabin structure—which is the same as the Aztec's—is wider than a Baron's, at 44 inches across), rugged construction, and reliable—not to mention miserly with fuel—Lycoming O-320 engines.

Today, 28 years after the Apache's introduction as the world's first true "light twin," the PA-23 is still in demand on the used market—largely because it holds the dubious distinction of being the least expensive used twin available. Doggy older versions of the twin can be had for under $10,000, while average-time, average-equipped 160-hp models can be bought (often with many STC'd options installed) for $15,000 to $20,000.

Whether the old bird is truly a bargain is certainly debatable, however. The Apache comes with a number of curious (and complex) mechanical quirks—not to mention a string of repetitive-inspection type ADs—resulting in upkeep

costs equivalent to those of a light twin costing upwards of $150,000.

History

To airplane genealogy buffs, it will come as no surprise to learn that the roots of the Apache's family tree lead not to Piper, but to Stinson. In 1952, Stinson built and flew a prototype "light twin" with two rudders (a la Ercoupe), a pair of Lycoming O-290-D2 engines rated at 135 hp, and retracting tricycle gear. The 3,200-lb. (gross) aircraft cruised at 130 knots, hauled 1,250 pounds of useful load, and was able to fly 625 nm on 72 gallons of fuel—outstanding fuel economy for a twin, even by today's standards. Target price for the Twin Stinson was pegged at $25,000, in 1952 dollars.

When the Stinson company fell on economic hard times, Piper agreed to take over the Twin Stinson design and—discarding its twin tail in favor of a single fin, and replacing the O-290-D2s with a pair of O-320-A1s—type certificated the airplane as the PA-23-150 "Apache" (the first of many Indian monikers to follow). In 1954 dollars, the original Apaches sold for $32,500 basic —$36,235 equipped.

The first 750 or so Apaches off the line—those built between 1954 and 1957—came with 150-hp engines and a 3,500-lb. gross weight (a

Even doted-over Apaches with shiny new paint jobs aren't worth much more than $15,000.

combination that was good for no more than 240 fpm rate of climb on one engine at sea level on a standard day). In mid-1957, the Apache got a higher-compression version of the O-320 engine with 10 additional horsepower; gross weight also went up, to 3,800 pounds. The bench-type rear seat was also replaced, in 1957, with two individual seats, and a five-place interior was offered as an option.

In 1959, the instrument panel (heretofore a crazy-quilt of dislocated gauges, switches, and boxes) got a facelift, with radios positioned in a center stack and flight gauges mercifully clustered on the left. The following year, a large third side window made its appearance with the debut of the PA-23G, which also featured a welcome increase in gear-down speed to 130 knots (from 109 knots) as well as an increase in flap speed to 125 mph (from the previous absurdly low 87 knots).

After a production run of only 28 airplanes in 1961, Piper reintroduced the PA-23 as the "Apache 235" in 1962. This version of the Apache was, in fact, merely a re-engined Aztec with carbureted, low-compression six-cylinder O-540-B1 engines. (It should be noted that the Aztec, which debuted in 1960, was originally an outgrowth of the Apache, and in fact shared the same basic type certificate.) Unable to sell more than a handful of the larger models, Piper axed the Apache 235—and with it, the Apache name —in 1965, having delivered at that time only 117 PA-23-235s (but more than 600 Twin Comanches).

Performance

Owners are divided on which of the Apache models (other than the large-engined 235) offers the best performance. Current hangar mythology holds that the early Apaches—with their 150-hp engines—are generally doggiest, with exceptionally low single-engine rates of climb (the book says 240 fpm at sea level). But in fact the higher gross weight of the 160-hp models resulted in a *higher* power loading (not to mention wing loading) for 1957-1961 models, and a *lower* single-engine climb rate (180 fpm). Single-engine performance is thus generally poor for the series—but no worse, on balance, than many other light twins. (In fact, the 150-hp Apache's engine-out climb rate is actually better than that of the Seneca II or Cessna's T303 Crusader.)

Everybody agrees on one thing: the Apache is not exactly overpowered. Speed simply is not the airplane's strong suit. The 1956 Owner's Manual claims a cruise speed of 152 knots at full throttle and 2400 rpm at 6,000 feet (roughly 75 percent power); but, as one owner remarked wryly, "The performance charts in the Owner's Manual were probably written by the marketing department." Owners typically report Skylane-like cruise figures of 135 knots true at 65 to 70 percent power, with fuel flows in the 15 to 16 gallon per hour range, for 150-hp models; about two knots more for the 160-hp versions (and up to 20 knots more for the highly modified, 180-hp turbocharged Geronimos). Economy cruise is in the 120 knot area, yielding 14 gph. These speeds are at gross weight, however, and owners claim that cruise figures go up about one knot for every 100 pounds of fuel or baggage offloaded.

Considering the airplane's respectable 1,250-lb. useful load and relatively tiny engines, the Apache returns fairly incredible short-field performance, with takeoff rolls of 990 feet at gross on a standard sea-level day (680 feet at 3,200 pounds), and landing distances of a mere 670 feet at gross (or just 600 feet at 3,200 pounds). These are no-wind figures. Obstacle-clearance numbers were not stated in the aircraft Owner's Manual. (Likewise, accelerate-stop distances had not been considered important in 1954.)

Once an Apache is airborne, a best rate of climb speed of 87 knots yields a creditable 1,350 fpm climb rate at gross (according to the book), diminishing to 1,000 fpm at 5,000 feet, with full throttle. And although single-engine rates of climb are poor at full gross weight, the offloading of 300 pounds of cargo and/or fuel results in a book climb figure of 330 fpm with one engine (we're not told which one) caged. Likewise, the single-engine absolute ceiling rises from 6,750 feet at 3,500 pounds gross weight (for the 150-hp Apache), to 8,000 feet at 300 pounds below gross, operating on the critical (right) engine.

Standard fuel capacity on the Apache was 72 gallons, in midwing fuel cells. Factory long-range tanks, installed in the outboard tips, however, boosted total fuel capacity to 108 gallons. For even more range, an owner can add STC'd Met-co-aire tip tanks, to give a grand total of 144 gallons of fuel—enough to make the airplane's endurance compete with the pilot's. (One owner tells of making nonstop flights from Wichita to the West Coast, bucking 20-knot headwinds.) With any more than 100 gallons of fuel on board, however, the Apache becomes a less-than-four-persons (assuming no baggage) airplane.

Handling Characteristics

What the Apache lacks in speed and sex appeal, it more than makes up for in comfort and easy handling, according to owners (who characterize the ship as "very forgiving," "a stable instrument platform," and "a delight to fly"). Control forces are light and well balanced, as twins go. Stalls, likewise, are docile, although one instructor-owner admonishes that plenty of right rudder will be required during power-on stall recoveries.

Docile demeanor aside, the Apache nonetheless displays several potentially irksome quirks in the air. Like the Aztec, the Apache has an annoying tendency to pitch up with the initial deploy-

Cost/Performance/Specifications

Model	Years Built	Number Built	Average Retail Price	Cruise Speed (kts)	Useful Weight (lbs)	Engine	TBO (hrs)	Overhaul Cost (each)
PA-23-150	1954	115	$13,500	148	3,500	150-hp Lyc. O-320-A1A	2,000	$ 6,000
PA-23-150	1955-57	626	$14,500	148	3,500	150-hp Lyc. O-320-A1A	2,000	$ 6,000
PA-23-160	1957-58	754	$15,500	150	3,800	160-hp Lyc. O-320-B3B	2,000	$ 6,500
PA-23-160	1959	368	$16,000	150	3,800	160-hp Lyc. O-320-B3B	2,000	$ 6,500
PA-23-G	1960	141	$17,500	150	3,800	160-hp Lyc. O-320-B3B	2,000	$ 6,500
PA-23-H	1961	28	$18,000	150	3,800	160-hp Lyc. O-320-B3B	2,000	$ 6,500
PA-23-235	1962-63	82	$20,750	166	4,800	235-hp Lyc. O-540-B1A5	2,000	$10,000
PA-23-235	1964-65	34	$22,000	166	4,800	235-hp Lyc. O-540-B1A5	2,000	$10,000

ment of flaps. (Piper finally got around to fixing this in 1976 and subsequent Aztecs. It was never corrected in the Apache.) And in pre-1960 models, the flap speed is fixed at a bothersomely low 87 knots, which requires quite a bit of nose-up trim to achieve in the first place. New pilots would be well-advised to anticipate the nose-up reaction as they reach down (way down on the center pedestal) to hit the flap lever.

In reaching for the trim, however, the new Apache pilot will face another quirky feature: the airplane's overhead crank-type trim knobs (a quaint Piper tradition with airplanes of the time). Let's see now, is it counterclockwise to trim nose-up, or clockwise? And which handle do we want? (There are two trim handles: one for rudder, another for pitch.) It's best to become thoroughly acquainted with this system on the ground, naturally, before tackling single-engine work—or pattern work, for that matter.

Another quirk: with the gear down, the rudder becomes heavier, since the shimmy dampener is a friction collar, which adds a lot of friction to the rudder pedals. This, according to one owner, takes some getting used to during crosswind landings.

The Apache's gear selector—located on the right side of the center pedestal—incorporates an effective (if infuriating to students) safety catch, a kind of thumb-switch that must be moved to the side before the gear lever can be moved upward. If the pilot attempts to yank the lever up without stowing the catch, the lever jams on the catch, and to be freed, the lever must first be lowered at least a half inch. Gear retraction thus takes some effort. (The catch constitutes a mechanical "squat switch," preventing inadvertent retraction of the hydraulic landing gear while on the ground.)

Despite the laudable attempt at making the gear handle difficult to raise while taxiing, Piper's designers for some reason decided to place the flap selector on the left

Aircraft Resale Value Chart

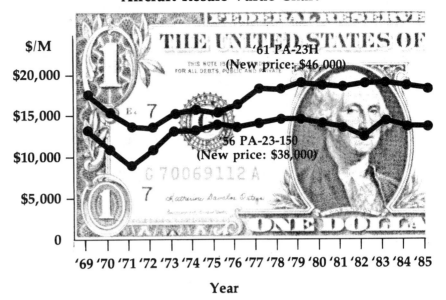

'69 '70 '71 '72 '73 '74 '75 '76 '77 '78 '79 '80 '81 '82 '83 '84 '85

Year

and the gear selector on the right—a nonstandard arrangement that subverts the original intent of the safety catch.

Another annoying gear problem: retraction time, at 11 seconds, is painfully long, particularly if you need the gear up fast in preparation for a single-engine climbout. Depending on which engine you lose, the gear retraction time could actually be 11 seconds or infinity; the hydraulic pump works off the left engine only, and while the pump will still function with the prop windmilling, the drag caused by the windmilling is more than enough to cancel any rate-of-climb gains that would accrue to raising the gear.

The bottom line: if you intend to hold altitude after the left engine fails, you'll need to feather the prop. (It will feather automatically in the event of oil pressure loss, but that's another matter.) At that point, however, you won't be able to raise the gear without pumping it up manually—30 to 40 strokes of the emergency pump handle (located in the center of the control pedestal). By Piper's own estimate, raising the gear this way takes 20 to 30 seconds. In an emergency, that may well be 19 to 29 seconds too long.

Since the flaps are hydraulically actuated, they, too, depend for proper function on the left engine's

turning. But at least here, selecting flaps up while airborne results in the wind blowing the flaps up. (Getting them down again would, of course, require manual operation of the emergency pump handle after left-engine failure.)

Standard equipment on the original Apaches included a single 35-amp generator driven by the left engine, and a single vacuum pump driven off the right engine. Fortunately, most Apaches were delivered with the optional dual generators and dual vacuum pumps, providing an acceptable measure of systems backup—an important part of what light twins are supposedly all about. Still, there are some single-generator, single-pump Apaches flying, and it behooves buyers to screen potential purchases carefully in this regard, particularly if serious instrument work is contemplated.

One other peculiarity that potential Apache buyers would do well to keep in mind: In a recently updated bird with lightweight digital electronics, the 30 pounds or so of avionics power supplies that came in the nose of the plane originally will be gone—leading to possible aft-c.g. loading problems. (The problem is aggravated by the absence, in the Apache and early Aztecs, of a nose baggage compartment. The Apache's baggage area is behind the rear seats.) What's more, the Apache, one owner

warns, does not fly well when tail-heavy.

Safety Record

In a special study by the National Transportation Safety Board of light twin engine failure accidents from 1972 to 1976, the Piper Apache fared very badly, ranking as the airplane (out of 24 light twins studied) having the worst incidence of accidents following engine failure. The actual rate of engine-failure accidents was found to be 6.91 per 100,000 flight-hours—more than triple that of the Twin Comanche, at 1.98 per 100,000 hours, and more than seven times that of the Aztec.

This is not to say that the Apache's *engine-failure rate* is high; there are no statistics on this, since—for one thing—nobody keeps records on how many engine failures occur that *don't* end in an accident. The NTSB study merely says that *if* you lose an engine in an Apache, your chances of crashing are higher than would be the case if you were flying almost any other popular light twin. Why is the Apache's engine-out accident rate so high? Apparently, it has little to do with the aircraft's Vmc (74 knots) or single-engine performance, which are nearly identical to the Aztec's. (The published single-engine ROC figures for the 1981 Aztec F and 1956 Apache 150 are 235 fpm and 240 fpm, respectively.) So why should the Aztec have one-seventh the engine-out accident rate of the Apache? The Safety Board laid blame to the Apache's high power loading (11.8 lbs./hp, versus the

Aztec's 9.6). We tend to think that the airplane's role as multiengine trainer has something to do with it, too.

An *Aviation Consumer* review of NTSB accident statistics covering a recent one-year period revealed that of 42 accidents involving Piper PA-23 aircraft, 16 (or 38 percent) were fatal. Of the fatals, about half involved continued VFR flight into adverse weather, with a surprising number of the pilots instrument-rated. (Three others involved pilot incapacitation for medical reasons.) The nonfatal accidents formed several distinct patterns. Among them: landing overshoots after engine failure (by far the largest category), loss of control after in-flight door opening, and accidents involving botched single-engine climbouts or go-arounds, where the aircraft simply wouldn't gain altitude.

Several gear-up landings were listed in the NTSB's recent records (one of them after total hydraulic failure combined with non-functioning of the emergency CO_2 blow-down system). Ironically, the PA-23's "half-in, half-out" wheel wells—designed specifically to allow tire rubber to cushion the impact of a gear-up landing and thus minimize damage—failed to keep these gear-up incidents out of the "substantial damage" column of the NTSB's accident printouts.

One accident (not fatal) involved a double engine failure over water as the pilot was descending on the auxiliary fuel tanks (which are placarded for level flight only).

Two hours of fuel were left in the mains when the engines quit. The aircraft sank off the coast of Florida.

Carburetor icing shows up with regularity in the NTSB's Piper PA-23 accident reports. The Apache's engines are notorious for breeding venturi ice in humid conditions, and more than one pilot has gone down after *both* engines have begun to run rough from carburetor freeze-up.

If there are lessons to be learned from the PA-23's accident record, they are: [1] Don't lose an engine. But if you do, be ready to land; and be current. [2] Don't even think about executing a go-around with one engine dead. One shot is all you've got. [3] Be ready for the door to pop open at any time—and don't let it bother you (just fly the airplane). [4] Don't climb or descend on auxiliary tanks. [5] Anticipate carburetor ice, and remember that if it comes, it will very likely affect both engines at once.

Airworthiness Directives

Like most aircraft of its vintage, the Apache has racked up quite a number of airworthiness directives over the years (23 on the airframe, nine on the O-320 engine, and sundry other ADs affecting accessories, such as the South Wind heater). Many of these ADs no longer apply. Some, however, are perpetual and repetitive. For example:

AD 63-12-02 requires repetitive 100-hour inspections of elevator butt rib P/N 17058-3 (and its doubler plate) for cracks, until a late-model, improved elevator assembly is installed.

AD 63-26-02 requires repetitive 100-hour visual inspections (and 500-hour dye penetrant inspections) of elevator and rudder castings for cracks. The replacement of affected castings with forgings eliminates the inspection requirement—but many Apaches still have the castings.

AD 71-12-01 mandates 100-hour inspections of a control pedestal support bracket until such time as an improved part is installed.

AD 78-08-03 requires 1,000-hour dye penetrant inspections of upper and lower rudder hinge bracket assemblies. No improved parts are available.

AD 80-18-10 requires 100-hour magnifying glass inspection of fuel control cable and valve assemblies, with mandatory 1,000-hour overhauls of the fuel control unit.

AD 80-26-04 required a beefup of the fuselage structure surrounding the cabin entrance step, with 100-hour inspections of the area thereafter. As it turns out, the portion of fuselage truss to which the cabin step bracket attaches also carries critical rudder cable pulleys; thus, when excess weight is placed on the cabin step, the structure deforms, causing misalignment of the rudder cable pulleys and binding of the rudder. (This AD applies to the Aztec as well.)

A sweeping AD on the PA-23 flap system (AD 81-04-05, revised February 5, 1982) requires repetitive 100-hour inspections of the flap-spar-hinge attachment areas and bellcrank for cracks, as well as one-time beefing up of the flap torque tube bearing block bracket in accordance with Piper Service Bulletin No. 671.

Where the Lycoming O-320 engines are concerned, the most important ADs are probably those affecting the oil pump. A 1973 AD required the replacement of Woodruff-key drive type oil pumps with square-drive components. In 1981, a controversial AD (81-18-04) required the replacement, at 2,000 hours after major overhaul or before, of sintered-iron type oil pump impellers. Almost every engine remanufactured by Lycoming (and quite a few of those overhauled in the field) between 1970 and 1980 got the sintered iron impellers, which have shown a tendency to crumble in extended

Stubby Apache is very unstable with aft center of gravity. Even NASA pilots found it tough to fly instruments under such conditions. Noseheavy, it's okay.

service. (They've been crumbling since 1970, but the problem was masked for years by the Woodruff key drive failures.) Compliance with these ADs is essential; check maintenance records carefully when considering a potential purchase.

Additional ADs have come out targeting combustion heaters made by Stewart Warner and Janitrol. Since all Apaches and Aztecs have either a Stewart Warner or a Janitrol heater, compliance with the repetitive inspection and overhaul requirements of these ADs is mandatory for any Apache owner. Figure on a $400 to $600 heater rebuild every 500 hours.

Parts and Service

Despite the Apache's age and its being out of production for practically two decades, owners report little or no problem obtaining replacement parts. One operator reports that when he needs an Apache part fast, he orders from Seguin Aviation (see below); when time is not of the essence, he orders from Piper.

Direct hourly operating costs in the $30 to $50 range (extremely low for a twin-engine plane) are frequently cited by owners, who lay much of the credit to the Apache's 2,000-hour-TBO Lycoming engines. These engines are, by industry standards, arguably the most reliable and economical to operate of any modern "flat, opposed" aircraft engine. (Note: The 2,000-hour TBO applies only to engines with half-inch valves. A few 7/16-inch valve engines are still in the fleet; these are limited to 1,200 hours be-

tween overhauls. Check engine records carefully.)

The engine cowlings, alas, are something else again. Due to what one owner calls "extremely poor cowl and baffle design," the cowls take a long time to remove for service, and are subject to repeated vibration cracking. Virtually every Apache cowling you come across is riddled with patches and stop-drill holes. (One operator suggests that perhaps this is how the Apache got its name: "You got a patch here, and a patch here, and . . .")

Access to the rest of the plane's systems is relatively good. An A&P owner of a highly customized Apache estimates that he spends 35 hours working on the plane for every 100 hours of flying time. Annuals range from $80 for the A&P-licensed owner with a no-squawks bird . . . all the way to $4,000, in the case of one M.D. who said he brought his many-squawks 1959 model to Seguin for its annuals.

The original Apaches came from the factory with Goodrich expander-tube brakes, which some owners characterize with Walt Disney adjectives. A sizable portion of the Apache fleet has since been converted to Cleveland brakes, however—a definite improvement, maintenance-wise.

The hydraulic power pack was mentioned by some owners as an item occasionally needing work. The most common failure mode involves sticking of the pressure relief valve, and bending of its retainer plates (with no loss of hydraulic fluid or danger of gear-up landing).

Mods and Clubs

A glance at the FAA's *Summary of Supplemental Type Certificates* shows no less than 157 approved STCs for the PA-23 series, covering everything from autopilots to dual brakes (most Apaches have brakes on the pilot's side only) to extra seats and emergency exits—not to mention such more-or-less standard mods as one-piece windshields, added side windows, square wingtips, full wheel enclosures, dorsal fins, long noses, bigger engines, and turbocharging.

The most important Apache modifiers are Nayak Aviation (206 East Terminal Dr., International Airport, San Antonio, Tex. 78216), which offers extra windows, baggage compartments, gross weight increase, and engine mods. J.W. Miller Aviation (P.O. Box 16203, San Antonio, Tex. 78216), with its dual brake mod, one-piece windshield, rear picture window, fiberglass nose mods, wheel well doors, and Franklin engine conversion . . . and, of course, Seguin Aviation (Rt. 1, Box 225, Seguin, Tex. 78155), home of the famous Geronimo conversion. Seguin will sell you individual STC'd kits, or a complete Geronimo treatment with 180-hp engines and a total airframe rebuild. If Seguin doesn't have it—you probably can't get it.

For camaraderie, there's the Flying Apache Association, Inc., 67 Brierbrook, Milton, Mass. 02186. The group, founded in 1978, has about 200 members.

Owner Comments

As the owner of an original Apache with 150-hp engines and no mods, I find the airplane inexpensive to own and operate. It burns 15 gph at what I call high cruise, 135 knots. When I'm not in a hurry, I use a low power setting, getting 117 knots and 14 gph.

The Apache is well known to be a two-engine twin, especially at gross, and I highly agree; however, with only two seats in use and no fuel in the aux tanks, it will actually fly the pattern on one engine (a big pattern), or climb 100 to 150 fpm at 6,500 feet in average temperatures.

The structure of the Apache (and its big brother, the Aztec) are something today's manufacturers have neglected to hold onto. One distinction I can claim, which I'm sure puts me in a small membership, is that I had occasion once to

Apache is notorious for lousy single-engine performance. In the real world, with any load aboard, an Apache will not maintain altitude on one engine.

smash the wings from an Apache (which had crashed in a forest) to dispose of them. My weapon was a 25-ton Northwest crane. Not owning a demolition ball, I used the weight of the crane to crush the wings—or tried to. To my amazement, the crane just crawled up on top of the wing and sat there. I had to be exerting 12½ tons, or half the crane's weight, as I could only get one track on the wing at one time. I stopped the crane, got off, and examined the wing. I hadn't dented it. I was amazed, to use the same adjective twice.

Piper, please don't throw away the fat Hershey-bar wing jigs. Maybe you could turn them over to Seguin Aviation.

I should mention the roominess of the cabin. It is one feature that I certainly enjoy. One bad feature that constantly bothers me, however, is the noise level in the cabin. (Without earphones, I couldn't take it.) I wish someone would come up with a cure.

●

My wife and I have owned a 1958 PA-23-160 since September 1976. We use it both for personal transportation and in our part-time flight instruction business. I am a licensed A&P, and perform almost all maintenance myself.

The most costly maintenance items I've faced, other than prop and engine overhauls, were a cracked engine mount, and welding required to beef up the truss structure in the area of the cabin entry step as required by AD 80-26-04. I have experienced a few problems

with the nosegear downlock mechanism, but I attribute these mainly to the fact that the plane is used as a trainer, cycling the gear all the time.

The hydraulic power pack malfunctioned once, when the main relief valve did not release the pressure surge at the end of the retract cycle and was forced out of its mounting hole, bending the retainer plates. According to John Dean of Midwest Piper in Wichita, that failure mode constitutes 90 percent of all power-pack failures in Apaches and Aztecs.

I purchased a new Southwind heater in 1979, and that unit has been a lemon, requiring repeated cannibalizing of the old heater to keep it going. Since glow plugs burn out quite regularly, it would be advisable to keep spares on hand.

Parts and outside labor probably average $7 an hour for me, and since I do all my own work my annual inspections run around $80 (for the IA to inspect the opened plane and sign the paperwork).

The performance charts in the Owner's Manual probably were written by the marketing department. Single engine performance is a far cry from the book figures (I estimate 70 fpm less than published); the only comfort is that the O-320-B3Bs have an outstanding reliability record, and shouldn't quit in the first place.

Cruise performance is approximately 135 knots true at about 10,000 ft. density altitude, with a fuel flow between 15 and 16 gph. It varies with weight, though, as in any airplane. Cruise increases about one knot for every 100 pounds less weight.

With the Metco tip tanks, the Apache is a two-seater with room for baggage and fantastic range. I've made several flights of almost 10 hours, going nonstop from Wichita to the West Coast bucking 20-25-knot headwinds. No-wind range is around 1,300 nautical, but you better stop at Sears and buy a Port-A-Potty.

Piper Twin Comanche

While it's been over a decade since Piper halted production of the PA-30 and PA-39 series, collectively known as the Twin Comanche, the aircraft continues to soldier on. All told, some 2,150 Twin Comanches rolled off the Lock Haven line in the years 1963-1972.

Anyone searching for a twin with the economics of a single almost — should give the Twin Comanche a closer look. As unveiled in 1963, the Twin Comanche was intended to fill the hole in the general aviation market created by the demise of the PA-32 Apache. In some ways the two aircraft are similar; sharing what was fundamentally the same 160-hp Lycoming O-320-B3B powerplant (except the PA-30's engine was designated the IO-320-B1A, due to the introduction of fuel injection).

History

The Twin Comanche could boast better speed and range with virtually identical cabin capacity as the Apache, and the buying public seemed to appreciate some of the sportier styling features of the new twin. The aircraft rested slightly aft on its tricycle landing gear, and the so-called "tiger shark" engine nacelles and optional wing tip tanks gave it a speedy look A top speed just over 170 knots enhanced the twin's sporty image. Accordingly, the airplane sold well to both private owner/operators and charter/flight school operations.

Tarnished Image

This image was soon to be tarnished by a series of fatal flight training mishaps, bringing to light what came to be called the "stall/spin syndrome." Flight schools came to regard the Twin Comanche as perhaps not the best light twin for training purposes.

Closer inspection revealed the real fault was an over-design of the airplane.

Rather than suffer from a lack of control at low speeds, the Twin Comanche suffered from almost too much. The originally placarded Vmc speed was quite low, due mainly to the airplane's oversized rudder, so low in fact that at low altitudes, Vmc and stall speed were nearly the same. Add to this the fact that FAA was recommending Vmc maneuvers be performed at as low an altitude as possible to take maximum advantage of asymmetric power and that the Twin Comanche's high aspect-ratio wing tends to dump all its lift at once in stall, and the reasons for the series of training accidents becomes clear.

In these low-speed conditions, symmetric lift could roll the airplane suddenly, with a spin a likely result, a maneuver that tends to be terminal at low altitude.

Piper's Fix

Piper took two steps to fix the problem, one voluntary, the other less so. An AD called for the placarded Vmc to be increased to 72 Knots. The company then developed a stall-strip kit which was offered to Twin Comanche customers at no charge. The strip gave more predictable stall performance by ensuring initial flow separation over the inboard wing sections. The strip became standard on the

PA-30 models like this one do not have counter-rotating props like the later PA-39 versions, which improve engine-out traits.

PA-39, the Twin Comanche variant with counter-rotating props.

The Stretch

The year 1966 saw the introduction of the PA-30B, an airplane that can't truthfully be called six-place for anything but the shortest flight because the addition of the extra seating eats up the baggage space and the useful load of 1,390 lbs. allows just a half load of fuel if all six seats are filled and a reasonably equipped instrument panel goes along. An additional window on each side gives these back seat flyers something to look out of.

Also new to the PA-30B were the factory-installed Rajay turbochargers, as was a 125-lb. boost in gross weight to 3,725 lbs. Tip tanks became standard on the turbo Twin Comanches. Rajay Turbochargers were used to normalize the engines' performance, that is, to restore sea-level manifold pressure, not to increase pressure above the normal 30 inches Hg.

The result is that the turbocharged airplanes are no more powerful than normally-aspirated ones and actually sacrifice a small amount of performance until altitudes are reached at which the normally-aspirated plane can no longer manintain 75 percent power. Turbo Twin Comanches are capable of cruise speeds of up to 190 knots at high altitude.

Turbocharging

The Rajay turbocharger installation is straightforward. Each turbo wastegate is controlled directly by a mechanical cockpit handle. A cheap, simple, and generally reliable system, the Rajay turbos impose additional pilot workload due to extra controls and the lack of an automatic controller, allowing major fluctuations in manifold pressure due to changes in airspeed, temperature, or mixture, or the presence of turbulence.

Some readers have reported turbocharger wastegate control cables burning out due to their proximity to exhaust heat. Whatever maintenance glitches turbo Twin Comanche owners do experience, it's a fact that they will have to overhaul their engines slightly more often than owners of their crafts' normally aspirated brethren. TBO is 1,800 for the turbocharged powerplants, 2,000 for the non-blown version.

Wending its way down the Piper production line in 1969, the PA-30C was different in incidental ways from its predecessors. The interior was cleaned up, most noticeably by a new instrument panel with offset radio rack and flight instrumentation in the venerated "sacred six" pattern.

End of the Line

The opening years of the '70s saw the eventual end of the Twin Comanche line. They also saw the creation of the final, and to a lot of Comanche fans, the finest of the line, the PA-39 series. New counter-rotating engines eliminated the critical engine, and marked the beginning of Piper's love affair with this configuration, which would later appear on both the Seneca and Navajo C/R series.

Older Twin Comanches can be converted into counter-rotating aircraft through the purchase and installation of the proper engines, props and related kits from the manufacturer. The prime caveat here is cost. Such an expensive conversion would only be really useful if the aircraft is to be used for instruction.

Performance

Prospective buyers can expect cruise speeds around 165 knots, with a fuel burn of 16-17 gph, although some Twin Comanche owners have reported even leaner burns. This puts the airplane in the same performance class as some single-engine models, all with the benefits of twin-engine flight, although some of those benefits may seem remote when engine overhaul time comes.

As introduced in 1963, the basic Twin Comanche was much like the single-engine Comanche of the period: four-place seating with baggage space aft of the rear seat. Four wing tanks held 90 gallons of fuel; tip tanks could increase that to 120 gallons, 114 of which is usable.

While overall handling for the Twin Comanche is conceded as good, many pilots report somewhat tricky behavior on landings. The airplane shows a marked resistance to greased landings, preferring to pay off with a jolt at the end.

Maurice Taylor, Twin Comanche enthusiast and de facto historian for the International Comanche Society, agreed that landing was often something different in this twin. "The airplane had funny landing characteristics that I think were partly due to its attitude on the landing gear. It sat back on the gear, sort of like a DC-3. That made it difficult to make it a good landing. It would be a safe landing but not a good landing, not a comfortable landing.

"Still, nothing has taken this plane's place. To build something comparable today, well, the cost would just be prohibitive."

Taylor doesn't hesitate when asked about the Twin Comanche's good side. "The airplane has a very good engine. The IO-320 is a reliable engine and one of the first with a 2,000 hr. TBO."

Pricing

Price performance for the Twin Comanche line has become predictable too. A 1969 PA-30C carried a price tag of $52,725. That same aircraft can be had today for about $38,000 inflation-weakened dollars. As shown on the accompanying graph, Twin Comanches have largely leveled off in terms of price in recent years.

When inflation is figured in, the aircraft seems to be trapped in a buyer's market, with sellers taking what they can get. The 1972 vintage PA-39C/R has proved to have

Cost/Performance/Specifications

Model	Year	Average Retail Price	Cruise Speed (kts)	Rate of Climb (fpm)	SE Ceiling	Useful Load (lbs)	Fuel Std/Opt (gals)	Engine	TBO (hrs)	Overhaul Cost (each)
PA-30	1963-65	$27,000	169	1,460	5,800	1,390	90/120	160-hp Lyc. IO-320-B1A	2,000	$8,500
PA-30B	1966-68	$33,000	169	1,460	5,800	1,350	90/120	160-hp Lyc. IO-320-B1A	2,000	$8,500
Turbo B	1966-68	$36,500	194	1,290	19,000	1,317	120	160-hp Lyc. 320-C1A	1,800	$9,250
PA-30C	1969	$38,000	172	1,460	7,100	1,330	90/120	160-hp Lyc. IO-320-B1A	2,000	$8,500
Turbo C	1969	$42,000	209	1,290	17,000	1,309	120	160-hp Lyc. IO-320-C1A	1,800	$9,250
PA-39C/R	1970-71	$41,000	172	1,460	7,100	1,370	90/120	160-hp Lyc. IO-320-B1A	2,000	$8,500
Turbo C/R	1970-71	$46,500	192	1,290	12,600	1,309	120	160-hp Lyc. IO-320-C1A	1,800	$9,250
PA-39C/R	1972	$43,500	172	1,460	7,100	1,370	90/120	160-hp Lyc. IO-320-B1A	2,000	$8,500
Turbo C/R	1972	$48,500	192	1,290	12,600	1,309	120	160-hp Lyc. IO-320-C1A	1,800	$9,250

Aircraft Resale Value Chart

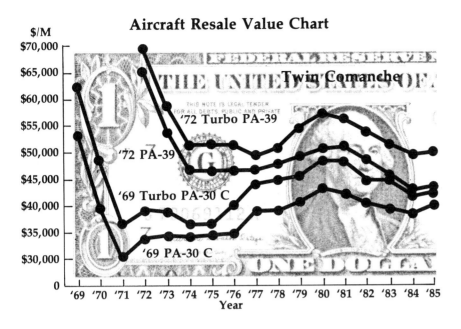

$/M

- $70,000
- $65,000
- $60,000
- $55,000
- $50,000
- $45,000
- $40,000
- $35,000
- $30,000
- 0

Twin Comanche

'72 Turbo PA-39

'72 PA-39

'69 Turbo PA-30 C

'69 PA-30 C

'69 '70 '71 '72 '73 '74 '75 '76 '77 '78 '79 '80 '81 '82 '83 '84 '85
Year

a fairly stable market value in recent years after taking a bit of a nose dive in the years immediately following manufacture. Costing $66,715 new, the 1972 model maintained a fairly steady price until 1984 when it dipped slightly into the low $40,000 neighborhood.

Safety Record

In terms of statistical safety, the Twin Comanche series stacks up as slightly better in some categories, slightly worse in others. In a NTSB study examining the safety performance of 20 light twin models over the years 1972-1976, the Twin Comanche emerged roughly average in terms of fatal accident rates at 1.91 per 100,000 flight hours. Engine failures resulting in fatalities are somewhat rare in this type, a testimonial to the reliability of the IO-320 engine. Just 0.14 deaths per 100,000 flight hours were reported due to engine failures.

On the dark side, however, the NTSB figures show the Twin Comanche well above average in terms of total accidents per 100,000 hrs., with 11.76 mishaps reported, compared to an average to 6.94. But when compared to the fatality figues, it looks like your chances of walking away from a Twin Comanche mishap are better than for a lot of other twins.

Of the 100 more recent Piper PA-

30/PA39 Twin Comanche accidents cited by NTSB between 1977 and 1982, 53 were attributed to conditions unrelated to aircraft systems; i.e pilot error. Of the remaining mishaps, 11 involved failure of the Twin C's landing gear due to mechanical failures of retraction tubes, bent or broken rod-end bearings on main gear, electrical systems failures blamed on excessive alternator wear, landing gear connecting arm failures, and overall electrical power failures.

Even when not beset by internal woes, the Twin Comanche's legs proved somewhat shaky in the sort of rough landings the aircraft is notorious for, with ground-loops, hard landings and over-shoots racking up 12 Twins. Gear retractions and collapses of undetermined cause resulted in seven more mishaps.

A handful of Twin Comanche accidents were attributed to miscellaneous causes. A fire in flight and a fire on the ground claimed an aircraft apiece, while engine-out situations downed five Twins. One broke up in a thunderstorm, while another became the victim of a triple threat: an alcohol-impaired, VFR-only pilot who took off into IFR conditions and broke up in a thunderstorm.

Airworthiness Directives

Indeed, evidence of the

powerplant's reliability is given in the small number of ADs dealing with it, even the turbocharged version. By far the bulk of Twin Comanche ADs focus on the airframe. In them are a number of potentially expensive structural notes, including replacement of the nose gear actuator tube, rebalancing of the stabilator, inspection/replacement of the stabilator torque tube bearings, and beefing up the aileron nose bulkheads. A 1983 AD calls for inspection of the lower spar cap for damage and possible cracks where the spar enters the fuselage at the lower wing root fairing.

Service Difficulties

As far as service problems go, the Twin Comanche has a number of trouble points that bear watching. Structural ADs have dogged the aircraft almost from its inception, and the situation bears even more careful monitoring as the fleet ages further. Reports from the field indicate the aileron spars are especially fragile components, with cracks developing under the hinge brackets.

An AD (77-08-01) deals with the problem, but cracks have been detected even after the notice has been complied with. That particular AD called for the fitting of replacement hinge brackets, after which the 100-hr. inspections are dispensed with. Reports would indicate, however, that continued examination of the area is the safest route to travel.

Watch Those Fuel Pumps

Fuel pumps seem to come and go quickly in some Twin Comanches. According to one report, a total of 15 pumps from six airplanes had to be replaced. One aircraft went through five pumps! Most failures happened within a few hours of overhaul, blamed on the lower parting surface on the pump, which leaks. One leaking pump resulted in an aircraft fire.

Similar complaints have come in from the field on fuel pumps in general. Frequent failures have been cited among pumps that apparently have been sitting on parts shop shelves for extensive periods—eight years in one case. While the shelf life of parts with rubber components depends to a large extent on the storage techniques, wise buyers will check the dates on both new and rebuilt parts.

Engine Mounts

Corrosion problems in engine mounts have become a serious matter, especially on the turbo Twins, where exhaust heat tends to waken the metal. Heat fatigue on engine mounts has been reported on the normally aspirated models as well.

Reports indicate a number of other spots to watch, such as: resin leaks on the magneto coil due to overheating; burned or cracked heat exchangers, the subject of an AD that requires a 500-hr. overhaul many Twin C owners find expensive and troublesome; and problems with the spinners on the Twin C's Hartzell props.

Useful Options

Among the most useful options are the tip tanks, prop de-ice (although prospective owners should be cautioned that the Twin Comanche is not certificated for flight into conditions of known icing), and avionics packages such as factory-installed three-axis fully coupled autopilots.

Miller Mods

J.W. Miller Aviation, Inc. at Horseshoe Bay Airport, Box 7757, Marble Falls, Tex. 78654, (512) 598-2556, is a major source for Twin Comanche mods, leading off with a 200-hp Lycoming powerplant to give the Twin a real kick in the pants: 174-knot cruise, 1,900 fpm climb along with 500 fpm single-engine climb. Price tag will come to $53,000 for the normally aspirated, $56,511 for turbos, and the mod comes with a dorsal fin and new cowlings.

Miller also offers a nose job for the Piper twin, only this one adds to the plane's proboscis, instead of subtracting from it. The new nose

Miller modification adds a swoopy new snoot and bigger 200-hp engines. Cruise speed is well over 200 mph.

affords seven cubic feet of baggage space capable of accommodating 130 pounds of baggage for $4,855. Nacelle baggage lockers from Miller can hold 75 pounds apiece, and cost $5,085 for both. Those who want to give a Twin Comanche longer legs can get the integral fuel tanks that boost fuel capacity by 38 gallons (19 gallons each in two separate tanks) while adding 180 pounds to the aircraft, and deducting $8,900 from the owner's bankroll.

R/STOL Systems

Up in Everett, Wash., R/STOL Systems offers a STOL mod that gives PA-30s and 39s some rather muscular capabilities, such as a 40 percent overall reduction in takeoff and landing rolls. Costing $9,000, the R/STOL mod allows a PA-30 to clear a 50-foot obstacle in 1,120 feet, a PA-39 in 1,050. Approach speeds can be as low as 65 knots, down from the standard 78 to 82 knots for this type. Vmc for the STOL-modified Twin Comanche is back where it once was, at 70 knots.

An earlier AD issued to R/STOL on the mod called for a cable to replace a bungee cord used for flap retraction. Piper used the bungee cord as original equipment but failure of the cord in a R/STOL mod left the aircraft in a dangerously symmetrical flap configuration. Failure of the cord in a stock Twin Comanche still leaves the aircraft with sufficient roll control in the eyes of the FAA.

Knots 2U

If Twin Comanche owners want to boost the performance of their

birds without resorting to brute force, they can turn to the service of Knots 2U, Inc., a company specializing in slicking up older airplanes. The Knots 2U mod comes in several parts, and all or part can be installed, either by the owner in kit form, or by professionals.

Gap seals for the ailerons and flaps cost $1,050 for the kit and will come to $1,450 installed. Wing root fairings are $355/kit and $425/installed and a removable dorsal fin hiding a pair of comm antennas is $1,080/installed or $895 for the do-it-yourselfer. Neither of these last two mods is approved for use on R/STOL twins. Installation of the antennae themselves is another $450.

Additional mods cover areas of high aerodynamic drag, such as the engine nacelle exhaust ports ($980/kit, $1,350/installed).

Knots 2U also has a one-piece windshield for the Twin Comanche that extends nine inches further into the roofline for better visibility. It is one-quarter-inch thick and tinted and costs $950 for the kit or $1,900 installed.

And what does all this buy the Twin Comanche flyer? Improved performance overall, some more docile behavior on landing, some eight to 12 knots better cruise speed, along with the better handling that entails a 200 to 300 fpm increase in climb speed, along with slightly better fuel consumption.

Knots 2U, Inc. is at 1941 Highland Ave., Wilmette, Ill. 60091, (312) 256-4807.

Maintenance Expert

Those looking for the ultimate maintenance guru for their aging Twin Comanche need look no farther than Robert Gift of Lock Haven Airmotive, Lock Haven, Pa., (717) 748-5820. Gift was service manager at Piper at the time of Twin Comanche production and is widely acknowledged as the expert in type.

The Society

For a good, eclectic (if not exactly impartial) information source on the Twin Comanche, get in touch with the International Comanche Society. While ICS's main concern is the single-engine cousin of the Twin, they also list a large number of Twin enthusiasts in their ranks. Home for the ICS is Box 468, Lyons, Kans. 67554. Telephone (316) 257-5138. Don't be put off if the person answering the phone doesn't immediately identify the place as the ICS; the organization shares office space with a print shop.

Owner Comments

I have owned a 1963 PA-30 for six years. It is by far the most reliable, cost effective aircraft I have ever owned or even been near. Cruise at 65 percent power, peak EGT, is 15 knots while burning 13.5 gph total. None of the new light twins can come close, and they are built like Spam cans; the PA-30 is solid. And it only cost me $27,000 in 1977! With the standard tanks (84 gals.) zero wind range is about 800 nautical miles with an hour's reserve.

If you are thinking of buying a PA-30/39 or a PA-24, you should join the International Comanche Society. Their monthly magazine, the *Comanche Flyer*, contains much useful information on both the

singles and twins. There is also a compilation of past information called "Tips" which can be purchased.

Keith F. Kelly, Jr.
Dallas, Tex.

Growing up in Lock Haven, I watched the development of the PA-30 with more than casual interest, spent a lot of time in them, was involved in the manufacture and new model refinements in the late '60s early '70s, disagreed strongly with the decision to curtail its production, and recently was a part-owner of a 1968 Turbo Twin Comanche.

Therefore, my comments might be somewhat prejudiced. However, I believe that the Twin Comanche remains one of the best airplanes every built by Piper; certainly one of the prettiest planes in the sky, fast, economical and a delight to fly, but it is not a toy. It is a small, high-performance airplane that must be flown as such.

For what it's worth, I've listed what stand out to me as the major pluses and minuses of the Twin Comanche:

Pluses:
Ecomony—both operating and maintenance. Quiet cabin—even by today's standards. Performance—especially cruise and takeoff performance. Appearance. Simple systems—fuel, landing gear, flaps, fresh air. Very solid construction, especially the wing spars. Easy access to the engines for maintenance. Flat, uncluttered floor. C.G. range and load carrying capability. Responsive, well-balanced controls. Convenient

Turbo Twin Comanche is beloved for high speed, economy, and purring quiet, but watch out for those pesky Rajay turboes.

storage areas under front seats. Stable platform for instrument flying. Range. Those sleek, low-drag cowls. Handy check lists and power setting charts on visors.

Minuses:
Landing characteristics, especially with full flaps. Lack of easy access to engines for preflight. Stall characteristics. Visibility, especially compared to newer aircraft. S/E performance. Heavy nose gear steering on ground. Props that don't like to stay in synch. The instrument panel is busy, crowded, poorly arranged in early models and has too many placards. Fresh air inlets are noisy and inadequate on hot days.

With regard to service and support, our experiences were that Piper still supports the airplane quite well with sheet metal and interior items. However, when we checked on buying new engine mounts, both the price and the lead time were prohibitive. The main problem areas, though, are vendor-supplied parts and systems, such as the STCd turbocharger, avionics and the heater.

After all these years, the Twin Comanche remains one of, if not the most, efficient twin-engine aircraft available. It has its faults and must be flown with respect. It is so clean that it can pick up speed quite rapidly in even a shallow dive, and with its abrupt stall characteristics, maintaining proper airspeeds on approach and in the pattern is a must. Nevertheless, it is a pleasure

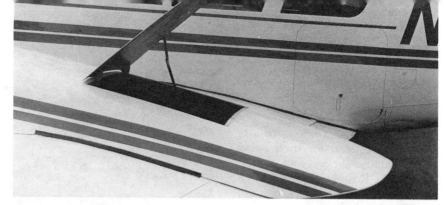

to fly and certainly one of the most economical and practical cross-country planes for one to four people ever produced.

John R. Piper
Culver, Kans.

I have been the owner of a 1971 PA-39 (counter-rotating prop) model for two-and-one-half years. This is my third Comanche over a 15-year period, starting in 1968 with the PA 24-180 model, upgrading to the 250 and then the Twin. My experience with Comanche Singles' excellent reliability, comfort, load carrying ability, simplicity of systems, and cost effectiveness continues, with the PA-39 Twin.

My aircraft has 1,530 hours total time, the cylinder heads have never been off, and the original engines are running perfectly with no less than 73 lbs. pressure per cylinder. Oil consumption is reasonable for engines with over 1,500 hours, averaging one quart (per engine) for every 10-12 flight hours.

In terms of range and flexibility, I've found this aircraft to be nothing short of fantastic. With 120 gallons total fuel capacity (tip tanks), practical range exceeds seven hours duration and 1,300 miles, leaving a reasonable 15-17 gallon fuel reserve. Maximum range (reflecting speed improvements due to the Knots-2U installation) is about 1,550 miles. Trying for max range is too much for my constitution, but it is nice to know when planning 1,300-mile legs that there's lots of reserve.

Regarding the Knots-2U installation, performed by Jim Bradshaw's group, the results are exceptional for what I consider to be a very fair installation price and quality workmanship. I spent approximately $2,000 to have the aileron/flap gap seals and the wing-root speed fairing installed in 1982. An accurate estimate of the increased airspeed is six knots. Together with a very capable 17,000-hour total time instructor, I have put this plane through its

Miller mod also offers nacelle baggage bins. No worries about balance; they're located very near the center of gravity.

paces in all flight regimens. As a result of the Knots-2U installation, it typically exceeds the manufacturer's specification by 30-40 fpm for single-engine rate of climb, and the power-off stall speed appears to be reduced by at least a knot or two.

Another important result of the Knots-2U installatiion is marked improvement of landing characteristics. While my total Twin Comanche time is only 250 hours, I have over 2,000 hours in single-engine Comanches which, with controlled release of manual flaps, could always be brought in for a smooth landing. The Twin Comanche, however, is somewhat more difficult to "grease in," particularly with full-flap settings. My instructor, and other high-time Twin Comanche pilots I know, either use half-flap settings to achieve smooth landing consistently or resign themselves to about a 50/50 chance of pre-landing stalls six to eight inches above the runway.

Dropping it in form a height of six to eight inches should have minimal impact on the longevity of the landing gear, but is not a great way to impress your passengers. As a consequence of the Knots-2U installation, I can count on a perfect landing 95 percent of the time with half flaps and with full flaps and careful speed control, ("a steady 82 knots on the final approach seems best"), I can get a greaser about 75 percent of the time. Prior to the Knots-2U installation, I had given up on full flap landings except in short-field situations where I was willing to accept the minor adverse consequences.

As to speed, I can consistently rely on 168-170-knot cruise speeds at 6,000-8,000-foot altitudes with a fuel burn of about 17 gallons per hour. For more range, I use lower power settings and get about 160 knots on 15 gph. I have met other Twin Comanche pilots who contend they get similar speeds burning up to two gallons per hour less fuel, but I do try to run the engines at 25%-50% below peak EGT.

I bought this aircraft for $42,000 in 1981 and have put approximately $18,000 of capital improvements into it for new paint, interior, avionics, etc. While I had expected to buy a set of new engines, my mechanic informs me that Twin Comanches typically run to their 2,000 hour TBO and advised me to stick with the existing engines since compression tests, oil analysis, and overall operating performance indicate that they are in perfect condition.

Considering the extra fun of flying a twin ("fist-full of throttles/macho syndrome"), the reliability of those little Lycomings, the high airspeed in relation to the horse-power/fuel consumption equation, etc., I am exceptionally pleased with the Twin Comanche. There is no new light twin on the market that can match the fuel economy, performance, range and flexibility even at three to four times my total investment. When you have something as good as the Twin Comanche, why switch? I would advise anyone interested in a PA-30 or -39 to hurry out to buy one before that flying public wakes up to their exceptional value, and the remaining number get bid up substantially compared to today's bargain basement prices.

Joseph E. Sichler
Simsbury, Conn.

Piper Seneca

As heir apparent to the Twin Comanche, the Piper PA-34 Seneca has been an enormous marketing success since it burst upon the scene in 1972. But used-plane buyers should be aware that there's a difference of night and day between the models that were built before and after 1975.

The first Seneca had normally aspirated Lycomings in blunt nacelles. Handling qualities were quite deficient.

The pre-1975 models had no turbo-charging and possessed an absurdly low single-engine ceiling along with what many pilots regard as abominable handling characteristics both in the air and on the ground. Coupled with short range and a lackluster payload, these qualities made the airplane ripe for a wholesale redesign.

Piper came through with just that in the 1975 model, by replacing the four-cylinder Lycoming IO-360s with turbocharged six-cylinder Continental TSIO-360s. This provided the Seneca with a more than respectable single-engine ceiling, a significant increase in payload — and better aesthetics, to boot, since the new powerplants were housed in much better looking streamlined cowls.

On top of that, the aircraft's control system was modified to eliminate its awkward handling characteristics.

Nevertheless, the newer Continental powerplants have not been without their problems, and they have received mixed reviews from owners and maintenance and overhaul shops.

The Early Models

The 1972 Seneca first on the scene was an ill suited adaptation of the Cherokee Six fuselage and wings to multi configuration. The nose gear steering was ponderously heavy, partly because the rudder was tied in with the aileron system, and every time the pilot kicked in left or right rudder, the ailerons responded as well, adding to the tug on the pedals.

This characteristic, engineered to satisfy the need to be able to raise a wing in flight with the rudders alone, gave the aircraft equally ponderous flight controls. The aircraft was at its worst in turbulent IFR work and in gusty crosswind landings, when the pilot could find himself banking left and right in great pendulum swings, as he attempted to keep the wings level.

Promoted as an ideal, simple step-up machine for single-engine pilots, the early Senecas were anything but that.

To make up for a serious deficiency in load-carrying ability, Piper in thh 1973 model pulled a mostly paper-work exercise that boosted the gross and useful load by 200 pounds, but it did so at the sacrifice of an already low single-engine ceiling — which dropped from 5,200 feet to 3,650 feet.

A Rash of Fixes

The pre-75 models also were plagued with potentially expensive fixes that unleashed a series of service letters, bulletins and Airworthiness Directives. The main landing gear support structure was hit with such an AD in '73 and the outer wing spars in '74.

Piper came out with kits allowing installation of skin and rib reinforcement doublers in '74 after "wing skin irregularities" were found under the wings outboard of the main landing gear wells in some aircraft. They also brought out a reinforcement kit to buttress the aft wing assembly after cracks were found at the juncture of the main landing gear with the aft false spar.

An exhaust system that turned up serious cracking problems was replaced in '73 by a completely new, "vastly superior" (said Piper) exhaust system of longer life, that eliminated the repetitive inspections required on the earlier system. This was offered as a retrofit.

During the first year of operation, some Senecas also were found to have loose balance weight assemblies on the stabilator tips, and an AD was issued on this. There have since been at least two, and possibly three Seneca crashes due to stabilator failure. (Incidentally, Piper's first prototype Seneca crashed during testing when the stabilator failed.)

In 1975 the usable fuel dropped form 95 to 93 gallons, and it was found that possible rough finish on the landing gear oleo struts might have been causing the struts to bind, putting extra load on the wing in landing, and causing wing cracks.

Buyers looking at the older model Senecas should keep all these pointers in mind during their inspection of the aircraft.

The New II — A Whole New Ballgame

The 1975 Seneca II wrought major changes in the flying personality of the airplane. The turbocharged Continentals removed the onus of the low single-engine ceiling and boosted it up to 13,400 feet. The powerful downspring that made the original Seneca awkward in the landing flare was replaced by a less potent one and a bobweight. Also, the rudder-aileron interconnect was removed, and a bungee smoothed out rudder steering during taxi. Furthermore, lateral control was improved by lengthening the ailerons.

Whereas the original Lycoming-powered model had seemed extremely noisy and vibration-prone, the new Continental package quieted and smoothed things down significantly. The "poor-man's" automatic turbo control also made its debut on this airplane. Equipped with a simple bypass valve and an overboost relief valve, it eliminated the need for a sophisticated automatic wastegate. However, at the same time, it demanded more attention from the pilot on takeoff to prevent excess spoolup as the throttles were advanced. In addition, the manifold pressure was extremely sensitive to minor changes in rpm, airspeed and altitude; consequently, precise

power management could be a real chore. This, of course, compounded the problems of pilots transitioning from singles, though the handling qualities of the aircraft were greatly improved.

Along with a jump in gross weight, the Seneca II offered an additional 186 pounds in useful load which the airplane desperately needed to take advantage of its truly commodious six-place cabin and 200-pound baggage capacity.

Pilots should be aware, however, that the Seneca II has a zero fuel weight limitation of 4,000 pounds. Therefore, anything above 4,000 pounds, up to the 4,570-pound gross weight must be in fuel only, not people or baggage.

In 1982, Piper spruced up the airplane once more and called it the Seneca III. Changes were not quite so dramatic as in the changeover from I to II, but the improvements were nevertheless worthwhile: an engine uprate that increased power from 200 hp to 220 hp, a 180-pound increase in gross weight, a wing beefup that increased the zero-fuel weight to a more reasonable 4,400 pounds, and a new windshield, along with other minor improvements.

Loading

A nice feature of the Seneca's baggage loading format is that half can be loaded in the nose compartment to ease weight and balance problems if need be. And everyone who talks about the airplane give high

marks to the both-sides, front-and-rear door configuration for loading and unloading of people and cargo. Also, club seating adds a little variety to the passenger format.

High Safety Marks

The National Transportation Safety Board's comparative accident figures show the Seneca to have the lowest fatal accident rate of seven popular classes of twins surveyed. Its total accident rate, however, placed it right in the middle of the pack.

If any one category of problem dominates the NTSB accident roster from 1971-1975, it is collapsing landing gear. Out of 57 reports, 15 dealt with this. Some of them were attributed to simple overload failures because of hard landings, or landing hot and attempting to turn off at too high a speed, but several were tracked to component failure.

The nose gear grag link bolt failed or was pulled from its fittings in two of these accidents.

The second largest problem area was related to engine failure or diminished power output from one or both engines — with 10 of those reported. On no less than four of these, dual instruction was involved, where the flight instructor yanked the mixture on one engine, and a problem developed on a go-around. In one case the wrong sparkplugs were used, and in another there was a problem relating to valves and plugs.

Cost/Performance/Specifications

Model	Year Built	Number Built	Cruise Speed (kts)	Rate of Climb (fpm)	S.E. Service Ceiling (ft)	Useful Load (lbs)	Fuel (gals)	Engine	TBO (hrs)	Overhaul Cost	Average Price
PA-34-200	1972	360	163	1,460	5,200	1,414	93	200-hp Lyc. IO-360-C1E6	1,400	$ 9,000	$ 29,000
PA-34-200	1973	353	163	1,360	3,650	1,614	93	200-hp Lyc. IO-360-C1E6	1,400	$ 9,000	$ 32,000
PA-34-200	1974	214	163	1,360	3,650	1,614	93	200-hp Lyc. IO-360-C1E6	1,400	$ 9,000	$ 36,000
PA-34-200T	1975	327	177	1,340	13,400	1,800	93	200-hp Cont. TSIO-360-E	1,400	$11,000	$ 49,000
PA-34-200T	1976	371	177	1,340	13,400	1,800	93	200-hp Cont. TSIO-360-E	1,400	$11,000	$ 54,000
PA-34-200T	1977	433	177	1,340	13,400	1,800	93/123	200-hp Cont. TSIO-360-E	1,400	$11,000	$ 59,000
PA-34-200T	1978	474	177	1,340	13,400	1,800	93/123	200-hp Cont. TSIO-360-E	800	$11,000	$ 67,000
PA-34-200T	1979	530	177	1,340	13,400	1,800	93/123	200-hp Cont. TSIO-360-E	800	$11,000	$ 78,000
PA-34-200T	1980	367	177	1,340	13,400	1,800	93/123	200-hp Cont. TSIO-360-E	800	$11,000	$ 87,000
PA-34-200T	1981	85	177	1,340	13,400	1,800	93/123	200-hp Cont. TSIO-360-E	800	$11,000	$105,000
PA-34-200T	1982	179	177	1,400	12,300	1,900	93/123	200-hp Cont. TSIO-360-KB	1,800	$11,500	$150,000
PA-34-200T	1983	115	177	1,400	12,300	1,900	93/123	200-hp Cont. TSIO-360-KB	1,800	$11,500	$180,000
PA-34-200T	1984	178	177	1,400	12,300	1,900	93/123	200-hp Cont. TSIO-360-KB	1,800	$11,500	$210,000

On the older Senecas two pilots were distracted enough by a cabin door opening in flight to crash. One occurred on an aborted take-off; the other forgot to put the gear down before landing. The newer Senecas have improved door latches.

Powerplant Record

The Seneca's II's weak spot is engine reliability. The Continental TSIO-360 with the fixed wastegate has not proved very reliable in the field, suffering a number cylinder and valve problems related to over-heating. (The same engine in the Turbo Arrow and Turbo Dakota has a poor record, partly due to the very poor cooling in those aircraft.) At high altitudes, it also suffers from magneto misfiring. (Piper steadfastly refuses to install pres-surized magnetos, as Mooney did with its 231, which also uses the TSIO-360.) And finally, the TSIO-360 has had more than its share of broken crankshafts and oil pump drives.

A review of FAA service difficulty reports showed that of the 135 Seneca engine problems listed in the FAA's tally (usually estimated to be about 10 percent of the total number of problems actually experienced in the field), the largest portion (26) were related to electrical system failures — like condensers, capacitors, leads, coils, etc. The second largest group was attributed to cylinder failures and cracks (16). The third stemmed from turbo problems with scrolls, housings, brackets, etc. (9). And the fourth was directed at scarred or damaged pistons (6). Four broken crankshafts were reported, but in 1977 the Piper factory issued a service bulletin calling attention to the fact that there had been 12 engine stoppages due to "techni-cally unexplained" crankshaft frac-tures. There were two reports of cracked crankcases on the Seneca IIs (out of a fleet of about 1,600 air-craft flying).

Dipstick Mystery

One strange problem that surfaced in connection with the Seneca en-

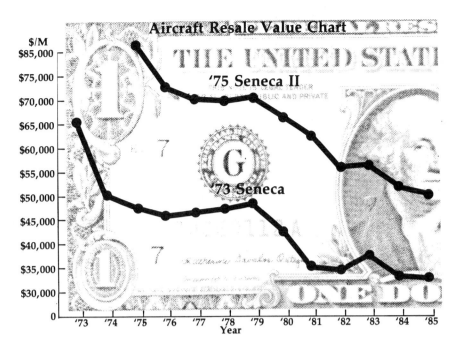

gines concerned oil dipstick cali-bration. Two Seneca II owners had notified us to complain that their dipsticks registered a quart and a half or so too little, which led ser-vice personnel to put in too much oil. Four reports of incorrect dip-stick calibration were also listed on the FAA's Service Difficulty run-down of Seneca IIs.

Each pilot who contacted us noted he had become involved with Piper and Continental in a heated discus-sion of the problem, and that they were concerned about engine dam-age from overloading with oil because of the incorrectly registered dipsticks.

One engine maintenance expert we contacted, however, volun-teered that the problem might stem from the fact that the Senecas have different dipsticks for left and right powerplants. This is because the wings have such a pronounced di-hedral; and since the dipstick is mounted on the left side on each engine, each has to measure a dif-ferent oil level.

He speculated that the engines might occasionally come from the factory with the wrong dipsticks installed.

As for whether too much oil could damage the engine or would simp-ly be thrown out of the breather harmlessly, our mechanic pointed out: "Too much oil is no good.

Your crankshaft thrashes around in the oil, and bubbles and aerates it, so the oil pump picks up air and oil rather than pure oil. You can burn up an engine by putting in too much oil, since air is not a very good lubricant."

Mechanic's Nightmare

The judgment of other mechanics and overhaul shops was that the TSIO-360 powerplant was, in general, a nice, smooth running engine. One powerplant instructor at an air university though, in-sisted that the design posed a prob-lem when things went wrong.

"It's a tough little engine to work on," he said. "It's cramped and nothing fits — it's just a mechanic's nightmare. If it starts giving you trouble, the repair bill looks like the gross national product."

He attributed the electrical acces-sory problems noted on the Service Difficulty list to the engine being "tightly cowled and tightly baf-fled, with a lot of heat built up in-side."

Some mechanics figured the cyl-inder and piston problems could be traced to pushing the engine too hard for prolonged periods under turbo boost. For that matter, fleet operators we talked to shared the opinion that the aircraft as a whole was not built ruggedly enough to be pushed too hard in commercial operations, though it seemed to stand up satisfactorily for personal use.

Among idiosyncrasies that turned up in our interviews was one complaint that the alternators put out too little power at low taxi rpms "to do the job," and the comment of one mechanic that it was necessary to reinforce the fiberglass area behind the spinner on the nose cowl because it seemed to have a tendency to crack.

Seneca II engines also are noted for cold-weather starting problems. To tackle this, Piper first issued special starting instructions for pilots, and then came out with an optional cold-weather priming kit for the aircraft.

Resale Value

As might be expected, the resale value curves for the pre- and post-'75 Seecas are quite different. The average '73 Seneca, for example, dropped almost $16,000 the first year whereas a '75 Seneca II could be expected, on the average, to lose only around $13,000. On top of that, where the '73 model bottomed in four years, the '75 model started back up in resale value after only three years.

Modifications

There are two major modifications available for the Seneca. Laminar Flow Systems, Box 8557, St. Thomas, U.S. Virgin Islands 00801 (809) 775-5515, sells an aerodynamic clean-up mod consisting of aileron and flap gap seals, flap track fairings, wing rivet fairings and wheel well fairings. The mod increases speed by 15-20 mph. (Speed gain is less if the airplane is equipped with de-ice boots, which prevents the use of the leading-edge wing rivet fairings.) The LFS mod can be applied to any model Seneca. Cost is $3,000 for the kit. Installation can run another $1,500 or so.

For the Seneca II and III, Turbo-plus, Inc., Gig Harbor, Wash. (800) 742-4202, sells an engine mod kit that includes an intercooler, im-proved induction system, pressurized ignition system and an uprate to the 220-hp standard for the Seneca II. It also sells speedbrakes. Cost for the complete mod is $15,210 installed, although it may be purchased piecemeal.

Owner Comments

We flew our Seneca 2,500 hours in three years with a total cost of $30,000 in maintenance costs. We lost six jugs; three were replaced under warranty, but we paid for the other three. At 1,400 hours, we lost the right engine. I examined it when it was torn down, and there had been detonation. Continental said those engines were over-boosted. We ended up rebuilding both, at a cost by Reading Air Service of $14,511. After that our engine maintenance went to nil.

•

We had problems with the dip-sticks reading incorrectly. To get the dipstick to read 6 1/4 quarts, you had to put eight quarts in the engine. This could be a real hazard because if you put too much oil in, you can bend the rods.

•

Lost nine jugs in 1,600 hours — average cost, $600 per jug.

Overall utility of my '77 Seneca II is superb. It handles well both on the ground and in the air. Control forces are quite well balanced. I like the way Seneca is off and running in short order, climbing at a solid 1,200 to 1,500 fpm. Landings require slightly more patience.

The not-so-good news includes difficulty maintaining level pitch attitude in cruise configuration. This is especially annoying when accompanied by moderate to strong winds and thermal updrafts. Level pitch trim is particularly elusive at high altitudes. The only other substantial 'handling' complaint is a tendency to yaw in turbulence — a particularly nauseating event for the rear-most passengers.

Also, zero-fuel weight limitation could be a problem for heavy haulers. Seating comfort is quite good with the exception of the rear-most seats (club configuration) which are much to 'low'.

Visibility in most directions (with the possible exception of rearward) is very satisfactory. All in all I'm very pleased with this plane's capabilities.

The bad news could be categorized under engine instrumentation and avionics interference, with the latter perhaps related to an alternator or voltage regulator. The most bothersome problem is the sensitivity and continuous discrepancy of engine instrument indications. Uneven surges in manifold pressure needles (even with slow, smooth power applications), and splits in fuel flow indicators are enough to drive even a seasoned pilot up a wall. Continuous engine adjustment and smooth power application seem to be an absolute must.

An incessant 'buzzing' drone on the ADF audio and also the radios (test mode) is currently among the trouble-shooting list items, with alternators and/or voltage regulators as chief suspects. Other irritants include heater malfunction, generator popping off line, voltage spikes (suspect strobe package), faulty operation of optional fuel primer button (for start-up), a precessing DG (suspect bad bearings).

Most of these items are being or have been 'diagnosed' by one or more fixed-base repair shops with limited corrective success. I've gotten fair to good cooperation from the factory on suggestions as to how to solve these glitches, but I'm becoming more impatient with each passing day.

For a new aircraft (375 hours), I've had more than my share of headaches. Were it not for my appreciation for the overal utility of this bird, I'd be driven stark raving mad!

Used Aircraft Guide

Cessna Skymaster 337

Cessna's most ingenious aircraft, the 337 Skymaster, is one of aviation's greatest paradoxes. As a used-plane, it's both a great buy and a washout. Conceived as the safest twin flying, the 337 is probably one of the biggest used multi bargains to be found, since prices are quite low. But as an investment, the Skymaster is a flop. Values don't level off and eventually rise with inflation; they simply slide down a great toboggan run. And maintenance complaints are fairly high.

Although the recipient of some of Cessna's most intriguing technical innovations — like centerline thrust and pressurization — the Skymaster somehow never made it as a smashing success, for reasons the company often pondered in the past. One popular theory is that so "safe" an airplane loses macho appeal to pilots.

Another theory is simply that the Skymaster doesn't go as fast as multiengines are supposed to. Since the 337 started life as a competitor to the Piper Twin Comanche with a mere 190-mph cruise as an economy twin, it has never been endowed with big enough engines to make it more of a demon speedster, and pull it out of the performance doldroms.

Aside from lackluster speed, the Skymaster suffers also from the lack of a genuine baggage compartment. The rear of the cabin can be devoted either to a fifth and sixth seat, or to baggage. A lower fuselage baggage pod can be added on at the cost of only a modicum of speed, but at the sacrifice of looks.

Centerline Thrust

The Skymaster's major rationale, of course, is elimination of the asymmetrical thrust problems of single-engine operation. Lose an engine on a Skymaster on climbout, and even at low speeds the aircraft won't twist irresistibly to one side or the other at high power settings. On one engine, however, the Skymaster at gross is no zephyr, even at sea level, since it will eke out a climb rate (on the normally aspirated model) of no greater than 235 to 300 fpm on the front engine, and slightly better on the rear one — provided the pilot feathers the right prop and cleans up the aircraft.

The shortage of muscle from just one engine to push the 337 around is impressed upon any pilot who puts the aircraft through its paces with one out, both in the air and on the ground. Lose a fan during taxi,

Skymasters should be the safest twins flying, but NTSB figures disclose a calamitous accident record. U.S. production of the aircraft stopped in 1980.

especially on the grass, and it takes a surprising blast of power on the live engine to keep the Skymaster's bulk moving.

This is not to suggest the Skymaster is a cumbersome, awkward airplane under normal circumstances with both engines operating. Though it takes a ponderous heave to rotate on takeoff, once airborne the aircraft has more facile ailerons than most twins though it possesses the usual heavy Cessna pitch pressures. Most pilots also come to regard the aircraft as a kind of poor-man's STOL, and the airplane is no slouch at getting in and out of tight spaces. Visibility is surprisingly good for a twin, since the wing is set back quite far from the pilot, and there are no engine nacelles out on the wings to obscure an airport on downwind.

Safety

As, theoretically, the safest twin around, the Skymaster received lots of unfavorable publicity and lawsuits a few years back when it was found that pilots were occasionally losing an engine (the rear one, usually) on takeoff roll, and continuing the takeoff attempt with awkward results, not realizing they'd lost a fan, or perhaps not caring.

Early models had a warning light to tell pilots when an engine had failed, activated by torque changes. Proper takeoff technique is to advance the throttle for the rear engine first to make sure everything's working, and then feed in the front engine. A placard mandated by an AD warns pilots not to take off on one engine, if they didn't know.

Another AD required raising the idle speed of the rear engine, so it would be less likely to poop out on takeoff, and pilots were told to taxi mainly by using the rear engine, to keep it warmed up and ready.

A 1979 National Transportation Safety Board study of light twin-engine aircraft accidents showed the Cessna Skymaster had the third worst fatal accident rate of 20 aircraft, after the Beech 18 and the Aero Commander 500, 520 and 560 series. In an attempt to isolate accident causes, we inspected a five-year rundown of accident briefs on the Skymaster from 1973 to 1977.

This examination showed that of the 29 fatal accidents reported during the period the greatest number — seven — were caused by weather related problems. One might reason that perhaps less-experienced pilots tend to migrate toward the Skymaster — supposedly a safe, easy stepup twin. The weather fatalities, however, suggest this is not so since most of the pilots involved had commercial tickets, were instrument rated and had lots of experience, but simply blundered into fog or ice they couldn't handle.

The next three accident categories that generated the highest frequency of fatal crashes did, however, involve the aircraft design. These were: engine failure on takeoff, fuel exhaustion and stall/spins.

Three fatal accidents were caused by loss of power on takeoff and climbout. Two of those involved failure of the rear engine. On one, witnesses had noted the rear engine running during taxi, but it had stopped during the takeoff roll. The aircraft stalled in climbout and then caught fire after impact. The private pilot had 516 hours total, 212 in type.

In another fatal accident, the rear engine failed on takeoff because of a plugged rear fuel pump vapor ejector; the pilot failed to abort and fire broke out after impact. The ATP pilot with 3,570 hours had three hours in type.

In the third fatal, both engines failed on takeoff, followed by a crash and fire. The private pilot had 1,800 hours, 94 in type.

There were two fatal accidents from engine failure because of fuel exhaustion, and two attributed to stall/spins. Most of the stall/spin or mush accidents appear unrelated to any particular aircraft deficiency. Of the two fatals, one occurred during a buzzing incident; the other was attributed to pilot fatigue.

Two nonfatals were related to engine failure. One pilot actually attempted to take off with the rear engine out, and the prop not feathered. He hit the trees. Another pilot stalled after he lost one engine from fuel starvation.

In a surprising number of instances, pilots who lost just one engine were unable to bring the aircraft back to a safe landing, despite the fact that the centerline thrust spared them the usual multi-engine problems of asymmetrical thrust and the traditional stall/spin threat with an engine out.

Skymasters also were plagued with a high rate of nonfatal accidents. Here the greatest toll was

Cost/Performance/Specifications

Model	Year Built	Number Built	Cruise Speed (kts)	Rate of Climb (fpm)	Useful Load (lbs)	S.E. Service Ceiling (ft)	Fuel Std/Opt gals	Engine	TBO (hrs)	Overhaul Cost Ea.	Average Retail Price
336	1964	195	150	1,300	1,580	8,200	93/131	210-hp Cont. IO-360-A	1,500	$ 9,000	$ 15,000
337	1965	238	167	1,200	1,565	8,300	93/131	210-hp Cont. IO-360-C/D	1,500	$ 9,000	$ 18,000
337A	1966	284	167	1,200	1,585	8,200	93/131	210-hp Cont. IO-360-C/D	1,500	$ 9,000	$ 18,000
337B	1967	226	167	1,250	1,685	7,500	93/131	210-hp Cont. IO-360-C/D	1,500	$ 9,000	$ 20,000
T-337B	1967	226	196	1,250	1,515	20,000	93/131	210-hp Cont. TSIO-360-A/B	1,400	$10,000	$ 23,000
337C	1968	207	166	1,200	1,750	6,800	93/131	210-hp Cont. IO-360-C/D	1,500	$ 9,000	$ 21,000
T-337C	1968	207	195	1,155	1,705	18,600	93/131	210-hp Cont. TSIO-360-A/B	1,400	$10,000	$ 24,000
337D	1969	199	166	1,200	1,745	6,800	93/131	210-hp Cont. IO-360-C/D	1,500	$ 9,000	$ 21,000
T-337D	1969	199	195	1,185	1,485	16,200	93/131	210-hp Cont. TSIO-360-A/B	1,400	$10,000	$ 25,000
337E	1970	122	166	1,180	1,820	6,500	93/131	210-hp Cont. IO-360-C	1,500	$ 9,000	$ 23,000
T-337E	1970	122	223	1,105	1,780	14,400	93/131	210-hp Cont. TSIO-360-A	1,400	$10,000	$ 27,000
337F	1971-72	132	166	1,100	1,935	5,100	93/131	210-hp Cont. IO-360-C	1,500	$ 9,000	$ 25,000
T-337F	1971	132	194	1,105	1,780	14,400	93/131	210-hp Cont TSIO-360-A	1,400	$10,000	$ 30,000
337G	1973-74	143	169	1,100	1,517	6,900	90/150	210-hp Cont. IO-360-G	1,500	$ 9,000	$ 29,500
T-337G-P	1973-74	194	204	1,250	1,533	18,700	151	225-hp Cont. TSIO-360-C	1,400	$10,000	$ 40,000
337G II	1975	64	169	1,100	1,517	6,900	90/150	210-hp Cont. IO-360-G	1,500	$ 9,000	$ 34,000
T-337G-P	1975	31	204	1,250	1,533	18,700	151	225-hp Cont. TSIO-360-C	1,400	$10,000	$ 49,000
337G II	1976	76	169	1,100	1,517	6,900	90/150	210-hp Cont. IO-360-G	1,500	$ 9,000	$ 37,000
T-337G-P	1976	31	204	1,250	1,533	18,700	151	225-hp Cont. TSIO-360-C	1,400	$10,000	$ 55,000
337G II	1977	66	169	1,100	1,517	6,900	90/150	210-hp Cont. IO-360-G	1,500	$ 9,000	$ 42,000
T-337G-P	1977	34	204	1,250	1,533	18,700	151	225-hp Cont. TSIO-360-C	1,400	$10,000	$ 62,000
337H II	1978	na	169	950	1,687	6,900	40/150	210-hp Cont. IO-360-G	1,500	$ 9,000	$ 49,000
T-337H II	1978	na	200	1,160	1,608	16,500	93/131	210-hp Cont. TSIO-360-H	1,400	$10,000	$ 56,000
337H II	1979	na	169	940	1,687	6,900	90/150	210-hp Cont. IO-360-GB	1,500	$ 9,000	$ 57,000
T-337H II	1979	na	200	1,160	1,608	16,500	93/131	210-hp Cont. TSIO-360-H	1,400	$10,000	$ 65,000
T-337H-P	1978	na	204	1,120	1,533	18,700	150	225-hp Cont. TSIO-360-C	1,400	$10,000	$ 72,000
T-337H-P	1979	na	204	1,120	1,533	18,700	150	225-hp Cont. TSIO-360-CB	1,400	$10,000	$ 86,000
337H II	1980	47	169	940	1,687	6,900	150	210-hp Cont. IO-360-GB	1,500	$ 9,000	$ 67,000
T-337H II	1980	30		1,160	1,608	16,500	150	210-hp Cont. TSIO-360-G	1,400	$10,000	$ 77,000
T-337H-P	1980	14	204	1,120	1,533	18,700	150	225-hp Cont. TSIO-360-CB	1,400	$10,000	$102,000

taken by simple fuel exhaustion — just running completely out of fuel. This happened no less than 13 times. Though Cessna likes to stress the high accuracy of the fuel gauges in the Skymasters, thanks to the capacitance type of measuring system, the location of both fuel gauges on the right side of the instrument panel cannot make fuel monitoring any easier for the pilot in the left seat. The fact that there are only two gauges for four fuel tanks — two mains and two aux tanks, also adds to the complexity of the task, since while any one set of tanks is in use, the pilot cannot see at a glance how much fuel remains in the other tanks.

Skymaster pilots have to switch from main to aux tanks for each engine.

Second biggest cause of nonfatal accidents in Skymasters was hard landings. Eleven of these were called out during the five-year period studied. Most involved propoising, and improper recovery from a bounced landing, often followed by a gear collapse.

Categories

There are four main classes of Skymasters. The aircraft was introduced in 1964 as a fixed-gear twin designated the 336. In 1967 the first turbocharged version was offered, followed in 1973 by the pressurized model. The clamshell door and smaller windows mandated by pressurization were carried over to the entire Skymaster line, except for bigger front-seat side windows for the non-pressurized models.

Note also that the pressurized version does not have a rear baggage door. Unlike most high-wing Cessnas, the Skymasters never had a left-side pilot's door. Entry is from the right front door.

With the pressurized model came a boost in horsepower from 210 each to 225 each. TBO for the powerful engine and the turbo 210 is 1,400 hours vs. 1,500 for the normally aspirated version.

Early models up through the '68 C version had TBOs of only 1,200

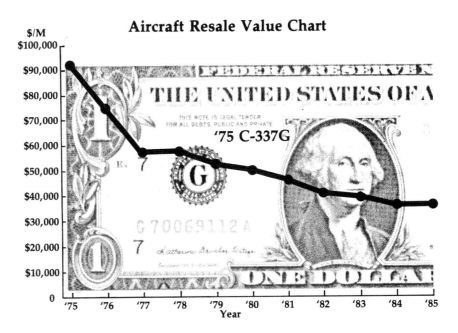

Aircraft Resale Value Chart

'75 C-337G

hours. This went to 1,500 hours with '69 models, thanks to the addition of nickel exhuast valves.

Gross weight on the Skymaster has risen from 4,200 pounds to 4,630 through the years, and to 4,700 pounds on the pressurized version.

Load Carrying

A 1972 model with a 4,630-pound gross and 1,935-pound useful load can handle a pretty good payload for a "light twin." With 150 pounds of optional equipment, the aircraft can heft full optional fuel of 131 gallons along with five adults and about 112 pounds of baggage. Range without reserve at 75 percent works out to about 1,060 sm, at 164 knots.

Maintenance

Skymaster owners report they have the most problems with the electrical system and the brakes. And a nearly universal complaint is that they can't seem to eliminate excess coating of the rear cowl and belly and horizontal stabiizer with oil.

Another dominant gripe among Skymaster owners is that "you can't get parts."

Airworthiness Directives

Aside for the aforementioned ADs

requiring a placard to warn aginst taking off on one engine and raising rear engine idle speeds, among other noteworthy ADs there was an AD requiring inspection of aircraft with over 5,000 hours of service for wing front and rear spar lower cap cracks. And another required checking flap actuator jacks for proper lubrication to forestall inadvertent retraction of flaps. Another AD required installation of a cooling duct for the fuel gauges, to prevent overheating and smoking.

Modifications

There are several STOL mods available for Skymasters from a host of companies. The most elaborate is R/STOL Systems', which installs drooped ailerons, recontoured wing leading edges, stall fences and flap actuated elevator trim springs. This mod also raises takeoff gross weight.

More modest STOL treatment, usually involving cuffing wing leading edges and modifying the wing tips and installation of vortex generators on the fuselage and fairings on the vertical tails is available on Supplemental Type Certificates issued to Horton STOL-Craft in Wellington, Kansas; Mid-America STOL in Wichita, Kansas, and Gus W. Simpson of STOL Aircraft Devices in Dallas, Texas.

A one-piece windshield STC is held by Beryl D'Shannon Aviation Specialties, Inc. in Leesburg, Florida, and an emergency exit door on top of the fuselage is STC'd by Floair, Inc. in Wichita, Kansas.

An electrically driven freon air conditioning system STC is held by JB Systems, Inc. in Longmont, Colorado, and DeVore Aviation in Albuquerque, New Mexico (505) 345-8713, installs recognition lights on the the trailing edge of R/STOL wing tips. Also, a Fiquench fire extinguishing system is approved for the cabin and engine area by Fike Metal Products Corp., Blue Springs, Missouri.

To accommodate wing-mounted weather radar, Renton Aviation in Renton, Wash. has an STC for installation of Bendix RDR 160 radar.

It should be noted that ownership of the above STCs, taken from the FAA's annual summary, may have changed hands in some cases.

Associations

At last word there was no association of Skymaster owners, though O.R. Whitaker (P.O. Box 1950, Liberal, Kansas 67901, (316) 624-2281) issues a newsletter periodically.

Owner Comments

I have owned a 1973 model 337G for about 18 months and have flown it 300 hours. It is roomy and comfortable for two couples, with plenty of baggage space. My wife likes it because it is easy to board and because there is a good view from all seats. The manufacturer didn't cheat any more than normal on owner's manual performance figures, and it comes pretty close to delivering the claimed performance when it is 800 pounds under gross.

I bought a Skymaster because flying terrifies me, and I think it is the safest airplane I possibly could be in — although its accident statistics do not bear this out. I got the opportunity to test its single-engine capabilities much earlier than desired. I had purchased the airplane in Kansas City, and 1:30 into the flight home, while IFR at 10,000 feet in VFR conditions above a solid undercast, I lost the front engine due to failure of the lube oil pump shaft. Flying to the nearest field and setting her down with only the rear engine running was no problem.

The airframe and engines had 800 hours on them at that time and Continental made a fair and reasonable adjustment on a factory-remanufactured engine — one that would make me want to do business with them in the future.

I could not be more pleased with the airplane itself. Unfortunately, the same is not true of the parts availability for the airframe or the Cessna avionics. Example: it recently took over eight weeks to get a replacement for the "ribbon assembly" — a wiring group which passes through the pilot's control column and connects to the autopilot disengage and electric trim switches on the yoke. Airframe parts availability hasn't been any better. Parts frequently must be re-ordered because orders are lost and never heard from and because wrong parts are shipped. It has been a real disappointment to find that a company like Cessna could do such an amateurish job of product support.

If I were to replace the airplane now, it would be a difficult decision as to whether to buy another 337. There is no other airplane I would rather fly in this size and price category. But I don't know whether I would be willing to get back into the service hassle with another 337.

●

Generally my 1968 Skymaster has met or exceeded book figures. We do have later style drooped wingtips, which may account for modest performance improvements.

The only outstanding irritation is the rear engine's oil leaks — not a serious problem, but who like a greasy rear engine cowl?

Passenger cabin room is excellent. The noise level can largely be controlled if close attention is given to getting the props synchronized.

Lack of baggage area is a pain, and the optional pod would seem to be a satisfactory solution at a nominal loss of speed. (Quoted as two or three mph.) Heater and cabin ventilation is good. Visibility is far superior to other twins.

Parts and backup have given me no problem.

I am currently spending about $40 per hour, which includes engine reserve, 100-hour engine inspection and radio maintenance. A fairly sizable amount is allocated for radios since they are older units. A noteworthy item is insurance cost. We received a better rate than most twins due to the centerline thrust safety factor.

Had one experience where the complete electrical system kicked out due to high load. A complete electrical system shutdown is required to reset alternators. This happened on final, IFR at night, which was disconcerting. I was told, however, that it is not an unusual occurrence on Skymasters.

Prior to the Skymaster I owned a Comanche 250, and had considered buying either a later Comanche or a 210. When I shopped the market, I discovered that Skymasters were a real bargain compared to the high-performance singles. The Skymaster offered good performance, safety and redundancy. It should be pointed out that redundancy goes well beyond just engines; i.e., alternators, voltage regulators, and vacuum systems. This is a tremendous consideration if anyone does much serious IFR flying. Fuel consumption is good for a twin. We usually get 18-19 gph at about 160 knots.

Overall, I think it is a 'super' light twin that didn't make it big because of its unusual appearance and the ego problems of many individuals looking into this class of plane.

Cessna 310

You've talked it over with your accountant (and presumably your psychiatrist), and you've decided that the time has come to trade up: You want to be able to tote a ton of useful load from one Loran chain to the next, at speeds that will have ATC confusing you with heavy iron, and do it with the (alleged) safety of two engines—all for less than the price of a new 172. The choices are few. You can buy a used Baron or Aztec (or possibly an Aero Commander, or a clapped-out Navajo). Or, you can do what more than 5,000 other light-twin buyers have done—and take home a Cessna 310.

As two-engine planes go, the 310 is singularly impressive—in appearance, if in no other category. (Who could fail to notice those Stabila tip tanks?) The George-Lucas-inspired design of the late-model (Roman-nosed) 310R leaves some pilots cold, admittedly. But despite the Baron-with-a-gland-problem appearance, the 310 proves itself a worthy contender in the six-place twin category, combining get-it-done-today performance with surprisingly docile handling, not to mention the load-carrying capacity of a light armored vehicle.

For every Indian head, there's a buffalo, however, and the flip side of aesthetic overachievement (in this case) is mediocre Dutch-roll stability, high V-speeds, and generally unflattering runway handling. (As one owner puts it, "A one-time flight will endear few pilots to the 310.") But what the 310 lacks in cockpit charisma, it makes up for in raw verve: Cob it, and the mother scoots. Topping 174 knots is no problem single-engine ROC is a creditable 330 to

440 fpm (depending on year/model), and the maximum *two-engine* climb rate will have you begging for ear surgery.

Fuel consumption, maintenance, and insurance costs for the 310 are substantial—but the same is true for any six-place twin. Owners point proudly to the 310's beer-hall cabin proportions, extra-tall (and wide) wheel stance, superb cockpit visibility (especially in later models), and logical panel layout as reasons for preferring a 310 to a Baron or Aztec. Another reason: price. In any given model year, 310s tend to underprice Barons by 10 percent (and more).

Model History

As any Sky King fan knows, the 310 (Cessna's first low-wing aircraft, not counting the wartime UC-78 "Bamboo Bomber"—which was *Sky King's* first airplane) began life as a snub-nosed, straight-tailed, tuna-tanked wonder in 1955. Approximately 1,200 tuna-tank models were delivered before Cessna—intent on enhancing the 310's dihedral stability and sex appeal in one bold stroke—introduced the now-familiar slanted tip tanks on the 310G in 1962. Wing lockers (and an underwing exhaust system) appeared two years later with the 'I' model. Total optional fuel was 133 gallons, carried in the tips (50 gals. each) and wing bladders.

The 1971 model had 260-hp engines and a short nose, but no rear window. Current value on the resale market: $40,000.

The 310K-N models (1966-68) were the first to sport double-wide "Vista-view" side windows. Optional fuel capacity increased to 143 gallons, flap speed (white arc) went from 122 to 139 knots, and three-blade props were offered for the first time. With the 1969 'P' model, optional fuel went to 184 gallons; the nose gear geometry was altered slightly; and the IO-470-V engine got changed to the IO-470-VO (the same as before, but with Nimonic valves, richer fuel injection, and piston oil cooling—all for better top-end life). A Turbo 310P model was offered as well, with more powerful TSIO-520-B engines (285-hp, versus the normally aspirated model's 260-hp).

The next big change came in 1972, when Cessna (wanting to rid the 310 of the "tunnel effect" that plagues many long-cabin aircraft) put a rear window in the fuselage of the 310Q. Rear passengers got three extra inches of headroom; the top of the one-piece windshield was extended a full nine inches aft; and the panel eyebrow was lowered. These changes brightened the interior environment indeed. Optional fuel capacity became 207 gallons, and gross weight was boosted to 5,300 pounds (from 5,200 in the 310P). Buyers should note that while all 310s built from 1970 to 1974 are 'Q' models, the rear-window and cabin-brightening mods first appeared in 1972, and apply only to serial number 310Q-0401 and up.

The last, and numerically most abundant, of the 310 models was the 310R, introduced in 1975. With the 310R, 285-hp IO-520 engines (1,400-hr. TBO if turbocharged; 1,700 hours otherwise) became standard, and baggage capacity went to a forklift-busting 950 pounds, thanks to a new 350-lb. cargo hold in the NASA-inspired nose. Max fuel stayed at 207 gals. Gross weight was boosted to 5,500 pounds, but useful load, equipped, remained in the 1,900-pound ballpark—about 200 pounds *less* than full-fuel-and-cargo (never mind pilot/pax).

It should be noted that Cessna made hundreds of minor (but important) changes to the 310 over the years; the forgoing discussion is necessarily cursory, and outlines only the most major changes.

Production of the 310 was terminated in 1981, to make way for the T303 Crusader, a clean-sheet-of-paper design that Cessna felt would better serve the light twin market into the 21st century. Actually, the 310's death was accidental; Cessna had not originally intended the T303 as a 310 replacement. Rather, the original T303 (*nee* "Clipper") was a 180-hp super-light twin aimed at the Duchess/Seminole market. Cessna wisely decided to withdraw from the "trainer twin" arena at the last minute, however, reconfiguring the T303 with 250-hp turbocharged powerplants. By default, the present Crusader—a lesser airplane than the 310 in almost every performance category—took away the 310's niche. The T303 survives; the 310, alas, is history.

Systems

In contrast to the Aztec, Aerostar, and Navajo, the 310 has no engine-driven hydraulics: Gear and flaps are all-electric, with juice supplied by 50-amp (standard) or 100-amp (optional) alternators on each engine. Cowl flaps are manual (unlike those on most Barons, which are electric). Brakes are Goodyear—which is to say, expensive to repair—and tires are odd-sized (6.50x10 on the mains—same as the Cheyenne), thus costly to replace.

It's perhaps worth noting that ARC 300-series avionics came as standard equipment on 310s (even the later models), although many owners have had King or Collins equipment installed. (Nonetheless, the 310 without an ARC autopilot is rare.) Check the black-box assortment carefully before you buy, and price each plane up or down accordingly.

If the 310 has a serious systems sore-point (and it does), it's the ludicrously labyrinthine fuel system, with its plethora of pumps, pressure switches, valves, vapor return lines, and underwing drains. (With the 207-gal. system, you can count on draining no fewer than 10 petcocks each morning: One for *each* main tank, aux bladder, 20-gallon locker, crossfeed line, and sump/strainer.) The fuel selectors read "on, off, aux, crossfeed"—simple enough, you say—but thereby hangs an invitation to disaster. Aux fuel can't be crossfed, for example, in a single-engine emergency. Nor can wing-bladder fuel be used in the event of failure of an engine-driven fuel pump, since the boost pumps are *inside the tip tanks*. (Also in the tips are *transfer pumps* to ensure that fuel from the front of the tank can be gotten to the rear—where the pickup line is—in steep descents. These pumps are wired to the landing-light circuit breakers and constitute go/no-go items.)

New 310 owners are often amazed to learn that their wing aux tanks—31 gallons each—are good for no more than 60 minutes' use in cruise (sometimes a lot less). That's because excess fuel is returned by the engine-driven fuel pumps not to the aux tanks (whence it came), but to the *tip tanks*. Accordingly, one must burn 60 to 90 minutes' worth of fuel out of the tips before selecting "aux." Otherwise, return fuel, arriving at already full tip tanks, will be pumped overboard out the vents.

Lockers are another story entirely. Some 310s have but one locker tank, in which case the drill is to burn fuel out of the mains, activate

Cost/Performance/Specifications

Model	Year	Average Retail Priced	Cruise Speed (kts)	Fuel (gals)	Useful Load (lbs)	SE Ceiling (ft)	Engine	TBO (hrs)	Overhaul Cost (each)
310A-B	1955-58	$18,000	178	133	1,740	8,000	240-hp Cont. O-470-M	1,500	$ 7,500
310C-F	1959-61	$21,500	191	133	1,795	7,450	260-hp Cont. IO-470-D	1,500	$ 8,750
310G-H	1962-63	$25,000	191	133	2,037	7,450	260-hp Cont. IO-470-D	1,500	$ 8,750
310I-J	1964-65	$27,000	194	133	2,037	6,850	260-hp Cont. IO-470-U	1,500	$ 8,750
310K-L	1966-67	$31,500	193	143	2,075	6,850	260-hp Cont. IO-470-V	1,500	$ 8,750
310N	1968	$34,000	193	143	2,030	6,850	260-hp Cont. IO-470-V	1,500	$ 8,750
310P	1969	$38,000	193	184	2,086	6,850	260-hp Cont. IO-470-VO	1,500	$ 8,750
310Q	1970-74	$39,000-49,000	192	207	2,086	6,680	260-hp Cont. IO-470-VO	1,500	$ 8,750
310R	1975-81	$55,000-147,500	194	207	2,047	7,400	285-hp Cont. IO-520-M	1,700	$ 9,250
T310P	1969	$43,000	226	184	2,108	18,100	285-hp Cont. TSIO-520-B	1,400	$11,000
T310Q	1970-74	$47,000-59,000	225	207	2,208	17,550	285-hp Cont. TSIO-520-B	1,400	$11,000
T310R	1975-81	$65,000-160,000	223	207	2,277	17,200	285-hp Cont. TSIO-520-B	1,400	$11,000

the locker transfer pump (which sends locker fuel to the adjacent tip tank), then crossfeed as necessary to balance the main-tank load. With dual lockers, you simply engage the transfer pumps when the mains have burned down to 30 gallons remaining (or less), and wait for two idiot lights to come on when the lockers are dry. (There are no quantity gauges.)

Obviously, the fellow who designed this system needs to have his bed made, and possibly his straps tightened. The rest of us, meanwhile, would do well to study the handbook carefully before (and after) buying or flying a 310.

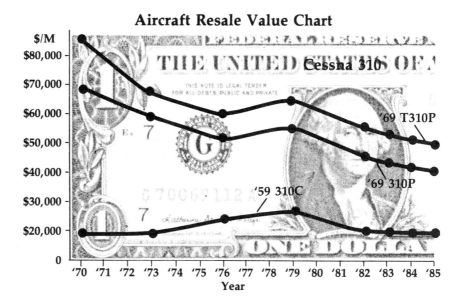

Aircraft Resale Value Chart

Comfort and Handling

Interior comfort is excellent in any model 310 (assuming you can abide the outdoor-patio grade carpets and fade-faster-than-memory seats), although noise levels are high enough to sterilize mice. Pilot and copilot sit miles apart, and rear passengers are pinched neither for leg nor shoulder room (except in the 5th and 6th seats, which are best occupied by Billy Barty types). And thanks to a generous array of baggage compartments (even the short-nosed 310Q can take up to 600 pounds in the lockers and aft cabin), no one is obliged to carry groceries on his—or her—lap.

In terms of handling, the 310 offers typical ''big mutha'' control response, with few or no unpleasant surprises. The ponderous roll response for which the 310 is famous has been overplayed somewhat by the airport-lounge lizards. Roll and yaw damping are poor at lower airspeeds, it's true, due to the concentration of mass in the wings (remember, each tip carries 600 pounds of petrol), and inexperienced pilots tend, as a result, to overcontrol on climbout or approach. The key is to keep a light touch. (One eventually learns to ''husband'' the plane's inertia, rather than fidget constantly with the yoke.) The 310 has a ''wallow'' mode, but so do other aircraft. More than one ATP has observed that ''there's no better training for a future Learjet pilot than a couple hundred hours in a 310.''

In cruise, the plane is a joy to fly. Stabila-tip models (310G thru R) exhibit little or no adverse yaw, and standard-rate turns can be done with feet flat on the floor. Extended hands-off flight does not result in tumbled gyros. Turbulence, however, produces a nauseous Dutch-rolling which can be quite pronounced at high fuel loadings, even in the post-1969 models with ventral-fin tail stingers. (This is where the $2,160 yaw damper option proves its worth.) Maneuvering speed (Va) is a high 148 knots.

Stalls in the 310 are preceded by mild bucking and shuddering (and steep deck angles, if any power is left on); the break and recovery, however, are straightforward and undramatic. Dirty, the stall comes at 63 KIAS; clean, 75.

Flaps are of the DC-3 (split) variety, producing more drag than lift— which is perhaps just as well, since the 310 is difficult to slow down without chopping power (and TBO). The standard slow-down drill is to squeeze off a couple inches of manifold pressure, then apply 15 degrees of flaps at 160 KIAS or below (139 KIAS in early models); then wait. Initial application of flaps is enough to slow the plane down to gear speed (140 knots), and with the gear down, power can slowly be bled off until—established on final

approach—17 inches of manifold pressure remain.

Landing a 310 with dignity calls for finesse (and, some would argue, retro-rockets). Power is best kept at 17 inches until over the threshold, at which time the throttles can *slowly* be brought back and the elevator trim readjusted. (Yoke forces are high in the flare.) The airspeed decay with power reduction is dramatic, and the plane ''pays off'' quickly. At moderate weights, the best landings seem to come about 9 knots above Vso, with some power still on. (If the stall horn sounds, you're in for a thumper.) At very light loadings, on the other hand, good ''stall horn'' landings are accomplishable with fair regularity. Just don't heave back heartily on the wheel after touchdown, or you're liable to pound the tail into the tarmac.

Performance

The 310 offers nosebleed-on-demand performance and thus is closer to the B55 Baron in all-around pep than to the Aztec. Owners of normally aspirated models typically claim 65-percent cruise speeds of 175 knots (at fuel flows of 22 to 26 gph) or 180 knots at 75 percent (burning 28 to 30 gph), at altitudes to 7,500 feet. Turbo models deliver blistering cruise speeds (up to 222 knots at 16,000 feet, burning 32 to 36 gph, at 75 percent), with top speeds of up to

238 knots—considerably better than the Turbo Aztec F (214 knots max) and dangerously close to Duke territory. Only one non-pressurized piston aircraft in current production is faster than the Turbo 310—viz., the Baron 58TC.

Almost all 310s were ordered with auxiliary fuel, and many have the full 207-gal. complement, which presents interesting possibilities for trip planning. Fill the cabin (six seats), and you can go 690 nm with reserves. Fill the tanks, and you can go 1,400 nm with reserves—although you'll be limited to about 450 pounds in the cabin. Fill the cabin, the tanks, and the baggage bays, and you'll be 1,400 pounds over gross.

On one engine, the normally aspirated 310 climbs 330 to 415 fpm; the turbo models 390 to 440 fpm. (The Aztecs deliver about 100 fpm less.) Single-engine ceiling is 17,000-feet-plus in the turbo models; a Baron-like 6,650 to 8,000 feet otherwise (depending on year-model). The 310s with the highest wing- and power-loadings (and therefore the lowest S.E. performance) are the 310K, L, N, P, and Q.

Safety

A special NTSB study of light twin safety covering the years 1972-76 showed the 310 ranking 10th in fatal accidents—and sixth-worst

Transport-like panel (painted battleship grey in later models) is a 310 trademark. Unfortunately, ARC avionics came standard. The panel shown here is from a 1975 model.

overall—out of 20 twin-engine planes studied. The 310 incurred 2.18 fatal accidents per 100,000 flight hours (versus 2.83 for the Barons and 2.60 for the NTSB's "Apache-Aztec" group, which unfortunately was not broken down further), while the total accident rate for the 310 came out to 9.81 per 100,000 flight hours (against 8.29 for the Barons and 7.54 for the "PA-23"). By comparison, the overall accident rate for general aviation as a whole, at the time of the NTSB's special study, was 9.42.

A more recent (October 1983) FAA computer-search of 310 accident statistics shows a grand total of 694 write-ups in the computer, going back to 1959. Major categories (and the number of incidents pertaining thereto) included: wheels-up landings, 139; gear collapses, 183; gear retractions on ground, 23; collision with ground (controlled), 26; collision with ground (uncontrolled), 28; stall, 31; spin, 1; fire in flight, 5; fire on ground, 6; "systems malfunction," 45.

Finally, an NTSB report analyzing accidents from 1978 to 1982 shows 213 total accidents in the five-year period, of which some 55 crashes—or 26 percent—were fatal. The single largest category of mishap (true to the plane's bag-of-bricks reputation): landing accidents.

Some 45 pilots landed their 310s wheels-up in the five-year period, many for reasons having to do with material failure and/or poor maintenance. Hard landings accounted for another 19 accidents (a surprising number of them non-injury);

gear collapses totaled 26. There was some overlap between "hard landing" and "gear collapse" categories, since NTSB allows more than one line in its type-of-accident description.

Interestingly, as many as a quarter of the wheels-up landings happened in conjunction with engine failure or malfunction (despite the fact that either of a 310's alternators—on either engine—will suffice to power the all-electric gear up or down). A typical scenario has the pilot noticing an engine irregularity, and aborting a departure, just after breaking ground and also just after selecting "gear-up." The plane subsequently settles onto the runway under complete control, wheels retracted.

In several cases, maintenance personnel apparently forgot to reconnect nose gear doors to actuator arms after performing required inspections of combustion heaters (which in early-model 310s are accessible only through the nose gear well). Jamming of the nose gear in the well—and/or breakage of retract arms—is the frequent result.

Many of the "hard landing" and "gear collapse" accidents involved arrivals in which the plane had accumulated some airframe ice; others happened as pilots unfamiliar with the 310 were being checked out by their instructors. In one case, a pilot making an ice-laden arrival, "dropped hard on all three wheels," after which "the right wing outboard of the engine nacelle buckled downward until the right tip tank struck the runway and was dragged along the ground."

The high number of gear-collapse incidents may be related to several factors, including poor maintenance, poor pilot technique, and outright underdesign of landing gear components in early (particularly pre-1970) 310 models. (Cessna issued numerous landing-gear service bulletins in the late 1960s and early '70s.) An aggravating factor, almost certainly, is the heavy torsional loadings placed on trunnions, struts, and brackets as a result of tip-tank "oversteer"

in taxi. (The inertia of the tanks is felt on the ground, as well as in the air.) Many gear-collapse accidents happen during high-speed turn-offs. *Caveat emptor.*

Engine failure or malfunction was a factor in 35 (or 16 percent) of the reported 1978-1982 Cessna 310 accidents, with fuel contamination, fuel exhaustion, and/or poor maintenance accounting, collectively, for over half the cases.

As light aircraft go, the Cessna 310 has a particularly perverse fuel system. Accordingly, one would expect the 310 to rate high in fuel mismanagement accidents. Not necessarily so, however: Only 13 out of 213 accidents (or a little over six percent of 310 mishaps) involved fuel-system-related brouhahas; and of these, several happened as pilots simply flew their airplanes beyond known endurance limits after exhausting all fuel from all tanks. In addition, fuel selectors were unaccountably found positioned between ''aux'' and ''main'' positions in several accidents.

Given the 310's high V-speeds, one might expect a disproportionate rate of stall-spin accidents. But the five-year record shows only eight such mishaps (out of 213 mishaps reported). By comparison, there were almost as many accidents involving marijuana overloads (some half a dozen in all).

Two of 55 fatal 310 accidents involved midair collisions. Another involved wake turbulence as a 310 attempted to land behind a Boeing 737 at Orange County Airport in southern California.

There were no airframe breakups listed in the 1978-1982 printouts.

What kind of pilot crashes a 310? PICs tend to be young (in their early 30s, most commonly)—but not inexperienced: Fully a quarter of all 310 accidents from 1978 to 1982 involved pilots with over 500 hours *in type.* (Only 54 of the reported 213 accidents came at the hands of pilots with less than 100 hours in type.) The vast majority—147 out of 213 (or 69 percent)—of aviators

involved in 1978-1982 Cessna 310 crashes had more than 1,500 hours in their logbooks; 53 (24 percent of the total) had more than 5,000 hours, while 23 pilots—more than 10 percent—had logged 10,000-hours-plus. One 310 fatal accident involved a 69-year-old commercial pilot with 30,087 logged hours. The crash in question occurred on an IFR air-taxi flight. (The pilot evidently became disoriented during a 400-and-one approach in fog and rain.) ''Pilot failed instrument check four days before accident,'' NTSB noted.

The moral: Don't underestimate the importance of proficiency—and good maintenance—in flying a 310 safely . . . regardless of the amount of time in your logbook.

For all-around single-engine safety, the 310 probably ought to be considered on a par with the Baron. The Aztec bests both planes for Vmc (69 knots vs. 75 for the 310, 81 for the Baron), but the 310 and Baron climb half again faster than the Aztec on one, and you don't have to reach to the ceiling to re-trim. The 310 and Aztec both have slow gear retraction times (about 13 seconds, versus the later Barons' four), which can be critical in an emergency. But at least the 310 has all-electric gear, and with an alternator on each engine you can be sure the gear is on its way up as soon as you hit the switch (conveniently and logically located above the upper left side of the power quadrant). Many Aztecs have but one hydraulic pump, on the left en-

The $19,000 R/STOL conversion substitutes ''back and down'' Fowler flaps for the 310's standard split flaps. Result: reduced stall speed, lower Vmc.

gine, and a port-engine failure means pumping the gear up by hand. Barons have fast-retracting electric gear, but the switch is in the wrong place.

The Aztec, Baron, and 310 all have emergency exits in addition to the entry door. In the 310, it's the pilot's side window; in the others, it's a back-seat window.

The 310 has one crashworthiness feature worthy of special note: namely, the tip tanks. Contrary to hangar mythology, aesthetics had little to do with locating the 310's main fuel tanks on the tips of the wings. According to one former Cessna engineer who was there at the time, Cessna felt in 1954 that many post-crash fires might be avoided if fuel were stored in detachable-on-impact external tanks. The 310, as a result, was graced with huge metal tunas, held on with quarter-inch bolts. The wisdom of this decision got an early test, as it turns out: One of the factory's first production prototypes crashed-landed wheels-up in a wheat field. The plane shed its tanks on touchdown; a major fire was averted; and the pilots walked away unscathed (and uncooked). External tanks remained a Cessna-twin trademark for many years thereafter.

Maintenance

Of the 310, Baron, and Aztec, the 310 is the clear winner in terms of the fewest number of Airworthiness Directives. Only eight airframe ADs affect the oldest 310s, and of those only one (on fuel-line inspection) is repetitive (every 50 hours). Turbo models have an additional repetitive-inspection AD of their own, requiring 50- and 100-hour look-sees of exhaust risers, slip-joints, ball joints, etc. (With the installation of Inconel parts, some of the 50-hour items are eliminated or rendered 100-hour items, however.) The Baron 58 has 14 airframe ADs; the Aztec, 24.

Some specific ADs to watch for include 69-14-01, which required installation of transfer pumps in the tip tanks of pre-1969 models; 72-03-07, inspection of main landing gear (the 310Q only); 72-14-08, the 50-hour fuel and oil hose inspection; and 76-04-03 and 78-11-05, requiring modification of ARC autopilot actuators.

A review of FAA Service Difficulty Reports on the 310 series going back six years reveals 1,300 reports covering a multitude of (mostly minor) sins. The single biggest category of complaint: landing gear problems (over 260 reports). Unfortunately, few generalizations can be made, as the reports refer to cracks in numerous locations (trunnions, torque links, rod-ends, brackets) on both main and nose gears, covering all models from 'A' to 'R.' One area that does stand out clearly is the nose gear idler bellcrank, P/N 08421022, which appears to break frequently on 310L-N models. (Also, nose gear drag brace doublers, P/N 081308930, crack on 310R models at upwards of 1,200 hours.) Fortunately, the median breakage time of landing gear components appears to be fairly high in most cases. Be wary of airframes that have racked up thousands of Part 135 hours.

Other problem areas suggested by our SDR printout: aileron bearing seizure in 310Rs; aft spar corrosion (from exhaust gases) in all models up through the 310Q; battery box corrosion (all models); leaking bladder tanks (all models with aux tanks); exhaust mufflers, bellows, and ball joints (turbo models in particular); and defective bearings in Prestolite ALV 9407 alternators (on 310R models).

Crankcase cracking appears to be less a problem with 285-hp 310s than with 285-hp Barons (the Baron 58 in particular). Our SDR listing showed up only 20 instances of crankcase crackage in IO-520-powered 310s in the past six years, versus more than 50 such reports for Barons 58s (IO-520-C) in a little over two years. The Baron fleet is older, on average; but it is also smaller. Thus it appears that the 310, by Baron standards, is relatively crack-immune. (Only four Turbo 310s showed up with cracked cases in our SDR printout.) The flip side of this coin is that the IO-470-powered 310 fleet, considered by many people "crack-proof," isn't. We counted no less than ten IO-470 case cracks in the printout (most at or beyond TBO, however).

Modifications

The 310 was the plane, of course, that rocketed Jack Riley to stardom.

In the early 1960s, Riley—having bought the Rajay turbocharger line from TRW— built up a pair of 290-hp turbosupercharged Lycomings and installed them on a 310D (along with pressurized magnetos, three-blade props, one-piece windshield, pointy radome, and King Faisal control yokes) to create the original Riley Rocket. Many of these 300-mph speedsters are still in service, and they occasionally pop up on the used market in the $29,000-35,000 price range. Most have been through the mill, however, and may be in need of considerable refurbishment. TBO is a short 1,200 hours.

Riley later outdid himself by putting 350-hp Navajo Chieftain engines on a few 1964 and later 310s, thereby creating the Turbostream. This mod is still available (for about $140,000) from Air America of Avoca, Pa., which purchased many of Riley's twin-Cessna STCs some years ago. Air America also does a healthy business installing auxiliary fuel tanks (up to 260 gals). Call Air America at 717/343-1228.

If you have a Turbo 310 or 320 made after 1965, RAM Aircraft Modifications of Waco, Texas (817/752-8381) has a 300-hp upgrade costing $32,500; a 310-hp engine swap which puts intercooled TSIO-520-NBs out front to give 253-knot cruise speeds and 550 fpm single-engine rates of climb ($64,000); and a unique 326-hp conversion that involves special RAM-built TSIO-520-NBR engines, for even more performance ($78,500). RAM does only first-quality work, and its STCs often include many worthwhile minor changes to ignition, cooling baffles, and exhaust systems; we can recommend their work highly.

If you own a 310F through Q (normally aspirated), and you want more power, but you don't want turbochargers, consider the Colemill Executive 600 conversion, which, for $38,500, gets you a pair

Here's the 310 instrument panel, circa 1972. Center console allows plenty of room on panel for avionics. Engine gauges are far from the pilot's eye, however.

of fresh 300-horse Continental IO-520-E engines with three-blade props. This is an excellent mod to have for better single-engine performance. Call Colemill at 615/226-4256.

Finally, R/STOL Systems, of Everett, Wash. (206/355-8702) can give your 310G, Q, or R, or T310P/-Q/R the runway performance (and Vmc) of an Aztec, roughly speaking, by replacing your split flaps with wing-widening Fowlers. The installation takes 15 working days and will set you back one C-bill less than $20,000.

Owner Comments

Since 1978, I have owned two Cessna 310s—a 1969 Turbo 310P with Robertson STOL, a 1973 Turbo 310Q with Colemill conversion. Overall, I think the 310 is an outstanding performer, with straightforward handling, excellent comfort, good parts availability and adequate factory support. Since my airplanes have been based at Crested Butte, Col., 8,850 ft. MSL, and the minimum enroute altitude to Denver is over 16,000 ft., high-altitude performance, especially climb performance, is vital in my operations, In this parameter the 310, especially the Turbo 310, performs admirably; however, at the cost of substantial maintenance expense.

A thorough 100-hour (or annual inspection) on a Turbo 310 by a shop experienced in maintaining turbocharged aircraft (and with all that complex, red-hot turbo exhaust machinery, you certainly want an experienced shop) always cost me at least $4,000.

The cost of properly maintaining the Turbo 310 is what drove me to try the Colemill conversion, which replaces the normally aspirated 260-hp IO-470 Continentals with normally aspirated 300-hp IO-520 Continentals. If you don't have to

In 1975, the 310 got a longer snout. Result: more baggage room up front and better landing characteristics, along with a sleeker look.

have the turbo, I strongly recommend this conversion. At mid-cruise weights, the Colemill will still climb at 500 fpm at 10,000-12,000 ft. MSL), and cuts the hourly maintenance cost of the turbo in half.

A couple of points: We have gotten excellent engine life by (I suppose this applies to any aircraft engine) using light power settings and extreme care on sudden temperature changes by gradual power reductions on descent. We have had no problems with cracking cases on the TSIO-520s. One of our cases is still an old "light case" and is performing very well.

The danger of overboost from cold oil is eliminated by using AeroShell Multigrade. We fly into Truckee, Calif., frequently the coldest weather station in the U.S. Cold starts are easy and we suspect engine wear is considerably reduced.

The 320E and F Models have the heavier gear of the 400 Series. If you can locate a clean 320 in the E or F model it can be an excellent buy.

John A. Linford
Oakland, Calif.

●

Our company has owned and operated Cessna 310s for 12 years—a 1967 "L" model for five years and a 1974 "Q" model with a Colemill

conversion (IO-520-E) for the remainder.

It is my belief that normally aspirated engines in the close-cowled 310 should not be operated at over 65 percent power. The small increase in speed with the increased maintenance and higher fuel burn does not justify going to 75 percent power. Our 310 cruises at altitudes of 5,000 and 12,000 at 187 knots at 27 gph. I have operated the IO-470 and the IO-520 engines to TBO and beyond using 65 percent as a maximum.

Tank management in the 310 was designed by somebody with a sense of humor who hoped to keep the pilot alert on long flights. The improved fuel gauges in the "Q" model are not as accurate or convenient as the gauges in the "L" model. When flying on the aux tanks, approximately 10 gph will be returned to the main tanks.

The wing lockers may be Cessna engineering's greatest claim to fame. Four suitcases, four sets of golf clubs, and all sorts of miscellaneous baggage can be loaded in the locker, very close to the c.g.

The annual inspections of the "Q" model have averaged $2,875. These have been higher than I would have anticipated, but they included some heavy maintenance items: i.e., complete rebushing of landing gear, AD on heater, and corrosion problems on wing flap push rods. The problem with the push rods was simple, but the labor to remove and replace the rods was incredible.

The annual maintenance cost has been just above $7.50 per hour. Approximately one-half of this cost has been in the replacement of vacuum pumps (covered in an earlier issue of *Aviation Consumer*) and three alternators that had to be replaced.

I do not believe that there is any light twin available today that has the speed, good looks, and reasonable price of the Cessna 310.

Art Silverman
McKees Rocks, Pa.

Beech 18

Battered by Airworthiness Directives, abused by midnight haulers and— some think—disinherited by its maker, the Beech 18 nevertheless represents one of the most intriguing buys in the used-plane market.

Imagine owning an aristocratic twin that will carry seven people 1,400 miles nonstop, and buying a creampuff example for an incredible $45,000.

Alas, some think that after a reign of over four decades and service in both military and civilian versions as a personnel carrier, twin-engine trainer, cargo carrier and corporate flagship, the Twin Beech is on its way out. The dwindling number of maintenance shops trained and equipped to handle the old Beech 18s say that the ranks are thinning. And there's not much action in used-plane sales because, frankly, there's not a lot of commission to be earned peddling the old dowager 18 when even a late model single will yield as much and more.

And the onus of devastating Airworthiness Directives in 1975 and 1980 weighs heavily on the old birds in the eyes of prospective buyers because the structural integrity of the wing is at stake. It was in '75 that owners were forced to begin a never-ending series of periodic inspections for possible cracks in the wing truss, or add a strap for backup security.

Latest Big AD

The latest major AD action by the FAA, which came in 1980 as a revision to the '75 AD, once again focused attention on the wing spars by demanding yet another check for cracks, within 75 hours, by removing and checking the security straps and making X-ray exams of the wing truss. Beech 18 owners howled in dismay, and some led by a West Coast pilot

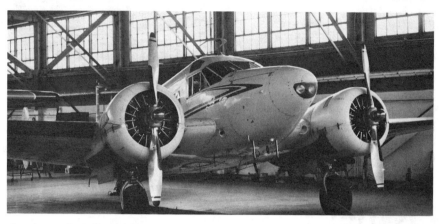

No hangar queen, this Beech 18 and others like it go out first thing each morning to make the overnight air freight business a workable proposition.

the late George Milligan, challenged the FAA move as unnecessary hassling not supported by the flight history of the aircraft.

But according to the FAA the AD revision was triggered by a pair of aircraft that had developed cracks and together suggested an unsavory scenario. In one, a crack developed in the wing structure of an ex-military model with 7,762 hours on it, in a location not previously pinpointed for inspection, right near the inboard juncture of the engine nacelle and the wing. And it occurred despite the presence of a strap. The second actually involved the cracking of the strap itself—a Dee Howard modification.

According to FAA engineer Ross Spencer in Wichita, Kans., the appearance of the two incidents almost simultaneously—good wing structure with a cracking strap on one airplane and bad wing structure with a good strap on another—made them realize the danger inherent in both situations.

Although a good wing strap theoretically should take the entire load in case of a wing structure failure, there was concern that a progressive failure might go undetected. And no one knows how long the strap could carry on before it, too, gave way.

Be that as it may, a glance through a five-year rundown of Service Difficulty Reports provided by the

FAA in Oklahoma City on the Beech 18 shows that many of the aircraft suffer from the cumulative effects of a low level of care and attention, and from old age.

History

The beginnings of the Beech 18 go back to 1938 when the aircraft, designated the C18, was powered by 350-hp Wright Wasp-Junior engines. During World War II and later it saw extensive use as C-45, AT-11 and SNB-1 military versions. It emerged from the war in 1946 as the D18 with the 450-hp Pratt & Whitney radials that have remained the stock powerplant to the present day, though in later years both AiResearch and P&W turboprops were hung successfully on the aircraft.

The D18 was succeeded in 1955 by the Super E18 in which the major change was a cabin level raised by six inches, giving the aircraft extra interior comfort. In 1960 the G18 arrived, and the tricycle gear originally developed as an STC by Volpar was offered by the Beech factory as original equipment. The angle of the horizontal stabilizer was changed slightly, upping cruise speeds correspondingly. Also, a longer wing with drooped tips was added, and this improved the climb rate and lowered the stall speed. An improved exhaust system is supposed to have boosted power output slightly.

With the final H model in 1963 came a few other touches like electric cowl flaps, in place of the manual ones, and fuel injection.

As the airplane evolved through the years, the gross weight was gradually raised from 7,500 pounds to 10,200 pounds. Prospective buyers should check this to make sure they're getting an aircraft with sufficient useful load for their needs.

Although U.S. production ended in 1966, we understand that Beech 18s were built for the Japanese military in the late 60's or early 70's.

Structural Problems

Many of the Beech 18's problems are obviously related simply to age and hard use. Some ex-military surplus models are reported to have as many as 20,000 hours on the airframe. Even before the big AD of 1975 requiring major inspections for wing spar cracks, there was concern about the possibility of cracks developing in the wing structure, and some nagging wing inspection ADs in 1972 and 1973. In about 1965 the Dee Howard Co. in San Antonio, Tex. came out with a supplemental strap that fastened

under the wing spar to strengthen the structure and safeguard against wing failures.

Subsequently, five other organizations, to our knowledge, came up with strap STCs for the Beech 18. They are: Aerospace Products, Inc. of North Hollywood, Calif.; Airline Training, Inc. of Ft. Lauderdale, Fla.; Canadian Aerocon, Ltd. of Mississauga, Ontario; Hamilton Aviation of Tucson, Ariz.; and Jourdan Aircraft of Raytown, Mo.

Although when Dee Howard first came out with its strap mod, the understanding was that it would never have to be removed for inspection, later events proved otherwise. Therefore, prospective buyers of Beech 18s might consider the type of strap installed since ease of removal can save time and money.

In this context, maintenance shops we talked to say the Dee Howard is the most difficult and time consuming to remove for inspection, and the Hamilton Aviation and Aerospace Products are probably the easiest.

It was Hamilton Aviation that came up with an exotic "depressurized" spar kit designed to point out cracks by means of warning gas leaks, as on some helicopter blades. Some 40 to 50 of these kits were sold, according to Hamilton, and they brought the spar lifetime way up to 3,600 hours.

Critical Event

Although the Beech 18s were developing a history of cracking wing components, and there were fatal in-flight structural failures, some say the critical event that precipitated the big '75 AD was the crash of a Twin Beech in Iowa, killing several VIPs from Washington. Following this, the FAA in Kansas City talked to Beech 18 operators and STC mod holders at a big meeting. And according to reports, one FAA representative told them all it was the agency's intention to "put these aircraft out of business."

Indeed, FAA spokesmen concede a notice of proposed rule making was under consideration that would for all practical purposes have ended the career of the old birds by requiring periodic wing spar replacements, presumably at great cost, rather than allowing the option of a supportive strap.

Nevertheless, in the ensuing hubub, the FAA person who issued the threat at the meeting was later transferred, but did not lose his job, as some contend.

Bad Feelings

The stage was set for a lot of bad feeling all around. And to this day, some Beech 18 operators feel they are unfairly harassed by the FAA via the AD route and, furthermore, many harbor great resentment for what they see as Beech Aircraft

Cost/Performance/Specifications

Model	Year	Number Built	Average Retail Price	Cruise Speed (kts)	Rate of Climb (fpm)	SE Ceiling (ft)	Useful Load (lbs)	Fuel Std/Opt (gals)	Engine	TBO (hrs)	Overhaul Cost
C18A	1938	NA	NA	NA	NA	NA	NA	NA	350-hp Wright R-760E-2	NA	NA
D18S	1946-48	NA	$22,000	183	1,200	7,750	2,980	206/286	450-hp P&W R-985-AN14B	1,600	$11,000
D18S	1949-51	NA	$23,000	183	1,200	7,750	2,980	206/286	450-hp P&W	1,600	$11,000
D18S	1952-54	NA	$24,000	183	1,200	7,750	2,980	206/286	450-hp P&W	1,600	$11,000
E18S	1955-57	NA	$28,000	187	1,250	8,400	3,150	206/286	450-hp P&W	1,600	$11,000
E18S	1958-59	NA	$29,000	187	1,250	8,400	3,150	206/286	450-hp P&W	1,600	$11,000
G18S	1960	91	$36,000	186	1,400	8,000	3,790	275/318	450-hp P&W	1,600	$11,000
G18S	1961	46	$37,500	186	1,400	8,000	3,790	275/318	450-hp P&W	1,600	$11,000
G18S	1962	20	$39,000	186	1,400	8,000	3,798	275/318	450-hp P&W	1,600	$11,000
H18S	1963	33	$40,000	191	1,400	7,900	4,055	198/318	450-hp P&W	1,600	$11,000
H18S	1964	61	$41,000	191	1,400	7,900	4,055	198/318	450-hp P&W	1,600	$11,000
H18S	1965	23	$42,500	191	1,400	7,900	4,055	198/318	450-hp P&W	1,600	$11,000
H18S	1966	8	$45,000	191	1,400	7,900	4,055	198/318	450-hp P&W	1,600	$11,000

Beech 18

239

Corp's abandonment of the old flagship. Beech, many "18" users maintain, would love to see the aircraft banished to eliminate a source of product liability discomfort and do away with yet another form of competition to new King Airs.

The Big AD

The Airworthiness Directive that brought matters to a head was 75-27-09. This imposed so-called "safe life limits" on all the Beech 18s, mandating one of two things: replacement of wing center sections and outboard wing panel parts that were older than those limits, or addition of a wing strap modification to cover the lower main wing spar tube. Since the cost of the first alternative was prohibitive, nearly everyone went the second route and installed the straps.

If a wing strap had already been installed, the AD required a never-ending series of X-ray inspections every 1,500 hours to check for corrosion, fretting, cracks or other defects.

The safe life limits for spar components if no strap were installed were pegged to the gross weight of the aircraft. The lower the gross, the longer the safe life limit. Hence, older aircraft certificated at a gross weight of only 6,700 pounds or less could go 3,500 hours before the big inspection or updating of wing parts. Aircraft with a gross of 10,200 or higher needed an inspection every 1,500 hours.

Do Beech 18s Break Apart?

Is the FAA's action on the Twin Beech justified? According to the agency, there have been nine fatal in-flight structural breakups of the Beech 18s involving wing failure. All but two of these, the FAA maintains, could have been prevented by adequate inspection.

According to the late George E. Milligan, the aircraft had been unfairly maligned, with the effect of greatly lowering its resale value. Milligan cited records showing that just six Beech 18s came apart in flight. But he said these ac-

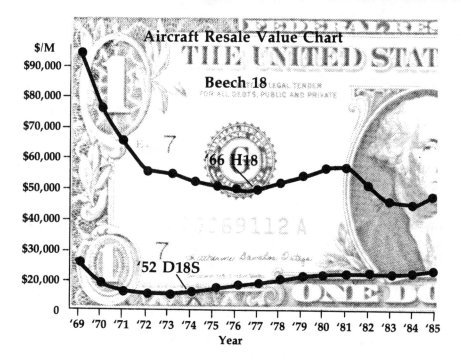

Aircraft Resale Value Chart

Beech 18

'66 H18

'52 D18S

$/M — $90,000 — $80,000 — $70,000 — $60,000 — $50,000 — $40,000 — $30,000 — $20,000 — 0

'69 '70 '71 '72 '73 '74 '75 '76 '77 '78 '79 '80 '81 '82 '83 '84 '85
Year

cidents don't reflect fairly on the civil fleet of Twin Beeches because most of them were military surplus, and at the time of the accidents were past their inspection time or over gross. To top it off, he claimed one was being used as a borate fire bomber when it hit a tree, but was back flying the next day when the wing came off.

Milligan also maintained and the FAA confirmed, that there has never been a failure in an airplane with the strap mod, which is designed to carry the entire load of the wing. And second, he claimed there's never been a crack in a tricycle-gear Beech 18, because the loads imposed by that configuration do not stress the wing spar.

Whether the AD severity is justified or not, the message is clear to the potential Beech 18 buyer. Many of the aircraft have been subjected to years of travail as military ships, cargo haulers and corporate machinery. The basic structure can be very old and very tired. It demands care and vigilance. With the wing strap attached and regular inspection, it would appear that the chance of catastrophic failure is remote.

Whether the economic burden of strap removal and elaborate, expensive X-ray inspections of wing spar components every 1,500 hours—plus an occasional emergency AD surprise like the one in

1980—make it worthwhile will have to be a matter of personal choice.

On the Other Hand ...

The other side of the coin, however, is that it conceivably could take quite a few inspection bills to balance out the intrinsic value of the Beech 18 as a mini transport hauler that costs no more than a fancily equipped "new" Cessna 152.

Owners rave about the comfort and style of the Beech 18s. How many other $50,000 aircraft can carry up to seven people plus 150 pounds of baggage and a full 320 gallons of fuel and cruise for 1,400 miles nonstop?

Said one operator: "My airplane carries nine people comfortably, and that's a pretty good-sized airplane. It's about four inches higher in the cabin and about two and a half feet longer in the cabin than a B90 King Air.

Performance and Handling

Pilots describe the Twin Beech as a real pussycat. "Better handling than a Baron" is a frequent characterization. "It's a hell of an instrument platform," said one owner. Pilots love the slow landing and takeoff speeds of the Beech 18—again, they say, slower than a Baron.

In cruise flight, the aircraft is also slower than a Baron. High cruise estimates in the real world range up to no better than about 179 knots at 58 percent power, while one figured he got no better than 143 knots at 55 percent.

"The only thing I don't like about it is that it's slow," said one owner. "We cruise at about 150 knots. Down and back to Savannah, Ga. from New York, I'll spend 11 hours in the plane." But, he says, "It's extremely comfortable, and our business is with corporations, and when you go into an airport, it's eye catching."

The tailwheel configuration also puts a bit more challenge into matters, especially since not too many of the newer pilots have taildragger experience. But owners adamantly downplay the difficulty of mastering the beast.

"As for tailwheel handling, it's like a standard shift on your car. Is that hard? It depends on what you're used to." Make wheelies or land three-point? Said one operator, "I land either way. It doesn't make much difference. But when you're landing three-point, you might catch hell on the tailwheel tire if you land slightly cocked while it's locked in the straightforward position. A lot of times I don't use the tailwheel lock on landing, depending on the winds. I let it castor."

Safety Record

The Beech 18 has a disastrous safety record. It logged the worst toll

On late models "power packs" improve the exhaust systems, but some mechanics report more difficult access.

for both fatal and nonfatal accidents among 20 different classes of light twins in a special study by the National Transportation Safety Board in 1979. The aircraft also had the worst rate of fatal accidents after an engine failure among that group.

A survey of Beech 18 accidents for a period of 26½ months (1977 through part of 1979) provided by the NTSB shows a total of 139 accidents for that period. Considering the fact that there are some 1,300 Beech 18s still flying, that means that some 11 percent of the entire fleet was involved in an accident in a little over two years.

As one might suspect, many of the accidents were related to extensive use of the aircraft as a commuter, air cargo ship and parachute jumping platform. A surprisingly small proportion of the accidents—nine were weather related. The dominant accident pattern—61, or about 44 percent—was related to problems encountered on the ground while landing, taking off or just taxiing. The second largest number—24, or 21 percent—stemmed from engine failures.

The ground-related accidents gave adequate testimony to the difficulty some pilots experienced handling the taildragger configuration of many Twin Beeches. Time and again the reports cited loss of directional control on either takeoff or landing, with resulting groundloops or swerves, along with improper recovery from bounced landings, often wiping out the landing gear.

The round-the-clock, fly-in-any-weather nature of air cargo operations took its toll on quite a few Twin Beeches, with aircraft running into snowbanks, or attempting to take off from slush- or ice-covered runways. Others managed to taxi into other aircraft, autos or other obstacles while trying to make their way around the airport at night, sometimes because no one cleaned the windshield. Several lost control on landing when a heavy cargo that was not secured shifted in the cabin. And there were quite a few in-

stances of operating well over gross and out of the c.g. range.

Poor maintenance showed up occasionally, with reports of failing brakes, severed control cables, failed tailwheel bolts or main gear mechanisms.

Among the engine-failure accidents, half a dozen or about 20 percent were attributed simply to the pilot running out of fuel because of mismanagement. There was no paricular trend among mechanical failures, which ranged from oil exhaustion to cylinder head breakage, malfunctioning prop pitch mechanism, turbo compressor failure and magneto and other ignition problems.

One Beech 18 crashed after taking off with a tank full of auto gas. And many of the pilots failed to make a successful landing despite the apparent full use of at least one engine—some failing to even feather the prop on the bad engine.

As a group, however, the Beech 18 pilots were no green tyros. Most had thousands of hours of flying time and lots in the Twin Beech. But this didn't prevent several from attempting to take off or land too close to big aircraft, and falling prey to vortex turbulence. One such crash cost the lives of nine people.

Among the bizarre accidents that befell the Beech 18 were a series related to buzzing for dope drops and several tail strikes by exiting parachute jumpers.

Maintenance

Operators claim maintenance problems—aside from wing spar troubles—are really not in proportion to the transport class of aircraft they are flying. Parts, even engine parts, appear easy to get—or at least no more difficult than for other contemporary general aviation aircraft.

"Ours is cheaper to fly than our Cessna 402," said one operator. "Number one, it's built to military specifications, so it's much more rugged. I would say our average

Deluxe configuration of the Larson cabin has four executive chairs in club-style seating, plus a two-place couch for a total capacity of eight, including crew.

annual wouldn't exceed maybe $700 or $800 at the most. And we're very cautious. We do our own maintenance.''

Indeed, most of the operators we talked to do the same; rarely did we find a party that farmed out the maintenance.

Said another operator, "In terms of maintenance, compared with a modern aircraft, I'd say the cost runs 50 percent less. I can get parts for the radial engines twice as quick as I can for my Bonanza. There's a firm in Tulsa (Southwest Aero Exchange) that has virtually every bolt, nut and rivet for the airplane.''

However, most of the owners we talked to said they shied away from Beech for parts support—though ironically at the same time they blamed the company for abandoning the aircraft. Said one, ''I wouldn't fool with Beech at all for parts. If Beech had them, they would cost an arm and a leg.''

This same party said his annual inspections ran from $1,500 to $4,000. "The highest I've paid was $7,000 at a Beech distributor," he added. "And then I brought it back home and got it fixed.''

Indeed, one of the growing problems for Beech 18 operators is that outside shops are less and less likely to have the specialized mainte-nance equipment for the aircraft and the radial engines.

Aside from the spar problems, we were able to log few chronic maintenance problems on the Twin Beech. One said he kept having trouble with the electric cowl flap motor, but added, ''I doubt if we've canceled more than one or two trips because of mechanical problems in a decade.'' Chronic problems tagged by others involved worn tailwheel tires and the older exhaust-type heaters that later were replaced by gas heaters.

Modifications

There is an endless list of modifications for this aircraft. There are stretched and turbopropped versions like the Hamilton Westwind. There is a single-tail model (the Tradewind) and a triple-tail model (the Dumod Liner). There are enlarged-window mods and double cargo door mods.

In the older airplanes there was a 77-gal. nose fuel tank along with four wing tanks. Some mods removed the nose tank and installed greater wing tank capacity, allowing useful items like radar to be installed in the nose.

Along with Hamilton Aviation, two of the best known modifiers are Volpar Inc. in Van Nuys, Calif. and the Dee Howard Company. But there are literally dozens of others.

Operators listed these other sources of Beech 18 parts: Howington Corp. of Daytona Beach, Fla.; Milford Aircraft Parts, Miami, Fla.; Courtesy Air Service, Glen Falls, N.Y. And of course Beech Aircraft Corp. is also supporting the aircraft, despite the sour expressions of disapproval from many.

Service Difficulties

In the five-year printout of problems there were many reports that the tailwheel shear bolt had failed during taxi or landing. One suggestion was the bolts be changed every 100 hours or even replaced with a stainless steel bolt.

Numerous problems were also reported with the radial engines, such as cylinder base studs broken, valves and cylinders cracked, superchargers failed. There also were many reports of cracked wing spar caps detected by X-ray inspection. According to an FAA spokesman, however, some of these are ''false calls,'' or manufacturing flaws that were accepted during the construction of the aircraft, but now are seen incorrectly as cracks. Also, some are minor flaws that might have opened up a bit but will go a long way before developing into any kind of a problem.

We also noted quite a few reports of cracked control columns or arms or yokes. There were also numerous reports of control cables frayed, rusted and broken. In a couple of cases there was a split flap situation when jackscrew threads were worn or pulled.

Investment Value

As an investment, the old Beech 18s have at least offered a certain drab stability in the past decade or so. Despite the devastating inspection ADs in the 1970's, the value of the aircraft held fairly stable and even rose a bit, though hardly enough to keep pace with inflation.

The last U.S. model—the H18, built in 1966—has remained roughly between $40,000 and $45,000 on the market for an entire decade. Its original bare price, incidentally, was $169,000—average equipped, $184,000.

The older D18—we tracked the 1952 model—sagged to a weary $15,000 in the early 1970's, but even it has slowly managed to climb back up in resale value to about $28,500 in 1981. This aircraft cost $87,000 bare when new and about $112,000 with average equipment.

There's no telling, of course, what effect further old age and repetitive nasty ADs will have on the aircraft, since it may have reached that plateau and status of the DC-3 in the minds of buyers. And everybody knows, that's indestructible.

Prospective Buyers

Any undeterred by the Beech 18's problems obviously would be wise to try to catch as late a model as possible—preferably a G or H model—with as few hours on the airframe as possible.

Although the military surplus models might be cheaper, many feel they've been put through the mill more than is desirable. And naturally, buyers should stay away from the fleet of night cargo ships plying the airways at a frantic pace, sometimes with insufficient care.

The best buys are those that have always been in corporate service, and the tricycle-gear models will spare the user some exciting moments and the need to be or find a qualified taildragger pilot. And remember to consider not only engine life left till TBO, but the number of hours left on the spar till the next 1,500-hour inspection. Naturally, high on the buyer's list of priorities should be evidence of a clean bill of health via the X-ray inspection route on the last strap examination.

Owner Comments

Our Beech 18 throws off a lot of oil. It's a loose-fitting engine. You've got to bear in mind that when you talk about the Beech 18 you're talking about several decades of airplanes. Mine (a '66 model) is four years newer than the King Airs. They cover a whole spectrum of time and usage.

For the hours it's flown and the way it's flown, the airplane does not have that bad an accident record. What they have done is to dump a bunch of military accidents in the accident reports. I think Beech has done just about everything they can to get the airplane grounded. I think it's one of the safest airplanes flying. But any time you gross one up the way some operators are doing and lose an engine on a hot day, it's about

like any other twin-engine airplane; it's not going to fly.

It's one of the easiest airplanes to fly. With the conventional gear, of course, if you let it get away from you, it's gone. But the tri-gear flies easier than a Baron. It's one of the most beautiful-flying airplanes, and ground handling is just perfect.

I can get parts for the radial engines twice as quick as I can for my Bonanza. One phone call will buy me any engine part I want out of Dallas. And not military surplus, but brand-new, even though they stopped making the engines about in 1950. There's a firm in Tulsa (Southwest Aero Exchange) that has virtually every bolt, nut and rivet for the airplane. I wouldn't fool with Beech at all. If Beech had it, it would be an arm and a leg.

In terms of maintenance, compared with a modern aircraft, I'd say the cost runs 50 percent less. First off, it's a hell of an airplane—it's a transport category airplane.

My airplane carries nine people comfortably, and that's a pretty good-sized airplane. It's about four inches higher in the cabin and about two and a half feet longer in the cabin than a B90 King Air.

I run around 42 gph fuel consumption with any octane from 80 up. At 55 percent power, that gives me about 200 mph true at 10,000 feet. We file 175 knots. With full fuel I can go about 1,200 nm without reserve, all the while carrying passengers and baggage to the tune of 3,000 pounds useful.

As for reliability, I've been flying behind those 450s since 1947.

Mine has thermostatic control of the oil temperatures, which is absolutely fantastic. I can crank up in zero degrees with 50 weight oil and by the time I get to the runway about half a mile from my hangar I have full operating oil temperatures.

I'd say the most chronic problem is the electric cowl flap motor. But I doubt if we've canceled more than

one or two trips because of mechanical problems in a decade.

The airplane has been highly maligned. Consider what's going on today with the Queen Airs and the Cessna 340 tails—airplanes still in production. There are no documented wing failures on a tri-gear model 18.

●

A lot of the Beech 18s have been put through the mill, and the majority of them, because they can carry so much weight, have been put through the 135 operation with cargo, coffins and everything else. You find that with 135 operations your maintenance is not up to par of that of corporate or airlines.

The 135 operators are trying to make dollars. They're flying nighttime, every day, and the airplane just can't be maintained as it should be.

The general handling of the airplane is beautiful. It's not heavy; it's very stable. And these Pratt & Whitney engines are really reliable. I've flown them where we blew a jug completely right off the engine, and you ride the manifold pressure and keep on truckin'. They swallow valves; they do all that good stuff, but you've got nine jugs out there, and they keep on goin'.

The problem with getting maintenance around the country is that the aircraft requires specialized tools for the radials. And not too many shops have them.

As for parts, if the FAA keeps going the way they are, putting all these airplanes in the boneyard, you'll never have problems getting parts. We have no problems. We have just as many problems getting parts for a Piper Arrow.

As for ADs, the nosegear had more ADs than the tailgear. I don't particularly care for it.

I can fly full fuel, three persons and stay up there for about 7½ hours.

As for pros and cons, you take the Beech 99 turboprop, with basically the same wing. The 99's having a lot of problems.

Beech Baron 55, 58, 58P

Beech's Baron is widely regarded as the "class" item among light twins — sort of a twin-engine Bonanza — with lots of performance, superb handling and a reputation for luxury and quality.

More than 5,000 Barons have been built over the past 25 years, ranging from the basic 260-hp 55 model to the pressurized 325-hp 58P. As an investment, the standard Baron has few peers, retaining a high proportion of its original value and, in most cases, appreciating steadily after a few years. For all its popularity and excellent reputation, however, some questions about safety and (in recent models at least) quality control deserve attention from the thoughtful used-Baron buyer.

History

The Baron was introduced in 1961 as an outgrowth of the Model 95 Travel Air series. That first Model 55 Baron had 260-hp Continental engines (up from 180-hp on the Travel Air) and a gross weight nearly 700 pounds higher than the Travel Air's. The 55 was Beech's answer to the very popular Cessna 310, which had been introduced six years previously.

The 1962 and 1963 Barons were called the A55, and offered a sixth seat as an option. The fuselage of the A55 was also 10 inches longer than the straight 55's. In 1964 it became the B55, a designation that lasted until production of the 260-hp Baron was suspended in 1983. In 1966, the gross weight of the B55 was increased from 4,880 to 5,100 pounds (actually, the higher gross weight applied to the last 11 of the 1965 models as well). With the gross weight came another nose extension to accommodate a larger front baggage compartment.

In 1966, the 260-hp B55 was joined by the 285-hp C55, which offered blistering performance (242 mph top speed) and 200 pounds more gross weight. The 1966 and 1967 big-engine Barons were the C55s, evolving to the D55 in 1968 and 1969, and finally to the E55 in 1970. Until the end of their production run in 1982, the 260-hp B55 and the 285-hp E55 remained virtually unchanged.

In 1967, the short-lived 56TC Baron was introduced. It was powered by monstrous turbocharged 380-hp Lycoming engines and a cruise speed of 284 mph was claimed. However, only 94 56TCs were sold over the next five years, and the airplane was discontinued after 1971. Apparently the lack of a large six-place cabin and pressurization doomed the airplane, and single-engine characteristics were reportedly, shall we say, challenging.

Taking up the slack from the unsuccessful 56TC in 1970 was the stretched 58 Baron, which at last provided a full six-seat interior instead of the four-plus-two arrangement of the standard-body Barons. It used the same 285-hp Continental engines as the big-engine 55 Barons, and had virtually the same performance as its short-bodied

Top of the Baron line are the 58s, here stacked up with the TC on top and the pressurized model on the bottom. The 58P has one rear left cabin door instead of double doors on the right side of the fuselage.

stablemate. The 58, with its wide double-door entry and club-car seating, has continued to be a strong seller.

In 1975, Beech introduced the pressurized 58P, with 310-hp engines. These were upgraded to 325 hp in 1979. In addition to the pressurization and bigger engines, the 58P has 100 pounds extra gross weight and a cruise speed that is 22 mph higher than the standard 58 (by the book, at least). A "non-pressurized 58P" was introduced in 1976, called the 58TC. The TC has the same engines as the P model, and got the boost to 325 hp at the same time, in 1979. Production was halted in 1982, however.

Investment Value

Like the Bonanza, the Baron is a real blue-chip in resale value in most cases. For example, a 1970 B55 originally cost $13,000 less than 1970 310, but today is worth $7,000 more. The big-engine E55 also looks good; a 1975 E55 cost $146,000 new and is worth $77,500 today (53 percent). A 1975 310 returns 40 percent, and is worth a fat $22,000 less than the E55 on the used-plane market. The 58 series does even better; a 1975 long-body Baron is now worth 56 percent of its original value.

The pressurized Baron 58P, however, doesn't seem to match the rest of the family in resale value. "The P-Baron has taken a real hit on the used-plane market," one big broker told us. Based on Aircraft Price Digest "Bluebook" retail figures, a 1976 P-Baron is today worth under 50 percent of its original price. For a straight 58 Baron, the figure is about 60 percent. "For the same money that a used 58P costs, you can buy a 421 that's just one year older. And the 421 is full cabin class, a hell of a lot more airplane," explained the dealer.

Another resale loser among the Barons is the ill-fated 56TC. The net value of those big engines over the years has been just about zero; a used 56TC is worth almost exactly the same as an E55 of the same vintage, which had non-turbocharged engines of 100 less horsepower each.

Performance

Here is the Baron's strong suit. The big-engine Barons are faster than any light twin except the Aerostar, and the 260-hp 55, A55 and B55 aren't too far behind. Owners report real-world cruising speeds of about 191 knots for the B55 and 195-200 knots for the E55 and 58 models. The turbocharged versions — 56TC, 58TC and 58P — are of course much faster at high altitude, with max cruise speeds rangin from about 209 knots for the 310-hp 58P and TC to well over 217 knots for the monster 56TC. The 325-hp 58TC and 58P, introduced in 1979, are listed by the books as about 9-13 knots faster than their 310-hp counterparts.

Standard fuel capacity in the small-body 55 Barons is normally 112 gallons (100 gallons usable), which gives a rather marginal endurance

of less than four hours, with no reserve. Many 55s have optional tanks that raise capacity to a more reasonable 142 gallons (136 usable), good for over five hours at moderate cruise power. The 285-hp airplanes burn about five gph more than the 260s, so even the 142-gallon tanks are not exactly generous. The 1973 and later E55s, however, have an optional capacity of 166 gallons, which is satisfactory for most IFR flying.

All the 58 models have standard 166-gallon fuel tanks, and most have optional tanks that raise capacity to 190 gallons. Obviously, a used Baron with long-range tanks is more desirable because of the greater flexibility for ultra-long-range flights with light passenger loads. (But extra tanks can be a mixed blessing from the maintenance standpoint. More on that later.)

Takeoff performance of the Baron is also excellent, particularly in the C, D and E55 models. Even at gross weight, an E55 needs little more than 1,000 feet to clear a 50-foot obstacle on takeoff (under standard conditions, of course). This requires some fairly extreme piloting technique that puts the airplane in the air below Vmc, however. With normal technique, takeoff distances under 2,000 feet are still possible at gross weight in the 55 Barons.

Handling

A major reason for the Baron's popularity and owner loyalty is the aircraft's superb handling qualities. The Baron is responsive and well-harmonized, a delight to fly. "The Baron is a beautiful flying aircraft, and it is just plain fun to handle on the controls," is a typical owner comment. There are no handling idiosyncrasies (such as severe pitch-up with flap deployment, as in the Aztec) we're aware of. "Real aviators" like the fact that there are no downsprings or aileron-rudder interconnects in most models of the Baron.

The other side of the "responsive" coin is, of course, sensitivity in turbulent IFR conditions. The same light control forces that win oohs and ahs from pilots demand more attention in the clouds, and a good autopilot is almost a necessity in a Baron flown IFR. One owner reports, "I have had several frightening moments because of its unstable flying characteristics in turbulence."

Like the Bonanza, the Baron is famed for its easy landings (except for the 58P), with a combination of pitch response and landing gear geometry that really boosts the egos of pilots. For many pilots, the way an airplane "feels" can overcome many performance shortcomings; the Baron's handling

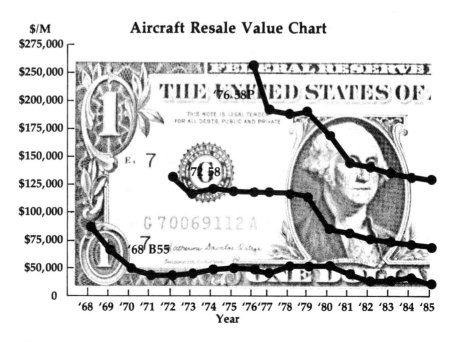

Aircraft Resale Value Chart

$/M

$275,000
$250,000
$200,000
$175,000
$150,000
$125,000
$100,000
$75,000
$50,000
0

'68 '69 '70 '71 '72 '73 '74 '75 '76 '77 '78 '79 '80 '81 '82 '83 '84 '85
Year

qualities have doubtless won over hundreds of piltos who may have been on the verge of buying something else.

Accommodations

The Baron pilot sits high, wide and handsome, with a plush, roomy cockpit and a professional-looking panel thankfully devoid of the plastic found in most other airplanes. Headroom is particularly good.

The 55 Barons are labeled "six-seaters," but the two rear seats are cramped afterthoughts, suitable only for kids or midgets on long flights.

The 58 models have the famous "club car" seating, which puts the back four passengers face to face in the style of the Orient Express. Although lacking Orient-Express roominess, the rear compartment of the 58 is adequate by light aircraft standards, and the fifth and sixth seats at least qualify as small-sized adult repositories.

The 58 models also have a big, wide double-door entrance to the rear compartment, a very nice touch. The 55s have the standard single

right-side pilot's door, which entails a certain amount of clambering for the hindmost travelers.

Baggage capacity is good, with front and rear compartments that allow reasonable balancing and good capacities in most models.

Up front, a couple of items on the panel are worth noting. First, the Baron's throttle quadrant is notorious for its reverse throttle and prop postions: the prop lever is on the left, with the throttle in the middle. An airplane could not be certified that way today, but Beech keeps on building them that way for some reason. Also, the gear and flap levers are reversed from their normal position in other aircraft, which could lead to the sound of

Throw-over wheel, reversed throttles and props, and aileron trim are standard on all the Barons. Only this 58P has the gear (left) and flap (right) levers in the standard position.

crunching metal when the pilot retracts the "flaps" during rollout after landing. (The 58P is an exception.) NTSB figures show many accidents of this type. The single throwover yoke is also an unusual feature, one that sometimes makes multi-engine instruction a tricky business (see "Safety" section for details).

Maintenance Checkpoints

The "Curse of the Cracking Crankcase" has depleted the bank ac-

Cost/Performance/Specifications

* TIO-540-E1B4   ** IO-520-C   *** IO-520-CB

Model	Year	Number Built	Average Price	Cruise Speed (kts)	Rate Climb (fpm)	Useful Load (lbs)	S/E Ceiling (ft)	Fuel Std/Opt (gals)	Engine	TBO (hours)	Overhaul Cost
56TC	1967-1969	83	$ 44,000	247	2,020	2,340	18,000	142/204	380-hp Lyc.*	1,600	$22,000
A56TC	1970-1971	12	$ 50,000	247	2,020	2,390	18,600	142/204	380-hp Lyc.*	1,600	$22,00
C55	1966-1967	451	$ 38,000	200	1,670	2,225	7,100	112/142	285-hp Cont.**	1,500	$ 9,250
D55	1968-1969	315	$ 44,000	200	1,670	2,225	7,100	112/142	285-hp Cont.**	1,500	$ 9,250
E55	1970-1971	82	$ 32,000	195	1,682	2,038	6,000	100/166	285-hp Cont.**	1,500	$ 9,250
E55	1972-1973	95	$ 61,000	195	1,682	2,038	6,000	100/166	285-hp Cont.**	1,500	$ 9,250
E55	1974	62	$ 70,000	195	1,682	2,038	6,000	100/166	285-hp Cont.**	1,500	$ 9,250
E55	1975	62	$ 77,000	195	1,682	2,038	6,000	100/166	285-hp Cont.**	1,500	$ 9,250
E55	1976	23	$ 85,000	195	1,682	2,038	6,000	100/166	285-hp Cont.**	1,500	$ 9,250
E55	1977	29	$ 97,000	195	1,682	2,038	6,000	100/166	285-hp Cont.**	1,500	$ 9,250
E55	1978	28	$111,000	195	1,682	2,038	6,000	100/166	285-hp Cont.***	1,500	$ 9,250
E55	1979	25	$130,000	195	1,682	2,038	6,000	100/166	285-hp Cont.***	1,500	$ 9,250
E55	1980	12	$150,000	195	1,682	2,038	6,000	100/166	285-hp Cont.***	1,500	$ 9,250
E55	1981	12	$172,000	195	1,682	2,038	6,000	100/166	285-hp Cont.***	1,500	$ 9,250
E55	1982	5	$200,000	195	1,682	2,038	6,000	100/166	285-hp Cont.***	1,500	$ 9,250

Cost/Performance/Specifications————————————————————

Model	Year	Number Built	Average Price	Cruise Speed (kts)	Rate Climb (fpm)	Useful Load (lbs)	S/E Ceiling (ft)	Fuel Std/Opt (gals)	Engine	TBO (hrs)	Overhaul Cost
55	1961	190	$ 28,000	191	1,630	1,920	7,600	112	260-hp Cont.*	1,500	$8,750
A55	1962-1963	309	$ 31,000	181	1,700	1,920	7,600	112	260-hp Cont.*	1,500	$8,750
B55	1964-1965	457	$ 35,000	196	1,670	2,025	7,600	112	260-hp Cont.*	1,500	$8,750
B55	1966-1967	76	$ 38,000	196	1,670	2,025	7,600	112	260-hp Cont.*	1,500	$8,750
B55	1968-1969	244	$ 42,000	196	1,670	2,025	7,600	112	260-hp Cont.*	1,500	$8,750
B55	1970-1971	124	$ 47,000	196	1,670	2,025	7,600	112	260-hp Cont.*	1,500	$8,750
B55	1972-1973	204	$ 53,000	196	1,693	2,025	7,600	100/136	260-hp Cont.*	1,500	$8,750
B55	1974	173	$ 59,000	196	1,693	2,150	6,400	100/136	260-hp Cont.*	1,500	$8,750
B55	1975	123	$ 66,000	196	1,693	2,150	6,400	100/136	260-hp Cont.*	1,500	$8,750
B55	1976	96	$ 73,000	196	1,693	2,150	6,400	100/136	260-hp Cont.*	1,500	$8,750
B55	1977	88	$ 82,000	196	1,693	2,150	6,400	100/136	260-hp Cont.*	1,500	$8,750
B55	1978	88	$ 91,000	196	1,693	2,150	6,400	100/136	260-hp Cont.*	1,500	$8,750
B55	1979	94	$100,000	196	1,693	2,150	6,400	100/136	260-hp Cont.*	1,500	$8,750
B55	1980	78	$115,000	196	1,693	2,150	6,400	100/136	260-hp Cont.*	1,500	$8,750
B55	1981	65	$136,000	196	1,693	2,150	6,400	100/136	260-hp Cont.*	1,500	$8,750
B55	1982	35	$165,000	196	1,693	2,150	6,400	100/136	260-hp Cont.*	1,500	$8,750

counts of more than a few 285-hp Baron owners. While crankcase cracks are rarely a safety-of-flight item, they can be expensive maintenance headaches. One operator of a fleet of Barons reports he spent over $70,000 in premature overhauls triggered by case cracks.

As you shop for used Barons, you may hear references to "light cases" and "heavy cases." Pre-1976 airplanes had cases which were particularly prone to cracking. Continental then introduced a beefier case which was supposed to lick the problem. It didn't. An *Aviation Consumer* survey in 1982 showed that, if anything, the "heavy" cases cracked a bit more often — and earlier in the engine's life — than the so-called "light" cases.

There have been so many permutations of IO-520-C crankcases that we can't advise one type as preferable to any other. As far as we can tell, they all are prone to crack. More important than case "heaviness" or "lightness" is heat-treating for stress relief. The crankcases are not heat-treated when they come from the factory, but some owners have their cases heat-treated during overhaul or when cracks are repaired. This ap-

parently reduces internal stress in the metal, dramatically reducing the cracking tendency. "I've heat-treated hundreds of IO-520 cases," one repair shop told us, "and not one of them has cracked that I'm aware of."

The bottom line: carefully check the crankcases of any 285-hp Baron considered for purchase. And count it a plus if the case has been heat-treated.

Despite the epidemic cracking crankcases, the Baron's owner loyalty is striking. One hyperenthusiastic 1974 Baron 58 owner wrote us, "Over a period of five years, my Baron operated flawlessly, with very minor problems, except the usual crankcase crack problems occurred at about 950 hours, necessitating the replacement of both engines at considerable expense . . .".

The other big maintenance headache for Barons is the rubber bladder-type fuel cells. The lifetime of these cells can be as low as three or four years, and 10 years seems to be about the maximum. The tanks of any used Baron should be carefully checked for leakage, and a buyer would be wise to set aside a bladder replacement fund for the

inevitable $3,500-plus wallop and accompanying downtime. Like the man in the cigar commercial says, "We're gonna get you. . .".

Some pre-1964 Barons may still have the so-called "light" cylinders, which proved troublesome and are subject to an AD requiring 20-hour inspections.

Other Baron problems to look out for: crazing windshields, unreliable Goodyear brakes, old B-series autopilots (very difficult to get service anymore), electric cowl flaps on pre-1974 models, 100-amp (Presto-Lite or Crittendon) alternators, and Airborne high-capacity vacuum pumps used for de-ice applications.

Safety

In terms of overall accidents, the Baron ranks about average among light twins. Fatal accident rate was also about in the middle of the pack. From 1972-76, the entire Baron/Travel-Air series scored 2.8 and 8.3, respectively, for fatal and total accident rates. The same group improved to 1.4 and 5.3 in 1977-82, for overall scores of 2.0 and 6.5 for the entire decade.

We decided to separate the 58 and

55 models out of the group to see if there was a difference between the long-body 58s and their smaller forebears. The answer: not much. For the period 1977-82 only, the 58 had a low 1.1 fatal rate, while the 55 was a not-quite-so-low 1.4. The 58 also had a better overall accident rate, 4.5 to 6.4

The Baron's accident rate might have been better without a bunch of stall/spin accidents. An earlier study commissioned by *Aviation Consumer* showed that for the years 1970-74, the Baron had a much higher stall/spin rate than other light twins. In fact, about a quarter of all fatal Baron accidents during that period were stall/spins. Eliminate those, and the Baron's accident rate would improve noticeably.

The Baron stall/spin rate has apparently declined in recent years, however, as more attention has been focused on the subject and Beech has mailed Baron owners

handbook supplements warning of the problem. That may be a big part of the Baron's improved accident rate during the last half of the decade.

A 1974 Army test report on the single-engine stall characteristics of the T-42A, the military version of the Baron, sheds some light on the subject. (The special test came after a series of fatal stall/spin accidents during Army training flights.) The Army test pilot reported that the T-42A would enter a spin within one second after a single-engine stall unless immediate anti-spin action was taken. Even if stall recovery was initiated within one-quarter second after the stall break, said the Army report, a split-S and 1,000-foot altitude loss resulted. The author of the report also criticized the T-42A operator's manual for not warning of the serious consequences of a single-engine stall, and not explaining, for example, that single-engine stall speed was up to 20 knots higher than the

listed stall speed under symmetric power conditions.

Later Baron manual revisions carry blunter warnings in the safety section, however.

Modifications

We know of just one Baron engine conversion, the Colemill "President 600," which replaces the 260-hp engines of the 55, A55, or B55 with 300-hp Continentals. It is reportedly an outstanding performer, with no major problems except the possibility of cracked crankcases in pre-1977 conversions.

Cosmetic mods, such as one-piece windshields and updated side windows are available from Beryl D'Shannon, Jordan, Minn.

We know of no owner's organization for the Baron, although the American Bonanza Society newsletter does occasionally

Cost/Performance/Specifications

* TSIO-520-L ** TSIO-520-WB *** IO-520-C

Model	Year	Number Built	Average Price	Cruise Speed (kts)	Rate Climb (fpm)	Useful Load (lbs)	S/E Ceiling (ft)	Fuel Std/Opt (gals)	Engine	TBO (hours)	Overhaul Cost
58P	1976	85	$130,000	207	1,424	2,115	13,220	190	310-hp Cont.*	1,400	$15,000
58P	1977	36	$140,000	216	1,529	2,115	14,400	166/190	310-hp Cont.*	1,400	$15,000
58P	1978	45	$152,000	214	1,529	2,115	14,400	166/190	310-hp Cont.*	1,400	$15,000
58P	1979	65	$170,000	232	1,481	2,200	13,490	166/190	325-hp Cont.**	1,400	$16,000
58P	1980	80	$202,500	232	1,481	2,200	13,490	166/190	325-hp Cont.**	1,400	$16,000
58P	1981	67	$235,000	232	1,481	2,200	13,490	166/190	325-hp Cont.**	1,400	$16,000
58P	1982	46	$270,000	232	1,481	2,200	13,490	166/190	325-hp Cont.**	1,400	$16,000
58P	1983	20	$350,000	232	1,481	2,200	13,490	166/190	325-hp Cont.**	1,400	$16,000
58P	1984	27	$450,000	232	1,481	2,200	13,490	166/190	325-hp Cont.**	1,400	$16,000
58TC	1976	34	$115,000	214	1,461	2,320	14,400	166/190	310-hp Cont.*	1,400	$15,000
58TC	1977	25	$122,000	214	1,461	2,320	14,400	166/190	310-hp Cont.*	1,400	$15,000
58TC	1978	24	$132,000	214	1,461	2,320	14,400	166/190	310-hp Cont.*	1,400	$15,000
58TC	1979	24	$150,000	232	1,418	2,412	13,450	166/190	325-hp Cont.**	1,400	$16,000
58TC	1980	23	$150,000	232	1,418	2,412	13,450	166/190	325-hp Cont.**	1,400	$16,000
58TC	1981	12	$210,000	232	1,418	2,412	13,450	166/190	325-hp Cont.**	1,400	$16,000
58TC	1982	4	$250,000	232	1,418	2,412	13,450	166/190	325-hp Cont.**	1,400	$16,000
58	1970-1971	174	$ 61,000	195	1,660	2,147	7,000	136/166	285-hp Cont.***	1,800	$ 9,250
58	1972-1973	209	$ 72,000	195	1,660	2,147	7,000	166	285-hp Cont.***	1,800	$ 9,250
58	1974-	139	$ 82,000	195	1,660	2,147	7,000	166	285-hp Cont.***	1,800	$ 9,250
58	1975	154	$ 90,000	195	1,660	2,147	7,000	166	285-hp Cont.***	1,800	$ 9,250
58	1976	92	$100,000	195	1,660	2,147	7,000	166	285-hp Cont.***	1,800	$ 9,250
58	1977	99	$112,000	195	1,660	2,147	7,000	136/194	285-hp Cont.***	1,800	$ 9,250
58	1978	99	$125,000	195	1,660	2,147	7,000	136/194	285-hp Cont.***	1,800	$ 9,250
58	1979	106	$137,000	195	1,660	2,147	7,000	136/194	285-hp Cont.***	1,800	$ 9,250
58	1980	113	$155,000	195	1,660	2,147	7,000	136/194	285-hp Cont.***	1,800	$ 9,250
58	1981	103	$175,000	195	1,660	2,147	7,000	136/194	285-hp Cont.***	1,800	$ 9,250
58	1982	57	$210,000	195	1,660	2,147	7,000	136/194	285-hp Cont.***	1,800	$ 9,250
58	1983	30	$267,000	195	1,660	2,147	7,000	136/194	285-hp Cont.***	1,800	$ 9,250
58	1984	39	$325,000	195	1,660	2,147	7,000	136/194	285-hp Cont.***	1,800	$ 9,250

publish material about the Baron. Also, the Barons and Bonanzas have enough in common that ABS membership might well benefit from Baron owners.

Owner Comments

Our company has owned three Barons in the past 12 years, and we hated to part with the first two. We purchased our present one, a 1974 B55, when it was a young demonstrator with about 80 hours. We have flown it 1,100 hours now.

Our '68 B55 performed perfectly for 800 hours when we swapped it for a newer '73 E55. A fine aircraft, but we had the usual problems with cracked cases on the 285 engines, noticeably more engine noise and about six more gallons per hour with only five knots or so more speed. A fine plane, but the B55 is even better.

Now take the B55 — responsive, economical (we use only 24 gallons per hour and cruise at 191 knots), very easy to handle in any type of crosswind, gentle in turbulent air, and the 260 Continentals are quiet. The B55 sits good. You are over the panel with a perfect view. Perhaps the cabin is not as dramatic as the 58 model Baron, but most of our flying is with only one or two passengers or alone.

The B55 is primarily a VFR light twin or mild IFR with no heavy weather. We've had ice a few times and it doesn't carry it very well. The Century 3 autopilot guides the B55 perfectly, and it is a fine night aircraft and good for normal instrument operations — but *not* for rough weather.

I took delivery of my new 1974 Beechcraft Baron 58 at the Beechcraft factory. I operated the aircraft for five years, and even though the aircraft was out of warranty, Beech continued to support certain items that they were not legally bound to support.

When I ultimately sold the aircraft,

Model 58P has depreciated much more than other Barons.

the value had held remarkably strong, even against used pressurized aircraft such as the Cessna 340. My depreciation was a mere 10 percent over a five-year period.

Over a period of five years, the Baron operated in a flawless manner with very minor problems, except the usual crankcase crack problems occurred at about 950 hours total time, necessitating the replacement of both engines at considerable expense. However, the airframe and component parts were all well within tolerances, except for the fuel gauges, which never were right.

It is an extremely efficient form of transportation and consistently flies at 190 knots. Over the five-year period it averaged approximately 30 gallons-per-hour at altitudes 8,000 to 12,000 feet.

●

I own a 1977 Beech Baron 55, which I purchased new in 1977. The aircraft now has 675 hours total time and has been piloted only by myself (4,000 hours) and a friend (1,000) who is also multi-engine and instrument rated.

I have been involved in aviation a long time and I had always felt that owning a Beechcraft would be the ultimate in aircraft ownership, but if this aircraft is an example of current Beech quality and workmanship, I would not recommend a Beech Baron to any friends that are contemplating buying an airplane.

In the first year of operation, I had literally scores of malfunctions,

and spent more than $1,000 just to rent aircraft to ferry me back and forth to the maintenance base after dropping off the Baron for repairs.

In addition, the following have happened to my Baron more recently:

1. 400 hours — the right vacuum pump failed.

2. 450 hours — the left magneto on the right engine failed.

3. 500 hours — the heater motor required replacement.

4. 500 hours — an oil seal in the right propeller hub failed.

5. 550 hours — left engine failed in flight.

6. 575 hours — new starter on remanufactured Continental engine failed.

7. 600 hours — nose gear door control mechanism failed.

8. The hot props do not work, and the wiring is again protruding from behind the spinner.

9. The yaw damper does not work properly.

The ease of handling in VFR flight makes the plane a delight to fly, but the same lightness of control can be hazardous in hard IFR. I have had several frightening moments because of its unstable flying characteristics in turbulence. I still feel that the Baron has the nicest landing characteristics, the best brakes, the best ground handling and the sleekest looks of any aircraft I have ever flown.

Piper Aerostar

Few aircraft have gone through such such dramatic highs and lows as the much-traveled Aerostar series. Although a hot performer, the aircraft has acquired a disastrous accident record.

As the brainchild of the late Ted Smith, the Aerostar was conceived as a kind of universal paradigm from which would spring all kinds of singles and twins, pistons and jets. Offered to and declined by the parent Rockwell company as a successor to the Aero Commanders (that, in turn, had been designed by Smith), the Aerostar project was then launched by the newly formed Ted Smith Aircraft Co., and the first Model 600 was certificated in 1967.

In one short year the aircraft was sold to, of all companies, American Cement. This relationship lasted a little less than two years before the aircraft was once again sold, this time to Butler Aviation. Shortly afterward, however, with the Aerostar name tainted by scandal and charges that the airframe was subject to corrosion because of improper manufacture, Ted Smith took over the airplane again to remove its scarlet letter and set it on a proper course.

This seemed a *fait accompli* when another uproar broke out in 1978 over the design of the Aerostar fuel system, and a number of double engine failures related to it.

Finally, Piper Aircraft Corp. took over the line and incorporated it as an avant-garde step-up from its aging, stalwart Aztec. This coup gave Piper the satisfaction of having acquired a trio of aircraft built on a common airframe, featuring a choice of normally aspirated, turbocharged and pressurized designs. It also presented Piper with the headache of coming up with a fuel system pilots could comprehend and live with.

The fuel system uproar finally died down by 1980, after FAA Airworthiness Directives required several changes. But in 1982, the Aerostar's stall characteristics came under FAA scrutiny. The result was another AD, this one restricting the center-of-gravity envelope unless the tail was modified to improve stall characteristics.

Piper introduced a couple of souped-up Aerostar versions of its own, but the Great Slump of the 1980s prompted Piper to halt production and put the whole Aerostar line up for sale. As this is written, in 1985, the Aerostar is in limbo, out of production and still on the auction block.

But despite their quirks, the Aerostars were the undisputed speed demons of the light-twin fleet.

Aerostars look fast; they fly fast. This means an astonishing 218 knots/251 mph on a normally aspirated pair of 290-hp Lycomings or 240 knots/277 mph with turbos and pressurization at 24,000 feet. By comparison, the old Aero Commander Shrike with the same normally aspirated engines yields only about 176 knots.

Investment Value

The Aerostar models — all three of them — appear to represent an unusually fine investment value, judging from the figures we obtained from tracking three early models.

After a sharp plunge in resale value in just one year, rather than the three to five in normal patterns, the 1970 normally aspirated 600 and the turbocharged 601 leveled off and began ascending. They did not begin to tail off until the early 1980s, when all aircraft values declined.

The 1974 pressurized 601P we tracked never did take the initial plunge most aircraft betray, but instead bounced up and down, pretty well maintaining its initial value until the early 80s.

Model Evolution

The design has undergone few changes of any significance since its introduction in 1969. In 1973, with the 600A and 601A models, a new so-called "K" crankshaft was incorporated in the Lycoming IO-540 engines. This reduced vibration and boosted the TBO significantly from 1,400 to 2,000 hours on the normally aspirated 600As and from 1,400 to 1,800 hours on the turbocharged models. This came about with serial number 0144 and up.

Non-turbocharged 600A was last built in 1981. It has shorter wings than 601 and 601P, but the engines are more reliable.

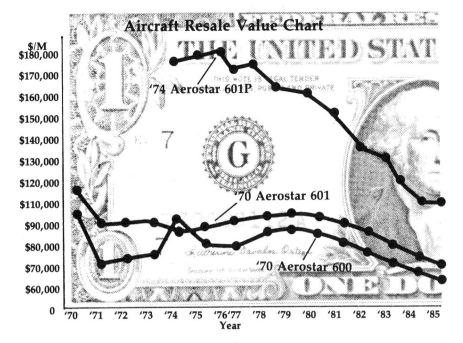

Aircraft Resale Value Chart

$/M

'74 Aerostar 601P

'70 Aerostar 601

'70 Aerostar 600

Year

The next big modification occurred in 1977 with the addition of 30 more inches in wingspan to the turbo models for better high-altitude performance. At the same time the gross weight was boosted by 300 pounds to 6,000 pounds. This began with serial number 213, designated 601B, and in effect brought the turbocharged model up to the same configuration as the pressurized model. The normally aspirated model kept its lower 5,500-pound gross and shorter wing.

Another significant change affecting all three Aerostars in '77 was a hike in the zero-wing-fuel limitation from 5,400 to 5,900 pounds. This eliminated what many felt was a serious payload shortcoming. Since it was a paperwork engineering exercise on the existing structure, it applied retroactively to the older Aerostars as well.

The year '77 was a good one for improvements in other areas as well. The flap extension speed was raised by 18 knots, making it easier to slow down the aircraft, and a positive down lock was incorporated into the landing gear handle to prevent inadvertent retraction of the nosegear on the ground. There is no squat switch on the gear itself, and in one instance the nosegear collapsed with the handle up and the engines running.

Pilots interested in the turbo-

charged Aerostars should note that several evolutionary changes were made. The first models had manual waste gate systems that worked off electric rocker switches. These were replaced on the B models with automatic systems. And in 1978 improved Piper waste gate systems were added, replacing the Rajays, giving much better high-altitude performance right up to 25,000 feet. It also boosted the critical altitude from 16,000 to 23,000 feet. Earlier models are described by pilots as going up to 25 grand when new, but then pooping out at lower altitudes after a few hundred hours' use. Dealers report a booming business on retrofitting these new waste gates to older model Aerostars at about $3,200 a set.

In 1981, Piper introduced the 602P, an improved version of the pressurized 601P. The new model had a Lycoming-designed integral turbocharger installation instead of the add-on Rajay units previously used, along with low-compression pistons. These changes were designed to combat the severe engine detonation problems resulting from the earlier jury-rigged turbo system. While offering much better reliability, the 602P unfortunately couldn't match the all-out performance of the 601P — cruise speed was about 10-15 knots slower.

Shortly after introducing the 602P, Piper dropped the unpressurized

600A and 601B models. In 1984, Piper brought out the 700P, with 350-hp engines, but only a couple of dozen were built before the whole line was folded and put up for sale.

Handling Characteristics

Despite its image as a hot ship, the Aerostar is regarded affectionately by most pilots in terms of handling. Control response is quick and deft; an aileron-rudder link allows almost feet-on-the-floor maneuvering. Pilots rave about engine-out characteristics such as an unusually mild yaw reaction with an engine loss during cruise, and a stall speed set above minimum control speed (Vmc) for added protection. Ted Smith like to boast that the aircraft really didn't need a minimum control speed, but the FAA required it.

Despite all this praise from pilots, however, there have been quite a few fatal Aerostar engine-failure accidents in which the pilot was unable to maintain control after losing an engine.

The takeoff perhaps give fliers the most cause for discussion. The aircraft, which rests on the ground with a negative angle of attack, tends to want to stay earthbound, and the heavy load on the nose-wheel calls for a real heave of the control wheel to get the machine rotated and flying. Some advise a partial easing back on the wheel, at 40 to 50 knots, and holding it there to ease the transition to final rotation.

On final approach the aircraft benignly tends to hold the airspeed determined by power setting, reacting hardly at all to variations in pitch.

In taxi operations, the pilot will have to become accustomed to steering not with the rudder pedals in conventional fashion, but by means of an electric rocker switch on the console beneath the throttle quadrant. It sounds eery, but works quite nicely and actually is great fun and allows unusually sharp manuevering on the ramp.

Piper Aerostar

One complaint that surfaces now and again about the Aerostars is vibration. Some blame it on the engines; some the props. One experienced Aerostar pilot has a theory he says he can prove every time. He maintains the problem is not related in any way to engines or proper, but to an idiosyncracy stemming from the heavier than usual skin gauge used in the wings and fuselage.

According to this theory, the vibration is triggered when the aircraft flies through light turbulence, as when ascending or dropping through a haze layer. This sets up a resonant, tuning fork-like vibration in the structure of the airplane that passes when the disturbance layer is passed.

The high wing loading of the aircraft typically handles normal chop with greater than usual aplomb and no abnormal vibration.

The designer's fondness for electric controls has given rise to the Aerostar moniker as an "electric aircraft." Indeed, the center console is home to a raft of unobtrusive electric switches — not only for steering, but for pitch and rudder trim — and even for turbocharging. A pair of rocker switches on the pre-B models allowed the pilot to close and open the waste gate by electric motor with little nudges of the switches. At least this eliminated the need for another pair of power levers on the throttle quadrant. It does leave the pilot is something of a bind, however, if the electrical system or the switches fail. Similarly, the fuel valve is electrically actuated. If the solenoid fails, the pilot may switch the fuel selector but not realize that the valve itself has failed to respond.

Cabin Comfort

With the constant-section fuselage, none of the up to six riders on the Aerostar can boast of more, or complain of less space, which is quite plentiful, with a small aisle between the seats. Though no conventional club-seating is available, there is a fold-out table arrangement for five seats.

Thanks to the big cabin windows, everybody has lots of light. Thanks to the mid-wing arrangement, though, only the pilots really have a great view of anything except the sky and the wing and engine nacelles. Pilot visibility naturally is fantastic.

The greatest discomfort burden Aerostarts have imposed through the years in one of terrible cockpit din, thanks to the droning of the props right outside the window. Pilots report the anguish diminished in stages with later models — especially the pressurized ones — as more and more soundproofing measures were taken.

Baggage

The Aerostars will carry a healthy amount of baggage — up to 240 pounds — but it must be heaved into a chest-high compartment accessible only from the outside rear fuselage. One loading quirk to look out for: the Aerostar is at its most tail-heavy with only a solo pilot aboard. This is because of the aft wing placement, which puts all the passengers ahead of the center of gravity. Unlike virtually all other aircraft, which have the c.g. position at about the pilot's seat, the Aerostar gets progressively nose-heavier as passengers are loaded.

Systems Engineering

Aside from the lack of nose-gear squat switch previously mentioned, which may result in inadvertent, unwananted retraction, the Aerostar lacks another feature in standard configuration that might result in failure to retract when it is most desired — on takeoff with failure of the right engine, housing the single hydraulic pump. An electric hydraulic pump is offered as an important option, however.

The shortcoming on which the most attention has been cast, of course, involves the fuel system. The Aerostars have a 44-gallon fuselage tank and wet wing tanks, each of which holds 66.5 gallons. Though everything is supposed to work automatically, with no need

Cost/Performance/Specifications

Model	Year	Cruise Speed (kts)	Useful Load (lbs)	SE Ceiling (ft)	Fuel (gals)	Engine	TBO (hrs)	Overhaul Cost	Average Price
600	1969-70	224	1,760	6,150	174	290-hp Lyc. IO-540-G1B5	1,400	$12,500	$ 59,000
600A	1973-75	224	1,760	6,150	174	290-hp Lyc. IO-540-K1F5	2,000	$12,500	$ 77,000
600A	1976-78	224	1,760	6,150	174	290-hp Lyc. IO-540-K1F5	2,000	$12,500	$170,000
600A	1979	224	1,760	6,150	174	290-hp Lyc. IO-540-K1J5	2,000	$12,500	$117,500
600A	1980	224	1,760	6,150	174	290-hp Lyc. IO-540-K1J5	2,000	$12,500	$127,500
600A	1981	224	1,760	6,150	174	290-hp Lyc. IO-540-K1J5	2,000	$12,500	$142,500
601	1969-70	233	1,950	10,800	174	290-hp Lyc. IO-540-P1A5	1,400	$12,500	$ 72,000
601A	1973-76	233	1,950	10,800	174	290-hp Lyc. IO-540-P1A5	1,800	$12,500	$ 85,000
601B	1977-78	233	2,040	9,300	174	290-hp Lyc. IO-540-S1A5	1,800	$12,500	$110,000
601B	1979	233	2,040	9,300	174	290-hp Lyc. IO-540-S1A5	1,800	$12,500	$127,500
601B	1980	233	2,040	9,300	174	290-hp Lyc. IO-540-S1A5	1,800	$12,500	$142,500
601B	1981	233	2,040	9,300	174	290-hp Lyc. IO-540-S1A5	1,800	$12,500	$157,500
601P	1974-75	230	1,950	9,300	174	290-hp Lyc. IO-540-S1A4	1,800	$12,500	$ 97,000
601P	1976-77	230	1,950	9,300	174	290-hp Lyc. IO-540-S1A5	1,800	$12,500	$110,000
601P	1978	230	1,950	9,300	174	290-hp Lyc. IO-540-S1A5	1,800	$12,500	$127,500
601P	1979	230	1,950	9,300	174	290-hp Lyc. IO-540-S1A5	1,800	$12,500	$140,000
601P	1980	230	1,950	9,300	174	290-hp Lyc. IO-540-S1A5	1,800	$12,500	$155,000
601P	1980	230	1,950	9,300	174	290-hp Lyc. IO-540-S1A5	1,800	$12,500	$175,000

to switch tanks, it is critical always to have fuel in the fuselage tank. Otherwise, inadvertent unporting of the supply line from either of the wing tanks to its respective engine, in a climb or dive, can result in engine stoppage. Line crews must always be advised to fill the center tank first.

However, in some situations, the fuselage tank does not feed evenly along with both wing tanks, as it should, and depletion of the center tank can trigger a single or a double engine stoppage.

Adding to the confusion was a fuel-monitoring setup that allowed the pilot to read either total fuel in all three tanks or fuel in the left or right wing separately. But he must calculate the amount of fuel in the fuselage tank. The fact that the fuel quantity gauge was located on the very right extreme corner of the instrument panel way out of the pilot's normal scan certainly did not improve the situation.

The first fix to preven inadvertent depletion of the center tank was an Airworthiness Directive mandating a low-fuel warning light for the center tank. Later, a sweeping AD required installation by Dec. 31, 1979 of a new triple fuel gauge showing fuel levels simultaneously in all three tanks. Or owners might install a single gauge showing a continuous readout of the center tank, with provision for switching to readouts on left or right wing tanks separately.

The AD also required a series of checks to insure a good seal of fuel filler caps and reduced the max usable fuel from 174.5 to 165.5 gallons (41.5 gals. in the fuselage tanks and 62 gals. in each wing tank). In addition, an overpressure relief valve

Aft wing placement puts all passengers ahead of the c.g. Aft limit is pushed with pilot only.

was ordered installed in the wing tanks.

The reason for the fuel cap checks was to prevent negative pressures from developing in the wing tanks, restricting fuel flow and causing premature depletion of the fuselage tank.

FAA tests made in connection with the AD also showed that it is rarely possible to fill the wing tanks to their full capacity unless the aircraft is dead level on the ramp and special fueling procedures are used. With normal fueling techniques, discrepancies up to nine gallons were noted. This is because of the configuration of the wing tanks and the lack of dihedral in the wings.

Safety Record

The Aerostar ranks dead last among light twins in safety. According to statistics compiled by *The Aviation Consumer*, it has a fatal accident rate of 4.4 per 100,000 hours — about double that of the typical light twin and more than triple the rate of the Beech Baron, a closely comparable aircraft. Total accident rate is 12.9, again much higher than the average light twin. The Baron's overall rate is 4.9.

Most of the Aerostar's fatal accidents are related to the design of the airplane, in our opinion. Weather played a surprisingly small role in Aerostar accidents, in contrast to most other aircraft. During the period 1978-82, there wasn't a single fatal IFR approach accident in an Aerostar and only about 25 percent of the Aerostar fatals involved weater. (By contrast, 75 percent of the Baron fatals involved weather.)

If weather isn't killing Aerostar pilots, what is? Forty percent of Aerostar fatal accidents followed engine failures of some sort; 35 percent resulted from stalls and/or spins. The pilots in fatal Aerostar crashes, although generally of broad flying experience, tended to

have few hours in the Aerostar. Median experience was just 70 hours in type, compared to 300 hours in type for pilots of fatal-crash Barons. For a detailed report on the Aerostar's accident record compared to the Baron, see the next chapter.

Other ADs

Other significant ADs included several in 1970 and '71 involving: installing a kit to prevent failure of the wing flap tracks and jamming the ailerons; inspection of fuel pressure indicators for ruptured diaphragms to prevent fuel discharge into the engine compartment and possible fire; inspection of the cabin door lock pins to prevent possible separation of the door; replacing the main landing gear side brace assemblies to prevent collapse of the gear.

The 1983 anti-stall AD restricted the aft center-of-gravity envelope when flaps are down. The restriction may be lifted if one of two tail modifications is made to improve the stall characteristics. One mod is the Piper factory fix, a moveable ventral fin connected to the rudder. (Its nickname is "the water rudder.") An alternative mod is a set of vortex generators on the vertical tail (along with stall strips and other wing mods) offered by Machen, Inc. in Spokane, Washington, a highly-regarded mod shop that specializes in Aerostars. According to pilots we talked to, the Machen mod is superior; try to find an Aerostar with this mod rather than Piper's.

Maintenance

Owners who reported to us seemed on the whole satisfied with their maintenance experience with the aircraft, and characterized it as average. They described factory backup with the Ted Smith organization as fair to good, but had not had sufficient experience to rate the new Piper management. However, one owner reported that he had misgivings. "My only reservations stem from the Piper takeover . . . and their distribution and service policies," he said. "One of my reasons for purchase of the Aerostar from Ted Smith was to avoid the problems with which I was plagued during my ownership of four different Piper aircraft."

No significant patterns of maintenance difficulty showed in owner comments, except we received several complaining about wing fuel tank leakage around the rivets.

The average cost of an annual inspection reported to us was $1,700.

As for parts availability, more owners rated it good or average than terrible, under Ted Smith's aegis, at least.

The brouhaha in 1970 over Aerostar corrosion problems was triggered when Butler Aviation International brought suit against American Cement Corp. in seeking to rescind its acquisition of the Aerostar line. The FAA, however, never grounded any Aerostars after inspecting more than 100 of the 130 or so built at that time. The agency said many of the aircraft showed no evidence of corrosion, though other had some, but none serious enough to ground the aircraft.

Summary

In all, then, the Aerostars might well be regarded as the cream of the owner-flown twins in terms of speed, looks and handling. They get much more performance out of 580 or so horsepower than any other airplane in their class.

Up until now the Achilles heels have been the fuel system and stall traits. The FAA-mandated modifications, however, should make the airplane more manageable and safer, provided the pilot knows the aircraft's idiosyncracies and how to cope with them.

Owner Comments

I selected my Model 601P Aerostar after owning a Piper Arrow 180D, an Aztec D and E and a Turbo B-Navajo.

Late-model 601B is the fastest of all the Aerostars, with a blistering 270-mph cruise.

After 350 hours' operating time, I cannot express sufficiently the satisfaction I have received from my Aerostar. No fuel problems have been apparent, and outside of minor waste gate controller adjustment, the aircraft has been free of any problems normally associated with a new aircraft and so evident in the ownership of my previous Piper aircraft.

●

My total maintenance, other than the normal oil filters and grease, has been as follows: brake shoes replacement at 275 hours; main landing gear tires at 275 hours; two ADs on fuselage drain and landing gear scissors; one hydraulic pump failure (warranty).

The interior appointments are outstanding, and the exterior paint has been subjected to severe weather involving heavy rain, snow, ice and hail, but remains in excellent condition.

When comparing all my previously owned aircraft, I find the Aerostar in a class by itself. The workmanship of the aircraft, as well as its performance, put it more in the class of heavy commercial aircraft. The heated windshield installation in the near future will complete my needs for this outstanding aircraft.

The performance data as outlined on the specifications sheets has been, in each case, easily achieved or exceeded.

My only reservations stem from the Piper takeover in May of 1978 and their distribution and service policies. One of my big reasons for purchase of the Aerostar from Ted Smith was to avoid the problem with which I was plagued during my ownership of four different Piper aircraft."

●

We have owned two 600As and have found both to be fantastic airplanes when compared to their competition.

They are truly the 'sportscars' of the recip aircraft — agile, responsive and fast on less fuel than an Aztec, Turbo 310 or C model Baron. The 600A has a range and performance ahead of any of these.

Like all aircraft, it has drawbacks, such as more than its share of AD notes. It's a little noisier than most of the competition, but a big plus is parts availability. We have bought both while they were damaged, and parts availability is unsurpassed in the industry.

We ordered and received all the parts and repaired the aircraft in less time than it took us to receive a left-hand gas tank for a V35 Beech Bonanza — AOG (three months and two days).

●

We purchased a 1974 600A Aerostar new, early in 1975 and have flowin it for 1,100 hours. I am extremely pleased with the Aerostar.

We have been lucky (I am told) with maintenance. We have experienced only two delays for mechanical reasons. One was for magneto problems (cracked magneto block), and one starter failure at a private grass airport.

We have experienced no problems with parts, since we have required few. The plane is a joy to fly. With our normal light loads we always get a true 210 knots from 10-12,000 feet and an average fuel burn of 28 gph. Our complaints are only two: noise level and vibration.

When all is said and done, I believe it is a great plane, and we would again buy the Aerostar today.

Pressurized Twin Roundup

The pressurized light twin—the *owner-flown* P-twin in particular—is one of few new, important genres to have come upon the GA scene in the past 15 years. From 1968, when the Beech Duke appeared, to 1984, an impressive 8,500 pressurized light twins were delivered, valued at well over $2.2 billion—of which almost half (3,800) are accounted for by the owner-flown models: the Cessna P337 and 340A, the Aerostar 601P/602P, the Beech Duke and the 58P Baron.

What with many recession-rocked companies bailing out of their piston aircraft (and with many remaining P-twin owners looking to move up to turbine equipment), a substantial portion of the past decade's "personal P-twin" production has suddenly landed on the used-plane market, and—trickle-down economics being what they are—more pilots than ever before are now asking themselves "Why not a used pressurized twin?" After all, for *half* the price of a new pressurized single (such as a P210 or Malibu), the canny used-plane shopper can nab a well-decked-out older Cessna 340A or Aerostar 601P—and achieve near-turbine performance on an avgas budget.

Used P-twin buying is not for the faint of heart, however—nor the thin of wallet. Pentagonian cost overruns are *de rigueur* in the operation of a pressurized aircraft, and cockpit workloads can be—in a word—trying (some experts, in fact, put the cockpit workload of a 340A-class aircraft above that of the average pure-jet). Billy Beer drinkers and VFR weekend pilots need not apply.

Price and Availability

Which owner-flown pressurized twin is best overall? The free market offers a telling bit of commentary: In roughly 15 years of sales, the market has "voted" the Cessna 340A the clear favorite overall, with 1,543 units shipped; the P-Aerostars (601 and 602 versions) a distant second, with 873 hulls sold; and the Beech Duke third, with 596 planes delivered. The Pressurized Baron (58P), having shipped 432 copies, appears a very distant fourth, but the 58P is actually a rather recent offering (the first unit came off the line in 1976), so the machine's popularity is not as weak as a casual review of the numbers might at first suggest. Cessna's Pressurized Skymaster, however, does represent a certifiable flop, with only 356 units moved in eight (troubled) years of production. More of that later.

The price of admission can hardly be described as low for any of these planes. Although blue-light-spe-cial shoppers will quickly spot the P-Skymaster as a tempting bargain, with entry prices as low as $40,000 (occasionally less), the P337's back-end costs more than make up for the lowball acquisition fee. After the Skymaster, the next-least-expensive P-twin is probably an early (1972) Cessna 340 with 285-hp engines, at $77,500 *Bluebook* (add $10,000 if the engines have been converted to 310-hp, as most now have), followed by a 1974 Aerostar 601P (coming in at around $110,000), and the P-Baron, at $135,000 for the earliest of '76 models. (These prices assume 600 to 700-hour engines, excellent paint and interior, a loaded panel, and most of the usual bells and whistles found on this class of airplane—which is to say, the full house of optional equipment.) A very early Duke can be had for $76,000 according to a 1984 *Bluebook*—some can be had for less—but any year-model Duke represents a quantum leap in operational cost and complexity over the other planes presented here, and for that reason we'll confine our discussion mostly to the 337P/340A/601P/58P group.

Suffice it to say that most first-time P-twin buyers gravitate toward the 340A or Aerostar; a few (seduced by the low initial cost) focus on the P337; and the cost-is-no-object bunch more often than not goes for the Baron 58P or Duke. (Some 250 or so Pressurized Navajos are also flying, and pressurized 400-series Cessnas abound—but most of these planes are in corporate service, and for this report, we're sticking to the predominantly owner-flown P-twins.) Since the flight envelopes are similar for each of these planes—all will let you fly 200 knots at 20,000 feet in shirt-sleeves—the decision of what to buy is as often based on such factors as engine brand loyalty, crea-

Aerostar 602P has low-compression engines that halt detonation woes of 601P.

ture comforts, and status-symbology, for example, as hard numbers performance comparisons. Some typical considerations follow.

Powerplants

If you're a Lycoming chauvinist, you have little choice—in this category of airplane—but to turn your attention to the Aerostars or the Beech Duke. None of the other P-planes is Lycoming-equipped.

The Aerostars boast the highest TBOs (1,800 hours) of any inflatable-cabin twin. But while both the 601P and 602P have 290-hp Lycomings, the engine models differ significantly. The 601P's IO-540-S1A5 engines are basically high-compression (8.7:1), turbo-normalized units (redlined at 29.5 inches) turning 2,575 rpm for takeoff. The turbo installation was conjured up by Ted Smith under an STC; Lycoming had nothing to do with it. The 602P's IO-540-AA1A5 engines, by contrast, are low-compression (7.3:1) and rely on a super-large AiResearch blower to develop 36 inches (at 2,425 rpm) for takeoff. The 602P engine/turbo installation was designed as a package, and the payoff (in terms of effortless low-rpm, high-altitude, high-speed cruise) is significant. This is something for prospective Aerostar purchasers to consider.

If the Aerostars' TBOs are high, so too are the attendant overhaul costs. Remanufactured IO-540-S1A5 engines list at $20,932 exchange each, minus turbochargers (for the IO-540-AA1A5, figure on $22,652 each). Field overhauls can be had in the $13,500 to $15,000 range, however.

The only other Lycoming-equipped plane in this fray, as we said, is the Beech Duke—and its monster TIO-541-E1C4 engines (1,600-hour TBO in the later versions; 1,200 otherwise) cost a minimum of $20,000 to overhaul properly. (Factory remans list at $35,368 each, exchange.)

The Baron 58P, like the Aerostar, comes with two flavors of engines depending on year model: early P-Barons had the 310-hp Continental TSIO-520-L engines (1,400-hr. TBO), while '79 and later planes come with 325-hp TSIO-520-WBs (1,600-hr. TBO). Both feature very expensive altitude-compensated Bendix fuel injectors, and a history of crankcase cracking; accordingly, overhaul prices are high (factory-reman -WBs list at $27,544 each, exchange) and life expectancy questionable.

The Cessna 340A's intercooled TSIO-520-NB engines (1,600-hr. TBO) are, like the P-Baron engines, Permold-crankcase Continentals; however, the 340A engines (particularly if updated by RAM Aircraft of Waco, Tex.) seem to perform reliably and economically over the long haul, with no special maintenance needs. The engine also has low parts costs, comparatively speaking (exhaust valves are $100 cheaper for the 340A engines than the Aerostar's) These factors, combined with a tolerably low replacement cost ($14,000 for field overhaul; $20,732 for factory reman), have endeared the -NB engine to many 340 owners as a "least evils" P-powerplant.

The Pressurized Skymaster's 225-hp Continental TSIO-360-C engines are the cheapest to replace of any P-plane's (if $14,724 for a fac-

tory rebuilt can be called cheap); but the engine has had a troubled service history (some 80 service bulletins apply) involving cylinder head loss, crankcase cracking, turbo and injector problems, etc.—and the official TBO of 1,400 hours is not to be taken seriously, particularly for rear-mounted engines, which suffer special cooling and vibration problems. What's more, peculiar installation geometries seem to add unnecessarily (i.e., grossly) to labor requirements for even the simplest maintenance chores. The prudent shopper will think long and hard about such things before buying (or not buying) a P337.

Flight Envelopes

Aerostar 601P/602P: True to reputation, the Aerostar is a bullet in cruise, with owners typically reporting 225 knots at 25,000 feet at 65 percent, or 233 knots at 75 percent (36 gph fuel flow). The cabin pressure differential of 4.25 psi is among the best of any piston P-twin, yielding an 11,000-ft. cabin at 25,000 feet. Getting there doesn't take long, either—max ROC for the 602P is 1,755 fpm (as good as any in its class). Range with full fuel (165 gals.) is a healthy 1,049 nm; but with a full cabin, that figure is cut to 426 nm. Plus points are clearly speed, fuel efficiency. Sore points: poor baggage accommodations (i.e., high rear fuselage hatch) and low single-engine ceiling (12,000 feet for the 602P; 9,300 feet for the 601P).

Baron 58P: The P-Baron isn't exactly a weak cruiser compared to the Aerostar—the later, 325-hp Beech 58P will, in fact, hit 300 mph if you flog it—but the Baron's fuel flow is substantially higher (the highest in

Cost/Performance/Specifications————————

Model	Years Built	Cruise Speed (kts)	Rate of Climb (fpm)	Useful Load (lbs)	SE Ceiling (ft)	Fuel Std/Opt (gals)	Engine	TBO (hrs)	Overhaul Cost (each)
Piper 601P	1974-81	235	1,460	1,944	12,900	165	290-hp Lyc.	1,800	$14,750
Piper 602P	1981-84	247	1,755	1,875	9,300	165	290-hp Lyc.	1,800	$13,500
Beech 58P	1976-84	232	1,475	2,190	13,490	166/190	325-hp Cont.	1,600	$15-$17,000
Cessna 340A	1972-82	229	1,650	1,806	12,100	102/207	310-hp Cont.	1,600	$14,000
Cessna P337	1973-80	204	1,170	1,516	18,700	150	225-hp Cont.	1,400	$10,000

its class, in fact), with 65-percent power resulting in 37 gallons per hour burned, and over 40 gph at 75 percent. Also, the Baron's cabin pressure differential (3.7 psi) isn't as good as the Aerostar's, giving a somewhat disappointing 12,500-ft. cabin altitude at 25,000 feet. The 58P will heft more Spam than the competition (useful load is 1,937 lbs. for the 58P, 1,717 lbs. for the 602P), but you need to carry more fuel anyway, so the issue is moot. Range with max fuel (190 gals.) is 946 nm; with full seats, 536 nm. Plus points: Speed and load capacity. Sore points: High fuel burn, hypoxic cabin.

Cessna 340A: Early 285-hp airplanes were real slugs, but the 310-hp 340A (and 326-hp RAM specials) offer reasonable performance, with real-world cruise speeds (65 percent) of 200 knots at FL 200, burning 30 gph. With the full optional 203 gallons installed (more can be obtained under STCs by Air America), an impressive 1,178 nm of range is available, although you'll be limited to around 300 pounds in the cabin. (Fill the cabin instead of the tanks, and range is a frighteningly low 259 nm. You takes your choice.) Baggage room is ample, and the 30,000-ft. operational ceiling—combined with a 4.2-psi cabin differential—means you can get over more weather, and perhaps ride stronger tailwinds, than Brand B. (You'll do it in less than bulletlike fashion, of course—but you'll also burn less fuel.) Strong points: Flexibility in cruise altitude, range, endurance. Sore points: Limited cabin payload, speed.

Cessna P337: Definitely an also-ran, this airplane's performance envelope is laughable even by P-single standards. Basically a P210 pressure vessel (3.35 psi) with an engine at either end, the P337 is a dismal performer (comparatively speaking, anyway), delivering no more than 189-knot cruise performance at 16,000 feet (65 percent power), with cabin altitude a mediocre 10,000 feet at FL 200—assuming the cabin isn't leaky, which older ones often are. The range with full tanks is 1,065 nm (with full seats, 340 nm), and single-engine ceiling is good

(18,700 ft.), as you would expect for a centerline-thruster. But that's where the good news ends. What you've got here, essentially, is P210 performance, on light-twin fuel flows. Strong suit: Range and single-engine controllability. (Engine-out ROC is not impressive, at 380 fpm, but it's the best of any of the planes presented here.) Sore points: You name it.

Systems

Aerostar 601P/602P: The Aerostars are often criticized as quirky airplanes, and not without some justification. Steering is by electric rocker switch; flaps and gear are hydraulic (motivated by a pump on the right engine); and the fuel system (with its oddball fuselage tank and many flapper valves) has developed a bit of a reputation—how shall we say?—for creating confusion (and silence). On the plus side, the Aerostar dispenses with cowl flaps (reducing pilot workload); the 24-volt electrical system uses two 12-volt batteries (much cheaper than using one 24-volt battery); and Cleveland brakes are standard (a definite maintenance plus). Little-known peculiarity: the 601P windshield is life-limited to 4,860 hours.

Beech 58P: Straight Baron systems all the way (electric gear and flaps), with moderate cabin workload. Unlike the Aerostar (which has wet wings), the Baron 58P has Goodyear fuel cells (three in each wing) which sometimes leak and can be hideously expensive to replace. Goodyear brakes are standard. The gear-driven Teledyne Crittenden and Prestolite alternators used on the P-Baron (and on the 340A) both suffer from checkered reputations, and neither is cheap to fix or replace. Likewise, vacuum pumps and magnetos seem to have relatively short lives on these high-flying planes, but that's nothing new. Prospective P-Baron buyers would do well to have a Beech shop do a thorough service bulletin search at the time of purchase, since the 58P is subject to scores of (labor-intensive, if minor) bulletins.

Cessna 340A: Most 340As come

Cost Comparison

Cessna 340/340A

Year	Number Built	Average Retail Price
1972	115	$ 77,500*
1973	135	$ 79,000*
1974	110	$ 85,000*
1975	185	$ 92,500*
1976	125	$116,500
1977	175	$126,000
1978	162	$135,000
1979	201	$152,500
1980	145	$180,000
1981	80	$235,000
1982	43	$350,000
1983	(none delivered)	

* Add $10,000 if engines converted to 310 hp.

Aerostar 601P/602P

Year	Number Built	Average Retail Price
1974	33	$105,000
1975	82	$110,000
1976	89	$122,500
1977	101	$135,000
1978	104	$147,500
1979	103	$160,000
1980	87	$177,500
1981	21	$205,000(601P)
1981	55	$235,000(602P)
1982	47	$310,000
1983	NA	$528,000**

** Deduct $500 per hour for every hour after 50 TTSN.

Cessna P337 Skymaster

Year	Number Built	Average Retail Price
1973	148	$ 37,000
1974	45	$ 43,000
1975	32	$ 50,000
1976	32	$ 57,500
1977	35	$ 65,000
1978	24	$ 75,000
1979	23	$ 87,500
1980	15	$107,500

Beech 58P Baron

Year	Number Built	Average Retail Price
1976	84	$135,000
1977	35	$145,000
1978	44	$160,000
1979	63	$187,500
1980	82	$225,000
1981	65	$265,000
1982	46	$325,000
1983	NA	$520,900***

*** Deduct $360 per hour for every hour over 50 TTSN.

Pressurized Twin Roundup

with aux tanks in the wings; these are bladders and should be watched for leaks. Goodyear brakes are standard, as with the Baron. If the 340A has a single notable systems flaw, it's the outrageously complicated fuel system, which—depending on the installed optional tankage—can incorporate locker tanks that won't crossfeed, aux fuel that's unusable in the event of engine-driven fuel-pump failure, aux-fuel overflow return lines going to the main (tip) tanks, double-duty fuel gauges, and as many as ten underwing drains, not to mention panel placards befitting a space orbiter. Study the handbook well, before— and after—you buy.

Cessna P337: Principal systems are all taken from the early P210 (or vice versa), with minor modifications. Mechanically, the plane is pure pandemonium. So Rube-Goldbergish and finicky-foo are the plane's systems, in fact, that not long after the P337's introduction in 1974, the factory recalled all airplanes (under ''Operation Care'') on general principles, to debug the fleet and thus head off an insurrection by disgruntled owners. (Landing gear, pressurization, and turbo-system problems were rampant.) The P337's biggest systems sore point may well be the electrohydraulic landing gear, a veritable plumber's tale-of-the-macabre. Rigging a Skymaster's landing gear has driven more than one A&P to the lunatic asylum, what with a not-so-grand total of 11 hydraulic actuators, plus solenoids that occasionally stick, thermostatic pressure relief valves, priority flow valves, etc. etc. Our advice is to safety-wire the gear handle in the down position—permanently. (You won't notice the performance change.)

Safety

Aerostar 601P/602P: The single biggest category of Aerostar accident appears to be fuel exhaustion/mismanagement, which has claimed at least 16 aircraft since 1971. (The number of aircraft that may have landed safely after fuel-flow irregularities, thus avoiding NTSB

scrutiny, isn't known.) In-flight door openings in pressurized models have led to serious controllability problems resulting in at least three accidents in the last four years (and several non-accidents). Aside from these two areas, however, no other pattern of mishap stands out—although certainly, there are areas of the Aerostar's envelope that bear careful scrutiny if safety is a concern (e.g., stall warning). Unfortunately, no one—including NTSB—has taken an in-depth, comprehensive look at the P-Aerostar's safety record since the 601P's introduction in 1974. Until such a detailed study is undertaken, we'll reserve judgment on the 601P/602P's overall record.

Beech 58P: In the most recent two-year period for which records are available (1978-79), there have been six P-Baron accidents, three of them fatal. In terms of overall accident rates, the Baron series ranks about average among light twins (with 8.3 accidents per 100,000 flight hours); but the fatal rate is somewhat higher than average. The 58P has yet to be sorted out from the 55/58 series' combined stats, however, so overall trends cannot be noted. Prospective purchasers should note the 58P's poor single-engine climb gradient (142 feet per nautical mile; 270 fpm), which is the worst of any owner-flown pressurized twin.

Cessna 340A: In a recent four-year

period there were 33 accidents involving 340-series Cessnas, five of them fatal. (One of the fatals was the Alaska tail separation that led to the emergency AD requiring replacement of the tails of some 1,000 aircraft.) Interestingly, only one accident resulted from fuel starvation. (The 340A has a complicated fuel system, on paper, but few fuel-related accidents; whereas the Aerostar—which has a simple fuel system on paper—suffers many fuel-related accidents.) Weather problems claimed a fairly large share of the 340A mishaps, including three of the five fatals mentioned above. Otherwise, the accidents were spread broadly among a wide variety of causes (including collision with wires, midairs, etc.).

Cessna P337: A special NTSB study of light-twin accident rates (1972-76) found the Skymaster series the 18th worst in total accidents out of 20 twins studied. (Total accident rate: 10.42 per 100,000 hours. Fatal rate: 3.06 per 100,000 hours.) Ironically, the Skymaster series has one of the worst engine-out accident rates of any twin—despite the fact that its centerline-thrust design was conceived for the sole purpose of reducing such accidents. The problem is twofold: One, the rate of climb is not that good on one engine (388 fpm), what with the relatively high power and wing loadings. Secondly, pilots are apt

Aircraft Resale Value Chart

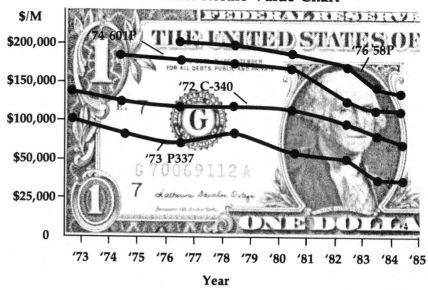

'74 601P
'76 58P
'72 C-340
'73 P337

$/M
$200,000
$150,000
$100,000
$50,000
$25,000
0

'73 '74 '75 '76 '77 '78 '79 '80 '81 '82 '83 '84 '85
Year

not to notice an engine failure (particularly a partial power loss) in the 337, since the usual aerodynamic cues (i.e., wild yawing) are simply not present. Weather, fuel exhaustion, and hard landings contribute heavily to the 337's overall accident record. Again, though, statistics for the *pressurized* 337 have not been culled and studied in depth, so we'll have to reserve judgment on the P-model's record.

Maintenance

Routine maintenance consumes vast amounts of capital for a pressurized twin; and sometimes maintenance is anything but routine. Turbochargers typically do not last the full engine TBO, for instance, and replacement costs are high ($1,200 to $2,500 per turbo). Also, most P-twin engines run hot and hard—cooling is poor in the rarefied air of the middle flight levels, and bleed air for pressurization is taken from the turbo compressor discharge (which adds to the workload of the turbo—and engine)—so top overhauls are frequent occurrences, and this must be added to already-outlandish overhaul reserves.

Operation in rarefied air is hard, also, on vacuum pumps, alternators, combustion heaters, and other accessories (cooling airflow is poor). And in this category of aircraft, boots tend to be used a lot; so figure on $5,000 to $10,000 worth of boot repairs (and/or replacement) every ten years or so.

The Pressurized Skymaster notwithstanding, P-twins tend to be heavy, hot ships. This, in turn, means long runway requirements —and inordinate demands on brakes and tires. Factor in a substantial budget addition for pucks, rubber, and oleos.

The P-twins are, in short, high-maintenance airplanes—it comes with the territory. Cessna's own flat-rate book shows a 100-hour (or annual) inspection requiring *50 man-hours* to complete for a Cessna 340A (45 hours for a P337). At the going $30/hr. shop rate, that's a *minimum* (no squawks) cost of $1,500 per 100 hours of operation,

for normal 340A inspection. (Figure a little less for the Aerostars—a little more for the P-Baron.) Add something for squawks—factor in parts—and you can begin to see how the average P-twin owner spends a *minimum* of $2,500 to $3,000 a year on maintenance. (We heard from one Duke owner who says he spent $30,000 last year on routine maintenance—with no major squawks other than a prop overhaul.) *Caveat P-twin-emptor.*

In Conclusion

As far as "bargains" go (to the extent that such a thing exists in the P-twin market), many brokers report that the Aerostars have taken a nosedive in price and salability. ("It's getting harder to sell an Aerostar," one well-known broker told us in 1984, adding: "And not only because of the recent tail AD, but because the Aerostar requires a very qualified pilot—it's hard for some guys to qualify for insurance.") A loaded, well-maintained 1978 or '79 601P, with all ADs (including the one requiring addition of a ventral rudder and/or flow generators to the tail) complied, strikes us as a relative bargain for $150,000—if speed is of some importance, and (more important) if one's piloting ability is equal to the machine.

If one's piloting ability is merely average to B-minus, however —and if 25 knots less cruise-speed doesn't make a lot of difference—the 340A appears to offer a tremendous transportation value. We'd look for a 1976-vintage 340A (with non-ARC radios, preferably),

The 310-hp Cessna 340A was a big improvement over the original 285-hp 340. Most 340s have been upgraded.

RAM-modified, in the $115,000 ballpark.

A well-maintained early Baron 58P might turn our heads if it could be demonstrated that all (or nearly all) service bulletins had been complied with, and if the price were below *Bluebook* high wholesale (i.e., something around $140,000 for a '78 model). But we would set aside several thousand dollars for the eventual, inevitable crankcase cracks. (The so-called "heavy case" is a non-solution where this engine is concerned.)

As for the P337: We simply cannot envision the circumstances under which we would buy a Pressurized Skymaster, unless it's as a jungle-gym for the children's playground.

Owner Comments

We have operated both the Aerostar 601P and the Beech 58P Baron. We operated a 1975 Aerostar 601P for approximately one year and 500 hours. This particular aircraft had numerous hydraulic problems and some turbocharger troubles. Some passenger complaints were: too much noise; not enough room; and not enough air-conditioning. From a pilot's standpoint the aircraft was

Beech 58P Baron has good performance, but maintenance bills can be awesome. A major culprit: cracking crankcases.

a delight to fly, but required a fair amount of runway for both takeoff and landing. The fuel flow was about 30 gallons per hour and with a TAS of about 215 knots in the mid-teens.

We traded this airplane for a 1976 58P (TJ-49). This aircraft has been very satisfactory for our company from the standpoint of reliability. We have, at this time, 2,879 hours on the aircraft. This usage has given us an opportunity to exchange four engines and experience several pressurization and air-conditioning problems. I must say that three of the engines made TBO, and one destroyed itself due to magneto arcing. Which brings me to what I feel is the weak point of these engines. I have had about 12 failures since we have had the aircraft, most with some indication; but four times there was no indication other than high CHT on takeoff. We fly about 600 hours per year and are on a 100-hour inspection program. The inspection costs approximately $1,400, not including parts and labor for squawks. The average bill is $3,000 per inspection. Fuel flow at 65 percent power is between 30-32 gph, at 75 percent power is between 36-38 gph, and 81 percent power is between 40-42 gph. All depending upon the altitude. Our direct operating cost is $110 per hour.

Contrasting the two aircraft, although my passengers like the speed of the 601P, they like the comfort and dependability of the Baron. From the pilot's standpoint,

the Baron is a very honest aircraft that is also very dependable.

Marvin M. Pippen
Wharton, Tex.

I have been the proud owner of a 1976 model 340A for over one year. I say the "proud owner" because I am pleased with the aircraft overall. I have had some difficulties with it, such as magnetos and auxiliary boost pump failures, maintenance difficulties with the aircraft other than the avionics, which cannot be attributed to the aircraft itself.

As you know, there are several AD notes which are applicable to the 340, the most significant of which deals with the tail change. Also, one should be certain that the 340 in which he is interested has the heavy case engines. The earlier lighter case engines are somewhat of a maintenance "headache." The average cost of an annual inspection, if no discrepancies are found, is approximately $1,500; based on a 40 man-hour time of completion at $31 an hour.

The performance of the aircraft is relative to the loading configuration. This aircraft is easily overloaded because of the amount of fuel it will carry. In my aircraft, I have a nacelle tank in the right nacelle in addition to the normal tanks and inboard auxiliary tanks. This makes for a delightful increase in range, but you are severely limited in passenger and baggage carrying capability. With an average load of approximately 100 gallons of fuel and four people on board with 150 pounds of baggage, there is an average climb of 800 fpm at 140 knots indicated, up to 10,000 feet. Above 10,000 feet the climb performance decreases gradually to around 300 fpm at 18,000 feet with that same load. I have had no difficulties with the performance of this aircraft at altitudes up to 24,000 feet, but it is weak when it gets there.

I would recommend to your readers that this aircraft, like any other tool, should be carefully fitted to the need. This is an excellent mid-

altitude range aircraft with good performance with three or four people on board and a respectable load of fuel. I would not recommend it for trips shorter than 250 to 300 nm because, in my experience, it is detrimental to these high-performance turbocharged engines to experience frequent temperature changes as in prolonged climbs, short durations at altitude, and high-speed descents. The average fuel consumption on my aircraft at 10,000-15,000 feet is 35 gallons per hour.

Frank Anders, M.D.
Ville Platte, La.

Although we had been nervous about the possibility of crankcase and crankshaft problems associated with the Continental 520-L turbocharged engines, based on previous reports, we had very little trouble with these engines in our P-Baron. The first set was exchanged for new engines at almost 1,400 hours, and the second set of engines will be coming up on the 1,400-hour TBO shortly.

The pressure system on our particular plane was great—smoother than a King Air's. However, from time to time the plane did develop pressure leaks—particularly around the door seal, but also occasionally in the bulkhead when avionics work was being performed, and once from the wheel wells.

The plane was a delight to fly—once you learned how to land it! It was very nose heavy, and the secret to a good landing with full flaps and a light load was to come back on the electric trim during the flare. (This problem was not noticeable with half flaps or no-flap landings.) Also, the flare had to be closer to the runway than one might think—a little like landing a Twin Comanche. There was no problem, by the way, with sudden go-arounds after full aft trim in the flare. The forward pressure was not that great while the plane was being retrimmed.

My only complaint with the P-Baron was its slow rate of climb, which was only 700-800 feet per

minute in the summer months. In Cincinnati, where we have a lot of hot weather and thunderstorms, I like to climb as fast as possible where I can see those storm cells with my eyes as well as on radar. Therefore, after a number of years of enjoyable flying in our P-Baron, we traded it in last winter for a Conquest 1, whose flying qualities are at least as gentle and whose climb rate is far superior to the P-Baron's.

John Laurence Jr.
Cincinnato, Ohio

The P-Skymaster is unquestionably the most capable airplane for the money in the market. What other airplane will cruise over 200 mph, with a range of over 1,000 miles in pressurized comfort on 23 gallons per hour?

I have a 1976 P-Skymaster with Robertson STOL and all King avionics. With all things, particularly airplanes, there are pluses and minuses. The major minuses with the P-337 are payload and maintenance. My plane came with six seats. The two rear seats were removed after my first look at the weight and balance. Baggage capacity is also limited by accessibility as well as gross weight. It is, however, very, very comfortable for up to four real-world adults.

Maintenance is continuous and expensive. It is a very complex airplane and requires all the care and maintenance of large P-twins. The engines are TCM's TSIO-360-Cs, those darlings of the aviation community, and AC's favorites. These engines operate under great stress at their rated 225 hp and require TLC. In my first 100 hours of ownership, the rear engine number four cylinder head separated from the barrel at 17,000 feet near Cleveland. I shut down and feathered, and flew home to Indianapolis on cruise power on the front engine, intentionally letting down about 200 fpm with no further difficulty. In over 500 hours, that is my only *engine*-caused shutdown. I've also lost the rear engine due to exhaust system separation, and the front due to turbo controller failure.

Cessna pressurized Skymaster is a high-maintenance dog that should be avoided if possible.

The centerline thrust of this unique airplane is a plus. In each case of engine shutdown it would be hard to describe the situation as an emergency. The airplane kept flying, behaved well, and was easy to reconfigure for SE cruise. It flies on one like a heavy single, and in each case, landing was simple . . . just use the same speed as normal and the landing is normal.

The airplane is heavy on the controls, and is remarkably solid at cruise speeds. Landings require precise speed control . . . a little fast and the powerful elevator will produce a long float . . . a little slow and there is no flare. Most airplanes behave the same way, though. It's just a matter of degree. The STOL modification reduces full-flap stall speed to about 45 knots, and maximum performance takeoffs are astonishing, to say the least; but for engine health should be reserved only for occasions of real need.

This is the airplane used to STC Bel-Ray Aero-1, and has just had its first annual since replacing the test engines with factory "rebuilts" with steel cylinders. The engines broke in at 35 hours, and stabilized on six hours/quart each. Now, after an additional 100 hours, it is using one quart (each) of Aero-1 in 19 hours and at annual all 12 cylinders were 78 or 79 over 80.

All in all, the P-Skymaster is a super cross-country machine and a real pleasure to fly. However, like so many other airplanes, the compromises made by the designers to accomplish a particular goal made some other aspect of the airplane undesirable and unacceptable to many and a market failure.

It's unfortunate that this excellent design has been discontinued.

Allan Abramow
Indianapolis, Ind.

I have owned a 1974 P337 Skymaster for almost three years now. During the first year of ownership a number of repairs were necessary to bring the airplane up to a satisfactory service level. After that period the airplane has required only routine maintenance of the type that would be expected for any twin-engine aircraft. I have experienced minor malfunctions, none of which have caused me any serious delays or inconveniences.

I'd have to say that my experience with the Skymaster has been a good one. After learning a few of the minor idiosyncrasies, I believe the plane is easy and safe to fly. Dollar for dollar it is hard to imagine a better airplane to fly.

Robert B. Edesess, D.D.S.
Indianapolis, Ind.

The Aviation Consumer has kept its readers well informed of the stall/ spin problems with the Baron. Some of us learned 40 years ago about stalls with an engine out and the rules haven't changed from that Lockheed Lodestar to the 747. The 58P is not even the same Baron as the 58 and I could not recommend it for the low-time, weekend pilot. I have, however, found it to be an honest airplane, comfortable and efficient for its class, with good range and speed. Mine has been dependable and trouble-free.

James Higby
Palos Verdes Estates, Calif.

TURBINE AIRCRAFT

Mitsubishi MU-2

Pilots browsing through the light turboprops as a natural stepup from a piston twin might be drawn to the Mitsubishi MU-2s by the lure of dazzling speed, unbeatable short-field work and a less-than-shocking purchase price. But the MU-2 has a very poor accident record and a reputation as a hard-to-fly, unforgiving aircraft that should make step-up pilots think long and hard before buying.

A glance at the roster of new pressurized cabin-class twins shows that aircraft like the Cessna 421 and Piper Mojave are going for around $750,000 new. Even smaller pressurized piston jobs like the Baron 58P go for $600,000-plus new. This makes a used 1977 Mitsubishi MU-2P, for example, a rather attractive alternative at around $370,000. Try to break into the turbine market with something else like a used King Air, even of the same vintage, and the ante goes up to around $500,000.

Naturally, there's a catch in the step-up to the MU-2; in fact, there are two. One is greatly increased cost of operation per hour; the other is aircraft handling and ease of pilot transition.

Though the MU-2s were among the earliest turboprops to appear on the market, they have always had what many would describe as avant-garde design features — such as a small-area, high-speed wing that sprouts nearly full-span flaps for landing and takeoff, and that uses spoilers instead of ailerons for roll control.

The MU-2s are the result of a true international amalgam. The airframe is built in Japan by Mitsubishi and shipped to the United States for assembly and addition of

AiResearch engines along with avionics and other systems. After an initial marketing relationship with Mooney Aircraft in 1965, Mitsubishi set up a wholly-owned subsidiary for assembly and sales in '69 (when Mooney went bankrupt).

Since the debut of the first MU-2B model, Mitsubishi has brought out nearly a dozen upgraded models, representing one major fuselage enlargement, two boosts in engine power and four jumps in gross weight.

Model Changes

The MU-2D followed the -2B, offering integral wet-wing tanks instead of bladder tanks, higher weights, higher pressurization and the four-position flaps.

The F model received engines of 665 shp, up from 575, and extra fuel.

The G was the first stretched version, with a cabin about five feet longer, with pods added to both sides of the fuselage to take the landing gear and allow the cabin to be enlarged.

In the J model the interior was redesigned slightly to provide another 11 inches of cabin room. Also, extra soundproofing was added to the later Js.

The L received bigger 715 shp engines, increased gross weight and pressurization.

Long-body Marquise is slower than Solitaire, but roomier.

The M boosted gross, pressurization, and certified altitude.

The N and P offered the engine slowdown and four-bladed props for sound reduction.

The Solitaire and Marquise with -10 engines boosted altitudes and speeds.

Investment Value

The MU-2's resale value has been uneven. Until a few years ago, the MU-2 held its value well. A 1968 F model, for example, cost $437,000 new but was still worth over $300,000 more than a decade later. However, the sharp fuel price increases of 1979 and the recession of the early 1980s hurt the MU-2 (and all other turboprops, of course), and that same 1968 F model today has a "bluebook" retail value of only about $200,000.

For comparison we tracked the 1968 Beech King Air B90 model and the '70 King Air 100, which might be considered comparable to the F and G Mitsubishis. The results showed the Beechcraft to represent a better investment value.

One broker we talked to said they tried to avoid the Mitsubishi Bs and Ds, though there was a "very warm market" for the F models.

The short F model was the first to receive the 151A engine with 90 extra shaft horsepower. In the long-bodied series, the L with its higher power rating would be preferred over the Js that preceded it.

The black sheep of the MU-2 family — as far as resale value goes — is the MU-2G, built in 1970 and 1971. It cost over half a million new, but commands barely $190,000 today. By comparison, the 1973 J model, only a year newer, is worth about $300,000. According to one used-plane dealer we queried, the main reason is that ''it's just underpowered.'' He went on to say that he usually sold MU-2Gs to first-time turboprop buyers not accustomed to great excesses of power.

Cabin Sound Levels

Perhaps the most significant improvement came only a few years ago, with the '77 P and N models, when a major effort was made to combat the aircraft's reputation for annoying cabin noise levels. A big change was made at that time by slowing down the engine rpm, adding a fourth prop blade and enlarging the prop diameters.

Owners say this hushes the cabin sound levels dramatically, by 10 dbA or so, though ironically the greatest din is still experienced during taxi, since the AiResearch Garrett TPE 331 engines are spooling up at around 65 percent rpm, unlike the P&W PT-6 turboprop engines, which idle in a more subdued, conventional fashion.

In fact, if there were one main complaint aired by MU-2 pilots, especially about the earlier models, it was the inescapable noise — and vibration — of the Mitsubishi aircraft.

One pilot for a 1975 M model said his company had taken sound level readings in the aircraft that showed extremely high decibel ratings in front, becoming progressively lower toward the back of the cabin. They recorded levels of from 95 to 102 dbA in the pilot and copilot seats, down to 87 to 90 dbA in the middle seats and 80 to 85 dbA in the rear seats — cruising at an altitude of 22,000 feet. He figured that later models with the engine slowdown dropped an average of 10 dbA across the board inside the cabin.

Cabin Room

Despite the apparent small cabin size when viewed from the outside, owners describe the interior as quite roomy and comfortable. The short models seat six in an executive configuration, the long ones eight, though more can be crammed in for air taxi hauling by eliminating facing seats and tables. The long models even come with private toilets and cabin-size baggage areas. The short ones have three separate baggage bays in back of the cabin, with the front one pressurized.

Two areas in which pilots were universally complimentary was riding comfort in turbulence and structural integrity. Thanks to the high wing loading on the MU-2s, the aircraft sails through chop with small discomfort. And everyone raved about the Sherman tank ''structural integrity'' of the Mitsubishi aircraft.

Payload

Payload appears quite good, especially on later models with higher-output engines not power limited by temperatures on warm days. The chief pilot of an organization that operated a short '75 MU-2 M model said he could fill the fuel tanks, allow 250 pounds for himself and his Jepps, etc., and still load on board five passengers and

Cost/Performance/Specifications ————————————————

Model	Year	Normal Cruise (kts)	Normal Altitude (ft)	Gross Weight (lbs)	Certified Ceiling (ft)	Engine	TBO (hrs)	Overhaul Cost	Average Retail Price
SHORT CABIN									
MU-2B	1967	240	15,000	8,930	25,000	575-shp TPE-331/25AA	2,000	$ 88,000	$ 105,000
MU-2D	1968	250	15,000	9,350	25,000	575-shp 25AA	2,000	$ 88,000	$ 110,000
MU-2F	1968-71	270	18,000	9,920	25,000	665-shp 151A	3,100	$ 92,000	$ 220,000
MU-2K	1972-74	300	21,000	9,920	25,000	665-shp 251M	3,000	$ 92,000	$ 300,000
MU-2M	1975-76	295	21,000	10,470	28,000	665-shp 251M	3,000	$ 98,000	$ 340,000
MU-2P	1977-78	290	19,000	10,470	28,000	665-shp 252M	3,000	$ 98,000	$ 390,000
Solitaire	1979	295	25,000	10,470	31,000	727-shp 10	3,000	$104,000	$ 470,000
Solitaire	1980	295	25,000	10,470	31,000	727-shp 10	3,000	$104,000	$ 490,000
Solitaire	1981	295	25,000	10,470	31,000	727-shp 10	3,000	$104,000	$ 550,000
Solitaire	1982	295	25,000	10,470	31,000	727-shp 10	3,000	$104,000	$ 635,000
LONG CABIN									
MU-2G	1970-71	240	16,000	10,800	25,000	665-shp 151A	3,100	$ 94,000	$ 190,000
MU-2J	1972-74	280	19,000	10,800	25,000	665-shp 251M	3,600	$ 94,000	$ 310,000
MU-2L	1975-76	280	19,000	11,5757	25,000	715-shp 251M	3,600	$ 98,000	$ 390,000
MU-2N	1977-78	275	19,000	11,575	25,000	715-shp 252M	3,600	$ 98,000	$ 480,000
Marquise	1979	295	23,000	11,575	31,000	778-shp 10	3,000	$104,000	$ 540,000
Marquise	1980	295	23,000	11,575	31,000	778-shp 10	3,000	$104,000	$ 585,000
Marquise	1981	295	23,000	11,575	31,000	778-shp 10	3,000	$104,000	$ 660,000
Marquise	1982	295	23,000	11,575	31,000	778-shp 10	3,000	$104,000	$ 750,000
Marquise	1983	295	23,000	11,575	31,000	778-shp 10	3,000	$104,000	$ 900,000
Marquise	1984	295	23,000	11,575	31,000	778-shp 10	3,000	$104,000	$1,300,000

214 pounds of baggage. His payload was 1,376 pounds.

When it comes to out-and-out speed, the Mitsubishis lead the pack and always have. The later models can be expected to yield over 300 knots (short models) and the long models only a whisker under that. Only the Swearingen IIIB comes close at 300 knots, and the Cessna Conquest at 293 knots. The small Beech King Air C90 trails way back at 222 knots and even the King Air 100 only makes it to 248 knots. The Piper Cheyenne I checks in at about 249 knots and the II and 283 knots.

A typical seats-full range on the later MU-2s works out at a bit over 1,000 nm, which is average for this class of aircraft, though it's overshadowed by some like the Conquest (1,232 nm) and Swearingen IIIB (1,393 nm).

The earlier model MU-2s (Bs, Ds and Fs from '67 through '71) had cruise speeds that were lower by 35 to 65 knots, and commensurately lower range.

Handling

When it comes to handling, there is common agreement that the MU-2s are more demanding for the stepup pilot than other turboprops like the Beech King Air and the Piper Cheyenne. The feel fo the aircraft is different because of the spoilers. And many confess that the other side of the coin relating to the MU-2's outstanding short-field performance is that the airplane can be a bear to land with finesse.

Pilots talk about descent rates on final as high as 2,000 fpm, if called for, with the props back in flight idle and 40 degrees of flaps hanging from nearly the full length of the MU-2 wing. The flare calls for a skilled touch to prevent slamming the aircraft on the runway. And even when the mains are on, the nosewheel is sure to fall like an axed tree no matter how the pilot tries to hold it off with elevator.

One owner complained that he was forever experiencing flight director failures which, correctly or

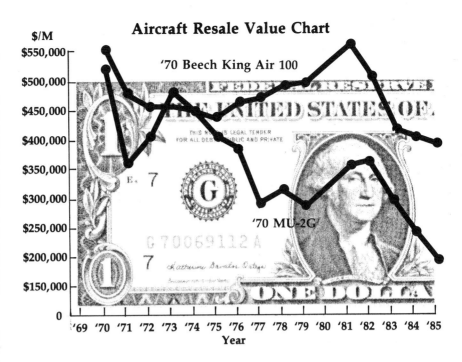

Aircraft Resale Value Chart

'70 Beech King Air 100

'70 MU-2G

not, he attributed to the pounding they took each time the nose slammed down on landing. And a professional pilot for a charter service is said to have frightened away customers from repeat business because of his tendency to hit down hard on every landing.

It is generally agreed that the short models are the worst in this regard.

One MU-2 flier offered this observation: "It wants to float down the runway, so you want to get it right down there on the flare. You don't want a 30-foot initiation of flare; you want it at three feet. And you want to keep the power on until touchdown.

"People transitioning into this aircraft tend to slow it up in the flare and get back to flight idle, trying to hold the nose off. It doesn't work. This airplane has to be flown onto the runway. Once you've got the mains on, the nosegear is going to plant itself. It seems abrupt to the pilot."

But this pilot said the aircraft could take the punishment. "That nosegear is tough," he said. "I don't know of any damage to the MU-2 nosewheels because of this characteristic."

The MU-2 is a high-workload airplane. It is not particularly stable, and every adjustment of power or speed requires retrimming in

pitch, yaw and roll. "Cleaning up an MU-2 after takeoff into IFR conditions is the busiest I've ever been in an airplane," one veteran corporate pilot commented. At high speeds, pitch stability decays, making it a challenge to hold altitude in high-speed cruise without autopilot.

Safety Record

To be blunt, the MU-2's safety record is bad. An *Aviation Consumer* study of the major turboprops showed that the MU-2 had a fatal accident rate of 61.5 percent per 10,000 aircraft-years — more than twice as high as any other turboprop and six times higher than the big King Airs. Engine failures and high-altitude loss-of-control accidents were especially deadly. Engine failures were also the leading cause of non-fatal MU-2 accidents, apparently more the result of the airplane's tricky engine-out handling than unreliable engines. For details on the MU-2's fatal accident rate and a look at its handling and workload problems, see the following chapter.

The FAA, however, gave the MU-2 a clean bill of health after a yearlong special certification review recommended by the National Transportation Safety Board. The FAA found that the MU-2 complied with all airworthiness rules, and that a special requirement for two-pilot operation, or a type rating, was not necessary.

However, the FAA required three minor changes in some MU-2s, in the trim tab, pitot heat and bleed air systems; also, Mitsubishi set about upgrading the MU-2 pilot operating handbooks. One FAA man commented that the early manuals "were skimpy at best."

After 60-plus hours of flight testing in both a short-body and long-body MU-2, the team of FAA experts concluded that the aircraft is no more difficult to fly than other turboprops.

The number two accident problem with the MU-2 models in a 13-year accident rundown (1965 through 1978) provided by the National Transportation Safety Board for *The Aviation Consumer* turned out to be hard landings. The number three problem area was undershoots — as might be expected in an aircraft that can be set up for a high sink rate on final, with the possibility of getting behind the power curve.

Of the nine pilots involved in hard landings or undershoots, only two might be considered to have low time in the MU-2. Pilot time-in-type for hard landing accidents turned out to be: 1,790 hours; 3,160, 51, 500 and 195. For undershoots, the pilot experience level in type went like this: 2,869 hours, 598, 37 and 435.

The leading probable cause for accidents in the MU-2 was engine failure. This also was blamed for the greatest number of fatal accidents in the MU-2 — three. On all three of these fatals, only one engine failed, but the pilot was unable to make a safe return with the remaining powerplant. One occurred on takeoff and climbout with snow, low ceilings and visibility; the others occurred in the landing pattern, and on final approach. A stall/spin was blamed in each case, with the pilots accused of "diverting attention" from flying the aircraft.

Similarly, on all four nonfatal engine failure accidents (or in-

cidents), only one powerplant was lost; nevertheless, only one of these pilots managed to bring the aircraft back to an unventful landing on an airport on the remaining engine.

A look at pilot experience in engine-out problems shows that all the fliers had thousands of hours of flying time, and most had at least a couple thousand in the MU-2. The lowest time in type, in fact, was 169 hours.

This might suggest that the loss of an engine, especially on takeoff and climbout and in the landing pattern, can be a serious cause for concern in the MU-2 aircraft. In fact, the only safe return with an engine out was made when the failure occurred during normal cruise and the pilot apparently had the time to sort things out and make it to an airport.

In another fatal MU-2 crash, the pilot had shut down one engine because of loss of oil pressure and apparently decided to abort an emergency landing and execute a missed approach, when he went in.

It should be noted that the six engine failure accidents (and one incident) were all evidently the result of some sort of malfunction. Another four engine failures occurred because of fuel exhaustion, caused, in turn, by pilot mismanagement; and three other fuel exhaustion accidents were the result of mechanical failures.

Though there are three main sets of fuel tanks in the MU-2, the moni-

toring system would not appear to be inordinately demanding. There is one main (segmented) tank in the central wing section into which outer wing tanks feed by electrical fuel pump and into which the tip tanks feed by pressurization from engine bleed air.

Since both engines feed from the center tanks, there is not even a need for crossfeed arrangement, and all the pilot has to do is monitor the transfer of fuel from the outer tanks into the center ones.

We noted no accidents from landings with asymmetrical tip loadings.

The last significant cause of MU-2 accidents disclosed in the NTSB briefs is gear-up landings. In the years surveyed there were seven of these altogether — and in four of these the pilot simply forgot to lower the gear.

Service Difficulties

Examination of the FAA's Oklahoma City Service Difficulty program on the MU-2 for 1974 through 1979 reveals several evident recurring problem areas. These involved thermal battery runaway (one of these caused a fatal accident), climate control system malfunctions, cracks and loose rivets in wing and stabilizer skins and in flap wells, and cracked landing gear wheels.

Short-body Solitaire model has hot performance, but owners complain that it's noisy.

One complaint aired by pilots we talked to involves the Bendix fuel control system introduced on the 251 series engine with the MU-2 K (short) and J (long) models. The Woodward fuel controller used on earlier models was much preferred. One operator said they had experienced "lots of downtime" as a result of Bendix breakdowns, though both Bendix and AiResearch picked up most of the repair tab, if not the fuel bills to fly back and forth for frequent repairs.

This operator converted its M model to the Woodward governor and has operated trouble free since then. An STC covers the conversion.

Another complaint centered on the climate control system after an "absolutely trouble free" AiResearch system was replaced with a new Hamilton Standard one that had a greater capacity, apparently, for both air output and temperature control problems.

How well does the MU-2 stand up to day-to-day use in commercial fleets, and what kind of backup support can owners expect. We encountered two vigorous complaints about what were described as aircraft chronic malfunctions and poor factory support. But by far the majority of the pilots and operators we were able to interview described the aircraft as reasonable to maintain and characterized backup support as good to excellent. Typical comments on maintenance went: "Not out of line," "pretty good," "routine," "virtually no squawks," and "we're pleased."

One subscriber, however, said that his MU-2 (a '79 P model) was "chronically defective" and a lemon that no one could seem to keep repaired. He complained of problems "with all systems," and 25 days of downtime in three months with 100 hours of flying time. And he claimed further that 15-20 hours were devoted to ferry time and maintenance flights.

The other protester finally "got rid of it" after he encountered what he said were terrible maintenance

Sleek lines of the MU-2 belie a very poor accident record.

problems. "There were no spare parts for anything." He reported chronic problems with O-rings on brakes, leaky fuel tanks, serious prop vibration and cracked wing skins. He finally went to a Beech King Air, which he described as a much more satisfactory aircraft.

Naturally, operators of large piston twins must brace for the quantum cost jump when they make the move to turboprops, but there are those who maintain that the fantastic speed of the MU-2 series will actually deliver a better cost per seat mile than the piston machines.

Nevertheless, an MU-2 operator can expect to lay out anywhere from $3,500 to $4,500 on the average for a 100-hour inspection. One chief pilot estimated the cost per hour, including everything fixed and variable from fuel to insurance and salaries worked out to $300 (based on 1,020 hours of flying time a year).

Another pilot estimated direct operating costs at $50 per hour plus fuel costs of $150 to $200/hour.

Airworthiness Directives

The brunt of the burden of Airworthiness Directives appears to

have fallen on the first, or B model MU-2. Perhaps the most critical AD called for checking wing flap actuator jack screws for cracks to prevent fatigue failure. Also, the nose gear actuating system had to be modified to prevent failure, and front windshields checked for cracks and optical distortion from discharge of unusually hot defogging air caused by an air conditioning system failure.

Other ADs on the B models called for inspection of control levers on prop pitch control units, and installation of heatproof insulation to prevent possible fire in the baggage compartment from engine bleed air tubing, along with a check of elevator trim tabs to prevent failure.

The most significant ADs on the AiResearch engines in the MU-2s involved checking engine oil filters for metal particles relating to problems with high-speed pinion gear shaft assemblies.

Owner Comments

The airplane is one of the hardest to fly I know of. It's almost impossible to make a good, soft landing, probably because of the high wing loading. You can't keep the nose off, either; it just comes down with a bang. On the rollout after landing, especially with full tip tanks, the plane sets up a rolling motion from side to side, and it's disconcerting because nothing seems to stop it — you can feed in opposite controls or even try to aggravate it and there's no difference.

On takeoff, you have to horse the nose off, and then when it does come off, it pops up. You might lift off at 100 knots and still have 30 or 40 knots go before single-engine climb speed, which is kind of a long wait. If you lose an engine, do not try to keep the airplane going straight ahead. If you do that, you will not be able to accelerate to single-engine climb. Instead, center the ball — that's the most important thing — but allow the plane to make a gentle turn, and then she'll accelerate. Once you get the speed, she'll climb fine on one engine.

It takes a strong man to fly the MU-2, and if you lose an engine, you'd better be mightly strong or quick with the trim. Funny thing, though — I've never heard a single complaint from the customers. Everybody riding in back think's it's a wonderful airplane.

We've been very pleased with the low maintenance on our G model. In the last two years the factory support has been outstanding. Historically, lacking a conventional distribution system, they did have some problems. Prior to '76 there may have been some delivery problems with parts, but I think Mitsubishi has identified that area today.

When we bought our airplane, they sent a man to handle all the service warranty matters. He carried with him all the materials, all the AOG (aircraft on ground) 24-hour service numbers, etc. Recently we lost a starter-generator on a Friday afternoon. They put one on Emery to us Friday evening, which we received Saturday morning. And that's a rather uncommon $7,500 part.

If the part is available through a Mitsubishi service center, they prefer you contact them. If the service center can't ship immediately, the factory will. Are there enough service centers — at 38? There are not!

The transition to a Mitsubishi would take a professional about five hours and a non-pro about 25 hours. If a doctor or attorney, to pick on the poor chaps, or a company executive were to buy the aircraft to fly single pilot, all-weather, he would be well-advised, one, to always fly with a safety pilot for the first 100 hours and, two, not to operate the aircraft unless he's flying it 10 hours a month.

•

The MU-2 is a beautiful bird once it's in the air and flying, but after 100 hours it won't fly. You simply cannot get spare parts, and that's why I got rid of it and got a King Air. I kept losing O-rings on the brakes, and had leaking fuel tanks they couldn't fix. We went through three flight directors because of the way the nose drops when you land the aircraft. We flew the short P model, and it's impossible to hold the nosewheel off after you touch down. It's very tricky to land, and I've had pro pilots in it who wouldn't go up again.

On top of that we had prop vibration that you wouldn't believe and cracked skin under the wing.

The sales people are nice and they try hard, but there's no backup for the company. I'm very happy with my King Air.

•

The strong point on the airplane is the airframe; it's built like a Sherman tank. The Garrett engines have been excellent, and we've found the maintenance to be not out of line.

•

We got an MU-2 because we wanted the fastest aircraft for the money. With our short model we get 300 mph at 75 gph vs. 230 mph in a King Air for the same fuel consumption.

HELICOPTERS

Robinson R-22

Hailed as the answer to a prayer for an inexpensive, easy-to-fly trainer, the Robinson R22 helicopter has had a tremendous impact on the chopper world and upset the name-brand pecking order with a single stroke. But it has also experienced a small number of devastating blade failures that have triggered a natural alarm response.

The FAA has reacted with a series of Airworthiness Directives mandating replacement of various defective main rotor blade types with new blades of improved design. At this point, with all the alphabetical blade series through W now discarded and replaced on every Robinson in the field, the R22s retain the latest Y and Z blades that have the FAA's longevity endorsement of a 2,000-hour TBO.

History

The blade problems experienced by the Robinson helicopter were especially poignant since the manufacturer had touted a blade life of 3,780 hours at the introduction of the R22 in 1979. Nevertheless, the little two-placer did come reasonably close to price expectations—originally ballyhooed at around $25,000 (granted, in 1975 dollars)— by cutting the cost of helicopters down to a base of $45,850. This represented a dramatic slash in price to about half that of other small new choppers like the Hughes 300 and the Enstrom F-28.

Since then, of course, prices on new R22s have gone up like everything else, to the point where the base figure for the 1985 Robinson is $82,850. That is still well under the price of a new Enstrom F-28F ($154,900) or a Schweizer/Hughes 300 ($132,250) of that year.

The clean, uncluttered design obviously contributes to the relatively high cruise speeds obtainable in the Robinson. The cockpit is cozy; there's no space for baggage.

The initial R22s brought out in '79 were powered by 150-hp Lycoming engines derated to 124 hp. The engine is basically the same as the old Cessna Skyhawk powerplant (though not the notorious H version), and has a phenomenal—for helicopters—TBO of 2,000 hours. Most small piston chopper engines come with much more modest TBOs. The Enstrom F-28C's is 1,500 hours, for example; the Hughes 300's is 1,200 hours, and the Hynes-Brantly's is 1,000 hours.

In 1981 the engine suffix went from the A2B to the A2C with a change in the magneto. Then in 1981 the HP model was introduced with a B2C engine carrying an extra 10 horsepower, bringing the total up to 160, though it continued to be derated to 124 hp. Nevertheless, the pilot can pull this power whenever he wishes. There are no artificial stops. And this provides extra performance in high density altitude situations.

In 1983 the Alpha model instrument trainer was brought out with

an increased gross weight—up from 1,300 pounds to 1,370 pounds, to accommodate the extra instruments. Changes were made in the structure and control system to widen the c.g. range. And the battery was moved from the nose to the engine compartment.

Safety Record

A survey of accident records provided by the NTSB and FAA reveals that nearly half of the accidents occurred during dual instruction, which might be expected in an aircraft primarily devoted to training. Furthermore, practice autorotations claimed a fairly large share of accidents—both dual and solo.

Another significant safety problem obviously is related to failure to maintain rotor rpm. In fact, that was the single largest accident group we were able to isolate.

Hard landings and rollovers also claimed a fair share of accidents, though of course sometimes these were related to the rotor rpm problem.

In an attempt to deal with low-rotor-rpm problems, the FAA issued an AD calling for immediate installation of low-rpm warning lights in those older R22s that still had not been equipped with them, to supplement the warning horns. The AD also required setting the alarms to go off at a slightly higher rpm to give a greater margin of warning.

Training Remedies

The Robinson Helicopter Co. set up a safety course for flight instructors designed to reduce the accident rate in R22s. This consists of 25 hours of ground instruction and one-and-a-half hours of flight instruction—all at the factory in Torrance, Calif. Special emphasis is given to reviewing helicopter training accidents and their cause and prevention.

To put the Robinson's safety record in perspective, a 1981 National Transportation Safety Board special study of rotorcraft accidents during 1977-1979 determined that for helicopter pilots in general, failure to maintain adequate rotor rpm or flight speed was the most prevalent cause or factor in accidents.

Main Rotor Failures

As for the dramatic, scary occasions when the main rotor blades on the Robinson failed, there were three accidents of this category in the period from 1979 through mid-1983 that we were able to scan. All of those were fatal. The first one occurred in 1980 at Rancho Palos Verde, Calif. during dual instruction. The FAA grounded the entire 33-ship fleet (then) of R22s until new rotorblades could be installed. A problem with the blade fabrication process (at an outside vendor, according to company head Frank Robinson) was blamed. Blade delamination caused the accident.

In 1981 another fatal accident involving main rotor blade failure occurred, this one at Granby, Conn. Fatigue failure of a root fitting was blamed for the crash, and the FAA once again grounded all the R22s— or at least all those with blades of over 300 hours in service. A strengthened W series blades came with a 1,000-hour service life. However, an emergency AD ordered removal from service of all Revision A through V blades.

The W type blades, in turn, came under the gun when an R22 crashed in July 1983 near Canton, Pa., killing the pilot and passenger after a W series blade failed from fatigue in the root area. The FAA at that time called for inspection of the 25 or so R22s still flying with the W blades and junking of blades with serial numbers up through 810. It later was clarified that this included all Revision W blades.

Accident Review

Our inspection of accident records from 1979 through mid-1983 showed a total of 16 fatal accidents—one in 1980, five in 1981, seven in 1982 and three in 1983. They are as follows:
'80—Rancho Palos Verde, Calif., main blade failure from delamination.
'81—Columbus, Tex., engine failure from fuel exhaustion, low rpm in the autorotation.
Near Fresno, Tex., low rotor rpm during practice autorotation; drug traces found in pilot.
Near Livermore, Calif., rotor blades hit the tail boom, the tail separated. The blades were bent excessively upward from overload. Cause undetermined.
Granby, Conn., main rotor blade failure from fatigue fracture.
El Paso, Tex., failed to maintain adequate rotor rpm, lack of familiarity with the aircraft.
'82—Ormand Beach, Fla., bad weather at night.
Spangler, Pa., hit power lines during patrol.
San Marcos, Tex., crashed out of control, probable cause not determined yet.

Nashville, Tenn., blades reportedly hit tail boom, probable cause not determined yet.
Cincinnati, Ohio, preliminary information suggests a hovering blade stall with low rotor rpm, but no probable cause has been determined yet by the NTSB.
There were two other fatal accidents about which we have no information.
'83—St. Louis, Mo., the rotorcraft is reported to have come apart in the air and crashed in the river. The wreckage and occupants were not recovered.
Sissetory, S.D., a crash reported in bad weather.
There is one other fatal crash about which we have no information.

Airworthiness Directives

By our count the Robinson R22 has been hit with 11 ADs so far: four in 1980, two in 1981, four in 1982 and one in 1983. A glance at the AD history of other similar small piston helicopters suggests that this is not an unusually large number. For the first five years of production, for example, the Enstrom F28A had 10 ADs, the Brantly B2B, 11, and the Hughes 269A six.

Three of the ADs on the Robinson, of course, dealt with inspecting and replacing main rotor blades of types involved in devastating accidents.

For Robinson owners these ADs have often had significant financial repercussions, since they were required to pay a portion of the cost of mandated replacements. One

Cost/Performance/Specifications

Model	Year	Number Built	Average Retail Price	Cruise Speed (kts)	Useful Load (lbs)	HOGE (ft)	Usable Fuel (gals)	Engine	TBO (hra)	Overhaul Cost
R22	1979	8	$32,000	94	538	4,500	19.2	124-hp (150-hp) Lyc. O-320-A2B	2,000	$6,000
R22	1980	41	$35,000	94	538	4,500	19.2	124-hp (150-hp) Lyc. O-320-A2B	2,000	$6,000
R22	1981	119	$42,000	94	538	4,500	19.2	124-hp (150-hp) Lyc. O-320-A2C	2,000	$6,000
R22HP	1981	56	$47,500	96	486	6,400	19.2	124-hp (160-hp) Lyc. O-320-B2C	2,000	$6,000
R22HP	1982	77	$55,000	96	486	6,400	19.2	124-hp (160-hp) Lyc. O-320-B2C	2,000	$6,000
R22HP	1983	36	$75,850	96	486	6,400	19.2	124-hp (160-hp) Lyc. O-320-B2C	2,000	$6,000
R22 Alpha	1984	76	$83,850	96	546	6,400	19.2	124-hp (160-hp) Lyc. O-320-B2C	2,000	$6,000

flight school operator who was one of the early R22 users told us he estimated he had paid out $9,000 to $10,000 over the past few years to comply with the ADs on each of his early model R22s. The bigger tabs involved replacement of the rotor blades and main transmission gears, main gearbox yoke and tail rotor driveshaft.

Naturally, it is not unusual for general aviation manufacturers as a group to let owners pay some or all of the cost of ADs, so the owner can just hope they are few and far between—and cheap. In most cases Robinson offered sizable discounts for the replacements, at least.

Service Bulletins

The same operator mentioned above, incidentally, estimated he had paid about $2,000 to cover the cost of non-AD-related Service Bulletins put out by the Robinson factory through the years for each of his older rotorcraft.

We have examined the Service Bulletins put out by the Robinson factory and agree with them that none could be regarded as optional, since all involve checks or part replacements that could have a critical effect on safety, even though they were not all coupled with ADs. Potential buyers of used R22s should get a list of these and make sure that all were complied with, or at least they should be aware of the possible safety ramifications.

The factory presumably can help identify which, if any, SBs might not have been complied with on specific helicopters being considered for purchase.

Examples of critical SBs: Install metal spring on old, worn cyclic boots to prevent interference with full travel of the cyclic control; replace lower actuator bearings, since several failed prematurely, and this could lead to failure of the main drive system; replace actuator drive screws with a special kit since some were not properly heat treated and could fail in service; install a special guard to pre-

Aircraft Resale Value Chart

'82 R-22HP

(y-axis: $/M — $70,000, $60,000, $50,000, $40,000, $30,000, $20,000, $10,000, –0)
(x-axis: Year — '82, '83, '84, '85)

vent V-belts from climbing out of the sheave grooves, etc. Naturally, these, and others, normally apply only to aircraft with certain serial numbers, not to the entire fleet.

Service Difficulty Reports

Inspection of SDRs showed three areas where repeated problems turned up, though none in large numbers. They included: cracked frames, especially in the tailcone area (seven); spalled bearings (11); and low-rpm sensor inoperative at high voltage (five).

Service Bulletins have been issued by the factory dealing with each of the problems.

Insurance

In an effort to cut insurance costs on the R22s, and supply insurance where operators were unable to find it, Robinson sponsored its own plan in January 1982. But this has triggered a controversy of its own. The company said the program was designed to "drastically" reduce the cost of insurance for R22 helicopter owners, and claimed that attractive, affordable hull rates would be provided, varying from six to eight percent, depending on use and pilot experience level. As the company correctly noted, these rates were far below those usually applied to piston-powered helicopters, which can run about 12 to 22 percent.

But it turns out that the plan, which is actually handled by Glacier General Assurance Co. out of Missoula, Mont., has several major qualifications that result in sharply increased cost to owners and, in effect, bring the six to eight percent rate much higher.

First, Robinson requires owners of damaged helicopters to pay for shipping the rotorcraft all the way back to the factory for repair or salvage. Naturally, this can cost up to $3,000 or so from the East Coast. Second, the company imposes a $7,500 deductible. Third, it subtracts five percent a year in chronological depreciation and $18 an hour of use time. Next, the owner must pay the pro-rated cost of replaced life-limited components like rotor blades. For example, if a 2,000-hour blade is replaced after it was in use for 500 hours, the owner must pay one-fourth of the price of a new blade.

And finally, Robinson requires owners of older helicopters of diminished worth to pay for coverage of the value of brand-new R22s, since the company claims that the cost of repair must reflect today's prices for parts and labor.

At least one owner of a crashed R22 helicopter has brought legal action against the Robinson company, claiming the insurance arrangement was in bad faith. He expected to be paid the face value of the policy, but when all the deductions and depreciation costs were applied, he said he stood to receive a much reduced portion.

The Robinson company says it tells applicants for insurance up front just how the program works and makes them read and sign an acknowledgement of terms beforehand. The form the factory sent us does explain about owner expenses in shipment back to the factory and pro-rating life-limited components, and it notes that the insured must pay ''the deductible specified in the policy...'' But it does not tell the cost of the deductible and does not say anything about the yearly or hourly depreciation deductions or that coverage is based on the cost of a new Robinson helicopter.

Performance

Among small piston choppers, the R22 is no slouch in the performance category. Though it has quite a bit less horsepower than the Hynes-Brantly, the Hughes 269/300 or the Enstrom F28C, for example, it can outcruise them all by four to 16 knots, and comes with a five- to 16-knot margin in never-exceed speed. This translates in the R22 to a 95-knot 75-percent cruise with a 103-knot Vne.

Hovering altitudes listed for the R22 HP version are also better than the competitors' by a considerable magnitude. The Robinson's hover altitude out of ground effect of 6,400 feet, for example, is more than twice that of the Hynes-

Brantly B2B (2,500 feet) and the Hughes 300 (2,700 feet).

The Robinson has no provision for a sling attachment, however, so is aimed strictly at training and personal transport.

Pilot Utility & Cabin Design

The most unorthodox aspect of the cockpit design is the cyclic control, which consists of a teetering handlebar arrangement mounted to a single control column sprouting from the floor alongside the instrument pedestal. This takes a bit of getting used to by fliers weaned on a separate cyclic for each pilot, but does reduce the parts count and complexity of dual cyclic control sticks.

The arrangement would seem to be awkward for the flight instructor, since when the student is resting his elbow on his knee to steady the cyclic, in conventional fashion, the handle on the instructor's side is teetered up a bit high for good control monitoring. Some instructors get around this problem by gently holding onto the central column.

As for the other controls, the collective provides unusually good coordination with throttle and requires less attention, we would judge, than in most other piston choppers. The Robinson also has a novel method of displaying rotor and engine rpm in a pair of fan-like

The single cyclic control has a teetering handlebar on top for dual instruction.

arcs that touch tengentially. This makes gauge interpretation quite easy and simplifies keeping the rpms in the green.

The cabin is smaller than that of many other helicopters—with one pilot likening it to a Cessna 152. And the two-per-rev blade beat is evident at higher speeds, which diminishes the feeling of comfort and security of nonchopper fliers on cross-country trips.

The aircraft is a less-than-ideal cross-country ship because aside from small crannies beneath the pilots' seats, there is no space for baggage.

Maintenance

Maintenance was characterized as not out of line for this class of rotorcraft by the users who responded to our survey. But some of them complained that parts shipment from the factory was slow. ''We were down two weeks waiting on parts,'' one owner said. A flight school operator, however, contradicted this statement, saying he was able to get parts shipped overnight when needed for grounded aircraft.

He reported normal maintenance was ''minimal,'' aside from problems on early ships with numerous electrical glitches caused by faulty voltage regulators and over-volt relays along with broken battery straps. He said the later R22 HP models eliminated the problems. This school operator reported their scheduled maintenance costs (for regular inspections, etc.) worked out to about $4.25 an hour and unscheduled costs (for unexpected repairs, etc.) came to about $2.50 an hour.

On the other hand, a 1983 hike in the price the factory charges for an overhaul from $24,000 to $36,000 has chilled the enthusiasm of some operators for the overall economy of operation of the Robinson R22. This is the price for overhaul of key life-limited components of the helicopter like main rotor transmission, rotor blades, etc.

Since there are no field overhaul

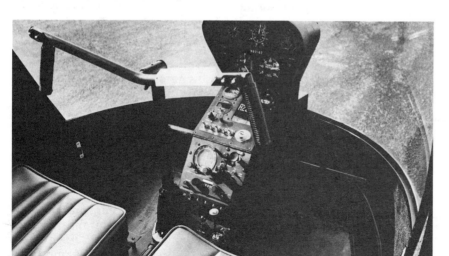

The four-cylinder Lycoming engine is mounted horizontally and comes with a phenomenal—for helicopters—2,000-hour lifetime.

facilities, owners once again face the expense of shipping the R22s all the way back to Robinson's California factory. And these rising overhaul costs are causing some operators to think that maybe the vaunted cost margin of the Robinson over the Enstroms and Hughes and Bell 47s and Brantlys may be vanishing.

Investment Value

The early R22s have held onto their value fairly well since the line was introduced in 1979. A '79 model that may have cost $47,000 or so equipped when new went for around $32,000 in 1985, according to the *Aircraft Bluebook Price Digest*. An HP model that sold for about $66,000 in 1981 was bringing around $46,000.

Buyers are well advised to be cautious about bargains they may encounter on the used chopper market. As Michael K. Hynes, head of Brantly-Hynes, Inc. mentioned in these pages a few years back, inexperienced buyers of used helicopters tend to be shocked at the maintenance costs of rotorcraft. And what looks like a marvelous "steal" will often haunt the owner in maintenance bills, because these should be budgeted on the basis of what new choppers cost, not old, depreciated ones.

The R22, then, has established a niche in the helicopter world as the most economical machine on the market—to the extent that anything having to do with rotorcraft is economical. Furthermore, it has dominated the training field by undercutting nearly all other dual chopper rates. The biggest black mark against the R22 is its history of traumatic rotor-blade problems. However, there have been no failures over the first two years of the surviving blade designs, the Y and Z revisions, and Robinson is banking on the future with them as it carries on an intensive series of instructional sessions with instructors that is reported already to have contributed to a lowered accident rate.

Owner Comments

I ordered my ship in the fall of 1975, and picked it up in February of 1981. The detail work on the hull is good, and it is fast and good-looking. The control feel is particularly nice, after one gets used to the unusual cyclic arrangement—kind of like driving a sports car. Mine cost about $52,000, plus options, and I was the second non-dealer owner. Like all helicopters, it takes a lot of concentration to fly safely. Unlike others, though, this one leaves zero margin for error during a touchdown autorotation in no-wind conditions. The rotor blades are so light that the rotor speed bleeds down below 100 percent before the airspeed gets to zero.

It is the smoothest machine machine I have ever flown, with practically no vibration at the controls.

The insurance situation turned out to be a big hassle. Only one carrier would quote on it, and the coverage was poor. During the first 144 hours, I spent over $6,000 replacing various things that weren't broken, thanks to a string of ADs. At the 144-hour mark, the main rotor hub bearings were found to be badly burned and deteriorating. Since I was the only pilot to use it, I knew that the history was good. The factory never did come up with any explanation. It looks as though the early owners did a lot of R&D on the R22 that the factory should have done. On the other hand, they are quick on the fixes. They are also quick on parts shipments and advice.

For a while there, I was pretty demoralized. The factory had catastrophic in-flight failures of three different blade designs, and my 3,700-hour blades are now 2,000-hour blades. I later heard that most helicopter manufacturers go through teething pains on their new designs. I hope Robinson is on the downhill side of the hump now, because I really like this little sports car.

Elliott Pisor
San Francisco, Calif.

I have been operating a Robinson R22 helicopter now for two-and-one-half years. Presently, I am the owner of two R22s, one of which is leased and one which I personally own, and I am half owner of a third R22 being used for helicopter service. I have accumulated more than 500 hours of flying time in Robinson helicopters and can happily report that it is the most well designed and useful tool that I have ever possessed. I have subjected my R22 to sometimes four or five startups, shutdowns, takeoffs, and landings a day, and it has never failed to perform admirably.

The parts availability and backup is sometimes time consuming because of the newness of the helicopter and the relatively small size of the factory where it is produced. This, however, is generally remedied on service bulletin modifications by allowing enough time for completion of the modifications and shipment of the parts. I personally have never had any difficulty with any of the helicopters I have operated. And all of the modifications since the initial purchase of my first helicopter have been minor with the exception of the blade change modification early on in the program, which was effected at a very low cost.

I would advise those reading this article that there have been many incidents and accidents which, I believe, have been related to the pilot's and owner's attitude regarding this helicopter. It has generally been viewed as a very elaborate toy, and this is a dangerous and sometimes fatal attitude. The Robinson helicopter is an excellent performer and should be treated with a great deal of respect and flown as it is placarded. If operated properly, I can assure you from many hours of experience that the R22 will be a joy and a pleasure to own and operate.

Frank Anders, M.D.
Ville Platte, La.

As the largest Robinson R22 dealer in the U.S. we feel well qualified to give valuable information to potential used R22 buyers. During the past three years NHI has operated up to 11 R22s, most of which were on leaseback for flight training. All things being considered, we feel that the R22 is perhaps the best buy on the market for an individual looking for both economy and reliability in a two-place helicopter. The following is a list of responses to your survey from an operator's point of view:

1. Performance — the R22 is capable of handling all operations within its flight envelope with ease. At sea level, full power is readily available even on the hottest days of the year, unlike the older (un-supercharged) recips of the past. Due to the derating on the Lycoming IO-320, the pilot has an additional power reserve of 25 hp if needed in a pinch. At higher elevations (5,000 feet) the R22 is still capable of producing full power due to the derated engine. (Although the pilot is not going to leap over tall buildings with a single bound at those elevations, he still has sufficient power at average payload to perform all normal operations with a margin for error.)

2. Handling characteristics — Although the R22 was built to be very quick and responsive, it is still a fairly easy helicopter to transition into, compared with most other helicopter trainers such as the Bell 47, Hughes 300 or Enstrom F-28. Students average about the same length of time to solo the R22 as they would a Hughes 300 and approximately the same number of hours to complete a course of instruction. As with most other helicopters, a first-time buyer should expect to obtain 45-60 hours of dual/solo instruction for his rating, but will normally require 75-100 flight hours before he becomes comfortable in the aircraft. During cruise flight the R22 handles more like an airplane, with the pilot workload being minimal thanks to a well balanced collective and corelated throttle control.

3. Comfort — Although small in comparison with other helicopters, the cabin area is about the size of a Cessna 152. The cyclic stick teeters so that the pilot can rest it on his leg during all flight operations. With the new tip-weighted Z blades, the aircraft flies relatively smoothly as speeds of up to 100 knots at average payload (pilot, passenger and full fuel), although the inherent 1:1 vibration is present at higher speeds, which is typical of most two-bladed systems. There is very little yaw effect at higher airspeeds during turbulent conditions, making for a fairly smooth ride for an aircraft of this size.

4. Maintenance — Although a few major problems were encountered with the R22 with the blade replacement costs and yoke replacement, normal maintenance has been minimal. Earlier ships (serial #001-075) had numerous electrical problems caused by faulty voltage regulators and over-volt relays. Broken battery straps also caused a few problems with the electrical system. The R22 HP model has incorporated a few minor design features which have eliminated these problems. The R22 HP has been equipped with a 160-hp rather than 150-hp Lycoming, allowing the higher-altitude performance, although it is still derated to 124 hp. The derating is accomplished by restricting manifold pressure limits the pilot can use during all flight operations. A manifold pressure chart is located on the cyclic and gives a pressure altitude/temperature combination to determine mp limits. The newer R22s have been virtually trouble-free with the exception of minor plug fouling problems during hot weather caused by carbon deposits building up on the valve guides. Design improvements in the R22 have eliminated most unscheduled maintenance problems, especially if the aircraft is used only for personal flying and not flight training.

5. Parts availability — Parts are readily available from the factory through any dealer in the U.S., and AOG service is available for a $50 handling charge. Most parts can be obtained and drop shipped anywhere in the U.S. within 24 hours. We have had parts shipped overnight when needed for a grounded aircraft and have had the part the next morning with only a few hours of lost flight time.

6. Operating costs — For the private buyer, the major cost will be insurance if hull insurance is carried. Most individuals insured through RHC's insurance program have found it difficult to obtain affordable rates on older aircraft ($25,000-$40,000 price range). Liability costs about $1,000/year for private usage based on pilot qualifications. Hull rates are about $6,000 for the same usage. Maintenance costs per hour according to Robinson Helicopter Co. are $3/hour for scheduled and $1.50 for unscheduled maintenance with an additional $18/hour reserve cost for major overhaul.

These figures, although fairly realistic for a new aircraft, are considerably lower than the costs that we have experienced at NHI, with the older serial numbers. Our maintenance costs have averaged approximately $4.25/hour for scheduled and $2.50/hour for unscheduled. Normally, a 10 percent increase in operating cost will occur if used for extensive flight training. The reserve for overhaul recently was increased from $12/hour to $18/hour, which came as an unexpected shock to dealers and private owners. This increased the cost of an overhaul at 2,000 hours from $24,000 to $36,000 with an additional cost of $5,000 to upgrade a standard R22 to an R22HP. A used buyer should be aware of this when purchasing a high-time aircraft (over 1,500 hours) even though it may look like a "steal." Another problem faced by buyers, especially those on the East Coast, is the fact that the entire aircraft must be returned to Robinson Helicopter Co. in Torrance, Calif.

for overhaul, which will add an additional $2,000-$3,000 to the overhaul cost.

7. Annual inspection — The cost of an annual inspection will be $450-$600, not $450-$600, not including parts that are worn and must be replaced. Although not required for a private owner, the RHC factory strongly recommends 100-hour inspections and 50-hour oil changes, which is typical of all helicopters. A 100-hour inspection will cost $300-$500, depending on age and condition of the aircraft. A buyer should check with his nearest dealer to determine if they have a flat rate for an R22 inspection. We have heard of at least one owner being charged an outrageous $1,400 for a 100-hour inspection on an R22 that had just been overhauled a few months earlier.

8. Idiosyncrasies — Although the R22 has displayed no unusual or noticeable idiosyncrasies com-

pared to other types of light helicopters, the new owner should be aware of a few minor problems that he may encounter when transitioning to the R22. First of all, it is strongly recommended that you find a CFI who is well qualified in the R22 to give you some instruction. Even the most experienced helicopter pilot is likely to get a surprise during his first attempt to hover the R22 since the cyclic control is on a teeter hinge which requires a few minutes to get used to. There is also a very noticeable change in c.g. and cyclic position when flying solo for the first time which could cause an unexpected roll-over for a novice pilot. The R22 is one of the few light helicopters that displays no unusual characteristics in high winds and is fairly predictable in any winds up to 25 knots once you get used to it.

Lawrence E. Durocher, Pres.
Northeast Helicopters
Ellington, Conn.